Rebecca S. Watson
Chaos Uncreated

Beihefte zur Zeitschrift für die alttestamentliche Wissenschaft

Herausgegeben von
John Barton · Reinhard G. Kratz
Choon-Leong Seow · Markus Witte

Band 341

Walter de Gruyter · Berlin · New York

Rebecca S. Watson

Chaos Uncreated

A Reassessment of the Theme of "Chaos" in the Hebrew Bible

Walter de Gruyter · Berlin · New York

♾ Printed on acid-free paper which falls within
the guidelines of the ANSI to ensure permanence and durability.

ISBN-13: 978-3-11-017993-4
ISBN-10: 3-11-017993-8

Library of Congress Cataloging-in-Publication Data

Watson, Rebecca Sally, 1971–
Chaos uncreated : a reassessment of the theme of "chaos" in the Hebrew Bible / Rebecca S. Watson.
p. cm. – (Beihefte zur Zeitschrift für die alttestamentliche Wissenschaft ; Bd. 341)
Includes bibliographical references.
ISBN-13: 978-3-11-017993-4 (cloth : alk. paper)
ISBN-10: 3-11-017993-8 (cloth : alk. paper)
1. Bible. O.T. Psalms – Criticism, interpretation, etc. 2. Theomachy in the Bible. 3. Dragons in the Bible. 4. Water in the Bible. I. Title. II. Series: Beihefte zur Zeitschrift für die alttestamentliche Wissenschaft ; 341.
BS410.Z5 vol. 341
[BS1430.6.T447]
221.6 s–dc22
[221.6]
2005028121

Bibliographic information published by Die Deutsche Bibliothek

Die Deutsche Bibliothek lists this publication in the Deutsche Nationalbibliografie; detailed bibliographic data is available in the Internet at <http://dnb.ddb.de>.

Printed in Germany

Cover Design: Christopher Schneider, Berlin

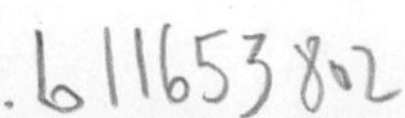

For my Parents,
In gratitude and affection

Table of Contents

Abbreviations

AJSLL	*American Journal of Semitic Languages and Literatures*
AKA	E. A. W. Budge and L. W. King, *Annals of the Kings of Assyria: The Cuneiform Texts with Translations, Transliterations, etc. from the Original Documents in the British Museum* (London: Trustees of the British Museum, 1902)
ANEP	J. B. Pritchard (ed.), *The Ancient Near East in Pictures Relating to the Old Testament* (Princeton, NJ: Princeton University Press, 1954)
ANET	*Ancient Near Eastern Texts Relating to the Old Testament* (Princeton, NJ: Princeton University Press, 3rd ed. with Supplement, 1969)
AOAT	Alter Orient und Altes Testament
AOS	American Oriental Series
ARI	W. F. Albright, *Archaeology and the Religion of Israel* (The Ayer Lectures of the Colgate-Rochester Divinity School 1941; Baltimore, MD: John Hopkins, 1942)
ARW	*Archiv für Religionswissenschaft*
BASOR	*Bulletin of the American Schools of Oriental Research*
BDB	F. Brown, S. R. Driver and C. A. Briggs, *A Hebrew and English Lexicon of the Old Testament* (Oxford: Clarendon, 1906)
BHS	K. Elliger, and W. Rudolph, (edd.), *Biblia Hebraica Stuttgartensia* (Stuttgart: Deutsche Bibelgesellschaft, 4th ed. 1990)
BHT	Beiträge zur historischen Theologie
BKAT	Biblischer Kommentar Altes Testament
BN	*Biblische Notizen*
BR	Biblical Research
BZAW	Beihefte zur Zeitschrift für die alttestamentliche Wissenschaft
CAD	I. J. Gelb et al. (edd.), *The Assyrian Dictionary of the Oriental Institute of the University of Chicago* (Chicago, IL: The Oriental Institute, Chicago; Glückstadt: J. J. Augustin Verlagsbuchhandlung, 1956-)
CBOT	Coniectanea Biblica Old Testament Series
CBQ	*Catholic Biblical Quarterly*
CHP	W. G. E. Watson, *Classical Hebrew Poetry: A Guide to its Techniques* (JSOT[S] 26; Sheffield: Sheffield Academic Press, 2nd edition reprinted with corrections, 1995)
CML	J. C. L. Gibson, *Canaanite Myths and Legends* (Edinburgh: T.

	& T. Clark, 2nd edition 1978)
CS, I	W. W. Hallo with J. L. Younger, Jr., *The Context of Scripture. I. Canonical Compositions of the Biblical World* (Leiden: E. J. Brill, 1997)
CTA	A. Herdner, *Corpus des tablettes en cunéiformes alphabétiques découvertes à Ras Shamra-Ugarit de 1929 à 1939*, 2 vols. (Bibliothèque archéologique et historique 79; Mission de Ras Shamra, 10; Paris: Imprimerie Nationale, 1963)
DCH	D. J. A. Clines (ed.), *The Dictionary of Classical Hebrew*, I-IV (Sheffield: Sheffield Academic Press, 1993-1998).
DDD	K. van der Toorn, B. Becking and P. W. van der Horst, *Dictionary of Deities and Demons in the Bible* (Leiden: Brill; Grand Rapids, MI: Eerdmans, 2nd extensively revised ed. 1999)
DIHG	J. C. L. Gibson, *Davidson's Introductory Hebrew Grammar – Syntax* (Edinburgh: T. & T. Clark, 1994)
ET	English translation
ExpT	*Expository Times*
FAT	Forschungen zum Alten Testament
FOTL	The Forms of the Old Testament Literature
GGG	O. Keel and C. Uehlinger, *Göttinnen, Götter und Gottessymbole: Neue Erkenntnisse zur Religionsgeschichte Kanaans und Israels aufgrund bislang unerschlossener ikonographischer Quellen* (Quaestiones Disputatae 134; Freiburg: Herder, 2nd ed. 1993)
GK	A. E. Cowley, *Gesenius' Hebrew Grammar as edited and enlarged by the late E. Kautzsch* (Oxford: Clarendon, 2nd ed. 1910)
HAT	Handbuch zum Alten Testament
Hrozný	F. Hrozný, *Sumerisch-babylonische Mythen von dem Gotte Ninrag (Ninib)* (Mitteilungen der Vorderasiatischen Gesellschaft 5, 8 Jahrgang; Berlin: Wolf Peiser, 1903)
HSAT	Die heilige Schrift des Alten Testaments
HSM	Harvard Semitic Monographs
HThKAT	Herders Theologischer Kommentar zum Alten Testament
HTR	*Harvard Theological Review*
HUCA	Hebrew Union College Annual
HZ	F.-L. Hossfeld and E. Zenger, *Die Psalmen: Psalm 1-50* (Die Neue Echter Bibel 29; Würzburg: Echter Verlag, 1993); *Psalmen 51-100* (HThKAT; Freiburg: Herder, 2000).
ICC	International Critical Commentary
IDB	G. A. Buttrick et al. (edd.), *The Interpreter's Dictionary of the Bible*, 4 vols. (Nashville, TN: Abingdon Press, 1962; Supplementary Volume 1976)
IEJ	*Israel Exploration Journal*
Int	*Interpretation*
JANES	*Journal of the Ancient Near Eastern Society*
JAOS	*Journal of the American Oriental Society*

JBL	*Journal of Biblical Literature*
JNWSL	*Journal of Northwest Semitic Languages*
JPS	Jewish Publication Society
JPSA	Jewish Publication Society of America
JQR	*Jewish Quarterly Review*
JSOT	*Journal for the Study of the Old Testament*
JSOT(S)	Journal for the Study of the Old Testament Supplement Series
JSS	*Journal of Semitic Studies*
JTS	*Journal of Theological Studies*
K	Cuneiform Tablets from the Kouyunjik Collection in the British Museum
KTU	M. Dietrich, O. Loretz and J. Sanmartin, *Die keilalphabetischen Texte aus Ugarit: einschliesslich der keilalphabetischen Texte ausserhalb Ugarits. Teil 1: Transkription* (AOAT 24; Kevelaer: Butzon & Bercker; Neukirchen-Vluyn: Neukirchener Verlag, 1976)
LXX	Septuagint
MT	Masoretic text
NCBC	New Century Bible Commentary
NEB	New English Bible
NIB	*The New Interpreter's Bible*, 12 vols. (Nashville, TN: Abingdon Press, 1994-1998)
NIDOTTE	W. VanGemeren, (ed.), *New International Dictionary of Old Testament Theology and Exegesis,* 5 vols. (Carlisle: Paternoster, 1997)
NRSV	New Revised Standard Version
n.s.	New series
OLP	Orientalia Lovaniensia Periodica
Or	*Orientalia*
OTG	Old Testament Guide
OTL	Old Testament Library
OTS	Old Testament Studies
OTT	G. von Rad, *Old Testament Theology*, 2 vols. (London: SCM, 1975)
PAP	M. D. Goulder, *The Psalms of Asaph and the Pentateuch* (JSOT[S] 233; Sheffield: JSOT, 1996)
PIW	S. Mowinckel, *The Psalms in Israel's Worship*, 2 vols. (Oxford: Blackwell, 1962). Revised and Translated from *Offersang og Sangoffer* (Oslo: Aschehoug, 1951)
PR	M. D. Goulder, *The Psalms of the Return (Book V, Psalms 107-150)* (JSOT[S] 258; Sheffield: Sheffield Academic Press, 1998)
PRU, II	C. Virolleaud (edd.), *Le Palais Royal d'Ugarit*, Vol. 2 (Mission de Ras Shamra 7; Paris: Imprimerie Nationale, 1957)
PSK	M. D. Goulder, *The Psalms of the Sons of Korah* (JSOT[S] 20; Sheffield: JSOT, 1982)
PsSt	S. Mowinckel, *Psalmenstudien*, 6 vols. (Oslo: J. Dybwad, 1921-4)

RB	*Revue Biblique*
REB	Revised English Bible
RHPR	*Revue d'Histoire et de Philosophie Religieuses*
RSV	Revised Standard Version
RTU	N. Wyatt, *Religious Texts from Ugarit: The Words of Ilimilku and his Colleagues* (The Biblical Seminar 53; Sheffield: Sheffield Academic Press, 1998)
SAYP	F. M. Cross and D. N. Freedman, *Studies in Ancient Yahwistic Poetry* (Biblical Resource Series; Grand Rapids, MI: William B. Eerdmans, 1997)
SBLDS	Society of Biblical Literature Dissertation Series
SBLWAW	Society of Biblical Literature Writings from the Ancient World Series
SBT	Studies in Biblical Theology
SEL	*Studi Epigrafici e Linguistici sul Vicino Oriente antico*
SKAI	A. R. Johnson, *Sacral Kingship in Ancient Israel* (Cardiff: University of Wales Press, 2nd ed. 1967)
StTh	*Studia Theologica*
Supp.	Supplement
Sym.	Version of Symmachus
Syr.	Syriac
Targ.	Targum
TAT	*Theologie des Alten Testaments*
ThSt	*Theological Studies*
ThZ	*Theologische Zeitschrift*
TWAT	G. J. Botterweck and H. Ringgren (edd.), *Theologisches Wörterbuch zum Alten Testament* (Stuttgart: W. Kohlhammer, 1970-)
UBL	*Ugaritisch-Biblische Literatur*
UF	*Ugarit-Forschungen*
Ug.	Ugaritic
UNP	S. B. Parker (ed.), *Ugaritic Narrative Poetry* (SBLWAW 9; Atlanta, GA: Scholars Press, 1997)
UT	C. H. Gordon, *Ugaritic Textbook* (Analecta Orientalia 38; Rome: Pontifical Biblical Institute, 1969)
UTT	O. Loretz, *Ugarit-Texte und Thronbesteigungspsalmen: die Metamorphose des Regenspenders Baal-Jahwe (Ps 24, 7-10; 29; 47; 93; 95-100 sowie Ps 77, 17-20; 114). Erweiterte Neuauflage von "Psalm 29. Kanaanische El- und Baaltraditionen in jüdischer Sicht" (UBL 2. 1984)* (UBL 7; Münster: Ugarit-Verlag, 1988).
VT	*Vetus Testamentum*
VT[S]	Vetus Testamentum Supplement Series
Vulg.	Vulgate
WAB	O. Keel, *Die Welt der altorientalischen Bildsymbolik und das AlteTestamentam Beispiel der Psalmen* (Neukirchen: Neukirchener Verlag; Zürich: Benziger Verlag, 1972)

WMANT	Wissenschaftliche Monographien zum Alten und Neuen Testament
YGC	W. F. Albright, *Yahweh and the Gods of Canaan: A Historical Analysis of Two Contrasting Faiths* (Jordan Lectures in Comparative Religion VII, 1965; London: Athlone Press, University of London, 1968)
ZA	*Zeitschrift für Assyriologie und verwandte Gebiete*
ZS	*Zeitschrift für Semistik und verwandte Gebiete*
ZTK	*Zeitschrift für Theologie und Kirche*

Biblical Books

Gen.	Genesis	Am.	Amos	Ru.	Ruth
Ex.	Exodus	Ob.	Obadiah	Cant.	Song of Songs
Lev.	Leviticus	Jon.	Jonah	Eccl.	Ecclesiastes
Num.	Numbers	Mic.	Micah	Lam.	Lamentations
Deut.	Deuteronomy	Nah.	Nahum	Est.	Esther
Josh.	Joshua	Hab.	Habakkuk	Dan.	Daniel
Judg.	Judges	Zeph.	Zephaniah	Neh.	Nehemiah
Sam.	Samuel	Hag.	Haggai	Chr.	Chronicles
Ki.	Kings	Zech.	Zechariah	Sir.	Sirach
Isa.	Isaiah	Mal.	Malachi	Macc.	Maccabees
Jer.	Jeremiah	Ps.	Psalm	Matt.	Matthew
Ezek.	Ezekiel	Pss.	Psalms	Cor.	Corinthians
Hos.	Hosea	Prov.	Proverbs	Rev.	Revelation

Grammatical terms

abs.	absolute	m.	masculine	Qr	Q[e]rê
f.	feminine	perf.	perfect	s.	singular
Hiph.	Hiph'îl	Pi.	Pi'el		
Kt	K[e]ṯîḇ	pl.	plural		

Preface

This monograph represents a revised and expanded version of a doctoral thesis written under the supervision of Dr. Paul M. Joyce at the University of Oxford. In its original scope it offered a reassessment of the theme of "chaos" in the Psalter. However, the results of that analysis, which suggested that the presence of "chaos" has been significantly overplayed in relation to this particular biblical book, clearly raised the question of whether the same conclusion is also applicable to the remaining instances in the Old Testament where this theme has conventionally been detected. An extra chapter has therefore been added in order to address this issue in relation to other key passages, but the original focus on the Psalter still remains in evidence in the shape and proportions of the monograph as a whole.

In the course of the present work, quotations from the Bible in English are taken from the RSV, and any deviation from this is indicated in the discussion; in exceptional cases, where it has been necessary to offer an alternative rendering for reasons of interpretation, this is clearly noted. Citations from the Hebrew Bible are taken from *Biblia Hebraica Stuttgartensia*, 4th edition, 1990, and those from the Ugaritic corpus, from S. B. Parker, *Ugaritic Narrative Poetry*. All biblical references are to the Hebrew text, which, of course, in the case of the Psalter often yields a verse number one higher than in the corresponding English versions. However, in respect of Job 40:25-41:26 (ET 41:1-34) and a small number of other instances where confusion might otherwise result, the verse number of the translation is given in brackets and marked "ET", as here. When citing secondary literature, I have given the full title in the first instance, and an abbreviated one thereafter, as may be expected; however, in the interest of clarity and brevity, for commentaries on the primary text under discussion at any point, only the author and page number(s) are cited, and the title omitted; references to Kraus' Commentary on the Psalms are to the 6th German edition, 1989, except when otherwise stated.

I have preferred to quote foreign language authors in English. Where an English edition of their work is cited in the bibliography, this is the source of the translation (though the page references are to the original); otherwise, translations are my own. An exception occurs where an author has rendered the Hebrew text of the Bible into his own language, in which case, for reasons of accuracy, this version is retained.

Use of the masculine singular form to denote an individual of either gender has a long history in the English language, as indeed in the Hebrew corpus under discussion. I have therefore employed this convention in preference to the more clumsy alternatives, trusting that as a female writer I am unlikely to be misunderstood as having a sexist bias.

An increasing weight of recent publications has been holistic in approach, focusing on the final form of the Psalter. Whilst this is an important development, it is tangential to my main diachronic and exegetical concerns, and therefore sparse reference is made to such works in the present context.

There are many people whose contribution to the writing of this monograph it is a pleasure to acknowledge. Among these I may mention my schoolteacher, Miss Elizabeth Edwards, whose enormous enthusiasm for biblical studies I found so infectious; and Dr. John Day, of Lady Margaret Hall, Oxford, who first introduced me as an undergraduate to the exciting world of dragons and "chaos" in the Old Testament. Although I have found myself disagreeing with his understanding of this theme at many points, the frequency with which I have referred to his book *God's Conflict* offers testimony to the fact that is probably the most often-cited work on the subject today, and I have turned to it as a conversation partner more than to any other. I am grateful also to my MA supervisor, the Revd. Dr. Tony Gelston, of Durham, who, besides proving a dedicated and supportive teacher, encouraged me to go on to further research; and to my D.Phil. supervisor, Dr. Paul Joyce, of St. Peter's College, Oxford, to whom I am particularly indebted. Without his disciplined deadlines, tempered by unfailing encouragement and good-humour, my thesis would have been very much longer in the making, whilst his wise counsel has improved it immeasurably on many counts. Dr. Gelston and Dr. Joyce have remained valuable sources of advice and feedback, and I owe much to both of them. I must acknowledge also the rôle of Dr. Terry Fenton of Haifa University, who very generously expended much time and paper discussing matters "chaotic" (or otherwise) and in making many helpful suggestions on matters of detail and bibliography.

I wish to offer my thanks to the English language editors of the BZAW series, Professors John Barton and Choon-Leong Seow, for accepting my manuscript for publication, and to Dr. Albrecht Döhnert for his assistance with innumerable formatting issues and his patience in awaiting the completed draft. I am particularly grateful to Professor Barton for his advice and encouragement during the final phase of the expansion of my original thesis.

I owe an enormous debt of gratitude to my parents for their self-sacrifice in funding my education over many years. Without them, the opportunity for postgraduate study would not have been available to me, and they have remained consistent in their support. I wish especially to record my mother's heroic contribution to the formatting of this manuscript, for which I am hugely grateful. I must acknowledge also the rôle of my parents-in-law, Drs. Lilla and Stanley Watson, who quite incredibly took on the task of contributing generously to my continuing education.

Not so long ago, a female scholar could preface her work by acknowledging the contribution of Messrs. Hoover, Kenwood et al. to her research.[1] I have the far greater pleasure, however, in thanking my husband, James, for sending me

1 M. Barker, Preface to *The Older Testament: The Survival of Themes from the Ancient Royal Cult in Sectarian Judaism and Early Christianity* (London: SPCK, 1987).

back to my books whilst he nobly wielded the inventions of the aforementioned gentlemen. More recently he and—even more so—our son Hugh have been subjected to the trials (and occasional benefits) of "relay parenting", with the two of them disappearing out for the day to allow me to work. I shall always be grateful for Hugh's parting wish that I should "have a nice time working" as he smilingly waved goodbye from the car each time, and I hope that he will one day think it was all worthwhile. I owe much to both of them.

There are many others whose smaller contributions have eased the way, among them Dr Francesca Stavrakopoulou and Mrs. Phyllis Williams, who offered invaluable advice on the vexed issue of formatting; Libby Birchall at the Theology Faculty Library in Oxford, who allowed me to renew my books without bringing them in; Helen Post, the student adviser at Lady Margaret Hall, who cheerfully agreed for me to pay my fees piecemeal over five years; and the administrators of the Watkins Hebrew Scholarship at Durham, whose award financed the computer at which I am sitting now.

I. Introduction

The purpose of this study is to subject those texts in the Hebrew Bible which have conventionally been associated with the theme of "chaos" to a thorough critical analysis, and to demonstrate that in many instances this traditional interpretation is in need of re-evaluation.[1] The prevailing approach is, I would suggest, fundamentally flawed insofar as it entails the imposition of a monolithic concept upon material which is so diverse as not to find any single unifying focus within the Hebrew language. Indeed, the so-called "chaos imagery" is expressed in such variable terminology, in so many different types of context and genre, and is juxtaposed with such a vast array of motifs drawn from so many areas of life, that the validity of clustering together such material under a single unifying theme must be called into question.

The present scholarly consensus has its origin in the discovery of the Babylonian text *Enuma elish*[2] and in Hermann Gunkel's seminal response, *Schöpfung und Chaos in Urzeit und Endzeit*, which was published in 1895. Gunkel maintained that the account of Marduk's victory over Tiamat and ensuing creation of the world was appropriated into an Israelite context, resulting in allusions to a battle between Yahweh and the sea or a dragon, known also as Rahab or Leviathan. Subsequent to the deciphering of the Ugaritic Baal myths, this position has been modified sufficiently to allow for a more immediate Canaanite derivation of the Israelite themes, without, however, the necessary and substantial reinterpretation of their significance taking place. This approach is typified by John Day's 1985 study, *God's Conflict with the Dragon and the Sea*:[3] he argues forcefully that the motif must have been mediated by Canaan, but otherwise adheres closely to Gunkel's position. Because the conceptions of chaos and creation do not appear together in the

---

1 Issues concerning the history of interpretation will be considered in the following chapter, and are therefore touched on only briefly here.

2 The first tablets were uncovered in excavations of King Ashurbanipal's library at Nineveh, conducted between 1848 and 1876; these were published in George Smith's book, *The Chaldean Account of Genesis*, in 1876. Further material later came to light in successive campaigns in Ashur (1902-14), Kish (1924-5) and Uruk (biblical Erech, 1928-9); see Heidel, *The Babylonian Genesis*, pp. 1-2.

3 Day's findings have been more recently summarised in *Yahweh and the Gods and Goddesses of Canaan* (Sheffield, 2000), pp. 98-107, but without significant modification. References in the present monograph are therefore to his original and more detailed work.

texts he considers, Day is compelled to supply the connection by pursuing a rather convoluted line of argument.[4]

However, it is becoming apparent that this interpretative strategy has resulted in a tendency to force the Hebrew material into a "*Chaoskampf*" straitjacket, and in particular to place disproportionate emphasis on comparisons with Babylonian and Canaanite (especially Ugaritic) mythology (so much so that concepts from these wider ancient Near Eastern backgrounds are arguably sometimes "read into" the Old Testament)[5]. This has resulted in an approach whereby a divine conflict with the sea, characteristically resulting in creation, is often assumed in passages where the presence of such allusions could hardly be supposed on the basis of the biblical text itself. Thus, a picture is drawn, according to which there are numerous references to Yahweh's battling with the waters of chaos and thereby bringing the cosmos into being, without there being any clear statement or account of such an idea in the Hebrew corpus, and despite the many inconsistencies between such a notion and much of Old Testament theology.[6] Hence, the association of chaos with each of these motifs—a battle and an act of creation—must now be contested,

---

4 Pp. 16-18. A brief allusion to the dragon (*tnn*) occurs at the end of the Baal-Mot cycle (in *KTU* 1.6.vi.51-53); since the myth appears to exhibit some form of seasonal correlation, Day suggests that its conclusion may have been associated with the close of the year. Then, presumably drawing on Mowinckel, he contends that, at this time, the impending New Year and hence "the battle with the dragon" would have been called to mind. He concludes that "since the creation of the world would naturally have been regarded as occurring at the time of the first New Year,... this provides evidence that the Canaanites may have associated creation with the conflict with the dragon". However, in the absence of a direct link between creation and either the New Year or *Chaoskampf* in Ugarit, this remains unconvincing: unless it can be assumed that there is an intrinsic connection between New Year and creation which exists independently of the putative chaos-creation connection or associated festal hypotheses (and this is doubtful), Day has merely presumed what he seeks to prove. His supporting assertion that "in any case,... the fact that the Old Testament so frequently uses the imagery of the divine conflict with the dragon and the sea in association with creation, when the imagery is Canaanite, leads one to expect that the Canaanites likewise connected the two themes" also risks circularity. This is especially so given that it is rare in the Old Testament for a clear allusion to creation to occur in proximity to the "chaos" motif; hence an intrinsic connection cannot be presumed even in Israel. Nevertheless, despite these difficulties, the resultant conclusion is crucial to Day's thesis.

5 Mowinckel virtually elevates this to the status of a methodological principle: see the discussion of the "comparative method" in Chapter 2.4 below.

6 In fact, the waters ordinarily appear in threatening guise only as a passive instrument effecting Yahweh's punishment, and never as a force opposed to him. Hence, rather than being inimical to the divine order, they are actively employed as a means of overcoming disorder—a point also made by Dennis McCarthy in his article "'Creation' Motifs in Ancient Hebrew Poetry" (*CBQ* 29 [1967] pp. 393-406, reprinted in B. W. Anderson, ed., *Creation in the Old Testament*, pp. 74-89). This is evident especially in the flood narratives, but also in arguably very early poetry, such as that of Ex. 15.

the former in every supposed instance, the latter, in the majority. Creation, I would suggest, is not the original or, indeed, the primary sphere of reference of the "chaos" imagery in the Hebrew Bible, and where the bringing of the cosmos into being does occur, it is not necessarily consequent upon Yahweh's action in relation to the waters.

It is therefore my intention to examine in turn each of the psalms which have conventionally been associated with "chaos", but without (at least in the first instance) having recourse to extra-biblical material,[7] or indeed attempting to seek a unifying theme, in order to allow the psalms' distinctive character to emerge. In this way, a picture of great diversity arises, where the oceans, deeps, rivers, dragons, Leviathan and Rahab may be appreciated as distinct entities, through which, alone or in different combinations, the psalms conjure up pictures of theophany, creation, exodus, conquest and death—a whole spectrum of human experience, individual, national or universal—yet all encompassed within the astonishing power of God.

It appears that at the root of all of these motifs is the prevailing Old Testament cosmology,[8] which was held in common with much of the ancient Near East. According to this, embraced within the created order were the waters of the primeval ocean, at present confined to their positions as the מַבּוּל above the firmament and תְּהוֹם beneath the earth. Evidently, there was an inherent potential for reversion, whereby the waters could once again engulf the earth. However, the biblical perception that the deeps were securely confined (swaddled,[9] kept behind bars and doors,[10] or the sand of the sea,[11] or commanded on the authority of the divine word "there shall your proud waves be stayed"[12]) is pervasive, for Yahweh is the Lord and Creator who is the guarantor of security and stability.[13] Moreover, it must be emphasised that, whilst Israel's apprehension of the universe, her cosmology, was largely determined by her chronological and geographical milieu, the understanding of the cosmogonic process attested by the Hebrew Bible was one which clearly distinguished her from her neighbours and contemporaries.

---

7 Implicit in the comparative method is the assumption that it may facilitate the discernment of what is not self-evident in the text itself; this can be as dangerous and misleading as it is potentially beneficial. It must be stressed that the occurrence of an image in two contexts cannot necessarily imply the same signification, as has often been supposed—or, indeed, the same level of significance. Hence, fascinating as any affinities may be, they cannot confidently be employed as a basis for interpretative judgments (especially when the Canaanite and Mesopotamian texts themselves are so imperfectly understood).

8 "Cosmology", the perception of the nature and structure of the universe, must here be distinguished from "cosmogony", the mythology attached to its formation.

9 Job 38:9.

10 Job 38:10.

11 Jer. 5:22; cf. Ps. 104:9 and perhaps 148:6.

12 Job 38:11.

13 Pss. 93; 46:2-4, cf. vv. 6-7.

For, I shall argue, nowhere in the Old Testament, still less the Psalter, is the sea manifested as a personal being, and nowhere does Yahweh engage in conflict with it. So great is his sovereign mastery over his creation, that sometimes he stirs up the sea so that its waves roar,[14] but elsewhere stills it;[15] he both "cleaves open springs and brooks and dries up everflowing streams".[16] So to the question, " Was thy wrath against the rivers, O Yahweh? Was thy anger against the rivers, or thy indignation against the sea?"[17] we must answer resoundingly with Habakkuk: no.[18] Rather, the anguish of the waters at the divine theophany is one in which they participate with the whole of creation,[19] just as elsewhere, they join in joyful praise of their maker.[20]

Nevertheless the potential threat of the cosmic deep to humanity and to life itself is especially evident when it is employed as a vivid image for the perils of death and Sheol, which is always ready to engulf the individual.[21] On a wider canvas, the imagery appears as a paradigm for endangered national stability or even for the fear of collective annihilation by the relentless onslaught of imperial expansionism.[22]

Fundamental to this study is the analysis and exegesis of the particular psalms which employ the imagery of "chaos". More broadly, the poetic material under discussion will be dealt with thematically, according to its

---

14 Isa. 51:15; Jer. 31:35.

15 Pss. 65:8; 89:10.

16 Ps. 74:15; cf. Ps. 114:8; Job 38:25-7.

17 Hab. 3:8.

18 The construction employed, אם ... הֲ, has been identified by M. Held as that of the "double rhetorical question" (*Eretz -Israel* 9 [1969] 71-79); it is essentially equivalent to a "rhetorical *Num?*" (BDB, p. 50, אם, 2.a.(*b*)(α)), to which "the answer *No* is usually expected" (BDB, p. 210, הֲ 1.d.). In fact, in every cited instance of this usage, not only here, but also in GK (p. 475 §150h; see also Gibson, *Davidson's Introductory Hebrew Grammar - Syntax*, p. 184 §153) the same oratorical force is evident; the repetition intrinsic to the disjunctive form serves solely for emphasis (GK p. 475 §150h) so that a combative or incredulous tone is often apparent (e.g., Gen. 37:8; Job 4:17; 8:2; Isa. 10:15). Hence, to interpret Hab. 3:8 affirmatively would impart an unparalleled nuance to the prophet's questions; it would, moreover, be inappropriate to the context (contra Roberts, p. 155, Watts, p. 149, and, implicitly, Eaton, *ZAW* 76, p. 161; cf. Albright, "The Psalm of Habakkuk", p. 11), since the verse directly follows a description of the affliction of the earth and nations at the divine epiphany (vv. 6-7; cf. vv. 12-13). In this respect the older commentators often have a sounder instinct; see, e.g., Stonehouse, p. 110.

19 Pss. 77:17-19; 114:3-7, in each instance, as a vivid portrayal of Yahweh's dramatic act of deliverance as manifested in the Exodus event; cf. 68:9-11; sometimes it is only the earth which trembles: Pss. 97:4-5; 99:1; 46:7; Am. 9:5.

20 Pss. 96:11; 98:7; 69:35.

21 Pss. 18:5; 32:6; 69:2-3, 15-16; 88:7-8, 17-18; 124:4-5; at times this seems to merge with the depiction of a human enemy, Pss. 18:17-18; 144:7.

22 Pss. 65:8; 46:3-7.

context and sphere of reference.[23] Sometimes a motif adheres to a particular genre—for example, praise of God's work in creation generally occurs in hymns,[24] depictions of Sheol as "the regions dark and deep"[25] in individual (or royal) laments or songs of thanksgiving—but the primary focus of enquiry will remain the consideration of its immediate rhetorical force.

Inevitably where a complex web of interrelated motifs emerges, there arises the task of determining their precise relation, whether on a literary, theological or chronological level. Literary relations are of course most evident in the case where there is a clear allusive or dependent relationship with other material in the collection (as in Ps. 18:3, 10-18 and Ps. 144:1-2, 5-7; Ps. 29:1-2 and Ps. 96:7-9) or in the broader Old Testament corpus (for example, Ps. 18 recurs in 2 Sam. 22; and Ps. 96 in 1 Chr. 16:23-33; there are also repeated references to the Exodus and Creation traditions, which may profitably be compared with extra-psalmic, often pentateuchal, allusions). The prime theological concerns when dealing with such diverse spheres of reference are: to decipher the significance of the various poetic images embedded in these passages; to attempt to discern some form of coherent relation between them; and to document the evidence for traces of conceptual development within the material. However, both of these exercises, the literary and the theological, look beyond themselves to the more complex and perhaps less certain issue of chronology. Admittedly, the effort to date particular psalms is notoriously difficult, and is fraught with potential pitfalls; nevertheless, it may be possible, with care, to discern certain chronological relations between them.[26] Hence, the present study may be thought of as being conducted in two primary dimensions, the conceptual and the developmental.

As a result, the whole interpretative task may profitably be framed along the twin axes of synchrony and diachrony. This antithesis was originally proposed by Saussure in the field of linguistics, synchrony being concerned with the study of the interrelation of terms within a self-contained, temporally-specific language-system. Diachrony, in practice, then refers to the examination of constituent elements as they are transformed and substituted over time. On the analogy of a chess game, "The value of the chess pieces depends on their position upon the chess board, just as in the language each term has its value through its contrast with all the other terms" (synchrony); on the other hand,

---

23 Thus, emphasis will be put on the wider units within which the "chaos" imagery features, and on the contribution of this type of language to the meaning of each psalm. This approach is to be distinguished from that adopted, e.g., by Wakeman (*God's Battle with the Monster*, 1973) or Day (*God's Conflict*), who tend to place the primary focus on the immediate section under consideration, at the risk of failing to take full account of its broader context. To proceed to conduct comparisons with other Old Testament and Ugaritic segments, on the assumption that they constitute allusions to or fragments from an independent but shared mythology of which only these traces remain, runs the risk of presupposing a certain type of result even before the analysis has commenced.

24 E.g., Pss 95:4-5; 104; 148:5-6; 33:6-9.

25 Ps. 88:7.

26 This issue will be considered in more detail in Chapter 3 below.

"the system is only ever a temporary one. It varies from one position to the next" (diachrony).[27]

Obviously, these respective methods are applied to biblical exegesis only in a transferred sense,[28] and consequently, there has been some inconsistency in their use. In relation to the present monograph, synchrony may be understood in three ways. Each is a legitimate approach, but their respective aims, presuppositions and limitations must be carefully distinguished. Firstly, the self-contained system may be provided by the individual psalm, and the interrelated terms which are to be analysed, by its content, as constituted by its vocabulary, theology, themes or motifs. The crucial factor in this type of interpretation as employed here is that it deliberately focuses on the time of composition.[29] As stated—perhaps overstated—by Saussure, the scholar "can enter into the state of mind of the language user only by suppressing the past. The intervention of history can only distort his judgment".[30] On the analogy of the chess game, "any given state of the board is totally independent of any previous state of the board. It does not matter at all whether the state in question has been reached by one sequence of moves or another sequence".[31] When applied to the study of "chaos" in the Psalter, it suggests a self-consciously limited and discrete exercise, entailing the exegesis of the psalm as a self-contained entity, irrespective of its literary development or relation to other texts; more importantly, issues of etymology and history of religions, and perhaps even its putative cultic background, are specifically excluded. This is

---

27 Ferdinand de Saussure, *Cours de Linguistique Générale*, ed. Charles Bally, Albert Sechehaye, with the collaboration of Albert Riedlinger (Paris: Payot, 1922), pp. 125-6.

28 Their employment in the sphere of Old Testament exegesis formed the substance of the discussion at the ninth joint meeting of het Oudtestamentisch Werkgeselschap in Nederland en Belgie and the Society for Old Testament Study held at Kampen in 1994. See J. C. de Moor (ed.), *Synchronic or Diachronic: A Debate on Method in Old Testament Exegesis* (Leiden: E. J. Brill, 1995).

29 As such, the communal aspect of discourse, involving both a speaker or author and his implied audience, may be kept in view, although the former (insofar as his rôle may be distinguished) is perhaps set in the foreground. Nevertheless, it may be observed in passing that an alternative perspective, placing the emphasis instead on the text's recipients, the readers, is also sometimes adopted by scholars. However, this may effectively distract attention away from the temporally-specific language-system employed by the original poet or narrator; it also requires further clarification, with regard to the audience's identity and context, and indeed, to the purpose of study. This point is illustrated by the fact that, e.g., for E. Talstra (*Solomon's Prayer*, pp. 20, 83), the "reader" is envisaged as a modern critical scholar engaging in a detailed literary-stylistic enquiry, whereas for E. J. van Wolde, the focus is placed on the "reader community" which was the recipient of the final (Masoretic) phase of the text (de Moor [ed.], pp. 227-244).

30 *Cours*, p.117. Thus, the genuine synchronic task, as focusing on the language-users as operating within a concrete period of time, is, paradoxically, strongly historical in nature, a point emphasised by J. Barr (in J. C. de Moor [ed.], pp. 1-14).

31 *Cours*, p. 126.

not to deny the value of such investigations in themselves; nevertheless, it is important that clarity be maintained between the various methods and their potential results. The necessity of differentiating between the prehistory of a text or motif and what it actually signifies is one which in relation to "chaos" themes is particularly in need of reaffirmation.

Secondly, and closer to Saussure's original intention, is the effort to take as a unit of comparison the literature of a particular period. This is a more exciting, but risky, enterprise—and one which transgresses, in practice, onto the diachronic. On a theoretical level, a language-state exists "synchronically", at a particular point in time; Saussure conceded that in practice, one should rather speak of "a period of time of varying length, during which the sum total of changes occurring is minimal";[32] but in relation to the psalms, dating efforts are usually tentative and often imply a possible range of two or three centuries. However, this is not to invalidate this particular application of the synchronic method. Linguistics is a subject area requiring a high degree of precision and attention to detail;[33] by contrast, our knowledge of the Hebrew language, culture, theology and cult is by its nature uncertain, approximate and subjective. The failure to date individual psalm texts accurately is symptomatic of the provisional nature of much of Old Testament study. Therefore, the effort to undertake a comparison of texts which seem, within the limitations of present research, to be contemporary, reflects this general feature of biblical studies. So long as the tentative nature of the results is acknowledged, some valuable insights may thereby be gained.

However, in some instances, it may be impossible to offer any conclusions regarding the dating of certain compositions. This is particularly the case, for example, in the individual lament or thanksgiving psalms employing the imagery of Sheol,[34] where a very closely related cluster of ideas occurs, often couched in stock phrases without any evidence of direct literary dependence.[35] The same difficulties also often pertain to the dating of hymnic praise of creation, albeit moderated by the circumstance that, on occasion, comparison of certain concepts or modes of expression may be drawn with texts outside the Psalter. Nevertheless, where it is impossible to discern different chronological strata within a particular genre, it may be beneficial to assume a third type of synchrony, a theoretical synchrony. Here, the intention is to adopt this approach as a conscious interpretative strategy, rather than as a judgment upon the

32 *Cours*, p. 142.

33 The biblical scholar should perhaps take comfort from the fact that even in this sphere, Saussure envisaged a span of "ten years, a generation, a century, or even longer" as the practical equivalent of the synchronous state (*Cours*, p. 142).

34 E.g., Pss. 42-3, 69, 88, and the "royal" psalms 18 and 144.

35 Rather, these psalms seem to be the product of a drawing from a rich and deep reservoir of tradition, from which individual strands cannot readily be distinguished. There is no discernible theological or thematic development between them; moreover, diachronic analysis is almost impossible in the case of psalms of the individual, where reflections of historical circumstance and indications of conceptual advance (a rather dubious basis for dating anyway) are particularly sparse.

diachronic task.[36] Thus, it may be valuable from a literary and theological perspective to compare instances of a certain group of "chaos" motifs (e.g., those relating to the underworld) or of their occurrence in a particular genre (here, usually individual lament and thanksgiving psalms), whilst remaining genuinely or heuristically agnostic regarding their date. This agnosticism may be justified on a methodological level, for example, by the impossibility of undertaking effective dating or source analysis of the Psalter, or by the existence of Masoretic Hebrew as a unique linguistic product from which earlier stages may never fully be abstracted.[37] However, the vital motivation for employing this type of analysis is that it may yield useful insights into the text itself, as long as the presuppositions of the method are recognised.

In the course of the present study, the first "synchronic" approach, centred on the individual psalm as a freestanding entity, may be applied in all instances; where possible, the broader synchronic task of comparing contemporary uses, will be employed; where this is impossible, it may be profitable to assume a theoretical synchrony, in order to implement an effective theological and thematic analysis of the core motifs.[38] It is to be noted that each of these methods is distinct, despite some possible overlap between them; moreover, their employment should not imply a denial of the literary, preliterary and contextual development which may underlie or be reflected in each of these psalms (though it may be indicative of a certain reluctance to assume that much may meaningfully be discerned of this history).[39]

Turning then to the diachronic task, this is more explicitly concerned with issues of chronology than the synchronic. It may be expected on an abstract level that this has to do with the evolution of systems over time; but, as already stated, as employed by Saussure, it was concerned merely with the succession

---

36 The term is fairly commonly applied in this manner: see, e.g., D. J. A. Clines, who argues that the Pentateuch should be regarded as a unity—"not in origin, but in its final shape" (*The Theme of the Pentateuch*, p. 5); and Polzin, who adopts a similar attitude towards the Deuteronomic History (*Moses*, p. 18); see also Talstra, *Solomon's Prayer*, p. 9; Kessler, "A Methodological Setting for Rhetorical Criticism", p. 16 n. 16; Clines and Exum, "The New Literary Criticism", p. 16.

37 On this, see E. Ullendorff, "Is Biblical Hebrew a Language?" in his volume of the same name, pp. 3-17.

38 It must be acknowledged that, on a more basic level, the same sort of theoretical synchrony is necessarily entailed in the treatment even of the individual psalm. Each composition may be the product of a long period of development and modification, the contours of which in most cases can no longer be discerned. Hence any employment of the term is necessarily qualified.

39 Contrast E. Talstra's effort to evaluate the limited section of material comprised by 1 Kings 8:14-61 (*Solomon's Prayer*, Kampen, 1987) both synchronically (as a completed composition) and diachronically (attempting to discern its underlying sources and redactional history); he adopts a similar approach in his article, "Deuteronomy 9 and 10: Synchronic and Diachronic Observations" (in de Moor [ed.], pp. 187-210). In this context, Kessler's virtual identification of diachronic analysis with source criticism ("A Methodological Setting for Rhetorical Criticism", p. 16, n. 17) may be noted.

of individual terms within the larger linguistic framework. The emphasis was placed on the process or events bringing about change, rather than on the examination of the resultant synchronic states. This limitation was, however, in many respects historically determined, since it was Saussure's intention to inaugurate and affirm the synchronic method over against its antithesis, as represented by traditional developmental linguistics.[40] Only once his systemic approach is accepted (and indeed recognised not to be inimical to the comparative task) does it become possible for the old dialectical opposition to find its synthesis in a thoroughgoing diachronic method, which builds both upon synchronic insights and linear diachrony. As with the putative synchronic state, there is a discontinuity between diachronic transformation as a philosophical construct and as an historical reality, since, in practice, linguistic (or textual, or theological, etc.) development is a gradual, irregular and multifaceted process. At best, one may seek only to capture snapshots, stills from a picture which is in fact always in continual motion.

Within the Psalter, temporally distinct material may be constituted either by individual compositions or by synchronic groupings of psalms. Specific elements which comprise the basis for comparison may be constituted by the content of this literature—its vocabulary, theology and motifs—or perhaps (adopting a more "static" perspective) by their mode of employment in the individual poetic unit. In practice, however, it is unwise to draw too close a distinction between the two, since the examination of a poem and of its content cannot readily be separated.

As is the case with synchronic analysis (at least as presented by Saussure himself), issues of dating are of crucial importance, and here indeed assume even greater prominence. A little has already been said about the limitations of the diachronic enterprise with respect to certain conceptual spheres and genres. Nevertheless, this type of analysis may profitably be attempted, with greater or lesser degrees of benefit and accuracy, with much of the material. Although psalms which may be dated with confidence to a specific period are very much the exception (Ps. 137 being perhaps the best example),[41] nevertheless, evidence may be gleaned in a variety of ways. Whilst no single factor may be decisive, often a cumulative case may be made with relative certainty. Such data may be stylistic or linguistic, such as the identification of archaic language (or deliberate archaisms) or, in the later period, of Persian or even Greek influence. Alternatively, if an affinity with certain strands of pentateuchal tradition, most typically regarding the creation or exodus, is identified, then this may perhaps be suggestive of a particular era of emergence, or it may at least facilitate the exclusion of another time of composition.[42] Likewise, sometimes "wisdom

40 It must be noted that for Saussure the two "are not of equal importance ... the synchronic view takes precedence over the diachronic, since for the community of language users that is the one and only reality" (p. 128).

41 The internal evidence points strongly to a *terminus a quo* of 587 B.C., and further, an exilic provenance seems to be implied.

42 Wellhausen's documentary hypothesis has been subject to increasing criticism in recent decades, being rejected, e.g., by R. Rendtorff, *Das überlieferungsgeschichtliche Problem*

influence" or, in the case of the divine kingship psalms, affinities with Deutero-Isaiah (though how this is to be interpreted is, of course, itself a matter for debate) may be identified, and again serve as a broad indicator of origin, especially in combination with other factors. Obviously, this method must be employed with caution, as the existence, and particularly the direction, of such dependence may prove difficult to demonstrate; nevertheless, if utilised with an awareness of its limitations, it may prove helpful.

Rather less certain, but sometimes beneficial if used cautiously, is the identification of ideas or motifs which are generally thought to be theologically or conceptually characteristic of certain times. This primarily applies as a rough indicator relating to either extreme of the chronological spectrum, on the axis "probably early / probably late". Obviously, this method carries with it the inherent risk of circularity; yet, when restricted to certain key concepts about which there is at least a degree of consensus,[43] it may be a useful tool, especially when used in conjunction with other methods. It is on this basis, for example, that the judgment is made that Ps. 29, which simply evokes Yahweh's manifestation in a storm theophany, is very early—an assessment which is reinforced by an observation of its stylistically archaic features, such as the threefold cumulative parallelism,[44] and by its conceptual (and, again, stylistic) affinities with Ugaritic Baal-hymns. Conversely, universalist or didactic concerns are often perceived to be "late": typical of the former is the call to all creation to praise Yahweh in Pss. 69:35; 148; 96:11-13 and 98:4-9; cf. Ps. 150:6. Perhaps indicative of the latter are the "moralising" tendencies of Pss. 32, 78 and 124. However, it cannot be overemphasised how easily such arguments slip into "circularity".

Of course, the most attractive (and elusive) type of evidence, is that of historical allusion to contemporary (or very recent) events. There are many psalms which refer back to the sacred traditions of the *Heilsgeschichte*, but terminate their recollections perhaps with the conquest or the entry into the land, or restrict historical reminiscences to a particular event such as the exodus. In either case, such narratives are in no way complete histories continuing up to the present day, but are confined to exempla, perhaps of Yahweh's חֶסֶד or Israel's faithlessness. As such, indications of provenance are once again circumstantial, relying on affinities to particular pentateuchal sources or on authorial perspective as an indication of the context of composition. For example, a very negative outlook focusing penitentially on Israel's sin, would be consonant with, though not necessarily indicative of, an exilic provenance, if

---

des Pentateuch (BZAW 17; Berlin: W. de Gruyter, 1977). However, it has been defended more recently by E. W. Nicholson, *The Pentateuch in the Twentieth Century: The Legacy of Julius Wellhausen* (Oxford: Clarendon, 1998), and it will be followed here, since it probably remains the best solution in a climate where no other proffered solution has yet been able to attract widespread support.

43 Preferably unconnected to the main theme which is the subject of the supposed developmental analysis.

44 Designated by Albright (e.g., "The Psalm of Habakkuk" p. 3) as "climactic" or "repetitive", and by W. G. E. Watson (p. 150) as "staircase" parallelism.

this was already inferred on independent grounds. Likewise, there may be a hint that God's promises would come to an end in the event of Israel's apostasy, or a possible eschatologising of her future hopes, which again, in conjunction with other factors, could assist in determining certain parameters within which to frame the dating discussion.

Potential or perceived sources of contemporary information are manifold, but unfortunately most prove on further examination to be ambiguous or elusive. It is here that the psalms' long history of development and adaptation becomes most evident, where sometimes even seemingly contradictory statements are piled together in a manner which is suggestive of so many situations—and none. This is particularly the case with individual lament psalms, where the petitioner seems both to be assaulted by his enemies on all sides and to be in prison, to suffer sickness and emotional exhaustion, and yet also to be accused. Even communal psalms having as their focus some form of national defeat or disaster, are perhaps not always entirely exempt from this phenomenon. For example, Ps. 89 seems to concern the end of the Davidic line[45]—yet also contains the words of the king.[46] This flexibility, which is of such virtue in hymnology and liturgy, is a source of frustration to the historian, but also a salient reminder of the limitations of his enterprise.

Thus, the dating of the psalms is often a limited and tentative exercise.[47] However, where conclusions concerning their origin may reasonably be made, the synchronic and diachronic analysis which consequently becomes possible promises to yield interesting results regarding the development and significance of the themes of "chaos" employed in the Psalter. For it is only when the psalms are viewed in the richness of their theological and historical interrelations that an appropriately balanced and nuanced appreciation of their diverse images may emerge. Hence, once the complex web of "chaos" motifs has been disentangled and its constituent elements set in thematic and (where possible) chronological relation, a twofold task remains. The first is to test the findings made in respect of the Psalter against the wider literature of the Hebrew Bible to assess whether the same conclusions may be made concerning the putative occurrences of the *Chaoskampf* theme found there. This will accordingly comprise the substance of the final chapter. If a consistent picture is obtained, this will, second, have important ramifications for the understanding of the history of the religion of Israel, not least as regards its relation to the wider ancient Near Eastern, and especially Canaanite, environment, and this will be considered in the Conclusion which follows.

---

45 Vv. 39-46, especially vv. 39-40, 45-6.

46 V. 51.

47 Incidentally, it should be acknowledged that within this monograph, attempts at placing psalmic material chronologically largely depend on an historical rather than a mythological or cultic approach, i.e. on the assumption that where the text refers, for example, to the despoliation of a city or desecration of the temple, in the absence of indications to the contrary, this is normally to be taken as alluding to an actual rather than a mythological or cultic event, albeit possibly poetically enhanced.

II. The Theme of "Chaos" in the Psalter: The State of the Question

The view that various passages in the Psalter reflect the idea of a divine combat with chaos resulting in creation is originally to be associated with Hermann Gunkel and his book *Schöpfung und Chaos in Urzeit und Endzeit*.[1] During the last century, there have been many more recent exponents, and a number of Gunkel's specific conclusions have been modified or challenged. As a result of the Ras Shamra discoveries in the 1930s, it is now also generally held that the more immediate background of the so-called "chaos" imagery is Canaanite, rather than Babylonian, as Gunkel had thought.[2] Another important innovation is Mowinckel's "enthronement hypothesis" (following Volz[3]), which placed the celebration of Yahweh's victory over chaos in the context of a New Year festival.[4] Nevertheless, the basic parameters of the present discussion are still framed—one might say "constrained"—by the conceptual framework laid out in the nineteenth century. The essential elements of chaos, creation and combat—and the comparative method on which they rest—all remain essentially intact, with only the creation-connection seriously being called into question.

However, if each of these four elements (that is, chaos, creation, combat, and the comparative method) are examined in turn, it appears that they may all prove to some degree deficient or inappropriate. It is therefore the purpose of the present chapter to highlight those aspects of previous research which point towards the need for a reassessment of the theme of "chaos" as currently perceived, and especially as it impinges on each of these four areas.[5] The cultic approach advanced by Mowinckel will then be examined in a further section.

---

1 Göttingen: Vandenhoeck & Ruprecht, 1895.

2 See, e.g., John Day, *God's Conflict with the Dragon and the Sea* (Cambridge: CUP, 1985) and Carola Kloos, *Yhwh's Combat with the Sea* (Amsterdam: G. A. van Oorschot; Leiden: E. J. Brill, 1986).

3 *Das Neujahrsfest Jahwes* (Tübingen: J. C. B. Mohr, 1912).

4 S. Mowinckel, *The Psalms in Israel's Worship*, 2 vols. (Oxford: Blackwell, 1962; revised and translated from *Offersang og Sangoffer*; Oslo: Aschehoug, 1951); *Psalmenstudien*, 6 vols. (Oslo: J. Dybwad, 1921-4), especially vol. 2 (1922), which is devoted to "Das Thronbesteigungsfest und der Ursprung der Eschatologie".

5 A more general summary of the results of psalms study to date is available in R. E. Clements, *A Century of Old Testament Study* (Guildford: Lutterworth Press, revised edition 1983), ch. 5, pp. 95-121, and in the briefer but more recent account of J. H. Hayes in S. L. McKenzie and M. P. Graham (edd.), *The Hebrew Bible Today: An*

1. "Chaos"

The term "chaos" derives from Greek cosmology, in which context it pertains to a world-view quite distinct from the Hebrew. From here, it entered the current of Western philosophy and literature from which Gunkel drew. However, the Old Testament itself lacks any overarching designation for the entities (dragons, the sea) classified by Gunkel as "chaotic", or any corresponding philosophical conception, so it thus seems to represent a superimposition from one matrix onto another.

The difficulty is compounded by the fact that both Greek and modern European definitions (which, of course, are anyway derivative upon the Greek) are very wide-ranging and inconsistent. Moreover, in most cases where the term is employed, no definition is offered at all. This situation is exemplified by the *Interpreter's Dictionary of the Bible*.[6] In Volume 1, T. H. Gaster states that it "must... be understood in the original Greek sense of 'void, empty space' (χαος), rather than as a synonym of 'confusion'".[7] Yet, in the Supplementary Volume, M. K. Wakeman begins her definition, "Chaos is a state of utter confusion...".[8]

At root, the Greek χαος seems to denote a "gaping void"[9] or "yawning abyss".[10] However, the most influential classical use of the term is by the Latin writer Ovid,[11] who describes the state of things before creation as follows:

> Before there was any earth or sea, before the canopy of heaven stretched overhead, Nature presented the same aspect the world over, to which men have given the name of chaos. This was a shapeless uncoordinated mass (*rudis indigestaque moles*), nothing but a weight of lifeless matter, whose ill-assorted elements were indiscriminately heaped together in one place.... Although the elements of land and air and sea were there, the earth had no firmness, the water no fluidity, there was no brightness in the sky. Nothing had any lasting shape, but everything got in the way of everything else; for, within that one body, cold warred with hot, moist with dry, soft with hard, and light with heavy.
>
> This strife was finally resolved by a god, a natural force of a higher kind, who separated the earth from heaven, and the waters from the

Introduction to Critical Issues (Louisville, KY: Westminster John Knox, 1998), pp. 153-166.

6 Ed. G. A. Buttrick et al. (Nashville, TN: Abingdon, 1962).

7 Vol. 1, p. 552.

8 *Supplementary Volume* (1976), p. 143.

9 H. J. Rose, "Chaos" in N. G. L. Hammond and H. H. Scullard (edd.), *Oxford Classical Dictionary* (Oxford: Clarendon Press, 2nd edition 1970), p. 226.

10 H. G. Liddell and R. Scott, *A Greek-English Lexicon* (Oxford: Clarendon Press, 8th edition 1897), p.1713; √χα; see Hesiod, *Theogony*, l. 116; Plato, *Symposium*, 178B, *Axiochus* 371 E; Aristotle, *Physics*, 4.1,7; Ibycus 26; Aristophanes, *Nubes* 424, 627, *Aves* 192, 693 sq.; LXX Mic. 1:6; Zech. 14:4; Oppianus C. 3.414.

11 43 B.C.—17 A.D., probably displaying the influence of Anaxagoras.

> earth, and set the clear air apart from the cloudy atmosphere. When he had freed these elements, sorting them out from the heap where they had lain, indistinguishable from one another, he bound them fast, each in its separate place, forming a harmonious union.... In this way the god, whichever of the gods it was, set the chaotic mass in order, and, after dividing it up, arranged it in its constituent parts.[12]

So, according to this view, it is the formless mass of confused and warring matter from which the earth was finally formed. The general similarity with the biblical creation account is an attractive one and for commentators well versed in classical literature, as most have been from Patristic through almost to modern times, the resonances were such that it was almost *de rigeur* to bring the idea of "chaos" to bear upon the discussion of Gen. 1:2.

Besides the Fathers,[13] the term occurs in Luther[14] and Calvin,[15] and in fact, many commentators (e.g., Delitzsch in 1852,[16] Bishop Colenso in 1863[17]) actually recast the Genesis account using the words of Ovid—*rudis indigestaque moles*.[18] It is as if the fact of the later convergence of Greek and Hebrew strains of thought in the corpus of formative texts underlying Western philosophy has overridden any consideration of their temporally, geographically and culturally diverse origins.

However, just as common as the assumption of parity is the denial that Gen. 1:2 conveys the notion of "chaos". This is especially characteristic of the Fathers (e.g., Hippolytus[19] or Clement[20]), but it also features amongst post-enlightenment writers. Herder, for example, stated that:

---

12 Ovid, *Metamorphoses*, 1:5ff.; translation from Mary M. Innes (trans.), *The Metamorphoses of Ovid* (Harmondsworth, Middx.: Penguin, 1955), pp. 29-30. This description of primordial chaos is not unlike that outlined in Plato's *Timaeus* 53 (fourth century B.C.), where, however, the term χαος is not actually employed; see also Lucian *Amores* 32.

13 See, e.g., "Genesis. (Authorship Uncertain)", ll. 1-5 in A. Roberts and J. Donaldson (edd.) *The Writings of Tertullian, Vol. III. with the Extant Works of Victorinus and Commodianus* (Ante-Nicene Christian Library, Vol. XVIII; Edinburgh: T. & T. Clark, 1870), p. 293; this fragment has been variously attributed to Tertullian, Cyprian and Salvian of Marseilles (*ibid.*, pp. xviii-xix).

14 J. Pelikan, *Luther's Works, Volume 1. Lectures on Genesis Chapters 1-5* (Saint Louis, MO: Concordia, 1958), p. 6.

15 J. Calvin, *Commentaries on the First Book of Moses Called Genesis*, I (Edinburgh: Calvin Translation Society, 1847), pp. 69-70; so also p. 74. Calvin's original edition was published in 1554.

16 *Die Genesis ausgelegt*, pp. 55-56.

17 J. W. Colenso, *The Pentateuch and Book of Joshua Critically Examined*, Part IV, pp. 96-97.

18 T. Fenton has traced the application of the phrase to Genesis 1:2 back to Johann Reuchlin, *de rudimentis Hebraicis*, 1506 (private communication).

19 "Refutation of all Heresies" Ch. 23 in J. H. Macmahon and S. D. F. Salmond (trans.) *The Writings of Hippolytus*, Vol. 1 (Ante-Nicene Christian Library, Vol. VI; Edinburgh: T. & T. Clark, 1868). See also Methodius, "Extracts from the Work on

[The Hebrews] know nothing for example of a chaos... a fiction, for which we are indebted to the Greeks.[21]

An indication of the difficulty of applying the concept to the Hebrew Bible occurs as early as Wellhausen. He repeatedly uses the term "chaos" in relation to Gen. 1, and then suddenly breaks off and remarks, "The notion of chaos is that of uncreated matter; here we find the remarkable idea that it is created in the beginning by God".[22] This he attributes to a conflict between the "religious spirit" with which the narrative is permeated, and the "nature of its materials"[23]—not to any impropriety in the attribution of this term to the creation account of Gen. 1 itself.

Later, it was a natural development for the earliest discussions of the parallels between the Babylonian *Enuma elish* and the Priestly account of Creation to incorporate the same terminology. Significantly, George Smith, who was responsible for the initial publication of the newly-discovered cuneiform tablets, was absolutely clear on this subject, as indeed the title of his work, *The Chaldean Account of Genesis*, indicates:

In the creation tablet the first existence is called Mummu Tiamatu, a name meaning the "sea-water" or "sea chaos"... It is evident that, according to the notion of the Babylonians, the sea was the origin of all things, and this also agrees with the statement of Genesis, I.2. where the chaotic waters are called תהום, 'the deep'.[24]

When Gunkel entitled his book *Schöpfung und Chaos*, he was therefore drawing on a long tradition of biblical interpretation of Gen. 1, as well as on

---

Things Created" (Photius: *Bibliotheca*, cod. 235; in A. Roberts and J. Donaldson [edd.] *The Writings of Methodius, Alexander of Lycopolis, Peter of Alexandria, and Several Fragments* [Vol. XIV; 1869], p. 179).

20 Clement of Alexandria, "The Miscellanies" Book V, ch. XIV, "'Greek Plagiarisms from the Hebrews" in W. Wilson (trans.) *The Writings of Clement of Alexandria*, II (Ante-Nicene Christian Library, XII; Edinburgh: T. & T. Clark, 1869), p. 274; cf. p. 276.

21 *Vom Geist der Ebräischen Poesie* Vol. 1 (Leipzig: Johann Ambrosius Barth, 1825), pp. 59-60.

22 *Prolegomena zur Geschichte Israels* (Berlin: Georg Reimer, 3rd. ed. 1886), pp. 310-311. The same sentiment is encountered also in A. Arnold, *Genesis*, 2nd edition, 1871, p. 13.

23 *Ibid.*, p. 310.

24 George Smith, *The Chaldean Account of Genesis* (London: Sampson, Low, Marston, Searle, & Rivington, 4th ed., 1876), pp. 64-65. The results of his research became available in a German edition later the same year (*George Smith's Chaldäische Genesis. Autorisierte Übers. von H. Delitzsch, nebst Erläuterungen von F. Delitzsch* [Leipzig, 1876]), and a comparable interpretation of *Enuma elish* shortly afterwards appeared in Schrader's *Die Keilinschriften und das Alte Testament*. (Schrader had already discerned the idea of a pre-existent chaos in the biblical Primæval History in 1863, in *Studien zur Kritik und Erklärung der Biblischen Urgeschichte: Gen. Cap. I-XI*, pp. 42-43.)

more immediate scholarly debate regarding its relation to *Enuma elish*. The presence of "chaos" in the Priestly creation account had for centuries variously been assumed, denied, or even reformulated—but seldom ignored. Gunkel's major innovation, however, was to derive the added ingredient of "combat" from Babylonian mythology, where there appeared to be a causal connection between a divine combat and the emergence of the created order from the "chaotic" sea or sea-monster. From this, he transposed the chaos-creation pattern onto biblical allusions which apparently also concerned such a combat. Once *Enuma elish* (with its themes of chaos-conflict-creation) and Genesis 1 (exhibiting the first and last of these) had been identified as widely separated instances of the same fundamental tradition, the motif of chaos was then immeasurably broadened by Gunkel to encompass all those intervening stages of transmission in which any combination of the same themes was exhibited. "Chaos" thus came to denote not merely the formless matter from which the cosmos was shaped, but specifically the sea, or a sea-monster, the opponent of God.[25] Thus the use of the idea of chaos actually came to involve a web of other related ideas, and ultimately a recognisable narrative sequence.

However, it is not only Gunkel's broader definition of "chaos", but even the original application of the term to the exegesis of Gen. 1:2—and especially to the description of the primæval earth as תֹהוּ וָבֹהוּ (rendered by the RSV as "without form and void")—which may be called into question. בֹּהוּ, which only appears in conjunction with תֹּהוּ, seems to denote "emptiness"; apart from Gen. 1:2, it is employed as a figure of the desolation following Yahweh's judgment (Jer. 4:23; Isa. 34:11). The root meaning of תֹּהוּ itself is uncertain, but it is commonly rendered by the versions as κενον, οὐδεν, ματαιον, *inane*, *vacuum*, *vanum*, all of which likewise seem to have the basic sense of "emptiness", whether literal or metaphorical, connoting vanity or worthlessness. When used literally, it often refers to the empty, uninhabited space of the wilderness (Deut. 32:10; Job 6:18; 12:24 = Ps. 107:40), or, similarly, to the desolation following Yahweh's judgment, as a result of which the ruined city will revert to its natural state (Jer. 4:23, Isa. 34:11, 24:10; cf. 45:18); however, the meaning of "emptiness, nothing" is particularly evident in Job 26:7. Thus, Westermann is probably right when he states, "תהו... is not a mythical idea but means desert, waste, devastation, nothingness.... And when תהו and בהו occur together there is no real difference in meaning".[26] Therefore any attempt to translate this vocabulary in terms of "chaos" would certainly require careful definition, and is best avoided.[27]

---

25 In fact, even the idea of creation as a "struggle" (specifically, with "the might of evil"; Delitzsch, *Die Genesis*, 1852, on Gen. 3, p. 117) was not entirely new to Christian hermeneutics. According to the "restitution hypothesis", which was advocated by Delitzsch in his 1852 commentary (pp. 116-118), but rejected in the 1887 revision (p. 52), the world reverted to chaos as a consequence of the fall of the angels, but was then restored as a new creation on the sixth day.

26 *Genesis*, I, p. 143.

27 The interpretation of Gen. 1:2 in terms of "absence" in specific contradiction to the notion of "chaos" has been urged by T. Fenton, ("Chaos in the Bible? Tohu vavohu" in

Further, if Ovid's mode of employment of the term is to be understood where "chaos" is predicated of Gen. 1:2—and this seems to be the general intention, even where it is not stated as explicitly as by Colenso and Delitzsch—this cosmological sense must be accompanied by a number of cautionary statements. Firstly, this particular application of the term *chaos* (here in its Latin form) is not the most common or obvious one, even in Classical literature. Therefore, if it is to be applied to the Old Testament, it cannot be employed without clear indications to the effect that this is the definition intended.

Secondly, this view of "chaos" is intrinsically bound up with creation: it has no place apart from primæval time. This was appropriate to the initial application of the concept to the cosmology of Gen. 1; however, when applied more broadly to the wider corpus of material considered by Gunkel and his successors, the intrinsic connection with creation has proved unnecessarily restrictive. Although a superficial analysis would suggest that this association suited Gunkel's portrayal, it is arguable that his cosmologically-bound interpretation actually rested on the *a priori* assumption that the presence of so-called "chaos" motifs fundamentally entailed a causal connection with creation, rather than *vice versa*.[28] In the course of the present monograph, it shall be shown that creation allusions comprise only a small proportion of the biblical "chaos" texts under consideration, and are in all likelihood confined to a fairly late period.

Thirdly, even the most fundamental supposed point of contact between the Latin and biblical texts under consideration—the idea of pre-existent, uncreated matter containing the ingredients necessary for creation—depends on a particular interpretation of Gen. 1:2,[29] entailing the reading of the verse as a description of the condition of the world prior to creation, rather than as a

---

G. Abramson and T. Parfitt [edd.], *Jewish Education and Learning: Published in Honour of Dr. David Patterson on the Occasion of his Seventieth Birthday* [London: Harwood Academic Publishers, 1993], 203-220), D. T. Tsumura, (*The Earth and the Waters in Genesis 1 and 2* [JSOT(S) 83; Sheffield, 1989], pp. 17-43, especially p. 43), and T. A. Perry ("A Poetics of Absence: The Structure and Meaning of Genesis 1.2", *JSOT* 58 [1993] 3-11); cf. R. Ouro, "The Earth of Genesis 1:2: Abiotic or Chaotic? Part 1" *Andrews University Seminary Studies* 35 (1998) 259-276, who also denies the presence of "chaos" in Gen. 1:2, though interpreting תֹהוּ וָבֹהוּ through the imagery of the desert: "uninhabited and unproductive" (p. 276).

28 A similar point is made also by Westermann, *Genesis*, I, p. 45.

29 For a fuller discussion of the issues involved, see W. Eichrodt, "In the Beginning: A Contribution to the Interpretation of the First Word of the Bible", in B. W. Anderson and W. Harrelson (edd.) *Essays in Honour of James Muilenberg* (New York: Harper & Brothers, 1962), pp. 1-11. The interpretation of the verse is further considered in I. Blythin, "A note on Genesis I 2" *VT* 12 (1962) 120-121; T. Perry, *JSOT* 58 (1993) 3-11; and R. Ouro, *Andrews University Seminary Studies* 35 (1998) 259-276.

portrayal of the state resulting from the first act in this process.[30] This evidently provided the most frequent source of tension in the application of "chaos" terminology to the Priestly cosmology prior to the publication of *Schöpfung und Chaos*. Gunkel himself seems to have embraced this approach, but only by maintaining that insofar as primordial chaos[31] contradicted the "Jewish concept of God as a 'freely-creating creator'"[32] it was indicative of the presence of ancient mythical material underlying the Priestly account. This he affirmed in conscious refutation of Wellhausen's assertion that the "chaos" must have been created by God. However, Gunkel's position is by no means universally accepted; nor may the notion of creation from pre-existent matter be applied in a thoroughgoing way to the account of Gen. 1 as a whole (e.g., to the acts of creation by divine fiat).

Finally, the "chaos" envisaged by Ovid (*rudis indigestaque moles*) is quite other than the understanding of הָאָרֶץ ... תֹהוּ וָבֹהוּ enunciated above as "emptiness, waste, nothingness". More importantly, if the discussion is broadened to encompass the mythical figures of Leviathan, tannîn, n^ehārôṯ, t^ehôm, etc., which writers since Gunkel have classified under this label, it becomes even more difficult to effect a reconciliation with Ovid's solid, immobile "chaos". The latter is a temporally limited, amorphous lump, containing all elements of creation, internally in turmoil, but exhibiting no aspects of personality, let alone opposition to the creator deity. By contrast, תְּהוֹם and related figures have personality attributed to them and may be identified or associated with the sea;[33] and as such they comprise only one element—and then a particularly vibrant one—of pre-existent matter, and persist in the present time in a confined form. They are also portrayed as having as their fundamental characteristic an opposition to the creator-deity, and indeed to creation itself. Moreover, instead of presenting themselves as a single mass, unsympathetic to ordering, the entities of chaos (תְּהוֹם, תַּנִּין, etc.) occur in a variety of identifiable forms, and revert to "chaotic" indistinction only in the hands of theological systematisers.

Thus the term "chaos" is unclear, inconsistently applied—and from the first, it was contested whether it accurately described the situation in Gen. 1.[34]

---

30 Moreover, the biblical record, unlike Graeco-Roman philosophy, displays no interest in the material from which the universe was formed; apart from this debatable and ancillary reference, it remains silent on the subject.

31 Understood as "Darkness and water at the beginning of the world" (*Schöpfung*, p. 7).

32 *Ibid*, p. 7.

33 Though among the Stoics, the "unformed matter" of chaos was conceived of as water (*School of Hesiod*; Plutarch 2.955 E).

34 The interpretation of Gen. 1:2 is still debated, the pre-existence of the primæval ocean being affirmed, e.g., by E. Speiser (*Genesis* [Anchor Bible Commentary; Garden City, New York: Doubleday, 1964], p. 9-13) and B. F. Batto (*Slaying the Dragon: Mythmaking in the Biblical Tradition* [Louisville, KY: Westminster John Knox, 1992] pp. 84, 213 n. 19), but denied, e.g., by A. Heidel (*The Babylonian Genesis*, 2nd ed. 1951, p. 129) and B. W. Anderson (*Creation versus Chaos* [Philadelphia, PA: Fortress, repr. 1987] p. 111). Perhaps more ironically, the term "chaos" is retained even by those

In fact, it seemed to enter the theological arena almost by default, and, more alarmingly, it formed an unrecognised part of the conceptual (or preconceptual) framework of the scholars seeking to understand the Hebrew text. Further, Gunkel and his successors have encompassed within the idea of "chaos" a number of images (Leviathan, תְּהוֹם, etc.) which have no obvious relevance to it in any attested form; even its relation to Gen. 1 depends on a very specific interpretation of that account's opening clauses.[35] Most importantly, the concept of "chaos" indelibly binds the biblical material considered under this banner to the theme of creation, so much so that it is often inferred that even where the motif of creation is not directly alluded to, it must somehow underlie any imagery associated with this idea. Thus, the application of the concept of "chaos" to the interpretation of biblical material often constrains, or effectively predetermines, the understanding of such passages.

2. Creation

Indissolubly connected to the motif of "chaos" is its counterpart, "creation". Despite the fact that one cannot speak of "chaos" in isolation from its antithesis, "cosmos", rather peculiarly, the propriety of interpreting "chaos allusions" in terms of creation has been challenged more often than the "chaos" terminology itself. Gunkel's assumption that the overcoming of chaos must necessarily result in creation has been questioned in relation to Babylonian, Ugaritic and biblical paradigms. For example, H. W. F. Saggs argues that "*Enuma Elish* is neither a paradigm for ancient Near Eastern creation myths, nor indeed early".[36] Rather, it represents a conflation of a number of earlier myths, with the purpose of glorifying Marduk (and, by extension, his city, Babylon) and claiming for him the attributes of his

---

who have denied the intrinsic connection between its constituent motifs and creation: see D. J. McCarthy, "'Creation' Motifs in Ancient Hebrew Poetry" in B. W. Anderson (ed.), *Creation in the Old Testament*, pp. 74-89; it is employed sparingly also by N. Forsyth (*The Old Enemy: Satan and the Combat Myth* [Princeton, NJ: Princeton University Press, 1987]).

35 Moreover, the possibility of inferring a "chaotic" notion of creation and primordial matter on the basis of a particular reading of the priestly narrative should be strenuously distinguished from the attribution of anything approaching this carefully formulated concept to its author. A helpful comparison may be provided by the Jewish and Christian insistence of the presence of the doctrine of *creatio ex nihilo* in these verses, which similarly owes more to postbiblical theological concerns (e.g., the controversies with Gnosticism) than to authorial intent.

36 *The Encounter with the Divine in Mesopotamia and Israel* (1978), p. 57. Compare similarly Lambert's assessment that "the *Epic of Creation* is not a norm of Babylonian or Sumerian cosmology. It is a sectarian and aberrant combination of mythological threads woven into an unparalleled compositum" ("A New Look at the Babylonian Background of Genesis" (*JTS* 16 n.s. [1965] 287-300, p. 291).

illustrious divine predecessors. Although motifs of theomachic combat[37] and of cosmic creation are elsewhere attested in Babylonian sources, there is no intrinsic connection between the two: creation frequently occurs by means other than *Chaoskampf*;[38] and battles between the gods do not necessarily result in creation. Besides, even in *Enuma elish*, these themes occupy a small proportion of the epic, and are of relatively ancillary concern.[39] Moreover, elsewhere in Babylonian sources, sea monsters are apparently envisaged as existing within historical time, and sometimes even as created beings rather than as adversaries of the gods.[40]

These findings are strongly supported by N. Forsyth's wide-ranging literary study, *The Old Enemy: Satan and the Combat Myth* (1987), in which he recounts a considerable number of ancient near Eastern myths in which combat comprises a major theme, but remains unconnected with creation. As a result, he repeatedly stresses the error of unthinkingly assuming this association must underlie every instance of a struggle between the gods, dismissing the whole issue as a "pseudo-problem".[41] This conclusion is further borne out by the Ugaritic tablets concerning the battles of Baal against Yam and Mot. Not only is it scarcely possible that Baal's (apparently consecutive) victories over these adversaries should in each instance result in creation (there are good reasons for believing that they are not simply variant versions of the same fundamental conflict)—in neither case is any act of creation described or even implied.[42] Moreover, there are numerous references

---

37 I.e., battles and strife among the gods.

38 See similarly Tsumura, *The Earth and the Waters in Genesis 1 and 2*, p. 49, and examples there. Westermann makes the further point that in the ancient Sumerian material, it appears that creation is never associated with a conflict, this connection being made for the first time in Babylon (*Genesis*, I, pp. 41-43). As a result, he states that it is "certain" that "the motif of the struggle with the dragon or with Chaos did not belong originally to the creation theme"(*Ibid*., p. 43).

39 See, e.g., Lambert, "Babylonien und Israel", *Theologische Realenzyklopädie* 5 (1980) pp. 71-2. Indeed, it is arguable that in *Enuma elish* Marduk is "superimpos[ed] ... as the creator upon a myth in which the world is already made by previous generations and divided into fresh and salt water" (Forsyth, p. 59).

40 Saggs cites I. Bernhardt and S. N. Kramer, "Enki und die Weltordnung", *Wissenschaftliche Zeitschrift der Friedrich-Schiller-Universität Jena* 9 (1959/60), 235, l. 184, in which "fifty monsters of the sea" are said to praise Ea, something which is in full accord with, e.g., Ps. 148:7— a passage regarded by Wakeman (following Cassuto, *Genesis*, pp. 49-51) as, like Gen. 1:21, "a deliberate effort to contradict the battle myth" (p. 78).

41 P. 92; see similarly Habel, *Yahweh versus Baal*, p. 65: "a dragon myth is not necessarily a creation myth".

42 Pertinent here is the opening statement of D. J. McCarthy's article, "'Creation' Motifs in Ancient Hebrew Poetry": "The Old Testament scholar should be surprised when he finds that Ugaritologists ordinarily deny that anything like a creation story has been found at Ras Shamra" (p. 74). The following examples may be cited: A. S. Kapelrud, "Creation in the Ras Shamra Texts", *StTh* 34 (1980) 1-11, p. 9; M. H. Pope, *El in the*

to El as cosmic creator[43] (including allusions in the Hebrew Bible[44]), but nowhere is this attribute claimed for Baal.[45] Ancillary details in each of these accounts also seem to presuppose the existence of the created order, insofar as they contain a number of allusions to humanity (*KTU* 1.6.ii.18; 1.6.v.24-5), animal life (1.1.iv.30-32; 1.6.i.18-29; cf. 1.2.iv.13-14, 15, 21, 24; 1.5.i.14-19;), and even ploughed fields (1.6.iv.1-3, 12-14) and vegetation (1.5.ii.5-6[46]). D. J. McCarthy is therefore probably right when he states, "The Ugaritic materials show that the so-called creation motifs borrowed from Canaan... do not really tell of a struggle against chaos and the formation of an ordered world consequent on victory over that enemy. At most they speak of a struggle for control of the world and of its organization."[47] They are not concerned with cosmic origins but with theomachic conflicts and the battle for supremacy among the gods.[48]

Ugaritic Texts (Leiden: E. J. Brill, 1955) p. 49; B. Margalit, "The Ugaritic Creation Myth: Fact or Fiction?" *UF* 13 (1981) 137-145; J. C. Greenfield, "The Hebrew Bible and Canaanite Literature" in Alter, R., and Kermode, F., (edd.), *The Literary Guide to the Bible* (London: Fontana, 1997) 545-60, p. 557; for further references, see Loren Fisher, "Creation at Ugarit and in the Old Testament" *VT* 15 (1965) 313-324, especially pp. 313-314. The absence of this theme from the Ras Shamra material is accepted even by such an advocate of the combat-creation connection as Day, who devotes a considerable proportion of the opening chapter of *God's Conflict* to the "problem ... of its non-mention in the Ugaritic texts" (pp. 7-18). Others have responded by seeking to redefine the nature of "creation" in this context, describing the Baal-Yam cycle as "cosmogonic" (e.g. Fisher, *op. cit,* R. J. Clifford, "Cosmogonies in the Ugaritic Texts and in the Bible" *Or* 53 [1984] 183-201, Grønbæk, "Baal's Battle with Yam—A Canaanite Creation Fight" *JSOT* 33 [1985] 27-44); for the evaluation of such interpretations, see M. S. Smith, *The Ugaritic Baal Cycle*, I (Leiden: Brill, 1994), pp. 75-87.

43 Especially in the common epithet ascribed to him, *bny bnwt*, "creator of creatures", *KTU* 1.4.ii.11; 1.4.iii.32; 1.6.iii.5, 11; 1.17.i.25; also *ab adm*, "father of mankind", *KTU* 1.14.i.37, 43, etc.

44 See Gen. 14:19, 22.

45 See further J. C. de Moor, "El the Creator" in G. Rendsburg et al. (edd.), *The Bible World: Essays in Honor of Cyrus H. Gordon* (New York: KTAV, 1980) 171-187.

46 Line 5 is probably to be translated, "Because he [Mot] was scorching the olive...", rather than merely as a simile: see *UNP*, p. 173 n. 162, *RTU*, p. 120, *CML*, p. 69.

47 P. 86, n. 5.

48 Such findings assume even greater significance when it is appreciated that biblical passages thought to relate to the conflict of the storm god with the sea may not only have their immediate antecedents in Canaan: it is at least possible that the motif itself may have originated among the western Semites (see, e.g., Jacobsen, "The Battle between Marduk and Tiamat" *JAOS* 88 [1968], p 107; Tsumura, *The Earth and the Waters in Genesis 1 and 2*, pp. 47-49) or be derived from a common prehistoric tradition (Lambert, "A New Look at the Babylonian Background of Genesis", Second Postscript (Sept. 1994) in *I Studied Inscriptions*, p. 111' cf. Wyatt, "Arms and the King" in *"Und*

As a result of these fresh insights, the biblical evidence adduced by Gunkel has been subject to more recent examinations. In this regard, Saggs points out the fragility of the connection originally perceived in the Old Testament between combat and creation. In particular, he illustrates how, although Gunkel succeeded in establishing a link between *Enuma elish* and various biblical allusions, he simply assumed a correlation between a battle and the emergence of the cosmos on the basis of the parallel, rather than seeking to demonstrate it in its own right.[49] In reality, the two themes occur in close proximity in only a minority of texts (Pss. 74 and 89 probably representing the only indisputable examples), and in neither of these is there any necessary causal connection. (In fact, it is fairly self-evident that in Ps. 74:13-14 the natural world is already presupposed). Saggs' conclusion is worth quoting here: "Where there is certain mention of God's victory, or assertion of control, over some monster (usually associated with the sea), there is no proved reference to cosmic creation as the sequel. On the other hand, in those passages where there is explicit mention of cosmic creation, there is no antecedent Leviathan, no dragon, no serpent, no Rahab. To create a marriage between the two series of mythic themes is to join together what Israelite thought kept asunder".[50]

Saggs' findings are corroborated by D. J. McCarthy's analysis of the use of "*Chaoskampf*" themes in ancient Hebrew poetry, in which he observes that they are employed in a variety of contexts, in combination with a number of different motif-spheres (such as those of mountain-, storm- and warrior-god).[51] They never appear as a fully-utilised, complete structure, but are applied with extraordinary versatility, so that the "chaotic" waters are as likely to represent an instrument of Yahweh (Ex. 15) as to indicate the nature of the psalmist's adversary, who is so easily suppressed (2 Sam. 22). He concludes that the imagery is always adapted in the service of demonstrating Yahweh's absolute kingship and awesome power, and of affirming his control of historical events for the benefit of his people. However, it is never employed in relation to creation. As a result, he suggests *Chaoskampf* themes held little power as a religious reality, but existed as a rich source of poetic imagery.

Day objects that McCarthy could have included for consideration other early texts, such as Ps. 93, where there is a connection between conflict and

---

Mose schrieb dieses Lied auf", p. 838). As a result, even the remote link with creation that an ultimate Babylonian derivation might afford becomes questionable.

49 *The Encounter with the Divine*, p. 54.

50 *Ibid.*, p. 56. A distinction between "chaos" and creation in Israel is urged by a number of other scholars: compare, e.g., Podella, "Der 'Chaoskampfmythos' im Alten Testament: Eine Problemanzeige" in M. Dietrich and O. Loretz, *Mesopotamica—Ugaritica—Biblica: Festschrift für Kurt Bergerhof* (AOAT 232; Kevelaer: Butzon & Bercker; Neukirchen-Vluyn: Neukirchener Verlag, 1993) 283-329, pp. 309, 319, Vosberg, *Studien zum Reden vom Schöpfer in den Psalmen*, p. 47, Görg, "'Chaos' und 'Chaosmächte' im Alten Testament" *BN* 70 (1993) 48-61, p. 50, and Kloos, *Yhwh's Combat with the Sea*, p. 85, and see the summary of scholarship in Kloos, pp. 70-74.

51 "'Creation' Motifs in Early Hebrew Poetry" in Anderson, *Creation in the Old Testament*, p. 83.

creation; and that the sample of material studied is too restrictive, since "quite often... the most striking parallels with Ugaritic come in relatively late texts".[52] Although Day's apprehension that the psalm is early is in fact probably correct, the putative connection with creation which he discerns therein is scarcely self-evident.[53] His admission that most of the passages in which this link is to be found are late, is striking, since it rather suggests that, even if it is present, it may be a secondary application of the imagery and not original to it.[54]

Nevertheless, despite overwhelming evidence to the effect that an intrinsic connection cannot be presupposed (even if in certain limited instances the possibility may be entertained), the argument is still frequently encountered that such a link underlies the biblical "chaos" allusions. By Mowinckel,[55] this was simply assumed and stated as if incontrovertible. It is asserted also by M. K. Wakeman,[56] though without detailed support, and recurs again in Day,[57] who is aware of the problems, but seeks to circumvent them.[58] Undergirding each of these studies is the assumption that a common "mythic pattern", entailing a theomachic conflict which results in creation, underlies various scattered Old Testament allusions as well as the often more complete material from Babylon (Mowinckel) and Canaan (Day);[59] it may even be abstracted from the basic

---

52 *God's Conflict*, pp. 3-4.

53 The date and interpretation of this psalm will be discussed in chapter 5 below.

54 Unfortunately, although Day affirms the presence of allusions to creation in Ps. 93 and "plenty of other passages", this is not elaborated in any further detail until a later section. Nor is it appropriate to discuss them further here. (From p. 19, it emerges that he has in mind Pss. 74, 89, 104, 65 and 93, all of which shall be given detailed consideration in the course of the present monograph).

55 In *The Psalms in Israel's Worship* and *Psalmenstudien*; see further the discussion of his work in section 6 below.

56 *God's Battle with the Monster* (Leiden: E. J. Brill, 1973), pp. 3, 59-62, etc.

57 *God's Conflict with the Dragon and the Sea* (CUP, 1985), pp. 1-61; so also F. M. Cross, *Canaanite Myth and Hebrew Epic* (Cambridge, Mass.: Harvard University Press, 1973), p. 16; P. Ricoeur, *Philosophie de la Volonté: Finitude et Culpabilité II. La Symbolique du Mal* (Paris: Aubier, éditions montaigne, 1960), pp. 167-198.

58 See chapter 1 n. 4 above.

59 Thus also L. Legrand, "La Création, triomphe cosmique de Yahvé", *Nouvelle Revue Théologique* 83 (1961) 449-470. Day actually claims that the Hebrew references to this mythology are dependent on Canaanite precedents mainly on the basis of linguistic factors rather than on grounds of content (pp. 4-7). E.g., noting that the Ugaritic form *thm* is equivalent to Hebrew *tᵉhôm*, he concludes that this "support[s] the view that the Old Testament term is Canaanite". However, demonstrating the provenance of the vocabulary does not explain the origin of its content or use. In fact, the Ugaritic word occurs in contexts where the supposed mythic pattern is not employed (*KTU* 1.23.30; 1.100.1; *thmt KTU* 1.3.iii.25; 1.4.iv.22; 1.17.vi.12; 1.19.i.45; 1.100.3); one is therefore left to conclude either that the Israelites expressed a mythic idea external to Canaan in familiar vocabulary, or that the supposed mythical overtones of *tᵉhôm* are foreign to both Israel and Canaan, and that claims that it should be so interpreted have been exaggerated under the influence of the now-discredited dependence on the

structure and constituent motifs of an assortment of selected accounts drawn from temporally and geographically disparate areas including Greece, Egypt and India, without it proving necessary even to demonstrate any line of dependence between them (Wakeman).[60] This presumed correlation therefore enables "missing links" to be supplied from supposedly "parallel" sources. However, it hardly needs to be stated that such circularity is scarcely defensible, especially if—as shall be argued—this structure is nowhere (or rarely) demonstrably attested in the Old Testament, and is also sometimes absent from the wider ancient Near Eastern sources. D. J. McCarthy goes so far as to demonstrate the inconsistency of such a pattern with the prevailing biblical evidence,[61] since, for example in J, "in the only instances when the waters do get out of hand... they do so not as a force opposed to the divine but rather as the passive instrument of divine punishment".

So how is Gunkel's original contention nowadays defended in the face of such arguments? Curiously, for proponents of the "mythical" viewpoint, such evidence as is adduced to suggest the absence of "chaos" motifs actually supports rather than contradicts their particular viewpoint. Saggs wryly draws attention to the assumption made by Wakeman[62] (but also encountered elsewhere) that: "The absence of particular details of the hypothetical myth where they might be expected is... taken not as a ground for querying the hypothetical reconstruction but, on the contrary, as proof of the accuracy of the reconstruction",[63] since a lack of reference to the myth is interpreted as evidence for its suppression.

Even where the focus is placed more directly on the interpretation of the biblical material, the motif of creation is often introduced only through great latitude in definition. For example, R. J. Clifford argues that ancient Near Eastern cosmogonies are not merely concerned with the genesis of the cosmos, but with the origin of the "'world' of human beings organised to serve the gods".[64] Hence, he defines as "cosmogonic" those psalms which are concerned with Israel's foundational story, whether exodus and conquest (e.g., Pss. 44, 78, 80) or the establishment of the Davidic dynasty (Ps. 89). However, it should be noted that, in this context, "cosmogony" and "creation" cannot be equated, so in a sense Clifford has succeeded merely in highlighting the "transhistorical" aspects of certain psalms, rather than in establishing the presence of creation motifs within them.

Therefore, a survey of relevant scholarship indicates that, at the very least, a causal connection between combat and creation can no longer be presupposed. However, whether it is exhibited in any or all of the specific instances in the Old Testament which are currently under examination, is keenly debated. As a

---

Babylonian *tiamat*. On this latter point, see further the discussion of Gen. 1:2 in Chapter 11 below.

60 *God's Battle with the Monster*, pp. 5-6.

61 In Anderson, *Creation in the Old Testament*, pp. 76-77.

62 *God's Battle*, p. 67.

63 *Encounter*, p. 56-7.

64 *Creation Accounts in the Ancient Near East and in the Bible*, p. 9.

result, any conclusion in this regard can only rest on a detailed consideration of each of the texts concerned.

3. Combat

The identification, under the influence of Babylonian mythology, of Yahweh's dealings with the dragon-figures and the sea in terms of combat has been particularly persistent, yet it is one which the evidence suggests is in need of review.

Fundamental to any "combat-myth" is the motif of the greatness of the struggle and of the genuine possibility of defeat. The combatants are generally fairly equally matched, an idea which finds especially vivid expression in the description of the struggle between Baal and Mot:

> They eye each other like fighters,
> Mot is fierce, Baal is fierce.
> They gore each other like buffalo,
> Mot is fierce, Baal is fierce.
> They bite each other like serpents,
> Mot is fierce, Baal is fierce.
> They drag each other like runners,
> Mot falls, Baal falls..[65]

Nevertheless, it is sometimes the case that it is the victor who is the weaker party, perhaps a quasi-human figure who succeeds by cunning or with the benefit of divine aid (e.g. Gilgamesh). Even Baal only achieves his eventual victory over Yam with the assistance of the craftsman-god, Kothar-wa-Khasis, who furnishes him with clubs of supernatural efficacy. Kothar-wa-Khasis addresses each of the clubs, Yagarrish and Ayyamarri, in turn with the words: "[May you] leap from Baal's hand, / like a raptor from his fingers. / Strike the torso/head of Prince Yamm..." (*KTU* 1.2.iv.13-14, 20-22). Gibson comments: "Apparently Baal was not himself strong enough to wield the weapon".[66]

The importance of genuine struggle taking place becomes especially clear if the various examples of combat myth are subjected to folktale analysis. Forsyth has compiled a "Schema of Combat Myths", in which he condenses in Proppian fashion the narrative features of the many myths which he considers.[67] It emerges from this that a prevalent feature is that of the "champions' [*sic*] temporary defeat", a motif which is described in terms of the "common sequence that involves the initial battle, defeat of the hero, enemy ascendant, hero recovers—itself an anticipatory form of the main combat sequence".[68] The elements concerning the temporary defeat of the hero emerge as defining features in the narrative sequence of combat myths.

65 *KTU* 1.6.vi.16-22.

66 *CML*, p. 44.

67 *The Old Enemy*, pp. 448-451.

68 *Ibid.*, p. 27.

How then does this pattern cohere with Old Testament allusions to the so-called "combat"? Rather surprisingly, although Forsyth confidently allocates four separate entries in his table to "the devil" (Semihazah-Asael, Mastema [Satan], Belial and Satan), he makes no mention of the struggle with Rahab, Tehom, and associated adversaries, despite the fact that a whole chapter of his book is devoted to "Combat at the Red Sea". Perhaps the reader is intended to consider it as a variant of the Canaanite "Yamm" pattern, since Forsyth includes under this heading a parenthetical note: "cf. Shilyat, Leviathan, Tannin". However, it probably also signals the difficulty—of which Forsyth cannot have been unaware—of fitting the numerous yet variable biblical "chaos" allusions into the scheme, since they seem to lack any clear statement of most of the required features.

More importantly, a "battle" or "combat" at its most fundamental level, and according to any definition, entails the engagement of two parties. Yet although there are allusions in the Old Testament to the waters fleeing or dragons being slain, there is no mention of the issuing of a challenge, of any attempt at the assault of God, or even of acts of self-defence by these agents. Their active opposition to God is nowhere unequivocally stated; nor is there any indication that God's destruction or "ordering" of them is a reaction to their behaviour.[69] Even in the case of Gen. 1, if the precreation waters were of their nature orderless or subject to subsequent ordering, there is no suggestion that this actually constituted what folktale analysis terms the "motivating incident" which necessitated God's creative action.[70] This is not to deny that the sea or a dragon may appear as an "enemy" of God, of the same order as the nations which they often represent; it may also be the case that the waters surrounding the earth have to be restrained by his power. However, it appears that the presence of "combat" themes in any or all of the biblical texts under consideration cannot simply be presupposed; any attempt to interpret the references concerned according to this pattern must therefore first be justified on the basis of detailed textual support.

4. Comparative Method

Turning then to the final aspect of Gunkel's enquiry, the comparative method, it may swiftly be perceived that this is the primary principle undergirding all of his findings—including the discernment of the themes of combat, creation and chaos—in the texts under consideration. A little has already been said about

69 This has already been recognised by certain scholars in respect of specific passages. For example, Mark Smith remarks of Ps. 104:5-9 that "there is no real battle to speak of"; indeed, "the waters... are changed from a negative, hostile force into a positive material of creation" (*The Memoirs of God*, p. 96).

70 Moreover, as Smith observes, "Genesis 1 evidently transforms creation by conflict into creation by the word ... Accordingly, Genesis 1 omits not only the conflict but also any personification of the cosmic waters. With no hint of conflict or even hostility, God speaks (not even rebukes), and the divine will is achieved " (*Ibid.*, p. 97).

this in relation to the discussion of the postulated connection with creation. Within the context of Gunkel's pioneering study, the establishment of a relationship between biblical and Babylonian themes was of immense benefit. However, although subsequent analyses have exhibited some development insofar as they have tended to place greater emphasis on correspondences with Canaanite material as opposed to that of Babylon, fundamentally, discussion of the Old Testament material has failed to outgrow this valuable starting-point. As a result, the distinctive voices of the biblical authors are in danger of being stifled.

Fundamental to the comparative method is the perceived contiguity of the Israelite material with the mythology and rites of her neighbours, such that the sparse Israelite references may be supplemented and interpreted in the light of the extant Canaanite and Babylonian texts. This presupposition is at times made explicit, as, for instance, by Mowinckel: "*A priori*, we could expect Israel ... to have a cult whose basic elements would be the same as those of neighbouring peoples ... In many cases then, where the Old Testament texts contain only casual and vague allusions ... the picture can be successfully completed by analogies from the cults of neighbouring peoples, which throw light on the allusions of the Old Testament."[71] Within the context of his work, this directly impinges on the interpretation of "chaos" imagery in the Psalter, since it is his declared presupposition that "the common oriental conception of creation as the basis of the kingship of the god would therefore be a matter of course for the Israelites. We may presume that even in Israel the mythical conception of creation as a fight against *dragons* and against the *primeval ocean* must have belonged to the ideas of the festival of enthronement from the beginning".[72]

However, even where less clearly stated, the supplementation of scattered biblical allusions with features derived from extra-Israelite occurrences of "the myth" pervades modern treatments of this issue. Wakeman, for example, speaks in terms of "read[ing] with an eye to *possible* allusions to the myth".[73] However, instead of simply assimilating biblical imagery to the Babylonian mythology and cult, as Mowinckel sought to do, Wakeman rather thinks in terms of a single myth which was manifested across a wide cultural area in a variety of forms, but which was nevertheless still felt as "the same myth".[74] This view is largely made possible on the assumption that the crucial aspect of the myth is its structure, which provides the key to its meaning, "regardless of the particulars".[75] Hence, the first part of her thesis consists of an attempt to

71 *PIW*, I, p. 16.

72 *PIW*, I, p. 145-6; his italics.

73 P. 65; her italics.

74 P. 4.

75 P. 5. She appears to suppose that "the myth" in all its manifestations, whether directly cited or merely evoked, everywhere retained the same essential structure and significance. Thus, she expresses her intention to discern "what the battle between monster and god is about" (p. 4). In this way, content and context are completely marginalised. The purpose of these myths (e.g., the glorification of Marduk at the *Akitu* festival, or some form of aetiology) and the importance of such distinctions as, for example, whether the

abstract from various narratives key features which were held in common. However, even this aspect of her research admits of a strong degree of subjectivity and circularity. Turning finally to Baal's battles with Yam and Mot (here considered to be different manifestations of the same general pattern),[76] she abandons herself to the inevitability that "any interpretation of the Ugaritic material must be highly speculative", and proposes to "start with the pattern derived from the myths summarised earlier, and using this as a hypothesis, see if an arrangement of the facts to fit it is plausible".[77] The same procedure is then repeated with the biblical material—with the proviso that the authors / editors sought to suppress "the myth" and that it is therefore necessary to "recover it in its original form".[78] Hence, her intention is not so much to interpret the biblical texts as they stand, or even to trace the development or transformation of any underlying mythology. Rather, it is to discover hints of the mythological model already created on the basis of extra-biblical texts, and to declare this as the background of the biblical material itself. The context of employment and intentionality of the author (except where he supposedly strives to "subvert" the pattern constructed by Wakeman) are simply ignored. The assumed priority of "the myth" in its fullest form over non- or quasi-mythological citations leads also to a complete disregard of the date and provenance of the texts in which they occur. For example, in her discussion of the nature of "Rahab",[79] she treats as primary the instances where "open reference to the myth" is made (i.e., Isa. 51:9, Ps. 89:10-11; Job 26:12-13, 9:13)—all of which are arguably exilic or post-exilic—and assumes that the "nickname" use of "Rahab" (referring to Egypt, Isa. 30:7; Ps. 87:4) is derivative (though it occurs in so-called First Isaiah).[80]

Nevertheless, it is noteworthy that where greater account is taken of the texts' context and significance, and of fundamental differences between them (as, for example, in the work of Forsyth, Saggs and McCarthy), this has

---

combatants are the "sea" and storm god or Mot and Baal, are completely overlooked. Nor is the possibility entertained that "the myth" may itself have been significantly adapted, transformed, reinterpreted, recontextualised or even applied in the service of purely literary or figurative interests.

76 The approach adopted also by Batto in *Slaying the Dragon*.

77 P. 37.

78 P. 3.

79 Pp. 59-62.

80 In addition to this broadening of the scope of "the myth", has been the perception of its enhanced significance, as manifested in Carola Kloos' examination of Ps. 29 and Ex. 15, *Yahweh's Combat with the Sea* (Amsterdam: G. A. van Oorschot / Leiden: E. J. Brill, 1986), from which she concludes that Yahweh had absorbed the characteristics of Baal, and that the myth of a battle with the sea had given rise to a historicising account of a battle at the sea. However, that the key element in her thesis should comprise the tracing of "A Canaanite Tradition in the Religion of Ancient Israel" (the words of her subtitle) illustrates how little the discussion of these texts has progressed since Gunkel defined his task as concerned "with the ... question of the relationship between the biblical and Babylonian creation accounts" (*Schöpfung und Chaos*, pp. 4-5).

prompted the questioning of certain received positions, especially with regard to the connection of "combat" and creation.[81] It is revealing that where a scholar such as Wakeman seeks to discern a common basic structure and fundamental identity in all instances where "the myth" occurs, she perhaps inevitably concludes that its influence is all-pervasive;[82] yet by contrast, Forsyth, in adopting a literary rather than a theological approach, and in concerning himself with the development, transformation and diversity of myths incorporating a battle, permits a greater openness to the individuality of the particular texts concerned. It is thus not merely coincidental that his work, perhaps more than any other, has revealed some of the deficiencies of the established assumptions governing current research into the imagery of "chaos".

5. Summary

To summarise the discussion so far, it has emerged that the fundamental principles of Gunkel's 1895 thesis—namely the hypothesis constructed on the basis of comparative study, of a combat with chaos cumulating in creation—continue to dominate and constrain any analysis of the biblical imagery under consideration. Nevertheless, all four aspects are in need of radical re-evaluation.

The employment of the term "chaos" to describe the figures of Leviathan, Yam, Rahab, tannîn, nᵉhārôṯ, tᵉhôm, etc. was apparently originally based on a fairly loose similarity of Gen. 1 with certain Greek cosmogonic myths, the essential element of which was the creation of the cosmos from pre-existent matter. Since Gunkel, the question of whether the darkness and deep were formed by God has continued to comprise a subject of debate, and there is no sign of consensus. The past century has also seen an implicit (though scarcely directly formulated) movement in the utilisation of "chaos" language towards a situation in which "chaos" is often primarily understood as the antithesis of cosmos, conceived of as "order". This corresponds to the most common non-specialist English usage.

Perhaps more significant than these semantic difficulties, however, is the very diversity of the figures encompassed within this terminology. The prevailing trend since the publication of *Schöpfung und Chaos* has been for the

---

81 The importance of discerning how an image functions within a particular society before conducting any external comparisons is well emphasised by M. Z. Brettler, *God is King*, p. 16; see also the perceptive comments of S. Talmon, "The 'Comparative Method' in Biblical Interpretation—Principles and Problems" (VT[S] 29, 1978) 320-356.

82 As Ricoeur perceives, (in a critique of the "Myth and Ritual" approach), the apparent pervasiveness of the "paradigm of the King and the Enemy ... is dependent on a certain method, more attentive to survivals than to new directions; once you have decided to explain the new by the old ... you will find everywhere, even in the most remote derivatives, the initial nucleus that you have decided to take as the basis of 'explanation'" (*La Symbolique du Mal*, p. 191).

vocabulary of "chaos" to be appropriated into the analysis of imagery (t^{e}hôm, Rahab, etc.) designated by Gunkel as connected with this theme, without there being any feeling that closer definition was required. As a result, it is now impossible to devise any collective noun to designate the entities under examination apart from this conceptual framework, despite its increasingly obvious unsuitability for this use. Indeed, if Rahab, Yam and their supposed confederates are once freed from this artificial constraint, it may well emerge that the difficulty is due to the impracticability of drawing together material which is too diverse and varied to submit to such an attempt. Certainly, it would be profitable to re-examine each of the relevant texts whilst consciously laying aside the idea of "chaos" and with it the subconsciously imposed and possibly artificial unity and creation-bias which this necessarily entails.

The motif of creation is the aspect of the present enquiry which has excited the most controversy. As scholars have become increasingly aware, there is no explicit mention of creation in the Ugaritic Baal-Yam cycle (or indeed in that concerned with the storm-god's struggle with Mot), and many would deny the connection of this theme with the combat described therein; similarly, the recognition that creation is not the primary focus of the Babylonian *Enuma elish* is one which is frequently encountered. This in turn has, in certain quarters, prompted a re-evaluation of some of the treasured presuppositions of biblical scholarship in relation to the Old Testament "chaos" texts. Once again, a careful examination of the evidence is required to establish whether creation is a necessary, or even merely an occasional, corollary of God's dealings with "chaos" figures. In this case, a diachronic aspect to the enquiry would, even if difficult, be especially valuable in ascertaining the probable sequence of development of the various spheres of allusion encountered in relation to the "chaos" motif.

Likewise, although the application of the term "combat" to "chaos" imagery has become axiomatic, nevertheless, there are indications that its appropriateness is by no means assured. Once again, only close textual analysis may reveal whether a combat can, properly speaking, be deemed to have taken place.

Finally, running as a continuous thread through all of these and many other interpretative issues is the rôle of comparative analysis. Valuable as this method of enquiry is, it is also clear that its use has often been overstretched beyond its helpful limit. Indeed, the very purpose of comparison is that it may point to a nuance, setting or reading which is not of itself self-evident or even clearly expressed in a text; it constitutes external data which may be brought to bear on a passage in order to offer a possible means of interpretation. What it does not do is to assist in teasing out the internal dynamics of a motif or expression as it occurs in context. If it is overemphasised, it can be at the expense of a sensitive appreciation of the individual characteristics of a particular passage or motif, as against all similar occurrences. It would therefore seem profitable to undertake an exercise in redressing the balance, by examining the internal biblical evidence without reference to external ancient Near Eastern data, and bringing the received body of "comparative" wisdom into play only once preliminary conclusions have been formed; obviously, proximity of language and meaning between biblical and extra-biblical material would support the comparative method, but the greater any discrepancy, the more the current mode of application of ancient Near Eastern "parallels" to the Old Testament is discredited. The results of this process may be no more definitive than those of analyses in which comparative data are heavily employed, but I hope it will at least provide a counterbalance (without swinging too far in the opposite direction) to this prevailing tendency.

Thus in all four instances, the same task presents itself: to undertake a careful exegesis of the relevant texts with an eye to the pertinent interpretative issues, and with a particular awareness of the conceptual boundaries established by Gunkel. These must be continually resisted if they are not to reassert their own version of "creative order" on the unorganised mass of material concerned.

6. Mowinckel's "Cultic" Approach

Finally, however, there remains to be considered the rôle of the cult, since it is often claimed that all or many of the psalms examined here were employed in the context of some form of autumn New Year Festival, in which the celebration of Yahweh's kingship had a central rôle. However, the very existence of the postulated ceremony has been strongly contested; even where it is assumed, it has been conceived of in such a variety of manifestations as to be scarcely recognisable from one reconstruction to the next.[83]

Since the debate originated with Mowinckel, and all other contributions are expressed in dialogue with him, any discussion of the issue must commence with an assessment of his ideas; conversely, insofar as the various festal

83 It has variously been characterised as an "Enthronement Festival" (Mowinckel, *Psalmenstudien* II, 1922; developed and defended in *The Psalms in Israel's Worship*, 1962), a "Covenant Renewal Ceremony" (Weiser, *Die Psalmen*, 5th edition, 1959), or a "Royal Festival on Zion", focusing on the election of Jerusalem and of David (H.-J. Kraus, *Die Königsherrschaft Gottes im Alten Testament*, 1951; *Gottesdienst in Israel*, 2nd edition, 1962). Mowinckel's thesis has been developed by proponents of the so-called "Myth and Ritual School", comprising the Englishman S. H. Hooke and a group of Scandinavian, mainly Uppsala, scholars, such as I. Engnell, G. Widengren and G. W. Ahlström. They claimed to have identified a common ancient Near Eastern "ritual pattern", entailing the enactment of the rôle of a dying and rising god (in Israel, identified with Yahweh) in the cult by the king, who was himself regarded as divine; a sacred marriage between the god and goddess was also, it is claimed, "realised" by the monarch during the festival. A medial, but still thoroughgoing, position is represented by A. R. Johnson ("The Rôle of the King in the Jerusalem Cultus" in S. H. Hooke [ed.], *The Labyrinth*, 1935, 73-111; *Sacral Kingship in Ancient Israel* [Cardiff, 2nd ed., 1967]) and J. H. Eaton (*Kingship and the Psalms*, JSOT, 2nd ed. 1986), who contend that the Davidic king underwent some form of ritual humiliation and vindication in the autumn festival, thus going beyond Mowinckel's original claims, but nevertheless refuting the "ritual pattern" outlined above.

hypotheses presuppose the "ritual method" which he pioneered, there is an extent to which the result of this critique must also impinge more widely on them as well. Essentially, his contention was that an autumn New Year Festival was celebrated at the feast of Tabernacles in pre-exilic times. At its heart was the enthronement of Yahweh, which dramatically re-enacted and made present his primordial defeat of chaos at creation, through which he first assumed the throne. It was thus primarily an occasion of re-creation and renewal. Yet in addition to this mythical act of salvation achieved at creation, Yahweh's corresponding deeds of deliverance in history—exodus, election, conquest and covenant—were also recalled and elided with the primal event. Mowinckel additionally associated features such as a procession of the Ark, emulating its first entry into Jerusalem under David (cf. Ps. 132), and a reconsecration of the Temple (comparing Ps. 93:5), with the ceremony, as well as seeking to retain the original harvest connection. Fundamental to this approach is his concept of the cult as creative drama, which both represents primordial events and vividly realises them in the present. It is supported by comparison with other ancient Near Eastern rites, notably the Babylonian *Akitu* festival.

However, there are numerous difficulties with Mowinckel's approach, not least with his methodology and presuppositions; it is with these in particular, rather than merely with his conclusions, that the following discussion must engage, even where it impinges on specific exegetical issues.[84] Firstly, the wide-ranging and comprehensive list of motifs which he attaches to the festival itself engenders suspicion (something which is not allayed by the fact that he consequently associates no fewer than 46 psalms with this single celebration). The primary basis for this connection is the supposed occurrence of these themes in the core group of "enthronement psalms". However, Mowinckel treats Pss. 47, 93, 96-99 (frequently supplemented by Pss. 95, 65 and 81, and where necessary, by other psalms which he believes—on the basis of their perceived affinity with the enthronement hymns proper—must also have been employed at the festival) as a single unanimous source: where a motif is discerned in one psalm, it is deemed to be implied—and certainly not controverted—elsewhere across the group. That they belong to the same liturgical setting is thereby assumed even before it is demonstrated. He likewise seems unconcerned to interpret each psalm as a coherent unit. Rather, he treats the Psalter as a source from which decontextualised segments may be removed, only to be reassembled in a fresh cultic patchwork, one that has been stitched together from a Canaanite pattern, and from which each element may derive an entirely new signification.

The flaws in Mowinckel's methodology are thus manifested most clearly in his interpretation of the biblical "source texts" for the reconstruction of the so-called "enthronement festival". For example, particularly crucial to his

84 For more general objections to his "enthronement hypothesis", see, e.g., Kraus, *Psalmen*, I, pp. 99-103, and the excellent critique by A. R. Petersen, *The Royal God: Enthronement Festivals in Ancient Israel and Ugarit?* (Sheffield Academic Press, 1998), especially chapter 2 (pp. 26-31). A survey of research is included in Lipiński, *Les Psaumes de la Royauté de Yahvé dans l'exégèse Moderne* (Louvain, 1962), pp. 241-272.

reconstruction of the enthronement festival is the claim that it entailed the celebration of creation, yet this theme is discerned only on the basis of Pss. 93:1b; 95:3-5; and 96:5.[85] Since, however, the most substantial of these references is drawn from outside the core group of psalms, and the motif of creation is otherwise employed only infrequently and in a subordinate rôle in the service of other themes, Mowinckel's postulation that the genesis of the cosmos was directly celebrated of itself, remains dubious.

Mowinckel's core theological claim that "the creation is depicted as a victorious struggle with the primeval dragon or primeval sea and its monsters"[86] will be considered in more detail in the ensuing chapters in the context of the discussion of each relevant psalm.[87] However, his reconstruction of the cultic features of the festival, no less than his interpretation of the psalms' theological content, is extremely dubious, at times relying on a somewhat disingenuous use of the source material. For example, the following assertion is typical, yet requires qualification at every remove: "Yahweh himself 'comes' (98:9), 'makes himself known' (98:2), 'goes up' (47:6) in a solemn procession to his palace, the temple, seats himself on his throne (93:2; 97:2; 99:1) and receives his people's acclamation as king (*tᵉrû'â*, 47:2 [*sic*.])".[88] However, there is an immense difference between Yahweh coming and revealing himself, and what Ps. 98 actually states—that he "has made known his victory / revealed his vindication in the sight of the nations", and (then) "comes to judge the earth". Drawing next from Ps. 47, Mowinckel translates Yahweh's ascension as present—despite the fact that it should most probably be understood as past—and then fails to provide any reference to support his claim that a procession is envisaged. Contrary to the claim that Yahweh "seats himself on his throne", Pss. 93:2 and 97:1 allude respectively only to the establishment of the throne "from of old" and to the fact that "righteousness and justice" are its foundation, whilst Ps. 99:1 describes Yahweh as יֹשֵׁב כְּרוּבִים. This is a very standard attribute, often reminiscent of his epiphany, but it has nothing to do with the action of sitting down (and, in fact, if Yahweh was invisibly borne in on the ark, then presumably he would actually have arrived enthroned). Finally, the תְּרוּעָה (Ps. 47:6) may be a battle-cry or alarm of war, or a (usually) religiously-motivated shout of joy; here, as in Pss. 33:3 and 27:6, it appears in the context of singing. There is no indication that it constitutes an acclamation of the divine king.[89] It may be noted that in Ps. 47, as in Ps. 98, Mowinckel translates the excerpted verses out of sequence in order to achieve his desired synthesis.

---

85 See, further, the discussion of these psalms in the ensuing chapters.

86 *PIW*, I, p. 108.

87 Mowinckel himself affirms this claim only on the basis of Ps. 93:3-4, though he seems to find an allusion to the same mythic struggle, for example, in relation to Ps. 98:1.

88 *PIW*, I, p. 107.

89 Num. 23:21, the only passage where a related association occurs, seems to refer to a rallying-call round the divine warrior, and certainly cannot be linked with any form of enthronement.

According to Mowinckel, Assyro-Babylonian ideas were mediated to Israel through a Canaanite context. This creates a further difficulty, insofar as Baal's defeat of Yam or Mot does not result in creation, whereas this consequence is attested in the Babylonian epic *Enuma elish* and is also claimed for Israel. A causal connection with creation is therefore supplied by two deeply unsatisfactory means. Firstly, it is suggested that it could have been transmitted directly from Babylon in the late-monarchical period (i.e. in c. 587 B.C.). Whilst this may have been the case, it could not account for the presence of the creation motif in an indigenous festival, in the context of which it constituted one of the most fundamental themes from its inception. The enthronement festival, if it existed at all in pre-exilic Israel, must have been celebrated long prior to this phase of contact with Babylonia. Alternatively, the problem is tackled by noting that, as well as adopting the mythical pattern relating to Baal's defeat of chaos, Israel came to identify other deities and their attributes with Yahweh. Among these was El, the Canaanite high god and creator. Hence, it is maintained, Yahweh came also to be recognised as creator. Mowinckel is probably justified in drawing this connection between Yahweh and El, but he then commits the error of transposing the El-attribute (creator) onto a Baal-pattern and concluding that kingship and creation must therefore have been the consequence of Yahweh's defeat of chaos. There is no justification in merging in this way separate traditions belonging to different deities, who were acknowledged contemporaneously and distinctly within the same culture.

More fundamentally, there is nothing actually to suggest from the biblical evidence either that New Year was an event which was cultically commemorated in Israel, or that "Tabernacles" included a specifically "new year" element in the Old Testament period.[90] The argumentation rests, rather, on the view that the feast of Booths coincided with the "turn of the year", coupled with the observation that a new year festival was held at this time in the post-biblical period; moreover, the existence of new year festivals is attested in other ancient Near Eastern cultures, in particular, Babylon, and this is adduced as corroboration of the hypothesis. The more detailed analyses in Mowinckel's work attempt to demonstrate the affiliation of motifs such as kingship and chaos, which he believes (mainly on the basis of Babylonian parallels) would form the content of such a celebration, with the time or content of the Feast of Tabernacles.

In fact, the only clear link between the themes which Mowinckel describes and Tabernacles is found in the late post-exilic text Zech 14:16. However, even here, the conjunction between kingship and this festival may be wholly incidental. The context concerns the eschatological "day" when Yahweh will vanquish the nations who assemble against Jerusalem and implement his ideal rule over the earth. Against this background, Booths is probably simply mentioned as the major pilgrimage festival in Jerusalem to which the nations would come. Moreover, even if the connection between Yahweh's reign and the

90 Indeed, accounts of the Feast consistently describe it as a specifically agrarian celebration, an element which runs deep from earliest times through to the post-exilic period. See de Vaux, *Les Institutions de l'Ancien Testament*, II, pp. 398-401, 404-407.

autumn festival were to be demonstrated as intrinsic to this passage, the legitimacy of transposing this link back into the celebrations of the pre-exilic era, let alone awarding it a pivotal rôle therein, remains questionable.

Similarly unsustainable is the claim that Zech. 14:17 reflects Yahweh's control of the waters which was primordially manifested in his battle with chaos at creation, as the provision (or withholding) of water is quite a different theme from the overcoming of the cosmic deep. Since the rainy season followed the Feast of Ingathering, there may well have been a petition for rain during the course of the festival; conversely, there may have been a belief that failure to give thanks for the harvest could result in the withholding of Yahweh's bounty in the future, perhaps especially in the course of the ensuing year. This would therefore support the traditional agricultural associations of Booths, even at this late stage, rather than imply a celebration of the type propounded by Mowinckel.

Yet if the affiliation between kingship and Tabernacles is uncertain, may a connection instead be drawn between Enthronement and New Year? This link is crucial to Mowinckel's argumentation, but, once again, may be called into question, since the evidence adduced is extremely late. This, in fact, belongs to two related spheres. First, it is noted that Yahweh's kingship was celebrated in post-biblical Jewish New Year ceremonies, which involved the reading of passages on this theme (the מלכיות), including Pss. 93:1 and 24:7-10, as well as the recitation of Pss. 47:5, 98:6 and 81:3. However, the earliest allusion to this practice is located in the Mishnah, *Rosh Hashshanah* 4.5. Secondly, it is also observed that the Septuagintal heading to Ps. 29 connects it with Tabernacles. However, without wishing to pre-empt the detailed exegesis of the following chapter, it appears that the connection with Tabernacles may in fact flow from the dominant theme of Yahweh's theophany in the thunder and storm which runs throughout this composition, and this would again cohere with the seasonal and agricultural connections of the Festival even at this late stage. On the other hand, the notion that Yahweh is here portrayed as assuming kingship or as defeating chaos is not sustainable. More importantly, the use of a psalm in the late Greek period cannot legitimately be adduced as evidence for liturgical practice in pre-exilic Jerusalem.

In fact, even Mowinckel's understanding of the *Akitu* festival has been called into doubt.[91] More serious is the absence of any clear indication that the New Year was celebrated in Canaan, or that the battle with chaos was there associated with creation. It is therefore perhaps not surprising that de Vaux has defended in detail the view that in Israel "under this name, and with these rites, the feast never existed in Old Testament times".[92] A further complication arises from the fact that the Babylonian New Year occurred in the spring, whereas the Jewish New Year festival (as attested in New Testament times and still celebrated today) is an autumn event, occurring in the seventh (Babylonian) month. This not only confuses the issue of dependence on Babylonian

91 See de Vaux, *Les Institutions de l'Ancien Testament*, II, p. 411.

92 *Ibid*. p. 407.

precedents—it is also unclear whether or when there may have been an autumnal new year in Israel in Old Testament times.[93]

The foregoing discussion thus calls into question the presence of the *Chaoskampf* theme within the Psalter and especially within the autumnal festal celebrations of ancient Israel, and this claim will be substantiated further in the ensuing chapters. Moreover, this silence may be recognised as hardly uncharacteristic of the Old Testament as a whole. There is, in any event, an immense gulf between the employment of an image in a poetic context as a vivid means of expression, and the physical embodying of that image in the cult as a literal and vital point of orthodox theology. Furthermore, as became apparent from the consideration of the "comparative method" (section 4, above), the validity of Mowinckel's methodology of "importing" extra-biblical, extra-Israelite material (especially from a rather different culture and far-removed age) to explain Hebrew references is questionable. In effect, to claim that the psalms can only be understood in the light of the *Akitu* festival, is tantamount to a "reading-in" of concepts from that context into material where they would otherwise be regarded as absent (or at least, imperceptible). Certainly, one should be sceptical of the ascription of such a large proportion of the psalms to a celebration for which there is no clear record, especially when the celebrated event is not even described in Israel's sacred scriptures. There is some truth in arguing that we should attempt to free ourselves from a late twentieth century occidental perspective and allow ourselves to enter into the festal atmosphere of the ancient Near East. However, this carries with it the risk of bracketing together a great diversity of cultures, smoothing out their variety, and then substituting this imperfectly understood amalgam for our own judgment, prejudiced in certain respects as the latter may be.

Finally, a related drawback of the type of approach practised by Mowinckel and indeed by all who enter into the perilous sphere of examining the evidence for ancient Israelite cultic practice is that it depends on an assessment of the psychology of this people, as viewed in its collective religious manifestation.[94] Obviously, there are few Old Testament scholars who are equipped to perform anything other than amateur inroads into this subject—perhaps an objective analysis is impossible anyway—and then on the basis of rather slender material. Comparison with other (perhaps even more superficially, or fancifully, comprehended) often far from contemporary ancient Near Eastern texts, or with anthropological studies of modern primitive societies, carries with it further risks.[95] Frequently, interpretations of "comparative" ancient material are themselves very far from certain, and often less is known about the societies,

93 See D. J. A. Clines, "The Evidence for an Autumn New Year in Pre-exilic Israel Reconsidered", *JBL* 93 (1974), 22-40.

94 See J. W. Rogerson, "The Hebrew Conception of Corporate Personality: A Re-examination", *JTS* 21 (1970) 1-16.

95 The danger of assuming cultural continuity across the ancient Near East is particularly highlighted by H. Frankfort, *Kingship and the Gods: A Study in Ancient Near Eastern Religion as the Integration of Society and Nature* (Chicago, 1948), especially pp. 337-344.

and especially about the cults, that produced them than about that in Israel. Moreover, the suitability of transposing concepts or practices from one culture to another is anyway highly tendentious. Often it is claimed that such comparisons are made only on the basis of a congruence of motifs or ideas between the two. Nevertheless, as soon as material from one culture is adduced to "illuminate" another, there is a concomitant risk of simply projecting ideas from the second back onto the first: indeed, it is on this process of transference that the method depends.

In any case, modern scholarship is often at its most subjective and is most vulnerable to accusations of projection in creating imaginative portrayals of the "ancient psyche", or conversely in the stubborn refusal to accept that the God of Israel could ever have been worshipped in a manner foreign to our own notions of how such worship should be conducted. Faced with this Scylla and Charybdis, it is difficult to imagine how to proceed, except with caution, and strictly on the basis of what the biblical text may, on its own terms and in its own context, reasonably be thought to convey. This is what is to be attempted in the following chapters.

III. Archaic Hebrew Poetry: Psalms 29, 68 and 114

Probably the earliest of the texts under consideration are Psalms 29, 68 and 114, the first two of which may derive from the pre-monarchical period. Here, the major interest is in Yahweh's theophany, in Ps. 29 this theme comprising the entire hymn. One may note in this context how the depiction of the theophany in the Song of Deborah (Judg. 5) and the Blessing of Moses (Deut. 33)—both generally estimated to be among the earliest poetry in the Hebrew Bible[1]—also displays a number of continuities with the present group of Psalms.[2] This sphere of imagery presumes a stable cosmos. It must be noted that, in each case, the emphasis is placed on Yahweh's incomparable power (e.g. in 29:1-2), which in turn causes spontaneous tremors throughout the earth. The mutual relation of these two aspects—Yahweh's action and attributes as manifested in the theophany, and the response of the earth to it—is especially worthy of notice. In the present group of psalms, they seem to act in a fairly organic relation, but elsewhere one element may be stressed above the other, or occur in isolation.

1. The Date of Psalms 29, 68 and 114

Psalms 29, 68 and 114 are by many scholars judged to be among the earliest preserved in the Hebrew Bible. However, a subject which elicits a still broader consensus is the difficulty surrounding any attempt to establish a reliable method for dating such poetry. A wide variety of dating criteria have been adduced as indicative of provenance, some perhaps more secure than others. Yet despite the uncertainties surrounding many of these indicators when considered individually, it is hoped that when they are attested collectively within a single

---

1 See B. Lindars (*Judges*, pp. 213-215), who, despite denying a very early date to the song of Deborah, still accepts that "some time in the early monarchy would be suitable" (p. 215), and compare D. A. Robertson (*Linguistic Evidence*, p. 155) and Cross and Freedman (*SAYP*, p. 3), who place it at the end of the 12th century. As regards the provenance of Deut. 33, A. Phillips (*Deuteronomy*, 1973, p. 210) assigns it to "a late date in the period of the judges", whilst R. Clifford thinks in terms of "an ancient poem, vv. 1-5 and vv. 26-29" framing the blessings which have been inserted between them (*Deuteronomy*, 1982, p. 177); see similarly Cross and Freedman (*SAYP*, p. 64), who advocate an 11th century date.

2 See especially Judg. 5:4-5, Deut. 33:2, 26-29; compare also Hab. 3.

composition, they may provide a cumulative basis on which to found a dating proposal, however tentative and imprecise that may be.

The data cited as relevant to the discussion may pertain to issues of content, such as factors relating to the history of ideas, theology, historical allusions, or reflecting certain attitudes—such as sympathy with or antipathy to certain groups or individuals—which may be associated with a particular period or situation. However, formal and linguistic phenomena, such as the presence of tricola or repetitive parallelism,[3] the prevalence of a particular divine name,[4] the utilisation of archaic orthography[5] or linguistic features,[6] or perhaps a propensity to employ certain vocabulary in preference to a more "modern" alternative, are especially frequently cited. Thus, it may be possible to calibrate the extent of archaic linguistic features and from this to derive tentative proposals regarding the relative probability that—or degree to which—a psalm may be regarded as ancient. Further corroboration or modification may then be supplied by data gleaned from the content or inner-biblical relations of a particular poem, and these in turn may serve to support or undermine the general validity of the linguistically and grammatically-derived diachronic model.

However, it must always be recognised, as acknowledged by Robertson and discussed more fully by Young, that such features may be archaising rather than genuinely archaic;[7] nevertheless, insofar as an archaising style might naturally be employed to express a content also perceived as ancient, it is possible that it might provide an indicator, if not of genuine antiquity, at least of the belief, even at the time of writing, that what is expressed here is "of the past". It is also probable that, notwithstanding any overlap between Archaic and Standard Biblical Hebrew (the latter of which Young dates from the time of David and Solomon), ABH is still in general most likely to occur at a relatively early date.

3 See Albright, *YGC*, pp. 4-25.

4 See D. N. Freedman, 'Divine Names and Titles in Early Hebrew Poetry' in *Pottery, Poetry, and Prophecy*, pp. 77-129 (reprinted from F. M. Cross et al (edd.), *Magnalia Dei: The Mighty Acts of God* [New York: Doubleday, 1976] 55-107).

5 A seminal work on this is Cross and Freedman, *Early Hebrew Orthography: A Study of the Epigraphic Evidence* (AOS 36; New Haven, CT: American Oriental Society, 1952). See however the cautionary analyses of Barr, *The Variable Spellings of the Hebrew Bible* (Oxford: OUP, 1989), especially Chapter IV, and Young, *Diversity in Pre-Exilic Hebrew* (FAT 5; Tübingen: Mohr, 1993), p. 122, cf. pp. 86-7.

6 See, e.g., the detailed analysis of D. A. Robertson, *Linguistic Evidence in Dating Early Hebrew Poetry* (SBLDS 3; Missoula, MT: Society of Biblical Literature, 1972) and the helpful summary in Kloos, *Yhwh's Combat with the Sea: A Canaanite Tradition in the Religion of Ancient Israel* (Amsterdam: G. A. van Oorschot; Leiden: E. J. Brill, 1986), pp. 130-2, together with the critical discussion in Young, *Diversity*, Chapter 5, especially pp. 122-130.

7 See Robertson, *Linguistic Evidence*, pp. 147-150, and Young, *Diversity*, Chapter 5. Young, moreover, highlights the strong Aramaic flavour of ABH, which is dropped in SBH (apart from in Wisdom contexts) and then resurfaces in some Late BH material (pp. 54-63).

Moreover, if it can be assumed (as seems reasonable) that the Hebrew Bible does contain material which is genuinely early, the criteria of clustering of early forms and (if it can be supposed that SBH features do not occur in ABH) a lack of characteristics which are typical of SBH, may also assist in distinguishing material which may be genuinely archaic from that which is merely "archaising".[8] The employment of further data which are not drawn from the linguistic sphere should in many cases also provide an important contribution to the judgment made in any particular instance.

i. The Date of Psalm 29

Despite the fact that Psalm 29 is frequently described as "archaic",[9] evidence for its antiquity is surprisingly sparse.[10] There is nothing in the vocabulary to suggest an early provenance,[11] nor is the grammatical evidence unequivocal, although the *yqtl - wyqtl* sequence in v. 9 may be noted, and there is a possible example of enclitic *mem* in v. 6.[12] In addition, the only divine name to be employed in the psalm is Yahweh,[13] which occurs no fewer than eighteen times in the short span of eleven verses. This therefore seems to place the composition firmly in the first phase of Freedman's tripartite chronological schema, that of "Militant Mosaic Yahwism", which he assigns to the 12th

---

8 See Robertson, *Linguistic Evidence*, pp. 135-150.

9 E.g., by Albright (*YGC*, pp. 19, 24) and Kraus, (I, p. 378). Like Dahood, (I, p. 175), Cross ("Notes on a Canaanite Psalm in the Old Testament", *BASOR* 117 [1950] 19-21) and Gaster ("Psalm 29", *JQR* 37 [1946/7] 55-65), Kraus follows H. L. Ginsberg's proposal that Ps. 29 is based on an earlier Canaanite hymn to the storm-god Baal ("A Phoenician Hymn in the Psalter" in *Atti del XIX Congresso Internazionale degli Orientalisti* [Rome, 1935], pp. 472-476; Kraus, p. 378). It is also assigned to an early date by Weiser ("a fairly early period", p. 176), Terrien ("the time of the Judges", p. 279), Anderson (10th century, I, p. 233), Freedman (not later than c. 1100 B.C., *Pottery*, p. 83) and Watson (c. 1150, *CHP*, p. 40). Nevertheless, there are contrasting voices largely emanating from the earlier critical tendency to date the contents of the Psalter late, e.g., Briggs ("subsequent to Nehemiah", I, p. 252) and Tournay (Hellenistic; "Recherches sur la Chronologie des Psaumes", *RB* 65 [1958], p. 324), though this view has been propounded more recently by Oeming (p. 178) and Loretz (*Psalm 29* [UBL 2, 1984], pp. 64-70), both of whom regard Ps. 29 as postexilic.

10 Robertson (*Linguistic Evidence*, p. 155) failed to find any "positive linguistic evidence" for the antiquity of the psalm.

11 Nor yet to preclude it. For example, reference to the "name" of God in Ps. 68:5 (besides Ps. 18:30 = 2 Sam. 22:30, Am. 2:7, and passages in Exodus conventionally attributable to J and E) calls into question Oeming's claim (I, p. 178) that this terminology is indicative of a late provenance.

12 The proposal that there is a further example in v. 1 (see Freedman, *Pottery*, p. 116) is probably to be rejected.

13 אֵל in v. 3 and אֵלִים in v. 1 apparently have generic force.

century.[14] This conclusion is supported by the second type of criterion employed by Freedman in assessing the relative antiquity of his selected poems, the use of the term עַם (which occurs twice in v. 11) in preference both to יַעֲקֹב / יִשְׂרָאֵל and to a concern with the human king.[15]

Perhaps the most conspicuous feature of Ps. 29 to be cited in relation to dating is the pervasive use of the "expanded colon".[16] Admittedly, within this pattern, Ps. 29 seems to exhibit a wider range of variations and verbal techniques and to deploy them more effectively than is evident in the extant Canaanite material,[17] but on the other hand, claims that it displays literary features such as inclusio[18] or an overarching chiasmus[19] must be rejected. Indeed, only a slightly different perspective is required to discern in the repetitive style and staircase progressions the substance of oral poetry.[20] In this regard, the continuities in vocabulary from verse to verse and the constant cross-allusions in language and motif should especially be noted, suggesting that we mistake the significance of these repetitions if we seek to attribute them to some grand overarching line-structure.

However, perhaps the aspect of Ps. 29 which has exercised the greatest influence on historians of Israel's prosody is its atmospheric—and to the modern mind, at least, unmistakably primitive—portrayal of the god of the thunderstorm. In fact, the divine theophany seems in general to predominate in psalms often recognised on other grounds as among the earliest in the corpus. In addition, the form of Ps. 29, and especially its focus on a single theme without obvious development or narrative progression, is without a clear parallel and defies form-critical classification. Moreover, scholars have pointed to the affinities of Ps. 29 to Ex. 15 and Judg. 5;[21] and its resonances with Ps. 68 may

14 See Freedman, "Divine Names and Titles in Early Hebrew Poetry" in *Pottery*, 77-129, especially pp. 78, 82-3.

15 *Ibid.*, pp. 83, 116-7.

16 See S. E. Loewenstamm, "The Expanded Colon in Ugaritic and Biblical Verse", *JSS* 14(1969) 176-196; "The Expanded Colon Reconsidered", *UF* 7 (1975) 261-264.

17 See Kloos, *Yhwh's Combat with the Sea*, pp. 104-5; cf. Loewenstamm, *JSS* 14, pp. 189-191, 194 and his concluding remarks on p. 196.

18 Watson, *CHP*, p. 284.

19 Watson, *CHP*, p. 207; he is followed by J. Hunter, "Theophany verses in the Hebrew psalms", *Old Testament Essays* 11/2 (1998), p. 260; cf. Freedman, *Pottery*, p. 9; Freedman and Hyland, "Psalm 29: A Structural Analysis", *HTR* 66 (1973) 237-256.

20 The importance of repetition and *Leitwörter* for creating rhythm and circles of meaning in oral composition is emphasised by S. Niditch in *Oral Word and Written Word* (London: SPCK, 1997), p. 13; see further her comments on formulae and epithets, pp. 14-17.

21 I.e., Freedman's other "Phase I" psalms; see Freedman, *Pottery*, pp. 82-3; Weiser, in keeping with his view of the origin of the divine epiphany, prefers to compare the Sinai traditions, p. 175, n. 3.

also be mentioned.[22] Obviously, such associations can be explained in terms of subsequence rather than precedence or contemporaneity. However, a clustering of motifs within a group of psalms identified on independent grounds as potentially among the earliest in the canon could reinforce the case for their common origin in antiquity.[23]

The other aspect of Ps. 29 which merits textual comparison is the almost verbatim recurrence of vv. 1-2 in Ps. 96:7-9. Once again, one cannot exclude their mutual dependence on a third source or the possibility that Ps. 29 may have "borrowed" from Ps. 96. However, the employment of the phrase מִשְׁפְּחוֹת עַמִּים in Ps. 96:7 where Ps. 29:1 has בְּנֵי אֵלִים is most plausibly explained as the product of a later discomfort with the polytheistic resonances of the latter expression. Obviously, it cannot be excluded that this occurred at a redactive stage, but the hypothesis that Ps. 96 is dependent on Ps. 29 may be defended on other grounds. Firstly, it is intrinsically more probable that the author of one hymn should quote the opening lines of another within the course of his "composition", than that he should commence with words borrowed from the midpoint of an earlier poem. Furthermore, Ps. 96 exhibits further points of contact with a variety of psalms,[24] though none of them have any obvious relationship to each other. It would certainly seem curious if so many poems should draw on different sections of Ps. 96, with no overlap in their selections, and none of them overtly citing its opening lines.[25] Moreover, since the majority of these parallel passages—especially those with the closest affinities to Ps. 96—are apparently pre-exilic, this would further suggest that this divine kingship psalm may be a relatively late and tradition-dependent work. If this assessment of the interrelations of Ps. 96 is correct, this would correspondingly strengthen the case for the pre-exilic origin of Ps. 29 as well.[26]

---

22 Compare especially Pss. 68:5, 33-35 (Yahweh's thundering voice); note also the parallels with 24:7-10 (God of Glory) and 114:4, 6 (the "skipping" effect of the divine presence).

23 Loretz has argued that certain key terms and concepts in the Psalm, such as בְּנֵי אֵלִים or כָּבוֹד, reflect a post-exilic setting (*Psalm 29*, pp. 70, 77-8, 85); however, although he has succeeded well in highlighting the divergences of this composition from the extant Ugaritic material, his placement of these developments so late remains questionable, as the mention of the כָּבוֹד of Yahweh in other apparently pre-exilic material (e.g., Ex. 33:18, 22, Isa. 6:3, Ps. 24) or the early identification of Yahweh both as a storm god and with El (e.g. in Ps. 68) attests.

24 Particularly notable are the similarities of v. 10 to Ps. 93:1, and of v. 4a to Ps. 48:2a (again it is the opening phrases which recur); more loosely, compare v. 9 with Ps. 114:7 (the final verse); v. 1a with Pss. 33:3a and 149:1b; v. 2a with Ps. 68:5; also vv. 2, 3 with Pss. 9:12 and 67:3; v. 11 with Ps. 67:5a; v. 10b with Ps. 67:5b (compare 96:11a with 67:4a); v. 10c with Pss. 9:9b and 67:5b (cf. 7:9a); and v. 6a with Pss. 104:1 and 111:3.

25 There is a passing parallel between Ps. 96:1a and Ps. 33:3, but no extended quotation.

26 Seybold's claim that the inclusion of material from Ps. 29 into Ps. 96 (and 1 Chr. 16 as well) did not occur long after it attained its final form (p. 122) is dependent on his theory of a second-Temple liturgical revision of the originally pre-exilic Psalm (on

Therefore, although the evidence for the dating of Ps. 29 is disparate and uncertain, it would appear that a pre-exilic origin is probably correct, and that there are certain lines of association which would tend towards grouping it with other prosodic material which is also often independently classified as among the earliest in the Hebrew corpus. Insofar as the הֵיכָל of v. 9 could allude to Yahweh's heavenly temple or indeed to any sanctuary, but does not necessarily presuppose the construction of a centralised national shrine, and since mention is likewise made only of the עַם and not specifically of Israel, there are no *a posteriori* grounds for excluding a pre-monarchical origin, although such a provenance cannot itself be demonstrated.

ii. The Date of Psalm 68

Psalm 68 is highly complex and ambiguous—or at least appears so to the modern interpreter.[27] The metre is irregular, and it lacks clear affinities to any other composition in the canon which would enable it to be classified with any confidence according to a recognisable genre. Moreover, the structure of the psalm defies systematisation, and many of the allusions are obscure—a problem which is exacerbated by the corrupt nature of much of the text and high frequency of *hapax legomena* and poorly-attested or disputed vocabulary. So great have these difficulties seemed that Albright abandoned all attempt to discern any logical coherence in its form and determined that it was not properly a psalm at all, but merely "a catalogue of early Hebrew lyric poems".[28] The effort by Mowinckel[29] and Gray[30] to relate its content to the disparate themes associated with the autumn festival, or of Seybold to explain it

---

which, see further "Die Geschichte des 29. Psalms und ihre theologische Bedeutung", *ThZ* 36 [1980] 208-219). However, it seems unlikely that the unusual archaic "staircase" rhythms of the psalm could chiefly have resulted through a process of expansion, or that the original core, comprising in the central section only affirmations concerning "the voice of Yahweh", should generally be so lacking in convincing parallelism. Similarly, the intrusion of scattered prose features in the Psalm may perhaps best be attributed to continuous use and to the especial popularity which the composition seems to have enjoyed in the post-exilic period, rather than to a specific programme of expansion at a relatively late stage in its history.

27 See, e.g., the opening remarks on this psalm in the commentaries of Tate (p. 170), Dahood (II, p. 133), Clifford (I, p. 314), Kraus (II, p. 628) and Weiser (p. 328) and Albright's observation that "Psalm 68 has always been considered with justice as the most difficult of all the Psalms" ("A Catalogue of Early Hebrew Lyric Poems (Psalm LXVIII)" *HUCA* 23 Pt 1 [1950] 1-39, p. 7).

28 *HUCA* 23 Pt 1(1950) 1-39. This position may be compared to that advocated by H. Schmidt (*Die Psalmen*, pp. 125-6, 127-131), who proposed that Ps. 68 comprised sixteen brief, independent compositions, collected together for liturgical use.

29 *Der achtundsechzigste Psalm* (Oslo: I Kommisjon hos Jacob Dybwad, 1953), e.g., p. 19.

30 J. Gray, "A Cantata of the Autumn Festival: Psalm lxviii", *JSS* 22 (1977) 2-26.

as the skeleton of a fragmented acrostic composition,[31] represent contrasting approaches to the same fundamental problem.

Nevertheless, there appears to be a considerable level of agreement concerning the essential antiquity of Ps. 68,[32] and there are a number of factors supporting this conclusion. First, v. 28 is most naturally to be understood as deriving from the time of the Saulide monarchy, when Benjamin, the "least" of the tribes, was "in the lead"[33] or, as Kraus renders, "klein, (doch) ihr Herrscher!".[34] A further aspect of interest here is the particular mention of Zebulun and Naphtali alongside the two tribes of the South, since four of the six occasions where the pair are mentioned in combination outside the more comprehensive tribal lists occur in Judg. 4-6.[35] These would seem to locate the notable activity of these two tribes in two successively recorded events deriving from the period of the Judges, i.e., from a time prior to, but perhaps not long antedating, the reign of Saul, the period to which allusion may be made in the first part of the verse.[36]

Second, there are indisputable affinities between Ps. 68 and Judg. 5, most evidently between Ps. 68:8-9 and Judg. 5:4-5.[37] However, there is nothing to suggest that the relation is one of literary dependence. Although the motifs follow the same underlying sequence, they seem to have been independently employed. A similar relationship may be discerned also between v. 18 and Deut. 33:2, v. 2 and Num. 10:35, vv. 34b-36 and Ps. 29, and v. 14a and Judg. 5:16a. Thus the evidence seems collectively to imply that Ps. 68 is steeped in the ancient theophany tradition of Israel, rather than being dependent on prior

---

31 Pp. 262-3.

32 See Gray (*JSS* 22, p. 26), Albright (*ARI*, p. 211 n. 104), Kraus (II, p. 629), Anderson (II, p. 482), Weiser (p. 483), and Tate (174). Even Gunkel (*Die Psalmen*, pp. 283-4) and Briggs (II, p. 96) temper their usual tendency towards late dating by recognising the influence of older traditions on the psalm.

33 Emending MT רֹדֵם, "their ruler", to קִדֵּם, Pi'el perf. קדם, "go / be in front".

34 II, p. 626; following MT. Goulder's claim that the reference is rather to the Benjaminite origins of David (*The Prayers of David*, pp. 208-210) varies only slightly from the early monarchic provenance advanced here.

35 Judg. 4:6, 10; 5:18; 6:35; the other occurrences are in Isa. 8:23 (reflecting a period of weakness for the region) and 1 Chr. 12:14 (exemplifying the remotest of the tribes).

36 There is a further possible connection between Ps. 68 and Judg. 4-5 in the sanctuary at Mount Tabor, though this is less certain. See especially Kraus, II, pp. 631-632, Gray, *JSS* 22, pp. 2, 5-7, and, for the argumentation behind regarding Tabor as a sanctuary, O. Eissfeldt, "Der Gott des Tabor und seine Verbreitung", *ARW* 31 (1934) 14-41, M. Noth, *Geschichte Israels*, p. 65. Note especially Judg. 4:12, 14; 5:13, and compare Ps. 68:16-17 with Ps. 89:13.

37 Note, e.g., the pairing of צעד and יצא in relation to the "march from the southland" in Ps. 68:8 and Judg. 5:4a (for which compare also Hab. 3:12-13) and the application of the verb רעש to ארץ in Ps. 68:9 and Judg. 5:4b (for which compare Ps. 18:8 = 2 Sam. 22:8, besides Ps. 77:19 and Joel 4:16). The commonality of the expression זֶה סִינַי and of the image of the heavens "dropping" or "dripping" (נטף) water in Ps. 68:9 and Judg. 5:4b-5 is particularly striking.

sources still discernible from the Hebrew Bible. This seems to be the only way to account for the commonality of the thematic threads running throughout the "parallel" passages, which points to a web of links between the various compositions, rather than merely a mutual relationship founded in Ps. 68. Moreover, although borrowing from earlier compositions, if it had occurred, would not facilitate the setting of a *terminus ad quem*, the fact that all the associated material, despite occurring in diverse sources, is apparently very ancient, reduces the probability that Ps. 68 could be anything other than very early in origin itself.

The linguistic evidence would seem to be generally in accord with this assessment. Stylistically, Ps. 68 is remarkably terse, even in comparison with the archaic passages to which it exhibits close affinities, its brevity sometimes almost verging on obscurity. It consistently lacks the standard prose features which in time tended to intrude into Hebrew poetry,[38] yet contains certain grammatical characteristics which are thought to be "survivals" from an earlier age, such as the relative pronoun זוּ (v. 29) or זֶה (v. 9), the form מִנִּי (explained as מִן + the old י of the genitive, v. 32), verbal terminations in וּן- (the so-called *nûn paragogicum*,[39] vv. 14, 17), the reassertion of a final י before an afformative beginning with a vowel in a final-ה verb (v. 32, though in this case, exceptionally, without a pause),[40] and the possible reappearance of a third person feminine plural suffix in ָה- (v. 14).[41] Admittedly, such features are by no means confined to, or even always especially characteristic of, the poetry of the Hebrew Bible which is commonly presumed to be archaic. However, in the present composition they are also set alongside various items of vocabulary which would appear to be limited to the earlier literature of Israel.[42] Possibly more significant for dating, though less subject to analysis and intertextual

---

38 Such as the relative pronoun אֲשֶׁר or object-marker –אֶת. Even the article -ה occurs just four times in its thirty-five verses, whilst the conjunction ו is permitted to open a line only twice. Although the masculine singular pronoun הוּא does feature once, it is notable that this is in the highly emphatic position afforded to the final word of the psalm, excepting the concluding בָּרוּךְ אֱלֹהִים.

39 GK §47m.

40 GK §75u.

41 GK §44m.

42 Note, e.g., the distribution of the combination צאר and יצא as applied to God (v. 8), and of the unusual term (מ)שפתים, which is confined, apart from v. 14, to Judg. 5:16 and Gen. 49:14. In addition, the use of the divine names יָהּ (vv. 5, 19) and שַׁדַּי (v. 15) may be noted, since both are apparently typical of some of the very earliest poetry, as well as of a later "archaistic" revival, the temporal separation between these different settings being quite considerable in the case of the latter title. Obviously, this type of evidence must be handled with great care, yet the apparent incompatibility of the remaining data with a late dating (and the conjoining of these appellations with other divine names weighs against regarding them as later editorial emendations) would tend to point towards the psalm's antiquity.

comparison, is the frequency of *hapax legomena*[43] and words of uncertain meaning which is probably unrivalled in the rest of the Psalter.

Nevertheless, despite the evidence pointing towards an origin in the time of the Judges or of Saul, the case for the early provenance of Psalm 68 should not be overstated, since there are also opposing factors to be taken into consideration. Especially weighty is the explicit mention of הֵיכָלֶךָ עַל־יְרוּשָׁלָםִ in v. 30, and of tribute from kings (vv. 30-32), which Gray suggests would best suit the time of Solomon.[44] One might, therefore, think in terms of an ancient pre-monarchical composition adapted to the circumstances of a cult centred in Jerusalem in the earliest phase of the monarchical period.

In addition, it must be conceded that the linguistic evidence does not uniformly point to the pre-exilic era as the setting for the psalm; on the other hand, examples of apparently late terminology are essentially confined to w. (6-)7 and 31, probably suggesting that, if they are late, they may be the product of localised editorial activity and that much of the psalm may have remained relatively untouched by such processes. Certainly, w. 5 to 8 would read very smoothly with the omission of v. 6-7, but since this psalm is not generally characterised by smoothness, this is hardly decisive. It may also be observed that vv. 30-32 are frequently regarded, on grounds of content, as potentially reflecting a later period than the rest of the composition, yet since the events alluded to are obscure, this does not permit of further chronological delimitation.[45]

Therefore, the evidence for dating Ps. 68, whether pertaining to its content and allusions, vocabulary, grammar, or use of divine names, seems to point to the conclusion that it is substantially very ancient, perhaps emanating from a period as early as that of the Judges or Saul. However, there is also a significant body of circumstantial detail which points to later redactional activity, perhaps initially reflecting the need to adapt the poem to the requirements of the Jerusalem temple, but also probably in part deriving from its incorporation into the Elohistic Psalter. Towards the end of the Psalm, in vv. 30-32, it is possible that historical circumstances which are now obscure to us but which reflect the Solomonic or (following the uncertain linguistic data) a later period may have left their imprint; similar activity may also have occurred in vv. 6-7, although the evidence is fragmentary and any confidence in this matter is elusive.

43 Or textual corruption? Where a term is not otherwise attested, it is often impossible to know with which we have to deal—or indeed, whether the one problem has precipitated and been compounded by the other.

44 *JSS* 22 (1977), pp. 4-5.

45 Suggestions range from the time of the exodus (viewed retrospectively; so Weiser, p. 333) to the fourth century (Gunkel, *Die Psalmen*, p. 287).

iii. The Date of Psalm 114

An immediately striking feature of Ps. 114 is that the masculine singular suffix of v. 2a has no obvious precedent, suggesting that the Psalm has lost its original opening. This implies that it could have originated as a liturgical extract, or that it has undergone fragmentation or reworking. In such circumstances, the feasibility of establishing a date (which date?) for the psalm must be particularly uncertain. Nevertheless, v. 2 may presuppose a capital in Jerusalem and probably also the temple, though it does not necessarily reflect the experience of a divided monarchy. Stylistic grounds, and probably also the mixed archaic and standard linguistic forms, may reflect a pre-exilic context, possibly but not necessarily prior to 721 BC. Possibly archaic linguistic features include the sequence *qtl-wyqtl-yqtl* in v. 3, and the appearance of ִי- and ו- terminations in v. 8,[46] whilst *waw compaginis*[47] occurs outside phrases involving the construct form חַיְתוֹ only here and in the Balaam Oracles of Num. 23:18, 24:3, 15.[48] In addition, both variant refrains (vv. 4, 6; 3, 5) and rhetorical questions (vv. 5, 6) are associated by Watson with an underlying orality;[49] the latter phenomenon may be compared also with Ps. 68:16 and with *KTU* 1.4.vii.38-9,[50] whilst the unusual "skipping" image of vv. 4, 6 resonates with Ps. 29:6. The use of expanded cola,[51] which is also frequent in Ugaritic,[52] appears in a relatively simple form in v. 7, and again, this could be consonant with an early provenance. Further, the notion of the earth trembling before the presence of Yahweh is a common feature of poetic representations of the divine theophany. Collectively, these points of contact suggest quite an early date (although secondary adoption of ancient motifs may also have occurred).

The parallelism of Judah and Israel in v. 2 has been subject to a variety of interpretations, all of which impinge on the origin of the psalm, yet although the verse tantalisingly hints at a specific historical background, it does not allow any firm evidence to be discerned. Nevertheless, it may be observed that, in marked contrast to the heavily Yahwistic focus of Ps. 29 (where the divine name occurs eighteen times, his unnamed עַם just twice at the end of the psalm), Ps. 114 opens with a fourfold mention of בֵּית יַעֲקֹב and יִשְׂרָאֵל, יִשְׂרָאֵל and יְהוּדָה (vv. 1, 2), while God is directly mentioned only twice, and then only by means of the appellations אָדוֹן and אֱלוֹהַּ יַעֲקֹב (v. 7), which apparently define him by his relationship to his people. This human-political perspective, and the bipartite emphasis on Judah-Israel as his sanctuary-dominion seems to suggest a focus

---

46 Robertson, *Linguistic Evidence*, p. 145.

47 Gibson, *DIHG*, p. 24 § 27 Rem 1.

48 These are assigned by Albright to the late 13th century (*YGC*, p. 29), by Freedman to the 11th century (*Pottery*, pp. 90, 118) and by Watson to c. 900 (*CHP*, p. 40).

49 *CHP*, pp. 295, 341.

50 Thus Gibson, *CML*, p. 65, n. 9.

51 Discussed above in relation to Ps. 29; Watson employs the term "pivot pattern" to describe the same phenomenon.

52 Watson, *CHP*, p. 217; it is discussed further in Dahood, "A New Metrical Pattern in Biblical Poetry", *CBQ* 29 (1967) 574-582.

on Israel (cf. v. 1) as one people, whatever the underlying reality may have been, and this may therefore perhaps best be placed after the foundation of the monarchy.

The history of traditions evidence may also make a tentative contribution, since the psalm does not necessarily seem to know of the tradition of the Red Sea crossing, which is well-developed in "P" but is not apparent in "J" and "E". This issue is complicated by the composition's evocative nature, but it is possible that the intermingling of the Red Sea and Jordan motifs in this Psalm or in the tradition to which it belongs may only later either have given rise to the idea that a crossing occurred at both the Sea and the River, or have been perceived as compatible with it. Thus, it could conceivably represent an ancient, probably independent, strand of tradition, and the possibility that it could be contemporary with, or even earlier than, J or E is not thereby precluded.[53]

Thus, the evidence which may be gleaned from this psalm would seem to be consistent with a pre-exilic provenance, and a few strands may actually be adduced in support of this. However, it is possible that a lengthy period of transmission has left influences from different eras, thereby inhibiting the effort to discern its origin.

2. The Theme of "Chaos" in Psalms 29, 68 and 114

i. The Theme of "Chaos" in Psalm 29

Psalm 29 is perhaps the "purest" example of the theophany motif, insofar as the epiphany of the deity comprises the subject of the entire poem, and appears primarily to function for its own sake. At its heart is the supreme God Yahweh, the king of heaven who is enthroned above the flood, and who manifests himself as the God of the thunderstorm, with great emphasis being placed on his mighty voice (vv. 3, 4, 5, 7, 8, 9). The references to thundering "upon many waters" in v. 3, and to the fact that "Yahweh sits enthroned over the flood / as king for ever" in v. 10, have widely been interpreted as alluding to a battle with chaos.[54] This approach is in part inspired by the general ambience of the psalm

53 Goulder, in contending that this composition represents a post-exilic elaboration upon the Pentateuchal portrayals of the Red Sea event (*The Psalms of the Return*, p. 165, following Gunkel, *Die Psalmen*, pp. 494-5; cf. Davidson, pp. 374-5), successfully indicates the differences between them, but fails to demonstrate how Ps. 114 demonstrates any knowledge of or dependence on these traditions. He moreover seems to underestimate the influence on this Psalm of ideas which are not necessarily directly manifested in the Sinai accounts but which are nevertheless fundamentally connected with the divine theophany, seeing them instead as enhancements of the Pentateuchal material.

54 Though note Davidson's perceptive statement that "Here, in Psalm 29... there is no such conflict" (p. 101).

and by the assumption of Canaanite influence.[55] However, it is also founded on a misconstrual of the imagery encountered in these verses, particularly in regard to the key terms מַבּוּל (v. 10) and מַיִם רַבִּים (v. 3).

The noun מַבּוּל figures outside Ps. 29:10 only in Gen. 6-11, in relation to the flood of Noah's time,[56] and hence it is frequently interpreted as a *terminus technicus* for the primæval Deluge. This has given rise to a variety of interpretations of Ps. 29:10, none of which has achieved widespread support. Essentially, there are three main possibilities, entailing reference to the Flood,[57] to Yahweh's victory over chaos,[58] or to a combination of these themes.[59] Rather disconcertingly, there is no clear relationship between the translations adopted and the corresponding exegesis, with particular confusion surrounding the issue of the temporal orientation of the verse, and of the force of the particle ל.[60]

However, it appears that despite the diversity of these readings, each is founded on a conception of מַבּוּל which may be mistaken. J. Begrich[61] has convincingly shown that the term actually refers to the heavenly ocean (cf. Gen. 1:7; Pss. 104:3a; 148:4; for the windows of heaven, compare Gen. 7:11; 2 Ki. 7:2, 19), as contrasted with the תְּהוֹם beneath the earth. Hence it is probably to be derived from the root יבל (perhaps, "flow, stream").[62] The cosmological significance of מַבּוּל is apparent not only from the present context in Ps. 29:10, but also from Gen. 7:7, 10 (J), where it occurs in the phrase מֵי הַמַּבּוּל; from the latter passage in particular, one might infer from this that they were not normally situated עַל-הָאָרֶץ. According to the Yahwistic source, the flood was caused by forty days of unceasing rain; thus, the מַבּוּל is to be located in the sky, the source of rainwater. If הַמַּבּוּל denoted the heavenly ocean, this would further explain the apparent familiarity with the term presumed by the employment of the article even at the first occurrence in each source (Gen. 6:17 [P]; 7:10 [J]). Unlike his predecessor J, P seems to portray a drastic image of complete inundation, entailing not only the opening of the fountains of the great deep (i.e., the waters under the earth; Gen. 7:11), but also the descent of the entire מַבּוּל onto the earth: וְהַמַּבּוּל הָיָה מַיִם[63] עַל־הָאָרֶץ (Gen. 7:6), וַיְהִי הַמַּבּוּל אַרְבָּעִים יוֹם עַל־הָאָרֶץ (v. 17). Thus, effectively, מַבּוּל has assumed the meaning

55 For the history of interpretation, see Loretz, *Psalm 29*, especially pp. 11-22.

56 Gen. 6:17; 7:6, 7, 10, 17; 9:11, 15, 28; 10:1, 32; 11:10.

57 Kissane, I, pp. 126, 128; Briggs, I, pp. 251, 255, Davidson, p. 103, Terrien, pp. 274, 278.

58 Dahood, I, pp. 175, 180; Girard, I, p. 511, Kraus, I, pp. 377, 383, Clifford, I, p. 156.

59 Craigie, pp. 282, 248-249.

60 Notwithstanding these difficulties, any exegesis which attempts to make sense of the expression לַמַּבּוּל is surely preferable to Loretz's methodologically dubious replacement of it with לכסאו, despite the lack of any textual support (*Psalm 29*, p. 96); cf. likewise Margulis, "The Canaanite Origin of Psalm 29 Reconsidered" *Biblica* 51 (1970) 332-48, pp. 334-5, 345 (reading למשל).

61 "Mabbul. Eine exegetisch-lexicalische Studie", *ZS* 6 (1928) 135-153.

62 Cf. the nouns יָבָל (Isa. 30:25; 44:4), יובַל (Jer. 17:8) and אוּבָל (Dan. 8:2, 3, 6).

63 מַיִם is omitted from the Greek.

"deluge" in P,[64] albeit in a derivative manner. מַיִם in Gen. 6:17, 7:6 is then to be regarded as a gloss inserted after the original significance of the term had been forgotten. The understanding of מַבּוּל advanced by Begrich has attained wide credence in Genesis scholarship,[65] but seems until recently to have evaded the attention of many psalms commentators.[66]

Thus, מַבּוּל seems to denote the waters above the firmament, on which were laid the foundations of Yahweh's heavenly temple (cf. Ps. 104:3), and from which were opened the windows of heaven to allow rain to fall, as (implicitly) in this theophany (cf. Ps. 104:13). However, מַבּוּל is never used in contexts where any form of divine conflict is implied, nor may extra-biblical comparisons be adduced. This has been shown especially clearly by Tsumura, who emphasises that:

> The Ugaritic term *mbd* "flood ocean"... is never used for describing an enemy of Baal like Yamm/Nahar who was conquered by Baal... There is thus no evidence for the theory that *mdb* refers to a conquered enemy in Ugaritic mythology... As far as the biblical evidence goes, Yahweh never fought against the "Deluge" (*mabbûl*); in the Flood story it was his instrument to destroy the [sic.] mankind. Therefore, it is not likely that the "Deluge" (*mabbûl*) in Ps. 29:10 is the conquered enemy on which Yahweh sat enthroned.
> ...Marduk also never sat enthroned over his defeated enemy, the sea-dragon Tiāmat, nor did Baal, his Ugaritic counterpart, sit enthroned over the sea-dragon Yamm after his victory. Even if one should recognize in Ps. 29:10 the motif of a divine enthronement over a conquered enemy, he should compare this rather with Ea's establishment of his abode over the conquered enemy Apsû:... (Enuma elish I 71). In this case, however, Ea's enemy is... the subterranean water and it is El, rather than Baal, who corresponds to the Mesopotamian Ea, a "creator" who resides at the watery abode.[67]

64 Gen. 9:11, 15, 28; 10:1, 32; 11:10; cf. Sir. 44:17.

65 See, e.g., Westermann, *Genesis*, I, p. 567, and von Rad, *Das erste Buch Mose: Genesis*, p. 105.

66 Exceptions are Anderson (I, p. 238), who mentions this as a possibility (citing E. Vogt, "Der Aufbau von Psalm 29", *Biblica* 41 [1960], p. 22), without devoting much attention to the issue, and Schmidt (p. 55), who relates it to the provision of rain. Kraus, quite appropriately, interprets v. 3 in the light of the reference to the מַבּוּל, the "sea of heaven" in v. 10 (I, p. 382), but rather surprisingly, fails to mention or take account of this in relation to v. 10 itself. More recently, Eaton has recognised here the allusion to the "throning of Yahweh above the heavenly ocean", but his association of this with the "subdu[ing] and ma[king] serviceable of the otherwise unruly cosmic waters" (p. 140; similarly Hossfeld in HZ, I, p. 185, Seybold, pp. 123-4) is not supported either by the Psalm itself or by the wider evidence for this symbolism, as will be shown in the ensuing analysis.

67 "'The Deluge' (*mabbûl*) in Psalm 29:10", *UF* 20 (1988) 351-5, pp. 352-3. Of course, no such tradition is known for El. Moreover, once Ea "had secured his triumph over his enemies", he "rested" "in profound peace" "in his sacred chamber", then "he named it 'Apsu,' for shrines he assigned (it). In that same place his cult hut he founded" (*Enuma

As a result, instead of being associated with the theme of "chaos", use of the term מַבּוּל must rather be recognised to cohere both with the thunderstorm imagery which pervades the psalm (thus relating to the provision of rain),[68] and with the allusion to the הֵיכָל in v. 9 (implied also by the invocation to the בְּנֵי אֵלִים to worship [הִשְׁתַּחֲווּ] Yahweh in vv. 1-2). According to the prevailing ancient Near Eastern temple ideology (the currency of which does not presuppose the existence of the Jerusalem temple), the heavenly and earthly abodes of God were not clearly distinct; the Temple constituted the meeting place of heaven and earth, "a place where the eternal and the earthly were one. In some respects the temple *was* the heavenly world ... The rituals of the temple were performed on earth but were part of an eternal, heavenly reality. Thus space and location were ambiguous".[69] This fluidity is evident in Ps. 29 in the transition from the heavenly realm, in which the בְּנֵי אֵלִים "ascribe to Yahweh glory and strength" (vv. 1-2), to the הֵיכָל where "all cry 'Glory!'" (v. 9); although the latter term encompasses both spheres, the focus in v. 9 is perhaps primarily on the earthly temple, as is evidenced by the human and national perspective of v. 11. The tendency towards the fusion of both realms is further exemplified by the parallel to Ps. 29:1-2 in Ps. 96:7-9, in which the בְּנֵי אֵלִים are transformed into מִשְׁפְּחוֹת עַמִּים.[70] Thus, there is good reason to believe that the reference to Yahweh sitting לַמַּבּוּל is not exclusively orientated towards the heavenly sphere, but may encompass the earthly temple also.[71] In any case, the parallels between the heavenly and earthly abodes of God are sufficiently established for one to expect that this concept may find expression in temple architecture and symbolism. In fact, the idea of enthronement "above the flood" seems to be supported in a variety of sources, perhaps most obviously in the molten sea of 1 Ki. 7:23-26 and 2 Chr. 4:2-6, which stood in the court of the temple.[72] It is therefore worth exploring this symbolism in order to illuminate the concepts of v. 10 more fully.

---

elish I.74-77; *ANET*, p. 61). It is these ideas, and not that of conflict, which pertain in the references to El's abode and in aspects of biblical Temple theology, as will be shown further below.

68 This imagery may climax with an allusion to the divine bestowal of water and its resultant benefits in v. 11: cf. שָׁלוֹם in Ps. 147:14, and ברך in Gen. 49:25, Deut. 28:12, 33:13, Ezek. 34:26 and Mal. 3:10b; and see further the detailed discussion of Kloos, *Yhwh's Combat with the Sea*, pp. 88-93, especially p. 93.

69 M. Barker, *The Gate of Heaven*, p. 61.

70 Compare also the mention of כָּל־הָאָרֶץ in Ps. 96:9.

71 Note also the structural links identified by Girard between vv. 1-2 and 9c-11, which support this identification (I, pp. 502, 504-5, 509, 512), and contrast Loretz, *Psalm 29*, p. 102.

72 One might compare also, in a far later context, Rev. 4:6, which describes how "before the throne [of God in heaven] there is as it were a sea of glass like crystal". The previous verse speaks of the "flashes of lightning, and voices and peals of thunder" which issue from the throne, which suggests a further point of contact with the imagery of Ps. 29.

Although the bulls supporting the molten "sea"[73] may be regarded as a sign of deity, "the lordly power of this deity apparently did not have to be shown by the use of depictions that portrayed his right to rule as being earned in battle ... Bulls appear only as resting beasts of burden."[74] Thus the paradigm of the *Chaoskampf* "apparently was treated as obsolete when it came to providing iconographic themes to decorate the Jerusalem Temple".[75] Instead, the imagery surrounding the bronze sea was entirely derived from motifs associated with the idea of fertility. This concern is encapsulated in the bulls themselves,[76] for, as Albright has observed, "The bull was one of the most popular symbols of fecundity in the ancient Near East; the animal was invariably associated with the rain-giver Hadad (Baal), but also appears in connection with the life-giving water of rivers and the underworld."[77] In addition, the employment of plant symbolism (note, for example, the decoration of the sea with gourds, and the description of the brim as made "like the flower of a lily") may be associated with themes of "life and regeneration"[78] and "ideas of continued blessing and prosperity".[79] According to Keel, the palm trees engraved on the stands for the lavers (1 Ki. 7:27-39) may, further, be symbolic of the tree of life,[80] a motif which is closely linked to that of life-giving water.[81] He cites, for example, a wall-painting from Mari entailing depictions of cherubim, bulls, palm trees and temple. "A stream with four branches (cf. Gen. 2:10) rises from the vessels held out by the deities. A stylised plant grows out of the stream. This is the place from which all life issues."[82] Thus, the Temple may be characterised as "a sphere of life"; the recurrence of the same features in the Jerusalem Temple and in the garden of Eden, and especially in the imagery surrounding the bronze sea and lavers, therefore indicates that the presence of the living God, whose blessings flow out to nourish the earth, may be represented here.

The absence of combat themes combined with the presence of more general motifs of regeneration and blessing finds a further correlation in the widely-held suggestion that the molten sea "cannot be separated from the

73 יָם, which, of course, as de Vaux (*Les Institutions de l'Ancien Testament*, II, p. 171) stresses, may connote "the sea, or a lake, or a large river (*e.g.* the Euphrates or the Nile), but which in later Hebrew also means a 'basin' or 'vat'"; so also Albright, *ARI*, p. 149.

74 Keel and Uehlinger, *Göttinnen, Götter und Gottessymbole* (Freiburg: Herder, 2nd ed. 1993), p. 195.

75 *GGG*, p. 196.

76 Keel, *Die Welt der altorientalischen Bildsymbolik* (Neukirchen: Neukirchener Verlag, 1972), p. 120.

77 *ARI*, pp. 149-150; cf. Albright, "Gilgameš and Engidu, Mesopotamian Geni of Fecundity" *JAOS* 40 (1920), pp. 316-7.

78 *GGG*, p. 195.

79 *GGG*, p. 413.

80 *WAB*, pp. 124-126.

81 *Ibid.*, p. 120.

82 *Ibid.*, p. 126.

Mesopotamian *apsû*, employed both as the name of the subterranean fresh-water ocean from which all life and fertility were derived and as the name of a basin of holy water erected in the temple".[83] However, this harmonious Temple symbolism, in which the fresh water features as a source of life and blessing and as an indication of the presence of the deity, must be rigorously distinguished from any idea of conflict with the salt-water ocean.[84] It is frequently stated in the context of discussions of the molten sea that it "represents the harnessed, subdued chaos from which the world arose".[85] However, this is misleading insofar as neither subjugation nor the motif of "chaos" are in any way implied by the description of the molten sea according to the Books of Kings and Chronicles, or by the evidence of comparable cultic artefacts and their portrayal in the wider cultural context. The archaeology of the ancient Near East attests to a vigorous iconographic vocabulary of combat, but it is not employed here. It is moreover ludicrous to suggest that just because a particular object is the product of creation, this theme must be implied wherever the same object is mentioned; this is surely nowhere more the case than in relation to such a multivalent entity as the sea.

The correlation between life-giving water and the abode of God, which is evidenced by the imagery of Ps. 29:10 and symbolised also by the bronze sea, is further manifested in the idea that the deity's house was located at the confluence of rivers. It is the source of the fertilising waters which flow out to nourish the earth (cf. Eden, Gen. 2:10; Ezek. 47:1-12; Joel 4:18; Ps. 46:5; Zech. 14:8; compare Ezek. 28:2; cf. also Rev. 22:1-2; 1 Enoch 26:2, and, more faintly, Pss. 65:10; 133:3; Isa. 8:6; the motif of the temple as the source of life and blessing may be reflected also in Hag. 1:9-11, cf. Hag. 2:9).[86] Although it might appear that the waters here depicted are merely subterranean, the apprehension of an identity between the celestial and terrestrial temples, and the obvious congruence of the heavenly and earthly oceans, militates against such a clear-cut division. One might note, for example, representations of the waters surrounding the earth in which those of each sphere are portrayed as obvious counterparts to each other, as interconnected, or simply collectively represented as a circle or frame; likewise, the Assyrian *apsû* could also variously denote either terrestrial, subterranean or supercelestial waters.[87] Thus, a cult basin from the Assur temple in Assur, cited by Keel, depicts "water-giving deities and

83 Albright, *ARI*, pp. 148-9; cf. de Vaux, *Institutions*, II, p. 158, May, *JBL* 74 (1955), p. 20.

84 Note also the absence of any correlation with combat themes in the practical purpose of the "sea", which, according to 2 Chr. 4:6, "was for the priests to wash in"; cf. Ex. 30:17(-21).

85 *WAB*, p. 120.

86 The idea of the waters separating into channels, attested in Gen. 2:10, Ps. 46:4, finds an interesting parallel in a seventh century Assyrian representation of the temple area, in which a river is similarly divided. Keel argues that if the bronze sea represented יָם / נָהָר, its channels may have been concretised in the immense lavers of the Temple (*WAB*, p. 124).

87 *WAB*, p. 120.

priests of Ea drawing holy water";[88] the presence of a number of water-sources in this image has understandably suggested to him the parallel with Gen. 2:10-14,[89] yet, in this case, their origin is apparently celestial.

The idea of the divine abode being situated over the flood, at the source of the life-giving waters, occurs also in Canaanite epic in relation to

> El at the springs of the Rivers,
> Amid the streams of the Deeps[90] (*KTU* 1.3.v.6-7; 1.4.iv.21-22).

An interesting outworking of the idea of life-giving water emanating from the temple may further be evidenced by the tendency for water to be stored in vast reservoirs under sanctuary precincts; as Keel has remarked in this connection, many temples had "not only basins, but sacred lakes and pools as well".[91]

However, perhaps the most direct confirmation of the notion of enthronement over the flood is provided by iconographic representations of exactly this idea. Particularly worthy of notice is a ninth century stone tablet recording Nabupaliddin's endowment of the sun temple at Sippar, and representing the presentation of this king before the enthroned deity Shamash (Figure 1), since "below the entire scene are wavy lines in which four stars are set, a representation of the heavenly ocean (*apsû*)".[92] Thus, the god is depicted, quite literally, as sitting "enthroned over the flood". Several aspects of this portrayal particularly merit attention. Most obviously, it does not celebrate the deity's enthronement over the flood *per se*, and it does not appear to be an issue which receives especial emphasis within the context of the picture as a whole. Rather, its purpose is the commemoration of Nabupaliddin's endowment of the temple and consequent presentation before Shamash. That the god should be depicted as enthroned, and that his seat should be "over the flood" is merely a corollary of this. Moreover, the heavenly ocean is, as Pritchard observes, represented by means of "wavy lines":[93] thus stylised, the waves exhibit no hint of personification or deification; nor is there any indication of interaction between them and the deity. It must therefore finally be stressed that the god's rule and the stability of his throne are here presupposed. The pillars of his throne are supported by two bull-men; he is surrounded by attendant deities, receiving homage from the king, wearing a multiple-horned

88 *WAB*, p. 121; the picture (no. 185) appears on p. 122.

89 P. 122.

90 *il mbk nhrm*
qrb apq thmtm.

91 *WAB*, p. 120.

92 Pritchard, *ANEP* p. 313. T. N. D. Mettinger further points out that this interpretation is confirmed by the fact that an inscription over the canopy explicitly indicates that Sin, Shamash and Ishtar are "above the ocean" ("YHWH SABAOTH—The Heavenly King on the Cherubim Throne" in T. Ishida, ed., *Studies in the Period of David and Solomon and Other Essays* [Tokyo: Yamakawa-Shuppansha, 1982] 109-138, p. 119); moreover, there appears to be a representation of the firmament below the waves.

93 The terminology employed also by Mettinger, p. 119.

mitre, a symbol of divinity, and holding in his right hand a ring and rod, connoting justice. Thus, all the indications are that enthronement over the flood is in this context an aspect of celestial geography rather than a consequence of theomachic victory or an object of cultic celebration.[94] A similar idea is conveyed in a more condensed verbal form in Ps. 104:3a, where God is lauded as the one "who hast laid the beams of thy chambers on the waters".[95]

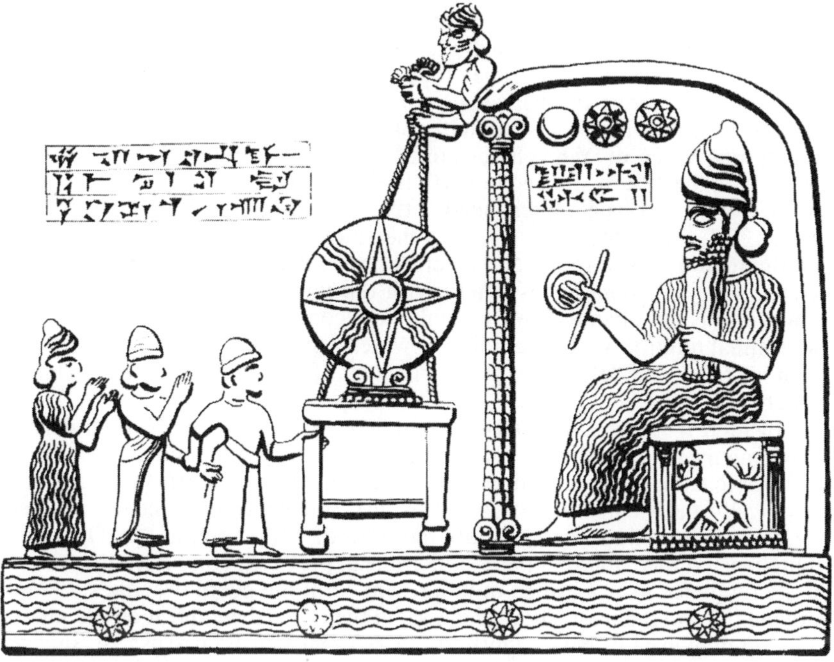

Figure 1: Stone tablet recording Nabupaliddin's endowment of the sun temple at Sippar, reproduced from O. Keel, *Die Welt der altorientalischen Bildsymbolik und das Alte Testament*, p. 153 (No. 239). (Reproduced with permission of Vandenhoeck & Ruprecht, Göttingen, Germany.)

94 A further aspect of the portrayal to be noted is that "the wavy lines extend over the entire breadth of the picture, thus indicating that both scenes—the presentation scene and the throne scene—take place above the celestial sea. The picture is a striking illustration of the mythical concept of space: the temple is the place where heaven and earth meet, or heaven on earth" (Mettinger, pp. 119-120; thus also Keel, *WAB*, p. 153).

95 One might, perhaps, also compare the reaction of Athirat to the news that a palace is to be constructed for Baal in *KTU* 1.4.v.6-9; here Baal's control over the water-reserves of heaven and self-manifestation in storm-phenomena seem to be consequent upon the establishment of his temple.

More importantly, if מַבּוּל signifies the "waters of heaven", this would also cohere with a contextual reading of v. 3, in which the voice of Yahweh is said to be "upon many waters": since the opening verse of Psalm 29 sets the scene in the heavenly realm, v. 3 should most naturally also be interpreted accordingly, as alluding to the waters of the same sphere. This approach is affirmed by the content of the verse, which intensely focuses on the thundering voice of Yahweh, presumably in the sky (compare especially Jer. 10:13; 51:16; cf. Ps. 148:4). Significantly, this conclusion is one to which the instincts of certain psalms scholars have already led, despite its essential incompatibility with dominant interpretative trends, and often with the general direction of their own exegetical leanings. Thus Kissane proposes that "*the waters* are most probably ... the 'waters above the heavens,' whose commotion caused the noise of thunder".[96] Likewise, Kraus explicitly asserts that "when v. 3 states that the thunderous voice of Yahweh resounds 'over the waters,' the reference is certainly to the מבול mentioned in v. 10. In the mythical-cosmological term מבול the 'sea of heaven' is comprehended ... המים are, in keeping with the definition in Gen. 1:7, המים אשר מעל לרקיע. This therefore means: in the highest heavens the thunderous voice (הרעים—קול) of Yahweh, the אל־הכבוד, is booming".[97] Kraus' analysis concurs absolutely with the interpretation advanced above; however it is not obvious how it should be reconciled with his discernment of the combat motif in v. 10, according to which Yahweh "has threatening chaos lie at his feet", and "elements of the theology of creation obviously are hinted at here".[98]

In fact, it is the *Chaoskampf* which is most commonly regarded as providing the interpretative key to both verses 3 and 10, although an excessively literalistic approach, entailing the discernment of a storm at sea (more specifically, the Mediterranean) in v. 3, is also sometimes encountered.[99] Often, the two contrasting readings are conflated, for example, in Dahood's apprehension that although the Mediterranean probably comprises the subject of the reference in v. 3 "since in its present form the poem describes a storm moving in from the west", nevertheless, "in the original composition the phrase *'al hammayim* may have signified... a reference to Baal's use of thunder against the chaotic waters".[100] In a similar vein, Craigie also contends that the storm imagery is "primary", yet emphasises that the "undertones of the language" must "reflect an adaptation of Canaanite / Ugaritic religious thought ... In Ps. 29:3, the Lord is described... as one victorious over the chaotic forces symbolized by the 'mighty waters'".[101] This interpretation is supposedly aided

96 I, p. 127.

97 I, p. 382.

98 I, p. 383.

99 Thus, e.g., Briggs, I, pp. 252-253; Terrien, pp. 276-7.

100 I, p. 176. In fact, Baal appears not to use thunder against Yam in the Ugaritic texts, but rather slays him with the clubs furnished by Kothar-wa-Khasis.

101 P. 247. He cites here *CTA* 3.D.36 (*KTU* 1.3.iii.39), where allusion is made to *nhr il rbm*, which he presumably understands as "Nahar the god of the great (waters)"; however, the translation adopted by Gibson, "Nahar the great god" (*CML*, p. 50;

by comparison with Ex. 15:3, 8, in which Craigie detects a further—and, one might infer, still more deeply submerged—allusion to Baal's conquest of Yam, where Yahweh "is described as using 'sea' (*Yam*) as a tool of conquest". However, one must question whether the discernment of such "undertones" is justified, when they are far from apparent or even recognisable from the text itself.

In fact the *Chaoskampf* interpretation of the verse seems rather to derive from two main external sources. The first is the assumption of Canaanite influence or dependence, which, despite its obvious circularity, has exercised a pervasive influence upon the psalm's exponents. The poem should initially be interpreted on its own terms, before the extent and nature of its relation to other traditions is assessed. This is imperative if the various nuanced possibilities of adaptation, dialogue, creative appropriation, parody or subversion, rather than merely straightforward plagiarism, are to be considered as potential modes of relation between the psalm and any prior material. The second is the perception of the "cosmic connotations of *mayim rabbîm*" set forth in a much-quoted but seldom-criticised article by H. G. May.[102] Consequently, a situation has arisen whereby it is possible for a scholar such as Dahood to offer a reference to this article as the sole comment on מַיִם רַבִּים in v. 3.[103]

Essentially, May's thesis was that "the 'many waters' are the chaotic, disorderly, insurgent elements which must be controlled".[104] He argued that a careful consideration of certain passages in which the expression appeared would indicate that it was employed to denote the enemies of Yahweh, of Israel, or of the pious individual.[105] The identification of the so-called "cosmic connotations of מַיִם רַבִּים" then relates to his claim that "the enemies are manifestations of the intransigent elements which had to be quelled by Yahweh before creation could begin, and which must ever be defeated by him as he continues his activity in history. The enemy defeated by Yahweh is... identified with the corporate whole of Yahweh's antagonists... There continues throughout history the kind of conflict which is posited at creation when Yahweh's wind blew over the watery abyss..."[106] Thus, "whether in the past, present, or future, the struggle is essentially one, the battle of God against the waters which threaten his rule. And after the conflict, he sits enthroned over the waters."[107] This last phrase provides an indication of the nature of May's treatment of Ps. 29, for he discovers a reminiscence of the *Chaoskampf* in v. 3,

---

followed by Smith in *UNP*, p. 111, Pardee in *CS*, I, p. 252, and Wyatt in *RTU*, p. 79), would seem more likely; cf., e.g., *KTU* 1.6.v.2, where *rbm* seems to constitute a collective appellative for the gods.

102 "Some Cosmic Connotations of Mayim Rabbîm, 'Many Waters'", *JBL* 74 (1955), pp. 9-21.

103 I, p. 177.

104 P. 10.

105 P. 12.

106 P. 11.

107 P. 12.

and apparently regards the action of v. 10 as consequent upon, or even indicative of, the divine victory.[108]

However, the picture which he projects concerning the significance of the expression מַיִם רַבִּים is somewhat distorted, insofar as many of the passages to which he awards detailed consideration make no use of it at all. Most notable is the emphasis he places on "Yahweh's struggle against the sea dragon ... most obviously in the allusions to Leviathan and Rahab"—a theme which he introduces in the first paragraph,[109] despite the fact that מַיִם רַבִּים never appear in connection with these figures. He then proceeds to bring his exposition of such passages as Pss. 74 and 89 and Isa. 51:9-10 to bear upon those properly meriting attention, and consequently imposes upon them "a suggestion of cosmic dualism"[110] and even the hint of pre-creation conflict alluded to above. מַיִם רַבִּים are thus swiftly identified as "the cosmic insurgent elements which may be manifest as the enemies of Yahweh, as the enemies of Israel ... or as the enemy afflicting the faithful individual." Yahweh's conquest consequently assumes the status of a "victory over cosmic evil and wickedness, over the demonic, or more properly the dragonic".[111] The key feature identified, however, is the theme of the combat against the waters.[112]

This lack of methodological rigour in distinguishing between different items of vocabulary and applications of imagery is especially evident in his account of Isa. 17:12-13, where he states: "The 'many peoples' are the 'many waters,' equals the 'seas,' as the enemies in Ps. 89:11 [10] are Rahab, and the enemies of Israel the 'many waters,' the seas and the dragon in Hab. 3."[113] However, in the passage concerned, מַיִם רַבִּים actually occurs in a simile, the point of comparison being the roaring of the nations and the roaring of 'many waters' (cf. Ezek. 1:24; 43:2). Thus, simply to assume an identity between the objects whose sound provides the focus of comparison, is equivalent to claiming that the waters are cherubim's wings or the advent of Yahweh (Ezek. 1:24; 43:2).

A similar laxity is exhibited in the use of putative cross-cultural parallels. Observing that "in the Babylonian creation epic Marduk mounts his storm chariot and uses the lightning and the winds", May concludes that "we may understand this wind motif as it appears in Ps. 18:11 (10) or as it is found in Gen. 1:2, where the wind of God moves over the face of the deep (*tehom*). It is the same wind which was sent by God and which 'caused the waters to subside' in Gen 8:1 after the flood, when the waters had once more ruled and re-creation became necessary."[114] However, whereas Marduk uses the four winds in order to distend Tiamat's body, leaving her mouth gaping open for him to deliver the fatal blow, in Ps. 18, Yahweh merely travels "on the wings of

108 P. 16.
109 P. 9
110 P. 11.
111 P. 12.
112 P. 12.
113 P. 11.
114 P. 14.

the wind": he does not necessarily generate, direct or control them here, but merely employs them as a mode of transport, not as an instrument of aggression. Moreover, Yahweh's "hovering" over the face of the deep in Gen. 1:2 is often thought to indicate a protective action; likewise the "clear-up operation" after the divinely-instigated Deluge is equally lacking in combative nuance.

Finally, the argument that the Temple was understood as a microcosm of the earth, with the sea of bronze in 1 Ki. 7:23ff. representing the "cosmic sea, the *tehôm*, as the subterranean ocean from which all fertility was derived",[115] though probably correct, in no way supports the "kind of cosmic reference presumed" by May.[116] This is not least the case because the fertility overtones of מַיִם רַבִּים, though a major sphere of allusion for this imagery, and consonant with the harmonic temple symbolism, are marginalised by May[117] in favour of a conflict-centred reconstruction, which if anything would be undermined rather than supported by this symbolism.

However, if May's reconstruction is to be rejected, it appears that a thorough re-evaluation of the significance of מַיִם רַבִּים is required. This is especially necessary if a proper understanding of Ps. 29 is to be achieved; moreover, the meaning of the expression will also prove to be a crucial factor in the interpretation of further passages to be considered later in the present monograph. The only means of establishing the likely force of the phrase is to submit the whole corpora of occurrences to a rigorous analysis, before returning to the issue of the interpretation of the specific verse under consideration, Ps. 29:3, once this has been accomplished.

The Meaning of the Phrase מַיִם רַבִּים

As is the case with many items of vocabulary which have conventionally been associated with the imagery of "chaos", the expression מַיִם רַבִּים is one which is not confined to a single sphere of allusion. As such, its significance cannot be identified in any absolute sense, but rather must in each case be determined by the context in which it occurs.

It is therefore perhaps fortuitous that מַיִם רַבִּים occurs as the vehicle (or "secondary subject") of a number of similes; although in each instance the tenor (or "primary subject") differs, it is the same fundamental aspect of the waters, epitomised by their roar / thundering, which forms the constant element of each image (Ezek. 1:24, 43:2, Isa. 17:12-13, Jer. 51:55). This may therefore be regarded as reflecting an important—and perhaps fairly broadly applicable—aspect of how מים רבים were perceived.

Their potentially dynamic nature is also revealed by such expressions as שֵׁטֶף מַיִם רַבִּים (Ps. 32:6) or חמר מַיִם רַבִּים (Hab. 3:15). Often, therefore, they are associated with the sea, sometimes being envisioned as the vehicle of maritime

115 P. 20.

116 P. 20. See the discussion of the significance of the "molten sea" above.

117 They are relegated to some concluding remarks on pp. 20-21.

commercial activity, e.g., in Ps. 107:23 and Isa. 23:3. Closely related in its sphere of imagery is the oracle against Tyre in Ezekiel 27, in which her downfall is portrayed under the image of a shipwreck. The story of the city's demise commences: "your rowers have brought you out onto מַיִם רַבִּים" (v. 26a); the wreck itself is then described as occurring בְּלֵב יַמִּים (vv. 26b, 27) and בְּמַעֲמַקֵּי־מָיִם (v. 34). Whether any significance should be accorded to this distinction is difficult to ascertain. However, in the presentation of the Red Sea event, the מַיִם רַבִּים are not envisaged as directly overwhelming the Egyptians (cf. תְּהֹמֹת, Ex. 15:5; יָם, v. 10; even אֶרֶץ, v. 12) but as the vast body of water into which they sank ("as lead", Ex. 15:10; "as a stone", Neh. 9:11); through the same מַיִם רַבִּים Yahweh miraculously made a path (Ps. 77:20; cf. Isa. 43:16, מַיִם עַזִּים [second exodus]; Isa. 51:10, מֵי תְּהוֹם רַבָּה) for the safe passage of his people. מַיִם רַבִּים thus seems to connote here the "great sea", a vast depth of water, its use the more strongly emphasising the immense salvific power of the God of Israel.

Elsewhere, there is a possible hint of the waters of the underworld, e.g., in the context of a further oracle against Tyre, Ezek. 26. Once again, she is commemorated as a "city renowned, that was mighty on the sea" (v. 17), and hence her downfall occurs "when I bring the deep over you, and מים רבים cover you" (v. 19). The train of thought continues in a clear allusion to Sheol: "then I will thrust you down with those who descend into the Pit..., and I will make you to dwell in the nether world ..." (v. 20). Thus, the audience is induced to reinterpret retrospectively its initial apprehension that מַיִם רַבִּים / תְּהוֹם simply relates to the maritime environment of Tyre; however, מַיִם רַבִּים does not of itself connote the underworld or its environs: rather it is subject to review in the light of the succeeding thematic development.

Again, in Ps. 32:6 (to be discussed in more detail in Chapter 4), it is not clear that anything more than metaphorical waters of affliction are implied. At least, proximate netherworld terminology, permitting a more definite interpretative strategy, is lacking, so the question must be left open, or resolved only by tentative comparison with the employment of similar vocabulary or themes within related contexts.

In Ps. 18:17 and the parallel in 2 Sam. 22:17, the connection with the underworld seems more definite,[118] but the motif of enmity is also introduced in the following verse (v. 18). This latter element also predominates in Ps. 144:7, a setting in which imagery apparently derived from Ps. 18 or a common source is recast so that the focus is transferred to the deliverance from the enemies, whilst the waters of the underworld recede from view (vv. 6-8).

However, in certain highly figurative poetic passages, often featuring the terrible theophany of Yahweh in the storm, attempts to identify the precise "geographical" location of מַיִם רַבִּים may be misplaced. Ps. 29:3 may conveniently be mentioned here since, in this context, there is ambiguity as to whether the waters of the sea or those of the heavenly ocean or storm clouds (cf. v. 10) are envisaged. However, perhaps the issue is irrelevant—for seas and

118 Note especially Ps. 18:5-6 and 2 Sam. 22:5-6; this imagery is probably also continued in v. 16.

deeps are interlinked and Yahweh is Lord of creation in its entirety, enthroned over the "cosmic" sea not only in heaven (note מַבּוּל, v. 10), but also representatively in his "microcosmic" Temple on earth (cf. vv. 1, 9c).[119]

Hab. 3:15 is similarly imprecise, forming part of a dramatic portrayal of the coming of Yahweh in a storm theophany. Since v. 8 clearly indicates that his wrath was not against the rivers or sea,[120] and since it is evident from v. 10 (cf. also vv. 6-7) that his coming is something to which all creation reverberates, it is not necessary to postulate any act of subjugation here. Indeed, the verse is perhaps to be linked with v. 9(-10), according to which Yahweh himself cleaves the earth with rivers.[121]

In Ps. 93:3-4, the waters appear to represent troublesome elements in nature (perhaps figuring potential foes of Israel) against which the order and rule established by Yahweh is absolutely secure and immovable (vv. 1-2); Yahweh "on high" is mightier far than they. There may be a possible progression from נְהָרוֹת to מַיִם רַבִּים to מִשְׁבְּרֵי־יָם, or they may all perhaps be regarded as aspects of the sea (נְהָרוֹת then being its channels: cf. Ezek. 31:4, 15, Ps. 24:2; compare Ps. 18:16 // 2 Sam. 22:16, Gen. 7:11); however, the point is hardly a significant one. More important is the fact that it is their voice, their roaring and thunder, which forms the basis of comparison,[122] thus epitomising tumultuous elements in all their sound and fury, but perhaps, in their practical effects, signifying nothing.

However, by far the most common mode of employment of מַיִם רַבִּים is to denote an abundance of fertile water that brings prosperity (Num. 24:5-7; 20:11; Jer. 51:13; Ezek. 17:5, 8; 19:10; 31:5, 7, 15; 32:13; 2 Chr. 32:4). Indeed, the words of Balaam's oracle in Num. 24:7 sound like the promise of blessing:

> Water shall flow from [Israel's] buckets,
> and his seed shall be in מַיִם רַבִּים,
> his king shall be higher than Agag,
> and his kingdom shall be exalted.

One might compare also the address to Babylon in Jer. 51:13. However, this sphere of imagery finds particularly full expression in the extended allegories of Ezekiel, in which the מַיִם רַבִּים, connected even with the deep, promote exceptionally abundant growth, allowing a plant to surpass all others, e.g., in 19:10, 17:5, 8, there in relation to Israel. However, to מַיִם רַבִּים are also to be attributed the strength and vigour of Pharaoh, depicted under the figure of a magnificent cedar (Ezek. 31:3).

> The waters nourished it,

119 Compare Keel's comment on the "molten sea" of the Temple: "Whether it represents the heavenly or the subterranean ocean is an irrelevant question, since both oceans (and the earthly ocean as well) originally and essentially belong together" (*WAB*, p. 120).

120 See the discussion above in Chapter 1.

121 For the connection between rivers and sea, compare the parallelism in v. 8, and the allusion to "waters" and the "deep" in v. 10, following the rivers of v. 9.

122 With which cf. Ezek. 1:24; 43:2; and Isa. 17:13, discussed above.

> the deep made it grow tall ..
> its boughs grew large
> and its branches long
> from מַיִם רַבִּים in its shoots. (vv. 4-5).

It may be noted that although these מַיִם רַבִּים may ultimately derive from the streams of the deep, in this context they may simply denote "plentiful water". Nevertheless, in v. 15, an association with channels or streams of water may perhaps be implied:

> When it goes down to Sheol, I will make the deep mourn for it, and restrain its rivers, and מַיִם רַבִּים shall be stopped...

Allusion to drinking water occurs again in relation to Egypt in the following chapter of Ezekiel (32:13-14), whilst the pragmatic value of מַיִם רַבִּים is well illustrated from two narrative contexts, the first being the incident at Meribah when, confronted by thirsty and rebellious Israelites,

> Moses lifted up his hand and struck the rock with his rod twice; and water came forth abundantly (וַיֵּצְאוּ מַיִם רַבִּים) and the congregation drank, and their cattle. (Num. 20:11).

However, its status as an invaluable resource was not only confined to the desert: see 2 Chr. 32:2-4, a picture which fully coheres with that of Num. 24:7 and Jer. 51:13.

Finally, distinct from all the above uses of the terminology of מַיִם רַבִּים, and probably in many ways somewhat ancillary to them, is the well-known truism of Cant. 8:7:

> מַיִם רַבִּים cannot quench love,
> neither can floods drown it.

Any attempt to discern the referential extent of the imagery employed here is heavily reliant on the subjective matter of interpretation. Insofar as the preceding verse describes jealousy (paralleling love) as "flashes of fire... a most vehement flame", the waters may be understood as a potential damper, quenching these flames; nevertheless, v. 6 also makes mention of death, another familiar sphere of allusion. In fact, there is no clear evidential basis on which to make a decision between these options, and aspects of each may be present. However, once again, the idea of a quantity of water may well be dominant.

Regarding the question of the unifying thread between מַיִם רַבִּים as thundering water, as the sea, or as "much / abundant water", one must, I think, conclude that it is essentially one of volume[123]—the huge volume (in both senses) of water hurling itself down a hillside or against the coast, the vast expanse and bottomless depths of the ocean, the delight in a plenteous abundance of fresh drinking water—all often conceived in a dynamic way. One

123 Hence perhaps Terrien's translation of מַיִם רַבִּים in Ps. 29:3 as "deep water" (p. 273).

might perhaps think then of מַיִם רַבִּים as an equivalent of the plural of local extension or amplification (the *pluralis intensivus*).[124] Insofar as מַיִם only occurs in the plural, supplementation with רַבִּים would perhaps have been necessary in order to convey the equivalent overtones of vastness or plenty (cf. the fairly frequent use of יַמִּים or תְּהוֹמוֹת in comparable situations).

Obviously, quantities of flowing water could be recognised as a valuable resource to be sought after and protected, as the basis of a vigorous, healthy nationhood, and essential to life. However, it may also properly evoke feelings of awe as a source of potential danger and unpredictability. This duality is well reflected in the ambivalence of the oracles concerning Tyre, since the sea was both the vehicle for her exceptional riches, but also her potential destroyer. Although this dangerous aspect of מַיִם רַבִּים elsewhere occasionally features in relation to the underworld or human enemies (cf. also allusions to the Egyptians at the Red Sea), the dominant emphasis in this sphere is Yahweh's absolute supremacy and safeguarding of his creation and people. High above the waters, absolutely secure, he is mightier far than they, untouched by their boisterousness, and well able to pluck his servant from their depths. Indeed, at the Exodus, he made a path through these waters, their volume no barrier to his ability to dry or divide them and lead his people safely through. Finally, not only are mighty trees and powerful kingdoms rooted in מַיִם רַבִּים —they may even conceivably underlie the throne of Yahweh himself.

Regarding the question of the interpretation of Ps. 29:3, the foregoing analysis does not permit a positive identification of the body of water designated by מַיִם רַבִּים. However, it does alert the reader to the prevalent fertility aspect of the motif and to the lack of evidence for the presence of an association with theomachic combat.[125] This would support an understanding of the verse which is congruent both with the identification of the מַבּוּל as the heavenly ocean, and with the self-evident correlation between Yahweh's manifestation in thunder and his presence above these waters. Moreover, the discernment of an association with the provision of rain in v. 3 is suggested by distinctive elements in the

124 GK, pp. 397-8, §124.

125 The difficulties with Kloos' contention (*Yhwh's Combat*, pp. 38, 52-5) that v. 3 refers to Yahweh's rising against מַיִם רַבִּים—despite the allusion to the provision of rain which this scholar recognises in v. 10—should be apparent. Not only does it have its basis in the doubtful identification of מַיִם רַבִּים as "the insurgent waters" (p. 55); it results in the opposed interpretation of two verses (vv. 3, 10) which in content seem to be very similar and closely bound up with the focus on the storm-theophany. It, further, raises the question of why Yahweh's real hostility to the sea should be indicated by a mere preposition, when the more circumstantial effect on the land is then detailed over five verses. Moreover, if Yahweh is depicted as Baal throughout this psalm, as Kloos contends (p. 93), it raises the question of why the enemy should be designated by the plural phrase מַיִם רַבִּים rather than by the singular name Yam, and why weaponry in thunder should be envisaged when the association between storm and *Chaoskampf* is not made in the extant Baal texts from Ugarit.

psalm as a whole.[126] Chief among these is the fact that Yahweh's epiphany appears simply as a manifestation of his power in the thunderstorm, and that it constitutes the theme of the entire psalm, without being subordinated to any other interest. It does not serve any particular historical purpose, though it does demonstrate Yahweh's power, supremacy (especially vv. 1-2, [3], 11), and ability to confer strength and peace on his people (v. 11). Notable also is the fact that Yahweh's epiphany has devastating effects on the surface life on earth, his destructive power explicitly being directed against the cedars (v. 5), Lebanon (v. 5-6), Sirion (v. 6), wilderness of Kadesh (v. 8), oaks (or calving hinds; v. 9) and forests (v. 9). However, the silences of the Psalm are as significant as what it proclaims, for although there is devastation on the earth at this magnificent theophany, there are no fleeing waters (later quite a common theme) and there is no resistance from any quarter. Nor is there any indication that the structure of the cosmos itself is disturbed,[127] or indeed that it causes any reaction among the nations. Thus there is no basis for discerning an allusion to "cosmic" conflict here.[128]

It appears also that any received Canaanite traditions utilised here have been reformulated anew as a vehicle for claiming Yahweh's absolute supremacy. Unlike Baal, his kingship is unchallenged, whilst thunderstorm motifs, as elsewhere in the Old Testament, have become absorbed into the spectacle of the theophany. They demonstrate his power and announce his coming, but there is no explicit interest in the bringing of rain. Finally, although it is not mentioned until the last verse, it is important that this God of power is the God of Israel: his strength is ultimately theirs.

It is this concluding motif which assumes predominance in the remaining psalms of the group. Here, perhaps in a discernible development from Ps. 29, the theophanies are concerned with Yahweh's manifestation for a purpose—to reveal himself and/or to redeem his people in the face of particular historical circumstances.

ii. The Theme of "Chaos" in Psalm 68

It is difficult to discern a wholly coherent structure in Psalm 68, a composition which, as has been argued, is probably very ancient, though it may have undergone some subsequent development. As noted above, it is steeped in the ancient theophany tradition, and certain elements in its concluding verses are especially reminiscent of Ps. 29: the voice of the Lord (v. 34), "ascribe to Yahweh / God" (v. 35), he gives strength to his people (v. 36, cf. 29:11). However, in many ways the two compositions must be distinguished. Most

126 Compare also the context of Jer. 10:13 = 51:16. Once again, it is the issue of Yahweh's creative beneficence and incomparable power which is at stake.

127 Perhaps the psalm predates an interest in cosmology—as may be said also of Gen. 2.

128 This conclusion applies even if a temporal allusion to "the Deluge" is advocated in respect of v. 10, as has been shown convincingly by Tsumura ("'The Deluge' (*mabbûl*) in Psalm 29:10", especially pp. 353-5).

obviously, although the epiphany is a recurrent theme, it now appears as a vehicle for a historical reminiscence; the perspective has been transferred from the acclamation of the sons of the gods in the heavenly sphere to the struggles between Israel and the nations. The psalm seems to open with the call accompanying the going out of God and his ark into battle (cf. Num. 10:35); and there is a concomitant stress on the deity's powerful, just and purposeful actions. He drives the wicked away, but causes the just to be joyful; he protects the defenceless, but causes the rebellious to dwell in a parched land (vv. 3-4, 6-7). Of particular interest is the reminiscence of vv. 8-11, 18-19, which, in typical theophanic language, recalls God's going forth before his people through the wilderness, probably from Sinai to the promised land (cf. Judg. 5:4-5, Deut. 33:2, Hab. 3:3) and ensuring their safe passage *en route*; Yahweh leads his people in victory (vv. 12-15, 18-22). Thus, intermingled with "holy war" themes is the rôle of God as judge and protector of the weak.

It seems that the divine epiphany here has two primary effects: first, and consistent with the historico-political concerns of the psalm, it causes the enemies to scatter (vv. 2-3, 12[-15]; cf. 19-24, 29-32). Second, in a manner close to the thunderstorm imagery of Ps. 29, it is stated that the "heavens poured down rain" (v. 9; cf. v. 10). This rain was shed by God in his goodness as a provision for the needy: it is a means of blessing and reviving his people (vv. 9-11; cf. v. 7). It is unclear whether the snow (v. 15) constitutes ammunition (cf. Job 38:22-23), fertile provision, a spontaneous reaction of creation, or simply a historical reminiscence. However, the allusion to "Israel's fountain" in v. 27 may also relate to the idea of the blessing of fresh flowing water.[129] The phrase מִמְּקוֹר יִשְׂרָאֵל has been variously interpreted,[130] and its meaning is not altogether clear. Cheyne understood here a reference to the temple, explaining that this particular expression was chosen "because the precious water supply connected with the temple ... had become a type of the temple itself, from which streams of living water were in the latter days to fertilise the earth (Joel iii.18 and parallel passages)"; thus the usage may be compared with Ps. 87:7[131] or Zech. 13:1. A more direct allusion to the spring Gihon has been inferred by Johnson,[132] who abstracts from the verse the itinerary of a sacred procession apparently accompanying the psalm,[133] translating, "In companies they greeted God, / Even Yahweh, from Israel's spring". Another alternative is that the reference may be to God himself, though this approach would necessitate deleting the מִן of מִמְּכוֹר in order to effect a transformation into a divine title.[134] Nevertheless, the solution which boasts the most immediate inner-biblical

129 Cf. Ps. 36:8-9.

130 Or emended: Kraus reads מִמִּקְרָאֵי, translating "aus Israels Festgemeinde" (II, pp. 626, 628); in a similar vein, Dahood, though respecting the MT, derives his rendering, "in the convocation of Israel" from מִן = בְּ, + מָקוֹר, "convocation", from a supposed √ קור "to call, convoke" (II, pp. 132, 148).

131 Cheyne, p. 91.

132 *SKAI*, p. 83.

133 See vv. 25-28.

134 So The Revised Psalter, 1964.

support is that the phrase מִמְּקוֹר יִשְׂרָאֵל addresses the people of Israel as descendants of Jacob, this patriarch being the common "source" of the nation;[135] as such, it is comparable with the description of Israel as עֵין יַעֲקֹב in Deut. 33:28. Significantly, the context in this latter passage has strong thematic resonances with Ps. 68: God is רֹכֵב שָׁמַיִם בְּעֶזְרֶךָ (Deut. 33:26b, cf. Ps. 68:5ff., 34), whose majesty (גַּאֲוָה)[136] is in the skies (Deut. 33:26c, cf. Ps. 68:34-35); he is the protector of his people, who thrusts out the enemy before them (Deut. 33:27-29; compare the force of much of Ps. 68, especially vv. 2f., 12-15, 19-24, 29-32, 36, though here the theme is independently executed); indeed, "your enemies shall come fawning to you, / and you shall tread upon their high places"[137] (Deut. 33:29; cf. Ps. 68:30-32); most importantly, the particular feature of Israel's blessedness (Deut. 33:29a) which is enunciated in v. 28, the verse in which the expression עֵין יַעֲקֹב appears, is that of fertility, with special emphasis on the gift of water:

So Israel dwelt in safety,
  the fountain of Jacob alone,
in a land of grain and wine;
  yea his heavens drop down dew. (Deut. 33:28; cf. Ps. 68:9-11).

It thus appears that, even if the motif of "Israel's fountain" refers most immediately to the people's common lineage from Jacob, it was also congenial to the related imagery of fertility, perhaps sharing a common heritage in the complex of ancient theophany traditions. Similarly, though the idea of Yahweh or the temple as a "fountain" may not be in the foreground, this is not to negate the resonances of the water-source imagery with motifs familiar from these spheres, and rightly identified by scholars who seek to discern their presence here. Rather, one might think of the operation of undertones of meaning which simultaneously chime in with the familiar and established associative spheres of the sanctuary and deity, thus enriching the primary allusion.

A motif familiar from elsewhere is that of the "pangs of creation": God's presence causes the earth to quake (v. 9); nevertheless, it is not here accompanied by a reference to a corresponding reaction in the waters of the sea or rivers.[138] Rather, as a corollary of the identification of the human foes as God's enemies against whom he sends out his hosts to victory, the nations are included within the "distress at his coming" theme. Like the earth, they melt

---

135 Cohen, p. 214, Goulder, *The Prayers of David*, p. 208; cf. H. Wheeler Robinson, *Deuteronomy and Joshua*, p. 244, who explains the idea in terms of "the succession of generations, streaming forth", comparing Isa. 48:1.

136 The term is applied to God only in these two verses.

137 For a more precise understanding of בָּמוֹת, see the discussion of Job 9:8 below in Chapter 11.

138 As in Ps. 114:3-6; Hab. 3:3-15; Nah. 1:3-6; cf. Ps. 18:8-16. The trembling of the earth or mountains occurs in isolation from the reaction of the waters in Pss. 68:8f; 97:4; 99:1; Judg. 5:4-5; cf. Ps. 46:7; Mic. 1:4.

and flee, but any enemies / waters parallelism is absent. Indeed, it appears that at this early stage, God as the all-powerful king and warrior are the primary themes, but the identity of the recipients of his terrible might is often non-specific and flexible; nor is there any stated opposition to the deity from this quarter. Their demise is simply a vehicle to demonstrate his power—although the effortless destruction of the foe was no doubt also of particular concern to Israel herself. In addition, the invocation of God to "rebuke" and "trample" his foes (v. 31) is reminiscent of the type of language encountered elsewhere, often in rather later poetry, in relation to Yahweh's terrible theophany.[139]

Despite indications that this psalm is, in the main, quite primitive, nevertheless, the attribute רֹכֵב בָּעֲרָבוֹת (v. 5, cf. v. 34) has the appearance of being a stock epithet; it may, of course, have been taken over from outside Israel as a familiar and typical aspect of divinity (e.g., from Baal).[140] In fact, the relation of the title to the appellation *rkb 'rpt* ("The Rider of the Clouds") ascribed to Baal in the Ugaritic texts has been much debated. Many scholars regard the expression in Ps. 68:5 as a direct equivalent to that attested in the Baal myth, explaining the consonantal difference between them as due to a natural development whereby one letter "mutated" into another (*p* into *b*), and therefore requiring no emendation. As Anderson remarks,[141] "it is possible that the appropriation of Baal's distinctive title reflects a deliberate religious polemic against the Canaanite beliefs. The Psalmist stresses that the giver of rain and prosperity is not Baal, but the one whose name is the LORD." Alternatively, one might imagine a sufficient continuity or elision of tradition that enabled "free-floating" epithets to be ascribed to more than one deity as appropriate, but without necessarily entailing the evangelistic or apologetic intent usually attributed to the biblical authors. Certainly, the ascription of rain-giving powers to Yahweh would well suit the present context and tone of the psalm,[142] and may particularly be compared with the description of God as "he who rides in the heavens" in v. 34.

Alternatively, one could adopt the straightforward understanding of עֲרָבוֹת as the plural of עֲרָבָה, "steppe, desert". According to this interpretation, Yahweh

---

139 The verb נער is associated with the theophany in Nah. 1:4, while the related noun features in such contexts in Job 26:11 and Pss. 18:16 (= 2 Sam. 22:16) and 104:7 (all of which concern the pangs of creation; one might compare also Isa. 50:2); cf. Isa. 66:15, Pss. 80:17, 76:7, in each of these contexts the divine appearance remaining in view. On the other hand, Ps. 68:31, the verse in which the verb רפס occurs, may be corrupt. There are only four further instances of the same verbal root in the Hebrew Bible (Prov. 6:3, 25:26, Ezek. 32:2, 34:18) and in these the usage is quite distinct. However, the notion of "trampling" the foe—if native to this verse—might be compared with Deut. 33:29 (דרך) and Hab 3:12 (דוש); "treading" (דרך) also occurs in connection with the theophany in Mic. 1:3 (cf. Job 9:8, Am. 4:13), and with reference to enemies in Judg. 20:43, Mic. 5:4,5, cf. Ps. 91:13; one might compare also the use of דוש in Isa. 25:10, and cf. Mic. 4:13, Isa. 41:15.

140 Cf. *KTU* 1.2.iv.8, 1.4.iii.18.

141 II, p. 484.

142 Note especially vv. 7, 9-11.

is depicted as riding through the deserts. This would cohere with the theme of the wilderness wanderings exhibited in the psalm, but perhaps has special relevance to the tradition hinted at in v. 18 of Yahweh's approach from Sinai to fight for his people, according to vv. 8-11, apparently at their head.[143] However, the two approaches need not be regarded as mutually exclusive, since, as Anderson proposes, the choice of עֲרָבוֹת may have been intended to encompass both "the title of Baal, the giver of rain (cf. v. [10]) and the Wilderness tradition (cf. v. [8])".[144] Indeed, according to vv. 8-9, in God's march through the wilderness (בְּצַעְדְּךָ בִישִׁימוֹן, v. 8), the heavens poured down rain (v. 9), so the two motifs there comfortably elide.

Regarding possible "chaos" allusions, Albright proposed that Bashan in v. 23 should be understood as referring to the Ugaritic *bṯn* = serpent, dragon,[145] and in this he has been followed by a number of subsequent scholars.[146] However, this interpretation sits oddly with the widespread recognition that "Bashan" is the name of a mountain in w. 16-17,[147] and it is commonly sustained only through often quite extensive emendation and repointing.[148] Even where the MT is retained by advocates of this type of approach, improbable readings tend to result. For example, Seybold's contention that the "primæval serpent", together with the "depths of the sea", may symbolise disaster and the underworld seems incompatible with the remaining references to serpents (or dragons) in the Bible: the waters of the underworld are elsewhere never identified as the "sea" (though the two may simultaneously or

143 Cf. vv. 2-3, and compare the reference to God coming from Sinai to the holy place in vv. 18-19.

144 II, p. 483.

145 W. F. Albright, "Catalogue", pp. 14, 27-28, 38.

146 These have been documented by Day, *God's Conflict*, pp. 114-5; more recent advocates include Seybold, pp. 261-2, 264, and (in an adapted form) Wyatt, *Myths of Power*, pp. 98-9.

147 See, e.g., Albright, "Catalogue", p. 37, Dahood, II, p. 142, Seybold, p. 264.

148 Albright's reading, "From smiting the Serpent I return, I return from destroying Sea!" (*HUCA* 23 [1950] 27-28), seems excessively reliant on such alterations (see similarly the critical comments of Tate, p. 167). To take another example, Dahood transfers the ב- of מבשן to the preceding word and dismisses it as an "enclitic *mem*"; his rendering of the revocalised word אָשִׁיב as "privative" hiphil from the root נשב ("to blow"), meaning "I stifled", he himself acknowledges as "doubtful"; and his repointing of אשבם to אֶשְׁבֹּם in order to bring it into conformity with the language of *KTU* 1.3.iii.38 is related to the translation "muzzle", which now seems difficult to substantiate (see J. Barr, "Ugaritic and Hebrew '*šbm*'?", *JSS* 18 [1973] 17-39; cf. also Dietrich and Loretz, *UF* 14 [1982] 77-81). Miller's proposal that אשבם should be emended to אֶשְׁבֹּם, "stifle, muzzle", in both cola (*Divine Warrior*, p. 110; "Two Critical notes on Ps 68 and Dtn 33", *HTR* 57 [1964] 240-3, p. 240) should be rejected on a similar basis: even if the verb were to be translated in the light of more recent interpretations of *KTU* 1.3.iii.38, this would impute to God the particularly improbable action of "lifting up" (thus Wyatt, *RTU*, p. 79; see further the literature cited in n. 48) or "binding" (thus Smith in *UNP*, p. 111, Pardee in *CS. I*, p. 252; cf. Driver, "captured", *CML* p. 50) the sea.

proximately be envisaged in such contexts as Jon. 2 and Ezek. 28), and serpents / dragons are not used to represent Sheol or such afflictions as are evoked (usually in contexts of individual laments) as pertaining on a personal level. Likewise, Wyatt's proposed interpretation,[149] again retaining the MT, is based on a series of conjectures which collectively seem difficult to sustain,[150] and similar criticisms may be levelled against Mowinckel.[151] Moreover, "Bashan" is not elsewhere employed in the Hebrew Bible to denote a serpent, though it is well-attested as a place-name; Hebrew already has a cognate term פֶּתֶן, whilst the *bṯn* of *KTU* 1.5.i.1-2 is in Isa. 27:1 referred to as a נָחָשׁ. In fact, the parallelism between Bashan and the depths of the sea seems simply to express the polarity between the extremities of creation, signifying the highest and lowest regions of the earth (cf. Am. 9:2-3, Ps. 139:8-9).[152] The presumed object may be the enemies, or the verse could presuppose some form of exile or dispersion of God's people (perhaps vv. 22-24 may be thought of as an addition). An association with human foes is given added strength by Girard's linking of vv. 22-24 with vv. 2-3, and indeed the dispersal of these hostile forces already occurs in w. 2-3a.[153] However, this further distances the passage from any presumed *Chaoskampf* association.

The invocation of v. 31 alludes to Israel's enemies under the figure of a beast dwelling among reeds (perhaps Egypt[154]), and as bulls. Eaton perceives here a reference to "the forces of chaos and death (personified as the monster of the marshes and her allies of bull-like demons)",[155] whilst Terrien refers even to "the Canaanite myth of Leviathan",[156] translating the first colon:

---

149 *Myths of Power*, pp. 96-8.

150 Following Neiman ("Gihôn and Pishôn: mythological antecedents of the two enigmatic rivers of Eden" in *Proceedings of the 6th Congress of Jewish Studies*, Jerusalem, 1977, 321-8), he links Pishon, the river of Gen 2, with פֶּתֶן and in turn with *btn*; then, in dependence on Del Olmo Lette ("Basan o el 'infierno' cananeo', *SEL* 5 1988, 51-60), connects Bashan with the underworld, since King Og, the last of the Rephaim (Deut. 3:11), dwelt at Ashtaroth and Edrei (1:4), which in *KTU* 1.108.2-3 are the dwelling-places of the underworld god Rapiu. Hence Wyatt argues for "the maritime, serpentine and cosmological character of the word" (*Myths of Power*, p. 98). The relation of Ashtaroth and Edrei to the underworld is interesting, though it remains questionable whether this association was intended in the more general reference to Bashan: it is certainly not applicable elsewhere. Moreover, to import a serpentine association as well, especially following the very tenuous hypothesis outlined above, seems a conjecture too far.

151 *Der achtundsechzigste Psalm*, pp. 47-8.

152 Thus many scholars, e.g., Johnson, *Sacral Kingship* (p. 73 n. 8), Hossfeld (HZ, II, p. 254), Day (*God's Conflict*, p. 115), Girard (II, p. 225), Tate (pp. 167, 182).

153 See Girard, II, p. 214.

154 "Reed" seems almost emblematic for Egypt in 2 Ki. 18:21, Isa. 36:6, Ezek. 29:6; cf. similarly the association of the Nile with reeds in Isa 19:6. Moreover, the rare verb רפס employed in the present verse is predicated also of the Pharaoh in Ezek. 32:2.

155 *The Psalms*, p. 250.

156 P. 496.

"Muzzle the beast that dwells in the marshes!"[157] However, the latter scholar offers no justification for this unusual rendering of MT גער, nor is there any basis for discovering mythological overtones in the language employed in this verse. אַבִּיר at root means "mighty", being applicable both to animals[158] and to people, in the latter case referring to "the powerful".[159] These two uses merge in the metaphorical denotation of a powerful enemy under the figure of a bull, most notably in Ps. 22:13,[160] in the present case, the aspect of rank also perhaps being present. בְּעֶגְלֵי is sometimes emended to (or understood to imply) בַּעֲלֵי,[161] but it seems more probable that the soldiers and perhaps also the general population subordinate to the אַבִּירִים are intended,[162] perhaps in a quasi-derogatory sense.[163] חַיָּה is a relatively common term for a "wild animal", in the great preponderance of cases being employed literally, save for that in the parable in 2 Ki. 14:9 = 2 Chr. 25:18, although a metaphorical use may be possible, if not very likely, in Jer. 12:9, Isa. 56:9 or Ezek. 34:28. However, what is evident is that the language employed derives in every case from the sphere of animal rather than mythological imagery.

Most scholars therefore identify the חַיַּת קָנֶה as Egypt,[164] and correspondingly relate this section to a period of strength for the region: Gunkel, for example, proposes the 4th century B.C.,[165] yet it can hardly be regarded as the only period which might be applicable. Others refer the allusion back to the Exodus and Red Sea crossing,[166] or simply regard the imagery as conveying a general sense of warlike strength without any specific nation being in mind.[167] However, there is a difference between being unable to determine

157 P. 487.

158 "Bull" provides the most relevant sense here: cf. Ps. 50:13, Isa. 34:7; but the term can also denote the horse: Judg. 5:22, Jer. 8:16, 47:3, 50:11.

159 As in Job 24:22, 34:7, Lam. 1:15, and with the sense "chief" in 1 Sam. 21:8. Compare its apparent use to denote angels in Ps. 78:25. A similar application of אַיִל, "ram", with the sense "chief", is evident in Ex.15:15, Ezek. 17:13, 31:11, 32:21, and עַתּוּד, "billy goat", with the meaning "leader", occurs in Isa. 14:9; cf. Ezek. 34:17, where both terms are employed metaphorically. Likewise, in *KTU* 1.15.iv.6-7, "bulls" and "wild deer" seem to be equivalent to "captains" and "chiefs" or the like: see *UNP*, p. 27 and p. 45 nn. 81, 82.

160 Compare similarly its application to the King of Assyria as one who brought down those who sat in thrones כַּאַבִּיר, Jer. 46:15.

161 See *BHS* footnote; Gunkel, *Schöpfung*, pp. 66-7, Kraus, II, p 628.

162 Thus Tate, p. 184; similarly Dahood, II, p. 150.

163 Cf. the reference to hired soldiers fleeing "like fatted calves" in Jer. 46:21.

164 This is not the only referent which has been proposed: Gray, for example, thought of the King of Hazor, who is mentioned in Judg. 4:2 ("Cantata", *JSS* 22, p. 20).

165 *Die Psalmen*, p. 287.

166 Weiser, p. 333, Terrien, p. 496.

167 Rogerson & McKay, II, p. 91, Davidson, p. 216. A contrasting permutation is for the חַיַּת קָנֶה, אַבִּירִים and עֲגָלִים to be interpreted as alluding to different nations (thus, e.g. Buttenwieser, p. 270, Briggs, II, p. 104), but it is doubtful if these beasts should be

the original reference, and in claiming that no particular nation(s) was intended; hence Girard is surely correct when he explains the subject of v. 31a as "supposedly Egypt or, in any event, a power which was politically hostile to Israel."[168] Thus the verses should almost certainly be assigned to a situation—now unidentifiable—when Israel felt itself to be under some specific threat, possibly, but not necessarily, from Egypt.

iii. The Theme of "Chaos" in Psalm 114

The theophany of Yahweh is clearly a key theme here, the climax of vv. 3-6, and possibly of the whole psalm, being the manifestation of the divine presence which causes the whole earth to tremble, in v. 7. This reaction of fear before the coming of the God of Israel is a familiar aspect of theophany imagery (cf. Pss. 18, 29, Nah. 1:4f.; Hab 3, etc.), and expresses the divine invincibility, indicating the terrifying might and kingship of the God who acts on behalf of his people, as manifested supremely when he led them on his march of conquest from Sinai into the promised land. However, there is no suggestion of conflict or even potential enmity here:[169] indeed, the mountains which now "skip" away before God like frightened sheep are characteristically an embodiment of permanence and stability, having been set in place by the divine decree.[170] The implication is that even what is strongest and most secure is cowed and weak before the mighty Yahweh; the sea then probably functions as the other fundamental element of creation, which also flees in terror. Thus nothing—neither mountain nor sea—would stand before him. Nevertheless, it is clear throughout that God does not act to intimidate or subdue nature: rather, it independently responds in fear to his presence. It is this "terror at his presence" which is the focus of interest here: the emphasis is on the Being of God rather than on his specific deeds.

However, the theophany which constitutes the climax of the Psalm is patently set within the historical context of a reminiscence of the Exodus events. Indeed, instead of opening with Yahweh's theophany (as in Pss. 29, 68, Judg. 5, Deut. 33, Hab. 3), the poem begins, "When Israel went out of Egypt" (v. 1). A

---

subject to such distinctions or indeed whether their precise referents can now be ascertained.

168 II, p. 220; cf. p. 230.

169 Contra those who would discern in the fleeing of the sea an allusion to "the suppression of primeval chaotic forces hostile to God" (Schaefer, p. 282; see similarly Gerstenberger, II, p. 282); often, however, this is seen as a mere "vestige" (Terrien, p. 769) or "echo" (Eaton, p. 394), Kraus even emphasising that "a real contest, a battle against chaos... never comes about at all. Here... a mythical complex is burst open and dissolved" (II, p. 958; cf. Anderson, II, p. 789, Allen, p. 103; Schaefer, p. 282).

170 Cf. Pss. 30:8, 65:7, 76:5. It is because this fleeing is fundamentally a response to the nature of the theophanic God rather than a reflection of the state of the elements that flee (cf., e.g., Ex. 19:18) that the assertion of Terrien that "the sea, the mountains and the hills are spoken to as personified villains" (p. 769) seems inappropriate.

concordant theme is the identification of Judah as "his sanctuary, / Israel his dominion" (v. 2); thus the cultic stress is transferred away from the heavenly realm (29:1, 10), the "sanctuary" (68:25-8, 36) or Sinai (68:9, 17, 18), onto the people, Israel and Judah.

Although the deeds of the *Heilsgeschichte* are clearly evoked, precision in identifying its components is difficult to achieve; certainly the emphasis is placed securely onto Yahweh's impact on creation rather than on the nations. V. 3 seems to allude to both the Red Sea and Jordan crossings, and v. 8 perhaps to the provision of water during the wilderness wanderings.[171] It is notable, however, that the receding of the waters before Yahweh is paralleled by the "skipping" of the mountains and hills,[172] although the latter element does not have a self-evident historical correlation, as the sea/river imagery does.[173] It nevertheless eloquently indicates that this response to the divine presence is common to all creation, no less to the land than the sea; this idea is reinforced further by the general invocation to the earth to tremble before Yahweh (v. 7; cf. Ps. 96:9), which likewise has no particular historical referent (possibly Sinai, if one wished to stretch the point). However, the language of fear and trembling which is sometimes in other contexts also applied to the reactions of human enemies to the coming of Yahweh (e.g., in Ps. 48:6-7, Ex. 15:14-16) is not present here. Perhaps the rain and tremoring earth are original components of the theophany (as in Ps. 68:9; the latter element is, of course, absent from Ps. 29) and the fleeing of the waters a secondary (though probably also very early) addition based on the fusion of these elements with the exodus tradition.[174] The emphasis on the divine might and salvific action with which this type of imagery is normally associated would also have cohered strongly with the Exodus events. However, it is interesting that Yahweh is depicted not only as the one who causes the sea to flee, but also as the one who brings forth water (cf. the rainstorm implications of Pss. 29 and 68). The fertility interest is thus

171 Although this represents a majority position, there are some dissenting voices: Dahood, for example, interprets the whole Psalm in relation to the events related in Josh. 3-5. Thus v. 3a is understood in the light of Josh. 3:14-16, and v. 4 is explained as a reference to Canaanite mountains, the abodes of the gods (III, pp. 135-6). Weiser, on the other hand, detects an allusion to "the quaking of the mountain at the revelation of God at Sinai" in this latter verse (p. 489), and the same view is propounded, e.g., by Goulder, *PR*, p. 164 and Girard, III, p. 194, Girard also offering a verse-by-verse schema in the same context.

172 The same verb recurs in the context of a remarkably similar image in Ps. 29:6 and thus belies the contrast drawn by Gerstenberger between "the uproar of primeval powers" and the "mountains and hills jumping like lambs… as an expression of joy" (II, pp. 282-3).

173 Unless the allusion is to the trembling of Mt. Sinai (singular), Ex. 19:18. However, the theophany motif manifested also, for example, in Ps. 29:6, must surely reflect a more immediate influence, and may even underlie the description in Ex. 19.

174 The mountains are mentioned together with rain in Ps. 68:9 and Judg. 5:4-5, while the combination of earth/mountain with sea/waters occurs in similar contexts in Pss. 18:16; 77:17, 19c; Nah. 1:4-5; and Hab. 3:6, 8-10; the mountains also stand alone in Pss. 97:4-5 and 99:1.

retained, and makes transparent the fact that Yahweh's action upon his creation is governed by his good purpose, not by automatic hostility towards certain of its components.

Finally, these events "of old" are not without their present significance, as indicated by the questions in vv. 5-6, which are stylistically akin to those in Ps. 68:17, and by the imperative in v. 7.[175] Thus the God who provided for them in the wilderness is a protective presence with them still.

3. Summary

The evidence of Pss. 29, 68 and 114 seems to indicate that the thunderstorm and provision of water motif is an early element of Yahweh's theophany, one which becomes less evident later on. Crucial also is the epiphany as the manifestation of Yahweh's power, in Pss. 68 and 114, as often, in specific circumstances of deliverance; this is summarised by the final verse of Ps. 68: " Terrible is God... he gives power and strength to his people..." (cf. 29:10). In Ps. 29, the epiphany has its impact on nature, but in Pss. 68 and 114, its effect is felt in the historical sphere; in Ps. 68, the quaking of the mountains is a subsidiary theme, but in Ps. 114, it is amplified by the fleeing of the waters. This motif corresponds well with the distress of the earth, and perhaps marks the beginning of a tendency to substitute it for the provision of rain. However, there is no allusion to the control of the sea as a feature of creation, or of anything which may be determined as a battle with chaos in these texts—or indeed in any of the earliest Old Testament poetry.

175 Unless the latter is to be emended to continue the sense of the preceding two lines.

IV. Individual Laments, Royal Laments and Related Thanksgiving Psalms: Psalms 18, 32, 42-3, 69, 88, 124 and 144

Psalm 18 displays a number of continuities with the compositions considered in the previous chapter, with regard both to its date (since it is frequently considered to be amongst the earliest compositions preserved in the Hebrew Psalter)[1] and also to its content, since it contains one of the most celebrated examples of the theophany motif preserved in the Old Testament. Nevertheless, despite these undeniable affinities with Pss. 29, 68 and 114, there are powerful motives for awarding Ps. 18 separate consideration. Firstly, as shall be shown below, it probably belongs outside the earliest phase of Hebrew poetic composition. Second, and perhaps as a corollary of this, it exhibits a number of important thematic developments from the earlier prosody, whilst a third, and related, aspect is that of genre. Although Pss. 29, 68 and 114 are notoriously difficult to classify,[2] they lack the individual and royal concerns which assume prominence in Ps. 18; similarly, their "hymnic" praise of Yahweh, despite the association with the Exodus events in Ps. 114 and with other more obscure historical happenings in Ps. 68, cannot properly be described as "thanksgivings" for a specific, recent act of deliverance, as can the content of Ps. 18.

However, perhaps even more significant than the ways in which Ps. 18 represents a development from Pss. 29, 68 and 114, especially in its exploitation of the theophany motif, are its undeniable thematic and generic affinities to Pss. 32, 42-3, 69, 88, 124 and 144, the individual and royal laments and thanksgiving psalms which comprise the substance of the present chapter. In the case of Ps. 144, this relationship is evidently one of direct dependence, either of one psalm on the other, or on common source material. Ps. 18 arguably exhibits the earliest and fullest example of a motif common to all of these compositions, namely that of the waters of the underworld, and the related idea of the waters as the embodiment of the psalmist's enemies. In the rest of the group, the motif is typically less dynamically portrayed, or commonly seems to focus on either the enemies or the underworld, but not both, perhaps encompassing the second only ephemerally; sometimes, it merely appears as one of a stock of images drawn from the suppliant's conventional repertoire,

1 See the discussion below.

2 A common consensus is that they are in various ways and to different degrees "hymnic", though both Pss. 68 and 114 have been ascribed "liturgical" significance, the former of these also sometimes being classified as a "song of victory" or related form.

and is thus awarded passing mention rather than detailed attention, the sphere of allusion presumably already being familiar to the hearer.

A further aspect of Psalms 32, 42-3, 69, 88, 124 and 144 which is worthy of mention, is their resistance to dating. The lack of any discernible historical references in laments or thanksgivings of the individual, combined with the conventional nature of much of their imagery and phrasing, renders the task especially uncertain. Moreover, the sphere of waters imagery which comprises the focus of the present analysis does not seem to reflect any particular course of development, but rather seems to recur in slightly differing forms without notable variation over time. Thus, it appears that there is little to be achieved from the diachronic endeavour, except the possibility of defining the parameters of the period during which the imagery recurs. Nevertheless, within the diachronic sweep of the monograph as a whole, there is good reason for placing this essentially "synchronic" chapter at the present juncture, since the key motif of the waters as Sheol or enemies is likely to derive from pre-exilic times (Ps. 18, at least, is probably pre-exilic), and to have provided an influence behind other, quite distinct, uses of "chaos" allusions from this time on. In addition, although some of the relevant material may potentially emanate from quite different eras and circumstances, the theme itself seems to have remained relatively stable throughout its possibly quite long use, and hence to have been resistant to the intrusion of later influences.

Ps. 18 shall here be awarded detailed attention, initially with the purpose of ascertaining its likely date, as an indication of the earliest known point of the appearance of the underworld and enemies imagery; then its content shall be analysed, both with a view to discerning its continuities with the archaic theophany psalms considered in chapter three, but also to establish the key areas of innovation. Once this has been achieved, the remaining psalms in the group shall be discussed according to their thematic content, the issue of dating arising only insofar as it may provide an indication of the persistence of the enemies and underworld motif into the post-exilic period.

1. Psalm 18: Yahweh's Deliverance of the Suppliant from the Waters of Sheol and from his Enemies

i. The Date of Psalm 18

Psalm 18 is sometimes thought to be among the earliest compositions in the Psalter, certain scholars even accepting the possibility that in its earliest form it may be attributed to David or to a poet of his court.[3] This perception is perhaps partly influenced by the Davidic ascription and by the setting of this psalm in 2 Sam. 22, which offer superficially appropriate details of the occasion for its

3 E.g., Dahood (I, p. 104), Craigie (p. 172), Weiser (p. 125), Berry, *The Psalms and Their Readers: Interpretative Strategies for Psalm 18* (JSOT[S] 153; Sheffield: JSOT, 1993), p. 60.

composition. Nevertheless, the poem bears indications of later features, which have sometimes been explained as due to redactional activity or supplementation.[4] A more substantial difficulty with the putative circumstances of its composition is the fact that the title apparently associates the psalm with a time prior to David becoming king, yet this contravenes the clear force of vv. 44-46, which "can hardly apply to one who is not king".[5] In addition, the psalm heading fails to differentiate between the various conflicts that characterised David's career, apparently classifying "all his enemies and... Saul" together;[6] though understandable from the perspective of historical retrospection, this hardly coheres with the psalm's content or with the implication of the title that it owes its composition to a specific act of deliverance. Yet if the original context ascribed to it is inappropriate, there seems no compelling reason to retain the Davidic connection.[7]

It is perhaps therefore not surprising that amongst scholars who have rejected the notion of Davidic authorship, the full range of dating possibilities is represented. Some still favour "the early part of the pre-exilic period",[8] whilst a fairly widely-held opinion is that in its final form, at least, it may owe something to the post-exilic age.[9] However, a sobering perspective is offered by Kraus, who emphasises that the psalm was subject to repeated use, as well as undergoing a transition from the royal to the congregational sphere. Thus "the gamut of frequently repeated conceptions basically reflects a changing history

---

4 See, e.g., Briggs, I, pp. 137, 140. Compare the twofold source-division advocated, e.g., by Schmidt (pp. 26-30; cf. Seybold, p. 80) and the more numerous independent elements identified by Oeming (I, p. 125) Hossfeld (HZ, II, pp. 119-121) and Terrien (p. 204). However, there is no agreement over the relative ages of its respective elements: Terrien maintains that vv. 2-20 may emanate from the tenth century B.C. and even King David himself, whereas Oeming and Seybold regard vv. 33-51 as the earliest, pre-exilic component, with the latter simply describing vv. 2-7, 17-20 as "very difficult to date". Hossfeld, on the other hand, assigns both vv. 2, 33-50 and vv. 3-20 to the pre-exilic era (p. 121). See further Kraus' arguments against partition (I, p. 285) and Berry's analysis of the many unifying thematic links between vv. 2-31 and 32-51 (*The Psalms and their Readers*, pp. 88, 92, 100-103).

5 Starbuck, *Court Oracles in the Psalms*, p. 118; note also v. 51.

6 Compare Dahood's emendation of שָׁאוּל to שְׁאוֹל in v. 1. This entails only a repointing of the M.T. and would admirably suit the content of the psalm, but is, however, conjectural and perhaps fails to distinguish adequately between the conventional modes of expression in psalmody and in psalm-ascriptions.

7 On the other hand, Eaton's claim that the psalm "reads as pure and intact myth" (*Kingship and the Psalms*, p. 115) relating only to a "liturgical salvation" (p.116) is far from self-evident, and necessitates reading vv. 33-46 as having a combination of present and future reference (p. 114).

8 Anderson, I, p. 153; a pre-exilic provenance is advocated also by Cheyne (p. 45), Gunkel (*Die Psalmen*, p. 67), Kittel (p. 62) and Oesterley (I, p. 162).

9 Anderson (I, p. 153), Hossfeld (HZ, I, p. 121), Briggs (I, p. 140), Wellhausen (p. 170), Gerstenberger (I, pp. 99-100), McCann (*NIB*, IV, pp. 746-7).

of tradition... All these interpretations grasp at phases of the tradition of Psalm 18".[10]

Yet despite the plethora of opinions and Kraus's scepticism, it is still possible to draw certain conclusions about the date of Psalm 18. At the very least, it seems to presuppose the existence of the Davidic monarchy,[11] and therefore a date of origin somewhere between the tenth and sixth centuries B.C. seems fairly secure, as Kraus himself tacitly acknowledges. Moreover, the linguistic evidence is compatible with this assessment, and indeed appears to offer further scope for narrowing the dating parameters.

The psalm lacks many of the prose features which tended to intrude into later poetic Hebrew, such as the object-marker -אֵת and relative אֲשֶׁר. Even the definite article, though occurring five times, is attached only to אֵל or an adjective modifying it, a use which Berry describes as "atypical of its standard prosaic employment."[12] On the other hand, it also manifests forty-four examples of colon-initial *waw*,[13] and this is consonant with the uncompressed style of the psalm, which stands in contrast to the compactness of much early poetry; the composition is accordingly dotted with phenomena such as suffixed pronouns or prepositions in contexts where a briefer verbal form may have sufficed, as well as terms such as עַל-כֵּן or כִּי. Corresponding to this is its lack of archaic forms; thus, Robertson lists Ps. 18 = 2 Sam. 22 as among "Poems that Resemble Standard Poetry", citing only the alternation of verb forms in past narrative as a potentially early feature.[14] Others who purport to have detected further archaic phenomena rely heavily on the reconstruction of supposedly lost and unrecognised features.[15] Nevertheless, such reconstructions remain speculative, and are considerably weakened by the lack of any preserved forms in the extant text.[16]

The impression that Ps. 18 is pre-exilic, but not especially archaic, is further reinforced by an examination of its vocabulary, which is generally attested across all periods, but is sometimes apparently confined to a "middle band" extending perhaps from the time of Isaiah and Micah to the early post-exilic age. There are some continuities with the early theophany tradition

10 I, p. 256.

11 Note especially v. 51.

12 *The Psalms and their Readers*, p. 24.

13 Cross and Freedman's advocacy of removing colon-initial *waw* in every instance where it lacks support in 2 Sam. or in one of the versions ("A Royal Song of Thanksgiving: II SAMUEL 22 = PSALM 18" in *SAYP*, 82-106) is needlessly self-justifying and circular, and carries with it the concomitant risk of removing motes rather than looking for the beams of later redactional activity of which they may be signals. Moreover, despite their efforts at elimination, there still remain twenty-two examples.

14 *Linguistic Evidence*, p. 139.

15 E.g., Cross and Freedman, *SAYP*, p. 83.

16 There is one instance of final *yod* in v. 32 (זוּלָתִי), which may be a remnant of an obsolete case-ending, yet further occurrences are attested only in "standard" Hebrew (Deut. 1:36, 4:12, Josh. 11:13 and 1 Ki. 3:18, 12:20); 2 Sam. 22:32 here duplicates the מִבַּלְעֲדֵי of the preceding colon.

discussed in the previous chapter,[17] and one example of the use of the verb מחץ (v. 39), which is confined, with one exception, to poetry often thought to be amongst the oldest in the Hebrew Bible.[18] However, more often, the language allies itself with later uses and, quite distinctively as compared with Pss. 29, 68 and 114, with the vocabulary and imagery employed to describe the appearance of Yahweh on Mount Sinai in the Exodus tradition.[19]

Similarly, the mention of Yahweh riding on a cherub in v. 11, though it resonates with apparently "primitive" images of the deity riding a storm cloud,[20] may be indicative of a period when the כְּרוּבִים, which may have been a Solomonic innovation in Israel, had become an established part of the religious and symbolic heritage of the nation. On the other hand, a late pre-exilic or post-exilic provenance is not demanded, since the dynamic portrayal in Ps. 18 / 2 Sam. 22 is highly distinctive, the idea of the כְּרוּבִים as living beings only actively being retained in Gen. 3:24 (J) and Ezekiel (1:5-28, 9:3, 10:1-20, 11:22).

Finally, evidence of direct borrowing in Pss. 144 and 116 is especially significant because it testifies to the enduring popularity and continued adaptation of the key motifs of Ps. 18 into the later period. There is a wide consensus that Ps. 18 is the source of quotation and allusion,[21] and this is indeed justified by indications of a late origin for both of the other psalms; this circumstance also further strengthens the case for a relatively early date for Ps. 18, whilst also warning of its likely adaptation over time.

ii. The Significance of the "Waters" Imagery of Psalm 18

As in the psalms already considered in Chapter 3, the divine epiphany constitutes an important theme in Ps. 18, but here various additional motifs are attested. Yahweh's dramatic manifestation in the thunderstorm is specifically to deliver his servant (depicted, according to the psalm heading and the framework provided for the parallel in 2 Sam. 22, as David); this may be thought of as a

---

17 Compare, e.g., רעשׁ הָאָרֶץ in Ps. 18:8 and 2 Sam. 22:8 with Ps. 68:9 and Judg. 5:4c. The theophany imagery is especially concentrated in vv. 8-16.

18 Outside Ps. 18:39 = 2 Sam. 22:39, it occurs only in Ps. 68:22, Judg. 5:26, Num. 24:8,17, Ps. 110:5,6, Deut. 32:39, 33:11, Hab. 3:13 and finally Job 26:12. Of these, the latter source is the only one not commonly subject to classification as among the earliest in the Hebrew Bible, though even here the frequently archaic style of the Book of Job must be acknowledged.

19 Into this category fall the motifs of smoke (v. 9), fire (vv. 9, 13) and thick darkness or heavy cloud (עֲרָפֶל, v. 10), and the idea that the deity descends (ירד) in theophany.

20 Cf. Ps. 68:5, 34, Deut. 33:26 and Hab. 3:8; the idea occurs also in Isa. 19:1, but the usage in Ps. 18 is in fact most closely comparable to that of Ps. 104:3, where the allusion to the cloud-chariot is paralleled with the description of Yahweh as הַמְהַלֵּךְ עַל־כַּנְפֵי־רוּחַ.

21 See, e.g., Starbuck, *Court Oracles*, pp. 118-9, Tournay, *Seeing and Hearing God*, p. 138.

development from the preceding theophany accounts, especially as regards its aims and reference, and the act of deliverance is set in the closer historical past. Thus, there is in this psalm a stronger sense of God participating directly in response to specific circumstances.

Although Yahweh's epiphany is in Ps. 18 the key element which facilitates a particular act of salvation, its effects are primarily seen in the earth, which "reeled and rocked" (v. 8; cf. v. 16).[22] However, there is more interest in the detail of the divine appearing than exhibited in the previously-considered psalms,[23] as well as in the purpose and method of deliverance enacted by Yahweh himself. Whereas in Ps. 29, Yahweh thunders from over the flood, and in Ps. 68 the picture is immediate and varied, Ps. 18 achieves a more comfortable synthesis: Yahweh is in heaven / his temple (v. 7), from whence he thunders and sends forth lightnings (vv. 14-15), but he also bows the heavens and comes down (v. 10), riding on a cherub (v. 11). The statement that he reached from on high to deliver his servant (v. 17) is slightly ambiguous, insofar as the petitioner is being drawn out of "many waters", the depths beneath. Hence, even the earth is (relatively speaking) "on high" from this perspective. However, the terminology also indicates Yahweh's transcendence, his distance from the shadowy realms below (Ps. 93:4 conveys a similar sense of Yahweh's innate and absolutely unthreatened superiority). The storm phenomena, thunder, wind and rain, now incorporate hailstones and coals of fire (vv. 13,14), thus functioning more directly as ammunition (v. 15). This is in keeping with the generally sharper focus of the psalm.

An important additional theme, not evident in the compositions previously discussed, is the employment of "torrents" as an image for Sheol[24] (v. 5b, here

---

22 Against Craigie's claim (p. 173) that הָאָרֶץ in v. 8 refers to "the underworld, realm of Mot" may be cited the apparent distinguishing of Sheol from the מוֹסְדֵי הָרִים in Deut 32:22 and the probable identification of the "mountains" with the "enduring foundations of the earth" in Mic. 6:2; moreover, the frequent paralleling of the trembling of the earth and mountains in connection with the divine theophany (e.g. in Judg. 5:4-5, Ps. 68:9; cf. Job 9:5-6). seems also to indicate that the thought is primarily of the terrestrial sphere. This is perhaps still more apparent in 2 Sam. 22:8, which has שָׁמַיִם for הָרִים, thus through the polarities of "heaven" and "earth" indicating the pan-cosmic trauma of Yahweh's theophany.

23 Pss. 29 and 114 are silent on the matter, whilst Ps. 68 has the quasi-titular allusion to God's riding on the clouds (v. 5) and through the heavens (v. 34).

24 בְּלִיַּעַל is conventionally explained as בְּלִי, "not, without", + יַעַל, "worth, use, profit" (e.g., BDB, p. 116), although the etymology advocated by Cross and Freedman, "*bal(i) ya'l(ê)* = '(place from which) none arises'" (*SAYP*, p. 97 n. 6, following earlier scholars) would well suit the context. In either case, the reference to the underworld is clear (contra Craigie, p. 173). However, a derivation from בלע, "swallow", to be understood as alluding to the nether world or even as a title of personified death (Curtis, p. 37, Eaton, p. 105, Davidson, p. 66; cf. Seybold, p. 81), is difficult to justify from the orthography of the word.

in combination with snares, v. 6b, and cords, vv. 5a, 6a),[25] and by extension, of the psalmist's enemies (מַיִם רַבִּים, vv. 17-18). Thus v. 16 may have a triple nuance: the exposing of the channels of (the) water(s)[26] and foundations of the world may be in part a reflection of the theme of "cosmic perturbation",[27] depicting a response to Yahweh's theophany. This image is all the more powerful for the fact that the foundations were symbolic of all that is enduring and unshakeable.[28] However, another aspect of the verse may be that it is in this nether region that the petitioner has been entrapped. Thus, the "torrents" also represent Sheol, which is at the foundations of the world (v. 16b, cf. Jon. 2:6-7). Finally, it is evident that those threatening the petitioner's death are also his earthly foes (vv. 15, 18) and may be encompassed by the imagery employed here. These strands cannot readily be separated, but they certainly caution against an ascription of *Chaoskampf* allusions in this context. In particular, the fact that the waters represent death (Mot) and not the cosmic sea (Yam) distinguishes the content of this psalm from Canaanite epic, both in substance and in essence. Various other features point in the same direction—the fact that the threat is against an individual human being and perhaps his nation, but not in any way endangering the cosmos; the deity's deliverance of that individual rather than engagement with the waters which engulf him; and so on. The imagistic rather than literalistic perception of the torrents is strongly implied by the breadth of their range of reference and by their employment alongside various other metaphors for death, some of which would be inconsistent with or contradictory to it, if understood as a depiction of tangible reality (e.g., Sheol as having "cords" or "snares").

Nevertheless, this is not to deny that the noun גְּעָרָה (v. 16), usually translated "rebuke", is quite strong; but against whom is it directed? The foe is

---

25 Many would "reinstate" here the parallel with מִשְׁבְּרֵי ("breakers, waves") in 2 Sam. 22:5, thus eliminating the twofold reference to חֶבְלֵי in vv. 5-6. In either case, the allusion to the underworld is clear.

26 Reading, with MT, אֲפִיקֵי מַיִם, a strikingly bland turn of phrase. However, it should perhaps be preferred over 2 Sam. 22:16, אֲפִיקֵי יָם, both as the *lexio difficilior* and because it is intrinsically more probable that the initial מ of מַיִם should drop out than that the same letter should be inserted from nowhere before יָם; Girard also cites a minor micro-structural advantage in its favour (I, p. 350). (Cross and Freedman, *SAYP*, p. 100 n. 41, propose that an unrecognised enclitic *mem* was transferred to יָם from the preceding word, but the otherwise total lack of archaic orthography in the composition renders this unlikely. Equally improbable is Berry's theory of the transference of the מ of an erroneous masculine plural absolute אֲפִיקִים onto the following word [*The Psalms and their Readers*, p. 39], since the context clearly requires a construct phrase.) In either case, subterranean (or submarine) channels seem to be intended, but the terminology employed should certainly caution against the ascription of a conflict with "chaos" here.

27 Thus also, e.g., Seybold (p. 81); the expression is Terrien's (p. 198). This response is shared by sea and land also in Ps. 77:17, 19c, Nah. 1:4-5 and Hab. 3:6, 8-10.

28 As the verbal root יסד, "establish, found, fix", and indeed the purpose of foundations, implies. Cf., e.g., Mic. 6:2, Isa. 40:21.

perhaps the most likely antecedent (v. 4; cf. v. 15), but Sheol may well also be secondarily implied (vv. 5-6). However, the parallelism and context of the present verse, as well as the employment of the verb גער elsewhere, would suggest that the term should primarily be understood to denote the roaring of Yahweh's thunderous voice (cf. "blast of the breath of thy nostrils", 16d; also v. 14).[29] Indeed, so vivid is the mythological and dramatic timbre of the passage that the articulation of a literal "rebuke", however stern, would seemingly only detract from the terrible spectacle of the epiphany of the God who descends in blazing wrath and fiery breath to deliver his servant.[30]

The reference to מַיִם רַבִּים in the following verse, v. 17, has for many commentators indicated an allusion to "chaos",[31] despite the fact that this is by no means an intrinsic aspect of the expression, as has been shown above in Chapter 3. The phrase is therefore best illuminated by its immediate context, namely the intersection of the language of cosmic distress at the divine theophany with the idea of the Psalmist being delivered from Sheol (cf. v. 16)[32] and from his "strong enemy" (cf. v. 18). Mention of מַיִם רַבִּים seems also to be the starting point for Day's attempt to relate the waters imagery of the Psalm to the theme of "chaos" whilst omitting to acknowledge any reference to Sheol.[33] However, this is achieved only through ignoring the use of similar language in the compositions considered in the present chapter, and interpreting it instead in the light of putative references to a suffering and vindicated royal figure which he associates with the autumn festival. In fact, all of these are of doubtful relevance: in Hab. 3:13, מְשִׁיחֶךָ is parallel to עַמֶּךָ, so the allusion is unlikely to be to the king; Zech. 13:7 occurs in a context of judgment; and the atoning or vicarious effects seen in Zech. 13:1 and Isa. 52-3 are wholly distinct from the experience of salvation celebrated in the present Psalm.

Equally lacking encouragement from the text itself is Clifford's relation of vv. 5-20 to "the installation of the king as viceroy after the Lord's world-establishing victory."[34] This thesis is based on the notion that "the Bible roots kingship... in the cosmic victories of Yahweh over Sea",[35] an assertion which is debatable even in respect of the divine sphere; it is here moreover transferred onto a human level, although this is without support from the biblical evidence.

---

29 As Hartley states, "*g'r* basically means 'a loud rumbling sound'" ("1721 גער" in *NIDOTTE*, I, 884-7, p. 884), citing *UT* 56, 23; see also J. Day, *God's Conflict*, p. 29 n. 82, p. 122, G. R. Driver, "The Resurrection of Marine and Terrestrial Creatures", *JSS* 7 (1962), p. 15, and P. Joüon, "Notes de lexicographie hébraique", *Biblica* 6 (1925), pp. 318-21; cf. also A. A. Macintosh, "A Consideration of Hebrew גער" *VT* 19 (1969), pp. 472-3, and S. C. Reif, "A Note on גער", *VT* 21 (1971), p. 243.

30 See further the discussion of this verb in connection with Ps. 104:7 in Chapter 8 below.

31 Thus, e.g., Kraus, I, p. 291, Hossfeld, HZ, I, p. 127, Curtis, p. 37, McCann, *NIB*, IV, p. 747.

32 The former motif is manifested also in v. 5 and the latter in v. 8.

33 *God's Conflict*, pp. 123-5.

34 I, p. 105.

35 I, p. 106.

Similarly, Clifford's statement, "that the Lord was in 'his temple' (v. [7]*c*) suggests he has already vanquished Sea and currently rules", is founded on the fact that "in the myths the god's palace (temple) was built after the battle to symbolize the cosmic victory."[36] However, he does not demonstrate why such mythology should be brought to bear in this instance, since it can hardly be assumed to be in mind wherever the Temple (or God's presence therein) is mentioned. This is not least the case when the only "waters" imagery utilised up to this point in the Psalm is related explicitly to the underworld (v. 5). In fact, when he turns from comparative methodology to exegesis of the psalm itself, he has to acknowledge that "the Storm God's immediate goal is not to annihilate Sea, however, but to rescue the king."[37] Hence his wider claims should be rejected.

The Sheol / waters imagery probably conceals a number of underlying concepts. Firstly, the image of death as drowning is a particularly vivid and powerful one; the appropriateness of the "water" imagery to a sudden experience of being engulfed by mortal danger is further illuminated by the rapidity with which a dry wadi could turn into a raging torrent. Then, the "underworld" was anyway cosmologically associated with the "waters beneath", a view no doubt reinforced by the possibility of experiencing rejection or punishment by being cast into a miry pit. Related to its position at the extremities of the cosmos, literally in the watery regions, far from God himself and possibly outside his domain, where the devouring monster Mot / Sheol holds sway, is the association with that which is frightening, threatening to life and an ordered existence and potentially able to engulf at any time. This is an inbuilt feature of the cosmos as it stands.

It is significant that the waters and the enemies are never actually directly compared, though both entities are brought into association with the Sheol imagery. In individual laments or songs of thanksgiving, the enemies are characteristically also individuals, who threaten the life (or, by extension, quality of life) of the psalmist, and thus are understood as parallel with Sheol. Here, that individual element is also present,[38] and then expands over into the military[39] sphere. Certainly, the images are very fluid, and distinctions not rigidly enforced. Thus, there is a blurring of the distinction between the enemies (v. 4) and Sheol (vv. 5-6), the latter in turn being experienced, amongst other images, as "torrents";[40] similarly, the way that the dramatic depiction of the laying bare of the foundations of the world and of the extraction of the suppliant from the מַיִם רַבִּים which lie beneath the earth (vv. 16-17) is framed by

36 I, p. 108.

37 I, p. 107.

38 Note especially vv. 21-25.

39 The foe may be Israelite: thus the superscription (v. 1), and perhaps also v. 42.

40 In addition, there are terminological links between the depictions of the spheres of enmity and the underworld (see Girard, I, p. 344); thus, "calling upon Yahweh" is related to salvation from enemies in v. 4, but follows on from engulfment by the powers of death in v. 7, whilst the verb קדם (Pi.) occurs in v. 6b in connection with the "snares of death" but in v. 19a with regard to the enemies.

Yahweh's "scattering" and "routing" of the enemy (v. 15) and his "deliverance" of the Psalmist from his "strong enemy" (v. 18) suggests that alternative perspectives upon the same events are here consciously being juxtaposed. Hence Sheol seems to be identified with both the enemies and the waters, and this combination may have led to the inference of parity between the waters and the foe, but there is no straightforward "chaos" waters-enemy transition.

In summary, the key features of Ps. 18 are the fact that the psalm as a whole takes the form of a thanksgiving celebrating Yahweh's deliverance of his servant, the speaker, through a specific act of intervention. The royal aspect of the psalm ensures that it encompasses both the personal and national sphere, but in genre and individual focus it represents a clear departure from the compositions considered in the preceding chapter. Though the theophany is depicted in unparalleled detail and magnificence, it is clearly anchored in a particular deed of salvation. This has two dimensions: on the historical plane, the circumstances are the routing of the petitioner's (i.e., probably the king's) foes; however, on a deeper and more mythological level, it may be understood as nothing less than a snatching from the clutches of death. However, although an aspect of the waters which is dangerous and threatening to the individual is implied, this is primarily (and perhaps exclusively) in connection with Sheol, and "chaos waters" *per se* do not feature.

2. Psalm 144: The Waters as Symbolic of the Psalmist's Enemies; Yahweh as Deliverer

Of the remaining psalms to be considered, the one bearing the closest relation to Ps. 18 is the prayer-song Ps. 144. Here, the imagery pertaining to the divine theophany has been formulated in considerable dependence on Ps. 18;[41] nevertheless, this prior material, which was originally crafted as an account of deliverance, has in Ps. 144 been selectively edited and transformed into imperatival petitions. The features of the divine epiphany itself have been retained relatively intact, but the underworld nuances have almost totally receded. Most notably, the vivid description of the channels of water/the sea being seen and the foundations of the earth laid bare at Yahweh's rebuke (18:16) has been excised. Nevertheless, the juxtaposition of מַיִם רַבִּים and the psalmist's foes has been retained. The general effect of these transformations, therefore, is a muting of the associations with Sheol which are evident in Ps. 18 and in the individual laments to be discussed below, but a corresponding simplification of the parallel between the treacherous waters and the alien enemy. The corollary of this is a heightening of national elements (political foes) at the expense of the individual (personal demise).

Therefore, the only verse of specific interest to the issue of "chaos" in the Psalter is v. 7, where the מַיִם רַבִּים of Ps. 18:17 resurface. Kraus's proposed

41 See the discussion of the dating of Ps. 18 above, and, briefly, of Ps. 144 below.

emendation, "Extricate me from mighty waters / and rescue me from the power of aliens" (transferring וְהַצִּילֵנִי from v. 7b to c), is unnecessary. The signification of the hostile foe, and perhaps also the underworld, by the "many waters" is indicated by the parallelism within the verse[42] (according to which מִמַּיִם רַבִּים and מִיַּד בְּנֵי נֵכָר seem effectively to be placed in apposition) and also by the context in Ps. 18:10, 15, 17, from which it borrows heavily; Pss. 46:3-4, 7 and especially 65:8 may also be compared. It is perhaps not merely coincidental that in the last-mentioned of these Psalms, like Ps. 144, the celebration of God's defensive capacities leads directly into an extended treatment of his gift of agricultural fertility and prosperity (Ps. 65:6-9, 10-14).

A distinctive aspect of Ps. 144 is the concluding petition for blessing and fertility in vv. 12-15, which has occasioned much surprise among contemporary exegetes. However, this is obviously consistent with the ancient theophany thunderstorm associations which have receded from any explicit mention, but a primary feature of which is the bestowal of rain (compare Pss. 68:9-11; 114:8). It also balances beautifully the opening beatitude acknowledging Yahweh as the one who gives victory and security to his king and people. Indeed, in its confident tone, Ps. 144 more closely approaches the tenor of the psalm of thanksgiving Ps. 18 than it does that of the laments to be considered in the course of the present chapter. Rather than pleading for deliverance from a situation of distress, the petitioner seems to be in a position where the paradoxical wonders of Yahweh's favour and support can be celebrated (see especially vv. 3-4; also vv. 1-2, 9-10) and further benefits beyond those gained on the battlefield (vv. 5-8, 11; cf. vv. 1-2, 10) may be sought (vv. 12-15). It is perhaps in accordance with this, then, that the human aspect of the enemies is uppermost, whilst the more terrifying prospect of Sheol seems almost to have receded from view. Of the psalms presently considered, the prominence of the enemies over the underworld is distinctive to Ps. 144. The confident presumption of Yahweh's support and concomitant victory is also striking in the mouth of a suppliant rather than of a victor offering his thanks to the deity who awarded him deliverance.

The theme of the intervention of Yahweh on behalf of the psalmist which is so conspicuous in Pss. 18 and 144 recurs in two more of the psalms to be considered, Pss. 124 and 69, and may be implied in a third, Ps. 32. The motif is clearest in Ps. 124, which seems to be a national thanksgiving in the wake of an "escape" (v. 7) from "men" who "rose up against us" (v. 2). However, less clear is the nature of the waters imagery employed in vv. 4-5, whether it has a purely human or a more sinister orientation, and this will now comprise the

---

42 This is recognised, e.g., by Anderson, II, p. 933, and Kraus, II, p. 1124. However, there is no contextual support for an allusion to "chaos", and hence even those who assume such a reference here are usually muted or indirect in their claims: thus Davidson describes מַיִם רַבִּים in terminology which is commonly applied to "chaos" but eminently appropriate to the underworld which it actually signifies (p. 464), whilst Eaton, having stated that the king has "fallen into the chaos-waters and the hands of abhorrent foes", has to qualify this by explaining, "these are the forces of death" (Eaton, p. 471; cf. Terrien, p. 899, Allen, pp. 287, 291).

subject of the following analysis, before the same issue is addressed in relation to Ps. 69.

3. Psalm 124: The Waters as Symbolic of Sheol and of the Psalmist's Enemies; Yahweh as Deliverer

In verses 3-5, a dual signification, encompassing both the foe and Sheol, may be detected.[43] On a superficial level, v. 3 continues the thought of the preceding verses in portraying the nation's adversary under the figure of a devouring monster,[44] but, more fundamentally, the metaphor resonates with the concept of Sheol as a monster with an insatiable appetite (cf. Prov. 30:15-16, Isa. 5:14, Hab. 2:5), its mouth open wide to receive its prey (Isa. 5:14, cf. Ps. 141:7).[45] Indeed in the Qal, relevant metaphorical uses of בלע apply not to political adversaries and rapacious superpowers, but to the jaws of death, since the motif of "swallowing alive" or "going down alive" is expressly confined to images for death.[46] A similar combination of ideas to that encountered in Ps. 124:3-5 occurs also in Ps. 69:16, where the Sheol referent is perhaps more pronounced, and the abysmal scene is evoked in strong colours. Yet even here the sphere of reference is hardly exclusive, since it is evident from the parallelism in v. 15 that the adversaries (especially perhaps against an individual) could manifest themselves also as the agents of Sheol.

---

43 Weiser urges here a further possible echo, that "of the tradition of the combat against the powers of chaos and of the primeval flood which had their place in the sacred tradition of the *Heilsgeschichte*" (p. 520); thus also, e.g., Anderson (II, p. 860), Goulder (*The Psalms of the Return*, p. 54) and Eaton (p. 430). On the other hand, others such as Tromp (p. 110), Seybold (p. 483) and Dahood (III, p. 212) emphasise the Sheol affiliations of the imagery, the first of these scholars to the exclusion of the adversarial aspect.

44 Cf. Ps. 79:7, Isa. 9:12, Jer. 51:34. It is improbable that the enemy is conceived of as a wild beast, as certain scholars, such as Kissane (II, p. 255) would claim (cf. v. 6; 7:3, 22:13-14), since it is portrayed as able to "swallow us alive", something which is more readily predicated of a supernatural creature. It is also unlikely (contra Girard, III, pp. 319, 320) that the thought of a consuming fire pertains to the whole verse, since "kindled anger" (v. 3b) is a common Hebrew idiom which operates independently of any surrounding metaphors, and בלע is not elsewhere applied to fire, despite its obvious devouring capacity (cf. Prov. 30:16)

45 Cf. the ironic statement in Isa. 25:8 that "[Yahweh] will swallow up [Pi. בלע] death for ever". For the motif of the hunger of death in a Ugaritic context, see *KTU* 1.4.viii.14-20.

46 Prov. 1:12, Ps. 55:16, and especially Num 16:30, 33; a related metaphor for death is the earth swallowing its victim, e.g., in Ex. 15:12, Num. 26:10; 16:30; Deut. 11:6. Only in Jer. 51:34 is the Qal verb applied to the action of an enemy towards a human subject, but there the notion of being consumed "alive" is not expressed.

Thus, the opening metaphor of Ps. 124 both encompasses established patterns for describing hostile enemy action and, even more strongly, connotes the nether realm, these spheres of reference continuing into vv. 4-5, even as the imagery is transformed into that of an onrushing torrent carrying all before it. Probably, observation of the sudden surge of floodwaters in a previously dry wadi after a storm would have inspired the image (cf. Judg. 5:21, Matt. 7:27). For the enemy as an overflowing river, epitomising the danger of being "engulfed" by an expanding superpower, compare Isa. 8:7-8, 17:12-13 and Jer. 47:2. There is a particular congruence between the key items of vocabulary—namely, מַיִם, נַחַל, שׁטף, עבר—in Ps. 124:4 and two of these references, namely Isa. 8:7-8 and Jer. 47:2a, where the overflowing waters function as a metaphor for military invasion and conquest.

Nevertheless, שׁטף also appears in close proximity to מַיִם (another of the key terms of Ps. 124:4) in Ps. 69:3, 16, in order to denote the sphere of the underworld;[47] in v. 16, the parallel motif is that of the deep "swallowing up" (בלע) its victim, a theme which has strong resonances with Ps. 124:2. A further possible connection between שׁטף and Sheol is manifested also in Isa. 28:15, 18. Thus, military campaigns and Sheol are dominant spheres of allusion for the destruction denoted by שׁטף; this is especially the case in contexts such as Jer. 47:2a, Isa. 8:7-8, Dan. 11:10, 40 and Ps. 69:3, 16, where the strongest affinities to Ps. 124:4—both in terms of vocabulary and imagery—are present.

Though the term נַחַל, "torrent, torrent valley, wadi" (v. 4) most frequently has positive connotations, as a source of water and fertility,[48] "an overflowing stream" appears in a simile for judgment in Isa. 30:28, whilst נַחַל שׁוֹטֵף denotes the invasion of an alien foe in Jer. 47:2, a passage which has already been shown to have numerous linguistic contacts with Ps. 124:4-5; no less significant is the parallelism between the נַחֲלֵי בְלִיַּעַל and the חֶבְלֵי־[מִשְׁבְּרֵי־] מָוֶת in Ps. 18:5 [2 Sam. 22:5]. However, in contrast to these passages, where the nature of the נְחָלִים is qualified, the נַחְלָה of Ps. 124:4 is free of adjectival definition, thus permitting a referential diversity which is further suggested by the context. Thus the operation of multiple spheres of allusion, in which terrestrial streams are linked by analogy to political or abysmal themes, cannot be ignored.

Though עבר (vv. 4b, 5a) is among the most common lexical items in Biblical Hebrew, three main referential possibilities present themselves: divine wrath,[49] military conquest,[50] and perhaps the breaking out of Sheol on its victim, as in Pss. 42:8, 88:17 and Jon. 2:4. The first option, divine wrath, is logically impossible; hence, once again, a bifarious signification, encompassing both the underworld and a national adversary, seems likely.

---

47 Note the proximate vocabulary: "deep mire", v. 3, "Pit", v. 16, etc.

48 Pss. 78:20; 104:10; 110:7; Isa. 35:6; Jer. 31:9; Ezek. 47; Gen. 26:19; Deut. 8:7; 2 Ki. 3:16; 1 Ki. 10:7; 17:4, 6-7; 18:5; Ps. 74:15.

49 Cf., e.g., Nah. 1:8.

50 Cf., e.g., Isa. 8:8, Dan. 11:10, 40.

The idea of overflow or of "overstepping" confines implied by עבר also touches on the motif of presumption or "haughtiness",[51] which is suggested by the adjectival hapax legomenon in v. 5, הַזֵּידוֹנִים. Translated as "raging waters" by the RSV,[52] it may communicate something of the essential nature of these waters,[53] which are, more literally, "proud"[54] or "presumptuous".[55] Hence, the adjective may perhaps denote turbulence in a physical sense (so "raging, foaming, seething," like Jacob's boiling pottage, Gen. 25:29) but possibly also seeking to transgress its bounds, of presuming (perhaps on its own initiative and against God's will) to attempt to sweep away Israel. Nevertheless, this does not permit a clear distinction between Sheol and the more immediate agents, the human foe, but finds its echo again with vv. 1-3, within which Israel openly acknowledges the competing spheres of influence, those of God and Man, which may act upon her.

The ambiguity of reference in the final clause of v. 5 then provides a bridge to vv. 6-7, in which the personal aspect of the enemy is allowed to predominate. Nevertheless, even here, the motif of being given "as prey to their teeth" (v. 6c) harks back to the imagery of v. 3a, the monstrous enemies / Sheol. Similarly, although snares appear frequently in connection with the wicked,[56] they and nets are often part of the armoury of Sheol, as is especially evident in 2 Sam. 22:6 = Ps. 18:6 and Ps. 116:3; compare Eccles. 9:12, Lam. 3:52(-58), Job 18: 9-10, 22:10.

Thus the motifs of vv. 6 and 7, the prey of wild beasts and the fowler's snare, are consonant with all the preceding spheres of allusion, including Sheol and the foe, yet also remain within the usual scope of imagery for an individual lament or thanksgiving. Accordingly, the actions of the enemy are depicted in language applicable to individuals rather than nations.[57] However, Yahweh's determination of Israel's destiny is also a dominating concern,[58] and this theme

---

51 Cohen, p. 425; Kraus, II, p. 1026.

52 So also, e.g., Allen (p. 162), Kraus (II, p. 1024, "tobenden Wasser"), Dahood (III, p. 211).

53 Militating against Kissane's contention that v. 4 refers to the "swollen torrent" and v. 5 to the "raging sea" are the close verbal links between these verses (מים, עבר; compare the echoing effect of vv. 1 and 2, and the chiastic arrangement of the four cola of v. 7, entailing repetition of Niph. מלט in the framing lines and פַּח in the central pair). Kissane's interpretation seems to be partially informed by his conjecture that the events of "Israel's supreme crisis", the Exodus, and hence the crossing of the Red Sea and Jordan, should comprise the subject of allusion here (pp. 254, 255).

54 For a similar idea, cf. perhaps Job 38:11. This translation is adopted by Cohen (p. 425) and Anderson (II, p. 860).

55 Anderson, II, p. 860.

56 E.g., in Pss. 119:110, 141:9-10, Job 22:10, Jer. 5:26, Hos. 9:8.

57 Notably, burning in anger (v. 3) and ensnaring (v. 7) are deeds characteristic of personal, rather than national, foes.

58 When enacted against a nation, the verbs cited in the previous note, anger and ensnaring, are primarily the preserve of God; hence their application to the enemies implies the improper assumption of a divine rôle.

finds universal expression in the theological summary of v. 8: Israel's help is in Yahweh, who made heaven and earth. Thus, he is the ultimate master of all creation and of the historical forces whose unfolding course is encompassed by his purpose.[59]

Finally, it is notable that there is no indication of a direct encounter between God and the waters, and no description of the means by which Yahweh subdued them. There is no interest in mythological detail, and the signification of human enemies by the imagery is made absolutely clear. Indeed, the foe is as nothing before God in such an unequal contest, for it is mere אָדָם.

In Ps. 124, then, it appears that both the foes and Sheol are kept directly in view, and there is a tension in the imagery which enables them to be held in balance as potential referents. In the individual laments to be considered, Pss. 42-3, 69 and 88, Sheol assumes greater prominence; though the foes and other manifestations of affliction feature in the course of these psalms, the waters imagery seems specifically to be focused on the underworld and the prospect of death. Admittedly, in Ps. 69, the enemies are permitted to appear in parallel with this experiential sphere; yet, even there, they seem to function as the indirect cause of woe. Thus, the Psalmist's predicament is expressed most tangibly as an encounter with the waters of Sheol, but there is a continued awareness that under its guise is concealed the agency of the foes.

4. Psalm 69: The Waters as Symbolic of Sheol; Yahweh as Deliverer

Verses 2-3 and 15-16 of this individual lament[60] exhibit an extraordinary confluence of waters imagery, the word מַיִם itself recurring four times in various combinations (מַיִם, v. 2; מַעֲמַקֵּי־מַיִם, vv. 3, 15; שִׁבֹּלֶת מַיִם, v. 16). Vv. 2-3 comprise a description of the psalmist's plight, and vv. 15-16 a plea for rescue, but both draw on common vocabulary and imagery. The suppliant is sinking in deep mire (vv. 3, 15; v. 3b adds "where there is no foothold"); he is in deep waters and the flood is sweeping over him (vv. 3, 15-16). In v. 2, the waters have come up to the petitioner's neck, but by v. 16 he is afraid that the deep may swallow him up and the pit close its mouth over him, like a threatening monster or beast. Another interesting feature of the second passage is the mention of the enemies: deliverance from the enemies and deep waters is paralleled with rescue from sinking in the mire.

The correspondences between vv. 2-3 and vv. 15-16 are striking, the only phrases lacking an obvious counterpart in the balancing section being the clauses at either extremity of the series employing waters imagery, in vv. 2b and

59 However, Kissane's assumption that a particular contrast is here implied between Yahweh and the "pagan idols", as in Ps. 115:3ff., is unnecessary.

60 It nevertheless has some national aspects: cf. vv. 36-7 and also v. 7, which may imply that the suppliant was a representative of the community.

16c.[61] Whereas the first of these, v. 2b, is as colourless as possible (employing terminology such as (מַיִם and בוא), the latter (וְאַל־תֶּאְטַר־עָלַי בְּאֵר פִּיהָ) exhibits perhaps the clearest affiliation with underworld imagery of all the expressions here encountered. In the intervening lines, the language ranges widely, from the mire (טִיט, יָוֵן) to flowing water (שִׁבֹּלֶת) to the deep (מַעֲמַקִּים, מְצוּלָה). While each of these touches on a different associative sphere, "mire", for example, normally being encountered in streets or pits, and "deeps" in the sea, topographical specificity (in the form of terms such as יָם, נָהָר, נַחַל, etc.) is eschewed. The physical unreality of the descriptions (the combining of the "mire" and "deep", for example) together with the absence of geographical indicators reveals the metaphorical character of the waters thus depicted and their identity as symbols of affliction and/or of Sheol. The ambiguous nature of the waters is apparent from the outset: once v. 2 has introduced the theme of the dangerous מַיִם, a term which leaves their more exact nature and location open, v. 3 opens with a reference to the "mire of the deep"—a combination which is, on a literal level, improbable.[62]

The noun יָוֵן, "mire", occurs only here in Ps. 69:3 and in Ps. 40:3, where it is conjoined with the apparent synonym טִיט; this same word stands in the place of יָוֵן in the counterpart to v. 3a in v. 15. The content of the two laments and their application of the "mire" terminology is so close that any cross-interpretation is at risk of circularity. Nevertheless, it is noteworthy that the phrase standing in parallel to טִיט הַיָּוֵן in Ps. 40:3 is בּוֹר שָׁאוֹן, a motif which is perhaps comparable to the mention of בְּאֵר in Ps. 69:16, and which has strong associations with the underworld.[63]

The noun with which יָוֵן stands in construct relationship in Ps. 69:3, מְצוּלָה, "deep", at first strikes one as rather incongruous. מְצוּלָה in the majority of cases appears in connection with the sea,[64] which is not normally associated with mire.[65] However, the association is once more illuminated by the concept of the underworld as a "pit", as the parallelism in Ps. 88:7 shows:

שַׁתַּנִי בְּבוֹר תַּחְתִּיּוֹת בְּמַחֲשַׁכִּים בִּמְצֹלוֹת׃

---

61 The only other significant divergence between the two sections is the mention of the enemies in v. 15b where v. 3b alludes to the lack of any foothold, as accords with the different emphases of the respective passages. In addition, v. 3a is split in a climactic fashion between vv. 15a and 16b, which frame the material derived from vv. 2-3; thus, reference to sinking in the mire in v. 15a is balanced in v. 16b by the more dramatic plea, "Let not the deep swallow me up", which in turn prepares the way for the climactic mention of the pit in v. 16c.

62 For a similarly anomalous pairing, compare בּוֹר שָׁאוֹן (literally, "pit of roaring [waters?]") in Ps. 40:3, which many have thought necessary to emend, e.g., to בּוֹר שָׁוְא, "pit of emptiness".

63 For the significance of בְּאֵר, see further the discussion of Ps. 88 below.

64 For references, see the discussion of Ps. 88:7 below.

65 Although in Isa. 57:20, the wicked are likened to the "tossing sea", whose waters "toss up mire and dirt", this is rather different from the idea of sinking in the mire of—and presumably therefore in—the deep.

This lament displays perhaps the greatest density of unequivocal netherworld images exhibited anywhere in the Psalter. The same combination of motifs is attested in Jon. 2:4, where the complaint "thou didst cast me into the deep" (מְצוּלָה) immediately follows a reference to Sheol (v. 3; cf. v. 7). Thus, the most plausible interpretation of the language of Ps. 69:3a would seem to be that it constitutes an experiential image for sinking into Sheol.

The combination יְוֵן מְצוּלָה (v. 3a) is in vv. 15-16 divided to provide a frame for further motifs drawn from v. 3, which then appear in sequence, the petitions closely echoing their descriptive counterparts. The יָוֵן of v. 3 (a word which, as has been seen, is attested elsewhere only once, and then in combination with טִיט) is replaced with the טִיט of v. 15a: "Rescue me from the mire, and let me not sink". Here, a parallel is furnished by Jer. 38:6, where the verb of Ps. 69:15, טבע, recurs in connection with טִיט: וּבַבּוֹר אֵין-מַיִם כִּי אִם-טִיט וַיִּטְבַּע יִרְמְיָהוּ בַּטִּיט. A further, and by now familiar, link with Ps. 40:3 and with Ps. 69:15-16 once more becomes evident: that of the pit (בּוֹר; cf. בְּאֵר in Ps. 69:16). Once again, therefore, it appears that the prime sphere of allusion indicated in Ps. 69:2-3a, 15a may be the underworld.[66]

In the following line (v. 15b), the phrase מַעֲמַקֵּי-מָיִם ("depths of the waters") exactly reproduces that of v. 3c, the initial experience of "coming into" the deep waters having its counterpart in the petition to be "delivered from" them. מַעֲמַקִּים does not seem to have a clearly-defined associative field and, in fact, its significance seems to vary according to its context and construct relation with other vocabulary.[67] However, it appears from the parallelism that it may now be the enemies which constitute the fundamental source of danger for the suppliant, and that they are merely figured by the מַעֲמַקֵּי-מָיִם. In this regard, the merging of Sheol and enemy motifs in the waters imagery of Pss. 124 and 18 may be compared; more commonly, one theme appears independently of the other, the underworld dominating in Pss. 42:8; 88:5, 7-8, 17-18, and the foes in Ps. 144:8.

שִׁבֹּלֶת, mention of which immediately follows that of מַעֲמַקֵּי-מָיִם in both v. 3d and v. 16a, then appears to constitute a further instance of a lexeme encountered in Ps. 69 for which a connection with a particular associative sphere, such as the underworld or enemies, is lacking.[68] Thus it appears that in the central core of vv. 15b-16a (and the parallel in v. 3cd) are encased relatively colourless, flexible "waters" images which of themselves contribute to the diversity of characteristics thereby connoted (i.e., depths, flowing [streams of] water), without, however, weighting the imagery towards a particular geographical or

66 Although the term טִיט in Job 41:22 precedes mention of מְצוּלָה // יָם (v. 23), it seems that the allusion is to Leviathan leaving an imprint from his sharp scales akin to that made by a threshing sledge, hence טִיט in this context must, as elsewhere, denote mud and is not something especially associated with the sea itself.

67 It occurs elsewhere three times, in Isa. 51:10, Ezek. 27:34 and Ps. 130:2, only in the last of these cases in the absolute, where it seems to denote a state of distress, though further delimitation is not possible.

68 It occurs outside Ps. 69:3, 16 only twice, in Judg. 12:6 and Isa. 27:12, neither of which can offer secure illumination on the meaning of the term.

associative sphere. Nevertheless, this apparent neutrality is counterbalanced by the force of the accompanying verbal ideas: besides the plea for "deliverance" from the deep waters (v. 15bc), the verb שׁטף, which recurs in both vv. 3 and 16 in relation to the שִׁבֹּלֶת, should especially be noted. The term has already been discussed in relation to Ps. 124:4, where it was shown that it is most commonly associated with the underworld and with the havoc wreaked by advancing military forces; this is especially the case where waters metaphors are employed (as here in Ps. 69, and in 124:4, Isa. 8:7-8, Jer. 47:2a and Dan. 11:10, 40). The connection with foes is pertinent to the situation in Ps. 69:16a, since the preceding line alludes to the שֹׂנְאִים of the Psalmist; hence the overtones of hostility sounded in v. 15b still resonate more faintly here. Nevertheless, a more conspicuous parallel afforded by Ps. 124 is the collocation of overflowing waters (מַיִם + שׁטף, 69:16a, cf. Ps. 124:4) with the motif of "swallowing" (בלע, 69:16b, cf. Ps. 124:3), a theme which is especially strongly associated with Sheol.

In fact, v. 16 as a whole seems to comprise a culminating sequence which gradually reveals the true identity of the perpetrator of the psalmist's woe. מְצוּלָה (v. 16b) is, of course, derived from the opening clause of v. 3, where it refers to the underworld, and here it provides the closing frame to the derivative material from v. 3, having its counterpart in the mire of v. 15a. Yet it also serves to reveal the fundamental identity of the perilous מַיִם, for they (in the guise of the מְצוּלָה) threaten to "swallow up" (בלע) their victim, which, as has been demonstrated, is a clear characteristic of Sheol.[69] This impression is then confirmed in the climactic line, "Let not the pit close its mouth over me" (v. 16c). Whilst this could indicate the mouth of a well, the context requires the meaning "pit", as in Ps. 55:24, Prov. 23:27; cf. Gen. 24:20.

Some have attempted to interpret these images literalistically, so that the "pit" is understood as referring to a punishment for an alleged crime (e.g., theft, vv. 5, 34b; cf. Jer. 38:6)[70] or even as the setting for a liturgical imprisonment;[71] if it was water-filled, this could explain some of the other descriptions. However, it is clear from the foregoing analysis that the language is far more imagistic, the "pit" and "mire" being particularly characteristic terminology for the underworld.[72] A minority of scholars have perceived a discontinuity between conceptions of the netherworld as "mire" and as "dust" (cf. Ps. 22:30, Job 7:21, 21:26, Isa. 26:19). Indeed, Dahood, though not denying that עָפָר ("dust") signifies Sheol, contends that it actually means

69 For the insatiable appetite of Sheol, compare Prov. 30:15f. and Isa. 5:14; for the "depths" as the underworld, see Ps. 88:7 and cf. Ps. 71:20 (there תהמות).

70 See Kraus, II, p. 643.

71 Thus Goulder, *The Prayers of David*, pp. 220-1.

72 For the pit, cf. e.g., Pss. 28:1, 30:4, 40:3, 55:24, 88:5, 143:7, Job 33:30 and perhaps also *KTU* 1.4.viii.11-12; for its clear synonymity with "going down to Sheol", see, e.g., Isa. 14:15, Ezek. 31:16; for the mire, cf. Ps. 40:3, and compare *KTU* 1.4.viii.12-13, 1.5.ii.15.

"mud".[73] Nevertheless, attempts to create a geographically consistent picture of the underworld are surely misguided. The metaphors employed are impressionistic, denoting the essential nature of that realm, not its physical characteristics. At root is the barrenness of its landscape—either as (dry) dust and desert or as the (wet) "mire" and deep, both of which are equally unable to support life.[74] G. R. Driver's proposal that שְׂנְאַי (v. 15b) should be emended to שָׁיִן ("mud"; adopted by NEB as "muddy depths")[75] for the sake of synonymity is equally misplaced, since on a metaphorical level, the existing parallelism is extremely apt.

The prevailing imagery conveys a sense of powerlessness and of the proximity of death. Anderson explains it thus: "'To die' means to go down to Sheol or to the Pit... and even one who is ill is already in the process of being overwhelmed by the deep waters of the underworld... he who is engulfed by *any* disaster, is actually in the sphere of death".[76] Thus, "Sheol was not so much a geographical location as a sphere of influence: wherever one finds the characteristics of Sheol, such as weakness, disease, misery, forsakenness, etc., there is Sheol also. The stricken man's experience of the underworld is partial, but it is none the less very real. Unless he was rescued from this situation by God, he would become fully dead and not simply 'like the slain' (88:5 (M.T. 6))".[77]

Thus, the underworld is an entity which, like the psalmist's enemies, functions as something personally threatening to him rather than to the rule of God. It must be recognised, then, that there is here no hint of a divine conflict with the sea.[78] Further confirmation of this occurs in v. 35, where the seas[79] and their inhabitants, together with heaven and earth, join in praise of their creator and lord. Moreover, although the poem employs many items of vocabulary ("waters", "deep waters", "deep", "flood") which also feature in various psalms to be discussed in later sections, the usage when applied in the

73 I, p. 140, following Gunkel, *Die Psalmen*, p. 128, who renders the term even more strongly as "Kot", i.e., "mire, filth".

74 See Tromp, *Primitive Conceptions*, pp. 132-3.

75 "Textual and Linguistic Problems of the Book of Psalms", *HTR* 29 (1936), pp. 184-185; *BHS* likewise recommends emending to שׁוֹאָה, "devastation, ruin, waste".

76 I, p. 315.

77 I, p. 241.

78 It is therefore perhaps not surprising that mention of "chaos" is only seldom made in connection with this Psalm. Perhaps the most notable advocate is Zenger (in HZ, p. 263, 269, 275; cf. Lindström, *Suffering and Sin*, pp. 344-5), yet even he acknowledges the underworld reference of v. 16bc; moreover, despite interpreting vv. 15-16a as employing the imagery of the "water floods of chaos", this follows his explanation of מַעֲמַקֵּי־מָיִם (v. 15c) as alluding to "death itself" in v. 3 (p. 270). This leaves only טִיט and שִׁבֹּלֶת מַיִם to bear the connotations he maintains, though no support for this may be garnered from elsewhere. Likewise Eaton, though making a brief allusion to "chaos" in his commentary (p. 256), fails to mention this theme in his earlier discussion of Ps. 69 in *Kingship and the Psalms* (pp. 51-3).

79 A term which is not employed in vv. 2-3, 15-16.

genre of individual lament is highly distinctive. First of all, creation and exodus language is understandably absent; but there is also no imagery of the floods being cut, divided, gathered, or rebuked, or of the waters fleeing. Nor is there any mention of the earth or mountains showing their fear. The only similarity which may be adduced is that of the parallelism of the "deep waters" with the psalmist's enemies (v. 15), which may be compared with the imagery of Pss. 46 and 65, which is to be considered in the next chapter. However, here these foes are apparently personal rather than national and are only secondarily implied.

Among the individual laments (as contrasted with the psalms of thanksgiving) under consideration, the convergence of the waters of the underworld and the threat of the suppliant's foes is distinctive to Ps. 69,[80] though, as has been stated above in comparison with the psalm of thanksgiving Ps. 124, the foes are not here fully identified with the waters. Thus Ps. 69 stands in mood somewhere between the psalms discussed above (Pss. 144, 18 and 124), where Yahweh's support seems to be assured and the foes are in proportionate measure in view, and those to be examined in the following section (Pss. 42-3 and 88), where the deity is regarded as the agent of affliction,[81] and the waters themselves assume dominance. It is as if the waters of the underworld are the primary object of the psalmist's fear but their underlying human agency and unacceptability to God can provide a basis for hope of deliverance. Nevertheless, it is significant that the fundamental aggressive function is, by implication, performed by something other than the waters standing in and of themselves. In this instance, it seems that the fundamental aggressor or destructive force is Sheol, a secondary and less direct referent being the foe.

5. Psalms 42-3 and 88: The Waters as Symbolic of Sheol; Yahweh as the Agent of Woe

In Pss. 88:8 and 42:8, in a clear departure from the Psalms so far considered, it is Yahweh who is perceived as the cause of affliction (possibly, but not self-evidently, as a punishment); in 88:7, it is even stated that "thou hast put me in the depths of the Pit,/ in the regions dark and deep". There is a positive aspect to this insofar as Yahweh has not simply abandoned the suppliant to the power of the underworld: the waters are apparently an instrument under his jurisdiction. Since God thus seems to have extended the sphere of his rule, any necessity for a grand rescue (still less "divine conflict") is obviated. The negative aspect of this is the distress that God is now experienced both as potential saviour and as present inflictor of pain. In any case, this experience is quite in contrast to that of Pss. 18, 144, 124 and 69, where the deity is called upon to deliver the psalmist from the "torrents of perdition" (18:5-7) and "deep waters" (69:2-3, 15-16) and the enemies and

80 Compare the discussion of Pss. 42-3 and 88 below.

81 Cf. v. 27.

waters are encountered as something "other" from which God could enact deliverance.

A noteworthy aspect of these psalms is the relative prominence of the enemies and Sheol motifs. Where the psalmist feels most confident of divine support, the former attains especial conspicuity, most notably in Ps. 144, where the underworld seems almost to have receded from view. However, the foes are also much in evidence in Pss. 18 and 124. Though they cease to be the direct object of the waters imagery in Ps. 69, and the distinctive aspects of Sheol loom in ghastly detail, the enemies do remain as implied agents, standing in parallel with features of Sheol. They are the human and physical counterparts to the world which hovers beneath ready to engulf the suppliant's life. However, in Pss. 42-3 and 88, the waters imagery seems to have shed its human aspect, in Ps. 88, perhaps the bleakest of all the psalms, the contours of Sheol being drawn in a startlingly uncompromising style. It is as if the psalmists could presuppose Yahweh's opposition to human enemies, those opposed to his governance or nation, but appreciated that when someone is consigned to Sheol, it is the work of Yahweh himself. The collective and individual aspects of these respective spheres is manifest, and correlates with the distinctions in genre and outlook between the various compositions.

However, it remains to be demonstrated how the depiction of the underworld is achieved in Pss. 42-3 and 88, and this shall now comprise the subject of the following analysis, before any further implications are drawn.

i. Psalm 42-43

Of particular interest is 42:8. There are four possible elements at work here:
1) The poet's supposed position by the upper reaches of the Jordan. As he looked on (or imagined) the raging torrents cascading down the hillside, it may have initiated a comparison with his personal situation (cf. Jer 1:13-14).
2) The painful conflict between the suppliant's faith and experience—his former life of praise in the temple precincts, sure of the steadfast love of the "rock" and "help" Yahweh, as contrasted with his present isolation from God, who has "forgotten" him and abandoned him to the taunts of his enemies. The "waves" and "billows" of Yahweh engulfing him would thereby form a fitting contrast with his thirsting for God "as a hart longs for flowing streams".[82] A further influence may be the traditional imagery of life-giving rivers flowing out of the abode of the deity,[83] which again is rudely shattered by his experience of being threatened with death, apparently at the hands of God.[84]

---

82 V. 2; note the appellation "living God" in v. 3, and compare the motif of Yahweh as מְקוֹר מַיִם חַיִּים, e.g. in Jer. 2:13, 17:13, cf. Ps. 36:9-10, even Rev. 21:6, 22:17.

83 Ezek. 47, Ps. 46:5, cf. Gen. 2:10, also *KTU* 1.4.iv.21-22, 1.17.vi.47-48.

84 A similar antithesis is also encountered in Isa. 8:5-8, where the "waters of Shiloah that flow gently" are set in contrast to the overflowing "waters of the River, mighty and many, the king of Assyria and all his glory" which are to advance into Judah.

3) The appropriateness of the imagery to the psalmist's situation—buffeted, submerged, engulfed and utterly helpless as he is carried along by the tide of his misfortunes.
4) The association of the "deep" with the underworld, the realm of death which renders him powerless in the face of adversity. The potential correlation of the netherworld with the deep is particularly evident in Jonah 2 (compare especially Jon. 2:4cd with Ps. 42:8cd, and the sense of being cast out of the divine presence in Jon. 2:5 with Ps. 43:2).

The metaphorical nature of the waters thus represented is further indicated by the illogicality of the description, when understood on a literal level. For instance, despite the putative setting by the Jordan, it is doubtful whether the river could itself be thought of as having מִשְׁבָּרִים or גַּלִּים,[85] still less that they could, properly speaking, be regarded as specifically those of Yahweh. Moreover, the claim that "all thy waves and thy billows have gone over me" should hardly be subjected to a literal interpretation; and this is still to leave aside the question of how exactly the deep could fit into the picture. Thus, it becomes evident that a superficial reading of the passage is inadequate, and that the description belongs to the symbolic, mythological world.[86]

An examination of the vocabulary employed in 42:8 may, however, facilitate the attempt to discern the prominent nuances of this imagery. צִנּוֹר, which is rendered poetically by the RSV as "cataracts", but more precisely by BDB as "(water)-spouts",[87] occurs elsewhere only in 2 Sam. 5:8 (where it is dubious if this is the correct reading) with reference to a "gutter, water course".[88] According to Dahood, "Ugar. *ṣnr* evidently denotes 'pipe, shaft'", an observation which is entirely consistent with this.[89] Thus, bearing in mind the

85 גַּלִּים, when referring to waves, is elsewhere associated with the sea, often explicitly: Isa. 48:18, 51:15, Jer. 5:22, 31:35, 51:42, Ezek. 26:3, Jon. 2:4, Zech. 10:11, Job 38:11, Pss. 65:8, 89:10, 107:25, 29; this link is less clear, though probable, in Jer. 51:55 (cf. v. 42), leaving Ps. 42:8 as a possible exception. מִשְׁבָּר tends to be employed in contexts where metaphorical overtones predominate (Ps. 42:8, 93:4, 88:8, Jon. 2:4, 2 Sam. 22:5), although a connection with the sea remains in Jon. 2:4 and Ps. 93:4.

86 On the other hand, this hardly necessitates the radical rewriting of v. 7 in order to replace the geographical setting with a direct allusion to the underworld, as Schmidt (pp. 79, 80), Dahood (I, pp. 254, 258-9) and Lindström (*Suffering and Sin*, p. 184) have thought.

87 Thus also Eaton, p. 179.

88 Briggs, I, p. 373; cf. Grätz, I, p. 311, Schmidt, p. 79, and Baethgen, p. 124, "[Wasser]rinnen".

89 It is therefore surprising that in the same context, he advocates the translation "thunderbolts", arguing that "it is the trident with which God strikes the sea and creates its breakers". How this corresponds with the cited derivation is difficult to discern. Also to be rejected is Kissane's translation, "floodgates" (p. 186), explained with reference to "the primeval Deluge, in which the abyss above the firmament joined the abyss beneath the earth and covered the earth" (pp. 189-190; cf. Wellhausen, pp. 42, 182, BDB, p. 857). No less dubious is Anderson's apprehension that it alludes to the channels of the

location by the sources of the River Jordan, an allusion to waterfalls[90] or (more likely) to water flowing along or emerging from underground channels, may be appropriate.[91] The latter would perhaps more accurately reflect the idea of an enclosed "watercourse" or "conduit" apparently described in 2 Sam., and as such, may connote the intrusion of the depths (and hence perhaps by implication Sheol) into this world to engulf the psalmist and carry him away.

The conclusion that the underworld may here be referred to is supported by an analysis of the significance of the "waves" and "billows" of Ps. 42:8. The former term, מִשְׁבָּרִים (√שׁבר, "break", hence more accurately rendered "breakers"), occurs almost exclusively in the group of texts presently under consideration, in 2 Sam. 22:5 (in the phrase מִשְׁבְּרֵי־מָוֶת),[92] Jon. 2:4b (exactly paralleling Ps. 42:8b) and Ps. 88:8.[93] In all of these passages, the context (lament or thanksgiving psalm) and surrounding imagery is very similar to that encountered here in 42:8, and the underworld is without exception explicitly mentioned in the cited or a closely proximate verse.[94]

The paired term גַּל, "heap, wave, billow", or perhaps better, "roller", is employed more diffusely and in a wider range of passages than מִשְׁבָּר. However, where "waves" (rather than a "heap" or other sphere of meaning)[95] are denoted, they are, in the majority of cases, specified as those of "the sea", and stand independently of any other parallel "waters" terminology.[96] This

---

oceans near the divine abode (I, p. 333; cf. *KTU* 1.4.iv.22; 1.6.i.34; 1.17.vi.48); what the psalmist was doing here when he was excluded from the temple is not explained.

90 So Girard, I, p. 702, Cohen, p. 132, Seybold, pp. 173, 174, 176, Broyles, *Conflict*, p. 203, and Briggs, I, pp. 370, 373.

91 Compare similarly Seybold's interpretation of תְּהוֹם in the light of Deut. 8:7 as alluding to such springs (p. 176, following Goulder, *The Psalms of the Sons of Korah*, p. 28). Goulder, further, quotes George Adam Smith's description of the source of the Leddan, one of the sources of the Jordan springing up near Mount Hermon (cf. v. 7), as "break[ing] from the bowels of the earth" (G. A. Smith, *The Historical Geography of the Holy Land* [London, 25th ed., 1931], pp. 472-3; Goulder, *PSK*, p. 27; cf. v. 7), and this too would provide a compatible interpretation.

92 Here, instead of being the instruments of God, the "waves" stand apart from him as an external threat to the psalmist, from which Yahweh intervenes to effect deliverance. The parallel in Ps 18:5 has חֶבְלֵי־מָוֶת, "the cords of death", but the reading in 2 Sam 22 is probably to be preferred, since חֶבְלֵי recurs in each version at the beginning of the following verse.

93 For its underworld signification, note especially the preceding verse and see discussion thereon below.

94 An exception is the remaining instance of the term, Ps. 93:4, where מִשְׁבָּרִים is applied more literally in relation to the sea, there in a hymnic setting where underworld and threnodic aspects are wholly lacking.

95 E.g., "spring(?)" in Cant. 4:12.

96 Jer. 5:22; 31:35; Isa. 51:15; Job 38:11; Pss. 65:8; 89:10; 107:25, 29; Ezek. 26:3; Jer. 51:42. The sole instance where the sea is not mentioned is in the metaphorical reference to the "waves" of Babylon in Jer. 51:55, whilst the imagery is slightly extended in the simile of Isa. 48:18 and in Zech. 10:11.

perhaps also accounts for the freedom with which the boisterous aspects of these "waves" are often vividly portrayed, sometimes being "stirred up"[97] or utilised[98] by God, elsewhere stilled[99] or confined[100] by him—or even both roused and calmed within the scope of a single Psalm.[101] Their lack of characteristically "mythological" associations facilitates a mode of employment which enables the powerful, even destructive, potential of the sea to be expressed in unequivocal terms. However, there are two very important, and closely related, exceptions to the foregoing uses of גַּל, in which the dramatic and threatening overtones are retained, but transferred from the "sea" to a more fundamental and personal threat: these occur in Ps. 42:8 and Jon. 2:4b. Quite in contravention to the observations made above, in neither instance are the waves simply those of "the sea", but in each case they occur at the culmination of a series of vocabulary evoking a more varied and darkly resonant sphere of "waters" imagery: in Jon. 2:4 after מְצוּלָה, לְבַב־יַמִּים, נָהָר and מִשְׁבָּרֶיךָ, in Ps. 42:8 after תְּהוֹם (twice), צִנּוֹרֶיךָ and מִשְׁבָּרֶיךָ. In Ps. 42:8, then, the sea is not even mentioned. Indeed, if anything, the Psalmist may have been prompted into his chosen form of expression by the vision of mountain torrents (v.7). This, again, would support the identification of Sheol as the locus for these waves, firstly because of the absence of a fitting setting in upland Palestine itself,[102] but also because of the coherence of this interpretation with the broader imagery of both Ps. 42-3 and Jon. 2. The verbal identity of Ps. 42:8b and Jon. 2:4b has already been noted; although the language in the opening line of each of these verses is otherwise quite distinct, the emphasis on God as the agent of affliction is sustained throughout the whole verse in each case.

The netherworld imagery is reinforced by the employment of the term תְּהוֹם.[103] Its spheres of allusion are more numerous but perhaps less diverse than those of גַּל, and many of them will be encountered again in the succeeding chapters of the present monograph, so detailed consideration is warranted. The

---

97 Jer. 31:35; Isa. 51:15.

98 Ezek. 26:3 (simile), Jer. 51:42 (metaphor).

99 Pss. 65:8; 89:10.

100 Jer. 5:22; Job 38:8-11.

101 Ps. 107:25, 29.

102 Cf. Cohen, p. 132, who, though admitting that "the words are usually connected with the sea", maintains that here they are "graphically descriptive of the Jordan in flood"; similarly also Briggs, I, p. 370, Weiser, p. 236 and Goulder, *PSK*, p. 32, the latter of whom merely takes these waves as "signs of divine life-giving power... pass[ing Israel] by". In what may be regarded as a compromise position, Craigie contends that the waves of the nearby ocean are also intended (p. 327).

103 Others assume that an allusion to chaos is required, e.g., Craigie (p. 327) and Kraus, for whom "the scene of the well-known torrents of the area of the headwaters of the Jordan and conceptions of the chaotic, destructive archetypal flood (cf. Akkadian *tiamat*) come together" (I, p. 476). This assertion is the more striking for the fact that it is immediately followed by the statement that, "Destructive forces emanating from Yahweh have stormed in on the petitioner"; thus the terrible cosmic forces of chaos become weapons unleashed by Yahweh against the hapless individual.

most common (and perhaps the most fundamental) of these concerns the nourishing fresh water which quenches thirst and bestows blessing and fertility;[104] related is the motif of the "fountains of the deep" being opened, together with the "windows of heaven" at the Flood.[105] It is thus envisaged as a sub-terrestrial (or sub-oceanic) reservoir, feeding the earth's water supply.[106] Consequently, the "deeps" are portrayed as within the sphere of Yahweh's rule,[107] and sometimes even as offering him their praise;[108] moreover they were created "by his knowledge"[109] and "established" like the heavens.[110] Indeed, Yahweh himself "set the earth on its foundations" and "didst cover it with the deep as with a garment".[111] The process of confining is then characteristically applied to the surface "waters"[112] or "sea".[113] Not surprisingly, the deep is also sometimes envisaged as participating in the general anguish at the divine theophany,[114] or as being touched by the Exodus events.[115]

Seybold's interpretation of the term in the light of Deut. 8:7, as alluding to a spring or source of a river, is plausible if the putative setting at the headwaters of the Jordan is taken into consideration in isolation from the wider context. However, a further possible nuance—and one which is particularly congruent with the continued imagery of the verse—may be inferred from Ex. 15:8: "They went down into the depths like a stone". Although on a literal level the drowning Egyptians sank to a watery death, on another, deeper plane, they "went down" to Sheol.[116] The same bifarious signification is evidenced on a more explicit level in Jon. 2:6 and Ezek. 26:19, where in each case, the immediate depiction of drowning or destruction blends into an unmistakable portrayal of Sheol. A similar sphere of imagery is also encountered more briefly in Ps. 71:20, where the Psalmist expresses the hope that God will bring him up again "from the depths of the earth" (מִתְּהֹמוֹת הָאָרֶץ).

---

104 Gen. 49:25; Deut. 33:13; Ezek. 31:4 (probably also v. 15) and context; Deut. 8:7; Am. 7:4; Ps. 78:15; Prov. 8:24; cf. Prov. 3:20; Ps. 33:7.

105 Gen. 7:11; 8:2; cf. Prov. 8:24, 28.

106 Perhaps compare also Ps. 33:7.

107 Ps. 135:6; Job 38:16, 30.

108 Ps. 148:7.

109 Prov. 3:20.

110 Prov. 8:27-8, cf. v. 24.

111 Ps. 104:6; cf. Prov. 8:24, 28 and Gen. 1:2, though the "createdness" of the deep in the latter reference is, of course, sometimes called into question.

112 Ps. 104:6-7.

113 Prov. 8:29; also Jer. 5:22; Job 38:8-11; though compare Ps. 33:7, where the distinction is not rigidly maintained.

114 Ps. 77:17; Hab. 3:10.

115 Besides the implied Exodus allusion of Ps. 77:17, note Ex. 15:5, in which the deeps "congealed in the heart of the sea", and Isa. 51:10; 63:13; Ps. 106:9, in which the Israelites are led through the depths.

116 Other, miscellaneous and ancillary, allusions to תְּהוֹם occur in Pss. 36:7; 107:26; Job. 28:14; 41:24 (English v. 32).

The affinities of the present lament (Ps. 42-3), and most especially verse 8, with Jon. 2 have, of course, already been mentioned with regard to גַּלִּים and מִשְׁבָּרִים, so it is especially remarkable to encounter a further correlation in imagery with the allusion to תְּהוֹם. So close have the similarities between the two passages been deemed to be that it is sometimes claimed that the prophet is dependent on the psalm.[117] The similarities of genre and putative setting (either in the sea or by a torrential river), as well as the sense of alienation from God and the Temple (Jon. 2:5, Ps. 42:10, 43:2-3; cf. also 42:2-7, 11-12; 43:4-5), may all be cited. However, most significant for the current interpretative task is the correlation of the Sheol / waters imagery. Mention of the deep (in Ps. 42:8 and Jon 2:6, cf. מְצוּלָה v. 4a) is in each case proximate with the complaint כָּל־מִשְׁבָּרֶיךָ וְגַלֶּיךָ עָלַי עָבָרוּ, discussed above as alluding to the underworld. That this region comprises the subject of allusion here is therefore fairly evident, and any allusion to the river sources of the upper Jordan must therefore (if present at all) be of secondary importance. In addition, Ps. 42-3 exhibits no clear correlation with any other recognisable semantic area surrounding the term תְּהוֹם, but points in its threnodic, alienated tone and in the employment of parallel images, to the nether world as its sphere of reference.[118]

It may therefore be concluded that the force of Ps. 42-3 seems to be to claim that Yahweh himself, the source of life (cf. "flowing waters... living God", 42:2-3, "the God of my life", v. 9), the rock (42:10), help (42:6, 12; 43:5) and refuge (43:2), has placed the suppliant in the sphere of death. The effect seems to be to give voice to this paradox, but not to offer any philosophical reflection upon it, or to provide any logical resolution. (This is reflected especially in the questions "Where is your God?" "Why?" etc.) Rather, comfort and hope can only be attained by turning to God; the one who is now experienced as afflictor is, nevertheless, affirmed by faith, tradition and past recollections as redeemer.

---

117 L. Alonso Schökel, "The Poetic Structure of Psalm 42-43" *JSOT* 1 (1976), p. 19; Lindström, *Suffering and Sin*, p. 172.

118 J. H. Patton's apprehension that the phrase תְּהוֹם־אֶל־תְּהוֹם is reminiscent of the Ugaritic dual *thmtm*, "the two deeps" (*Canaanite Parallels in the Book of Psalms*, p. 46; thus also Dahood, I, p. 259, and, tentatively, Lindström, *Suffering and Sin*, p. 183 n. 21), seems to be somewhat misplaced, since in that context it was associated with the abode of the deity El (*KTU* 1.4.iv.22; 1.100.3), and not with the opposing realm of Sheol. By contrast, in the extant Hebrew tradition, although it is the fertility aspect of תְּהוֹם which is numerically dominant (see discussion and references above, and cf. *KTU* 1.19.i.45), it is nevertheless apparently only rivers which are envisaged as flowing out of Eden, the Holy City or "mountain of God". Conversely, the total linguistic content of Ps. 42:8 indicates that Sheol constitutes a primary sphere of allusion for תְּהוֹם (as Dahood would acknowledge, e.g., on p. 262), yet this is far from being confirmed by the Ras Shamra tablets.

ii. Psalm 88

Psalm 88 is pervaded with the deepest gloom, lacking any clear expression of trust in Yahweh[119] or vow of praise; nor is there any mention of enemies or of guilt, as is usual in individual laments. Instead, the Psalmist's suffering is attributed entirely to God (vv. 7-9, 15, 16b-19). A closer examination further reveals that although the suppliant repeatedly cries out to God in prayer, there is no explicit petition for deliverance;[120] he seems beyond hope indeed. So overwhelmingly and disturbingly negative is this psalm felt to be, that a number of scholars have maintained that a concluding section, perhaps expressing trust or anticipating thanksgiving on deliverance, must have been lost.[121] However, whilst this is possible, there is no evidence to support the claim; certainly, the composition was thought worthy of preservation as it stands.[122] It appears that the psalmist is presented as someone who had long endured great suffering, and for whom death had become inevitable.

In accordance with this, unmistakable underworld imagery dominates this psalm (vv. 4-8, 11-13), which explicitly speaks of "Sheol" (v. 4), "the Pit" (vv. 5, 7), "the dead" (vv. 6, 11), "the grave" (vv. 6, 12), the "Shades" (v. 11), "Abaddon" (v. 12) and the "land of forgetfulness"[123] (v. 13, cf. v. 6). These, then, are the "regions dark and deep" (v. 7), and they are presumably also the sphere of encounter with Yahweh's overwhelming waves (v. 8); his "dread assaults" are experienced as a flood which, like the approach of death, first surrounds the psalmist and then closes in upon him altogether (vv. 17-18).

It is interesting to note the (apparently inconsistent) juxtaposition of assertions that in Sheol the dead are outside Yahweh's sphere of interest and protection (vv. 6, 11-13) with descriptions of the waves of the underworld as God's instrument of wrath. Yahweh is seemingly forcibly separating the dying man from himself and actively putting him in the Pit (v. 7); he thus hides his face from the petitioner and casts him off (v. 15). Although this process is

---

119 Except possibly in the opening colon, v. 2, but אֱלֹהֵי יְשׁוּעָתִי is often emended to אֱלֹהַי שִׁוַּעְתִּי (e.g. in the RSV). Goulder's interpretation of v. 14 as articulating the psalmist's "expectation of imminent deliverance" (*PSK*, p. 208; cf. p. 203) ill-fits the negativity of the surrounding verses and is dependent on a highly speculative cultic reconstruction.

120 Contrast Broyles' apprehension that the absence of any petition for intervention "may suggest that the form of deliverance required is self-evident from the lament itself" (*The Conflict of Faith and Experience*, p. 207); however this perhaps takes inadequate account of the distinctive formal characteristics of the psalm.

121 E. g., Wellhausen, p. 200; this interpretation may be traced back to the Targum and Rashi.

122 Cohen's assertion (p. 288) that, despite the Psalm's dark ending, a "note of hopefulness... may be implied in the conviction which pervades the psalm that the sufferer is all the time in the hands of God", also seems unwarranted. The uncomfortable reality is rather that God has acted to cut the suppliant off from these very hands (v. 6), in the process not only turning his back on his pleas (v. 15), but actively working to afflict (vv. 8, 16-18) and isolate him even from human companionship (vv. 9, 19).

123 Or perhaps "forgottenness": it is where "one forgets and is forgotten" (Cohen, p. 287).

presented as rejection, the "wrath" (vv. 8, 17) and "dread assaults" (v. 17) are not explained in practical or moral terms, nor is there any admission of guilt.[124] Rather, they appear simply to express the experience that it is Yahweh who is taking the psalmist to his fate, not some external agent from whom rescue could be sought, and therefore there is no hope for him.

Especially pertinent to the present investigation is the imagery of vv. 5, 7, 8 and 17-18. The term בּוֹר, "pit", features in both vv. 5 and 7, the latter occurrence being in the expression בְּבוֹר תַּחְתִּיּוֹת;[125] in each instance, the allusion to the underworld is self-evident, both on the basis of the immediate context[126] and by comparison with the wider Old Testament usage. The phrase יוֹרְדֵי בוֹר (v. 5) is a conventional means of referring to the dead,[127] and indeed is employed exclusively in relation to this semantic sphere. Likewise, בּוֹר occurs in parallel or close proximity with שְׁאוֹל not only in Ps. 88:5, but also in Ps. 30:4. Isa. 14:15, Ezek. 31:16, and Prov. 1:12; one might compare also Ezek. 26:20; 31:14; 32:18, 23, 24.

However, this is almost certainly a derivative application of the word, since בּוֹר (and the related nouns בְּאֵר and בֹּאר) primarily denotes a "pit", a term which encompasses both wells (dug down to water) and cisterns (for water storage). Insofar as the nature of man-made pits is likely to have suggested the metaphorical depictions of the underworld under the same imagery,[128] it is perhaps therefore necessary to outline some of their key features as they may have impinged upon portrayals of Sheol. In this regard, one must be aware that the employment of a metaphor may also stimulate a continued dialogue between first and second subject, with further points of affinity later being recognised and exploited. Thus the idea of the underworld as "Pit" may stand in its own right, but could also have prompted the employment of related concepts in the succeeding lines of the poem.

---

124 This aspect of the Psalm is developed further by Lindström, *Suffering and Sin*, pp. 196-217.

125 Literally, "in (the) pit of the lowest places"; cf. the paraphrases of Cheyne ("Hades which is below the earth", p. 241) and Anderson ("the netherworld in the depths [of the earth]", II, p. 626). The same expression is attested elsewhere in Lam 3:55. In addition, תַּחְתִּי occurs in conjunction with שְׁאוֹל in Deut. 32:22 and Ps. 86:12; in the distinctive expression אֶרֶץ תַּחְתִּיּוֹת, "the land of 'lowest places', the netherworld" in Ezek. 26:20; 31:14, 16, 18; 32:18, 24; and in the phrase תַּחְתִּיּוֹת הָאָרֶץ, "the 'lowest places' of the earth", in Pss. 63:10; 71:20, all in clear reference to the realm of the dead; cf. תַּחְתִּיּוֹת אָרֶץ, Isa. 44:23, Ps. 139:15.

126 Note especially the colon immediately preceding the initial reference to the pit in v. 5: "my life draws near to Sheol", v. 4; and the entire contents of v. 6.

127 E.g., in Pss. 28:1, 143:7, Isa. 38:18, Ezek. 26:20, and Prov. 1:12; cf. יוֹרְדֵי עָפָר, Ps. 22:30, and the oft-repeated motif of "going down" (ירד) to Sheol, e.g., in Num. 16:30, Ezek. 32:27, Ps. 55:16, and Job 7:9.

128 This seems to be assumed also by Broyles, who proposes that the image is "of one in a cistern, a place dark and mucky with no means of escape" (*Conflict*, p. 207); see also Keel, *WAB*, pp. 60-62.

בּוֹר seems at its most basic level to denote a hole dug to contain or reach down to water; hence, when referring to an empty pit, the biblical authors often deemed it necessary to add the explanatory statement that "there was no water in it".[129] However, pits also had a more dangerous aspect. Left uncovered, they could constitute a hazard for man[130] or beast;[131] indeed, sometimes they were employed as traps[132] or as prisons,[133] בּוֹר on occasion being utilised to denote a "dungeon".[134] Jer. 41:7, 9 attests to the idea that a "pit" could also provide a convenient means of disposal for murdered corpses. Whilst the circumstances described here may be exceptional, it must be acknowledged that it was also into a pit (פַּחַת) that the body of Absalom was cast, before being covered with stones.[135] It is perhaps this type of burial which could partially be in view also in Isa. 14:19, again in relation to the ignominious death of "the slain, those pierced by the sword",[136] and on a different plane, to the fate of the usurper who aspired to the highest office, yet was cast down in shame to the depths.[137]

Thus, there are several points of congruence between the בּוֹר and the underworld, since both could be manifested as a trap, prison, or grave,[138] the victim entering through its "mouth".[139] Moreover, the miry depths of a "pit"

---

129 Gen. 37:24, Jer. 38:6; cf. Zech. 9:11.

130 Ps. 7:15-16, Prov. 28:18; cf. Gen. 14:10 (בֶּאֱרֹת חֵמָר) and Lam. 3:47 (פַּחַת; בּוֹר in vv. 53, 55).

131 Ex. 21:33-34; cf. perhaps Lev. 11:36.

132 See Prov. 23:27 (בְּאֵר); also Jer. 48:43-44 = Isa. 24:17-18 (פַּחַת; though N.B. בּוֹר in Isa. 24:22); there is often no clear distinction between this and the "pit" as a more general hazard. For Sheol as a trap (usually under the imagery of snares and nets), see the discussion of Ps. 124.

133 Jer. 38:6-13; cf. Gen. 37:20-29; בּוֹר אֵין מַיִם בּוֹ appears also as a symbol of the captivity of Exile in Zech. 9:11; for Sheol as a prison, cf. perhaps Job 40:13, Ps. 18:6 and parallel in 2 Sam. 22:6, Ps. 18:5, Jon. 2:7. In addition, prison seems to belong to the stereotypical imagery of the lament, where it symbolises affliction, though often whether it is intimately connected to Sheol is less clear: see Job 36:8, Lam. 3:7 (note v. 6), Ps. 107:10-17 and, of course, Pss. 88:9 and 69:34.

134 E.g., in Gen. 40:15, 41:14, Ex. 12:29, Isa. 24:22 and Jer. 37:16.

135 2 Sam. 18:17.

136 Cf. also Ezek. 32:17-32, in which there is perhaps a distinction between those who were "uncircumcised, slain by the sword", who go down to (the uttermost parts of) the Pit or netherworld, and the "mighty chiefs" or "mighty men" (vv. 21, 27) who descend to Sheol. Perhaps the mass graves of battle are in view in Ezek. 32 and Isa. 14; cf. also Ps. 88:6.

137 Besides Isa. 14:15, 19, cf. Ezek. 31:14, 16.

138 Anderson interprets בּוֹר simply as denoting "either Sheol or the grave which, in a sense, forms the entrance to the netherworld, and as such may suggest the whole" (II, p. 625; so also Kraus, II, p. 193).

139 "The pit... was imagined as a vast subterranean cave with a narrow mouth like a well" (G. A. Cooke, *Ezekiel* [ICC, 1936], p. 293). For the "mouth" of a well, see 2 Sam. 17:19, Gen. 29:8 (בְּאֵר). For that of Sheol, see Isa. 5:14, Ps. 141:7; compare also allusions to the mouth of the pit (underworld) in Ps. 69:16; and the mouth of the earth

were not only a potential hazard—they also comprise a further feature which appears to have much in common with presentations of life-threatening danger or Sheol itself.[140] Obviously, it is not always possible to claim a simple identity between imaginative portrayals of the netherworld and common aspects of "pits". Nevertheless, ideal circumstances for the transference or integration of motifs would have been provided by the existing imagery of Sheol as a trap or prison, and by the idea that the underworld was located beneath the earth with the "subterranean deep". The double associations of the Pit / grave and Pit / abode of the dead is perhaps apparent in Isa. 14:19, whilst the pit / trap and Pit / underworld themes converge in Lam. 3:53-55.

The continuing imagery of Ps. 88:7 is certainly compatible with both of the spheres of allusion connoted by the term בּוֹר—water-pit and the Pit of death—, מַחְשָׁךְ being applied to the underworld in Lam. 3:6, Ps. 143:3, as well as in Ps. 88:19.[141] Although מְצֻלוֹת, "deep places", without exception connotes watery depths,[142] the occurrence in Jon. 2:4 would seem to have double associations, encompassing both the ocean and the nether realm, whilst the underworld would seem to be in view also in Ps. 69:3, 16. Both of these passages find an echo in Ps. 88:7, the parallelism between מְצוּלָה and the "pit" recurring also in Ps. 69:16; cf. Jon. 2:7. This parity, and the obvious contiguity of Ps. 88:7b with the numerous and often explicit allusions to the underworld in adjacent cola (coupled with the commensurate lack of any obvious relation to the sea) therefore indicates that the phrase בְּמַחֲשַׁכִּים בִּמְצֹלוֹת should likewise be understood as having Sheol as its primary sphere of reference.[143]

The notion that we are dealing here with a tightly woven matrix of netherworld motifs is further enhanced by the appearance of כָּל־מִשְׁבָּרֶיךָ in the following verse, since exactly the same expression has already been encountered in very similar circumstances in Ps. 42:8: כָּל־מִשְׁבָּרֶיךָ וְגַלֶּיךָ עָלַי

---

which opens to swallow those who "go down alive into Sheol", Num. 16:30, 32; cf. also Deut. 11:6 and Ex. 15:12. Reference in the Ugaritic texts to the mouth of Mot may also be noted: *KTU* 1.4.viii.18; cf. 1.5.i.7.

140 Notably in Ps. 40:3; for a cistern as miry, see Jer. 38:6; and compare also Job 9:31 (of a pit, שַׁחַת); the same imagery is applied to Sheol in Pss. 69:3, 15-16; 40:3. In a Ugaritic context, see *KTU* 1.4.viii.11-14. For a correlation between the deep (תְּהוֹם) and the Pit, see Ezek. 26:19-20. Compare also Pss. 42:8, 32:6, and especially Ps. 18:5-6, 16-17 and its parallel in 2 Sam. 22:5-6, 16-17.

141 For the darkness of the grave, see also Job 10:21-22.

142 This consideration, as well as the allusion to the מִשְׁבָּרִים in the following verse, cautions one against accepting the possibility advanced by Cheyne that here "the reference to water has vanished" (pp. 199, 245); his alternative suggestion, that the "subterranean waters encircling Sheol" (p. 245) may be intended, seems overly precise and lacks clear foundation.

143 LXX ἐν σκοτεινοις και ἐν σκιᾳ θανατου apparently presumes the Hebrew וּבְצַלְמָוֶת for MT בִּמְצֹלוֹת. Even if this reading is not original, it probably indicates the sphere of allusion anticipated by the copyist, not least given the familiar nature of the term מְצוּלָה and the absence of צַלְמָוֶת in a proximate line.

עָבָ֣רוּ, and, of course in the parallel in Jon. 2:4, mentioned above in relation to מְצוּלָה. Like מְצוּלָה, מִשְׁבָּר also has its natural environment in the sea,[144] but it is chiefly applied to the waters of death, as is evidenced by 2 Sam. 22:5, Jon. 2:4 and Ps. 42:8, besides the present verse, Ps. 88:8.[145] These latter three texts are further united in the important aspect that they ascribe the destructive waves to Yahweh himself.

However, despite the strong nominal links between Pss. 88:8, 42:8, Jon. 2:4 and 2 Sam. 22:5, there is in the present verse a significant verbal deviation in the use of מִשְׁבָּר: here it is stated that it is with his breakers that Yahweh "bows down" the sufferer or "afflicts" and "humbles" him (ענה), a term applied to the discipline or chastisements of Yahweh, as experienced especially in hardship and oppression. Thus, as one is pushed down under a heavy burden, the suppliant sinks—or, rather, is submerged—under כָּל־מִשְׁבָּרֶיךָ. The verb suggests the hidden reality of the Psalmist's suffering, even while the noun exposes its epitomisation in the waters of the underworld; nevertheless, both terms point beyond themselves to their source in Yahweh, the God who "humbles" and "afflicts" his servant with his "waves".

Striking nominal-verbal combinations are employed to similar effect in vv. 17-18, which comprise an impressive pattern of interlinked images: in v. 17a, the verb עָבָרוּ, used in Ps. 42:8 of the "waves", is instead uncharacteristically applied to God's wrath sweeping over the Psalmist. Thus, the content of v. 18, which speaks of the actions of the מַיִם, is already implied before it is stated. Conversely, it is the parallel term, Yahweh's "dread assaults" (v. 17b), which is said to "surround me like a flood [מַיִם] all day long; / they close in upon me together" (v. 18). The experience of divine hostility is thus portrayed as (flood)waters surrounding the suppliant and then closing in around him, ready to inflict the final blow which is suggested by v. 18b. Dramatic intensity is here powerfully conveyed by the progressive parallelism: סַבּוּנִי... הִקִּיפוּ, and by the corresponding transition from כָּל־הַיּוֹם, connoting continuation, the watchful waiting of the besieging enemies, to יָחַד, perhaps indicating a sudden co-ordinated effort to effect a stranglehold, before the final annihilation is accomplished (v. 18b). Thus, whereas v. 17 conveys the idea of the force and fatality of Yahweh's wrathful attacks, v. 18 emphasises that their threat is also constant, co-ordinated, and as irresistible as rising waters. Nevertheless, the subtle interweaving of the nominal and verbal pairs permits both aspects to be held the more strongly in tension.

The imagery of v. 18 could be explained entirely in terms of the natural world, and this is the approach adopted by Anderson, who simply comments that "the misfortunes surround the distressed man like the flood waters... and they threaten to overwhelm him."[146] Yet in the same context he also ventures to

144 Cf. Ps. 93:4, Jon. 2:4.

145 There is therefore little foundation for Goulder's speculative and literalistic application of this terminology to a Danite underground stream (*PSK*, p. 202). For Ps. 88:8b as alluding to "the metaphorical waters of the abyss", see also Anderson, II, p. 627, Eaton, p. 315, Clifford, II, p. 88.

146 II, p. 630.

refer back to v. 8b, a setting in which he openly acknowledges the allusion to the "waters of the abyss,"[147] so he apparently does not entirely exclude the possibility of a connection with the underworld. By contrast, Broyles boldly claims that, "The psalmist experiences the consequences of [Yahweh's] wrath as those (burning!) waters of death which overwhelm him (vv. 8, 15-16)";[148] yet at the same time this assertion is aided by the inclusion of v. 8 as a supporting reference. In fact the presence of netherworld imagery in vv. 17-18 is far less obvious than in v. 8. In the latter, it is anticipated by the language of the preceding verse, whereas here in the former, the primary force of the simile relies on the known nature of floodwaters, without necessary reference to their precise location. Nevertheless, the obvious continuities of the waters imagery with v. 8, and indeed with Ps. 42:8, Jon. 2:4 (both עבר), Ps. 124:4-5 (מַיִם + עבר), Ps. 18:5 and the parallel in 2 Sam. 22:5 (the idea of water surrounding the sufferer), all of which seem to have the underworld in view, imply that this nuance may also be present here. This interpretation is further supported by the references in the preceding lines to death (v. 16) and destruction (v. 17)

Finally, it may be observed that the most violent waters of the Psalm appear to be the metaphorical "waves" of God (v. 8), but that the מַיִם of the simile (v. 18) are perhaps less dramatic, though still exerting a potentially fatal hold over the suppliant. However, the more concrete idea of the "Pit" is decidedly static: it cannot close in upon an individual, still less "sweep over" him, but rather exists as a hole into which he must "go down" (v. 5) or be cast by other agencies. That agent is, characteristically for Ps. 88, God (v. 7).

iii. The Significance of the "Waters" Imagery of Psalms 42-3 and 88

The contrast between the stark portrayal of Yahweh as the agent of woe in Pss. 42-3 and 88, and the more familiar presentations of his deliverance of the psalmist from the waters in Pss. 18, 144, 124 and 69, gives rise to the question as to whether there is an underlying diachronic development towards a perception that God is the cause of both "weal and woe",[149] or whether the difference may be accounted for in terms of situation or genre. Certainly, if there is an underlying pattern of evolution, it is not now discernible; however, this may be as much a consequence of the extreme difficulty of dating the psalms concerned, as a feature of the texts themselves. In any event, the question of context appears more promising, since it is noticeable that God is envisaged as the agent of misfortune only in individual laments, whereas in psalms with a royal or national orientation, it is he who effects deliverance.

There may be two principal factors governing this: the first is the distinction between laments and thanksgiving psalms. In the latter, God's

147 II, p. 627.

148 *Conflict*, p. 208; he presumably cites vv. 15-16, in error, intending vv. 17-18.

149 And back away from it again? Though post-dating Ps. 18, Ps. 42-3 seems, as far as may be discerned, to be one of the earliest psalms here considered, Pss. 69 and 124 possibly rather later. See the summary of dating issues below.

mighty and gracious act of deliverance is proclaimed, and grateful songs of praise offered by the beneficiaries, or the congregation as a whole. In the atmosphere of renewed faith and gratitude following an experience of redemption, the anguished cries for mercy uttered on the dark night of distress are forgotten and transformed into the praise of the God who defends his people and forgives those who turn to him. It could never be said that he has merely deigned to withhold his torments—for he has actively saved (and by implication confirmed) the suppliant.

The second contributing factor is the function (as well as the underlying assumptions) of royal and/or national psalms, i.e., in circumstances of supplication, it is hoped or assumed that Yahweh will bestow victory and blessing on his people, and especially his king, thus setting himself against the foe. This is perhaps also reflected in the tone of accusation and disorientation which is typical of national laments uttered after defeat ("Thou dost not go forth, O God, with our armies", Pss. 60:12, 108:12, cf. 44:10). Certainly, after the victory has been won, the ensuing songs of thanksgiving can confidently proclaim Yahweh as the one who effects deliverance for his king and people.

Within individual laments, however, the rationale behind the depiction of God either as the agent of woe or as deliverer is harder to account for, not least because of the difficulty in ascertaining the precise nature of the Psalmists' troubles. One may hazard that personal circumstance or mental attitude, possibly the distinction between the admission or denial of guilt and wrongdoing, may constitute contributing—or even decisive—factors. Perhaps it may be the case that a king or national leader praying for deliverance from a political foe, or an individual who felt that he was suffering persecution for his religious zeal, could adopt the terminology of the enemy as "other"—whereas someone undergoing personal misfortune might assume that his own culpability (or perhaps even, *in extremis*, God's injustice, as in Job) and hence divine punishment was at work.[150] This could offer an explanation of the difference in tone between Ps. 69 on one hand and Pss. 42-3 and 88 on the other, since national elements are clearly prominent in Ps. 69:36-7, which may support the view that the psalmist should be regarded as a leader of the people. In addition, vv. 8, 10 seem to imply that the suppliant was suffering persecution for his religious views, and he may have been a representative of a particular group within Judaism (v. 7). The precise circumstances surrounding these illusions are now irrecoverable, though conjectures have not been lacking.[151] However, they suggest a context in which the psalmist could have been more than usually hopeful of divine intervention on his behalf, and especially inclined to have viewed his opponents as the natural objects of divine wrath.

---

150 A view strongly contested by F. Lindström, *Suffering and Sin: Interpretations of Illness in the Individual Complaint Psalms* (CBOT 37; Stockholm: Almqvist & Wiksell, 1994).

151 It is sometimes suggested that the suppliant may have sought to initiate some form of cultic reform which had met with opposition (v. 10; see Tate, p. 192), or that he may have been someone who actively sought the restoration of the Temple in post-exilic times (Kraus, II, p. 642, Schmidt, p. 133).

The final Psalm to be considered, Ps. 32, offers the briefest allusion to the waters, and is arguably the least precise in its signification. Equally ambiguous is God's rôle vis-à-vis the waters, whether they are his agent or something "other" from which he may effect deliverance. However, even the possible diffidence of the psalm in this respect can offer an insight into the way in which God's activity in the persecution or salvation of the sufferer may have been perceived.

6. Psalm 32: Freedom from the Waters Attained through Prayer

Of especial interest is v. 6d, which contains an allusion to the שֶׁטֶף מַיִם רַבִּים. Unfortunately, the preceding clause, v. 6c, is probably corrupt. Literally, "at a time of finding only", it has been subject to a number of proposed emendations, so no interpretative weight may be placed on it as a potentially illuminating parallel term.[152] Nevertheless, it seems fairly evident that a situation of distress is here depicted in terms of raging floods. The image is perhaps derived from the rapidity with which dry wadis could be transformed into threatening torrents carrying all before them,[153] or from the sea.[154] The waters of the underworld (cf. Ps. 18) and the cosmic waters of the deep are not obviously in view. Nevertheless, insofar as v. 3 seems to suggest that the

152 JPSA understands it as indicating "in a time when thou mayest be found"; thus also Kraus (I, 400), Weiser (p. 189), Terrien (p. 291) and Cohen (p. 93), who compares Isa. 55:6; perhaps cf. also Isa. 49:8. Most modern translations presuppose the emendation of MT to לְעֵת מָצוֹק, ("at a time of distress": RSV; Wellhausen, p. 29; Briggs, I, p. 276; Craigie, pp. 264, 267), explaining that "if the *waw* was written erroneously as *resh*, the *aleph* in MT may have been introduced to resolve the anomalous form" (Craigie, p. 264; cf. Briggs, I, p. 283). Dahood's offering, "when an army approaches" (I, p. 193) is typically idiosyncratic, relying on emendation and on unconventional translations of familiar vocabulary. Also doubtful is Girard's repointing of רַק as רֵק, i.e., as defective for רֵיק, meaning "the void" (I, p. 555), which is without clear parallel elsewhere in Hebrew usage. Other possibilities are cited in Kraus, I, p. 400.

153 This is the most common view, which is advocated, for example, by Anderson, I, p. 258, Craigie, p. 267, and Kraus, I, p. 405.

154 Cf. Cohen's description of "the godly man... like one standing upon a high rock safe from the waves which dash against it below" (p. 93). For the dangerous nature of מַיִם רַבִּים or "overflowing" (√שׁטף) water, compare Ps. 18:17, Isa. 8:7, 17:12, 28:2 (מַיִם רַבִּים) and Isa. 28:17, 30:28, Nah. 1:8 (שֶׁטֶף). Often whether rivers or the sea are envisaged is uncertain, and this frequent ambiguity should be respected (torrents are alluded to in Isa. 8:7; 30:28, and the sea in Isa. 17:12, though in the latter context the primary emphasis is on the roar of the water). However, the noun שֶׁטֶף is never explicitly associated with a river, and flooding on an oceanic scale is apparently envisaged in Isa. 54:8-9; indeed, since its root meaning is "overflow", and the verbal form is sometimes applied to the efforts of the sea to "break bounds", there seems no reason to impose our perhaps more limited concept of what constitutes a flood onto the Hebrew environment.

psalmist was suffering from a serious illness, and since this is the only description of his plight in the entire thanksgiving, it may be that the proximity to death suggested by his situation finds a faint echo here also in v. 6.

The particular vocabulary employed, שֶׁטֶף מַיִם רַבִּים, is resonant with a number of passages discussed above. The verb שטף has already been considered in relation to Ps. 124, where it occurs in connection with הַמַּיִם (v. 4); as has been seen, it characteristically connotes the overflowing or overwhelming action of floodwater. An association with the waters of Sheol nevertheless seems to be implied for this term in Ps. 69:3, 16 where, as in Ps. 124:5, the abundance or force of the water is also stressed;[155] this motif is of course also echoed (though in different terminology) in the מַיִם רַבִּים of Ps. 32:6. However, the nominal form, שֶׁטֶף, encountered in Ps. 32:6, besides denoting an "overflow", or "flood", of water, also in the majority of cases appears in relation to wrath,[156] usually that of God.[157]

The close association between שֶׁטֶף and the outpouring of (the especially divine) anger is, of course, pertinent to the interpretation of Ps. 32:6, since the sin-forgiveness-relief dimension of deliverance is explicitly drawn out in the preceding verses. Before the psalmist declared his sin "thy hand was heavy upon me" (v. 4), but relief was subsequently granted after a process of confession and forgiveness. Therefore, although the "rush of great waters" is not explicitly stated to be from God, the motif certainly occurs within a contextual framework within which peril seems to be the result of (unconfessed) wrongdoing, and in which distress can only be alleviated by turning to God in penitence and trust: Yahweh alone has the power to offer forgiveness and consequent salvation. Thus, even if God is not understood as the direct agent of misfortune, he is perceived as its ultimate cause, if only by withholding his protection and blessing; he is also consequently the sole and sure means to its removal. This sense of divine causality is subtly advanced in v. 6 by the distinctive vocabulary of שֶׁטֶף which, besides introducing the established motif of the waters of distress which sweep over their victim, at the same time eloquently imparts the nuance of the wrath of God which has already been implied in the preceding verses.

Yet if divine causality is in v. 6d indicated only by a subtle allusion, the possibility of the involvement of Sheol is perhaps less certain still.[158] Though, as has been seen, "waters" imagery (including the root שטף) is often employed within individual laments and thanksgiving psalms to convey a sense of proximity to death, a situation perhaps suggested also by the description of the psalmist's plight in v. 3-4, there is no concrete indication that this sphere of

---

155 מַעֲמַקֵּי־מַיִם, Ps. 69:3; שִׁבֹּלֶת מַיִם, Ps. 69:16; הַמַּיִם הַזֵּידוֹנִים, Ps. 124:5.

156 Prov. 27:4.

157 Isa. 54:8, Nah. 1:8, and perhaps Dan. 9:26. Cf. Cohen's explanation of the clause (translated as "when the great waters overflow") as "a symbol of Divine retribution upon the wicked, suggested by the Flood." (p. 93).

158 Contra Brueggemann (*The Message of the Psalms*, p. 97) and Tromp (*Primitive Conceptions*, p. 110, n. 53), the latter of whom includes even Pss. 65:8; 77:17; and 106:11 in this category.

reference is actually engaged here. The noun שֶׁטֶף is not elsewhere associated with the netherworld, whilst any connection between מַיִם רַבִּים and this sphere is infrequent and context-specific, as well as operating exclusively within the realm of double entendre.[159]

It is therefore perhaps significant that שֶׁטֶף מַיִם רַבִּים, i.e., the great volume[160] of (overflowing) floodwater (v. 6), has no active verb attributed to it; nor is it explicitly stated to be manipulated by God. This great, destructive force, whose key behavioural feature is rapid, irresistible movement, paradoxically has no stated impulse behind it: it is just there, as an ever-present existential possibility. The very suddenness and unselectivity of the torrent eloquently speaks of the experience of misfortune, disease, death; these the religious man cannot avoid, but his hope and salvation is in prayer.

As well as standing at the culmination of the sequential narrative complex of vv. 3-5, which functions according to the sin-affliction-confession-relief dynamic, v. 6b also effects a transition to the more positive perspective afforded by v. 7. In the latter verse, in a manner which may perhaps be regarded as characteristic of psalms of thanksgiving, the Psalmist gratefully acknowledges Yahweh as his protector and deliverer. Thus the initial recollection of forgiveness, the lifting of the heavy hand of wrath, has now been transformed into a more expansive acclamation of Yahweh as the one who preserves from harm, and who effects deliverance. As a consequence, the "trouble" threatening the psalmist has also been translated into the realm of the "other", which is opposed not only to the suppliant, but also to God's intention for him. V. 6 may therefore be regarded as the pivot on which this important transformation of perspective turns.[161] The movement is effected not only by the verse's neutrality on the subject of the agency of the waters, but also by its entry on one note ("let everyone... offer prayer to *thee*", i.e., turning to God, one might imply in penitence, as the key to relief) and exit on the other ("*they* shall not reach him"—the great waters, the agents of distress, as other).

7. A Note on Dating

None of the psalms here considered contain identifiable allusions to historical events which may assist in the attempt to place them chronologically. Ps. 69:36-7 could feasibly presuppose the events of 587 B.C.,[162] but the position of these

159 In Ezek. 26:19 (sea / underworld); Ps. 18:17 = 2 Sam. 22:17 (underworld / enmity; here the underworld is dominant); and perhaps Ps. 144:7 (though here Sheol has rather receded from view).

160 See the discussion of מַיִם רַבִּים in chapter 3 above.

161 Contrast the contention of Hossfeld that v. 6 (together with vv. 9, 10) belongs to a secondary redactional layer which "can scarcely be integrated" into the rest of the Psalm (HZ, pp. 200-201).

162 Or possibly of 589 B.C., since the saving of Zion is mentioned alongside the rebuilding of Judah, which may suggest that Jerusalem had not yet fallen, although other Judaean towns had suffered much destruction.

verses at the end of the poem, and their lack of any intrinsic connection with what precedes, cautions one against simply assuming that they necessarily provide an indication of the time of origin of the composition. However, since it is not here maintained that a particular course of development is exhibited within Pss. 18, 32, 42-3, 69, 88, 124 and 144, it is only of interest to demonstrate the apparent longevity of the "waters" imagery exhibited within them. It has already been shown that Ps. 18 may derive from the monarchical period, and, in fact, Ps. 42-3 may also be pre-exilic (note the probable existence of the Temple, 43:3-4, and the direct approach to the altar, 43:4, besides the "chiefly classic or early"[163] language). On the other hand, evidence may be adduced for the post-exilic provenance of Ps. 88 (particularly the use of late vocabulary, including a wide variety of terms to denote the sphere of death and Sheol), Ps. 69 (for instance, the conception of a "book of life", v. 29, cf. Dan. 12:1, and the affinities of v. 35 to some of the hymns of praise found in the latter part of the Psalter, e.g., Ps. 148, especially v. 7) and possibly even Ps. 144 (note especially its anthological character[164] and its use of apparently late vocabulary, e.g. the Aramaism קְרָב, "war", v. 1[165]). However, rather than discussing the limited evidence pertaining to each of these psalms in turn, attention will be devoted to Pss. 124 and 32, for which marginally more data are available, as providing examples of thanksgivings for which a post-exilic dating is plausible; though inevitably tentative, such an exercise may, at least, serve to illustrate the possible prevalence of the underworld motif over a sustained period.

The absence of historical references means that one can only rely on linguistic or conceptual evidence for dating. However, such data often fail to assist in narrowing the parameters beyond the conjecture that a composition is unlikely to predate the late pre-exilic era or perhaps cannot belong to the latest phase of post-exilic composition. Indicators drawn from the "history of ideas" must be handled with still greater caution, because of the risk of circularity. Nevertheless, a few tentative observations regarding the provenance of Pss. 32 and 124 may be offered.

---

163 Briggs, I, p. 366; a pre-exilic origin is supported also by Kraus, I, p. 473. Contrast, however, the post-exilic setting commended, e.g., by Gerstenberger (I, pp. 181-2) and Zenger (HZ, I, p. 266).

164 Most obvious are the connections with Ps. 18 (or 2 Sam. 22) vv. 47, 35, 3, 48, 10, 15, 17-18, 45-6, 51 which are evident in vv. 1-2, 5-7, 10, 11; compare also v. 3 with Ps. 8:5, v. 4 with Ps. 39:5, v. 5 with Ps. 104:32, v. 9 with Ps. 33:2-3 and v. 15 with Ps. 33:12.

165 This common Aramaic word, which is however rare in Hebrew, replaces the standard term מִלְחָמָה ('war'), used in the 'host' passage, Ps. 18:35a, and seems in general to be confined to later settings; hence it answers the criterion of "linguistic opposition" identified by Hurvitz ("The Chronological Significance of Aramaisms in Biblical Hebrew", *IEJ* 18 [1968] 234-40, p. 239; see Young, *Diversity*, pp. 63, 94). See further the examples of late language in Ps. 144 documented by Goulder, *PR*, p. 271.

The wisdom influence underlying Psalm 32,[166] as well as the language in which it is couched, would imply that it is fairly late.[167] The transmigration of notions deriving from the wisdom tradition into the psalms seems unlikely to have occurred before at least the late pre-exilic period and possibly rather later. Perhaps in accordance with this, Kraus places Psalm 32 towards the end of a process during which the emphasis on teaching in thanksgiving psalms gained increasing prominence.[168] Likewise, the Psalm's emphasis on the distinction between the righteous (חָסִיד, v. 6, צַדִּיקִים and יִשְׁרֵי־לֵב, v. 11) and wicked (רָשָׁע, v.10)—who appear now to be groups within Israel, rather than external to it—and the extensive vocabulary with which notions of sin, confession and forgiveness are conveyed, would seem to be particularly reminiscent of later Jewish piety.[169] However, it is difficult to be more specific.

Issues of genre are relevant also to the dating of Ps. 124, since, despite its superficial appearance as a national thanksgiving, "not a single idiom, not a single word or image of Psalm 124 is typical of psalms of the people or the community,... but many of them are expressly typical of psalms of an individual. For a number of them it is significant that they are applied also to external enemies only in prophetic language".[170] Similarly distinctive is the psalm's didactic intent, which governs the transformation of the conventional offer of thanksgiving into a moral exhortation to the assembled congregation, a feature which lacks any clear parallel in the Psalter.

Particularly striking is the way in which vv. 1-5 comprise a single sentence. Here there is no simple *parallelismus membrorum*, but a progressive narrative line, full of relatively complex and, for the Psalter, unusual grammatical structures, like the repeated extended conditional. Instead of declaring what Yahweh is or has done, the psalm points to what would have happened had divine intervention not been forthcoming. The attempt to draw a direct correlation between these features and any particular period of composition can only be made on an intuitive basis, and must therefore be resisted. However,

---

166 See Donn F. Morgan, *Wisdom in Old Testament Traditions*, pp. 125-132, who highlights many correspondences between the concerns of the post-exilic period and those of the wisdom psalms, which are largely to be dated to this era. Although his emphasis on the theology of retribution at this time should perhaps be reformulated in the light of the conclusions of K. Koch regarding the built-in consequences of actions (*ZTK* 52 [1955], 1-42), this does not affect the fundamental veracity of his dating assessment.

167 So also Anderson, I, p. 254, Gerstenberger, I, p. 143. Briggs contends that an original core, vv. 1-6, was composed during the Persian period, and further additions, namely vv. 7, 8-9, 10-11, later grafted on (I, p. 276).

168 I.e. "fairly late", p. 402.

169 Hence there is no need to draw a distinction between an original wisdom-influenced core and later redactional material, as Hossfeld has attempted to do (HZ, p. 201). Also to be disregarded is the traditional view that the Psalm was composed by David in the wake of his adultery with Bathsheba (Ewald, *Die Dichter des Alten Bundes*, I, pt. 2, p. 34; Cohen, p. 92).

170 F. Crüsemann, *Studien zur Formgeschichte*, p. 166.

there is reason to believe that the grammatical markers with which this structure is accomplished may be especially characteristic of the later literature. According to BDB,[171] usage of the relative particle שֶׁ (vv. 1, 2) is limited to "late Hebrew and passages with N. Palest. colouring"; in fact all of the instances in which it occurs seem to be fairly late, whilst the specific combination לוּלֵי...שֶׁ, "except that", which is comparable with Aramaic, may be particularly consonant with "later language".[172] The accompanying adverb אֲזַי is peculiar to Ps. 124:3, 4, 5; however, the usage here is perhaps analogous to the employment of אָז in the apodosis after לוּלֵי, which occurs in Ps. 119:92, probably a late Torah psalm.[173] It is perhaps therefore not surprising that Ps. 124 is generally regarded as "relatively late",[174] and one might concur with Oesterley in considering a late post-exilic date to be possible,[175] insofar as the relatively slender evidence permits a conclusion to be drawn.

Thus, despite the many uncertainties involved in attempting to date these compositions individually, one can be relatively confident in asserting that the imagery of the waters as symbolic of the underworld and of the enemies persisted into the post-exilic period. Many of the psalms here considered seem to be fairly late; however, the pre-exilic origin of Ps. 18, and the likelihood that Ps. 42-3 also may predate the exile suggest that the chronological parameters of this usage were fairly broad.

8. Summary

It may be concluded that there are two primary aspects to the imagery here under examination, namely, the entity signified by the waters, and the rôle performed by Yahweh as persecutor or deliverer. These variables may be viewed in either synchronic or diachronic perspective. The latter approach has already been shown to be unhelpful in relation to the rôle of Yahweh, since no clear pattern may be determined. However, as regards the waters imagery, in the earliest of the psalms considered, Ps. 18, the chief referent is Sheol, though the enemies are also present as counterparts and confederates of the underworld. A similar situation pertains in Ps. 69, whilst in Pss. 42-3 and 88, Sheol is presented as the sole direct cause of the suppliant's engulfment. By contrast, Ps. 144's reworking of material from Ps. 18 results in the predominance of the

171 P. 979.

172 Thus BDB, p. 530. This not entirely clear, however, since although Ps. 106 may well be post-exilic (see further Chapter 9 below), the dating of Ps. 27 is uncertain.

173 Briggs (II, p. 452) even cites שֶׁ(הָיָה) (vv. 1, 2) and אֲזַי (vv. 3, 4, 5) as evidence that "the language is of the Greek period". See Goulder, *The Psalms of the Return*, p. 54, for further examples of apparently post-exilic linguistic features.

174 Kraus, II, p. 1025. A post-exilic provenance is commended by the great majority of scholars, e.g., Seybold, p. 483, McCann, *NIB*, IV, p. 1189, Terrien, p. 821, Goulder, *The Psalms of the Return*, p. 54.

175 II, p. 510; cf. Clifford, II, p. 230, Briggs, II, p. 452.

enemies, to the extent that the netherworld cannot be said to be incontrovertibly in view. Likewise, in his subtle depiction of an occasion of national distress, the author of Ps. 124 skilfully draws upon images common to both spheres and melds them into a portrayal in which the physical and psycho-mythical aspects of the nation's torment are integrated to form a presentation of profound realism.

Though the issue of dating individual laments and thanksgivings is controversial, it is perhaps not unreasonable to suggest that in these psalms Sheol was the primary and original referent of the waters imagery. Pss. 124 and 144, in which allusion to the enemies is made, may well both be post-exilic, the transition from the original sphere of allusion perhaps having been suggested by inference from Ps. 18, and by the reality of circumstances of need (the situations of life-threatening magnitude which the imagery of Sheol graphically portrays may often, in reality, have entailed a literal threat from human foes); it may have been further reinforced by the influence of the imagery to be examined in the following chapter. It would be foolhardy to suggest that Pss. 124 and 144 are the latest of the compositions here considered; the evidence is too fragile to support such a claim. Any transition towards the idea of the waters representing the enemies was probably by no means monodirectional and absolute, and the motif of Sheol no doubt persisted into the late period (perhaps, for example, in Pss. 69 and 88). However, the emergence of the enemies motif does seem to be later, and may be derivative upon that of Sheol.

From a synchronic perspective, the individual and communal dichotomy is illuminating. Sheol dominates in individual laments (Pss. 42-3, 69 and 88), whereas in situations of national crisis, the rôle of the enemies is more evident (Pss. 124 and 144). Ps. 18, as a royal psalm, displays aspects of both, whilst Ps. 69, which has some national elements, may also be distinguished from the other individual laments here considered as regards the parallelism which it perceives between the foes and Sheol. If the action of Yahweh is added to the equation, further subtleties emerge, since he is experienced as the "agent of woe" only in individual laments; where communal aspects and mention of the enemies feature, he is regarded as the source of salvation. There may therefore be some form of general correlation between Yahweh's rôle as afflictor and cases of internal suffering (sickness and/or sin), and between his action as agent of justice against enemies and cases of external threats (persecution or warfare). This model may find corroboration in the ambiguities of Ps. 32, where relief is the direct result of forgiveness of sin, but the exact nature of Yahweh's involvement oscillates from the lifting of the heavy hand of wrath to setting the suppliant on high out of the reach of external torments.

V. Songs Relating to the Protection of Zion: Psalms 24, 93, 46 and 65

Probably rather later in origin than the tradition of the theophany are the hymns which exhibit an overriding interest in Yahweh as the supreme guarantor of the stability of the cosmos, and of the holiness and security of Zion. Effectively, these psalms seem to reflect the concern: How secure is this stable order? Will it be maintained?—and offer in answer a resounding affirmation of Yahweh's strength and supremacy. This is manifested throughout Ps. 93 and typified by Ps. 24:2: "...he has founded [the earth] upon the seas, / and established it upon the rivers." The imagery is also employed in relation to the nations, as in Pss. 46 (implicit through wordplay) and 65.[1]

Though the psalms here considered may exhibit a concern with enemy nations, even paralleling them with the roaring of tumultuous waters, this imagery is probably to be regarded as essentially independent from that examined in the previous chapter. Particularly noteworthy are the distinct spheres of application, Pss. 24, 93, 46 and 65 being hymnic[2] and having a national or cosmic orientation, in contrast to the personal tone[3] and threnodic or thanksgiving orientation of the psalms analysed in Chapter Four. As a corollary of the communal / individual dichotomy, the experience of divine deliverance can clearly be differentiated in each situation. Whereas Yahweh may reach from on high and draw a suppliant out of the underworld, often in a dramatic act of rescue, protection from the cosmic ocean depends on his strength to uphold the world order. This latter sea can only be constrained or subdued, and is a feature of the cosmos as it stands. Nevertheless, a common aspect of both groups of psalms is that the waters may signify something beyond themselves. In the laments and thanksgiving psalms examined in the previous chapter, it was seen that the threat of the underworld could denote anything adverse to an ordered and healthy existence, which diminishes the quality of an individual's life and draws him near to the sphere of death. Likewise, the issue of cosmic stability encountered in the present group of psalms fundamentally concerns the maintenance of a stable world, and this impinges on the social, political and moral orders. Thus, the two uses are probably to be regarded as reflecting contrasting spheres of experience without any close interrelation existing between them. Although they may be partially contemporary, that examined in

---

1 Though v. 8c, the clause in question, may be an addition (see below).

2 Ps. 24 has, of course, been described as a liturgy, yet this does not detract from the hymnic tone and content of this composition, but rather clarifies its possible use.

3 This, of course, pertains even to the royal Psalms 18 and 144, and to Ps. 124, which, as has been observed, adopts the language and imagery of a psalm of the individual even while its explicit interest is a national one.

the present chapter is the more dynamic and subject to change, whereas the enemy / Sheol sphere of imagery discussed above apparently remained fairly constant over a long period of time.

The presence of the *Chaoskampf* motif has been particularly vehemently defended in relation to Psalms 24, 93, 46 and 65, not least because these compositions are deemed to reflect Israel's peculiar contribution to the history of the "chaos" theme, namely its transference onto the political sphere. Certainly, Pss. 24, 93, 46 and 65 do seem to be concerned with the maintenance of a secure cosmos, as a result of which, the "world... shall never be moved" (Ps. 93:1). However, in the absence of explicit mention of cosmic combat in these psalms, it has to be questioned whether it is legitimate to infer this theme as the background to the imagery employed therein. It is therefore methodologically necessary to establish the place of the cosmology described in these psalms within its wider context, before embarking on a detailed treatment of each of these compositions in turn.

Essentially, the language employed relates to the complex of ideas undergirding the common ancient Near Eastern world-view, according to which the earth was a flat disc supported on pillars, under and around which was the ocean from which it had emerged and which could potentially subsume it once more. Likewise, above the earth, and again supported on pillars, was the firmament which supported the heavenly ocean. Through the sluices of this firmament and the "fountains of the deep", rain and floodwater would issue forth. Completing the picture were the heavens above and the underworld probably beneath the respective oceans (though Sheol is sometimes almost identified with the seas, e.g., in Jon. 2, and on other occasions depicted as directly under the earth). Thus, the surrounding waters could be experienced in a threatening guise, and the maintenance of a stable order on the earth be perceived as a fragile process, of which the guarantor was God (or the gods). However, the Israelite tradition clearly attests the view that this structure was something which could absolutely be trusted, so much so that the pillars of the earth were axiomatic for firmness and stability.

It cannot simply be presumed from the fact that Israel shared the cosmology of her neighbours, that she participated in (any one of) their cosmogonies. Common to all was their perception of the structure of the cosmos; far more variable was the mythology attached to its formation. Hence, reference to the *Chaoskampf* in these psalms cannot simply be assumed. In Israel, as elsewhere, the surrounding oceans must have been perceived as a potential threat. However, it is stated that Yahweh made the seas (Ps. 95:5), and there is clarity in the idea that he consigned the sea to its limits, set bars and doors, and commanded, "there shall your proud waves be stayed" (Job 38:10-11). The waters are powerful; their waves roar—yet Yahweh on high is mightier far than they. His power over them is an affirmation of stability, order, safety, security. So much is this the case, that, as has been seen in the theophany psalms considered in Chapter 3, it is Yahweh's coming that causes the earth to shake on its foundations. This communicates the terror and unimaginable כָּבוֹד (heaviness / glory) of his appearing—but also perhaps implies the ability of the earth to withstand such tremors.[4] Thus, one would have to examine the content of the psalms very carefully before asserting the presence of a conflict with the waters, and then to do so strictly on the basis of the available evidence.

No less important than creation is the maintenance of order. In Canaan, this was apparently a volatile affair, dependent on the relative ascendancy of various warring junior gods, watched over by El, the semi-otiose head of the pantheon, who would interfere only to curb their worst excesses, or to ensure the correct balance in the annual cycle.[5] The picture is therefore one of conflict, instability, cycle and change. With this must be contrasted the options available to the mono- or henotheistic position which is advocated by the biblical literature. Yahweh functioned, like El, as creator and guarantor; on him "cosmos" depends. Since there is no room for variation as occasioned by warring underlings, the picture is one of stability. It is non-cyclical and perpetuated by the activity of one God. He it is who provides the rains, the seasons and plenty. Accordingly, the prevailing approach of the Old Testament is to interpret climatic irregularities and national disasters as instruments of Yahweh's punishment.

But if the stable mono- or henotheistic Israelite view must be contrasted in its implications with that of the unstable, polytheistic Canaanite outlook, the prevailing agricultural existential concerns of the latter must also be contrasted with Israel's historical, political preoccupations.[6] It must be stressed that the occurrence of an image in two contexts cannot imply the same signification, as has often been supposed—or, indeed the same level of significance. In Israel, the imagery of the control of the waters is characteristically employed poetically in the context of other concerns and as an expression of them—as an evocation of political or personal anxieties, or of Yahweh's absolute supremacy, as in the present group of psalms. It was only used perhaps more literally in relation to creation—though even then, metaphorical language is apparent,[7] and suggests that this operated on a far from straightforward "factual" level. It is employed in passing allusions, in relation to something else, and never loses its earthly orientation. In Ugarit, although theomachic struggles may have had consequences in the terrestrial sphere, the extant descriptions of such conflicts occur in self-contained, mythical accounts concerned at an explicit level only with the behaviour of the gods: the imagery is not interwoven with other—e.g.,

4 As A. G. Hunter states in respect of Ps. 24, "as long as God is in control there is no danger—except from God's own strength" (p. 135).

5 See Lowell K. Handy, *Among the Host of Heaven: The Syro-Palestinian Pantheon as Bureaucracy* (Winona Lake, IN: Eisenbrauns, 1994), who builds a convincing case for regarding El and Asherah as the "authoritative deities" standing at the apex of the Canaanite hierarchy of gods, above the "active deities" such as Baal and Mot, but performing a vital rôle in maintaining order and regulating the activities of the other gods (pp. 75, 92).

6 This should not be stated too strongly: the provision of food and political independence must have been vital concerns in each, yet in terms of what is expressed in the extant texts, this antithesis seems to stand.

7 E.g., swaddling (Job 38:9), and the use of various images to describe the process of creation (separation, word, forming, making, etc.).

prophetic or historical—material as in Israel, but operates within its own sphere of reference. This is a significant difference, especially in gauging the level of literal concern and belief expressed in language of cosmic stability. The absence of any genuine suggestion of a struggle between Yahweh and another being, and the considerable flexibility of the image, its lack of clear connection with any crucial event (historical or mythical), and the passing contextualised references in which it is expressed, further mitigate against any suggestion of a cultic celebration (of what, exactly?).

Thus, in Israel, quite distinctively, the imagery of cosmic stability, and in particular the concerns it embodies, passes over into the historical. Sometimes this is implied even where it is not stated (for example, in relation to Zion); elsewhere, it appears in similes and metaphors for Israel's enemies (e.g., in Isa. 17:12-13, 8:5-8, and often in the Psalms). The transition is an obvious one: the threat of engulfment by floodwaters readily merges into that of an expanding superpower sweeping all before it. However it is difficult to see this as much more than a lively and apposite image, at once expressive and familiar. Yet there is no indication that the sea itself is deified: in contrast to Ugaritic practice, it is not bestowed with titles, and is referred to by an immense variety of terms. This is particularly confirmed by comparison with the employment of the image in relation to the Red Sea and Exodus, where the waters may function as Yahweh's instrument, not as his foe.

1. The Date of Psalms 24, 93, 46 and 65

The application of sociological principles may in this instance prove illuminating. Rainer Albertz, in his history of the religion of Israel, has distinguished the function of ancient Near Eastern state religions in "legitimating rule and stabilizing the existing social order"[8] from the circumstances surrounding the emergence of Yahwism, "the liberation process of an oppressed outsider group".[9] He proposes that, as a consequence, "Yahweh was not originally a god who could be drawn into the world through an image as a guarantor of the existing social order, but a god who with his promise of liberation transcends the existing world in the direction of a new world and a better order".[10] Thus, the early religion of Israel naturally has a far more dynamic emphasis on the salvific action of the god as experienced through historical events. If this dichotomy has any validity in relation to the internal development of the religion of Israel in the pre-exilic period, and perhaps especially regarding the transitional process associated with the establishment of the monarchy and a centralised state, this is perhaps nowhere more clearly reflected than by a comparison of the theophany Psalms 29, 68, 114 and 18 with the "Psalms of Zion" which comprise the subject of the

8 *Religionsgeschichte Israels in alttestamentlicher Zeit*, I (London: SCM, 1994), p. 78.

9 *Ibid.*, p. 78.

10 *Ibid.*, pp. 102-3.

present discussion. The former group celebrates Yahweh's purposeful approach in clouds and thunder, from heaven[11] or from the southland,[12] his self-manifestation in a terrible theophany, and the resultant disruption of the natural order.[13] These hymns are thus concerned with intervention, change, action and disturbance. In the latter group, by contrast, the emphasis is on security, stability, and certainty. Yahweh's permanent abode is on his eternal mountain, whose preservation he ensures; his kingship, the holy mountain and city, and the cosmos itself are all secured from of old. Rather than causing the mountains to shake and flee, he ensures that they can never be moved; rather than revealing himself in fearsome epiphany, he may be approached in his temple (through established ritual); far from devastating nature, he bestows fertility and plenty.[14] This security is built into the foundations of the cosmos.

This difference of emphasis may reflect distinct social circumstances and perhaps the changing historical environment in which the respective groups of psalms originated. Of course, although the motif of the divine theophany seems to have appeared very early,[15] and indeed had its antecedents in the wider ancient Near Eastern environment, it persisted for many centuries in Israel, and its presence cannot be employed in any absolute form to determine a psalm's origin. However, the concern with Yahweh's election and protection of his holy city is more temporally restricted, most probably being confined to the period of the monarchy—i.e., after the establishment of Jerusalem as David's capital, and prior to its destruction in 587 B.C. Although the city was never completely abandoned, and a building programme was initiated after the return of the exiles, it seems reasonable to suppose that after the conspicuous failure of the divine promises and Davidic covenant manifested by its fall, trust in the inviolability of Zion could never again fully be restored. The pervasive concern with the stability of established structures would also appear as most characteristic of the period of the monarchical state. Thus, many writers have, with good reason, envisaged this period as providing the context for the songs of Zion.[16]

i. The Date of Psalm 24

Psalm 24 is lacking any obviously archaic linguistic features. "Prosaic" elements include the article ה, which occurs in the opening phrase and in the divine title מֶלֶךְ הַכָּבוֹד (vv. 8-10); the relative pronoun אֲשֶׁר (v. 4); and many instances of colon-initial *waw*. In addition, this composition lacks the conciseness of early poetic style, as is evident from the use of emphatic pronouns and demonstratives.[17] However, the dialogic liturgical background of

11 Ps. 18:10.

12 Ps. 68:8, 18; cf. Ps. 114:1.

13 Pss. 29:5-9, 114:3-7; cf. Ps. 68:9.

14 Ps. 65:10-14.

15 Cf., besides the psalms considered in Chapter 3, Judg. 5 and Deut. 33.

16 See the discussion of the date of Ps. 87 in the following chapter.

17 הוּא, vv. 2, 10; זֶה, vv. 6, 8; הוּא זֶה, v. 10; and אֲשֶׁר, v. 4.

the psalm may account for the adoption of a slightly colloquial idiom suitable for congregational delivery, whilst the repeated demonstratives serve also to create emphasis, for example, on the person of Yahweh (vv. 2, 8, 10; cf. זֶה דוֹר, v. 6).[18] Indeed, the repetitive style of vv. 7-10 has been judged to be characteristic of the earliest poetry.[19]

A positive indication for the early origin for the psalm is perhaps provided by the phrase אֵל־הַכָּבוֹד in Ps. 29:3, which offers the closest biblical parallel to the otherwise unattested expression מֶלֶךְ הַכָּבוֹד of Ps. 24:7-10.[20] Another title which would seem to have its closest parallel in the earliest phase of Hebrew poetry is גִּבּוֹר מִלְחָמָה (v. 8c), which may be compared with Ex. 15:3, אִישׁ מִלְחָמָה, the only other occasion in which מִלְחָמָה functions as an attribute of Yahweh.[21]

Nevertheless, in general, the distribution of the varied titles which occur in Ps. 24 would tend to imply at the very least a monarchical origin for the psalm,[22] as is particularly the case with יהוה צְבָאוֹת (v. 10).[23] The psalm likewise seems to presuppose the existence of a centralised shrine, the מְקוֹם קָדְשׁוֹ, which either possesses gates or is located in an urban setting, and which has established conventions for entry. This seems to require the centralisation of Israelite worship, and perhaps therefore the construction of the Jerusalem Temple. Mention of the הַר־יהוה[24] and interrelated themes is also fully congruent with the Zion theology attested in the rest of the present group of psalms. One might naturally associate the composition's triumphalistic celebration of Yahweh as the divine warrior returning in victory to his city with the successes of the united monarchy as it established its mini-empire under Solomon, and possibly indeed with a relatively primitive stage in Israelite

18 See further the structural analysis of Hunter, p. 134.

19 Cross, *CMHE*, p. 93, Seybold, p. 105, Hossfeld, HZ, I, p. 157.

20 The article is employed in each case, perhaps to facilitate the recognition of the construct relationship.

21 Compare also 2 Sam. 22:35 = Ps. 18:35 and Ps. 144:1, where Yahweh is credited with endowing the king with warlike skills, as well as the timbre of Judg. 5, an apparently ancient song of victory.

22 See D. N. Freedman, "Divine Names and Titles in Early Hebrew Poetry" in *Pottery, Poetry, and Prophecy: Studies in Early Hebrew Poetry* (Winona Lake, IN: Eisenbrauns, 1980) 77-129 (reprinted from F. M. Cross et al [edd.], *Magnalia Dei: The Mighty Acts of God* [New York: Doubleday, 1976] 55-107).

23 See T. N. D. Mettinger, "YHWH Sabaoth—The Heavenly King on the Cherubim Throne" in T. Ishida (ed.), *Studies in the Period of David and Solomon and other Essays* (1982) 109-38 and Albertz, *Religionsgeschichte Israels,* I, pp. 200-3, both of whom stress the title's strong links with the temple cult and paucity in or absence from traditions of northern origin; nevertheless, Tournay's contention that the use of the title indicates a post-exilic date cannot be substantiated (*Seeing and Hearing God*, p. 127). For an opposing view, tracing the title back to the traditions of Shiloh, see, e.g., Kraus, I, pp. 85-6, 315-6, and Hossfeld, HZ, I, p. 161.

24 Attested elsewhere only in Mi. 4:2 = Isa. 2:3 and Isa. 30:29 (and in Num. 10:33 [JE] in relation to Horeb); Isa. 2:3 = Mic. 4:2 may be redactional additions, but are unlikely to post-date the sixth century B. C.

theology, the warlike attributes of God being especially the subject of celebration in Ex. 15:3, Judg. 5 and, via the king, in Ps. 18 = 2 Sam. 22.[25]

However, it seems that arguments favouring a late origin are without substance.[26] In view of the identification of heavenly and earthly sanctuaries, it cannot simply be asserted that the ascription "ancient" implies that the temple building had long been founded, as Gunkel maintained.[27] Similarly, the entrance qualifications in vv. 3-6 need not reflect late Torah piety, since they lack the didactic tone found in later wisdom-style psalms, and are very general in their demands. The requirements may belong to an ancient tradition of regulations for admission to various sanctuaries, for which there are a number of ancient Near Eastern parallels.[28] Nor is it clear that v. 1 reflects "a late, cosmic theology",[29] as the following exegesis and comparison with the other psalms in the group, especially Ps. 93, attests.

It is sometimes claimed that Ps. 24 "would contain individual pieces of a liturgy that accompanies the cultic act of bringing in the Ark at the sanctuary".[30] If entry to the Temple is envisaged, this would necessitate a dating in at least the time of Solomon, a conclusion which is consonant with the findings made so far. However, there is no direct evidence for the Ark being carried in liturgical processions, or indeed for it being transported at all after its installation in the Temple.[31] As Craigie points out, "once the Ark was

25 Cf. Briggs, I, pp. 213-4.

26 The Maccabean provenance advocated by M. Trèves ("The Date of Psalm 24" *VT* 10 [1960] 428-437) and B. Duhm (p. 102) is now, in the light of the Qumran discoveries, difficult to sustain for any part of the Psalter, but perhaps even more for one in the body of Book I. Terrien's allocation of Ps. 24 to the exile (pp. 249-250), on the other hand, is dependent on an eschatological interpretation which overemphasises putative similarities to Isa. 33-35, 40-66 (e.g., Isa. 65:17, 23), whilst Gerstenberger's attribution to the second temple period derives from his (questionable) perception of an "apparent confessional organization of the worshipping community" reflected in vv. 3-6 (I, p. 118). Likewise, Oeming's proposal that the disparate elements of the Psalm find their unity in the didactic purposes of the Hellenistic wisdom schools (I, p. 160) may fail to do justice to the form of the psalm as a whole, and particularly to that of vv. 7-10.

27 *Die Psalmen*, p. 104; cf. Wellhausen, p. 174, and Trèves, p. 428. Contrast Kraus, I, p. 347, who understands the reference as pertaining to the gates of the heavenly temple (cf. Gen. 28:17), from which the earthly counterpart was virtually indistinguishable.

28 Cf. Ps. 15, a composition which is also frequently assigned to the pre-exilic period, and the references in Kraus, I, p. 254. The alternative is to regard Ps. 24:3-6 as a later formalised version of the requirements for entry (Anderson, I, p. 200); however, the general movement seems to be towards greater elaboration rather than compression in the post-exilic era.

29 Contra Gerstenberger, I, p. 117.

30 Kraus, I, p. 343; it is associated with the transposition of the Ark at an annual festival, e.g., by Anderson, I, pp. 200, 204, Mowinckel, *PIW*, I, p. 178, and Cross, *CMHE*, p. 93.; cf. Hunter, pp. 137-8.

31 D. R. Hillers, "Ritual Procession of the Ark and Ps 132" *CBQ* 30 (1968) 48-55, is doubtful whether the Ark was used in regular festal worship; see similarly Weiser, p. 158, and A. Cooper, "Ps. 24:7, Mythology and Exegesis" *JBL* 102 (1983) 37-60, p. 41; compare also Loretz, *Ugarit-Texte und Thronbesteigungspsalmen* (UBL7, 1988), pp.

established in Jerusalem, it tended to lose its practical function; the development of the Ark traditions became more and more literary in character ... Thus it remains possible that Ps. 24, in its present form, is essentially a hymn... within which ancient liturgical materials have been... united into a fine literary structure".[32] Indeed, the middle section of the psalm, taken alone, would suggest a concern for the conditions in which pilgrims could enter Yahweh's "holy place" where he was already present, rather than an attempt to gain access with the Ark itself.

This then raises the question as to whether the transitions in the psalm are due not to liturgical movements, but to the juxtaposition of originally independent sources.[33] In this respect, it may be remarked how the psalm falls into three easily identifiable sections: vv. 1-2, 3-6 and 7-10, each of which have a distinct metre, form and content.[34] At the same time, Ps. 24 also seems to maintain an overall coherence,[35] and it lacks linguistic indicators which might suggest a very significant discrepancy in date between the respective phases. It may, therefore, be the case that Ps. 24 witnesses to the creative utilisation of earlier material. One might tentatively suggest in this instance that the double attestation of the article in v. 1 (which, as has been stated, appears elsewhere in the psalm only in the divine attribute הַכָּבוֹד, as in Ps. 29), the superfluous הוּא in v. 2, and the more prosaic and conventional (though not typically ancient) language in vv. 1-2 could be congruent with an underlying separation in the content of the psalm, especially between vv. 1-2 and vv. 7-10; these sections may thus represent respectively the latest and earliest parts of the psalm. The apparent inconsistency in the worshippers petitioning for entry (probably to the temple) prior to the return of their divine King might support a further division between vv. 3-6 and vv. 7-10; in any case, the possible incongruity may also imply that the psalm as a whole would not in its present form have accompanied

---

268-9, who, despite stressing that the presumed connection with the Ark has no evidential basis, proposes that the symbolisation of Yahweh's presence with a throne or "throne-wagon" is reflected in vv. 7-10.

32 P. 212.

33 A composite origin is defended by W. S. McCullough et al. (*Interpreter's Bible* IV, 1955, p. 131), Hossfeld, HZ, I, p. 156, and Briggs, the latter of whom assigns vv. 1-6 and v. 7-10 to "widely different periods" (I, p. 213; cf. similarly Loretz, *UTT*, pp. 268-9). Nevertheless, most critics (e.g., Kraus, I, p. 343) treat it as a unity. Weiser's is a typical mediating position (p. 156): he remarks that each section is clearly delineated from the others in its style and subject matter, and yet suggests they probably collectively arose out of the same cultic tradition.

34 Verses 1-2 are hymnic, whilst liturgical elements, perhaps employed antiphonally, are evident in vv. 3-6, a Torah liturgy (Kraus, I, p. 342; Anderson, I, p. 200), and vv. 7-10, an Entrance or Gate Liturgy (Kraus, I, p. 343).

35 For a careful analysis of the unifying features of the Psalm, see Hunter, pp. 133-4; cf. also Girard, I, pp. 446-451. However, although Girard's reading may broadly succeed on a retrospective synchronic level, it offers little which might persuade the reader of the original unity of the composition (contra his claim on p. 451), especially as regards the inclusion of vv. 1-2.

The evidence, assessed cumulatively, would therefore seem to favour the monarchical era, though some of the incorporated material (notably vv. 7-10) may derive from the earliest period in this bracket (or earlier, though not apparently in its present form, since the use, for example, of the title יהוה צְבָאוֹת may not strictly allow this); the other sections may be somewhat later, although there seems no reason to place even the final composition after the mid-monarchy.[36]

ii. The Date of Psalm 93

Psalm 93 has conventionally been dated in conjunction with the other so-called "divine kingship psalms" or "psalms of Yahweh's enthronement",[37] by the older commentators being regarded as subsequent to and dependent on Deutero-Isaiah,[38] and by Mowinckel and certain of his successors as deriving from a pre-exilic "enthronement festival".[39] However, more recent scholarly treatments of the "divine kingship psalms" seem to acknowledge the importance of awarding each separate diachronic consideration. In fact, it is unlikely that this group of psalms should be regarded as comprising a distinct genre, since they lack obvious formal coherence.[40] Similarly, despite certain affinities in content, which pertain especially between Pss. 96 and 98, notably the acclamation of Yahweh as king, it is far from self-evident that they should

---

36 Cf. Hossfeld's advocacy of a "great age for almost all four parts" of the psalm (HZ, I, p. 156, taking v. 6 as a later addition).

37 These are Pss. 47, 93, 96-99.

38 So Briggs, who treats Pss. 93, 96-100 as originally comprising a single song of praise (II, p. 299), cf. Cheyne, p. 261. Often these psalms were interpreted eschatologically: see Gunkel, *Ausgewählte Psalmen* (Göttingen, 1904, 1905, 1917, e.g., 1904 pp. 161-2 re Ps. 97) and compare the modification of his arguments in *Einleitung*, § 3, subsequent to the appearance of Mowinckel's *Psalmenstudien* of 1921-4.

39 See his seminal 6-volume work, *Psalmenstudien* (Christiania, 1921-4); his position was restated and defended in *The Psalms in Israel's Worship* (Oxford, 1962). The pre-exilic provenance of these psalms has been advocated more recently, for example, by A. R. Johnson (*SKAI*, e.g., p. 61; cf. J. Day, *OTL*, pp. 71-73). However, despite later polarisations on this issue, Mowinckel himself in his commentary of 1955 retained the traditional post-exilic dating for Pss. 95-99 and made no attempt to date Ps. 93 (thus Eaton, *Psalms of the Way and the Kingdom*, p. 83); even in *PIW*, he went no further than to state: "I feel convinced that it will not be possible to give cogent *proof* of the post-exilic origin of any one of the enthronement psalms" (I, p. 117). Compare likewise Gray's realistic assignment of a late date to Pss. 96 and 98 (*Biblical Doctrine*, p. 67) despite his general concurrence that the "enthronement psalms" have their prototype in the liturgy of the pre-exilic autumn festival.

40 Note Westermann's discussion of the "Songs of the Enthronement of Yahweh" in *Lob und Klage*, pp. 110-115, especially his comment on p. 111: "The enthronement Psalms do not constitute a category, nor are the Psalms so designated united by regular marks of a category"; see again p. 114.

be interpreted collectively, or treated as a self-contained group.[41] Indeed, for the purposes of the present study, at least, many of Ps. 93's leading motifs, especially its emphasis on cosmic stability, resonate more closely with Pss. 24, 46 and 65 than with Pss. 96-99—hence its consideration in this chapter. This treatment is already paralleled in Lipiński's classification of the psalm as a "Song of Zion".[42] It is in any case methodologically unsound to attempt to date and interpret any group of psalms on the *a priori* basis of their perceived collective coherence; rather, each should be awarded independent consideration, and only then if compelling evidence for their chronological and thematic unity is revealed, should it prove necessary to account for this. Such an approach is nowhere more important than in regard to perceived cultic or eschatological relations, since their identification is so subjective and contentious.

Thus, a consensus seems to be emerging, despite sometimes considerable disparities, that Ps. 93 is early pre-exilic, Ps. 99 probably also pre-exilic (with dates ranging from Solomon to Deuteronomy), Pss. 96 and 98 (early) post-exilic and derivative upon Deutero-Isaiah, and Ps. 97 late post-exilic, possibly even Hellenistic.[43] This is a topic which has excited an unusual degree of interest, yet the high degree of unanimity regarding the (early) pre-exilic origin of Ps. 93 may especially be noted, this dating being maintained on a general basis by Kraus,[44] but substantiated by the more detailed analyses of Dahood,[45] Lipiński,[46] Howard[47] and Gray,[48] and by studies of ancient Hebrew poetry, such as those by Albright,[49] Freedman[50] and Robertson.[51] The reader is

41 The phrase יהוה מָלָךְ is not confined to—or even present in all of—these psalms, being absent from Ps. 98, but attested (in the imperfect) in Ps. 146:10; compare Mic. 4:7c, Isa. 24:23b and Isa. 52:7e, the close association with Zion in all of these instances being unmistakable. The verb מלך is moreover applied to God in Ex. 15:18, Ezek. 20:33 and 1 Sam. 8:7, whilst יהוה מֶלֶךְ in Ps. 10:16 would in the original unpointed text have been indistinguishable from the verbal phrase יהוה מָלָךְ; cf. also among the present group of psalms Ps. 24:7-10. It has even been claimed that "the declaration '*YHWH malak*' involves a vision of reality that is the theological centre of the Psalter" (J. L. Mays, "The Centre of the Psalms", in Balentine and Barton [edd.], *Language, Theology and the Bible*, p. 245).

42 Together with Pss. 46, 48, 76, 84, 87 and 122; Lipiński, *La royauté de Yahwé dans la poésie et le culte de l'ancien Israël* (Brussels: Paleis der Academiën, 1965), p. 153.

43 See, e.g., the treatments of these psalms by Kraus (*Psalmen*), Lipiński (*Royauté*) and Jeremias (*Königtum Gottes*).

44 According to Kraus, "We can hardly go wrong if we date Psalm 93 in the early time of the kings. The transmissions are archaic; the conceptions are ancient." (II, p. 816).

45 Who advocates a tenth century date, II, p. 339.

46 *Royauté*, pp. 163-172; he locates the psalm in the period of Solomon or one of his immediate successors (p. 172).

47 *The Structure of Psalms 93-100*, pp. 184-9; he proposes a 10th century origin, whilst conceding that it may have been composed as early as the 12th.

48 For whom "the cumulative evidence for a date in the early monarchy is impressive" (*Biblical Doctrine*, pp. 46-7).

49 W. F. Albright, *YGC*, especially Ch. 1, "Verse and Prose in Early Israelite Traditions", pp. 1-46.

therefore referred to these earlier treatments, especially the very thorough discussion by Lipiński.

However, one proviso needs to be added: despite the preponderance of evidence pointing to an early pre-exilic origin for Ps. 93, v. 5 has by a number of scholars been regarded as a late addition.[52] Even among those who argue for its authenticity, there has often been a failure to integrate this verse fully with the interpretation of the main body of the psalm.[53] The vocabulary of the verse would actually seem to lend some support to this view. For example, the verb נאה (parsing נַאֲוָה as Pi'lel) occurs elsewhere only in Isa. 52:7 and Cant. 1:10; if the term is understood as the feminine singular of נָאוֶה, the rather more frequent appearances of this adjective cannot support a derivation prior to the late pre-exilic era.[54]

Nevertheless, the evidence is not unequivocal. For example, though it is sometimes assumed that a concern with holiness and the law suggests a late setting,[55] holiness, in particular, is actually a theme which recurs repeatedly in early poetry, e.g., in Ex.15:11; Ps. 68:18; Deut. 33:2; the concern with ethical criteria as the basis for any relationship with God is also evidenced in Pss. 24:3-6 and 18:21-27.[56] Nor is it entirely certain that reference is actually made to the law (a supposedly late concern) in v. 5.[57] Moreover, Ps. 93:5 has been carefully composed in a metre and style which are consistent with that of the preceding verses, the avoidance of prose-style particles, in particular, being consistently maintained. Therefore, although the contribution of v. 5 to the dating of the psalm is uncertain, it cannot be precluded that it is original to this early hymn.

iii. The Date of Psalm 46

The style of the psalm is congruent with a pre-exilic provenance, but not with an especially early date within this bracket. It has no specifically archaic features, and the article -ה, colon-initial *waw* and the relative אֲשֶׁר each feature once. The

---

50 D. N. Freedman, *Pottery, Poetry and Prophecy: Studies in Early Hebrew Poetry* (Winona Lake: Eisenbrauns, 1980).

51 D. A. Robertson, *Linguistic Evidence in Dating Early Hebrew Poetry* (SBL Dissertation Series 3; Missoula, Montana: Scholars Press, 1972). Compare also the scattered remarks on the subject in Watson, *CHP*.

52 E.g., by Briggs, II, p. 197, Seybold, p. 370, Jeremias, *Königtum*, pp. 25-6, and Hossfeld, HZ, II, pp. 645-6.

53 Most spectacularly, by Westermann, *Lob und Klage*, p. 114; cf. Tate, p. 480.

54 It is confined to Cant. 1:5; 2:14; 4:3; 6:4; Prov. 17:1; 19:10; 26:1; Pss. 33:1; 147:1; and Jer. 6:2.

55 See, e.g., Jeremias, *Königtum*, pp. 25-6, re עֵדוֹת.

56 Note especially the legal language of Ps. 18:23.

57 For alternatives see Kissane, II, p. 115, Lipiński, pp. 148-9, Weiser, p. 424, Gunkel, p. 411, and Dahood, II, p. 343. The legal force of עֵדֹתֶיךָ is however retained by Briggs, II, p. 303, and Kraus, II, pp. 815, 819, whilst the compatibility of its use with an early dating has been urged by Howard, *Structure*, p. 40.

diversity of divine names attested within its eleven verses[58] likewise seems to place the psalm outside the earliest phase of Hebrew poetry, and the titles עֶלְיוֹן and יהוה צְבָאוֹת further reinforce the links with the Jerusalem temple tradition indicated by the content of the hymn. The vocabulary of the psalm does not otherwise permit greater specificity.[59]

However, affinities with Isaiah of Jerusalem are detectable: compare v. 11 "be still and know" with Isa. 30:15; "Yahweh Sebaoth is with us" (vv. 8, 12, cf. v. 6) with "Immanuel", Isa. 7:14, 8:8,10 (though it is also quite widespread elsewhere); the "river whose streams make glad the city of God" (v. 5) with Isa. 8:6, 33:21; the comparison between the roaring of the nations and the sea (vv. 4, 7) with Isa. 17:12-14; God "in the midst of her [Zion]" (v. 6) with Isa. 12:6; and God as the only true source of security (vv. 2, 8, 12, cf. v. 11) with Isa. 28:15,17, 30:2.

Also potentially illuminating is a comparison with Isa. 2:2-4 = Mic. 4:1-3, these verses probably providing the earliest biblical attestation of hopes for universal peace and harmony, besides being rooted in a Zion theology closely akin to that exhibited in the present group of psalms. Especially notable are the interest in the primacy of Zion above all mountains (Isa. 2:2-3 = Mic. 4:1-2), its establishment (Isa. 2:2 = Mic. 4:1), and the concern with ethics (Isa. 2:3 = Mic. 4:2) and the inclusion of the nations (Isa. 2:2-4 = Mic. 4:1-3). The application of these key themes would seem to be more developed than those of Ps. 46, most notably in the fact that Ps. 46:10 seems to express hope for peace as being achieved through the destruction of enemy forces. It was customary for a victorious army to destroy enemy weapons,[60] and the general tenor of the psalm, especially of vv. 9, 11bc, would support an allusion to this practice here. Further, the incoming of the nations in Isa. 2:2-3 = Mic. 4:1-2 would seem to surpass the horizons of Ps. 46, and stand closer to Pss. 65[61] or 96 and 98. As Sweeney observes in relation to his late sixth century dating of Isa. 2:2-4:[62] "whereas both the Zion psalms (Psalms 2; 46; 48; 76) and the Isaiah texts (Isa 8:9-10; 29:1-4; 31:4-5) emphasize YHWH's defeat of the nations and the breaking of their weapons prior to peace and their acknowledgment of YHWH, Isa 2:2-4 portrays the nations as voluntarily submitting to YHWH, seeking torah, and refashioning their weapons into agricultural implements.... Such peaceful submission to YHWH and pilgrimage to Zion by the nations does not

---

58 אֱלֹהִים (vv. 2, 5, 6, 6), אֱלֹהֵי יַעֲקֹב (v. 8), עֶלְיוֹן (v. 5), יהוה (v. 9) and יהוה צְבָאוֹת (v. 8).

59 On the other hand, Gerstenberger's claim that the first person plural form (used in the present Psalm, apart from the refrain of vv. 8, 12, in vv. 2-3) is "a marker for identifying late liturgical compositions" is belied by its occurrence in Ps. 44, which may be pre-exilic, and Pss. 74 and 137, which almost certainly reflect the events of 587 B.C. and shortly thereafter. Moreover, the unusual focus on the threat of cosmic upheaval at an early point in this psalm, in connection with which this form is used, may well be sufficient to account for the communal perspective here expressed.

60 Cf. Josh. 11:6, 9; Ezek. 39:9-10; also Hos. 2:20; Ps. 76:4.

61 On which see below.

62 Its Isaianic authorship is defended by Wildberger (*Jesaja*, I, p. 80; cf. von Rad, *TAT*, II, p. 306), but most modern commentators would regard it as a later addition to both settings (e.g., Kaiser, *Das Buch des Propheten Jesaja, Kapitel 1-12*, pp. 61-63).

appear in biblical texts until the exilic or early postexilic periods".[63] Once again, the similarity of Ps. 46 with certain Isaian passages is significant; it is also possible that the ambiguity of Ps. 46 in proclaiming a message of triumph or of peace may perhaps reflect a transitional stage of thought antedating that of Isa. 2:2-4 = Mic. 4:1-3.

Therefore, there seem to be grounds for drawing a broad association with the message of First Isaiah. Accordingly, although the Psalm cannot be directly attached to any particular historical circumstance, and it may perhaps be located in a more general cultic background,[64] a connection with the events of 701[65] (or with the Syro-Ephraimite crisis, c. 733-732 B.C.) may not be wide of the mark. Alternatively, one may think of the prophet's dependence on earlier cultic precedents, and place the time of its composition slightly earlier.

iv. The Date of Psalm 65

Psalm 65 falls naturally into two sections, vv. 2-9 and vv. 10-14, which are sometimes claimed originally to have been independent;[66] this could be supported by the fact that the former has a predominantly 3+2 metre, the latter mainly 3+3. Nevertheless, the psalm has a coherent theme in the good things of God as it stands, and it should probably be regarded as a unit.

There is nothing to indicate the date of this psalm, and assessments of its origin vary considerably, with estimates ranging from the pre-exilic period[67] through to the post-exile,[68] Buttenwieser even associating vv. 2-9 with the deliverance from Babylonian exile, [69] whilst claiming of vv. 10-14 that "there is nothing so primitive as this anywhere in the Psalter".[70] However, Tate is probably correct in perceiving that "the portrayal of Zion as the rallying point for all mankind ('all flesh'; note Isa. 40:5; 46:26 [*sic.; cf. 49:26*]; 66:23; Jer. 32:26 [27]; Ezek. 20:48; Zech. 2:13; etc.) and the availability of the temple to all those whom Yahweh chooses to bring near relates well to passages like Isa.

---

63 M. A. Sweeney, *Isaiah 1-39* (FOTL 16, 1996), p. 93. Contrast Zenger, HZ, I, p. 285, who, unusually, detects in Ps. 46:10 an allusion to Yahweh as a "universal peacemaker", again making comparison with the same Isaiah-Micah passage; however, his interpretation of the verse leads—on the same principle—to the conclusion that v. 10 (or 10ab) may be a post-exilic expansion.

64 It is associated with the Autumn enthronement festival by Schmidt (pp. 88, 89), Zenger (HZ, I, p. 284) and Mowinckel (*PIW*, I, pp. 141-2; cf. Anderson I, p. 355); and with a "Zion festival" by Kraus, I, p. 497.

65 Thus also Cohen, p. 144; cf. Zenger, HZ, I, p. 285, Podella, "Der 'Chaoskampf-mythos'", p. 318, and (more obliquely) Dahood, I, p. 282.

66 Thus Gunkel, *Die Psalmen*, p. 272, Kraus, II, pp. 609-610.

67 Kraus, II, p. 610, Anderson, I, p. 465, Weiser, p. 314, Terrien, p. 474, Cohen, p. 201, Hossfeld, HZ, II, p. 219.

68 Tate, p. 139.

69 P. 346.

70 P. 50.

2:2-4; 56:7; 1 Ki. 8:41-43—all exilic or post-exilic passages".[71] The inception of the idea of the nations coming into Jerusalem and participating in her blessings cannot be placed at the earliest before the late pre-exilic period, and is probably (at least in its fuller expression) better located after the exile.

The impression that Ps. 65 requires at minimum a late pre-exilic date and may even be post-exilic is in general supported by the linguistic evidence. The hymn lacks obviously archaic features: there is one ן- termination, but only on a verb whose use outside Ps. 65:12, 13 is apparently confined to the exilic or post-exilic periods.[72] In addition, the definite article is employed twice, and colon-initial *waw* seven times, whilst various items of vocabulary seem to be predominantly confined to the later period. For example, the expression כָל-בָּשָׂר (v. 3) is especially characteristic of P, besides featuring in Deuteronomy, Job, Isa. 40-66, Jeremiah, Ezekiel, Joel, Zechariah and Pss. 136,[73] 145[74] and 65; one might cite also the Pi'el of קרב I (v. 5)[75] and קְצָת, "end" (v. 9),[76] whilst apparent Aramaisms also seeming to have a late pattern of distribution include the adverbial form רַבַּת meaning "much, exceedingly" (v. 10) and the verb עטף (v. 14).[77]

Nevertheless, these data are balanced by some evidence resisting a very late dating. רְבִיבִים, "copious showers" (v. 11) occurs elsewhere only in apparently pre-exilic contexts,[78] whilst כֹּחַ (v. 7) is applied to the power of God in creation elsewhere only in Jeremiah.[79] More importantly, the language of v. 8 has close affinities with certain passages in Isaiah and Jeremiah, which would again be consistent with a late pre-exilic provenance. The confluence of motif and vocabulary in Isa. 17:12-13 is especially notable, and Jer. 31:35 may also be compared. Nevertheless, the possibility of dependence cannot be excluded, and even as regards these parallels, the case even for a very late pre-exilic provenance must not be overstated, since many common terms are attested into the post-exilic period.

Thus, although the date of Ps. 65 remains uncertain, it does seem unlikely that it antedates the late pre-exilic period, and it may well owe its origin to the early post-exilic era.

---

71 P. 139.

72 רעף, Job 36:28, Prov. 3:20, Isa. 45:8 (the latter in the Hiph.).

73 See the discussion thereon in Chapters 8 and 9.

74 Ps. 145 is acrostic; Oesterley describes it as "one of the latest in the Psalter" (p. 572).

75 Which is employed elsewhere in Ezek. 37:17, 36:8, Job 31:37, Isa. 41:21, 46:13 and Hos. 7:6, the last of these, however, being emended by most commentators.

76 Which is otherwise confined to P (Ex. 38:5; plus the *k^{e}tîḇ* of 37:8 and 39:4), Neh. 7:69, and Dan. 1:2, 5, 15, 18.

77 רַבַּת is otherwise confined to the Psalms of Ascent 120, 123 and 129, which are likely to be post-exilic; the evidence is more slender for עטף, since it occurs elsewhere only in Ps. 73, but this psalm is also commonly assigned to the post-exilic era.

78 Deut. 32:2, Mic. 5:6, Jer. 3:3, 14:22 and Ps. 72:6.

79 Jer. 10:12, 32:17, 51:15.

2. The Theme of "Chaos" in Psalms 24, 93, 46 and 65

i. The Theme of "Chaos" in Psalm 24

Of particular interest is the simple cosmological statement in v. 2 that Yahweh has founded / established[80] the earth upon the sea / rivers.[81] There appear to be no mythological or combative overtones:[82] rather, the picture expresses the common ancient world-view, according to which the earth was supported on pillars (the bases of the mountains) which rested on the waters of the underworld.[83] This conception is in no way dependent on a specific religious background or cosmogonic myth. That the earth was founded on the waters was universally accepted;[84] here the declaration is made that Yahweh has achieved this, but a particular means of so doing is not presupposed. The significance drawn from this statement within the psalm is expressed in v. 1: because Yahweh has established (i.e. created) the world, it is his in its entirety[85]—structure and contents, and all its inhabitants. As creator, Yahweh is Lord of all the earth (cf. Pss. 89:12, 97:5).

The theme of kingship is further elaborated in the final section in language clearly borrowed from Holy War imagery, in which God's triumphal entry as a conquering king is portrayed: Yahweh is strong and mighty in battle (cf. Ex. 15:3), the Lord of Hosts, the King of Glory (cf. Ps. 29:9). The title יהוה צְבָאוֹת is often associated with the Ark, the embodiment of the deity's victorious appearance in early Israel (1 Sam. 4:4, cf. Num. 10:35-6); even when the Ark is not mentioned, the protective presence of God is often still implied by the term (cf. Ps. 46:8, 12). Thus once again, as in the theophany hymns considered in Chapter 3 and in Ps. 18, the epiphany of Yahweh appears at the climax of a pre-exilic psalm. However, in this instance, it appears that it may be the Ark which is envisaged as representing the deity, or at least that his entrance is ritually conceived. The terrifying aspects of the storm-god and the features of his dramatic theophany, along with associated cosmic traumas, are lacking and have been replaced by an assumption of the protective benefits of his presence, and of the ethical requirements for entry. It is as if the epiphany has been "demythologised" and tamed for practical use.

The question however presents itself: how closely related are the opening and closing sections of this tripartite psalm? Is it legitimate to infer a link between the kingship and military themes of vv. 7-10 and the motif of creation in vv. 1-2, and to abstract from this the assumption that a battle to bring the

---

80 Although the verse is often rendered with the simple past tense, the imperfects here may denote continual action; cf. Hunter, p. 129, p. 273 n. 1.

81 For נְהָרוֹת as referring to subterrestrial waters, cf. Isa. 44:27.

82 Contra Weiser, p. 157, Seybold, p. 104, Hossfeld, HZ, I, p. 159, Girard, I, pp. 443-4.

83 Cf. 1 Sam. 2:8, Jon. 2:7.

84 Cf. Ps. 136:6, Ex. 20:4, Job 26:10.

85 An idea which perhaps reflects Canaanite claims about El (see Hossfeld, HZ, I, p. 156), rather than concepts relating to the rather different attributes of Baal.

ordered cosmos into being is envisaged?[86] On the basis that the respective units may have originated independently, that they are in any case separated by an intervening section which has quite a different emphasis, and that there is no cross-reference between them, to the extent that some scholars even believe that there are two independent psalms here, one would certainly have to exercise great caution in so doing.[87] Although there is clearly—or there was surely perceived to be—a coherence in the poem as it stands, and there is a manifest link between the roles of Creator and King,[88] the battle imagery should not automatically be transposed back onto the opening hymnic statement. It is a fairly common feature of Hebrew poetry for a logical linear progression to pass through various stages, where the connection between each element may sometimes be as insubstantial as a mere linguistic affiliation, and the thematic or logical overlap between separated units may be non-existent. One should therefore resist the temptation to create a totally unified "package" only to blur the colour and contrast which lends this ancient literature its character. As a result, the connection between creation and divine warrior should only be drawn if it is regularly or explicitly indicated in comparable literature of the period.

Nevertheless, one unified theme may perhaps be detected, which is suggested by the closing line of the related composition, Ps. 15: "He who does these things shall never be moved". This motif of stability is manifested in a cosmic capacity in v. 2 and is implicit in the notion of the "hill of the Lord" (v. 3); those who maintain the moral order shall also "never be moved". The reassurance for this is the kingship of Yahweh, the Lord of Hosts. There can also be a darker side to this concern for stability, although it does not feature prominently here (cf. Pss. 46, 65, 93), namely its manifestation in the historical sphere, which in reality is often threatened by war and conflict. Nevertheless, the psalm asserts that "God, the Creator of order,... is also the Warrior of Israel, subduing the military threats... that undermine Israel's orderly existence. Order in creation, and victory and peace in historical existence, are part and parcel of the same concept: God is King. And both evoke from Israel the worship that belongs to God."[89]

86 Mythic overtones are discerned in vv. 7-10 by Cross, *CMHE*, pp. 91-99, who claims that these verses "can be fitted into a Canaanite pattern" (p. 93), despite acknowledging in the same context that "the normal locus of holy warfare is discovered in the Exodus-Conquest, not in the primordial battle with creation" (p. 100; see similarly Seybold, p. 106). Even less persuasive is Cooper's reference to a descent of the "high god... to the netherworld to combat the forces of death" ("Ps. 24:7" *JBL* 102, p. 53), on which see further the critical comments of Loretz (*UTT*, pp. 265-7).

87 A similar point has already been made by Loretz, who argues for the absence of the *Chaoskampf* motif here on the basis that such an interpretation is founded on the assumption of the unity of vv. 1-2 and 7-10, which he regards, probably correctly, as mistaken (*UTT*, pp. 255, 267). In addition, he highlights the fact that, if v. 8 is to be interpreted in the light of the Ugaritic material, it should most likely be associated not with a battle with the sea, but rather with the Baal-Mot conflict (*ibid.*, p. 255).

88 Cf. Ps. 95:3-5.

89 Craigie, p. 214-5.

Crucially, it is the establishment of the created order which provides the foundation for and assurance of stability in other spheres, since the firmness of the earth epitomises that which is established and immovable. However, Ps. 24 shows little explicit awareness of any underlying tension between theological reality and historical experience.[90] Here there remains an affinity with the early ark imagery encountered in Ps. 68:2 // Num. 10:35, and Yahweh is apparently welcomed back into his city as a conquering hero, "Yahweh strong and mighty, Yahweh mighty in battle,... Yahweh of hosts" (vv. 8-10). The tone is one of ebullient confidence, untroubled by the defensive attitude which is especially evident in Ps. 46, and equally untouched by the universalist vision of Ps. 65. Consonant with this is the fact that the foundation of the cosmos is apparently unquestioningly assumed to be secure. Nor is there any interest in the wider consequences of creation, for example, the conclusion that Yahweh is king over all nations or the only God. Indeed, the lack of any mention of other peoples is noteworthy, whilst the central positioning of the conditions for entry perhaps also reflects the relative insularity of the community which produced this psalm.

ii. The Theme of "Chaos" in Psalm 93

Psalm 93 celebrates Yahweh as the King, Lord of the creation and fount and assurance of all stability, whose eternal, unchanging rule is as firm as the pillars of the earth. The world-view reflected here is of תֵּבֵל, i.e. the habitable part of the earth as opposed to the ocean, as established and immovable but threatened by נְהָרוֹת. These are conventionally translated "floods", though the term normally signifies "streams, rivers", even "canals". In the present context, however, they seem to denote the subterranean channels of the deep, which feed its water supply.[91] This is suggested by their apparent threat to the establishment of the world (and of Yahweh's throne), the earth being set upon pillars which separate it from the waters beneath.[92] The continuation of the imagery of v. 3 with the mention of מַיִם רַבִּים and מִשְׁבְּרֵי־יָם in v. 4 would also seem to support this interpretation, since these terms are apparently inappropriate to rivers, but amply convey two key aspects of the deep, namely its vast capacity (which is often, but not exclusively, experienced in its subterranean nourishing aspect) and its more immediate and fearsome manifestation in the sea. Yet the assertion is made, mighty and terrible though these waters may be, Yahweh is still greater. The poetic motif of the cosmic structure potentially wavering and the waters presenting a threat is encountered in Ps. 46:3-4 (cf. vv. 6-7), whilst the tottering of the earth is brought into association with the issue of equity among the nations in Pss. 96:10 (// 93:1c) and 75:4.

---

90 Cf. Hunter's deconstructive description of the deity of vv. 7-10 as "a military hero without enemies" (p. 138).

91 Cf. Ps. 24:2, Ezek. 31:15, Jon. 2:4 (in the singular); the "channels of the sea" (אֲפִקֵי יָם) are mentioned in 2 Sam. 22:16 (Ps. 18:16 has אֲפִיקֵי מַיִם).

92 For the earth as founded on water, cf. Pss. 24:2, 136:6, Job 26:10, Prov. 8:27.

There could be an element of anti-Canaanite polemic here. Yahweh's eternal, unchangeable kingship is the guarantee of stability, perhaps encompassing cosmic catastrophes or climatic cycles, or even the earthquakes to which the region was vulnerable. However, the tumult of the nations, conflicts and uprisings and threats to Israel's security may also be in mind: compare, for instance, Ps. 46, and also Isa. 17:12-14. The rule of Israel's God is not subject to cyclical changes, to periods of supremacy alternating with humiliating defeat and even death. Moreover, there is no reference to a primeval battle: quite the reverse, for he is King "on high", far above the waters of the deep, robed in splendour and strength, supreme in sovereign majesty and not involved in the business of conflict.[93] Thus, "the mythical conceptions of the struggle with chaos are fully cast off".[94]

Two issues have proved especially important in discerning the significance of this Psalm. The first is the force of the opening declaration יהוה מלך, which may be understood either duratively ("permansively": "Yahweh reigns / is king")[95] or ingressively ("inchoatively": "Yahweh has become king").[96] It has been the focus of particular debate,[97] because the second translation has come to be closely associated with Mowinckel's enthronement hypothesis, and hence has been perceived to require a corresponding cultic interpretation and

93 Compare Hossfeld's perception that the battle between the gods has been replaced by a struggle with the powers of nature, "but the victor is certain from the outset" (HZ, p. 647). Moreover, as he emphasises (*ibid.*, pp. 647-8, quoting Jeremias, "Die Erde 'wankt'", in R. Kessler et al. [edd.], *"Ihr Völker alle, klatscht in die Hände!" FS E. Gerstenberger* [Münster, 1997], 166-180, p. 169), "the great respect for the power of the waters serves to describe the danger they present from human perspective, as is clearly shown by the angst-filled vocative, 'Yahweh', in v. 3a."

94 Kraus, II, p. 818, in relation to v. 4. Rather anomalously, he juxtaposes an explanation of how v. 1b is resultant upon the combat with chaos with the clearly contrasting statement: "but this is now the hymnically celebrated fact: by the God-King Yahweh (v. 2), who rules eternally and unchangingly, the world is firmly established down to its foundation" (II, p. 818). However, whereas the latter part of his discussion represents the explicit agenda of the passage, the former is merely a questionable assumption imported by the reader. A similar tension is discernible in Weiser's analysis, since, despite speaking of a "considerably softened" allusion to the battle with chaos in v. 3, he emphasises that the verse "nevertheless does not sound a note of fear,... but rather rings with joy at the roaring of the seas" (p. 424). A reference to primeval chaos is urged also, e.g., by Koenen, *Jahwe wird kommen*, p. 62, Jeremias, *Theophanie*, p. 27, Mowinckel, *PIW*, I, p. 145, Seybold, p. 369, and Schmidt, p. 174, whilst Dahood even maintains that in v. 4 the conquest of Baal is envisaged alongside that of Yam (translating בַּמָּרוֹם as "than high heaven", II, p. 342).

95 Thus, e.g., Kraus, II, p. 814, Koenen, *Jahwe wird kommen*, p. 60, Dahood, II, p. 339, Seybold, pp. 367, 368-9, RSV, JPSA.

96 Thus, e.g., Schmidt, p. 174, Mowinckel, *PIW*, I, p. 107, Cohen, p. 307, Weiser, p. 421, Girard, II, p. 536, Loretz, *UTT*, p. 279.

97 For a survey of some of the issues, see, e.g., Kraus, II, p. 817, and A. G. Gelston, "A note on יהוה מלך", *VT* 16 (1966), 507-512, and note the extensive bibliography in Howard, *Structure*, p. 36.

setting for the psalm as a whole.[98] However, the inconclusivity of the standard grammatical arguments, as well as of Lipiński's thorough comparative work,[99] has been demonstrated by Brettler.[100] In reality, proffered translations are often anyway derivative upon the interpretation adopted for the psalm as a whole, and indeed this issue can only be determined contextually.[101]

Nevertheless, since Yahweh's "throne ascension" has often been regarded as consequential upon his victory over chaos, it remains to be considered whether such an event is represented in v. 1. Certainly, it is highly debatable whether Yahweh's assumption of kingship over Israel was ever conceived of as an event which was rooted in a particular occasion or imbued with special significance, still less that it should have attained a pivotal position at the heart of the nation's chief religious festival. Yet even apart from this, it is evident that the general tenor of the psalm seems to lie elsewhere, since the emphasis is consistently placed on Yahweh's kingship "from of old" (v. 2,[102] cf. v. 5). The primary concern of this hymn therefore seems to be with the everlasting rule of Yahweh[103]—and it is his eternal unbroken power in maintaining order which is the subject of celebration.[104] This fact is dismissed by proponents of the ritual hypothesis on the basis that the realisation of a crucial past event as present in the cult—as in the cry, "Christ is risen" uttered on Easter morning—in no way undermines the uniqueness of the original salvation-historical occasion. Of course, understood as a theoretic principle, this statement is eminently reasonable. However, it cannot appropriately be applied to Ps. 93, since the celebration of a past event, either expressed in the "historic present" or in the simple past tense, must be distinguished from the perspective which focuses on a continuous state, as is the case in Ps. 93:2. There is a severe incompatibility in entering imaginatively into a past event as present and yet interrupting this with retrospectives placing the event against its distant historical background; in claiming a state as new and yet eternal and unchanging. Indeed, the "paradox" created by the juxtaposition of Yahweh's eternal kingship (v. 2) with the

98 It has been associated with a festival of Yahweh's enthronement, e.g., by Mowinckel, *PIW*, I, p. 106 (and frequently; see especially *PsSt II*), Schmidt, p. 174, Gunkel, *Einleitung*, §3, ¶9, and Weiser, p. 422.

99 *Royauté*, pp. 336-91.

100 *God is King*, pp. 141-4. Compare now Hossfeld's "ingressive-durative" understanding, "YHWH has assumed the kingship and rules since then as king" (HZ, II, p. 646), which is expressed in the translation "JHWH ist König (geworden)" (*ibid.*, p. 643), and thus consciously leaves open both the temporal setting of the cry, and whether it expresses a proclamation or homage.

101 Cf. Brettler, p. 144.

102 This is subject on which all commentators seem to agree, e.g., Weiser, p. 423, Kraus, II, p. 818, Cohen, p. 307, Terrien, p. 659, Hossfeld, HZ, p. 647.

103 Thus also Anderson, II, p. 666; note similarly Brettler's appreciation that "firmness is clearly the *leitmotiv* [*sic*] of Psalm 93" (*God is King*, p. 145), since it is both manifested in various spheres (vv. 1, 2, 5) and temporally enduring (vv. 2, 5).

104 Cf. Pss. 9:8, 10:16, 29:10, 145:13, 146:10. The ongoing activity of Yahweh's rule, guaranteeing the preservation of the world in past and future, is well emphasised by Seybold, p. 369.

presumed conquest of the sea (vv. 3-4) and assumption of his reign (v. 1) is perceived by Brettler to be so great that he proposes that v. 2 is a later addition inserted to "undercut[] the Canaanite myth" alluded to in the adjacent verses of the psalm.[105] Thus, the durative perspective of the composition requires the reading, "Yahweh reigns / is king", in preference to the ingressive rendering of the phrase יהוה מלך.

The second issue of contention also concerns a problem of translation, in this case, the force of the Hebrew verb-sequences. In particular, the *qatal—qatal—yiqtol* series in v. 3 has been a source of especial controversy, and has consequently given rise to highly divergent interpretations of the actions of the נְהָרוֹת here. Proposed renderings include "have lifted ... have lifted ... lift",[106] "lift(ed) ... lift(ed) ... would / will lift",[107] "lift(ed) ... lift(ed) ... are lifting (continually lift)".[108] However, the significance of tense-sequences in Hebrew prosody is not always clear, since variations do not always seem to reflect an obvious temporal transition. Hence, Ugaritic parallels, in which the force of the opening perfects seems to be carried throughout the sequence, have also sometimes been adduced as offering a further model of translation.[109] As is the case with the debate over the expression יהוה מלך, the

105 *God is King*, p. 146. A closely parallel interpretative process is evident in Loretz's treatment of this composition. In common with Podella ("Der 'Chaoskampfmythos'", pp. 314-5), he maintains that the theme of *Chaoskampf* is not expressed here but is nevertheless presupposed (i.e. in vv. 1ab, 3-4; *UTT*, p. 290). However, like Brettler, he appreciates that his "chaos"-inclusive assessment of the Psalm is undercut by the declaration of the eternal kingship of Yahweh in vv. 1c-2b, and he, too, seeks to explain this with the hypothesis that these cola are a secondary addition to the original core of the Psalm (vv. 1a-b, 3-4; *ibid.*, p. 291). However, since he regards both sections (minus v. 2b, which he considers to be a later insertion) as having their roots in Canaanite religion (*ibid.*, pp. 291-2), there seems to be no justification for attributing to them chronologically divergent origins.

106 JPSA, Briggs (II, p. 297), Cheyne (p. 261), Girard (II, p. 536); cf. Weiser (p. 422) and Wellhausen (p. 99).

107 See Anderson, II, p. 668: "The Hebrew imperfect may... imply that the floods (symbolizing the elements hostile to the present world-order) would still like to return and cover the earth, but this they are unable to accomplish because Yahweh reigns, and has set a limit which they cannot pass (104:9)." The third colon is translated in the future by Codex Alexandrinus.

108 Thus the English translator of Kraus, II, p. 231 (cf. German, II, p. 815), probably rightly (note Kraus' reference to destructive, rebellious forces "still at work", II, p. 818), Podella ("Der 'Chaoskampfmythos'", p. 314) and Hossfeld (HZ, II, p. 644).

109 Dahood translates "raised" in each colon (II, p. 339), citing Ugaritic practice (p. 341); see likewise Lipiński, p. 97, Mowinckel, *PIW*, I, p. 145, Seybold, p. 367, and M. Held, "The *YQTL-QTL* (*QTL-YQTL*) Sequence" in *Studies and Essays in Honor of Abraham A. Neuman* (Leiden, 1962) 281-290, p. 281. This approach is adopted also by Tate, who offers a trifold "roared" (p. 471; see his notes on pp. 472, 480); yet contrast Jeremias, who maintains the perfect throughout, but only on the assumption of a presumed textual error (*Theophanie*, p. 27). Further permutations include Terrien's employment of the present tense for all three cola (p. 657), and Loretz's rendering,

ambiguous linguistic situation can only be resolved by a contextual analysis of the passage concerned.

It is sometimes claimed, for example, that if the subject is the primeval waters, the allusion could be to the *Urzeit*, and then, in the imperfect, to a present[110] or perhaps thwarted ("would lift")[111] threat, or possibly to their rising and defeat in the *Endzeit*, on which would be based the establishment of Yahweh's kingdom.[112] However, in the absence of any clear chronological transitions or markers ("then / now / when / but" etc.), dramatic contrasts between past and present, present and future, or past and future are best precluded. The verse is more likely to indicate the progress or succession of the waves, "they lift ... lift ... are lifting / still lift". Just as Yahweh's kingship is "from of old", so the waters have always been there; just as Yahweh is now worshipped as a mighty king, girt for action, so they continue to lift their voice—but in the present situation offer no threat to the mighty Yahweh.[113] Such a translation would acknowledge the tense change, whilst avoiding a massive transition, thus achieving a resolution which balances both the need for differentiation and the recognition that the distinction between the tenses may be very faint or even indiscernible.[114]

Thus, it appears that the psalm concerns Yahweh's eternal kingship, reference to an event through which he "became king" being precluded by the dominant focus on his "everlasting" reign. His incomparable might is

---

"erheben sollen" (*UTT*, p. 279, cf. p. 286), which again is sustained throughout the verse.

110 See Kraus, II, p. 818.

111 Anderson, II, p. 668.

112 Though presently realised in the cult; see Weiser, p. 424.

113 On the other hand, Loretz's categorisation of vv. 3-4 as containing an invitation to the "floods" to praise Yahweh, comparable to Ps. 98:7-8 (*UTT*, pp. 284, 290), seems inappropriate, given the comparison with Yahweh's greater strength in v. 4: some level of tension is evident here even if it is not indicative of cosmogonic strife.

114 Attempts to read the whole of v. 3 as referring to the past (i.e., to primeval time) are equally unsatisfactory for very similar reasons, since they merely result in the transposition of jarring tense changes into different sections of the psalm, despite the lack of any supporting linguistic indicators. Thus, for example, Dahood begins his translation in the present, ending v. 1 in the future ("no more shall it totter"), but after imposing a disjunctive transition into the past at the beginning of v. 2, and a move to the present in v. 2b ("you are from eternity"), he returns to the past in vv. 3-5a, before concluding with the future in v. 5bc. Tate's rendering is similarly tortuous, entailing the sequence: present (v. 1aα), past (v. 1aβ-b), present (v. 1c), past (v. 2a), present (v. 2b), past (vv. 3-4), present (v. 5); though the temporal fluctuations are less extreme than those advocated by Dahood, since at least the future is not encompassed, it seems intrinsically unlikely that they should both exceed the number of verses in the composition, and fail to correspond to the few tense changes which do occur in the Hebrew. Nevertheless, this type of approach is by no means confined to those advocating a ritual interpretation of the Psalm; Westermann, for instance, treats vv. 3-4 as "a clear allusion to the primeval struggle with chaos", interpreting v. 3 "almost as a lament" and v. 4 as "the account of deliverance", though the conclusion of this verse "is to be understood in an eschatological sense" (*Lob und Klage*, p. 114).

epitomised as greater even than the thunder of many waters, for he is "on high", mighty above, and not embroiled with, the forces below. As a result, the attempt to discern an allusion to the battle with chaos cannot here be substantiated, since it depends on importing it as a presumed background to the situation described. Though such a backdrop may be possible, it runs counter to the explicit agenda of the composition, and the effort to locate a more concrete allusion to the *Chaoskampf*, e.g., in vv. 1c-2 or v. 3, merely creates a series of awkward and unsupported temporal transitions, which in some reconstructions outnumbers the verses in the psalm.

iii. The Theme of "Chaos" in Psalm 46

In this hymn, the use of duplicated verbs serves to effect an implied correlation between the "shaking, tottering" (מוט) of the mountains (v. 3), of Zion (v. 6) and of the kingdoms (v. 7), and also between the "roaring, raging" (המה) of the sea (v. 4) and of the nations (v. 7). The threat of instability is thus placed in the historical realm, and the nations are implicitly correlated with the sea on which the earth rests, and which may threaten to engulf it. Here, the archetype of the most impossible and dreaded scenario is that the foundations of the world should crumble, and the tumultuous waters topple what had previously been synonymous with absolute stability. The emphasis on mountains rather than the earth (which is however mentioned in v. 3a) as potentially vulnerable (vv. 3b, 4b), though not uncommon,[115] well suits a Zion hymn celebrating Yahweh's holy mountain which was hoped to be inviolable above all else.

Nevertheless, faith paradoxically asserts that even if the world should be shaken, Israel will still trust in its Lord. This is a remarkable statement: elsewhere, the fact that Yahweh is the creator and upholder of the cosmos provides the basis for faith in its utmost stability and in his strength as the supreme God (cf. Pss. 24, 93), yet here it is declared that even should the cosmic order which Yahweh had formed appear to weaken or be under threat, nevertheless, there are still grounds for trusting in his protection in the historical realm. The particular focus for hope now is Yahweh's peculiar presence in the midst of Zion with its people (vv. [5], 6, 8, 12).[116] The world may shake, but Zion "shall not be moved".

This assurance is partially communicated by the waters imagery employed within the psalm. It is evident from Pss. 24 and 93 that closely associated with the sub- and periterrestrial seas (יַמִּים, 24:2; יָם, 93:4) were נְהָרוֹת (24:2, 93:3), normally perennial "rivers", but there apparently ocean channels.[117] In Ps. 46,

115 Cf. Jer. 4:24, Nah. 1:5 (רעש); Judg. 5:5 (repointed), Isa. 63:19, 64:2 (זלל); Isa. 5:25, Ps. 18:8 (רגז); and Ex. 19:18 (חרד). מוט appears in the statement that "Mount Zion... cannot be moved" in Ps. 125:1.

116 Cf. Joel 4:17, Mic. 3:11, Zeph. 3:15.

117 This meaning is adopted by Dahood for v. 5 (transferred by him to the end of v. 4), which he explains as signifying "the ocean current" (I, p. 280), an interpretation which is doubtful both contextually and in the light of the singular form.

this association is harnessed to powerful effect, since it is asserted that the waters of the sea roar and foam, making the mountains tremble at their swelling[118] (vv. 3-4), yet, in complete contrast, "a river [there is], its streams make glad the city of God"[119] (5a; the positioning of נָהָר is emphatic).[120] Here, instead, the idea seems to be that of the nourishing waters of the deep providing an assurance of blessing and of the beneficent presence of the deity (v. 6a) through life-giving streams.[121] The picture, then, is of order, peace and blessing emanating from Yahweh. The symbolic nature of this image is underscored by the reality that Jerusalem has only one modest stream, the Gihon: thus, the picture is fundamentally a theological one.[122] The implicit message seems to be that even if all is in tumult, either in neighbouring states or in Judah itself, God may still be trusted to protect his holy mountain, the streams providing assurance of his presence and blessing.

The people are, further, exhorted to "be still" (v. 11) and trust in this God who was known from his great theophanies, associated with terrible works of destruction and tremendous victories (vv. 9-12).[123] However, the divine epiphany has become a general attribute of the deity rather than a focus of interest. Yahweh is the one who "utters his voice, the earth melts" (v. 7).[124] He is the "Most High" (v. 5), but his power now has the practical function of providing reassurance for his people that he will protect Zion.

Scholars have sometimes detected a reference to the combat with chaos in Ps. 46, especially in vv. 3-4,[125] v. 7 sometimes, further, being perceived as a

---

118 Though גַּאֲוָה may mean "majesty, pride" in certain contexts, the root meaning for גאה is "rise up", hence, in respect of waves, "swelling, rising up": cf. Ezek. 47:5 (גאה), Ps. 89:10 (גאות), and see the more detailed discussion in respect of Job 38:11 in Chapter 11 below.

119 Translation mine.

120 Hence Gerstenberger's apprehension that "the violent waters of v. 4 have been domesticated... to bring life to the 'city of God'" (I, p. 192; cf. Goulder, *PSK*, pp. 141-2) does not do justice to the separation, and even antithesis, set between them, or to the distinction in the vocabulary employed (יַמִּים and נָהָר).

121 A closely comparable contrast is effected also in Isa. 8:6-8, whilst the protection of God is also likened to a river in Isa. 33:21, in a context where a strikingly similar web of associations is activated as in the present passage.

122 Cf. the discussion of Ps. 29 in Chapter 3, and the image of rivers flowing out of Eden (Gen. 2:10-14) or from the sanctuary or city of God (Ezek. 47:1-12, Joel 3:18, Zech. 14:8); a similar idea may also be reflected in the Zion Psalms 87:7 and 65:10; cf. *KTU* 1.3.v.6, 1.4.iv.21-22.

123 Compare Dahood's rendering of v. 9b, "who has put fertility in the earth" (I, p. 277), שַׁמּוֹת being explained as the antonym of מִלְחָמוֹת and identifiable with Ugaritic *šmt*, from *šmnt* (I, p. 281; cf. Anderson, I, p. 359). This would correspond well with the imagery of the river which gladdens the city of God (v. 5), but it is uncertain whether the focus of the third stanza would support that meaning here.

124 The voice of Yahweh in thunder is a widespread theophany motif: see Pss. 29, 18:14, Ex. 19:16, Isa. 30:30, and compare Job 37:2-5. For the earth melting (מוג) before God, see Am. 9:5, Nah. 1:5; cf. Ps. 97:5, Mic. 1:4 (מסס).

125 E.g., Mowinckel, *PIW*, I, p. 87, Anderson, I, p. 356, Seybold, p. 189, Dahood, I, p. 279, Weiser, p. 248; cf. Zenger, HZ, I, p. 287. Other spheres of allusion have also been

"historicization" of this myth.[126] However, as has already been indicated, although the common ancient Near Eastern view of the cosmos, entailing the possibility of the encroachment of the waters, is presupposed, there is no clear interest in the originating act of creation, either in the temporal orientation of the hymn, or in its thematic scope; most importantly, the psalm does not touch on themes of God's engagement with or separation of the waters, still less on direct combat with them.[127] Thus, any reconstruction of such a background to this hymn remains conjectural, and lacks any direct support either within the composition itself, or from the wider corpus of psalms so far considered within the present investigation. Rather, it seems that God's undoubted, and most impressive, control in the cosmic sphere serves to provide reassurance in the historical realm, the implied comparison being underscored by the wordplay between the evocations of the two arenas of activity (vv. 3-4 and 6-7).

The congruence of the waters and the psalmist's enemies which is manifested in this composition is also already familiar from Ps. 124, where the foes are presented as the life-threatening forces of Sheol, from which Yahweh has delivered his grateful servant (Ps. 124; cf. Ps. 18:4-5, 15-18). A very similar pattern may also be discerned in Ps. 144, where a more direct correlation is drawn between the enemies and the waters.[128] As in these prayer and thanksgiving psalms, Yahweh is also perceived in Ps. 46 as the source of protection. Nevertheless, a proposal of Dahood[129] would create an even closer link between the two groups of compositions, since he interprets בְּהָמִיר (v. 3) in the light of Ugaritic *bmhmrt*, which he translates as "into the jaws";[130] hence Ps. 46:3a is rendered: "Therefore we will not fear the jaws of the netherworld", אֶרֶץ being taken by Dahood, as elsewhere, to refer to Sheol. This translation is

---

suggested, such as an earthquake and resulting tidal wave (Kraus, I, p. 498, re vv. 3-4; cf. Dahood, I, p. 280, re v. 4, and Girard, I, p. 760, re vv. 3a, 7b), perhaps as an expression of the divine theophany (Brettler, "Images of YHWH the Warrior in Psalms", *Semeia*, 61 [1993], p. 144), or alternatively the cascading water at the source of the Jordan at Dan, representing the waters of Sheol (Goulder, *PSK*, p. 140; cf. Smith, *Historical Geography*, pp. 472-3).

126 Thus Weiser, p. 250, Anderson, I, p. 358; similarly Zenger, HZ, I, p. 288. Mowinckel speaks of a "mutation of the chaos myth into a myth about the fight against the nations" who surround Jerusalem (*PIW*, I, p. 152), whilst Terrien refers to "the end of the world" in which "the natural world returns to chaos, but the Lord of hosts remains in control: he utters his voice and the earth vanishes" (pp. 372-3); cf. also Gerstenberger, I, p. 192.

127 A similar lack of evidence also hampers Podella's proposal that the *Chaoskampf* is not here or in Ps. 93 recounted but is presupposed ("Der 'Chaoskampfmythos'", pp. 313-8).

128 See the discussion of these psalms in Chapter 4 above.

129 I, pp. 278-9.

130 Perhaps, better, "miry depths": see *KTU* 1.5.i.6-8 (*CTA* 5.i.6-8) in Gibson, *CML*, p. 68, and cf. Ug. *hmry*, "Miry, Muddy" (*KTU* 1.5.ii.15; thus Gibson, *ibid.*, and Whybray, *RTU*; cf. Smith in *UNP*, "the Pit"); in an Old Testament context, compare Ps. 140:11, מַהֲמֹרוֹת (RSV "pits"; BDB "flood, watery pit, place of flowing waters") and Job 17:2b, וּבְהַמְּרוֹתָם (Clines, *DCH*, II, p. 572, "and in their slime pits [of the underworld]").

possible: the alternative, the "changing" of the earth, is not attested elsewhere, and is emended by some commentators.[131] Nevertheless, Dahood's proposal seems to create greater problems than it solves, since the parallelism between the earth and mountains, and the trauma apparently endured by each of them, is logical and well-attested, even if the particular verbal combination is otherwise unknown. Moreover, although the spheres of "water" imagery encountered in relation to Sheol and to the present group of Psalms would seem relatively close (especially in their concern with enemies, God's protection and even sometimes theophany phenomena and subterrestrial waters) the two *Wortfelder* would seem to be fundamentally distinct, and there is no clear instance of merging. As was indicated above, whereas God may reach from on high and draw a suppliant out of the underworld (Ps. 18:17), protection from the ocean depends on his capacity to uphold and establish the cosmic order. The former group of psalms may perhaps be regarded as stemming more directly from the theophany tradition (though representing an important development from it), whereas Ps. 46 represents a more static, defensive Zion theology. Thus, in Ps. 46, Yahweh is portrayed as the source of strength and stability, the preserver of the *status quo* and averter of trouble; he makes wars cease to the ends of the earth and will protect his sacred mountain. However, he is not envisaged as going forth to enact deliverance, nor is the term "enemy", still less underworld imagery, actually used.

iv. The Theme of "Chaos" in Psalm 65

It is vv. 6-9 which are of especial relevance here—the dread deeds of Yahweh which provide assurance of salvation and which excite fear[132] and joy throughout the earth. Verses 7-8 may be understood as an elaboration upon v. 6: God is the hope both of the ends of the earth and of the farthest sea (or "seas", following Syriac).[133] In the former sphere, there is assurance of the steadfastness of the mountains, the symbol of all that is firm and enduring, which God has established by his might. Here, warrior-style imagery is evident: Yahweh is girded with strength (cf. Ps. 93:1), though there is no indication that the founding of the mountains entailed any form of combat. Balancing this, in

131 Schmidt also discerns a reference to the underworld here, emending to הַמְּרוֹת and translating "die Tiefe sich erhebt" (p. 87); for alternative readings, see Kraus, I, p. 495, and Seybold, p. 189.

132 "Fear" need not connote the cowering of enemies; rather, it often indicates reverent awe at his power and mighty deeds, and at the resulting realisation that he is God: see the discussion of this term in *NIDOTTE*, II, 527-533. Contrast Mowinckel's insistence that—contrary to the understanding of the author of v. 8c—"the dwellers at the end of the earth" are "the demonic powers of the *tehom* around the earth, 'the helpers of Rahab' (Job 9:3), whom Yahweh at that time conquered" (*PIW*, I, p. 162).

133 There is no need to emend to וְאִיִּים (with BHS footnote, Kraus, II, pp. 608, 609, Seybold, p. 252; cf. Targum, *wngwwt ym'* = וְאִיֵּי יָם): the use of "earth" and "seas" indicates the universality of Yahweh's salvation and blessing, but need not require that they are inhabited by man, cf. Ps. 96:11-12a, 98:7-8.

the latter sphere, that of the sea, it is the bringing of stillness that is emphasised. This may be compared with Ps. 89:10; elsewhere, it is made clear that Yahweh also stirs up the sea so that its waves roar (Jer. 31:35, Isa. 51:15), this also being part of the fixed order of creation (Jer. 31:36); both aspects of this divine activity are encountered in Ps. 107:25, 29, where they, too, are seen as manifestations of his "wondrous works" (Ps. 107:24). It is therefore difficult to see why special significance should be attributed to this routine aspect of God's work, requiring an explanation in terms of a background of theomachic combat, as certain scholars have urged.[134] Terrien seems rather to come closer to the truth when he states that "the psalmist... avoids any explicit allusion to a triumph over chaos. He may not even have had in mind more than the smoothing of the roaring waves."[135]

The comparison with the nations (v. 8c) may well be a late addition,[136] which disrupts the bicolonic rhythm of the stanza. If so, this would provide clear evidence of a later explicit historicization of "roaring waters" language during the process of its development in an Israelite context, possibly in dependence upon the similes of Isa. 17:12-13 or like material. In either case, it is clear that vv. 7-8 express grounds for trust in God at his well-ordered and secure universe—the steadfast mountains, the still sea, the quietened nations, all established according to his purpose.

The stilling of the roaring of the seas and tumult of the peoples in v. 8 may perhaps within the present group of psalms be compared with Ps. 46:10, "makes wars cease". However, here in Ps. 65, the perspective is more clearly focused on universal blessing and harmony, as is especially evident from vv. 3, 6, 9, (10-14). Viewed contextually, therefore, it seems most probable that v. 8c is to be regarded as a "stilling" exercise, the bringing of peace.[137] Thus, although Ps. 65 goes beyond Ps. 46 in drawing a direct parallel between the roaring seas and tumultuous peoples, Yahweh's action in relation to the nations has undergone a transformation from defence and probably triumph in battle, to ensuring peace. Perhaps further expressive of this transformation is the fact that Ps. 65 transcends the essentially comparative, probably traditional Zion, rôles and titles attested in Pss. 24, 93 and 46 (Most High God or King of a heavenly court) by affirming the strongly monotheistic view that God is the focus of the hope, prayer and fertility of the whole earth. It is as if the corollaries of creation have now been worked out to their fullest extent. Nevertheless, the positive

134 E.g., Mowinckel, *PIW*, I, pp. 162, 188, II, p. 30, Schmidt, p. 122, Dahood, II, pp. 109, 112, 113, Kraus, II, pp. 610, 612, Anderson, I, pp. 464, 469, Hossfeld, HZ, II, p. 217, Girard, II, p. 185. Some, however, are quite muted in their claims: Gunkel, in his commentary, for example, merely refers to the "stilling" of the sea as "an originally mythological concept" (p. 273).

135 P. 473.

136 Thus *BHS* footnote, Gunkel, *Die Psalmen*, pp. 272, 275, Mowinckel, *PIW*, I, p. 162, Kraus, II, p. 612, Schmidt, p. 121, Anderson, I, p. 469, Briggs, II, p. 82; cf. Weiser, who removes the second colon, p. 313.

137 Similarly, rather than merely being described as mightier than the roaring waves (Ps. 93), and more terrible (louder?, Ps. 46:7), or even as an immovable stronghold when all else is in tumult (Ps. 46:2, 6, 8, 12), God here stills the roaring (v. 8).

universalist aspect of the hymn should not be overstated, as deeds of salvation, implicitly for his people ("us", v. 6) are also mentioned.

The awareness of the dependence of "all flesh" on Yahweh (v. 3, cf. vv. 6-9) perhaps derives from the concern for God as the beneficent creator, who provides all good things for his creatures (vv. 10-14, cf. Ps. 104); thus, the specific aspect of creation as to do with provision, care, fertility and growth is present. The tone appears to be a positive, joyous declaration of the different aspects of divine blessings and protection in various spheres of life. It is noteworthy that the variety of divine benefits "showered" on the earth in vv. 10-14 all apparently depend on the most fundamental and essential gift of all—that of water. Indeed, this hymnic section commences: "Thou visitest the earth and water it, / thou greatly enrichest it; / the river of God is full of water..."[138] (v. 10), and continues with the use of such images as that of God "water[ing] ... furrows abundantly ... softening it with showers" (v. 11). Even his "[wagon] tracks overflow with richness" (NRSV v. 12) and "the pastures of the wilderness drip" or "overflow" (v. 13). Mention of "tracks" probably reflects the idea of God riding on the storm clouds as if in a chariot (cf. Pss. 18:11, 68:5, 34, *KTU* 1.4.iii.18, 1.2.iv.8), which is again associated with water provision. Clearer confirmation could not be found for the fact that water in the Old Testament may be an immensely positive and valuable force, bestowing all manner of blessings, and deriving from God.

3. Summary

The psalms here considered are clearly concerned with the stability of the created order established and upheld by God, its firmness and immovability providing reassurance in the historical sphere. Nevertheless, the language of conflict is lacking and, moreover, the process of formation underlying the cosmos does not seem to feature in the explicit agenda of any of these psalms. Scholarly attempts to posit retrospective recollections of a struggle with chaos have simply created awkward tense-transitions which are not supported by the grammatical structure of the psalms, and require reading against their rhetorical flow, as is especially evident in the case of Ps. 93.

138 Probably an allusion to rain (thus Cohen p. 203) or, more precisely, to the channel cleft for its passage (cf. Job 38:25), akin to the "windows of heaven" (Gen. 7:11, 8:2); thus Anderson, I, pp. 470-1.

Obviously, there is an extent to which to speak of "order" awakens the possibility of its antithesis, "disorder", "dissolution" or, as one might term it, "chaos". However, it is a logical fallacy to equate the content of such ideas with an originating struggle with chaos, both on temporal and conceptual grounds. It seems that scholars are in danger of being so dazzled by the difference of "the ancient world view" from our own as to become incapable of distinguishing the more subtle variations between its various manifestations and to assume that such cosmologies must be dependent on the same fundamental cosmogony. However, although there are a number of references to Yahweh having set bounds for the sea (Jer. 5:22, Job 38:10, Ps. 104:9,[139] perhaps 148:6[140]), it is in no instance made clear that this formed part of an originating conflict:[141] indeed, according to one image, the sea emerged from "the womb" to be clothed and swaddled by God (Job 38:8-11[142]). This is not to diminish the magnificence of God's restraining power, nor the destructive capability of the sea, but to suggest that it cannot merely be assumed that this had to be achieved through theomachic combat, or that the majority of such references have an "urzeitlich" (or indeed "endzeitlich") nuance.

For moderns, to speak of the maintenance of the cosmic order may imply its inception and a certain view of how this was achieved. However, it cannot be supposed that claims that Yahweh upheld the *status quo* had always necessarily been accompanied by a clearly thought-out expression of how creation itself had been achieved, and the multiplicity of the forms of creative action attributed to God within the Israelite tradition precludes dogmatism on this subject. Nevertheless, even were the possibility that the *Chaoskampf* could form the implicit background to the present group of psalms to be granted, it is nowhere made explicit, and the burden of proof must be placed on those who would wish to presuppose it here.

139 See Chapter 8 below.

140 See Chapter 7 below; here, the context is of joy at the createdness of the waters and at their establishment for ever.

141 The same may be said with regard to the peoples, to whom he also assigned their place, Ex. 23:31, Deut. 32:8.

142 See further Chapter 11 below.

VI. National Laments: Psalms 77, 74, 89 (with 87) and 44

The psalms to be considered in the present chapter, Pss. 77, 74, 89 and 44, are all national laments,[1] each of which is characterised by a sense that God has forgotten his promises, renounced his covenant, or even turned against his people, the pain of rejection being articulated in the questions, "How long?",[2] "Why?",[3] and by pleas for God to act in the face of the taunts of neighbouring peoples. Nevertheless, these psalms also frequently provide the context for "calling to mind the deeds of Yah" (Ps. 77:12), a heightened recapitulation of the great acts of deliverance enacted by God on behalf of his people during the formative period of their history, especially in the exodus, and by a recollection of his great promises of old (as in Ps. 89:4-5, 20-38). The incorporation of such retrospective elements simultaneously functions both to express the painful paradox of the contrast between Yahweh's former acts of salvation as set against his present inactivity, and yet also as the basis of its resolution in the hope of a renewal of his חֶסֶד (Pss. 77:16-21; 74:12-17; 44:2-9). This emotionally-charged crisis-situation for Israel's faith and the contrast between God's former great deeds of salvation / victory as compared with his nation's present rejection and defeat also provides the context for some of the most heightened poetic depictions of Yahweh's deliverance of his people "of old", in Ps. 77 this being portrayed in terms of a magnificent theophany and accompanying phenomena, whilst Pss. 74 and 89 provide the contexts for the mention respectively of the "dragon" Leviathan and of Rahab.

All of these psalms would seem to demand a situation of grave national crisis, the experience of defeat and territorial annexation at the hands of the Babylonians in c.587 B.C. being the obvious setting for this. The allusions to the destruction of the Temple in Ps. 74 and to the renunciation of the Davidic covenant in Ps. 89 would seem especially to point in this direction. Nevertheless, this position cannot simply be presupposed, since it has occasionally been maintained on one hand that Pss. 77 and 89 (or sections thereof) are very archaic, or conversely that Ps. 74 hails from the Maccabean

1 Although Psalm 77 appears to take the form of an individual lament, the communal aspect predominates, especially from v. 6. For this reason, probably the most apposite overall designation for the psalm is that of the national lament.

2 Pss. 74:10, 89:47, cf. the Asaph psalms 79:5, 80:5.

3 Pss. 74:1, 11, 44:24, cf. 79:10, 80:13; alternative forms of question occur, e.g., in Pss. 77:8-10, 89:50.

era. It therefore seems necessary to establish the likely background of each of the psalms before addressing issues of interpretation.

1. Psalm 77

i. The Date of Psalm 77

Psalm 77 lacks any clear indication of provenance.[4] However, it is widely assigned to the exilic era.[5] The experience of corporate rejection at the hand of Yahweh which it reflects, entailing a sense of estrangement from him, and precipitating a questioning of his continued power and promise, would seem best to suit this period. This position is supported not only by the depth of the crisis of faith which the disaster has precipitated, but also by indications within the Psalm that the situation has pertained for some time (vv. 8-9, perhaps v. 3).[6] Moreover, it shares many affinities with other communal laments which may with greater confidence be regarded as testifying to the events of 587/6 B.C.[7]

Nevertheless, reference to "Aaron," like that to "Joseph" in v. 16, is sometimes attributed to a northern provenance, the Psalm then commonly being associated with the fall of Samaria.[8] However, whereas in E, Aaron is not presented as the partner of Moses, and sometimes indeed acts in opposition to him, here the two leaders are paired, as perhaps first in Mic. 6:4 and sometimes in Deuteronomic literature or subsequently. Indeed, Aaron only really attains prominence as Moses' helper in post-exilic literature,[9] as is congruent with the exilic dating here advanced. The independence of this pairing from the northern kingdom seems further to be supported by its occurrence in the Book of Psalms only in compositions which are either thought to be post-exilic (Pss. 105, 106) or which, though probably earlier, specifically mention Zion (Pss. 99), whilst the name "Moses" is also, apart from Ps. 77:21, restricted in the

4 An observation made by both Norin (*Er spaltete das Meer*, p. 119) and Weiser (p. 361).

5 So, e.g., the early Kraus (*Psalmen*, 1961, I, p. 530), Norin (*ibid.*, p. 119, 121), Day (*God's Conflict*, p. 187), Hossfeld (HZ, II, p. 406) and Anderson (p. 556), though sometimes the possibility of a post-exilic origin is accepted (thus Kraus, 1989, II, p. 694, and Tate, p. 274).

6 Such questions are very typical of a number of national laments which are commonly dated around the time of the Exile: compare Pss. 74:1, 9-11; 79:5; 44:24-5; 89:47.

7 Some of these have already been adverted to above; others will be explored more fully below. Cf. the comparison made by Hossfeld with the wider corpus of exilic literature (HZ, II, p. 406).

8 Thus Leslie advocates an origin between 733 and 721 B.C. (p. 238), and Goulder, from 732-722 (*PAP*, p. 35), whilst Terrien (p. 557) allows any time during the duration of the northern Kingdom.

9 See T. M. Mauch, "Aaron", *IDB*, I, 1-2.

Psalter to the fourth book.[10] Interest in "Joseph", on the other hand, seems to be a peculiarly Asaphite trait (Pss. 78:67, 80:2, 81:6; cf. 105:17), which is often associated by scholars with the influence of northern traditions. This connection is certainly possible, but since the reference in Ps. 78 seems to betray a Judahite hostility to "the tribe of Ephraim", and as traditions from the north would not have ended with the Kingdom of Samaria, the issue of dating is better resolved on other grounds.[11]

The argument is also sometimes encountered that Ps. 77, especially vv. 17-21, exhibits features which point to an early origin.[12] H. G. Jefferson[13] has attempted to demonstrate that there is a high concentration of words attested in Ugaritic literature in vv. 13-15, 17-20, and of terms featuring in pre-exilic literature in the remainder of the Psalm. From this, she concludes that "the whole psalm may have a pre-exilic date, but there are two sections which seem very early: vv. 17-20 which is related to Ps. xviii 8-16, and vv. 14-16 which is related to Ex. xv 11-13."[14] However, there are serious difficulties in her presentation, since she fails to distinguish between the earliest occurrence of a lexical feature, and its period of use, something which is evidenced by her assumption that the recurrence of a term in Ugarit is demonstrative of its antiquity, irrespective of its attestation in Israel, and by her apparent ignorance of the distinction between "old or Canaanite influenced psalms".[15] This seems to result in the allocation of certain comparative texts which are by no means universally regarded as pre-exilic, to an early period—notably Pss. 89 and 96, both of which she believes (following Albright) to be Canaanite-influenced.[16]

In fact, the supposedly early occurrences of each term only ever constitute a small proportion of the total number of instances, and nowhere is Jefferson able to claim a predominantly early provenance.[17] By contrast, whilst Ps. 77 is

---

10 Besides Pss. 99:6, 105:26, 106:16, in Pss. 90:1, 103:7, 106:23, 32.

11 Cf. Hossfeld and Seybold, who, despite thinking in terms of "a 'northern' background" (Seybold, p. 300, cf. p. 302) or "the continuing effects of traditions of the northern kingdom" (Hossfeld, HZ, II, p. 410), still ultimately attribute an exilic origin to the psalm (Hossfeld, II, p. 406, Seybold, p. 299).

12 See e.g. Dahood, II, p. 224, Albright, "The Psalm of Habakkuk", p. 9.

13 "Psalm LXXVII" *VT* 13 (1963), 87-91.

14 P. 91. One might compare the view that vv. 14-16, 21, and within them, vv. 17-20, constitute insertions of older hymnic material within an exilic psalm (Seybold, pp. 300, 301-2; cf. re vv. 17-20 Hossfeld, HZ, II, p. 405, Gerstenberger, II, p. 90, and Loretz, *UTT*, p. 394). However, note Clifford's arguments in favour of the unity of the composition (II, pp. 38-9) which, together with the structural and verbal analysis of Girard (II, e.g., p. 335) and the thematic links between the respective sections outlined by Hossfeld (*ibid.*, p. 405), provides a strong case against source division.

15 P. 88.

16 Albright, however, in exactly the same context, rightly stresses that "we cannot ... establish any definite correlation at present between the date of a Psalm and its Canaanite content" and acknowledges that sometimes those psalms with "recognizable Canaanite material are undoubtedly post-exilic" (*ARI*, p. 128).

17 She mentions the singular of אֹמֶר, but excludes those occurrences with suffixes, of

lacking in items of vocabulary which are confined either to the pre- or post-exilic eras, there are nevertheless many features which exhibit an overwhelmingly exilic pattern of distribution. In addition, a number of grammatical traits would seem to be inconsistent with an early provenance, thus corroborating Briggs' judgment that it is couched in a "classic" style.[18]

It is occasionally claimed that the employment of tricola (vv. 3, 17-20) is an ancient feature,[19] but, in fact, this structure, which tends to occur rather haphazardly in Ugaritic literature, is attested in a wide variety of biblical poetry,[20] and the ability to sustain it over a series of verses may be a sign of sophistication.[21] More commonly encountered is the perception that the "repetitive" parallelism of vv. 2 and 17 may be indicative of an early provenance. Sometimes, indeed, this seems to be the case (e.g., in Ex. 15:11, Pss. 29, 93:3), but it is not exclusively so (compare, e.g., Pss. 124:1-2, 129:1, Prov. 31:2,4, Eccl. 1:2, Cant. 4: 9, 5:9, 7:1), and in fact the device in both vv. 2 and 17 serves to demarcate a fresh section (the former of which is rarely considered to be especially early). Although the structure of v. 17 may impart an archaic flavour to the depiction of God's ancient act of deliverance, it does not of itself constitute compelling evidence for the antiquity of the verse.

Finally, the relation of Ps. 77 to the texts with which it is rich in affinities, namely Ex. 15, Ps. 18 (= 2 Sam. 22) and Hab. 3, must be taken into account; if a likely dependence should be established (whether operating in one direction or the other), this could be indicative of the time of composition. Such parallels are in fact confined to vv. 14-21, this passage as a whole, as Norin has observed, being particularly reminiscent of Ps. 74 in terms of its structure and blending of apparently deuteronomic, priestly and mythical material.[22] In the case of Ex. 15, the points of contact essentially pertain to the general attributes of Yahweh manifested particularly in ancient times,[23] which are frequently alluded to in a number of deuteronomic and prophetic sources and especially in certain psalms which incorporate reminiscences of the Exodus.[24] It may

---

which many are in Job.

18 II, p. 172 (re vv. 2-16; he considers vv. 17-20 to be very much later, perhaps emanating from the Greek period).

19 Jefferson, p. 87.

20 E.g., Pss. 24:7-10; 119:48, 62, 64, 75, 145, 176; Job 19:29, Nah. 1:11, 3:18a.

21 Cf. Pss. 99:5-9; 100. Admittedly, a series of tricola is encountered also in Ps. 24:7-10, a psalm which is frequently considered to be pre-exilic. However, the rhythm is there maintained primarily by means of close repetition (v. 7 is replicated in v. 9, whilst v. 10 remains close to v. 8), in which little thematic development is shown.

22 *Er spaltete das Meer*, p. 119. Further correspondences between Pss. 74 and 77 are noted by Goulder, *PAP*, p. 97.

23 Relevant correspondences between the two compositions are detailed by Goulder, *PAP*, pp. 103-4, and McCann, *NIB*, IV, p. 984; in addition, the former includes mention of תְּהֹמ(וֹ)ת, and the latter cites further waters imagery, but such points of contact should be attributed to the general context, in each case the specific usage being distinct.

24 E.g., the incomparability of Yahweh (Ps. 77:14; Ex. 15:11) is acclaimed also in Pss. 86:8, 89:7-8, 95:3, 96:4-5 and 97:7, 9; עֹשֵׂה פֶלֶא (Ps. 77:15; Ex. 15:11) occurs in Ps. 78:12 (cf. v. 4); 88:11 (cf. v. 13) and Isa. 25:11; whilst God's rôle as the redeemer of

therefore be concluded that the affinities between Ex. 15 and Ps. 77:14-21 are by no means indicative of an early provenance for the psalm, and indeed would be in keeping with an especial resurgence of interest in Israel's sacred traditions around the time of the Exile. This is particularly supported by the fact that none of the correlations pertain to the central theme of the Red Sea event, and there are radical differences between the content of the miracle in each case, so that it is difficult to imagine how they could have emanated from circles close to each other. Thus, the primary focus of the Song of the Sea is on the drowning of the Egyptians, whereas in Ps. 77, the dominant theme is the crossing of the sea, a distinction which corresponds to that between the two main narrative strands of Ex. 14, usually identified as J and P.[25] Although it is often the case that "P" preserves ancient traditions, in the present instance, it appears that the dividing of the sea constitutes a development of the earlier understanding of the miracle. This would cohere with the view that the Song of the Sea is indeed a poem of possibly quite considerable age, but that Ps. 77 may better be classified among rather later literature.

Correspondences have also been detected between vv. 17-20 and Ps. 18:8, 12-17,[26] whilst vv. 17-18 exhibit such close affinities to Hab. 3:10[27] that, on occasion, they have been employed to reconstruct this prophetic text.[28] However, the only point of contact between the comparative texts themselves, Hab. 3:10 and Ps. 18:8, 12-17, is the expression נתן קוֹל (cf., e.g., Am. 1:2; Jer. 25:30; the same phrase is attested also in *KTU* 1.4.vii.29). This might indicate that they do not stand in common dependence on Ps. 77, but that it may rather

---

Israel (Ps. 77:16; Ex. 15:13) is attested in Ps. 74:2; 78:35, 42, as well as being especially prevalent in Deutero-Isaiah. Likewise, the 'arm' (Ps. 77:16, Ex. 15:16) of Yahweh appears in connection with the Exodus mainly in Deuteronomy, Jeremiah, Deutero-Isaiah and in Pss. 44:4; 79:11; 89:11, 14, 22; 98:1. Moreover, the "leading" of the people like a flock has closer parallels in Pss. 78:52-53a, 80:2 and Isa. 63:11, 13 than in Ex. 15, the relationship between Yahweh and Israel also being expressed in ovine imagery in Pss. 74:1; 79:13; 95:7 and 100:3; whilst references to God's "right hand" (Ps. 77:11; Ex. 15:6, 12) and חֶסֶד (Ps. 77:9; Ex. 15:13) are innumerable. For the correspondences between Ex. 15 and Deuteronomic and other literature, see further Martin L. Brenner, *The Song of the Sea: Ex. 15:1-21* (BZAW 195; Berlin: de Gruyter, 1991).

25 This distinction is observed in relation to the Pentateuch by a number of scholars, e.g., Childs (*The Book of Exodus*, pp. 220-1; see further his summary of scholarship on pp. 218-220), de Vaux (*Histoire ancienne d'Israël*, I, pp. 358-9) and Eakin ("The Reed Sea and Baalism" *JBL* 86 [1967] 378-384, pp. 379-380).

26 See Norin, *Er spaltete das Meer*, p. 120 n. 31, for a comprehensive list.

27 The similarities may be presented as follows:

Ps. 77:17a, b	רָאוּךָ מַּיִם אֱלֹהִים רָאוּךָ מַּיִם יָחִילוּ	Hab. 3:10a	רָאוּךָ יָחִילוּ הָרִים
Ps. 77:18a	זֹרְמוּ מַיִם עָבוֹת	Hab. 3:10b	זֶרֶם מַיִם עָבָר
Ps. 77:18b	קוֹל נָתְנוּ שְׁחָקִים	Hab. 3:10c	נָתַן תְּהוֹם קוֹלוֹ
		cf. Ps. 77:17c	אַף יִרְגְּזוּ תְהֹמוֹת
Ps. 77:18c	אַף־חֲצָצֶיךָ יִתְהַלָּכוּ	Hab. 3:11b	לְאוֹר חִצֶּיךָ יְהַלֵּכוּ

28 As in Gray, p. 132; cf. Wakeman, p. 121. Briggs (II, p. 171) and Duhm (p. 297) commend the opposite direction of dependence.

have drawn independently from one or both of these sources or from material underlying them. This is also perhaps suggested by the extended nature of the theophany depictions in Ps. 18 and Hab. 3, in which those parts displaying similarities to Ps. 77 are in close continuity with the surrounding material, whereas in Ps. 77, as has been noted, there is an evident transition in style and metre in vv. 17-20. It is, further, interesting that the past imperfects in vv. 17-18 have sometimes been seen as isolated indicators of archaic style, despite the fact that the psalm possesses characteristics which tend to militate against an early provenance. This anomaly would, however, be resolved if vv. 17-18 were to be regarded as dependent upon their parallels in Habakkuk, or on material closely underlying both. However, insofar as Hab. 3 is notoriously difficult to date (it may be an earlier independent psalm incorporated into the work of the probably late seventh century prophet), and since the parallels are confined to one verse, which could at one stage have been free-floating,[29] only limited conclusions may be drawn. Nevertheless, if the assessment that Ps. 77 may be dependent on Hab. 3:10 is correct, it would in general corroborate the dating arrived at on other grounds, namely that it is most likely to be a product of the exile or a time close to it.

ii. The Theme of "Chaos" in Psalm 77

It is commonly asserted either that Ps. 77:17-21 constitutes a presentation of God's battle with the waters, such that it is reapplied in "demythologised" form to the deliverance enacted at the Red Sea,[30] or that these verses (or part of them) maintain an active reference to the struggle with chaos at creation.[31] So widely is this type of approach assumed, that nowhere is the rationale behind it articulated, and rarely is evidence offered in its defence.[32] Indeed, the absence

---

29 Cf. the recurrence of the expression of Ex. 15:2 in Ps. 118:14 and Isa. 12:2.

30 E.g., Day (*God's Conflict*, p. 97); Brueggemann (*Israel's Praise*, p. 138); similarly Jeremias (*Theophanie*, p. 95), Gray (*Biblical Doctrine*, p. 71-72).

31 "Creation" is specifically mentioned, e.g., by Gunkel (*Schöpfung*, p. 108), Weiser (*Psalmen*, II, p. 362), Kraus (II, pp. 696-697) and Dahood (II, p. 231), Dahood awarding especial prominence to this theme. The exodus and creation interpretations are sometimes not clearly distinguished, (e.g., Tate, p. 275; von Rad: creation and redemption "can almost be looked on as one act of dramatic divine saving action in the picture of the struggle with the dragon of chaos", *TAT*, I, p. 142).

32 There are only two instances in which I have encountered a direct comparison between an aspect of Ps. 77:17-21 and an extra-biblical text. Jeremias cites Assyrian parallels to the motifs of the trembling of the earth and of the deep before the deity (*Theophanie*, p. 89), but these merely pertain to aspects of *Theophanieschilderungen* and no claim is made in this context with regard to the *Chaoskampf* theme. Similarly, although Dahood mentions *KTU* 1.4.v.8 in connection with a discussion of the content of vv. 17 and 19 (II, pp. 232-233), again the correspondence relates to the depiction of the theophanies of Yahweh and Baal, and it is not of direct relevance to the putative battle with chaos, since the emphasis seems to be placed on Baal's rôle as the provider of rain. More

of supporting data is sometimes almost tacitly acknowledged, for example in von Rad's admission that the Psalm does not actually explicitly draw a connection between *Chaoskampf* and creation,[33] or in the characteristic explanation that here the motif is "demythologised".[34] Nevertheless, I would submit that analysis of the text indicates that "conflict" motifs are absent, and that the entire passage may readily be explained by reference to the *Heilsgeschichte* and storm-theophany traditions, with which the Psalm is rich in allusions.

There seems to be a near-consensus that the Exodus comprises the subject of the debated verses (or at the very least of vv. 20-21),[35] and this interpretation is supported by the fact that vv. 12-16 display various features which are characteristic of hymnic introductions to the recitation of Yahweh's saving acts, whether in structure and content (cf. Pss. 74:2, 12; 89:2-9) or in vocabulary.[36] It is further strengthened by the affinities of the passage to the Song of the Sea (discussed above), whilst the allusion to Moses and Aaron (v. 21) and the image of God leading his people[37] like a flock[38] also cohere particularly closely with the Exodus theme.

Nevertheless, vv. 17-19 do not of themselves self-evidently draw on the traditions of the Red Sea.[39] Rather, the passage seems primarily to derive from the storm-theophany motif, and may be illuminated by comparison with those other texts with which it stands in close relation.[40] Significantly, the "fear" and "trembling" of the waters in v. 17 (cf. the similar types of image in Ps. 114:3, 5, Hab. 3:10) is balanced by the "trembling" and "shaking" of the earth in v. 19 (cf. Ps. 114:4, 6, Hab. 3:10).[41] This distress of the whole cosmos at the

---

importantly, there is no hint of any conflict either in these lines from the Ugaritic tablets or in the broader context in which they are set.

33 *OTT*, I, p. 151, n. 24; not included in the first German edition (p. 155, n. 21).

34 Tate, p. 276; Dahood, II, p. 233, Norin, *Er spaltete das Meer*, p. 120.

35 Though cf. Terrien, pp. 556-7.

36 E.g., "deeds", vv. 12, 13, cf. Pss. 44:2, 4; 66:5; 78:4; 105:1; "wonders", vv. 12, 15, cf. Pss. 78:4; 89:6; Isa. 25:1; "of old", v.12, cf. Ps. 143:5; Isa. 45:21; 46:10; "arm", v. 16, cf. Pss. 44:4; 98:1, and often in Deutero-Isaiah; "redeem", v. 16, cf. Pss. 74:2; 107:2, and often in Deutero-Isaiah.

37 Cf. Pss. 78:14, 52-3; 80:2; 106:9; Isa. 63:13, 14.

38 Cf. Ps. 78:52-3; 80:2; also 74:1; 68:11.

39 Contra Lauha ("Die Geschichtsmotive in den alttestamentlichen Psalmen", p. 68), who considers vv. 18-19 to be the product of a further poetic shaping of the J account (Ex. 14:24). However, the similarities would not be obvious without the benefit of the context to inform the comparison.

40 Namely Hab. 3:3-15; Pss. 18:8-16 (= 2 Sam. 22:8-16); 97:2-5; but also Pss. 29; 46:7; 68:8-10, 33; 99:1; 114; 144:5-7; Judg. 5:4-5; Deut. 33:26-8; and, more loosely, Isa. 30:17-33; 59:15b-20; 63:1-6; Mic. 1:3-4; Nah. 1:3b-6; Zech. 9:14.

41 Indeed, as Hossfeld has recognised (HZ, II, pp. 405, 410), vv. 17-19 may collectively serve to underscore the divine mastery of the whole tripartite cosmos. This Hossfeld defines as primeval waters, i.e., underworld (v. 17), heavenly ocean (v. 18) and circle of the earth (v. 19). However, it may be preferable to think chiefly in terms of phenomena in the visible world of earth, sea and sky, since to envisage the waters of v. 17 as solely subterrestrial may be too restrictive.

divine epiphany is perhaps the most prevalent theophany motif,[42] and is expressed in a variety of forms. Sometimes, indeed, it is applied merely to the "earth" and "mountains"[43] (Pss. 97:4-5; 99:1; 46:7; 68:8f.; Judg. 5:4-5; Mic. 1:4), but often both earth and waters participate in the general woe (Hab. 3:3-15; Ps. 114:3-6;[44] Nah. 1:4-5; cf. Ps. 18:8-16).[45] The same type of imagery is employed also to evoke the "terror" and "dread" of the nations (often in the same context: Pss. 99:1; 46:7; Hab. 3:7; cf. Ex. 15:14[-16]; Ps. 97:3; Isa. 63:1-6; Nah. 1:5; Zech. 9:15) and even of the worshipping community (Ps. 96:9; cf. also Ex. 19:16,18), for it is the fundamental response of creation to the "presence of Yahweh" (Ps. 114:7; when God or his activity is "seen", Pss. 77:17, 97:4, 114:3, Hab. 3:10; or "heard", Ex. 15:14). However, the universality of this reaction, and in particular, the pairing of the "trembling" (רגז) of the deep with that of the earth,[46] seriously undermines Anderson's perception that the deep "was agitated because of its desire to revolt against God, as well as because of awe and fear".[47] Thus, v. 17 seems to fit most

---

42 Jeremias describes this "Aufruhr der Natur" theme as one of the two crucial elements of the original bipartite theophany form (*Theophanie*, p. 151).

43 By contrast, the distraught reaction of the sea is only ever described in conjunction with a terrestrial parallel.

44 However, only the earth is invoked to tremble at the presence of Yahweh in v. 7.

45 This wide biblical attestation of the trembling of the earth at the divine appearance (especially as it often appears in conjunction with the shaking of the mountains) cautions one against following Dahood's proposal that v. 19c should be read "the nether-world quaked and shook" (Dahood, II, p. 232; similarly Gray, *Biblical Doctrine*, p. 73).

46 In fact, the verb רגז is most naturally applied to the earth (Ps. 77:19; 1 Sam. 14:15; Am. 8:8; Joel 2:10) and its mountains (Isa. 5:25; Ps. 18:8 = 2 Sam. 22:8) or to peoples (Ps. 99:1; Ex. 15:14; Hab. 3:7; Joel 2:1; Deut. 2:25; Isa. 64:1; Jer. 33:9). חול (77:17) is likewise often employed in relation to the earth (Pss. 114:7; 97:4; 1 Chr. 16:30; Ps. 96:9), the mountains (Hab. 3:10) and the nations (Deut. 2:25; Joel 2:6; Zech. 9:5; Ezek. 30:16), and even Israel (Jer. 5:22), but not, however to the sea (except, in a rather different context, metaphorically of childbirth, in Isa. 23:4). Jeremias' contention that the substitution of the waters for the mountains as the object of these verbs indicates the fusion of the *Chaoskampf* motif with the theophany portrayal in v. 17 (*Theophanie*, pp. 27-28) is undermined by his own consistent attribution of the terminology of "trembling" to the "Aufruhr der Natur" aspect of the original theophany form; it is further weakened by the fact that the "deeps" are not merely substituted for the earth, but stand in close proximity to it as the object of the same verb, a pattern which is mirrored elsewhere in the Old Testament and in extra-biblical literature (e.g., *AKA* No. 96, Col. 1, l. 3-4).

47 II, p. 560. Similarly dubious is Gray's explication of the "mixture of Canaanite and native tradition" in these verses, since he quotes vv. 17-19b as hailing from "the province of Baal" and vv. 16, 20ab, 21 as relating to the Exodus (*VT* 11 [1961], p. 9), but completely passes over v. 19c, translated by RSV as "the earth trembled and shook". This is surprising, because although Gray assigns to the preserve of Baal "God's victory over the waters and his control of rain, thunder and lightning", he seems to overlook the fact that the quaking of the earth is also associated with the deity's thunder (*KTU* 1.4.vii.31). However, it is only by effecting an artificial division between the theophany

naturally in the context of the divine theophany, and may be explained entirely in this light.[48]

The "pouring out" of the water (v. 18) is likewise an ancient motif associated with the thunderstorm (cf., e.g., Judg. 5:4; Deut. 33:28; Pss. 18:12-13; 68:9, 10; 114:8; Hab. 3:9), and it is employed here despite its absence from the core Red Sea traditions. In its current setting, it takes its place among the other storm phenomena which are described in vv. 18-19 in terminology which bears particularly close similarities to Ps. 18:14-15. However, despite the linguistic resemblances between these passages, their content and rhetorical force must be carefully distinguished. In Ps. 18:15 and its parallel in Ps. 144:6, the meteorological weaponry is explicitly directed against the suppliant's enemies (as represented also by the waters) in an act of purposeful warfare. By contrast, in Ps. 77:18-19, the storm phenomena, and not God as protagonist, comprise the subject of the poetic statements, and any hint of a potential target is excluded. In fact, the only objects affected by the storm in these verses are the תֵּבֵל and הָאָרֶץ, terms which (especially in combination) serve to underscore the generality—and indeed the universality—of the effect of the divine manifestation. It thus becomes apparent that the pouring down of water in v. 18 is a feature of purely meteorological significance, which could perform no practical military function. It rather serves to emphasise the awesome nature of the theophany *per se*, eloquently revealing God's power and presence as he protectively guides his people.[49]

That the thunder and lightning are not here presented as the weaponry of God,[50] but as manifestations of his awesome presence and as an indication of the magnitude of his redemptive action, is further supported by comparison with Ex. 15. In the Song of the Sea, the content of the event is summarised in the claim that "Yahweh has triumphed gloriously. The horse and the rider he has thrown into the sea"; i.e., its essential element is the victory over the Egyptian foe, whereas the crossing of the sea is nowhere unambiguously referred to. By contrast, in Ps. 77:17-21 it is the "path through the waters", Yahweh's protective leadership of his people through the Red Sea, which constitutes the climax of this hymnic section, whilst there is silence on the matter of the routing of the adversary. Yahweh's theophany dramatically reveals his power and imminent, active involvement on behalf of his people, showing forth "the mighty deeds" of the "God who ... hast manifested thy might

---

and the terrified response of the cosmos in this way that the *Chaoskampf* hypothesis may be sustained in relation to Ps. 77:17-21.

48 In addition to the biblical references mentioned above, *KTU* 1.4.vii.28-37, 1.4.v.6-9 may also be compared.

49 Thus, wholly in contravention to the *Chaoskampf* interpretation of vv. 18-19, the thunder and lightning of vv. 18bc and 19ab are framed by reference to the pouring out of water, which is of purely theophanic-meteorological significance (v. 18a), and to the trembling of the earth (v. 19c), whereas no aquatic or marine reaction is recorded.

50 Contrast Mowinckel's contention (*PsSt*, II, p. 250), which is presumably to be understood with reference to the lightning, that in v. 19 "the divine fire consumes the enemies of God".

among the peoples". However, his lightning-arrows fly hither and thither,[51] illuminating the world, rather than homing in on a specific target.

Yet if the psalm is silent on the matter of the routing of the Egyptian foe, mention of the drying or dividing of the sea is also absent (cf. Pss. 78:13; 106:9; 136:13-14). Furthermore, מַיִם (77:17; מַיִם רַבִּים, v. 20) is probably the least mythologically laden term which could have been employed to denote the sea,[52] whilst יָם in v. 20 appears only in its "everyday" sense.[53] This sits uncomfortably with the view that Yahweh is here envisaged as engaging in combat with Yam or his equivalent,[54] as indeed does the quiet pastoral image of an invisible guiding of the flock of Israel through the sea (v. 21).

Nevertheless, the word תְהוֹם (v. 17c) is often considered to be resonant of the primordial chaotic deep with which Yahweh supposedly engaged in combat at creation;[55] sometimes such overtones are imported into translations of the verse.[56] However, if תְהוֹם is a potentially stronger term than its rather colourless parallel מַיִם,[57] it is nevertheless employed of the waters when they are in their weakest state, in a description exposing them in their trembling vulnerability. Thus, if the latent danger of this body of water is at all implied, the allusion is drawn only to be emphatically quashed; what might have been is held up only to highlight with greater intensity the dramatic otherness of what actually was. In reality, however, if all the occurrences of the plural תְּהֹמוֹת are analysed, it emerges that in the majority of cases, it is employed in the context of the Red Sea deliverance (besides Ps. 77:17, in Ex. 15:5, 8; Ps. 106:9; and Isa. 63:13), although in none of these can mythological overtones readily be identified.[58] In Ps. 78:15, the term immediately follows a presentation of the same event, although it more directly alludes to the provision of water in the wilderness, a use with which Deut. 8:7 may also be compared. In addition, it features in a couple of hymnic settings which, again, are devoid of mythological content

---

51 Hithpa'el הלך, a form which often characterises wide-ranging or multi-directional movement; cf. Job 1:7; 2:2; 1 Sam. 30:31; Judg. 21:24.

52 Moreover, as Loretz has already observed in respect of v. 17, this is combined with a lack of characteristic *Chaoskampf* terminology (*UTT*, p. 392). מַיִם רַבִּים (v. 20) is discussed in Chapter 3 above.

53 Thus Norin, *Er spaltete das Meer*, p. 120 (on the basis of the parallelism with מַיִם).

54 In fact, the inclusion of the definite article in the prefixed preposition precludes the interpretation of יָם as a proper name, unless it is to be repointed.

55 See Dahood, II, p. 231, Anderson, p. 560, Kraus, p. 696; such scholars would appear to be guilty of importing notions derived from the Babylonian monster Tiamat whilst often simultaneously disclaiming any direct relation between this figure and the biblical תְהוֹם (note especially Dahood's remarks on p. 231).

56 E.g. Kraus (II, p. 693), Weiser (II, p. 360) and Jeremias (*Theophanie*, p. 26).

57 Interestingly, the term תְהוֹם may have been drawn from Hab. 3:10, a verse to which Ps. 77:17 is very closely related; by contrast, מַיִם occurs where Habakkuk refers to הָרִים.

58 It is stressed by a number of scholars who would advocate the *Chaoskampf* interpretation of Ps. 77 that in the Song of the Sea the conflict occurs at rather than with the sea (e.g., Day, *God's Conflict*, p. 97).

(Pss. 135:6; 148:7), as well as in the hymn to Wisdom in Prov. 8:24. Less promising support for a notion for תְּהֹמוֹת as representative of primordial, uncreated chaos could scarcely be found. The word occurs once again in the context of creation in Prov. 3:20 and, finally, in Ps. 107:26, in a poetic description of the fate of mariners caught in the peaks and troughs of the waves at sea. Therefore, it may be concluded that none of these examples offer any support for the view that some form of battle is implied in Ps. 77:17.

It has nevertheless been proposed[59] that דֶּרֶךְ in v. 20 may retain the overtones of domination which (according to some) may occasionally adhere to the verbal form of that root, Dahood even claiming that "perhaps ... the verbal element of *derek* is more prominent than the nominal". However, the text provides no support for this assertion, as is evidenced by the parallel members ("path" and "footprints"), for which a combative application would be scarcely possible. Moreover, in distinction to contexts where this sense has been claimed, Yahweh's path is here described as being "through" (בְּ) not upon (עַל), still less עַל-בָּמֳתֵי,[60] the sea.

Therefore, it must be concluded that Psalm 77 offers no support for the claim that it constitutes a recollection of a battle with "chaos", howsoever demythologised. God's guidance of his people was indeed a "wonder", a miracle demonstrating the extraordinary fact of his election and protection of Israel, manifested in the fearful spectacle of his storm theophany. But above all, God's epiphany shows forth his power in and over the mightiest forces of creation, so much so that it causes even the sea to tremble and the earth to quake; it also reveals his ability to transgress the natural order in guiding his people through the waters of the Red Sea. Obviously, in such a context, the dangerous aspect of the sea could not be ignored, and the representation of dire distress through the image of encroaching waters (for example, in Ps. 18, with which it has so many resonances), could not be entirely excluded. However, these overtones are not directly implied, and it is the more fundamental aspect of the event—Yahweh's astonishing redemptive power—which is awarded prominence.

2. Psalm 74

i. The Date of Psalm 74

The most obvious *Sitz im Leben* for this psalm is in commemorative ceremonies of lamentation held after the destruction of the Temple on the site of its ruins, or some comparable occasion of great national mourning and defeat,

---

59 By Dahood, II, p. 233, and Wakeman, *God's Battle*, p. 120-121.

60 As in Job 9:8; cf. Deut. 33:29, Am. 4:13, Mic. 1:3, Hab. 3:19.

as reflected in Jer. 41:4-5, Joel 1:13-14, Zech. 7:3-5, 8:19 and 2 Chr. 20:1-19.[61] Here, fasting and ritual expressions of grief would be accompanied by prayers and confessions of national guilt. Interestingly, 2 Chr. 20 incorporates an oracle delivered by "a Levite, one of the sons of Asaph" (2 Chr. 20:14-17; with which compare the title and plaint of v. 9 of the psalm), whilst the prayer of Jehoshaphat in the same context (2 Chr. 20:5-12) presents a number of interesting parallels to the content of the present lament.

As regards the specific occasion which gave rise to Ps. 74, investigators are fortunate that it contains an unusually lengthy description of the situation of plight experienced by the suppliants, who are presumably to be understood as representative of Israel (vv. 3-9, 18-23). Two main situations are proposed: the Fall of Jerusalem in c.587 B.C., and the desecration of the Temple by Antiochus Epiphanes in 167 B.C.[62] The latter is generally favoured by the older commentators,[63] the former by more recent critics.[64] However, even if the psalm was originally composed in the aftermath of the Babylonian victory, it would doubtless subsequently have been reinterpreted in the light of the Jews' later sufferings, particularly during the time of the Maccabees. It is partly in appreciation of this that some scholars have ventured into the precarious task of attempting to identify second century interpolations into an originally exilic psalm.[65]

In fact, the evidence seems to point more directly to an exilic provenance, although—as may be expected from a composition which presumably remained in use until the formation of the canon and beyond—it contains nothing which is jarringly inconsistent with the Maccabean era. The destruction (v. 3; perhaps

---

61 Nevertheless, a radical "Myth and Ritual" hypothesis has been put forward by F. Willesen (*VT* 2 [1952], pp. 289-306), who suggested that the situation of distress is purely a product of the cult, and that the psalm should therefore be located in an annual ritual involving the profanation and purification of the Temple during the course of the New Year Festival. This is not a view which has attracted much support. Compare also Bouzard's analogy with the use of Mesopotamian *balag* / *eršemma* texts at the demolition of temples prior to renovation and "as a means of pacifying the gods over unknowingly committed offenses" (*We Have Heard with Our Ears*, p. 207; cf. pp. 174-180).

62 A few other possible *Sitze im Leben* have been advocated by a minority of scholars, among them the pillaging and burning of the shrine at Bethel during the invasions of 732-722 (Goulder, *PAP*, p. 63), a conjectural attack on Jerusalem by Orophernes, a general of Artaxerxes Ochus in 344 B.C. (Buttenwieser, pp. 609-612) and an Edomite destruction of Jerusalem in c. 485 B.C. (J. Morgenstern, *HUCA* 27 [1956], 101-79, especially pp. 130-1).

63 E.g., Gunkel, *Die Psalmen*, p. 322, Wellhausen, pp. 194-5; this view may be traced back to the Targum, in which נָבָל in v. 18 is rendered "the mad king", apparently in allusion to Antiochus Epiphanes, who was dubbed by his opponents Epimanes, "madman".

64 E.g. Kraus, II, pp. 678-9, Seybold, p. 287, Mowinckel, *PIW* II, p. 152, Terrien, p. 538, Spieckermann, *Heilsgegenwart*, p. 126.

65 E.g., Briggs, II, p. 150.

v. 7b) and igniting (v. 7a) of the Temple would clearly be most consonant with the events of c.587 B.C. (2 Ki. 24:13; 25:9, 13-17; cf. 2 Ki. 18:16), rather than with the actions of Antiochus Epiphanes some four hundred years later, which may have involved plunder and damage to the interior of the building (1 Macc. 1:21-24; 4:38; 2 Macc. 5:16, 21; 8:33), but still required that the Temple be left sufficiently complete for the "desecrating sacrilege" of the statue of the Greek god-king to be erected in the sanctuary (1 Macc. 1:44-50, 54; 2:7, 12b; 2 Macc. 8:2, 17).

It is nevertheless sometimes objected that the silence of the lament on the matter of the Exile seriously damages the case for a sixth century authorship.[66] However, it must be countered, firstly, that the argument from silence, especially regarding a composition couched in condensed poetic form, is a weak one. The section describing the historical situation requiring Yahweh's urgent intervention comprises a series of "snapshots" centred around the Temple itself and the actions performed against it, rather than being directly concerned with the unfolding of a longer chain of political developments and their consequences. The focus is primarily, if not always explicitly, on the indignity perpetrated against Yahweh himself and his need to restore his "name" in the face of such assaults on his Temple. Furthermore, if the lament was composed by those left behind in "the land", it would not be entirely surprising if the removal of their former leaders who had led them into disaster is not recalled as one of the worst features of Jerusalem's fall. Nevertheless, the exile could perhaps be reflected (remotely) in v. 9bc, especially 9c.[67] That the psalm was composed by the "remnant" in Jerusalem is perhaps indicated also by v. 20, which should most naturally be translated as referring to the "dark places of the land".[68]

Sound evidence may also be advanced against specific interpretative points adduced in support of Maccabean dating;[69] perhaps most damaging to this

---

66 E.g., by Gunkel, *Die Psalmen*, p. 322, Goulder, *PAP*, p. 62; see also Wellhausen, p. 194; Gunkel advances the same argument in regard to the destruction of the whole of Jerusalem, p. 322. Of course, not everyone considers that the Psalm is silent on the matter of the deportation to Babylon; see Briggs (II, pp. 154, 157 re vv. 8a, 20).

67 Amongst the great prophets of the Exile, Jeremiah was carried off to Egypt and Deutero-Isaiah evidently wrote in Babylon among the Exiles, this being the location also for the visions of Ezekiel.

68 This is commonly understood as a reference to fugitives' hiding places, where "the enemies have perpetrated their violence by slaughtering the helpless refugees" (Anderson, II, p. 546; thus also Cohen, p. 240, Weiser, p. 352, Kraus, II, p. 676).

69 E.g., אֹתוֹת in v. 4b most probably refers to military standards, rather than constituting a veiled (and somewhat obscure) allusion to the statue of Zeus. Similarly, v. 8b need not refer to synagogues, since the completeness of Josiah's reform can hardly be presupposed (cf., e.g., 2 Ki. 23:9, 1 Macc. 2:1, 3:46). In any case, the Hebrew מוֹעֲדֵי may be understood as referring to the *times* rather than *places* of meeting, and this interpretation is supported by the versions (LXX, Targ., Syriac). Finally, rather than reflecting a situation when it was accepted that prophecy had ceased (cf. 1 Macc. 4:46,

position is the reality that the Psalter must have been complete some time before the Qumran psalm texts were created in the first century B.C., and thus it is unlikely that the book, and perhaps especially a composition embedded at almost its exact midpoint, should contain material from so late a period. More generally, it must be allowed that, although assaults upon Jerusalem and especially upon the Temple treasures were not confined to any particular era,[70] c.587 B.C. is the only occasion for which there is evidence for the complete destruction of the building itself.

The linguistic data offered by the psalm would seem to cohere with this conclusion, since, like Ps. 77, its language seems in general to be attested throughout a broad chronological range. Quite distinctively, however, it seems to include a few elements of vocabulary which would seem to be predominantly pre-exilic or exilic[71] and others which are generally exilic or post-exilic,[72] and this would seem further to confirm a median (i.e., exilic) date. Furthermore, the intertextual evidence provided by its points of contact with Lamentations and Psalm 79 (vv. 6-7 of which are in turn "quoted" in Jer. 10:25, whilst the rare phrase "the sheep of your pasture" recurs outside Pss. 74:1 and 79:13 in Jer. 23:1) would seem consonant with this conclusion.[73]

The thesis that Ps. 74 most probably reflects the destruction of the Temple by the Babylonians therefore seems to be one of the firmer conclusions in the dating of the Psalms. However, that it is not absolutely specific in its present intention, and may have been subject to modifications in transmission, should be recognised. Finally, the dating in relation to c.587 B.C. also requires further clarification. Since there are a number of allusions suggesting that the ruination of the Temple has pertained for some time (vv. 1, 3, 9) it appears not to have

---

9:27, 14:41), v. 9b clearly constitutes a cry of desolation, articulating a feeling of alienation from God, comparable with Lam. 2:9 and Ezek. 7:26. Indeed, the verse is perhaps best illuminated by comparison with 2 Chr. 20:14-19, which demonstrates the expectation that on the occasions when the nation "assembled to seek help from Yahweh" (2 Chr. 20:4) an oracle may be given offering consolation or advice; the absence of such a response from God would no doubt have been a particular source of grief.

70 E.g., 1 Ki. 14:25-26 (Egypt); 15:18 (Syria); 2 Ki. 14:13-14 (Israel); 16:8 (Assyria); 24:11, 13 (Babylon).

71 E.g., קַרְדֹּם (v. 5, which occurs elsewhere only in 1 Sam. 13:20, 21, Judg. 9:48, Jer. 46:22) and אֵיתָן, "perennial", of flowing water, which is exclusive to Ps. 74:15, Am. 5:24, Ex. 14:27 (J), Deut. 21:4, cf. 1 Ki. 8:2.

72 E.g., תַּנִּין as a "dragon" or "great sea-creature", which occurs in v. 13, Gen. 1:21 (P), Isa. 27:1, 51:9, Jer. 51:34, Ezek. 29:3, 32:2, Ps. 148:7, Job 7:12, Neh. 2:13. Note also the distribution of לִוְיָתָן, which is peculiar to v. 14, Isa. 27:1, Job 3:8, 40:25, Ps. 104:26; and that of מָאוֹר as a "luminary" (not of eyes as a lamp), v. 16, which features five times in Gen. 1:14-16 (P) and in Ezek. 32:8; it also occurs with the meaning "lamp" frequently in P.

73 See further Hunter, p. 147, who emphasises also the significance of this Psalm's location in the third book of the Psalter, which, "taken as a unity in some significant sense", would seem to have "a particular *raison d'être* in the context of the immediate post-exilic period." If correct, this observation would impact similarly on the dating of Pss. 77 and 89, also considered in the present chapter.

been composed in the immediate aftermath of the Fall of Jerusalem.[74] Thus Briggs suggests an origin for the psalm prior to Deutero-Isaiah but subsequent to Ezekiel,[75] whilst Kraus locates it "closer to the year 520 than the year 587".[76] In any case, a date of composition within, but not necessarily in the latter part of, these limits is to be preferred.

ii. The Theme of "Chaos" in Psalm 74

Structurally, the hymnic middle section in which the putative "chaos" imagery occurs (vv. 12-17) has a pivotal rôle: prior to it, the petitions are cast in terms of Yahweh's rejection of his people, and there is much insistence on the activity of the foe. However, it is only after the hymnic recollection of vv. 12-17 that, in the longest supplicatory section of the psalm (vv. 18-23), Yahweh is finally called upon to act. This progression is especially evident in the transformation of the primary structural markers which likewise pivot around vv. 12-17, particularly conspicuous being the rhetorical adaptation of the linguistic data framing the hymnic core of the psalm from v. 10 to v. 18. The mere request to God to "remember" his people in v. 2 is similarly transformed into an urgent plea for action: "remember ... how the enemy scoffs, and an impious people reviles thy name" (v. 18), whilst "the foe" and "the enemy" (vv. 10, 18) finally become "thy foes", "thy adversaries" (v. 23).

Yet besides having a pivotal rôle within the structure of the psalm as a whole, the central hymnic section vv. 12-17 is also one of the most crucial texts in any study of "chaos" imagery in the Psalms or, indeed, in the entire Old Testament, since here the myth of Yahweh crushing the dragon is alluded to more explicitly than anywhere else in the Psalter. In addition, the passage is distinguished by containing one of the two allusions to Leviathan in the collection (the other being in Ps. 104:26), as well as by the considerable debate surrounding its interpretation. Its significance has characteristically been understood in terms of the polarity: does it allude to Yahweh's slaying of a "chaotic" dragon in order to bring creation into being,[77] or to his salvific action during the events of the Exodus and wilderness wanderings,[78] or perhaps to both?[79]

---

74 This would further explain the (possible) silence of the psalm on the matter of the Exile.

75 II, p. 152.

76 II, p. 679.

77 This possibility was propounded by Gunkel, primarily on the basis of the putative dependence of the section on Babylonian precedents (*Schöpfung und Chaos*, p. 42-5, *Die Psalmen*, pp. 321, 324-5), and has subsequently been maintained, e.g., by Schmidt (p. 142), Lauha (*Die Geschichtsmotive*, p. 13), Emerton ("'Spring and Torrent' in Psalm LXXIV" VT[S] 15 [1966], pp. 122-3, 130-3), Lelièvre ("YHWH et la mer dans les psaumes", *RHPR* 56 [1976], pp. 256-63), and Seybold (p. 289).

78 This option is attested in the Targum and Rashi (Gruber, p. 342), but has been

The first principle to be established is that the section which has become the focus of attention must be interpreted within the context of the psalm as a whole. Certainly it seems that creation is alluded to in vv. 16-17. The important issue, however, is how these verses cohere with what precedes. It is unacceptable simply to assume that since an act of creation seemed to ensue from Marduk's defeat of Tiamat, the same causal connection must automatically pertain here. This is not least because of the absence of any such link in the Ugaritic texts,[80] and indeed in the biblical material examined so far,[81] but more importantly because of the general methodological unsoundness of making such an assumption. Likewise to be treated with caution is John Day's statement that "since we have other passages in which the creation is associated with a conflict between Yahweh and the primordial sea or with Yahweh's control of the sea, e.g., Ps. 104:6-9, Job 38:8-11, Prov. 8:29" and "since this sea could be personified by the dragon (e.g., Is. 51:9-10), it is only natural to suppose that we similarly have a conflict with the dragon at the time of creation here".[82] The psalms considered so far, which pertain only to Yahweh's dealings with the sea, and which include all of those which may with any degree of confidence be dated prior to Ps. 74, yield no picture of a combat with chaos or resultant act of creation. Moreover, it is not clear that the dragon and the sea should be identified;[83] hence, the conclusion which Day draws is itself somewhat dubious. It therefore seems to be mistaken to assume that "creation" is the original and normative context in which this type of imagery may be attested, and in the light of which all other occurrences must, if possible, be interpreted. More importantly, in the texts to which Day appeals (Ps. 104:6-9, Job 38:8-11, Prov. 8:29), although the confining and assigning to limits of the sea is indeed seen as part of the process of creation, the relation between the two is not—as in the putative myth—sequential; rather, the containment of the

---

advocated in modern times, e.g., by Franz Delitzsch (pp. 538-9), König (pp. 350-1, 670-1), Heidel (*The Babylonian Genesis*, p. 109), Norin (*Er spaltete das Meer*, pp. 112-114) and Briggs (II, pp. 152, 155).

79 A dual signification has been perceived here by Kraus (II, p. 681), Weiser (p. 354), Girard (II, pp. 303-4, 310) and Kissane (II, pp. 9, 15); cf. also Hunter, pp. 152-4.

80 The claim that the defeat of Leviathan should be associated with creation (e.g., by Day, *God's Conflict*, p. 23, Oesterley, II, p. 348, Anderson, II, p. 543) is a misconception which substantially derives from the transposition of the conclusions of Gunkel's study of the Babylonian myth *Enuma elish* (*Schöpfung und Chaos*, 1895) onto both the Ugaritic Baal epic and the Old Testament. A manifest difficulty for the creation interpretation of the Ras Shamra material is that El is normally presented as the high god and creator within the Canaanite pantheon. Even in the Baal tablets, he appears to perform a balancing role in relation to the warring younger gods, so that a semblance of order is maintained. Moreover, no mention of the cosmogonic process occurs in the extant Baal texts, and it seems particularly unlikely that this consequence should adhere in relation to the relatively marginal combat with Ltn, as opposed to the more substantial conflicts against Mot and Yam.

81 Not that this should of itself become an informing interpretative principle, either; cf. Norin, *Er spaltete das Meer*, p. 112.

82 *God's Conflict*, p. 23.

83 As Day himself admits, p. 14.

waters is one among many acts of ordering performed by God within (and not prior to) the creative process. This is not depicted in terms of the crushing of a dragon, the image which is attested in Ps. 74. Nor can the works of separation encountered here accurately be described as combat; hence even Day speaks in terms of "Yahweh's conflict with or control of the primordial sea".[84] In fact, it seems rather to be implied in these texts that the deeps and seas are created (Prov. 8:28, Ps. 104:5-6, Job 38:8-9).

In Psalm 74, a situation within historical time, i.e., subsequent to creation, seems to be presupposed, as is indicated by the allusions to יְשׁוּעוֹת בְּקֶרֶב הָאָרֶץ (v. 12)[85] and to עָם לְצִיִּים (v. 14). Day's assertion that the latter "need not imply that the battle occurred after Yahweh's effective work of creation had taken place"[86] evidently requires clarification before it may be considered as a serious possibility. On the other hand, there is an undeniable representation of some of Yahweh's acts of establishing and fixing the cosmic order in vv. 16-17, and the sequence of these verses from vv. 12-13 certainly needs to be explained. It may therefore provisionally be observed that v. 12 has a present orientation: the allusion may be to Yahweh's continual nature and acts beginning in primordial time, but the focus remains on the current situation of need. A similar transitional and retrospective function is performed also by v. 16, where the reflection לְךָ יוֹם אַף־לְךָ לָיְלָה leads into a recollection of Yahweh's creative acts. Moreover, the primary interest is clearly not on the event of creation, but on the deity's lordship over space, time and seasons, and on the resultant firmness and order,[87] which provide hope in the present situation. It therefore appears from the structure and phrasing of vv. 16-17 that these lines may be logically rather than chronologically sequential to vv. 12-15, and that v.

84 *God's Conflict*, p. 3.

85 As will be indicated further below, mention of salvation seems to presuppose the existence of a beneficiary (and this applies even where the sense "victory"—not even listed in *DCH*—may be applicable); hence the plea that הָאָרֶץ could be employed to denote the earth in its pre-created state, as in Gen. 1:2, is of limited relevance.

86 *God's Conflict*, p. 23.

87 Notice the concern with "boundaries" (v. 17a) and polarities (day and night, summer and winter), and in "fixing" (v. 17a) and "establishing" (v. 16b). For the interest in the polarities of creation, compare especially Jer. 31:35-36a, where its "fixed order" is enunciated in similar terms to Ps. 74:16 (cf. also v. 15); and Gen. 8:22, where the same concern is evident in the mention of "summer and winter, day and night". The aspect of powerful control over day and night, waters and constellations is further illustrated, e.g., by Am. 5:8. Moreover, although Hiph. נצב is not elsewhere applied to the creation of the natural world, the phrase יַצֵּב גְּבֻלֹת עַמִּים in Deut 32:8 resonates closely with Ps. 74:17a (אַתָּה הִצַּבְתָּ כָּל־גְּבוּלוֹת אָרֶץ: possibly as an equivalent expression); the context is again an appeal for action based on the historic relationship between Yahweh and his people (here addressed to Israel) and wrought in the aftermath of the same or a similar disaster. The correlation of language between Deut. 32:6c-9 and Ps. 74:2, 16-17 is especially notable and may be indicative of a common circle of ideas.

16 may hark back to or continue the thought of v. 12a.[88] This would certainly cohere with the rhetorical focus of the psalm, in which Yahweh's kingship and salvific acts performed "of old" are painfully contrasted with his present inactivity, and appeal made on this basis for him to intervene to resolve the current crisis.[89]

Thus, it emerges that the psalm may only properly be understood when it is considered as a unit. In fact, if vv. 12-17 are to be interpreted sensitively, it must first be recognised that appeal has already subtly been made to Israel's "special relationship" with God, forged at the Red Sea, in vv. 1-2. Indeed, at the heart of the psalm is the paradox that Yahweh, her God who had from the beginning manifested himself in great deeds of deliverance, and had subsequently been relied upon to protect her, had now "cast us off" (v. 1a). Hence, Yahweh's protective activity, fundamentally revealed at the Exodus, through which he effectively became Israel's God and they his people, is invoked in the opening section of the poem. This is achieved especially through the terminology of "the sheep of thy pasture" (v. 1), "gotten / acquired" (קָנָה, v. 2a)[90] and "redeem" (גאל, v. 2b), all of which allude powerfully to this essential tenet of the Hebrew faith, as an examination of the applications of these motifs shows.

The pastoral image of Yahweh as the shepherd of Israel (v. 1b) is encountered primarily in relation to the Exodus and wilderness wanderings (cf. Pss. 77:21; 78:52-53a), and often, as here, it forms the basis of an appeal for deliverance, as in two other Asaph communal lament psalms, Pss. 79:13 and 80:2.

The "getting" (קָנָה) of the congregation "of old" (v. 2a) likewise "[refers] to the Exodus from Egypt and entrance into the Holy Land".[91] The Song of

---

88 See similarly Podella, "Der 'Chaoskampfmythos' im Alten Testament: Eine Problemanzeige" in M. Dietrich and O. Loretz, *Mesopotamia—Ugaritica—Biblica* (AOAT 232; Kevelaer: Butzon & Bercker; Neukirchen-Vluyn: Neukirchener Verlag, 1993) 283-329, pp. 306-7.

89 One might compare the frequent appeal to creation made by Deutero-Isaiah as a basis for hope in God's salvation, the sequence of thought from (new) exodus to creation being apparent in 40:11-12, 51:11-13. (On Isa. 51:9-11, see further Chapter 11 below).

90 This is the commonest meaning of the term in biblical contexts, often with the sense "purchase": cf., e.g., Ex. 15:16, 21:2, Isa. 11:11, 24:2, Ps. 78:54, Prov. 1:5. For Ugaritic *qny* as "possess, acquire", cf. *KTU* 1.19.iv.58, and see e.g. Cunchillos, "Peut-on parler de mythes de création à Ugarit?" in L. Derousseaux (ed.), *La Création dans L'Orient Ancien*, 79-96, p. 87 and references there.

91 Briggs, II, p. 152. This is a very widely held opinion: see also Kissane, II, p. 12, Cohen, p. 236, Hunter, p. 150, Goulder, *PAP*, p. 64, Spieckermann, *Heilsgegenwart*, p. 128, all of these scholars further recognising the same sphere of allusion in the verb גאל, whilst Spieckermann adds the statement that "קדם 'primeval time' is the time of the Exodus"; קָנָה is also interpreted in relation to the exodus, e.g., by P. Humbert, "'Qânâ' en Hébreu Biblique" in Baumgartner, W., et al. (edd.), *Festschrift Alfred Bertholet* (Tübingen: J. C. B. Mohr, 1950), p. 260, Weiser, p. 353, and Oesterley, II, p. 348, contra Kraus, II, p. 679.

the Sea may particularly be compared here, since the verb קנה in Ex. 15:16 is merely one of many elements from the terminological cluster appearing also in Ps. 74:2-3. There too it appears in conjunction with "the people whom thou hast redeemed" (Ex. 15:13, cf. Ps. 74:2b) and with allusions to the "sanctuary" and parallel terms (Ex. 15:13, 17, cf. Ps. 74:2c, 3ff.). Similarly, the context of קנה in v. 54 of the Asaphite Psalm 78 is unmistakably in reference to the exodus and settlement, with further thematic points of contact with Ps. 74 occurring in the motifs of the people as "sheep" led by God (78:52, cf. 74:1b), the "holy land" (גְּבוּל קָדְשׁוֹ, v. 54a; cf. "sanctuary" [קֹדֶשׁ], 74:3b) and "mountain" (v. 54b; cf. "Mount Zion", 74:2c), and the activity of Yahweh's "right hand" (יָמִין, 78:54b; cf. 74:11).[92] Indeed, in support of this interpretation of Ps. 74:2, even the verb which opens this verse, זכר, "remember", invokes a previously-existing relationship and harks back to the election traditions.

For Exodus as redemption (v. 2b), simply note the many references in BDB I. גאל Qal 3.b.,[93] which relate to the deliverance of "Israel, from Egyptian bondage".[94] In fact, the verb is only otherwise used of God as subject in relation to individuals, so the Exodus remains the sole supported referent of the allusion here.

Finally, the mention of Mount Zion in v. 2c continues the same pattern of Yahweh acquiring, redeeming and leading his flock, and bringing them to his holy mountain, as seen especially in Ex. 15. It is the culmination of his redemptive acts manifested from the Exodus through to the entry into the land. This particular colon also simultaneously acts as a bridge into the enunciation of Israel's predicament in vv. 3-11, which is centred on the Temple, traditionally the special focus of his protection.

It is thus evident that the Exodus is stated as an opening theme in the psalm, and is of crucial theological importance to the suppliant. Moreover, although a description of the present predicament is interposed in vv. 3-11, this initial appeal to Yahweh's former acts of salvation is resumed again in vv. 12-17. Thus, logically and structurally, the central hymnic passage under particular consideration here must be understood as a continuation of the initial plea of vv. 1-2.[95] Even more importantly, the link between vv. 1-2 and 12-17 is apparently cemented by the complaints of vv. 9, 11 that "we do not see our signs" and "you hold back your hand... keep your right hand in your bosom", since they

---

92 One might compare also Isa. 11:11, where the verb קנה is employed of Yahweh "recover[ing] the remnant which is left of his people" in the second exodus, and. 32:6-7, where Israel is invoked to "remember the days of old"(v. 7a, cf. Ps. 74:2a) and described as Yahweh's "heritage" (v. 9, cf. Ps. 74:2b) in a passage concerned with the gift of the land.

93 P. 145.

94 Cf. also c. "from exile".

95 See further the structural correspondence discerned by Girard between the historical retrospectives of vv. 2 and 20aα, which are focused on the exodus and covenant formation, and that of vv. 12-17 (II, pp. 309-310).

seem to reverse the Deuteronomic "manifesto" of the Exodus, according to which this event was accomplished with "signs and wonders, the mighty hand, and the outstretched arm" (Deut. 7:19; cf. 26:8, 5:15, Ex. 6:6). Hence God's great deeds of power manifested in the exodus events are called to mind directly before the hymnic recollection of vv. 12-17.[96]

This section itself is introduced by a declaration of faith: "Yet God my king is from of old, working salvation in the midst of the earth" (v. 12), which is a classical example of a confessional introduction to a recitation of the salient events of the *Heilsgeschichte*. This is immediately apparent, firstly, on the basis of its position within the structure of the psalm: a recitation of Yahweh's mighty acts of deliverance is typical of communal lament psalms, and naturally follows on from the description of the suppliants' plight and their questioning pleas for aid.[97] But it is also evidenced by the formulation of the verse. Note the opening "(וְ)אַתָּה"[98] and the traditional idioms מֶלֶךְ, מִקֶּדֶם and יְשׁוּעָה. Yet it is also couched in a sufficiently general language of hymnic declaration that it almost demands clarification in the following lines. Of course, primary among the "salvation-working" enacted by God on behalf of his people was the Exodus, a theme which has already been exposed in v. 2. However, even without recourse to its context, the following clause, v. 13a, "Thou didst divide the sea by thy might" (cf. Ex. 14:21), is manifestly resonant with the Exodus tradition.[99] Therefore, it is almost impossible to deny that its subject is the crossing of the Red Sea.

Likewise, the cleaving open of springs and brooks and drying up of ever-flowing streams (v. 15) recall the traditions of the provision of water in the wilderness (Ex. 17:6; Num. 20:8; Pss. 78:15, 16, 20; 105: 41; Isa. 48:21; and probably also Ps. 114:8)[100] and descriptions of the entry into the land across the Jordan (Josh. 3:16-17; 4:23; 5:1; cf. the Red Sea crossing, Ex. 14:21-22, 29; Josh. 2:10, 4:23)[101], and so they naturally flow on from the allusion to the

---

96 The thought may then continue beyond this hymnic recollection to the appeal to the covenant in v. 20, since, as Hunter has indicated (p. 150), its formation at Sinai/Horeb constituted the consummation of the drama of the exodus; this interpretation is supported also by the structural observations of Girard summarised in the previous note.

97 Hence there is a "theological expectation[] postulating the exodus tradition" as the subject of reference in this section (Gerstenberger, II, p. 78) even before it is realised.

98 To be assumed on the basis of the phraseology of the following verse, and conjecturally added in *BHS* footnote and by many commentators (e.g., Gunkel, *Die Psalmen*, p. 320, Anderson, II, p. 543, Kraus, II, pp. 676, 677, 681, Day, *God's Conflict*, pp. 21, 24). That v. 12 introduces a new section is also indicated by the change of person.

99 The same sphere of allusion pertains if one follows Greenfield's translation of פּוֹרַרְתָּ, "you made flee", based on the Ugaritic *prr* (*KTU* 1.19.iii.14, 28), as this is comparable with Ps. 114:3, 5, which also refers to the Exodus ("*'attā pōrartā bĕ'ozkā yam* [Ps. 74:13a]" in Balentine and Barton [edd.], *Language, Theology and the Bible*, 113-119, p. 118).

100 Thus Briggs (II, p. 155), Cohen (p. 239) and Weiser (p. 354).

101 Cf. also Isa. 19:5; Jer. 51:36; Joel 1:20; Zech. 10:11; an allusion to the fording of the

Exodus. However, it also leads into the thought of Yahweh's power over the extremities of creation: he both provides fresh sources of water and dries up existing streams,[102] just as he is lord also of day and night, summer and winter (vv. 15-17). Nevertheless, Emerton's interpretation of the verse,[103] which entails that the springs and brooks are opened to provide drainage to remove water from the face of the earth at creation, whilst the drying up of ever-flowing streams constitutes a further assault upon the powers of chaos represented by Leviathan and the sea, is difficult to justify. In particular, there is no indication that springs (מַעְיָן) could be considered capable of draining water away in the opposite direction from their wonted flow: it is fundamental to their nature that they bring water up. This distinction seems to be evident in the apocryphal flood narratives which Emerton cites in support of his interpretation, since in each case it is said that "abysses", rather than "springs", open up to drain the water away. It is also debatable whether the mechanism by which the waters were removed from the surface of the earth was an issue given even transitory consideration in exilic Israel, or whether it would be conceived of in such a technical way. Certainly the process described by Emerton seems to be at variance with the biblical record, which is consistent in painting a picture of command and compliance (Prov. 8:29, Job 38:10-11, Gen. 1:9, Ps. 104:7-9; cf. Ps. 33:6-9), the movements described in Ps. 104:8 being especially incompatible with his portrayal.[104] Further, if מַעְיָן וָנָחַל are "springs" and "wadies, streams", as acknowledged by Emerton,[105] נַהֲרוֹת אֵיתָן should also most naturally refer, not to "the currents of the cosmic ocean", but to inland waterways. This, in fact, is the most usual sense for נְהָרוֹת, but, more importantly, where נְהָרוֹת (or נָהָר in Jon. 2:4) is applied to "cosmic currents", it seemingly always occurs in conjunction with the sea or deep, which does not happen here.[106] In any case, although אֵיתָן is meaningfully applied to rivers to

Jordan is recognised here by Cohen (p. 239), Briggs (II, p. 155) and Weiser (p. 354), and to both the Red Sea and Jordan crossings by Kissane (II, p. 15). Spieckermann also acknowledges the exodus reference of v. 15 (*Heilsgegenwart*, p. 130), but since he relates vv. 13a, 14a (deleting vv. 13b and 14b as secondary, *ibid*, p. 125) to a primeval divine conflict (*ibid*, p. 130), he is left with what he himself describes as a "strange sequence" in vv. 12-17 (*ibid*, p. 131), so this is scarcely satisfactory.

102 Similarly also, e.g., Kloos, *Yhwh's Combat*, p. 80.

103 "'Spring and Torrent" in Psalm LXXIV 15" in *VT[S]* 15 (1966) 122-133.

104 Of course, still further to be distinguished are the traditions which speak of the sea as made by God (Pss. 95:5, 146:6, 148:5; cf. Prov. 8:28), so that it broke forth (Prov. 3:20, of the deeps) or came to birth (Job 38:8-9), the earth then either temporarily being clothed with the deep (Ps. 104:6), or being spread out (Ps. 136:6) or founded (Ps. 24:2) on the waters / seas (cf. also Prov. 8:27b, עַל־פְּנֵי תְהוֹם).

105 *Ibid.*, p. 127.

106 In Isa. 44:27, mention is explicitly made of the נְהָרוֹת of the deep; in Ps. 24:2, the term stands in parallel to יַמִּים, and in Jon. 2:4, parallel to מְצוּלָה and לְבַב יַמִּים; the loosest connection occurs in Ps. 93:3, where, following the theme of the foundation of the world (i.e., implicitly on the sea, v. 1c), reference is made to נְהָרוֹת in each of the verse's three colons, with מַיִם רַבִּים and מִשְׁבְּרֵי־יָם then occurring in v. 4ab. A similar sphere of allusion is also sometimes claimed for Pss. 89:26 and 46:5, where, however,

indicate a consistent flow (cf. Am. 5:24, Deut. 21:4), thus distinguishing them from the variable wadies, the term has no such relevance to the sea. The only exception is in the extraordinary event of the Red Sea crossing, where in Ex. 14:27, it is stated that the sea "returned to its wonted flow" (לְאֵיתָנוֹ), with אֵיתָן thus denoting a norm for הַיָּם but, as might be expected, not qualifying it directly. Moreover, Emerton's reconstruction is founded on the explicit presupposition that the passage must refer to a hostile act by God against the waters enacted in primordial times; in other words, he begins with the conclusion, and then attempts to devise a means of moulding the Masoretic text into his framework, even when this is achievable only on the basis of general comparisons with post-biblical material not concerned directly with creation. However, his proposal cannot be upheld on the basis of normal Hebrew usage.[107]

Thus the results of the foregoing analysis indicate that the events of the *Heilsgeschichte* are clearly invoked in v. 12, and further alluded to in the succeeding verses. By contrast, in the context of the present psalm (and indeed in the historical traditions as a whole), it is particularly doubtful whether creation is to be regarded as among these crucial saving deeds.[108] After all, יְשׁוּעָה "suggests vindication of faith and release from suffering as well as victory over enemies".[109] The assumption behind 74:12 is that Yahweh, as

---

this is doubtful (see thereon below and in Chapter 5 respectively), but in any case the same close connection with the sea is again discernible. The pairing is also strongly attested in Ugaritic, classically in the description of the abode of El (*KTU* 1.3.v.6-7, 1.4.iv.21-22) and in the title of Yam (*KTU* 1.2.i.8-9, 16, 21, 23, etc.); cf. also *KTU* 1.3.vi.5-6, 1.4.ii.6-7.

107 The difficulty of sustaining a thoroughgoing *Chaoskampf* interpretation throughout this section is further illustrated by Anderson's discussion. Regarding v. 15b, he offers little more than a general assertion that "the allusion is to the mythical rivers", referring to Ps. 46:5, and notes that נָהָר corresponds to the Ugaritic *nhr*, a title of Yam, thus implying the continuation of the putative combat theme here (II, p. 545). However, this type of signification is, of course, excluded in the present verse by the use of the plural and qualification by אֵיתָן, whilst the fruitful rivers of Ps. 46 have entirely different connotations as a "symbol of God's presence", as his discussion of them shows (I, p. 357, cf., e.g., *KTU* 1.6.i.33-4). As for v. 15a, one might note Wyatt's deletion of this colon, since it appears to be "a generalisation into a broader account of the natural world" and not compatible with the mythological terminology which he looks for here (*Myths of Power*, p. 91).

108 See further Saggs' cogent arguments against seeing a causal connection between God's dealings with Leviathan and creation here (*Encounter with the Divine*, pp. 54-56) and the broader discussion of this issue in Chapter 2 above.

109 Rogerson & McKay, II, p. 128. Thus, "the creation of the cosmos by Yahweh was essentially *not* a liberating act" (G. M. Landes, "Creation and Liberation" in B. W. Anderson [ed.], *Creation in the Old Testament* 135-151, p. 138): indeed, "the relationship between Creation and redemption consists in a polarity. The attempt is nowhere made to bring both under one notion" (Westermann, *Schöpfung*, p. 166). Contrast von Rad's "soteriological interpretation of the work of creation" in relation to Ps. 74 ("Das Theologische Problem des alttestamentlichen Schöpfungsglaubens" in P. Volz et al., *Werden und Wesen*, 1935, p. 143) which, however, encounters a number of

King, gives victory to his people—to which may be compared especially Ps. 44:5, and indeed the military connotations of Ps. 74:22 (cf. 44:27). This conclusion is reinforced by the many thematic and linguistic affinities which Ps. 74 has with a number of other compositions in the Asaph collection, especially 78 and 79, but also 77 and 80, since they seem to share a concern with God's activity in history. Common motifs, besides those intimately connected with the lament form, such as various types of questioning and allusions to the anger of God, his remembrance of his people, or the scoffing of the nations, include: sheep / flock (צאן and parallels: see above); acquire (קנה: 74:2; 78:54); redeem (גאל: 74:2; 78: 35; 77:16; cf. 78: 42 [פדה]); heritage (נַחֲלָה: 74:2; 78:55, 62, 71; 79:1) Mount Zion (הַר־צִיּוֹן: 74:2; 78:68; cf. יְרוּשָׁלַםִ 79:1, 3); sanctuary (קֹדֶשׁ, 74:3; מִקְדָּשֶׁךָ, 74:7; מִקְדָּשׁוֹ, 78:69; הֵיכַל קָדְשֶׁךָ, 79:1; גְּבוּל קָדְשׁוֹ, 78:54); hand, right hand (יָד, יָמִין: 74:11; 77:11, 80:18; זְרוֹעַ: 77:16, cf. v. 21); salvation, save (√ישע: 74:12; 78:22; 79:9; 80:3, 8, 20); "of old" (מִקֶּדֶם: 74:12; 78:2 [מִנִּי־קֶדֶם]; 77:6, 12); Egypt (מִצְרַיִם: 74:13 [implied]; 78: 12, 43; 80:9); Red Sea (יָם etc.: 74:13; 78:13; 77: 17-21); bodies as food (מַאֲכָל) for beasts (74:14; 79:2-3); water being "opened" (בקע) in the wilderness (74:15 [נָחַל]; 78:15, 16, 20 [נְחָלִים]); and the covenant (בְּרִית: 74:20; 78:10, 37). It is particularly to be observed that the only historical themes to be invoked belong to the periods of the exodus and wilderness wanderings; these, however, occur across the entire group, with the exception of Ps. 79, which nevertheless ends with an appeal to Israel's status as "your people, the flock of your pasture".[110] By contrast, nowhere in these psalms does creation or even the orderly division between universal opposites feature.

It is therefore particularly interesting to observe how the "historical" framework of vv. 13a, 15, whilst unmistakably alluding to the Exodus, is also couched in language consonant with the more mythic intervening section. For example, the division of the sea is not followed by any direct reference to the crossing of the people of Israel, as is elsewhere so often the case, so the mythic tone is maintained throughout. On the other hand, it would be extremely unusual for there to be a mention of the separating of the waters without any allusion to its underlying salvific purpose, which, of course, was twofold, the second key Red Sea theme (besides the crossing) being the drowning of the Egyptian foe. However, an awareness of the axis between convention and originality operating here may facilitate the recognition of the implicit nuances underlying the poetic core of this section.

Egypt and Pharaoh are elsewhere described as a dragon in an extended metaphor (Ezek. 29:3-6; 32:2-8), and the name "Rahab", which is sometimes used as a synonym for the proper noun "Egypt" (Ps. 87:4; Isa. 30:7), is elsewhere employed of a draconic figure which is probably to be regarded as more-or-less equivalent to Leviathan (Rahab: Ps. 89:11, Job 9:13; 26:12; Isa. 51:9; cf. Leviathan: Isa. 27:1; Ps. 104:26; Job 3:8; 40:25-41:26). Indeed, it is the opinion of BDB that in Ps. 74:14 the latter term is to be understood as

---

difficulties.

110 Ps. 79:13.

"figurative of Egypt as all-engulfing".[111] It is an interesting question whether the name "Rahab" (only attested in Israel and meaning "proud", "arrogant") was originally devised to apply to Egypt, a nation of legendary hubris,[112] and perhaps came to develop prosaic and mythical uses from this "nickname".[113] That the description of Egypt as a crocodile or dragon was originally intended with derisory connotations is especially indicated by Ezek. 32:2: the implication is that it may be a dangerous and aggressive creature, but it is also foul, unclean and deserving of an ignominious end. It is also worth bearing in mind that Hebrew did not have an independent word for "crocodile",[114] a beast which was so characteristic of the Nile and thus of Egypt itself; in many cases, therefore, the distinction between the mythological and natural is very tenuous.[115]

"Heads", v. 13b, continues this dual signification: *Ltn* in Ugaritic literature is portrayed as having seven heads (*KTU* 1.3.iii.42, 1.5.i.3; cf. Rev. 12:3, 13:1, 17:3), but רָאשֵׁים may also represent the military leaders of Egypt. Perhaps the latter is more likely in the view of the plural "dragons".

The phrase מַאֲכָל לְעָם לְצִיִּים may be compared with Ps. 79:2,[116] which describes the fate meted out to Israel by its enemies, and understood as alluding to the ignominious nature of death, unburied on the battlefield, and its dire consequences (cf., e.g., Ezek. 28:8, and the fate of Jezebel, 2 Ki. 9:10). With this may be compared especially the gruesome picture of Ezek. 29:5; 32:4(-6), describing the punishment awaiting the dragon Egypt. In the present context, it could possibly derive from the tradition of the casting up of the bodies of the Egyptians onto the seashore, Ex. 14:30.[117] However, the reference presents difficulties for the *Chaoskampf* view, especially if an allusion to creation is presupposed, since the body of the slain monster is consumed rather than employed as the raw material for creation; hence Wyatt even dismisses vv. 14b-15a as "clearly intrusive" chiefly on the basis of the content of v. 14b.[118]

If the battle between Baal and Yam signified some form of conflict involving the sea and storm, and that between Baal and Mot involved rain (or flood) and drought, v. 15 clearly rises above such a division of rôles—Yahweh both opens and dries up watercourses, just as day and night, summer and winter, and

111 P. 531.

112 See, e.g., Ex. 18:11; Jer. 46:7-8, 17; Ezek. 30:6, 18; 31:10; 32:12; Neh. 9:10.

113 See the discussion of this issue below in relation to Ps. 89.

114 כֹּחַ, Lev. 11:30, apparently refers to the "'monitor,' any of a family (Varanidae) of large, carnivorous lizards", which is to be distinguished from the crocodile itself (W. S. McCulloch, "Land Crocodile", *IDB*, Vol. 3, p. 66).

115 See especially the depiction of Pharaoh as a monster of the Nile in Ezek. 29, 32 and the detailed description of Leviathan in Job 40:25-41:26, which many commentators have regarded as a mildly embellished portrayal of the crocodile; the latter passage is discussed in Chapter 11 below.

116 Cf. also Ps. 63:11: "food for jackals".

117 Thus Kissane, II, p. 15, Briggs, II, p. 155, Cohen, p. 239.

118 *Myths of Power*, p. 91.

indeed "the boundaries of the earth" are his preserve. These polarities reinforce the idea of divine ordering—and hence of moral and social order, the purposefulness of history, and Yahweh's ultimate righteousness and care. But it also emphasises his omnipotence, and, as in Deutero-Isaianic thought, God's power over the extremities of creation demonstrates his absolute sovereignty (cf. "King", v. 12a) in the historical sphere as well: it was the prerogative of a king to impose order on his kingdom. This paralleling between control over the forces of nature and over political powers, between waters threatening to burst their boundaries to engulf the land and world empires who aspired to do the same, is familiar from elsewhere,[119] but here the mythic is the more strongly stated element (even if the historic is more emphatically implied), for here we have moved from simile and metaphor into symbol.

It was noted in relation to Ps. 46 that where the establishment of Zion and unshakability of the physical cosmos are spoken of, the city's inviolability and protection from the fear of attack are primarily implied. Now, in Ps. 74, in the context of the anxieties concerning the physical desolation of the holy place, a similar process comes into operation, whereby God's activity in nature is employed to convey political assurance. Hence, whilst Yahweh's cleaving of the dragon is described, his deliverance in the events of Exodus and entry may be understood. Both elements are undeniably present, closely intertwined and mutually enriching. As a result, it would appear that there is no need to impose a logical dichotomy between myth and history onto the poetic imagery, for the latter is related through the medium of the former.[120] The recounting of the destruction of the dragon is the vehicle through which the tenor of the *Heilsgeschichte* is conveyed. In so doing, the psalmist has moved beyond the use of mere poetic metaphor into the realm of symbolism, in its specific literary sense. Correctly speaking, "a symbol is a specially evocative kind of image..., that is, a word or phrase referring to a concrete object, scene or action which also has some further significance associated with it... The symbolic... remains mysteriously indeterminate in its possible meanings. It is therefore usually too simple to say that a literary symbol "stands for" some idea as if it were just a convenient substitute for a fixed meaning: it is usually a substantial image in its own right around which further significances may gather according to different

---

119 See the discussion of Pss. 93, 46 and 65 in the previous chapter, and compare also Isa. 8:7-8; 17:12-13; cf. Jer. 51:34.

120 Compare Hunter, pp. 153-4, who thinks in terms of a juxtaposition of history and myth in a culture that drew no sharp dividing line between them; as a result "the broken body of Leviathan, scattered as food for the creatures of the wilderness, is one and the same as the broken power of the Pharaoh and the shattered bodies of the Egyptians, left to rot in the desert" (p. 154). Kraus, in framing the question in terms of Creation / Exodus, also recognises that "this is hardly a matter of an either-or". However, it is his view that "both complexes have mutually impinged upon each other" "even though the mythical elements unquestionably predominate" (II, p. 100).

interpretations".[121] Thus, the relationship between vehicle and tenor is a mutually enriching one.

As for the form of the myth as it was known in Israel, nothing of any significance can be determined. This is also the case in Ugarit, where among the extant texts there are merely passing allusions to the defeat of Ltn by Baal[122] and of "the dragon... the wriggling serpent, the tyrant with seven heads" by Anat, the latter appearing in the midst of a list of the goddess' conquests.[123] In each instance, there is merely an allusion to a presumably well-known story whereby the deity kills a dragon, variously known as Lotan, Leviathan, Rahab, or simply *tannîn*. Whether this constituted mere folktale, or a detailed myth of profound theological significance in either case can only be conjectured. All that can be said is well expressed by Donner, namely that "on the Palestinian-Syrian land bridge inhabited by Canaanites there was a repertoire of mythical conceptions which at various times, under various conditions, and in various places were able to constitute themselves variously... Israel drew on this repertoire in the same way as the Ugaritic mythical poets of the North did. Therein lies what they have in common."[124]

It is possible that in Israel, where the story was adopted and retold, it was appreciated simply on that level, as a story. Ps. 74 provides evidence that it was employed as a rich source of poetic imagery,[125] but whether its significance transcended this, is difficult to determine. Quite probably it retained all its mythic power but was crucially adapted to a new situation, with concomitant transformations in content and significance.[126] Crucially, however, in contradistinction to a polytheistic worldview, it was the Israelite position to

---

121 C. Baldwick, *The Concise Oxford Dictionary of Literary Terms* (Oxford: OUP, 1990), pp. 218-219.

122 *KTU* 1.5.i.1-3.

123 *KTU* 1.3.iii.40-42.

124 H. Donner, "Ugaritismen in der Psalmenforschung", *ZAW* 79 (1967), 322-350, p. 344; quotation as in English translation of Kraus' Commentary, II, p. 101.

125 Eichrodt (*TAT*, II, pp. 72-73) suggests that the myth of the *Chaoskampf* was "of no consequence for Israel's understanding of the world", but that it belonged "to the treasure-house of poetry, on which poets and prophets liked to draw in order to clothe their thoughts in rich apparel". Contrast Anderson's contention that "the appropriation of foreign myths and their reinterpretation was...an expression of...theological vitality. The primary purpose of this takeover was polemical" (II, p. 543).

126 The meaning of the struggle with "chaos" may in this case be understood as operating on two levels, the first being a very broad underlying one, which may be thought to apply in all instances (e.g. "the God overcomes his enemy as a manifestation of his supremacy"), and the second being specific to the individual reference (in this case, the overpowering of the Egyptian foe as a reminiscence of God's past salvific action as it pertains to the present challenging situation). If this is the case, to speak of the "original" meaning of the myth may be mistaken: rather, each retelling (or allusion) retains the same basic force as its predecessors, but is reforged afresh in each new situation without necessarily carrying with it the specific meanings which pertained in previous applications.

affirm the absolute power of Yahweh over all creation. In Ugarit, conflict between relatively equally-matched deities could cause frightening and dangerous phenomena on earth. By contrast, in the dominant voice in the literature of Israel, it was declared (especially following the crisis of c.587 B.C.) that Yahweh was the only God (Ps. 89:7-9, Isa. 45:14, 18, 21, 22 and often in Deutero-Isaiah), and that everything was governed by his power and righteous will. He it is who both cuts openings for springs and torrents and dries up the ever-flowing streams. This is closely reflected in the second part of the passage, concerning cosmic ordering, in which it is affirmed that the polarities which were separated and ordered within the cosmos at creation have a place within his righteous purpose. Thus, when the myth is adopted as a means of retelling the saving event of the Exodus and expounding Yahweh's omnipotence, it is imparted with a radically different meaning than would have adhered in a Ugaritic context. Indeed, it is a great paradox that it was at the nadir of the Hebrew faith—when it must have appeared to many that Yahweh was weaker than his foreign rivals and that the pagan deities should be worshipped in his stead—that the terminology of the mythology attached to such deities was employed in Israel, and then in order to provide consolation and renewed hope in the divine salvation.[127]

---

127 It is interesting to consider whether, if the psalm was intoned by those who were left behind in the land after the exiles had been taken away (cf. v. 20; and perhaps also the repeated allusions to the poor and downtrodden, vv. 19, 21), it is possible that this reflects more of popular religion than is customarily the case in the psalms. This could have occurred through a combination of factors: the elite "opinion-formers" had been removed, and only the lower strata remained; there was probably a deep need within people to give expression to their spontaneous, heartfelt response to a disturbing situation; and there may have been a recognition even among official priestly circles of the danger of people turning away from Yahweh to other gods. So it may have been that this lament was couched in popular language to express popular sentiment, whilst at the same time emphasising Yahweh's absolute supremacy and uniqueness over the cosmos, other nations and other gods.

3. Psalm 89

i. The Date of Psalm 89

Psalm 89 has been subject to a variety of dating proposals, including attempts at source-division.[128] However, although it may readily be divided into three main sections,[129] the structure and central themes of the psalm transcend these boundaries. Thus, the motifs of Yahweh's steadfast love and faithfulness and his promises to David which are stated in the opening hymnic address (vv. 2-5) are resumed in the concluding petitions, vv. 50-52. The intervening hymn (vv. 6-19), enunciation of the Davidic promises (vv. 20-38) and counterposed description of Yahweh's renouncing of his covenant (vv. 39-46), simply elaborate upon this.[130] Moreover, the simple juxtaposition of joyful praise in the God of supreme power and steadfastness who had committed himself in covenant love to his "son", with the utter renunciation of his election of David and degrading reversal of the expected blessings, poignantly exposes a painful paradox: the utter irreconcilability of Yahweh's past promises with the present plight of his people and their king. Thus, the subtle poetic transitions within the psalm as it stands militate against outright fragmentation. Another indication of unity is the fact that the promises to David as enunciated in vv. 20-38 seem exaggerated in comparison with 2 Sam. 7, so that the "steadfast love" is now unconditional (vv. 34-38), and the Davidic realm intended as a universal empire, spanning from the Mediterranean to the Euphrates.[131] This implies that the

---

128 Indeed, certain commentators have regarded the psalmist more as a compiler than a poet; arguments for a composite origin have been advanced, e.g., by Gunkel (*Die Psalmen*, pp. 389, 392, 396), Norin (*Er spaltete das Meer*, pp. 116-7), Schmidt (pp. 165-6, 167-8), Mowinckel (*PsSt*, III, p. 37), J. M. Ward ("The Literary Form and Liturgical Background of Psalm LXXXIX" *VT* 11 [1961], pp. 338-9), Goulder (*PSK*, pp. 212-3) and Lipiński (*Le poème royal du Psaume LXXXIX, 1-5, 20-38* [Cahiers de la Revue Biblique 6; Paris: Gabalda, 1967]). However, the resulting variations in dating and in the proposed patterns of growth for the psalm, and even over the identification of the earliest section, suggest rather that the various models have been prompted by the presupposition that transitions in mood must reflect source divisions, and not by concrete indications of divergent origin present within the material itself.

129 Vv. 2-19, 20-38 and 39-52, besides the concluding doxology to the third book of the Psalter in v. 53.

130 Yahweh's חֶסֶד is specifically mentioned in every section but vv. 50-52, in each case in conjunction with אֱמוּנָה (vv. 2, 3, 25, 34, 50) or a cognate term (אֱמֶת, v. 15; אמן, v. 29). Another keyword is כִּסֵּא, which is likewise attested across the main divisions of the lament, once in relation to the kingship of God (v. 15), but otherwise referring to the Davidic throne (vv. 5, 30, 37, 45). Further links between vv. 2-38 and 39-52 are enumerated by Broyles, *The Conflict of Faith and Experience*, pp. 169, 251 n. 69.

131 V. 26. Thus Cohen, p. 293, Wellhausen, p. 182, Goulder, *PSK*, p. 232, Veijola, "Davidverheißung und Staatsvertrag", *ZAW* 95 (1983) 9-31, pp. 22-4; cf. Gen. 15:18,

section may not directly derive from this earlier source or indeed from pre-exilic traditions, but reflect an idealisation which was only concretised when the covenant had come to an end.[132] In addition, the metre would seem to confound all attempts at fragmentation, since the metrical transitions of the psalm transgress its logical divisions, the opening and closing verses (vv. 2-16, 47-52) being mainly 4+4, and the central portion (vv. 17-46) predominantly 3+3.

More significantly, the linguistic evidence provides no support for a composite origin, but rather suggests that the composition as a whole emanated from the same, exilic or even early post-exilic, period.[133] Like Ps. 74, the data are not wholly biased either to the pre- or post-exile, yet, distinctively, any pointers to the early period are weak and sparsely attested, in contrast to the far more substantial indicators favouring the exile or shortly thereafter. Among these may be cited תִּפְאָרָה as an attribute of Yahweh (v. 18);[134] קָדוֹשׁ as referring to a heavenly being (vv. 6, 8);[135] the verb ערך with the meaning 'compare, be comparable' (v. 7);[136] I. דמה, 'be like, resemble' in the Qal (also in v. 7);[137] III. חלל, 'pollute, defile, profane' of violating a covenant (in the Pi'el, v. 35);[138] and עֲלוּמִים, 'youth' (v. 46).[139] Moreover, מִצְוֹת (v. 32) denotes the divine commands

---

Deut. 1:7, 11:24, Pss. 72:8, 80:12. Nevertheless, alternative proposals have been made: see Schmidt, p. 168, Kissane, II, p. 97 (the Tigris); Gunkel, *Die Psalmen*, p. 393, Leslie, p. 277 (the Nile). One interpretation which must surely be rejected, however, is that signifies "the 'currents' of the cosmic sea" (Johnson, *SKAI*, p. 27), so that "the king is declared to be the universal victor over chaos" (Kraus, II, p. 791; see also Heim, "The [God-]Forsaken King of Psalm 89" in J. Day [ed.], *King and Messiah in Israel and the Ancient Near East*, p. 315, Wyatt, *Myths of Power*, pp. 82-4, and Hossfeld in HZ, II, p. 593). Even should the attribute of victor over chaos be accepted for Yahweh himself (which, as has been seen, is debatable in respect of the psalms so far considered), it seems most unlikely that it should be transferred to the human king, as has been recognised by most commentators.

132 Of course, it could rather stem from a time of ebullient optimism and encapsulate genuine hopes and expectations, but if so, it has not left its mark elsewhere in the Old Testament, except in post-monarchical eschatology.

133 An exilic dating for the psalm is advocated, e.g., by König (p. 492), Cohen (pp. 289, 295, 296), Heim ("The [God-] Forsaken King of Psalm 89", p. 298), Tournay, (*Seeing and Hearing God*, p. 202) and Day (OTG, p. 95, correcting his earlier pre-exilic dating, *God's Conflict*, p. 26), and for its final form by Norin (*Er spaltete das Meer*, p. 117) and Seybold (p. 350), whilst Gerstenberger classifies it as exilic or post-exilic (II, p. 154). Veijola even describes its setting in exilic ceremonies of lamentation as "as good as certain" (*Verheissung in der Krise* [Helsinki: Suomalainen Tiedeakatemia, 1982], p. 210). Only marginally to be distinguished is Goulder's dating of the completed psalm to "the years after 597" (*PSK*, p. 218).

134 Occurring elsewhere only in 1 Chr. 29:11, 13, Ps. 71:8, Isa. 60:19, 63:12, 14; cf. Ps. 96:6, Isa. 60:7, 63:15, 64:10, where it is applied to God's house or sanctuary; distinctively, in Ps. 78:61, which may be earlier, it seems to denote the Ark.

135 Job 5:1; 15:15; Zech. 14:5; Dan. 8:13, 13. (This is assuming קְדֹשָׁיו of Deut. 33:3 are, as the parallelism implies, human).

136 Isa. 40:18; Ps. 40:6; Job 28:17, 19.

137 Ezek. 31:2, 8, 8, 18; Isa. 1:9; 46:5; Pss. 102:7; 144:4; Cant. 2:9, 17; 7:8; 8:14.

138 Mal. 2:10; Ps. 55:21; cf., of the חקות of God, Ps. 89:32.

139 Job 20:11; 33:25; Lam. 54:4.

in predominantly late contexts;[140] in Ps. 89:31-32, it is combined with חֻקָּה, תּוֹרָה and מִשְׁפָּט, a factor which increases the statistical probability of late origin.[141] In addition, Veijola has documented the many overlaps in theology and vocabulary between this Psalm and deuteronomistic and exilic or post-exilic texts, such as Lamentations and Deutero-Isaiah,[142] whilst Gerstenberger and Crüsemann have drawn attention to the hymnic style of vv. 10-14 (characteristically "you" plus perfect verb) as "a distinct mode of praising Yahweh in the late periods of Israel's congregational worshipping".[143] This evidence would appear cumulatively to point both to the substantial unity of the psalm and to a likely exilic or early post-exilic dating.

The conclusion arrived at on linguistic grounds is supported also by the content of the Psalm, since the lament of vv. 39-46 would seem most closely to fit the crisis of c.587 B.C.[144] In fact, it is difficult to imagine "what other catastrophe would invite the conclusion that God was not merely punishing a disobedient king, but that he had broken his promise 'I will not renounce my covenant' (verse [35])".[145] The situation reflected by the passage—the apparent end of the monarchy (vv. 40b, 45) and perhaps even the death of the king (v. 46),[146] besides military defeat (v. 44), the breaching of walls (v. 41a), the ruination of strongholds (v. 41b), and the plunder of cities and their inhabitants (v. 42)—seems to demand this setting and a consequent exilic dating.[147] However, such an interpretation encounters a difficulty insofar as vv.

---

140 Note BDB's analysis: 'not used before D and Je; in Je only of man's commands; not Ez or Minor Proph., exc. Mal' (p. 846). The examples are, however, too numerous to list here.

141 The combination שְׁאוֹל // מָוֶת, v. 49, may also be of a similar order: cf. Prov. 5:5; 7:27; Cant. 8:6.

142 *Verheissung*, pp. 48-59.

143 Gerstenberger, II, pp. 149-50; Crüsemann, *Studien zur Hymnus und Danklied*, pp. 292-4.

144 This is, of course, to assume that historical events are reflected in these verses, in contradiction to the contention of G. W. Ahlström (*Psalm 89: Eine Liturgie aus dem Ritual des leidenden Königs* [Lund: C.W.K. Gleerup, 1959]), A. R. Johnson (*SKAI*, pp. 112-3) and Eaton (*Kingship and the Psalms*, pp. 121-2; see also Day, *God's Conflict*, p. 26) that the Psalm reflects the ritual suffering or humiliation of the king in the annual new year festival. This theory not only requires the transference of a Babylonian "dying and rising god" mythic prototype onto an Israelite matrix, but it also ignores the strongly national nature of the king's affliction, which is quite in contrast, for example, to the individual and vicarious nature of the suffering of the עֶבֶד יהוה in Isa. 52:13-53:12; see further Mowinckel's critique of Ahlström's work in *JSS* 5 (1960), pp. 291-298.

145 Rogerson and McKay, II, p. 196.

146 Or at least the premature curtailment of his young and vigorous rule, as was suffered by Jehoiachin (thus Goulder, *PSK*, p. 235).

147 Other situations have been proposed, but have failed to attract widespread support. Weiser seeks to blend cultic and historical approaches by arguing, perhaps rather incongruously, that the psalm was used in the pre-exilic cult "in times of a grave

51-52 appear to be spoken by the king. It is obviously hard to conceive of any situation in which the end of the monarchy (vv. 40b, 45) and premature death or incapacity of the king (v. 46) could be accompanied by a speech by him: the psalm seems to be inherently contradictory. There are nevertheless various ways in which scholars have attempted to resolve the apparent inconsistency:

1) Jehoiachin may have been perceived as the bearer of the divine promises in Exile after the fall of Zedekiah and the destruction of Jerusalem, 2 Ki. 25:27-30 being expressive of such hopes.[148] If, as seems likely, Jehoiachin himself was unable to participate in any festivals of lamentation, perhaps someone else would take his part and speak on his behalf.

2) The Davidic promises may have been focused elsewhere. It is not impossible that Gedaliah may have been of the royal household (after all, he must have been regarded as someone who was equipped for office by those who appointed him) but perhaps was only awarded the position of Governor by his overlords as a sign of subjugation. Even without any official recognition, some individual or family may have been regarded as the heir of the Davidic line (compare modern Eastern European and Russian parallels). In a state so monarchically aware as Israel, in which the king was wrenched from them by a hated aggressor, it would not be surprising if their aspiration lived on, embodied in certain individuals.

3) The sense of "continued promise" and the hope of restoration is especially embodied in Hag. 2:20-23 and Zech. 4:6-14, 6:12-13, there centred on Zerubbabel as the scion of the Davidic line. In fact, Deissler proposes that the psalm may actually have been composed in c. 520 B.C., in the context of a renewed hope that the Davidic king might be reinstated.[149] The distinctive participation of the "family of the house of David" on an occasion of mourning in Jerusalem is, further, anticipated in Zech. 12:12.

4) The other possibility is that the psalm was actually intoned on the eve of the Fall of Jerusalem or capture of the king, when her fate had become inevitable, and the treatment meted out to foreign kings who had resisted the Babylonian advance was well known. Thus, the defiling of the crown had effectively happened: the course of events was advancing inexorably to the end (indeed effective government throughout Judaea must have long been impossible in siege conditions anyway) and yet the king was still available to add his voice at the culmination of a last, desperate plea.[150]

---

national disaster... at the covenant festival" (p. 403), whilst Kraus locates it between the death of Josiah and the exile (II, p. 784; cf. Terrien, who relates it to the defeat of 609 B.C., p. 639). Broyles (*The Conflict of Faith and Experience*, p. 168) and Mowinckel (*PIW*, II, p. 152) also place its composition in the pre-exilic era, without, however, being more specific.

148 Goulder makes the converse claim that "we should have a resolution of the difficulty if it is Jehoiachin who has been deposed and Zedekiah who is still there as Yahweh's anointed" (*PSK*, p. 235). However, vv. 40b, 45 and perhaps 46 weigh against this.

149 II, p. 182.

150 An alternative approach favoured by Wellhausen (pp. 95, 200) and certain older scholars, to interpret the reference to "thy anointed" in v. 39 as collective (cf. Ps. 28:8) and then to delete v. 50b, seeks to erase rather than to solve the problem, and lacks textual

Perhaps one of these last two situations, just before or some time after the Fall of Jerusalem, are the most attractive; the linguistic evidence (and perhaps also form-critical considerations) would seem to favour the latter option. However, c.587 B.C. remains the most certain historical point of reference.

ii. The Theme of "Chaos" in Psalm 89

As regards possible *Chaoskampf* allusions, vv. 10-11, which occur within the central hymnic section, are of major interest. Particularly worthy of attention is the mention of "Rahab" in v. 11, since many have discerned here on the basis of a comparison with Isa. 51:9 a reference to a dragon, with which God engages in battle.[151] However, the term recurs apart from Isa. 51:9 and Ps. 89:11 once more in the Psalter, in Ps. 87:4, as well as in Isa. 30:7 and twice in Job (9:13, 26:12).[152] Although the references in Job would appear to be mythological, Ps. 87:4 and Isa. 30:7 clearly employ "Rahab" as an appellation of Egypt, and the allusion in Isa. 51:9-11 is also, at least in part, to the Exodus. Obviously, therefore, it cannot simply be presupposed into which category Ps. 89:11 should fit, since Rahab is not there specifically stated to be a dragon. More importantly, the respective uses of Rahab raise the issue of the origin and development of this figure, and in particular of the crucial aspect of these apparently diverse applications which lends them cohesion.

As regards the question of whether Rahab as a nation-name precedes or succeeds more mythological usages of the term, it may be observed that Ps. 89:11 and Isa. 51:9 emanate from around the time of the exile, whilst Job 9:13 and 26:12 may be rather later. Isa. 30:7, however, is most probably pre-exilic.[153] If Ps. 87 were pre-exilic also, this would suggest that the national use may be prior to any mythological developments (which, however, does not

---

support.

151 Hence, in the opinion of many commentators, Rahab is a personification of the "powers of chaos... tak[ing] the form of the primeval sea rebelling against God" (Weiser, p. 403), "the primeval chaos-monster" (Johnson, *SKAI*, p. 108; so also Kraus, II, p. 787-8), "either another name for the chaos waters or one of the marine monsters" (Anderson, II, p. 636), "the sea dragon... who with his helpers, the enemies (v. 11), constitutes the powers hostile to God" (Seybold, p. 352).

152 A minority of scholars have also interpreted רְהָבִים in Ps. 40:5 as the plural of רַהַב (thus Gunkel, *Schöpfung*, p. 40; Dahood, I, p. 245, translating "pagan idols", p. 243). However, the existence of such a plural is semantically improbable, since Rahab would appear to be a proper name, and the allusion to עֹזְרֵי רָהַב in Job 9:13 would further confirm that Rahab himself, even if accompanied by others, is singular. The more commonly accepted translation, "the proud", would, further, provide a more suitable parallelism within that context: see Day, *God's Conflict*, p. 6, n. 11.

153 Day (*God's Conflict*, p. 90) describes Isa. 30:7 as "almost certainly dating from the period 705-1 B.C.", a conclusion to which Sweeney (*Isaiah 1-39* [FOTL 16, 1996], p. 397) assents, adding that "most scholars do not contest this point"; thus even Kaiser attributes it to "the year 701 and to the prophet Isaiah" (*Der Prophet Jesaja Kapitel 13-39*, p. 230).

imply that every national use is early, since the two forms may have been employed concurrently).[154] Such a view would be consistent with the fact that "Rahab" (or any cognate form) is unattested outside Israel as the name of a dragon. However, the designation would be appropriate as an appellation for proud Egypt,[155] the hubris of whom, as far back as the exodus, was notorious.[156] The negative personification of Egypt at a later stage as a dragon would also be readily explicable, since the Nile, the country's best-known feature, was inhabited by crocodiles, creatures which were both fearsome and unclean. The motif could thus have derisory connotations, whilst aptly conveying Egypt's dangerous aggression: compare especially Ezek. 32:2.

More importantly, this projected course of development would seem to cohere with the dating of the relevant texts, including that of Ps. 87, as shall now be shown.

The Date of Psalm 87

Psalm 87 appears somewhat cryptic, so much so that it is widely perceived to be disordered, and has prompted many attempts at reconstruction.[157] It certainly raises many awkward questions of interpretation: In what sense can the nations be claimed to "know" Yahweh? What is the significance of the references to places of birth? How is the assertion that "all my springs are in you" (v. 7) to be understood?

The first of these issues, concerning the interpretation of v. 4 ("Among those who know me..."), impinges directly on the dating of the psalm. The verb ידע most probably implies acknowledgment of Yahweh's power, and perhaps also the pledging of loyalty to him, and has conventionally been regarded as permitting three possible settings for the verse, namely either that the nations listed signify diaspora Jews[158] and / or proselytes[159], or that the reference is

154 It is difficult not to be aware that, were it not for the preservation of Isa. 30:7, an argument for the opposite line of development could be sustained. But then one would have to account for how the notion of a dragon called Rahab arose and how it came later to shed its mythological connotations completely and become a straightforward designation for Egypt.

155 The root רהב means "act stormily, boisterously, arrogantly" (Isa. 3:5, Ps. 138:3, Prov. 6:3, Cant. 6:5), hence the adjective רָהָב (Ps. 40:5), "proud, defiant", and nouns רֹהַב (Ps. 90:10), "pride", and מַרְהֵבָה (Isa. 14:4 [emended]), "boisterous, raging behaviour". Thus רַהַב seems to connote, literally, "arrogance"; cf. T. H. Gaster's translation of Ps. 89:10: "Thou it was crushed the Dragon Proud..." (*Thespis*, p. 419).

156 Relevant references are cited above in relation to Ps. 74:14.

157 See, e.g., Kraus, II, pp. 765-6; Seybold, pp. 341-2; Weiser, p. 394; Gunkel, *Die Psalmen*, p. 378; Schmidt, p. 163; NEB.

158 Thus Kraus (II, p. 769), Schmidt (p. 164), and Anderson (II, p. 619), who includes proselytes among them.

159 Thus Weiser, who envisages the scene for the inspiration of the psalm as one of the

expressive of the hope of a future eschatological reconciliation.[160] Hence, the psalm would have to belong to the exilic[161] or the post-exilic[162] periods.

The diaspora interpretation is typified by Kraus, who asserts[163] that dating Ps. 87 presents "no difficulties. In v. 4 the presupposition is that Israel is scattered throughout Egypt and Babel. Accordingly the Babylonian exile is the terminus a quo". However, this conclusion depends on his reordering of the poem, especially his concentration of Zion imagery in the preceding verses[164] and the conjoining of vv. 4b and 6b to form the couplet, "'This one is born here, that one there...'",[165] so that "the trend of Yahweh's words that culminate in v. 5a" (itself significantly emended[166] in favour of Kraus' interpretation) seem to "lean toward" this outcome.[167] In addition, his apprehension that "the names of the foreign nations indicate the broad area of dispersion of postexilic Israel"[168] is misleading, since Philistia had ceased to exist as an independent nation by this time, its population having been deported[169] and the territory incorporated into the province of Ashdod. Similarly, "Babel" could in the post-exilic era signify only the contemporary Mesopotamian sphere of governance, or the city of that name, since the Neo-Babylonian Empire proper came to an end in c.539 B.C.[170] More importantly, one has to account for the choice of nations mentioned, despite their depleted state, in this period. However, these difficulties could be alleviated if both the most natural sense of the Hebrew of v. 4 (namely, that the peoples of themselves, rather than diaspora Jews or proselytes, comprise the subject of the verb) and the consequent possibility of a pre-exilic setting were admitted, and in fact, this would cohere with such evidence as may be extracted from the Psalm.

Linguistically, Ps. 87 lacks exceptionally archaic or distinctively late features. However, it shows little sign of the intrusion of prose elements, exhibiting only one occurrence of the article -ה, and then as attached to אֱלֹהִים, as sometimes occurs even in the poetry identified as ancient; similarly, colon-initial *waw* intrudes only in vv. 5ac, 7a, but אֶת־ and אֲשֶׁר are absent. This would

---

great pilgrimage festivals, when incomers from all over the world would throng the temple (p. 395); cf. Kittel's title, "Pilgrimage Song of the Proselytes" (p. 288).

160 Thus Cohen, p. 283, Kissane, II, p. 80, Zenger, HZ, II, pp. 557-8.

161 Oesterley, p. 390.

162 Kraus, II, p. 769; Anderson, II, p. 619; Cohen, p. 283; Schmidt, p 164; Zenger, HZ, II, p. 555.

163 II, p. 767.

164 He adopts the sequence 1a, 2, 1b, 5b, 7, 3, 6a, 4b, 6b, 4a, 5a.

165 II, p. 766.

166 To וּלְצִיּוֹן אֵם אֹמַר, "But Zion I call mother", II, p. 765.

167 II, p. 769.

168 II, p. 769.

169 See E. F. Weidener, "Jojachin, König von Juda, in babylonischen Keilschrifttexten" in *Mélanges Syriens offerts à M. René Dussaud*, II (Paris: Paul Geuthner, 1939) 923-35, pp. 928, 935.

170 As Kraus himself acknowledges (II, p. 769). Others, however, recognise that "the mention of Babylon v. 4 implies the Babylonian period" (Briggs, II, p. 239).

be consistent with a moderately early provenance, but cannot support a post-exilic origin for the psalm.

The hymn apparently lacks vocabulary which is elsewhere confined to a particular period. Nevertheless, the expression (בְּ)הַרְרֵי־קֹדֶשׁ, which is otherwise unique to Ps. 87:1, is almost certainly to be restored also in Ps. 110:3,[171] which "may well be one of the oldest poems in the Psalter".[172] In addition, the verb I. חול [חִיל](v. 7)[173] is employed of people dancing only in relation to the pre-exilic period: 1 Sam. 18:6[174] (singing and dancing there also being conjoined)[175] and Judg. 21:21, 23;[176] alternatively, if the form חֹלְלִים is parsed as the Qal participle plural of II. חלל, "pipe", 1 Ki. 1:40 serves as the only other occurrence of this verb.

However, more important than the linguistic criteria is the situation which Ps. 87 implies. Firstly, it is a Zion hymn,[177] the most natural, and almost certainly the original, milieu for this form being the monarchical era.[178] It certainly draws on ancient motifs belonging to this tradition: Seybold,[179] in his discussion of the "Psalms of Zion" 46, 48 and 87, lists among the "older themes... "the city of YHWH'... (46,4 [5]; 48,2 [3]),[180] "the Holy Dwelling Place" on the "Holy Mountain" (46,4 [5]; 48,1 [2]; 87,1), "the River of God" (46,4 [5]; cf. 87,7; 65,9 [10])'. He could also have mentioned the appellation עֶלְיוֹן (v. 5; cf. 46:5), which, though not confined to the earliest period, is obviously very ancient and seems to derive from the same Jerusalem tradition, perhaps dating back to pre-Israelite times.[181] Likewise, Kraus states that "Psalm 87 is related to Psalms 46 and 48, but especially to Psalm 132 and Ps. 78:67ff... These parallels... put the total picture of the songs of Zion into proper relief"[182]—a relief which, it might be added, seems otherwise to be pre-exilic.[183]

---

171 MT has בְּהַדְרֵי־קֹדֶשׁ, but the emendation, adopted in the apparatus of *BHS* and by many modern translations, including RSV, is supported by the Cairo geniza, many Hebrew manuscripts, Symmachus and Jerome.

172 Anderson, II, p. 767.

173 Taking MT חֹלְלִים as a Po'lel participle with the initial מ omitted (for מְחֹלְלִים).

174 Reading הַמְּחֹלְלוֹת with LXX in place of MT הַמְּחֹלוֹת.

175 In a context similar to that of Ex. 15:20.

176 In Ps. 96:9, though the verb may be translated in this way, it occurs in a poetic invocation to "all the earth" to dance (or "tremble") before Yahweh, which appears to be a recollection of the old theophany theme of cosmic perturbation, and hence is noticeably different in tone and orientation from the other occurrences.

177 According to Mowinckel, "the most characteristic Zion-hymn", *PIW* I, p. 90, the others conventionally thus classified being Pss. 46, 48, 76, 84, 122, and sometimes also 132.

178 See S. E. Gillingham, *The Poems and Psalms of the Hebrew Bible*, pp. 212-3, 251, especially her remark on p. 213, "the Zion hymns... suggest the time of the monarchy".

179 *Introducing the Psalms*, p. 132.

180 Presumably he omits to mention 87:3 only in error.

181 See also the comments of Kraus on vv. 1b, 5b (II, p. 768).

182 II, p. 766.

183 The dates of Pss. 46 and 78 are considered in Chapters 5 and 9 respectively. For the settings of Pss. 48 and 132, see, for example, Kraus I, pp. 511-2, II, pp. 1056-1061;

Such indicators are not decisive in determining a *terminus a quo* for the composition, whatever their bias towards the earlier period. However, v. 2 seems to presuppose the division between the Northern and Southern Kingdoms which pertained from c.922 B.C.[184] The Hebrew מִשְׁכְּנוֹת has been subject to various interpretations, since it may refer either to cities or to sanctuaries.[185] Proponents of an exilic or post-exilic provenance have suggested that Jewish settlements of the Diaspora are the subject of the reference—yet this is hardly the most obvious interpretation, unless this type of allusion were to be expected on other grounds, and it begs the question of why such a divine preference might be assumed, especially in a psalm which otherwise seems so inclusive in its horizons. Kraus proposes that, despite the fact that it belongs to the same historical context as Ps. 78, the spheres of reference are to be distinguished, Ps. 78:67 being directed against "the sanctuary of northern Israel", but Ps. 87:2 referring more generally to "all the other temples in Israel".[186] However, this sounds like special pleading, and raises the problem of how many "other temples" there were in Israel in the post-exilic era. Similarly, the notion that the allusion constitutes a veiled criticism of the Temple on Mount Gerizim still fails to account for the plural, although it could be far more simply overcome by the acceptance of a pre-exilic provenance for the psalm.

In fact, it may be that the allusion is primarily to cities,[187] since שַׁעֲרִים is sometimes employed synecdochically in this way,[188] and "Zion" is also a city-name, despite its sacred connotations. The declaration is a natural expression of Yahweh's preference for Judah over against the northern tribes, and finds its closest parallel in Ps. 78:67-68, another psalm which may emanate from the pre-exilic period:[189] note how, in each case, the verb אהב is utilised to convey Yahweh's special commitment to Zion, and the rhetorical intent seems to be the same.[190] One might think, more specifically, of a situation demonstrating this

---

and Anderson, I, p. 377, II, pp. 879-80. Compare also Dahood's remark (II, p. 298) that Psalm 87 "bears marked resemblance to Pss xxiv and xlviii", Ps. 24 also usually being recognised as pre-exilic (see the discussion in Chapter 5 above). Of course, the pre-exilic dating of Ps. 87 would still apply even if Goulder (*PSK*, pp. 170-172) and Seybold (p. 341) were correct in their contention that it may betray signs of an earlier, Danite, origin; see however Tate's critique of Goulder (p. 388).

184 Following, with Bright (*A History of Israel* [3rd ed.], p. 229), the chronology of Albright ("The Chronology of the Divided Monarchy of Israel" *BASOR* 100 (1945) 16-22); the chief alternative schema is that presented by J. Begrich (*Chronologie der Könige von Israel und Juda*, BHT 3, 1929) and adopted, for example, in the *Geschichte Israels* of M. Noth (p. 206).

185 It is also occasionally employed to denote Yahweh's elected sanctuary (Pss. 43:3, 84:2, 132:5, 7), but that is unlikely here, since a contrast is implied between Zion as a religious site and other places of comparable significance.

186 II, p. 767. So also Anderson, II, p. 620, Eaton, *Psalms*, p. 214 (in respect of Ps. 87:2 only).

187 So Cohen, p. 283; Dahood, II, p. 299; Briggs, II, pp. 239-40; Tate, p. 392.

188 See Isa. 14:31; 1 Ki. 8:37 // 2 Chr. 6:28; this usage is especially frequent in Deuteronomy (e.g., 12:12, 15, 17, 21), where it occurs some 22 times.

189 See Chapter 9 below.

190 It refers to his election and protection of Zion; see, e.g., Kraus (II, p. 767), Anderson

divine preference, for example, the fall of the Northern Kingdom as contrasted with Judah's continued independence,[191] or an occasion when Jerusalem was in particular danger during the years between the fall of Samaria and that of Jerusalem itself. Such a setting would cohere closely with the characteristic concerns of the Zion psalms—namely, the election and protection of the holy city by God.[192] Indeed, it is open to question whether this belief, which is probably implied by v. 2, remained a live hope and could have been presumed upon sufficiently to be employed in a presently-orientated saying after c.587 B.C.

But if the monarchical period seems to present a number of advantages over the exilic or post-exilic eras championed by certain scholars,[193] how is v. 4 to be understood? Evidently, the most straightforward sense of the Hebrew is that the nations themselves are alluded to. Probably the only period in which all five, together with Judah, were active agents in the arena of history as it pertained to the fortunes of Syro-Palestine was that of the maximum extent of the Empire of Assyria, when Egypt (under the 25th, Ethiopian, dynasty) and Babylon presented the chief challenges to its hegemony.[194] More specifically, historical records reveal one particular occasion when precisely this combination of nations, with Judah as a leading agent, conspired together to throw off the Assyrian yoke, namely at the accession of Sennacherib in 704/5 B.C., though it was not until c. 701 B.C. that he undertook his famous campaign in Syro-Palestine to restore his authority.[195] This would give direct point to the unfavourable comparison with Jacob in v. 2, since it had, of course, already fallen in 722/721 B.C.[196] It would also explain the sense of identity with the

---

(II, p. 620).

191 Cf., e.g., 2 Chr. 30:7.

192 Compare the implied contexts of Pss. 24, 46 and 65.

193 "An early date" is advocated by Gillingham (*The Poems and Psalms of the Hebrew Bible*, p. 251), and is commended also by Dahood, who proposes that the contrast between Egypt and Babylon, and the omission of Assyria implies a 7th or 6th century date, whilst "the reference to Cush suggests the period of Ethiopian ascendancy in Egypt under the Twenty-fifth Dynasty (ca. 715-663 B.C.)" (II, 298). In a similar vein, Briggs locates its composition in "a peaceful time, such as the early reign of Josiah", stressing that "there is no internal evidence of late date" (II, p. 239), whilst Goulder even relates it to ninth-century Israel, "a powerful country" at whose festal worship "foreign nations were welcome" (*PSK*, p. 171).

194 See similarly Dahood (II, p. 298). Briggs' placement in the reign of Josiah explains the prominence of Babylon and Egypt, and the inclusion of Philistia and Tyre as "the nearest nations to Israel, and in a like situation with her in relation to the two great world powers" (II, p. 240). Nevertheless, it fails to account for the mention of Cush, which he deletes as a later editorial gloss—a problem which could, of course, be avoided if the psalm were placed only three generations earlier, in the reign of Hezekiah.

195 See Noth, *Geschichte Israels*, pp. 240-243 and Bright, *A History of Israel* (3rd ed.), pp. 284-5.

196 Alternatively, the reference could be to the many Judaean cities which capitulated before the Assyrian advance, whilst only Jerusalem, with a few others (such as Lachish), held out: see Bright, *A History of Israel*, p. 286; Noth, *Geschichte Israels*, pp. 242-3.

other members of the confederation who "knew" Yahweh and together[197] obeyed his will, and on whose continued co-operation the future of Jerusalem depended.

The allusion to "springs" (מַעְיָנִים) in v. 7 is slightly strange, though the motif of the streams of the garden of paradise as a source of blessing is familiar from elsewhere,[198] and many commentators resort to emendation.[199] However, the slight awkwardness of expression, despite the familiarity of the motif, may be accounted for if it functions as a *double entendre*. Hezekiah combined his rebellion with the precaution of securing his defences, and especially the water-supply of the capital. As 2 Chr. 32:2-4 records, "when Hezekiah saw that Sennacherib had come and intended to fight against Jerusalem, he... stopped all the springs (אֶת-כָּל-הַמַּעְיָנוֹת) and the brook that flowed through the land, saying, 'Why should the kings of Assyria come and find much water?'." 2 Chr. 32:30, like 2 Ki. 20:20, further, makes reference to the famous Siloam tunnel: the upper outlet of the Gihon spring was closed, and the waters were redirected along the tunnel to a pool in the lower part of the city, so that they could be accessed from within the walls. Thus, for the first time, and much to the general reassurance, it could indeed be said of the city that "all my springs are in you".

Such a reconstruction is, like any other, inevitably conjectural, but it does at least cohere with the available evidence relating to the date of the psalm and respects the most natural implications of its language. It thus seems to offer the most satisfactory solution to the problem, and seems less reliant on special pleading and emendation than the alternatives.[200] Even apart from these specific proposals regarding its context, the evidence would at least seem to suggest a pre-exilic origin for the psalm, whilst clear indicators pointing to the post-exilic period are lacking.

From this conclusion regarding the dating of Ps. 87, it therefore appears likely that the original usage of the name "Rahab" in an Israelite context[201] is

---

197 Note the final conjunction עם encompassing the last-mentioned of the nations within the list "together with" the others.

198 See Gen. 2:10, Ps. 46:5 and the discussion of this motif in relation to the imagery of Ps. 29 in Chapter 3 above. There may also be an allusion to it in Ps. 36:10, and perhaps even in Ps. 68:27.

199 A preferred solution amongst certain German scholars is that of H. Gressmann, as quoted in H. Gunkel *(Die Psalmen*, p. 380: שָׂרִים וְחֹלְלִים כֻּלָּם עֹנֵי בָךְ) and adopted also by Kraus (II, p. 765) and Schmidt (p. 163). Contrast the proposals of Kissane (II, p. 81), Seybold (p. 341), and Dahood (II, p. 300).

200 Also attentive to the present form and likely date of the psalm is Gerstenberger's explanation that it is an "admission pronouncement" for foreigners in Jerusalem, which legalised their right to residence and participation in worship (II, pp. 139-140). However, the absence of evidence for such ceremonies, and the resultant vagueness of the references in vv. 2, 7, may weigh against it.

201 It is not apparently paralleled elsewhere. Norin proposes a derivation from the Egyptian *ḫ3b* ("crooked, bent", which he argues was transformed by a series of rather convoluted transitions into Semitic *hab*) + *r3* ("serpent", vocalised *ra* or *ro*) = "Rahab" (*Er spaltete*

as a prosaic nation name for Egypt, since this meaning is clearly demanded both here, where רַהַב is utilised alongside customary designations of other peoples, and in Isa. 30:7, where it stands in parallel to מִצְרַיִם.[202] The derivation of this appellative befits the legendary pride of this nation, and may well account for its origin.[203] In later literature, Rahab is described as a תַּנִּין (Isa. 51:9) or (as would appear from the parallelism in Job 26:12-13) נָחָשׁ בָּרִיחַ, and it is possible that it was in due course envisaged as embodied in this form. As has been seen in relation to "Leviathan" in Ps. 74 and to the imagery of Ezek. 29:3-5 and 32:2-8, this is consistent with the portrayal of Egypt in the exilic period, and would cohere also with the context of Isa. 51:9-11, where the allusion is indisputably, at least in part, to the Exodus; it is in any case a development which scarcely requires explanation.[204] The more naturalistic (as opposed to historical) contexts of Job 9:13 and 26:12 may reflect a further stage in the evolution of this motif, but this is not of immediate concern at present.[205] Rather, it remains to be discussed how the content of Ps. 89 relates to this pattern of evolution and to the possible variants in usage.

Returning then to the content of Ps. 89, and in particular to the disputed verses 10-11, various interpretations are possible, although it is difficult to decide between them. Perhaps elements of each are implied.

1) Vv. 6-19 concern the incomparability of Yahweh over other gods, perhaps reflecting a response to a crisis within Yahwism at the failure of the divine promises. The necessity of worshipping Yahweh above all other deities is implicitly elaborated in the succeeding lines. Not only is he immeasurably greater than the (nameless) "sons of gods" (v. 7), and feared by them (v. 8), but he is the God of all creation (v. 12), including the "heavens", the contents of which were so frequently the subject of worship. "Zaphon" is both "the north" paralleled with "the south",[206] but also the name of the Holy Mount

---

das Meer, pp. 74-5), but this combination is seemingly not attested in an Egyptian environment.

202 The contents of these passages thus militate against the view that "Rahab" is there employed only metaphorically for Egypt, as proposed by Norin, *ibid*., p. 72.

203 The personal meaning "proud one" would also cohere well with the masculine gender of the noun רַהַב, which agrees with that of the founding ancestor (and hence nation) מִצְרַיִם (Gen. 10:6, 13, 1 Chr. 1:8, 11; see *DCH*, V, p. 454). Variations in the gender of מִצְרַיִם may be attributed to the fact that where a land or city is denoted, nations tend to be feminine (a construct with אֶרֶץ fem. or עִיר fem. perhaps being understood), but when conceived chiefly as a people (cf. עַם masc.) or as a collection of individuals, they are understood as masculine (see e.g. מִצְרַיִם Ex. 12:33; cf. Gibson, *Davidson*, §17a). Such transitions in focus are evident in Isa. 30:7, where m.pl., f.s., and m.pl. are employed in succession, the last plural confirming the conceptualisation of Rahab, in this early instance, as a group of people rather than as a personified dragon.

204 Cf. Jer. 51:34 (in relation to Nebuchadnezzar).

205 These passages are considered in Chapter 11 below.

206 Or, perhaps better, the name of an archetypally high mountain coupled with the sea (יַמִּים or יָם): see further below.

where Baal resided.[207] "Tabor" is mentioned in Hosea 5:1, probably as a site where syncretistic practices were perpetrated, whilst "Hermon" is elsewhere (Judg. 3:3) prefixed with Baal's name. Yet, despite the worship of other deities that many occur on their surface, these mountains praise only Yahweh's name (v. 13). צֶדֶק וּמִשְׁפָּט (v. 15) are the particular attributes of the sun deity (cf. אוֹר־פָּנֶיךָ, v. 16), but they are also sometimes divine beings in their own right. Here, they are not only the seat of Yahweh's just rule: God's own special covenant attributes of חֶסֶד וֶאֱמֶת go before him like attendant angels. It is no wonder, then, that his people are especially "blessed", for he is the "glory of their strength". Seen within this polemical context, vv. 10-11 may be understood as the deliberate adoption of the attributes of other deities (especially his main rival, Baal) and their transformation into vehicles of his glory. The famed "mighty deeds" of Yahweh are thus reformulated in such terms as unequivocally to surpass his main rivals.

2) In contexts of hymnic praise within lament psalms, the saving acts of the *Heilsgeschichte* are invoked so often that this could be the case here. "Rahab" is elsewhere known as an epithet of Egypt (Ps. 87:4; Isa 30:7; 51:9-11), or to have dual signification (cf. Leviathan in Ps. 74:14); as such, the section vv. 10-11 "alludes to God's victory over the Egyptians... at the exodus"[208] and would naturally follow on from Yahweh's control of the sea.[209] This is particularly suggested by the parallelism of the singular "Rahab" with the plural "enemies", which could readily imply the metaphorical embodiment of the Egyptian troops in the dragon: the same singular-plural combination occurs also in Ps. 74:13a-14b, apparently again in reference to the exodus, whilst the denotation of Egypt / the Pharaoh as a "dragon" is especially clear in Ezek. 29, 32. However, a literal reference to Egypt is equally possible. In addition, the passage sounds a number of verbal echoes with the "Song of the Sea" (Ex. 15)[210] as well as broadly mirroring the structure and content of Ps. 74:12-17,[211]

---

207 See, e.g., *KTU* 1.3.i.22, 1.5.i.11.

208 Rogerson and McKay, II, p. 191; thus also, e.g., Norin (*Er spaltete das Meer*, p. 115), König (*Die Psalmen*, p. 485) and Cohen (p. 290); cf. Hossfeld (HZ, II, p. 591). However, Kissane's additional discernment of allusions to the conquest in vv. 13-15 (II, pp. 95, 96) is to be rejected.

209 Nevertheless, the view that God is envisaged as actually overcoming the Red Sea in battle, as advocated by Rogerson and McKay (II, p. 191), is not supportable.

210 As recognised also by Norin (*Er spaltete das Meer*, pp. 115-6), Cohen (pp. 290-291) and Dahood (II, p. 311). In addition to specific correlations (the incomparability of Yahweh among the gods, his right hand, etc.), the similarity of perspective, focusing on the destruction of the foe rather than on the deliverance of the Israelites, is especially notable.

211 As in Ps. 74, key motifs of the Deuteronomic Exodus "manifesto", such as "wonders" (v. 6), "feared" (v. 8), "mighty arm" (vv. 11, 14) and "high ... right hand" (v. 14) may also be identified (cf. Deut. 7:19, 26:8 and the discussion of Ps. 74:9, 11 above).

whilst the correlations with Ps. 77:12-16 are still more impressive.[212] This would seem to require that a corresponding sphere of reference should be alluded to here.[213] It is not valid to suggest that because creation (vv. 12-13) is chronologically prior to the Exodus, the crushing of Rahab must allude to Yahweh's victory before the constitution of the cosmos. Logically, the argumentation: Yahweh controlled and crushed Egypt: indeed, the whole world is subject to his power—is perfectly cogent, and indeed, reflects the line of development of Israel's theological consciousness, exodus back to creation.[214] Moreover, one might note also that the topic is introduced by a reference to Yahweh's אֱמוּנָה, "faithfulness" (v. 9), which suggests that the events described must be understood not in relation to creation, but as manifesting God's fidelity to his promises.[215] Finally, the frequent recitation of the Exodus events in association with celebrations of the Davidic kingship, perhaps because of a common rooting in the concept of election, must also be brought into consideration.[216]

3) However, it is also possible that v. 11 should be regarded as expressive of a myth regarding Yahweh's material rather than metaphorical slaying of a dragon. This is not an inevitable aspect of the verse, and it cannot be assumed that it was actually intended, since there is no clear indication that the apparently original use of "Rahab" as a nation name is transcended. On the other hand, once the identification between Rahab and a dragon had been made, the verse

---

212 Cf. "wonders", 77:12, 15a, 89:6a; "holy", 77:13a, 14a, "holy ones" 89:6b, 8a; "What God is great like our God?" 77:14, "Who among the sons of god is like the Lord... greatly terrible above all that are round about him?", 89:7-8; "arm", 77:16a, 89:11b, 14b; חֶסֶד, 77:9a, 89:2, 3, 15; לְדֹר וָדֹר, 77:9, 89:2; יָמִין, 77:11, 89:14; עֹז, 77:15, 89:18.

213 Thus even Seybold acknowledges that the motif of Yahweh's strong hand in v. 14 "belongs primarily to the Exodus tradition" (p. 352), despite advocating a *Chaoskampf* interpretation of v. 11b, where the same idea recurs.

214 In fact, Rahab is elsewhere sometimes mentioned after evocations of Yahweh's creative power, notably in Job 9:13 and 26:12. In Isa. 51:13, another passing creation allusion is separated from mention of Rahab (v. 9) by references to the exodus (v. 10) and return (v. 11) and by the opening of the oracle of assurance (v. 12) in which it is contained. This variable pattern of combinations suggests that the motifs are not sequential elements in a fragmentarily preserved creation account, but that they are rather bound together as manifestations of Yahweh's extraordinary power: only thus can the anti-creation behaviour of God enunciated in Job 9:5-7 (cf. perhaps also 26:5-6, 9, 11), again in proximity to the mention of Rahab, be explained. With respect to Ps. 89 itself, the discernible divisions in content and structure between vv. 6-11 and 12-19, despite their overarching thematic unity within the triptych vv. 2-19, is brought out especially clearly and persuasively by Girard (II, pp. 472-3, 477-490), and offers further confirmation of the interpretation adopted here.

215 See Kissane, II, pp. 95-6, and compare Mitchell's insight that vv. 6-19 "develop the themes of vv. 2-3", just as vv. 20-28 represent an expansion of vv. 4-5 (*The Message of the Psalter*, pp. 253-4).

216 See Norin, *Er spaltete das Meer*, pp. 114-5, and cf. 1 Sam. 10:18; 2 Sam. 7:6, 23; 1 Ki. 8:16, 21, 51, 53.

would appear open to this reading, and it is indeed encouraged by the similarities between vv. 10-11 and Isa. 51:9, in which Rahab is apparently explicitly identified as a dragon, as well as by Job 26:12 (cf. also Job 9:13), which clearly has a mythological reference and seems to attribute to Rahab the epithet "serpent"; hence this level of meaning may even be original here. Nevertheless, the view that the activity of defeating the dragon is to be associated with the time of creation,[217] remains questionable. The hymn describes in a long series the attributes of the incomparable God, and this provides a strong unifying focus for its constituent elements; however, a corollary of this is that there is not necessarily an obvious logical or chronological link between its sequential motifs.[218] For example, it is not clear how Yahweh's "mighty arm" and "high... right hand" (v. 14) have a direct connection with "creation" (vv. 12-13) or with his "righteousness and justice" (v. 15), except through his rôle as most high God and king.[219] In fact, the thesis that vv. 10ff. present a chronological account of a divine combat culminating in creation meets the difficulty that unless Rahab is actually to be identified with the sea,[220] the supposed logical series culminating in creation in v. 12 already seems to be undermined by the calming of the sea in v. 10, before the dragon has been slain and creation brought into being.[221] Moreover, the ruling of the raging waters appears to be one of many features of Yahweh's lordship over the entire cosmos, and part of his ongoing work. It is this "cosmic control" which is also to the fore in v. 12, since the concern is with the "foundation" of heaven and earth, the security of the divinely-ordered world. The ends of the earth (v. 13), then, were created by him and so now continually praise him. The ongoing assurance of Yahweh's power in an harmonious universe is then continued by direct affirmations of his might (v. 14) and justice (v. 15), i.e., his ability and will to maintain that order. Therefore, it may be concluded that Ps. 89:10-13 does not seem to be concerned to recite the sequential events of creation.

Which aspect of the presentation of the slaying of Rahab—polemical, historical, or mythical—is uppermost here, is difficult to determine objectively, and elements of each may be present. However, a clearer understanding of the

---

217 As advocated by Gunkel (*Die Psalmen*, p. 387; *Schöpfung*, pp. 33-36) and many subsequent scholars.

218 Particularly notable in this connection is the syntactic independence of v. 11: see Podella, "Der 'Chaoskampfmythos' in Alten Testament" in *Mesopotamica—Ugaritica—Biblica*, p. 305; see similarly Vosberg, *Studien zum Reden vom Schöpfer in den Psalmen* (Beiträge zur evangelischen Theologie 69; Munich: Chr. Kaiser, 1975), p. 46.

219 See again Podella, *ibid*., pp. 305-6.

220 This is unlikely: the dragon and Yam are separate entities in Ugarit, and it is difficult to imagine how a beast of the sea could also embody the sea; nor could such an equation claim clear support from the Old Testament.

221 The "seas", which are portrayed as the work of the third day of creation in Gen. 1:10, are apparently to be distinguished from the primeval "waters" or "deep" which preceded them; hence יָם nowhere seems to denote the precreation ocean.

imagery of vv. 10-13 may be obtained through a close analysis of the language in which it is couched.

The noun גֵּאוּת (v. 10) is often translated in a manner reflecting the *Chaoskampf* interpretation of the section, for example, as "raging"[222] or "tumult".[223] However, such terminology does not best accord with the root meaning of the Hebrew. The verb גאה means "rise up"; hence גֵּאוּת is, literally, "lifting up, rising", or sometimes, by extension, "majesty, pride". Thus, the most natural sense of v. 10a, as suggested by the parallelism with שׂוֹא גַלָּיו,[224] is that it alludes to the "swelling"[225] of the sea, and to God's power over the tides or over the building up and falling of the waves. This action is encompassed within his rule (משׁל), and should probably be understood in conjunction with the allusions to his might and faithfulness: the regulation of the sea illustrates the enormous scale of God's work, but it also an aspect of his steadfastness and ongoing commitment to the world.[226] שׁבח, "still", or perhaps "hush, soothe",[227] in the parallel colon is, like משׁל, not a confrontational term implying domination and harsh control.[228] This thus appears to be an ongoing feature of Yahweh's governance of the world, not a form of combat.[229]

Turning to the disputed v. 11, it must first of all be observed that the verb דכא is somewhat open-ended: it may be used in a generalised sense of humbling,[230] or oppression (for example, that of the enemies in an individual lament psalm), but in relation to physical injury, its significance may range from "bruise" (the translation frequently adopted in Isa. 53:5b) to the destruction of an individual or nation (cf. Job 6:9). However, it is never employed literally,[231] and is applicable either to an individual or to a group; hence, it must be distinguished from terms denoting slaying or wounding,[232] since these are

---

222 Leslie (p. 275), RSV.

223 Kraus, II, p. 778 ("Aufbegehren").

224 Literally, "lifting up", hence the frequent translation "(a)rise, rise up" (e.g., JPSA; Johnson, *SKAI*, p. 108); cf. Gaster, "surge" (*Thespis*, p. 419).

225 Kissane, II, p. 91; "swell", Johnson, *SKAI*, p. 108; "surging", Day, *God's Conflict*, p. 25, Kloos, *Yhwh's Combat*, p. 78.

226 In fact, משׁל is employed of the "execution of control or dominion" by God only in a positive sense (P. J. Nel, "5440 משׁל", *NIDOTTE* , p. 1137).

227 Thus J. N. Oswalt, "8656 שׁבח", *NIDOTTE*, 26-7, p.26.

228 It occurs elsewhere in Ps. 65:8 (in the Hiph.), there in relation to the roar of the seas (on which, see Chapter 5 above), but the only other attestation in the Pi'el is in Prov. 29:11, of "stilling, calming" a temper.

229 Contrast Anderson, II, p. 635: "Yahweh is the ruler of the raging sea because he is its conqueror". The "natural" (as opposed to mythological) interpretation of this verse is, however, apparently advocated by Cohen, p. 290.

230 E.g., Jer. 44:10 (Pu'al).

231 A point made in BDB, p. 194.

232 Of which there are a multiplicity in Hebrew—e.g., הרג, מות (Hiph.), חלל, דקר, שׁחט, נפל (Hiph.). Note how the verb of v. 24, כתת, "beat, crush by beating", is far stronger than that employed in the present verse.

concrete terms appropriate to an individual or individuals but not to a collective entity. Thus, דכא is unlikely to refer to a literal "crushing" of a single being, but is more probably employed metaphorically, perhaps of a collective object; this would cohere with the impression arrived at on other grounds that "Rahab" may refer to Egypt, but would be rather curious if it was simply intended to allude to the physical slaying of a dragon (contrast Isa. 27:1 and, in a theomachic context, *Enuma elish* IV.101-2).

As regards the expression כֶּחָלָל (v. 11a), it appears that—as often in Hebrew— it is not the verb (דִכִּאתָ) which serves as the point of comparison, but its object, here רָהַב. There are two possible interpretations of the colon, then: either that Yahweh crushed Rahab as one might crush one already pierced or slain (cf. Judg. 14:6, where the verb is actually repeated), i.e., with as much ease as if he were already dead or wounded, thus emphasising the helplessness and lack of effective resistance on Rahab's part;[233] or, alternatively, it may indicate that he was crushed "like unto death", so that he became as one fatally wounded.[234] Once again, the collective (Egyptian) interpretation would be preferable, since an individual reading would empty the comparison of its point: Rahab, if he was a living being, would not become "like one slain", but would actually be slain.[235] Moreover, that "crushing" refers to the military defeat of the Egyptian foe is further suggested by the parallelism of the following colon: בִּזְרוֹעַ עֻזְּךָ פִּזַּרְתָּ אוֹיְבֶיךָ.

Finally, it may be observed that LXX has in v. 13a the reading βορραν και θαλασσας (other Greek versions have την θαλασσαν),[236] i.e. "north (wind) and seas / the sea". If it is original,[237] this would seem further to undermine the notion that some form of primordial cosmic conflict is envisaged here, since the sea is affirmed to have been brought into being by God, the verb בְּרָאתָם, further, standing in parallel to בְּשִׁמְךָ יְרַנֵּנוּ. It seems likely, then, that at some stage there was a confusion between יָמִין and יַמִּים[238] or יָם, though which is original is difficult to determine. The parallelism in the extant Hebrew text might appear

---

233 Thus apparently most commentators, perhaps most vividly Kissane, who translates, "Thou didst crush Rahab as one slain" (II, p. 91), explaining, "like those slain in battle, who are trampled on by the victors and left unburied" (II, p. 96).

234 Compare Day's translation: "You did crush Rahab with a mortal blow" (*God's Conflict*, p. 25).

235 It is also possible that there may be a wordplay here on the other meaning of חָלָל, "unhallowed, profane": Yahweh crushes Rahab as befits one that is unclean, meeting an end deserved by one who is an offence before God. This would perhaps be comparable to the thought of Ps. 44:20. Of course, the slain were anyway unclean (Num. 19:18; 31:19; cf. Ezek. 31:18; Jer. 25:33), so the statement would have a further double edge to it.

236 Alexandrinus and the Lucianic recension, besides the Latin codex Parisinus.

237 As urged by Norin, on the basis that it is the *lectio difficilior* (*Er spaltete das Meer*, pp. 115-6); see similarly de Savignac, "Le sens du terme Ṣâphôn", *UF* 16 (1984) 273-8, p. 275).

238 Cf. Ezek. 29:3 and 32:2, where תַּנִּים seems to stand for תַּנִּין.

smoother than that of the Greek, but in fact, as Mowan has indicated, Zaphon is nowhere in the Hebrew Bible attested parallel to יָמִין, "south".[239] Moreover, any awkwardness in the Septuagintal pairing is much alleviated in the Hebrew, whether the reading יָם (i.e., "west") is accepted as original[240] or, perhaps better, if צָפוֹן is understood as alluding to the name of the highest of the mountains, and יָם to its opposite, the sea.[241] This latter reading would balance the mention of the word-pair שָׁמַיִם and אֶרֶץ in the preceding verse (v. 12), but there is an additional aspect to this possible parallelism, as "Zaphon" in the Ugaritic texts denotes the abode of Baal,[242] whereas that of El is "at the source(s) of the rivers, amid the springs of the oceans".[243] Still more interesting if the psalm is concerned with engaging with Canaanite mythic material (and it has already been observed above that it is apparently polemical in character), is that "Zaphon" may possibly stand for Baal himself (cf. *KTU* 1.19.ii.35),[244] just as "Yam" is, of course, the name of one of his chief opponents in the Ugaritic texts. The polysemic statement that Yahweh created both Zaphon / Baal and the sea / Yam would thus take up the claim for his supremacy among the gods which was trumpeted at the beginning of the hymnic section (vv. 6-9); thus, within the polemical context of the psalm, it would serve, rather in the manner of the oracles of Deutero-Isaiah, to challenge the fears of the wavering exilic community, for whom Yahweh's apparent lack of power to intervene on their behalf was an impetus to apostasy.

Turning, then, to overview the content of vv. 10-13, it transpires that a close analysis of its key terms confirms the preliminary indications that the theme of "chaos" is absent here, as well as supporting the relation of v. 11 to the defeat of the Egyptians at the Red Sea. This would seem to cohere with the developmental model advanced above, according to which Rahab originated as a designation for Egypt, possibly as a "nickname" referring to its legendary

---

239 See O. Mowan, "Quattuor montes sacri in Ps. 89, 13?" *Verbum Domini* 41 (1963), p. 13. As he explains, although the combinations "north and south" and, less commonly, "left and right" are acceptable, the hybrid "north and right" or "left and south" is not; hence this would constitute the sole instance of the former, whilst the latter is nowhere attested.

240 Cf. Ps. 107:3b.

241 Cf. Ps. 68:23, Am. 9:3, in each of which a specific mountain—Carmel or Bashan—is coupled with the sea. A different interpretation of the same pairing is maintained by de Savignac ("Le sens du terme Ṣâphôn", p. 275), who, in accordance with his understanding of צָפוֹן, translates, "Tu as créé le ciel nuageux et les mers", thus obtaining a contrast between the upper and lower waters. If his proposal is correct, there is much justification for his suggestion that an original Hebrew יַמִּים was corrupted to יָמִין once the significance of צָפוֹן here was no longer recognised.

242 E.g., *KTU* 1.3.i.22; 1.5.i.11.

243 *mbk nhrm qrb apq thmtm*, e.g., *KTU* 1.3.v.6-7; 1.4.iv.21-22.

244 See, e.g., de Savignac, "Le sens du terme Ṣâphôn", p. 275. Another possibility is that it denotes another Canaanite deity or is tantamount to "the gods"; see Wyatt, *RTU*, p. 301 n. 229 (an "umbrella deity"), Gibson, *CML*, p. 116, ll. 84-5 and n. 7.

pride; the appellative may later have been understood as a personification embodied in a draconic form, perhaps especially in relation to the exodus, so that in due course the motif of the overcoming of the dragon Rahab became a freestanding entity in its own right. Wherever Ps. 89:11 stands on this line of development, the lack of a clear link to the theme of *Chaoskampf* would be understandable. However, the Rahab motif may have been viewed as a prime embodiment of the Yahweh's conquest of "the enemy" and have been regarded as manifesting the deity's power and supremacy in a particularly impressive way (both of these aspects being true also of hymnic recollections of the exodus, especially as employed in a lament setting); moreover, there may also have been a polemical aspect to the claiming of a draconic conquest for Yahweh. It is also possible that the motifs of the overcoming of Rahab and of Leviathan, though probably originating independently and being transmitted as discrete entities without specific identification being made between them, may have came to absorb some of each other's theological content and to exercise a mutual influence. This might be indicated by the relation of the dragon Leviathan to the exodus tradition in Ps. 74, and the graduation of the nation Rahab to independent draconic status in Job.

The foregoing analysis can therefore claim certain points of agreement with the "chaos"-oriented interpretation. It has been observed that the hymnic section may have mythological overtones; that the psalm seems to exhibit polemical aspects; that "Rahab", in time, came to designate a dragon; and that it may own something of that quality here. On the other hand, more impressive is the fact that the fundamental elements of *Chaoskampf* are absent, as may perhaps helpfully be demonstrated by a comparison with the account of the hymn offered by an exponent of this interpretation. According to this latter, and most prevalent, perspective, it concerns:

> the mighty deeds of the Lord at the creation of the world. It tells how He mastered the defiant, chaotic waters which were roaring against Him and stilled them; how He crushed the terrible dragon of the primeval watery deep as an unclean, arrogant, and abusive monster which had challenged His lordship... This monster of the primeval sea is an evil being... But the might of the Lord broke the rule of this dragon and proved God to be the mightiest of divine beings... By this great act He opened the way to the present order of the world.[245]

However, as has been shown above, it is far from certain that the verses under discussion concern the originating events of creation; the foregoing account, further, fails to distinguish between the dragon and the sea, which is surely of critical importance (in Ugarit as in Israel), whilst the designation of "the dragon" as "evil" and as "ruling" the world prior to creation, though not

245 Leslie, p. 275; see likewise Johnson, *SKAI*, p. 108, Weiser, p. 403, Kraus, II, pp. 787-8. Even some who would identify Rahab with Egypt still discern "an allusion to the monster of chaos destroyed by God before the work of creation" (Kissane, II, p. 96).

peculiar to this cited instance, owes more to the merging of the dragon and Satan in the early Christian era, as reflected in Rev. 12:9, than to the Old Testament. Moreover, one must take issue with the presumption that Rahab and the sea challenge God or exhibit aggression, since, as has been shown, this is not reflected in the passage under examination. Such an approach, further, fails to acknowledge the rhetorical and historical context of the psalm, which is fundamentally concerned with Yahweh's current ability to intervene in world events for the protection and restoration of his nation; nor does it take account of its antecedents in the lament form,[246] its polemical force[247] or the wider use of the name "Rahab". Thus, the *Chaoskampf* interpretation of the Psalm is to be rejected in favour of a more nuanced approach which enables the mythic, historical and polemical to find their voice in an evocative web of traditional associations, whilst directly addressing the challenges of a new and frightening situation. This conclusion is entirely consistent with the results of the analysis of the psalms so far considered, but that it may be supported on so many different bases in this most contentious case does much to confirm the general thrust of the present thesis.

Finally, concerning the interpretation of the "creation" content of Ps. 89:6-19 and of Ps. 74:12-17, the other psalm which is of crucial interest here, a few further summarising remarks may be in keeping. Through the foregoing discussion, it has emerged that both are intense and multifaceted poetic passages, in which the mythic and polemical is blended with the historical. Nevertheless, these hymnic interludes are primarily concerned to demonstrate God's ability to act on a global scale, whether through the deliverance from Egypt (89:11, 74:13-15) or the regulation of the tides and times (89:10, 74:16-17), or his lordship of all creation (89:12-13, 74:17), since the fundamental issue at stake is that of Yahweh's capability to intervene on the world arena (89:14, 74:12) and his commitment so to do (89:15; see also 74:1-2, 20, and 89:9, where both are envisaged). However, the context does not require, and nor does the imagery suggest, that some form of hymnic recitation of the originating events of creation is systematically explored here. The providential focus of the imagery of God's action in nature is rather concerned to demonstrate his regulatory and possessory work throughout the whole cosmos, and not to relate his engendering of it. This interpretation is especially confirmed in relation to Ps. 74 by the allusion to the עָם לְצִיִּים in v. 14 and by

246 Leslie, like many other commentators, seems not to look beyond the immediate context, which is designated as a "hymn" and sometimes treated as having a former independent existence. However, the fact that it constitutes a recognisable element of the lament form—the recollection of Yahweh's past deeds of might and faithfulness (v. 9)—and performs a rhetorically significant function within this wider structure, strongly cautions against such a narrow approach.

247 Leslie even interprets Mounts Tabor and Hermon as "the chief sanctuaries of the worship of the Lord in the poet's home region of Israel" (p. 275), which can claim only the slenderest support and is damaging to the natural force of the Psalm (see the discussion above).

the reference to the cleaving open of springs and brooks and drying up of ever-flowing streams in v. 15, which cannot be matched with any recognisable act in creation. Similarly, the opening declaration of 89:12-13, that the whole cosmos is Yahweh's, expresses the chief rhetorical concern of these verses, which is then simply supported by the claim that he created תֵּבֵל וּמְלֹאָהּ and graphically illustrated by the notion that even seats of worship for rival gods are in reality offering him willing praise. Thus, the intention in each psalm is the demonstration of Yahweh's sole power in heaven and on earth, not the relation of creation *per se*, and hence the allusions to Yahweh's work in nature are in general presently-oriented and concerned with his ongoing work: they do not constitute the major focus of the hymnic sections of either composition. Finally, it must be noted that Yahweh's engagement with Leviathan and Rahab does not properly amount to a theomachic combat, since there is no indication of their near equality with God, still less of their hostile action or resistance to him. This is a situation in which Yahweh remains the sole significant agent throughout, and in Ps. 89, the incident is apparently passed over quite briefly, without much emphasis. Thus, although these psalms may be dependent on earlier mythic accounts through the vehicle of which the defeat of the Egyptian foe at the Red Sea is symbolically and graphically related, the theme of a battle with "chaos" at creation does not apparently implied here even at an underlying level.

4. Psalm 44

i. The Date of Psalm 44

As is the case with the psalms already considered in the present chapter, Psalm 44 is a communal lament belonging to a situation of national crisis; thus its *Sitz im Leben* is probably to be found in a time of fasting and prayer called by the leaders of the nation to appeal to God for help. As in 2 Chr. 20, the psalm would most likely have been recited by an individual, perhaps the king or some other national representative, on behalf of the people, hence the occasional first-person singular declarations (vv. 5, 7, 16) in a primarily plural-voice psalm.

The particular historical circumstances of crisis are, in this instance, apparently harder to discern than the cultic, and accordingly dating proposals range from c. 609 B.C.,[248] or even "from the end of the northern kingdom",[249] through the time of the exile,[250] to the post-exilic era,[251] with some scholars

248 I.e., the death of Josiah; thus Anderson (I, p. 337). He considers Sennacherib's invasion of Judah during the time of Hezekiah (c. 701 B.C.) to be an alternative, though less likely, possibility.

249 Goulder, *PSK*, p. 90, suggesting more tentatively the time of King Hoshea.

250 Mowinckel places its composition shortly after the catastrophe of c. 587 B.C. (*PIW* II, p. 152), Terrien in the years prior to it, i.e. c. 605-587 B. C (p. 361).

even advocating a composite origin.[252] The nature of the affliction depicted includes military defeat (v. 10), pillage at the hands of the victorious foe (v. 11), mass slaughter and exile or slavery (vv. 12-13), and humiliating derision from neighbouring peoples (vv. 14-15). However, this does not permit of chronological specificity: the allusion to the dispersal of the people among the nations does not demand an association with the events of the exile, any more than the reference to suffering "for thy sake" in v. 23 presupposes a background of persecution, as occurred during the Maccabean period. Nor is there any other detail confining the date of composition to a particular time, and the linguistic data are similarly unilluminating.[253] Even the similarities to the language of Jeremiah to which Terrien has drawn attention[254] are difficult to assess, since one context is that of judgment, the other of lament; hence one composition may be cross-referring to conventional language exhibited in the other, earlier source.[255] Moreover, there is nothing in the Psalm to link it specifically with Jerusalem or the Judahite cult; the self-reference of the nation as "Jacob" (v. 5), the location of the composition within the Elohistic Psalter, and even perhaps the image of the "sleeping" of Yahweh, analogous to Baal (v. 24; cf. 1 Ki. 18:27; contrast Ps. 121:4) opens the possibility of a northern provenance.[256] One must further be aware that the lament may have been both adaptable and actually adapted to different circumstances, perhaps especially if it owed its origins to the northern kingdom and had later been appropriated by the Judahite community. Thus a precise date is not attainable.

ii. The Theme of "Chaos" in Psalm 44

The presence of "chaos" language here depends on the emendation of the MT of v. 20a. The extant text בִּמְקוֹם תַּנִּים is comprehensible in itself, and is normally understood to indicate the abode of jackals, i.e., the wilderness or uninhabitable, desolate places of ruin and destruction, which are often associated with defeat

251 Thus Schmidt, who considers it at the earliest to be Persian (pp. 83-83; cf. Gerstenberger, I, p. 186), Oesterley (late post-exilic but not Maccabean, I, p. 245), Leslie (c. 351 B.C., p. 227) and Gunkel (Maccabean, *Die Psalmen*, p. 187).

252 E.g. Zenger, HZ, I, p. 272.

253 Some items of vocabulary are predominantly attested in the pre-exilic or exilic periods, others in the exilic age or subsequently, with perhaps a marginal bias towards the later period. On the other hand, the composition is consistently lacking in later prose features; though colon-initial waw occurs fifteen times, it never features at the beginning of a line, and the article -ה occurs only in the phrase כָּל־הַיּוֹם (vv. 9a, 16a, 23a). From this little may be deduced, except perhaps that the lament is unlikely to derive from a time subsequent to the early post-exile.

254 P. 361.

255 Equally difficult to evaluate is the language and theology of vv. 2-3, which Gerstenberger adjudges to be deuteronomistic and late (I, p. 183), whilst Zenger regards it as deuteronomic and reflecting the time of Josiah (I, p. 272).

256 Both Seybold (p. 180) and Goulder (*PSK*, e.g. pp. 85-7) associate the psalm with Dan.

(Isa. 13:22, 34:13, Jer. 9:10, 10:22, 49:33, 51:37, Lam. 5:18, Mal. 1:3).[257] It would thus allude either to the ruinous state of the land, or to the uninhabited regions to which the defeated remnant have been compelled to flee (cf. Jer. 4:29, 1 Macc. 1:38f., 2:29). Nevertheless, Gunkel[258] proposed emending MT תַּנִּים, "jackals", to תַּנִּין, "dragon",[259] and interpreted בִּמְקוֹם as "instead of, as", comparing the thought of the verse with that of Job 7:12, where, however, the sea and תַּנִּין are only said to be "watched".[260] If Gunkel is correct, the dragon would here be indicative of the enemy of Yahweh which should be crushed and destroyed.[261] It would constitute a rare and exceptionally direct allusion to some form of divine conflict as encountered in Canaanite (and Babylonian) literature, and as such would be highly significant. It may claim some support from the Peshitta, which seems to presuppose the Hebrew בִּמְקוֹם תַּנִּין; LXX and Vulg., however, read respectively ἐν τόπῳ κακώσεως ("in place of ill-treatment, damage, misfortune") and *in loco afflictionis* ("in [the] place of affliction"), presuming a derivation from the root ינה, "oppress, maltreat",[262] whilst the Targ. seems to require the Hebrew תַּנִּים.

More importantly, Gunkel's proposed rendering of בִּמְקוֹם is itself dubious, claiming its only support from a debatable translation of Hos. 2:1.[263] Yet if the more natural, local, sense of the Hebrew, "in the place (i.e., region) of" is accepted, as seems necessary, the emendation to תַּנִּין is insupportable.[264]

---

257 Although the precise expression מְקוֹם תַּנִּים is not replicated elsewhere, one might compare מְעוֹן תַּנִּים in Jer. 9:10, 10:22, 49:33, 51:37 and נְוֵה תַנִּים in Isa. 34:13, 35:7.

258 Following the early lead of Olshausen (*Die Psalmen*, pp. 197-198), who understood תַּנִּין as alluding to the crocodile. See Gunkel, *Schöpfung und Chaos*, pp. 70-71, *Die Psalmen*, pp. 184, 186, 188; his interpretation was subsequently adopted by Mowinckel (*PsSt* II, p. 340), Leslie (pp. 229-230) and Day (*God's Conflict*, pp. 112-113).

259 Cf. the confusion of תַּנִּין for תַּנִּים in Lam. 4:3 and, conversely, of תַּנִּים for תַּנִּין in Ezek. 29:3, 32:2.

260 The resultant translation, "Denn du hast uns geschändet anstatt des Drachen" (*Schöpfung und Chaos*, p. 70; cf. *Die Psalmen*, p. 184: "daß du uns wie den Drachen mißhandelt"), also entails an abnormal rendering of the verb דכא, which means "crush", not "defile" or (following the proposal in *Die Psalmen*), "maltreat, afflict", as Gunkel's approach requires.

261 According to Olshausen (p. 198), the "crocodile" is representative of the King of Egypt in an allusion to the Red Sea miracle. Day also considers the dragon to "symbolise the enemy nation defeating Israel", perhaps Babylon or Egypt, or possibly Assyria (*God's Conflict*, p. 113).

262 Or perhaps, as Goulder proposes in respect of the Greek, this is simply an interpretation of the Hebrew, understood as referring to the cities which "have been stripped of human inhabitants, and taken over by jackals" (*PSK*, pp. 265-6 n. 16).

263 See G. I. Davies, *Hosea* (NCBC, 1992), pp. 60-61 and J. L. Mays, *Hosea* (OTL, 1969), p. 30, both of whom reject this reading as without valid parallel. As Mays indicates with reference to Hos. 2:1, "the problem is contextual; what 'place' could the text have in mind?" (p. 30).

264 Oesterley (I, p. 246) retains the conventional translation of בִּמְקוֹם in conjunction with תַּנִּינִים, but this is only achievable by a further emendation, of דִכִּיתָנוּ to הִדַּחְתָּנוּ, resulting

Besides, the implied error of judgment on Yahweh's part in destroying his faithful people instead of his (or their) foe—which is absent from Job 7:12 and is not paralleled elsewhere—renders this an especially dubious reading. It is perhaps not surprising that it is rejected by the majority of modern commentators.[265]

Nevertheless, the conventional understanding of the verse, while substantially correct, should perhaps be slightly refined, since מָקוֹם need not accurately denote the 'home, abode' of a person or creature, but may be employed more generally of a 'haunt, lurking place' (cf. 1 Sam. 23:22, 2 Sam. 17:9, 12). Thus, ominously, the Israelites were crushed in a place where jackals were already present. This does not, as has sometimes been supposed, require that the defeat took place among ruins, since jackals hunt and scavenge both in the open countryside and near to human habitation, where they are known as agricultural pests. Rather the significance of these animals lies in the fact that, as carrion-eaters, they are natural harbingers of death, like vultures, possessing an uncanny ability to home in on a kill. Their spine-chilling howls and nocturnal habits further contribute to their wholly negative sphere of association.[266] Thus the allusion suggests their readiness prior to the battle to enjoy the impending feast; the fate of the Israelites, however, is one of progressive, but total, oblivion - crushed on the battlefield, consumed by the hungry awaiting jackals[267] and then "covered over", i.e., almost "closed over"[268] by צַלְמָוֶת, a term frequently associated with Sheol,[269] and possibly equating to "dark shadow of death", צֵל + מָוֶת.[270] Thus, the existence of the victim is entirely obliterated. The frequent mention of jackals in relation to ruined cities is probably a secondary reflection of their association with death

---

in the reading: "Yet thou hast thrust us into the place of dragons"; whether this rather obscure allusion merits a double emendation (entailing five consonantal changes) of MT, or even that it represents an improvement upon it, is questionable. The same objection also applies to NEB/REB: "Yet thou hast (/you have) crushed us as the sea-serpent was crushed".

265 Thus Schmidt, p. 82, Kraus, I, pp. 479, 480, Anderson, I, p. 343, Goulder, *PSK*, pp. 256-6 n. 16. By most modern scholars it is not even mentioned, though implicitly dismissed: Weiser, p. 238, Seybold, pp. 179, 183, Zenger (HZ, I, p. 277), Briggs, I, pp. 375, 381, Cohen, p. 138, Buttenwieser, pp. 749, 753, Craigie, pp. 331, 334 and Dahood, I, pp. 264, 267.

266 Cf. Mic. 1:8, Isa. 13:21-22.

267 Cf. Pss. 63:11, 74:4b.

268 Cf. Num. 16:33, Ps. 106:17 (// בלע, 'swallowed up').

269 An association with the darkness of death is advocated or implied by Gunkel (*Die Psalmen*, p. 186), Weiser (p. 238), Anderson (I, p. 344) and Craigie (pp. 207, 331).

270 See further the discussion in relation to Job 3 in Chapter 11 below. A connection with death is apparent in Job 10:21, 22, 38:17 and probably also Job 3:5, whilst an association with the desolation of the wilderness may be inferred from Jer. 2:6. However, צַלְמָוֶת is never linked with precreation darkness. Leslie's attempt to interpret Ps. 44:20 in the light of the 'Semitic theology of creation', explaining that 'the Lord has dealt with His people as He maltreated and trampled the monstrous and evil dragon' and 'overwhelmed them with the abysmal darkness that belonged to that monster's reign' (comparing Gen. 1:2; p. 229), is therefore untenable.

and decay, and as an eerie and disturbing creature of the night.[271] Thus, the MT of the verse would appear to be internally coherent and well-integrated into its context, exhibiting a 'progressive' parallelism, in which the second colon offers the narrative sequence to and an intensification of the first.[272]

5. Summary

The national laments Pss. 77, 74, 89 and 44 form a continuum with the Zion psalms examined in the previous chapter, insofar as the increased anxiety concerning Israel's political fortunes which may be traced throughout the monarchical period reached its culmination with the disaster of the exile. Yahweh's past salvific actions, in which he redeemed his people "of old", are painted in increasingly extravagant colours; the gulf between Israel and the nations, God and the foe, is ever more decisively drawn as his desperate people plead for intervention or explanation.

The presence of negative, threatening forces within the world and the sometimes unresolved nature of Yahweh's kingship—has he broken his covenant, or forgotten his people, or is he unable or unwilling to act?—comes to the fore in these psalms of lamentation, where disaster has apparently taken hold and yet the expected salvation "as of old" has not (yet) been forthcoming. Here the ardent desire for God to engage in direct divine conflict with the nation's tangible historical enemy invites the employment of "dragon" imagery—Yahweh has / will destroy(ed) Leviathan / Rahab (74 / 89), crushing it or its heads like a carcass and leaving its body to be preyed on in the wilderness—and therefore, faced with a crisis of Exodus proportions, he must surely do so again.

Thus, the impetus of these laments lies firmly in the historical realm. On the other hand, it may readily be noted how much more "mythological" the Red Sea descriptions of the laments are as compared with the hymns.[273] This indicates that the literary context and rhetorical usage are as important in determining the force and type of image as the date of composition; neither does the subject of an allusion intimately govern its strength. This suggests a further very important corollary, namely that the respective genres do not so much reflect opposing visions of reality or radically divergent understandings

---

271 One might note that in the wider Ancient Near Eastern context, Anubis, the Egyptian deity who was believed to conduct the souls of the dead to the underworld and to preside over mummification and funerals, was represented as a jackal or as having a jackal's head.

272 For this dynamic quality of Biblical poetry, see Robert Alter's analysis of 'The Dynamics of Parallelism' in *The Art of Biblical Poetry*, pp. 3-26.

273 Compare especially Pss. 66 and 114 as well as the psalms to be discussed in Chapter 9 below (Pss. 78, 106 and 136).

of the events they describe, so much as harness contrasting means of expression as befits the context, mood and authorial intent of their use.

VII. Songs of Universal Praise: Psalms 96, 98, 148 and 135

The psalms considered in the present chapter are joyful hymns of praise in which the entirety of creation, including הַיָּם (Pss. 96:11b, 98:7a) and נְהָרוֹת (98:8a), תַּנִּינִים וְכָל־תְּהֹמוֹת (148:7b), is enjoined to "sing to Yahweh a new song" (96:1, 98:1) and "praise [his] name" (148:5; cf. 135:1-3, 19-21). As regards their thematic resonances with the remaining psalms discussed in the present monograph, Pss. 96 and 98 stand in continuity with the "songs relating to the protection of Zion" examined in chapter 5 above, Ps. 96:10b even replicating Ps. 93:1c, whilst Ps. 98:7b parallels 24:1b. This issue will be explored in more detail in the discussion of the psalms' content below. In addition, Ps. 148 exhibits an interest in the laudation of Yahweh as creator of the world, the listing of all elements of the created universe being especially striking; the same motif occurs also in a more muted form in Ps. 135:5-7 and in the universalist concerns of Pss. 96 and 98, notably in the call to praise of Pss. 96:11-12 and 98:7-8. In this respect, these compositions, though not properly "creation psalms", display certain affinities with the hymns specifically dedicated to this theme, which shall be discussed in chapter 8 below. For the present purpose, however, the main focus of interest in Pss. 96, 98 and 148 is the universality of the offered praise in which the whole cosmos is joyfully and harmoniously united, since it seems powerfully to contravene the notion that any form of divine conflict is here in view.

1. Psalms 96 and 98

i. The Date of Psalms 96 and 98

The dating of Psalms 96 and 98 has already been adverted to above, where doubt was cast both on the reliability of the evidence which has been thought to demonstrate the association of these psalms with an autumn enthronement festival (Chapter 2), and on the attempt to date the so-called "divine kingship psalms" (Pss. 47, 93, 96-99) *en masse* (Chapter 5). Rather, it emerged that where, in more recent studies, each has been awarded separate consideration, the results have been broadly consistent. Psalms 96 and 98 are perhaps alone among this group in exhibiting close affinities to Deutero-Isaiah,[1] the

1 See Jörg Jeremias, *Das Königtum Gottes in den Psalmen* (Göttingen: Vandenhoeck & Ruprecht, 1987), who even structures his discussion on a chronological basis, with Pss. 96 and 98 alone being classified as "Deutero-Isaianic" (p. 6); note also the summary of scholarship on this issue in J. H. Eaton, *Psalms of the Way and the Kingdom*, p. 118.

dependence of these two hymns upon the prophet being urged by Jeremias,[2] Koenen,[3] Kraus,[4] Hossfeld,[5] Loretz,[6] Westermann,[7] and even Gray.[8] The evidence for this will be discussed further below.

However, this does not provide the sole basis for claiming the dependence of Pss. 96 and 98 on earlier precedents. As has been demonstrated in relation to the provenance of Ps. 29 (a hymn on which Ps. 96 seems to draw),[9] Ps. 96 exhibits points of contact with a variety of psalms, which nevertheless seem to have no derivative relationship to each other, and which also fail to duplicate significantly between them any of the material held in common with Psalm 96. Since the majority of these psalms are apparently pre-exilic, and since the parallel passages exhibiting the closest similarity to sections of Ps. 96 are opening verses,[10] it is difficult to avoid the conclusion that Ps. 96 must have drawn on earlier cultic material.[11] It is intrinsically more probable that the author of one hymn should quote the opening lines of another within the course of his composition, than that a poet should have commenced with phrases borrowed from the midpoint of an earlier hymn. For so many poems to draw on different sections of Ps. 96, with no overlap in their selections, and none of them overtly citing its opening lines[12] would, moreover, seem incredible. The composite origin of the Psalm is, further, supported by its irregular metre.[13]

The conclusion that Ps. 96 may be a relatively late and tradition-dependent work is reinforced by the way some of the apparent source-materials are adapted and utilised. For example, the replacement of the phrase בְּנֵי אֵלִים from Ps. 29:1 with מִשְׁפְּחוֹת עַמִּים may probably most satisfactorily be accounted for as the result of a later discomfort with the polytheistic resonances of the former,

2 *Das Königtum Gottes*, pp. 121, 126-131 (re Ps. 96); 133-4 (re Ps. 98).

3 *Jahwe wird kommen*, e.g., p. 116.

4 II, p. 846 (on Psalm 98) and p. 835, where he describes Ps. 96 as "later than Isaiah 40-66".

5 II, pp. 670, 690.

6 *UTT*, p. 358 (on Ps. 98); cf. pp. 328-9 (on Ps. 96).

7 *Lob und Klage*, pp. 111-112.

8 P. 35 n. 88 and p. 67; see also Gunkel, *Einleitung*, §3, ¶11, and Terrien, pp. 676-7, and note especially Cohen's statement that "modern scholars... are unanimous that [Psalm 96] is post-exilic" (p. 315; see similarly his comments on Ps. 98, pp. 320-1).

9 See Chapter 3 above.

10 Ps. 29:1-2 (recurring in Ps. 96:7-9); Ps. 93:1c (in Ps. 96:10b); Ps. 48:2a (in Ps. 96:4a). There are less direct resemblances between Ps. 104:1c and Ps. 96:6a, whilst Ps. 96:9b corresponds to the penultimate verse of Ps. 114 (v. 7).

11 The only verse which is not paralleled elsewhere in the Psalter is v. 5, which has every appearance of a quotation from Deutero-Isaiah.

12 There is a fleeting parallel between Ps. 96:1a and Pss. 33:3, 149:1, but no extended quotation.

13 Kraus classifies the metre of Ps. 96 as 3+3 in vv. 1, 3, 6 and 13; 4+4 in vv. 2, 7 and 8; 4+3 in vv. 4, 5, 9, 11 and 12; and 4+4+3 in v. 10 (II, p. 834).

rather archaic, expression.[14] Similarly, although apparently ancient notions, also encountered in Canaan, such as divine King concepts, entailing supremacy over all other gods, may be reflected in Ps. 96, they have metamorphosed into a more mature form. The description of all other gods as mere אֱלִילִים is, in fact, especially characteristic of Proto-Isaiah,[15] but the insistence that they are devoid of all significance and power indicates that "the message of Deutero-Isaiah is to be presupposed".[16] Moreover, the wider theological interests of Ps. 96 also tend towards a universalistic and monotheistic stance. A particularly striking feature is its sustained inclusivism, which is explicit in vv. 1, 3, 7, 9, 10 and 13, the thought of many of these verses also often being continued into the following lines, as well as being mirrored in the inclusion of all the spheres of the natural world in vv. 11-12. This is quite in contrast to the passing phrases which occur in the psalms on which it seems to draw, which are frequently ambiguous regarding this matter as well as often being juxtaposed with more nationalistic sentiments.

In addition, the content of vv. 12-13 recurs only in the closely related Ps. 98. The timbre and universalism of the passage, which is characteristic of Ps. 96 as a whole, would seem to point to an eschatological interpretation as the primary context for the psalm.[17] Yahweh's rule over all the earth is proclaimed, and its final consummation in recognition by the nations also anticipated. If the discernment of a universalistic eschatological interest here is correct, this would seem to provide a further indication of lateness.

Ps. 98 also exhibits a number of inner-biblical parallels, though its relation to passages from within the Psalter is less marked than in the case of Ps. 96. Nevertheless, the phrase תֵּבֵל וְיֹשְׁבֵי בָהּ (98:7b) is paralleled by Ps. 24:1b,[18] the relationship, once again, being with a composition which is almost certainly fairly early, as well as from its opening verse. In addition, 98:9 may be compared with 9:9, and 98:4a with 66:1,[19] whilst 98:8b-9 has slightly looser affinities with 67:5. Psalm 98 is also often deemed to stand closer to Deutero-Isaiah than Ps. 96, and this issue will be discussed further below. It scarcely needs to be added that the two hymns Pss. 96 and 98 are evidently related,

---

14 Compare Jeremias' contention that "Ps. 96:1-9 on the whole wants to be a modern exegesis of Ps. 29:1f." (*Königtum*, p. 125)

15 See Isa. 2:8, 18, 20; 10:10-11; 19:1, 3; 31:7; it does not occur in chapters 40-66. (The remaining occurrences are in Ps. 97:7, Lev. 19:4, 26:1, Ezek. 30:13 and Hab. 2:18, besides the parallel to Ps. 96:5 in 1 Chr. 16:26.)

16 Kraus, II, p. 836; cf. Isa. 40:19-26, 44:12-20. For Gray, too, this is a particular mark of lateness, indicating that Ps. 96 "is even more mature than Ps. 98" (*Biblical Doctrine*, p. 68); Seybold, on the other hand, though with the same consequences for dating, thinks of the depotentisation of the "gods" as chiefly propagated by the deuteronomistic writers (p. 381). Contrast Weiser, p. 431, and cf. Hossfeld's dismissal of the verse as redactional (II, p. 667).

17 Though not necessarily the exclusive one: it may have been celebrated in the cult.

18 The same phrase recurs also in Nah. 1:5.

19 Cf. also Ps. 100:1.

particularly close parallels occurring between Ps. 96:1a and 98:1a;[20] 96:11b and 98:7a; 96:13 and 98:9; and, more generally, between 96:11-12 and 98:4, 7-8. Nevertheless, whether they were composed contemporarily, perhaps by the same author, or whether their relationship is otherwise to be explained,[21] cannot be deduced on the basis of the parallels themselves.

In addition, both Pss. 96 and 98 exhibit various characteristics of vocabulary and phraseology which would seem to point to a relatively late provenance, though there is nothing in this aspect to suggest the priority of one over the other.[22] The expression שִׁיר חָדָשׁ, which is common to the opening line of each, recurs elsewhere only in psalms which would appear to be late and probably post-exilic (i.e. Pss. 33:3,[23] 40:4,[24] 144:9[25] and 149:1),[26] as well as in Isa. 42:10. More specifically, the invocation שִׁירוּ לַיהוָה שִׁיר חָדָשׁ is peculiar to Ps. 96:1a,[27] 98:1a, 33:3a,[28] 149:1 and Isa. 42:10. Further, although the lexeme חָדָשׁ is, as may be expected, not confined to a particular period, the anticipation of a new era in the relationship between Israel and her God and of a fresh beginning which it here conveys is especially characteristic of exilic and post-exilic writers.[29]

There are also various types of linguistic usage occurring either in one of Pss. 96 and 98 which seem to be confined to the exilic and post-exilic periods, for example מִיּוֹם־לְיוֹם (96:2),[30] תִּפְאָרָה (96:6)[31] and זמר of playing musical

20 Cf. Ps. 33:3a.

21 For example, by a common cultic setting and liturgical influences, as advocated by Weiser (p. 436).

22 Yet cf. the remarks of Gray (*Biblical Doctrine*, p. 68) cited above in relation to the theology of Ps. 96:5; the priority of Ps. 98 is asserted also by Jeremias, *Das Königtum Gottes*, p. 135.

23 The date of which will be considered in the following chapter.

24 See, e.g., Anderson, I, p. 314, Kraus, I, p. 460, Zenger, HZ, I, p. 253.

25 See the discussion in chapter 4 above.

26 Contra Day, OTG, p. 72, who concludes from these references that "the words... are characteristic of psalmody rather than prophecy" and therefore antedate Deutero-Isaiah.

27 It is omitted from the parallel in 1 Chr. 16:23.

28 The MT reading is שִׁירוּ־לוֹ שִׁיר חָדָשׁ, but a few Hebrew manuscripts and Targ. have לַיהוָה; in any case, it refers back to an antecedent יהוה (vv. 1, 2).

29 Jer. 31:26, 31, Ezek. 11:19 (emended in line with a few Hebrew Manuscripts, Syr. and Targ.), 18:31, 36:26, Isa. 42:9, 43:19, 48:6, 62:2, 65:17, 66:22. See H. W. Wolff, "Prophecy from the Eighth through the Fifth Century" *Int* 32 (1978), pp. 24-5. For שִׁיר חָדָשׁ as the proper response to God's renewed action, see Isa. 42:9-10.

30 Although the combination יוֹם יוֹם is not always late, the prefixing of prepositions to either or both of the nouns is restricted outside Ps. 96:2 to Chronicles, Nehemiah, Ezra and Esther, with just one exception, 1 Sam. 18:10, where כְּיוֹם בְּיוֹם has the peculiar force of "according to daily habit".

31 For its attribution to Yahweh, see on Ps. 89; it is by extension applied to his sanctuary, besides Ps. 96:6, in Isa. 60:7, 63:15 and 64:10.

instruments.[32] חֲצֹצְרָה, "clarion" (98:6) exhibits a markedly late pattern of distribution, being employed as a sacred instrument only in 2 Ki. 12:14, P, Chronicles, Ezra, Nehemiah and Ps. 98:6, and parallel with שׁוֹפָר in 2 Chr. 15:14, and with קוֹל שׁוֹפָר in 1 Chr. 15:28 (besides Ps. 98:6). The verb מחא, "strike, clap" (98:8) is apparently an Aramaic form of II. מחה,[33] occurring also in Isa. 55:12 and (in the Pi'el) in Ezek. 25:6.

In addition, there are many sparsely-attested items of vocabulary in each psalm which are otherwise confined to Deutero-Isaiah and occasionally also to other compositions from the Psalter. However, these shall be considered in the context of the broader question of the relationship between these two sources, and to this issue we shall now turn.

ii. The Relationship of Psalms 96 and 98 to Deutero-Isaiah

Despite extensive discussion and confident claims by both sides,[34] very little which may be considered as determinative has been said. Some contributions suffer from the weakness that they presuppose uniformity amongst the "divine kingship psalms" and attempt to demonstrate their collective precedence or subsequence to Isa. 40-55.[35] Nevertheless, it must be emphasised that the case for the late origin of Pss. 96 and 98 has not been answered by Mowinckel, since he simply approaches the problem by attempting to demonstrate Deutero-Isaiah's dependence on earlier cultic material, without addressing the issue of his relation to the divine kingship psalms now extant.[36]

Clearly, the fact of a relationship between two literary entities is not always decisive, despite its tantalising aspects, since any dependence could operate in either direction, or indeed derive from a mutual source. Another possibility is that such similarities may indicate contemporaneity, rather than dependence in either direction: it is conceivable that both passages emanated from a common and roughly contemporary culture and thought-world where certain concerns, ideas and motifs were current, perhaps in the Temple-community of a certain era. Affinities may then be due, not so much to "borrowing", as to a common

---

32 Confined to Pss. 98:5, 33:2, 144:9, 71:22, 147:7 and 149:2, all of which would seem to be post-exilic. Further examples of late linguistic usage in Ps. 96 are cited by Hossfeld in HZ, II, pp. 668, 670.

33 Itself restricted to Num. 34:11 (P).

34 For Westermann, "the priority of Isa. 52:7-8 can be clearly shown" (*Lob und Klage*, p. 111), whereas for Mowinckel, "there is clear evidence that... exactly the opposite is true" (*PIW*, p. 116; cf. Day, OTG, p. 72).

35 See, for example, Westermann, *Lob und Klage*, pp. 111-115 (asserting the priority of Deutero-Isaiah), and Day, OTG, pp. 71-73 (arguing for a pre-exilic dating of the Psalms).

36 *PIW*, I, pp. 116-8.

"phrasing mentality", to borrow Martin Brenner's terminology.[37] Thus, in the attempt to define the nature of the relationship between the two sources, it may prove helpful to distinguish between verbal reproduction, such as may have occurred through dependence on common cultic formulae or through literary transmission, perhaps over an extended period of time, and shared themes and concerns. These may sometimes be less precise in their affinities, but may occasionally—especially in connection with such a seismic theological shift as occurred in connection with the exile—point to a proximate origin or even to a greater level of development in one context than in the other.

As has been seen, Pss. 96 and 98 are both composite, Ps. 96 in particular sometimes depending very directly on earlier poetry. However, their relationship with Deutero-Isaiah is generally far less close, and often described in terms of shared "conceptions and images"[38] or "characteristic themes".[39] Amongst these may be cited the worthlessness of foreign gods (Ps 96:5, cf. Isa. 40:18-20, 41:23-4, 44:6-20), the evidence of creation for Yahweh's power (Ps. 96:5, 10, cf. Isa. 40:22, 42:5, 44:24, 45:12); the conviction that the nations will know Yahweh (Pss. 96:1-3, 7-10, 98:2-3, cf. Isa. 45:5-6, 22-3, 49:7, 56:3-8, 60:9, 66:18-19) and witness his salvation (Ps. 98:2-3, cf. Isa. 52:10; compare Isa. 40:5 and 66:18 of seeing his glory); the appeal for all nature to join in his praise (Pss. 96:11-12, 98:7-8, cf. Isa. 42:10, 44:23, 49:13, 55:12); the call to "sing to Yahweh a new song" (Pss. 96:1, 98:1, Isa. 42:10, cf. Ps. 98:4-5, Isa. 52:9, 51:3); and the advent of God, often in connection with his righteousness, judgment and/or the nations (Pss. 96:13, 98:9, cf. Isa. 40:10, 59:19-20, 60:1, 62:11). These are all arguably late themes, which are either not attested in such a full form, or are perhaps absent altogether, in the pre-exilic period. Nor do many of them—especially the type of monotheistic, universalistic issues tackled by Deutero-Isaiah in the wake of the exile—have the appearance of simply having been drawn from Israel's cultic traditions: rather, the evidence of the Bible as a whole suggests that they emerged in response to the disaster of exile, and in the consequent rethinking and rapid evolution of Israel's core theological beliefs. It may be that such radical ideas were initially articulated by such a theological giant as Deutero-Isaiah himself, though doubtless reflecting the anxieties and indeed the insights of many of his contemporaries; it is, in any case, in his prophecies that they are first clearly attested.

Thus, certain affinities between the respective texts may be due to their reflecting a common *Zeitgeist* rather than to direct literary borrowing. For example, the theme of "newness", and indeed the sense of the potentialities of a new beginning seem, as has been argued above, to be rooted in the exilic age and to have extended from there into the post-exilic period. This may have been reflected in the cultic creations of the time and/or have been adopted into the cult rather later, as part of the continued process of reception and evolution. If

---

37 *The Song of the Sea: Ex. 15:1-21* (BZAW 195; Berlin: Walter de Gruyter, 1991). His ascription of the Song of the Sea to the post-exilic era draws heavily on the perceived presence of such relations.

38 Kraus, II, p. 834.

39 Anderson, II, p. 681.

Pss. 96 and 98 are to be thought of as eschatological, this might provide an example of the type of reapplication of this prophetic tradition which might have occurred in a later period.

In addition, Ps. 98 shows a stronger tendency than Ps. 96 to echo the language of Deutero-Isaiah, for example, in the motif of Yahweh's arm ("holy arm" in Ps. 98:1 and Isa. 52:10) bringing him victory (Hiph. ישׁע; 98:1, Isa. 59:16, 63:5),[40] or in the pairing of Yahweh's צְדָקָה and יְשׁוּעָה (Ps. 98:2, Isa. 51: 6, 8, 56:1, 59:17). The correlations in the language associated with music-making (e.g., in Ps. 98:5 and Isa. 51:3; Ps. 98:4 and Isa. 52:9; and Ps. 98:8 and Isa. 55:12) are unlikely simply to be attributable to a common cultic background, since they are exclusive to their present contexts.[41] One might add also that פָּצַח, "break forth (with)" is confined (in the Qal) to Isa. 44:23, 49:13, 52:9, 54:1, 55:12, Ps. 98:4 and Isa. 14:7.[42] Moreover, with regard to Ps. 96, אֶרֶץ as the subject of the verb גִּיל, "rejoice",[43] מְלֹא, "fullness, that which fills", in connection with יָם[44] and עֲצֵי־(הַ)יַּעַר, "trees of the wood",[45] may all be cited. Thus, there may be a closer relationship between the two contexts than at first appears, either through a common emanation from proximate circles, or through the pervasive (but not necessarily direct and literary) influence of one source upon the other.[46] The exclusivity of the parallels to these two contexts militates against a broader cultic background, but suggests that the psalmist(s) must have been influenced by the prophet.

The conclusion of dependence is further confirmed by the fact that there is a close parallel between Isa. 42:10ab and Ps. 96:1 (as between Isa. 42:10a and Ps. 98:1a), and then between Isa. 42:10c and Ps. 98:7a (as between Isa. 42:10c [emended] and Ps. 96:11b). Similarly, Isa. 52:10a and Ps. 98:1d share the only reference in the Hebrew Bible to זְרוֹעַ קָדְשׁוֹ; this is then followed in Isa. 52:10b by the clause לְעֵינֵי כָּל־הַגּוֹיִם (cf. Ps. 98:2b, which omits the כָּל, but is otherwise identical), and in v. 10cd by the assertion that וְרָאוּ כָּל־אַפְסֵי־אָרֶץ אֵת יְשׁוּעַת אֱלֹהֵינוּ; this is replicated in Ps. 98:3cd but for the initial *waw*.[47] Thus some have seen here a declaration of the fulfilment of the prophetic hope,[48] or perhaps its transcendence into eschatology. Here, once again, it is to be noted that each context seems to be expressive of the same hope and ideal, one which does not seem to be attested prior to Deutero-Isaiah.

---

40 Cf. Ps. 44:4.

41 The verb מחא occurs also in Ezek. 25:6, in a malicious sense, but in the Pi'el, and in conjunction with יָד.

42 The last of these has been dated variously between the times of Sargon and Alexander the Great: see e.g. Sweeney, *Isaiah 1-39*, p. 232.

43 1 Chr. 16:31 = Ps. 96:11, Ps. 97:1, Isa. 49:13.

44 1 Chr. 16:32 = Ps. 96:11, Ps. 98:7, Isa. 42:10.

45 1 Chr. 16:33 = Ps. 96:12, Isa. 44:23.

46 A similar type of interaction is perhaps suggested by Ps. 96:5, which despite its strikingly Deutero-Isaianic sentiments, is clothed in its own distinctive phraseology.

47 Notice how the nature of the relationship between Isa. 52:10 and Ps. 98:1-3 naturally requires that in discussion the Isaiah material is awarded priority.

48 Cf. the RSV translation of Isa. 52:10cd in the future and 98:3cd in the perfect.

In conclusion, it appears, on the basis of the linguistic, theological and comparative evidence, that Psalms 96 and 98 both originated in the very late exile or in the post-exilic period, and this seems to be one of the firmer conclusions in the dating of the Psalter.

iii. The Theme of "Chaos" in Psalms 96 and 98

Mowinckel closely associates the so-called "enthronement psalms" with his postulated autumn enthronement Festival,[49] an important aspect of which, according to his reconstruction, was the defeat of "chaos". He has accordingly conjectured that the mention of the "victory" in Ps. 98:1ff. alludes to the "mythical conception of creation which may be termed the Primeval Struggle Myth or the Fight with the Dragon Myth".[50] Others have similarly proposed that the subjugation of chaos may constitute an element of the "salvation" or "deliverance"[51] celebrated in Ps. 96:2,[52] or that it may undergird the allusion to creation in Ps. 96:5.[53]

However, it is doubtful whether creation was ever regarded as an act of salvation; more importantly, it has to be acknowledged that the conflict motif is not implied, directly or indirectly, by the agenda of Pss. 96 or 98 themselves.[54] In fact, both seem to present a wholly unified and positive view of creation, which seems to accept the ultimate consequence of a thoroughgoing monotheism, that God is the Creator, Judge and King of all the cosmos, and that his righteous purpose and just rule encompasses all, even as the whole world is united in joyous praise.

This perspective is eloquently conveyed in Ps. 96 in the series of imperatives employed in vv. 1-3, 7-10: שִׁירוּ ("sing", vv. 1ab, 2a), בָּרֲכוּ ("bless", v. 2a), בַּשְּׂרוּ ("announce good tidings", v. 2b), סַפְּרוּ ("declare, relate" the glory and marvellous deeds of Yahweh, v. 3), הָבוּ ("ascribe" glory

---

49 In this he is followed, e.g., by Weiser (pp. 430, 436), Schmidt (pp. 178, 180), Oesterley (II, pp. 422, 427) and Day (OTG, pp. 69, 73-5).

50 *PIW*, I, p. 108; cf. Terrien, p. 683.

51 The same noun, יְשׁוּעָה, is employed in v. 2 of each of these psalms.

52 Thus Anderson, II, p. 682; similarly, Gray considers that cosmic conflict, though not specifically mentioned in 98:1ff., may be reflected in the allusions there to God's יְשׁוּעָה and צְדָקָה (p. 68).

53 See Anderson, II, p. 683; Weiser, pp. 430-431.

54 Cf. Brettler on Pss. 96-99: "There is no trace of an image of God ascending the throne after a mythological victory" (*God is King*, p. 157); similarly Loretz: "a connection between Ps. 98 and the Ugaritic texts concerning a battle between Baal and Yamm is *de facto* not possible" (*UTT*, p. 357); and Gray: "Ps. 96 does not... reflect the cosmic conflict in which Yahweh vindicates His Kingship. It is a call to praise Yahweh as King and to proclaim his effective power to the peoples... Here as in Ps. 98, Sea has become the sea, which with all the rest of creation is called upon to praise God"; likewise, in Ps. 98, "there is no mention of the cosmic conflict... Nor is there any reference to the homage of God's vanquished enemies" (*Biblical Doctrine*, pp. 67-8).

and strength to Yahweh, vv. 7, 8a), שְׂאוּ ("bring" an offering, v. 8b), בֹּאוּ ("come", v. 8b), הִשְׁתַּחֲווּ ("worship", v. 9a), חִילוּ ("tremble", v. 9b) and אִמְרוּ ("proclaim" the kingship of Yahweh, v. 10a). The verb חול (or חיל) can, of course, have negative connotations, and convey the fearful reaction of Yahweh's foes.[55] However, trembling is also the natural and proper response of his worshippers and all who acknowledge his incomparable power and rule, so it frequently occurs as an aspect of the theophany motif,[56] but it can, as here, reflect human awe at his presence.[57] It is thus elicited by the "contemplation of his awesome majesty";[58] as Weiser expresses it, "the experience of God's presence entails that fear and trembling and rapturous joy are here interwoven, indicating the peculiar character of the mood and attitude of a man who is deeply stirred by the greatness of God".[59] Alternatively, the verb חיל could, as Briggs proposes, concern dancing; he translates "whirl before him", explaining the colon as "a universal summons to take part in the sacred pilgrim dance in the temple".[60] This rendering is certainly possible (cf. Judg. 21:21 and Judg. 21:23 [Po'lel], and probably Ps. 87:7 and 1 Sam. 18:6) as well as being consistent with the mood and proximate vocabulary of Ps. 96:9. However, "tremble" may better reflect the nuance of reverent acknowledgement of Yahweh's power, especially if this is to be understood in the light of his theophany; it is also more open to the universal and cosmic aspects of אֶרֶץ which may be implied here.

This positive and general human participation in Yahweh's praise undermines a further pillar of Mowinckel's thesis, that the deity's victory over "chaos" corresponds with that over the other gods and over the nations, so that it may be asserted that God "has... conquered [the heathen] with his coming".[61] In fact, although the reality underlying the psalm is indeed well-integrated, it is quite contrary in its impact since, as Gerstenberger states, "the universal outlook of… the total psalm is quite obvious."[62] Thus the imperative calls for the participation of all people in Yahweh's praise (vv. 1-3, 7-10)[63] are balanced by jussives encouraging the whole of creation, the heavens and the earth, the sea and the open countryside, even the trees of the forest, to יִשְׂמְחוּ ("be glad", v. 11a), תָגֵל ("rejoice", v. 11a), יִרְעַם ("roar", v. 11b), יַעֲלֹז ("exult", v. 12a) and יְרַנְּנוּ "sing for joy" (v. 12b). It has occasionally been proposed that the "roaring" (רעם) of the sea may comprise a reminiscence of its former chaotic state, even if the verb now appears as an expression of its participation in the general joy. However, it seems more likely that the choice of

55 E.g., in Deut. 2:25; Zech. 9:5.

56 E.g., in Pss. 77:17, 19, 97:4, 114:7, Hab. 3:10.

57 Cf. Jer. 5:22, Ps. 99:1 (רגז + נוט).

58 Cohen, p. 316.

59 P. 431; cf. the convergence of these motifs in Ps. 99:1, 3 and indeed in Ps. 96:4 itself.

60 II, p. 304.

61 *PIW*, I, p. 108.

62 II, p. 189.

63 As Brettler notes, the call to praise is in this psalm never addressed specifically to Israel, but only to the nations (*God is King*, p. 147).

language in this context simply conveys the notion that the ocean is vocalising its impulse to praise and celebrate, and it achieves this in a manner most befitting its nature, whilst contributing an impressive and "thunderous" note to the universal chorus of praise. The same idea recurs in Isa. 42:10,[64] which again seems devoid of any "chaos" associations.

It has already been stated that "trembling" may often occur in connection with the theophany, but there are also further indications that a divine epiphany may be anticipated here. Kraus has explained הֲדָרָה, v. 9a, in the light of evidence from the Ugaritic text *KTU* 1.14.iii.50-51, where *hdrt* stands parallel to *ḥlm* ("dream, vision"), seemingly with the meaning "appearing, theophany"[65]; this interpretation is, he contends, further strengthened by the appearance of מִפָּנָיו in the parallel colon.[66] Thus, he translates, "Prostrate yourselves before Yahweh at his holy appearing!"[67] In addition, though no more tangibly, the motif of the presence of the deity may be reflected in v. 6, his עֹז and תִּפְאֶרֶת apparently being employed in reference to the Ark in Ps. 78:61; one might compare also the attributes of Yahweh celebrated in Ps. 29:1-2, 4 in connection with his theophany. The "coming" of God as judge is also anticipated (or, according to the cultic interpretation, acclaimed) in v. 13,[68] which has been the subject of considerable debate.

The primary matter of contention here is naturally whether the advent of Yahweh is to be understood as the product of the poet's vivid imagination, to be interpreted eschatologically,[69] or perhaps as an event which was somehow realised in the cult.[70] Of course, the two alternatives are not mutually exclusive: Weiser, who regards both Pss. 96 and 98 as liturgies of Yahweh's enthronement employed at the "covenant renewal festival", nevertheless

---

64 Emending יוֹרְדֵי הַיָּם וּמְלֹאוֹ in line with Pss. 96:11b and 98:7a, with RSV and most modern commentators (e.g., R. N. Whybray, *Isaiah 40-66*, p. 77, and C. Westermann, *Das Buch Jesaja Kapitel 40-66*, pp. 84, 85).

65 Citing C. H. Gordon, *Ugaritic Handbook*, III, p. 225; thus also Dahood, I, p. 176, III, pp. 356, 358, and Cross, *CMHE*, pp. 152-3 n. 28, and compare likewise Gibson, *CML*, p. 86, where it is translated "visitation". Wyatt (*RTU*, p. 198) and Greenstein (*UNP*, p. 18) prefer the meaning "vision" which, however, is not necessarily incompatible with the assumption of some sort of theophanic appearance: see again Cross, and Tate, p. 511, yet contrast Craigie, pp. 242-3 and note further the bibliography cited there.

66 II, p. 834. This approach is adopted also by Anderson, II, pp. 684-5.

67 II, p. 833.

68 This judgment is aptly explained by Weiser as "serv[ing] to restore his order in the world. This order manifests itself as much in the realm of Nature as in that of History; as much in the blessing of the fertility of the earth as in the blessings bestowed upon the nations" (Weiser, p. 431; cf. Cohen, p. 317; Cheyne, p. 268).

69 Thus Kraus, II, p. 838 (on Ps. 96), p. 848 (on Ps. 98); Gray, pp. 67-8; Koenen, p. 68; Tate, p. 512 (on Ps. 96), p. 525 (on Ps. 98).

70 Weiser, pp. 430-431 (on Ps. 96), p. 436 (on Ps. 98).

recognises the eschatological and unrealistic aspects at least of Ps. 98;[71] likewise, even if they are predominantly eschatological in concern, it is scarcely beyond question that they were sung in the context of the Jerusalem cult.[72] Nor can the presence of cultic or eschatological features objectively be determined: as Kraus has emphasised, the issue "whether Psalm 96 should be understood strictly cultically or eschatologically cannot be answered on the basis of form criticism".[73]

For Kraus, the late origin of the psalm "alone justifies the exegete in taking an eschatological understanding as its basis".[74] This claim is perhaps a little extravagant. Nevertheless, the eschatological approach may be supported by the content of the psalm. The central theme of the unification of all peoples and creation in praise of their lord Yahweh, and the motif of God's advent to judge the earth can scarcely be correlated with a specific historical occasion, though it may have been anticipated as an imminent or prospective reality. Moreover, Hossfeld has drawn attention the context provided by Ps. 97 as evidence for a future-eschatological understanding of Ps. 96;[75] although such an understanding may in principle only apply at a later, redactional, level, the thematic correspondences within the series including Pss. 96-98 are so conspicuous that many commentators have sought to interpret them as a unit.[76] Hence the present sequence may well antedate the final compilation of the Psalter, and it is not impossible that certain of its components may have been composed specifically for their present location. Once again, however, it indicates the blurring of the distinction between eschatology and the cult.[77]

The translation of the verb בָּא itself is difficult, since it may either be a participle ("he is coming, he comes") or third person masculine singular perfect ("he has come, he comes"). The former would support the

---

71 As indeed do Gunkel (*Einleitung* §3 ¶4) and Oesterley (II, pp. 422, 424 re Ps. 96; pp. 426, 427-8 re Ps. 98); see Weiser, p. 436, and compare his remarks on p. 431 re Ps. 96.

72 Cf. the setting of the psalm in 1 Chr. 16:23-33 and the title ascribed to it in the LXX.

73 II, p. 834. Compare similarly H. Schmidt's apprehension that eschatology cannot be identified on the basis of the form or terminology of the psalm (*Die Thronfahrt Jahwes zum Fest der Jahreswende in Alten Israel*, 1927, pp. 5-6). At the same time, despite the lack of certainty in this matter, there may be some strength in Hossfeld's contention that in 96:12b, which comprises an introduction to the climactic affirmation of v. 13, the conjunction "then" is most naturally to be interpreted as providing a clear demarcation from the preceding jussives; with the following verb then interpreted as indicative, as seems most likely, this would tend to support a future orientation (HZ, II, p. 670).

74 II, p. 835.

75 HZ, II, p. 670.

76 Though with different parameters: see, e.g., Tate (96-99; pp. 504-509) and Briggs (93, 96-100; II, pp. 296-313), and cf., from the perspective of the final form of the Psalter, Howard (93-100; *Structure*, e.g. pp. 20-1; see further the bibliography cited on p. 21) and Koenen (Pss. 90-110, *Jahwe wird kommen*, especially Part IV).

77 Indeed, compare the context for the citation of Ps. 96 in 1 Chr. 16:23-33, where it is associated with the bringing of the Ark into the city of David.

eschatological view, but may be incompatible with the type of cultic position advocated by Mowinckel, which entails that Yahweh's arrival would somehow have been enacted.[78] A perfect verb, on the other hand, though conventionally associated with a cultic understanding of the verse, would not exclude the eschatological interpretation—Westermann and Gunkel speak of the use of the "prophetic perfect" in such contexts, which would entail the description of something actually in the future as having already occurred, so certain is its eventuality deemed to be.[79] However, the cultic celebration of an event which is wholly or primarily futuristic seems doubtful, though, of course, the cult may encompass eschatological elements in its celebrations. Both the context and wider Old Testament usage of Yahweh as the subject of the verb שׁפט[80] in association with his theophany or active intervention would tend to suggest that a specific occasion of judgment ("he has / will come"), rather than characteristic action ("he comes"), may be intended; the evidence, which is mainly derived from prophetic sources, suggests this is most likely to be prospective rather then retrospective. Such a future, eschatological, interpretation may claim the support of the Septuagint,[81] as indeed of most modern translations.[82] However, in a situation where the rendering of the Hebrew into English is expressive of an interpretation, rather than its basis, the focus of discussion should rightly be placed elsewhere.

Psalms 96 and 98 may also be understood as representing the end-point of the trajectory traced from the Zion Psalms 24 and 93 through 46 and then 65, in which an increasing hope of world peace and cosmic blessing is envisioned in conjunction with the motifs of Yahweh's kingship, incomparability and holiness. The motif of the immovability of the world in Ps. 96:10b is expressed in exactly the same terms as in Ps. 93:1c. However, the basis for hope is no longer simply that "thy throne [i.e., God's powerful and effective rule as king and also perhaps secondarily as judge] is established from of old", but rather that of Yahweh's equity,[83] his fairness and integrity, in governing or judging all his creatures. The onus is thus transferred from a continuous, unchangeable state which has pertained "from of old,... from everlasting" to his future and universal action (Ps. 96:10c, cf. Ps. 98:9). Accordingly, in the last phase represented by Pss. 96 and 98, the eminence of Zion is not explicit,[84] and the

78 See, e.g., *PIW*, I, p. 109.

79 See Westermann, *Lob und Klage*, p. 112; Gunkel, *Einleitung*, §9 ¶16.

80 Except, of course, in its participial form.

81 I.e. ἐρχεται, "he is coming, he comes"; Vulg. *venit* mirrors the ambiguity of the Hebrew, since it may be present or perfect.

82 "He is coming" (NRSV, New JPS); cf. RSV, REB, "he comes". For a survey of scholarship on this issue, see Koenen, p. 68, n. 56.

83 Cf. Ps. 75:3-4.

84 Though, of course, his מִקְדָּשׁ is mentioned in 96:6 and his חַצְרוֹת in 96:8; the temple would also seem to be implied setting for the address to the assembled congregation in 96:1-3, 98:1, 4-6. A close association with Zion is, further, presumed by the setting bestowed on the psalm in 1 Chr. 16:23-33, where it is cited in connection with the celebrations surrounding the bringing of the Ark into Jerusalem.

requirements of purity for entry into the sacred precincts have been transmuted into an all-embracing vision which is nevertheless contained within the absolute justice, righteousness and equity of God.

Turning then to Psalm 98, it emerges that vv. 1-3 are broadly equivalent to Ps. 96:1-6, whilst vv. 4-9 correspond to 96:10-13, sometimes, as in the case of 98:7-9 and 96:11b-13, very closely.[85] As in Ps. 96:1-2, the occasion for giving praise with a "new song" is that of Yahweh's "salvation" (יְשׁוּעָה, 98:2, 96:2); this act of deliverance on behalf of Israel has "revealed his righteousness in the sight of the nations" (v. 2b), so that "all the ends of the earth have seen the salvation of our God" (v. 3c). This apparently provides the occasion for their conversion. Many commentators have seen here an allusion to the miracle of the second exodus, through which the vision of Deutero-Isaiah attains its fulfilment (cf. Isa. 40:5; 52:10).[86] Certainly, the verbal similarities with Isa. 52:10 are especially close: it contains the only reference outside Ps. 98:1 to זְרוֹעַ קָדְשׁוֹ, this appearing in conjunction with the phrase לְעֵינֵי כָּל־הַגּוֹיִם (cf. Ps. 98:2b), and the parallel colon being the declaration וְרָאוּ כָּל־אַפְסֵי־אָרֶץ אֵת יְשׁוּעַת אֱלֹהֵינוּ (compare Ps. 98:3cd). The opening verse of the oracle (Isa. 52:7) also employs terminology such as בשׂר (which occurs in the equivalent section of Ps. 96, v. 2b), יְשׁוּעָה (cf. Ps. 98: 2a, 3d; 96:2b; see also 98:1c) and מָלַךְ אֱלֹהָיִךְ (compare Ps. 98:6b; the keynote expression recurs in 96:10a, where it is to be said בַגּוֹיִם); this is then followed by allusions to joyful singing in vv. 8 and 9 (note especially רנן, v. 8,[87] and פצח + רנן in v. 9).[88]

Although the imperatives in vv. 4-6 do not specifically mention whether Israel or all the nations are invoked to participate in praise of Yahweh, the direct antecedent remains כָּל־אַפְסֵי־אָרֶץ, and indeed the listing of תֵּבֵל וְיֹשְׁבֵי בָהּ ,הַיָּם, נְהָרוֹת and הָרִים (vv. 7-8) certainly suggests a universal application. Similarly, the phrase יֹשְׁבֵי בָהּ in v. 7b most obviously includes—indeed, primarily denotes—the human occupants of the world. תֵּבֵל (v. 7b) most commonly appears in parallel with (ה)ארץ, but relatively infrequently in preference to it; however אֶרֶץ could simply have denoted the "land" (i.e., of Israel), so תֵּבֵל is perhaps utilised here to avoid ambiguity. The universality of the invited praise is, further, suggested by the fact that Yahweh's anticipated righteous and truthful judgment is of the whole earth (v. 9)[89] and indeed by the description of Yahweh as "the King" (v. 6) without any possessive qualification (our King, King of Israel, etc.). It seems that it is his universal sovereignty and, in particular, his impending advent, which is acclaimed.

---

85 The structural similarities between the psalms are emphasised by many scholars, e.g., Koenen, p. 72.

86 "All nations (again in keeping with the proclamation of salvation in Deutero-Isaiah) are to be witnesses of the final activity of the worldwide theophany of the God of Israel" (Kraus, II, p. 847). See also Cohen, p. 320 (and note his comments on Ps. 96:1, p. 315), Koenen, p. 72, Jeremias, *Königtum*, pp. 133-4, and Hossfeld, HZ, II, p. 689.

87 The verb features also in Ps. 98:4b (with פצח), 8b and 96:12b.

88 Cf. Ps. 98:4b.

89 Though cf. Pss. 9:9, 82:8, 94:2 and context, where this seems to be in Israel's favour.

The invocation to praise in vv. 4-6 is as colourful and varied as that in Ps. 96:7-11a, though in this instance focusing on musical celebration. Thus, the same conclusions may be drawn as in relation to Ps. 96 as regards the absence—indeed contravention—of any notion of cosmic conflict here. The notion of the roaring sea (v. 7a), which has already been discussed in relation to Ps. 96:11b, is further supplemented by the image of the נְהָרוֹת ("rivers, streams") clapping their hands. Clapping in Hebrew may sometimes be a gesture of derision or malice,[90] but the sense here is obviously one of enthusiastic applause, as in Isa. 55:12 and Ps. 47:2, and this is confirmed by the parallel image of the hills singing for joy. All creation is thus united in praise and celebration of its Lord.

2. Psalm 148

Psalm 148 has every appearance of being a very late hymn,[91] like Psalm 150, simply consisting in the extended call to praise.[92] Features which would seem to be late include הַלְלוּ יָהּ (vv. 1, 14);[93] מַלְאָכִים as among the permanent body of the heavenly host offering praise (v. 2);[94] the description of the people of Israel as "his saints" (חֲסִידָיו, v. 14); the personification of the astral bodies (v. 3) which in an earlier period would have risked implying that these were deities; and the psalm's self-assured universalism (which is evident from v. 11 in particular). If correct, its possible dependence on Egyptian nature wisdom[95] or

---

90 See, e.g., Lam. 2:15, Ezek. 25:6, Nah. 3:19.

91 This is a subject about which the commentators seem to be unanimous, the psalm being designated as post-exilic, e.g., by Kraus (II, p. 1141), Anderson (II, p. 949), Oesterley (II, p. 581), Goulder (*PR*, p. 213), Terrien (p. 922) and Gunkel (*Einleitung*, §2 ¶66). However, the claim that v. 14 alludes to the return from exile (Cohen, pp. 475, 476, Wellhausen, p. 216, Allen, pp. 313, Kissane, II, p. 330) is very uncertain.

92 See Westermann's theory of the degeneration of the hymn form resulting in this type of psalm (*Lob und Klage*, p. 99, especially n. 85); see also F. Crüsemann, *Studien zur Formgeschichte von Hymnus und Danklied in Israel* (WMANT 32; 1969), pp. 72-3.

93 Which is confined to the fifth book of the Psalter and the Chronicler. See J. Hempel, "Hallelujah", *IDB*, II, 514-5, who points out that "there is no clear example of the use of the verb הלל with 'Yahweh' as its object before Deutero-Isaiah and that 'Hallelujah' is to be found only even later" (p. 514).

94 Contrast the בְּנֵי אֵלִים of Ps. 29:1; Kraus speaks of "the glaring demotion of the בני אלים to מלאכים" (I, p. 381); the increased prominence of angels in exilic and post-exilic theology, including that of Ps. 148:2, has been detailed by von Rad, "מַלְאָךְ im AT" in G. Kittel (ed.), *Theologisches Wörterbuch zum Neuen Testament*, I (Stuttgart: W. Kohlhammer, 1932), pp. 77-78.

95 See von Rad, "Hiob 38 und die altägyptische Weisheit", *VT(S)* 3 (1960), pp. 293-301. Note in this connection the strong affinities of Ps. 148 to "The Song of the Three Young Men", Dan. 3:52-90 (Greek), and cf. also Job. 38, Sirach 43; the presence of

on the creation account of Gen. 1[96] may also point in the same direction, as may the high frequency of prose particles.[97]

In tone and in many aspects of content, it has affinities with Psalms 96 and 98. However, in Ps. 148 the traditional tripartite universe has apparently been superseded by a bipartite view,[98] encompassing only heaven (vv. 1-6) and earth (vv. 7-14),[99] each populated by a variety of beings (vv. 2-3; 7, 9-12) and each with its own ocean (vv. 4, 7). Thus, the seas are here assumed to be fully integrated members of the created order, participating in the universal praise of their lord and maker, but not attaining to the status of one of the major "zones" of creation. Indeed, the listing of the "creatures" is arranged chiastically, with the respective oceans placed centrally (vv. 4, 7), but prime position being awarded to the heavenly beings (vv. 1-2) and human worshippers (vv. 11-13a, 14b), whose invocation to praise frames the psalm. This is entirely appropriate, since human and divine praise is the most fundamental form of laudation,[100] whereas the expansive list encountered in Ps. 148 (as in Pss. 96 and 98) is due to poetic elaboration, added for emphasis and totality. It is difficult to conceive of a picture less conducive to the idea of cosmic conflict.

The motif of the heavenly ocean has already been discussed in chapter 3 in relation to the imagery of Ps. 29. There may be gradations here in the celestial realm: the heavens (v. 1), the "heaven of heavens"[101] (v. 4a) and then the "waters above the heavens" (v. 4b) above all else. Nevertheless, it is possible

---

such connections has, however, been called into question by D. R. Hillers, "A Study of Psalm 148" *CBQ* 40 (1978) 323-334.

96 As advocated, e.g., by Gunkel, *Die Psalmen*, pp. 618-9, Goulder, *PR*, pp. 213, 294-5, Rogerson and McKay, III, pp. 184-5.

97 Note especially אֲשֶׁר (v. 4b), fourfold אֶת and sevenfold הַ.

98 Contra Kraus, II, p. 1143 and especially Dahood, III, p. 352.

99 Unless הָאָרֶץ in v. 7 is to be understood as an allusion to the underworld; see Dahood (III, pp. 351, 352, 353, following Cross and Freedman, "The Song of Miriam", *JNES* 14 [1950], p. 247). Yet even he admits that it "does appear singular... that the psalmist dedicates only one verse to the subterranean beings after having given six verses to celestial bodies, and reserving the next seven for terrestrial creatures" (III, pp. 353-4). In fact, תַּנִּינִים cannot naturally be classed among the inhabitants of the nether world; contrast also the thought of Pss. 6:6, 30:10, where the inhabitants of the underworld are said to be unable to praise God. Rather, הַלְלוּ אֶת־יְהוָה מִן־הָאָרֶץ corresponds structurally to הַלְלוּ אֶת־יְהוָה מִן־הַשָּׁמַיִם in v. 1, each introducing the praise of one of the two main spheres of creation. See likewise Anderson, II, p. 494, Gerstenberger, II, p. 447, Girard, III, pp. 526-7, Goulder, *PR*, pp. 294-5, Tsumura, *The Earth and the Waters in Genesis 1 and 2*, p. 75.

100 Cf., e.g., Ps. 29:1-2, 9 (together with v. 11).

101 A "superlative... very likely the higher sphere of heaven, above which the waters of the ocean of heaven are stored" (Kraus, II, 1142-3; see Cohen, p. 475, Dahood, III, p. 142); for a possible distinction between הַשָּׁמַיִם and שְׁמֵי הַשָּׁמַיִם cf. Deut. 10:14, 1 Ki. 8:27, 2 Chr. 2:5 and Sirach 16:18. The idea of successive strata in heaven is reflected in later Christian and Jewish literature, e.g., 2 Cor. 12:2, Testament of Levi 3:1-8.

that this portrayal is not to be understood too literally,[102] since Ps. 104:3 seems to indicate that the abode of God was above the heavenly ocean, and this is reinforced by the imagery of Ps. 29:3, 10.

Corresponding to the celestial sea are כָּל־תְּהֹמוֹת, which are paired with תַּנִּינִים (v. 7). The latter would seem to denote "the great creatures of the sea, or marine animals in general",[103] and as such is comparable with Gen. 1:21. It scarcely needs to be stated that to the ancient Hebrew the demarcation between mythology and natural history, especially as regards ocean life, was not as self-evident as it is to modern commentators. The decoration of mediaeval maps with "sea-monsters" and the obvious zoological errors of, for example, the Hereford Mappa Mundi, are testimony to how long traditions regarding the inhabitants of the sea or distant lands remained the preserve of folk-legend, hearsay and conjecture; nor was there yet the available vocabulary (let alone biological conventions for species-classification) to enable such creatures to be identified more precisely. In any case, the context of Ps. 148:7 indicates that תַּנִּינִים is an all-embracing term, just as all trees and animals are swiftly encompassed by the designations in vv. 9 and 10: all are called to join in praise of their lord and maker. The association of תְּהֹמוֹת with the blessing of fertility has already been mentioned in connection with Pss. 42:8 and 77:17;[104] as the (sub)terrestrial reservoir it provides the obvious counterpart to הַמַּיִם אֲשֶׁר מֵעַל הַשָּׁמָיִם in v. 4. Such a background obviates the need to discern an echo of some kind of mythic battle here, as certain scholars have proposed, either in relation to תַּנִּינִים[105] or, occasionally, to תְּהֹמוֹת as well.[106] In fact, even Kraus, one of the strongest proponents of such a view, concedes that "it could also be that in v. 7 the thought is only of the sea (cf. תהום in Ps. 107:26) in which the 'great sea animals' live (Gen. 1:21)",[107] and it is this interpretation which is allowed to predominate in the commentaries of Anderson,[108] Cohen[109] and Kissane.[110] In any case, the context of universal praise of Yahweh by all creatures who are made and sustained by him can scarcely be denied, and "chaos" is thus excluded from the conscious agenda of the psalm.

It is therefore especially interesting to discover the common notion of an established universe recurring in v. 6 in relation to the heavenly ocean, since this would seem to confirm the impression that these waters comprise an aspect of God's gracious provision, and are created and maintained by the divine decree,

---

102 Thus Anderson, II, pp. 494-50, J. Gray, *I and II Kings*, p. 205.

103 Anderson, II, p. 544.

104 Cf. Ps. 78:15, Deut. 8:7, Prov. 8:24 and probably 3:20; see also M. H. Pope, *El in the Ugaritic Texts* (VT[S] 2, 1955), p. 63.

105 Thus Weiser, p. 580, and Dahood, II, pp. 205-6.

106 Kraus, II, p. 1143, Terrien, p. 921.

107 II, p. 1143.

108 II, p. 950; see also II, p. 544.

109 P. 425.

110 I, p. 332; see also C. Westermann, *Genesis*, I, p. 191; J. Skinner, *A Critical and Exegetical Commentary on Genesis* (ICC; Edinburgh: T. & T. Clark, 1930), p. 28, and the careful analysis of Tsumura, *The Earth and the Waters*, pp. 74-77, especially p. 77.

just as is the earth (cf. Pss. 93:1c, 96:10b) or Zion itself (Ps. 46:6). The emphasis here thus seems to be on the fixed and secure nature of Yahweh's creative work, that its elements should never pass away (v. 6a). The interpretation of v. 6b is more complex, since although the verbal suffix in v. 6a is masculine plural, referring back to the waters or perhaps to the entire antecedent list of Yahweh's creations, the verb of v. 6bβ is masculine singular. This difficulty is compounded by the ambiguity of the term חק itself, since it essentially denotes "something prescribed", but this may be manifested either as a statute or (more seldom, but perhaps most appropriate here) in a spatial sense, as a geographical boundary. The latter force would well suit the present context, and would be comparable to the usage of Jer. 5:22, where חק appears in connection with the same verb, עבר;[111] however, in that setting, the emphasis is on the inability of the waters to "pass over" the boundary, but this meaning, if transferred to Ps. 148:6b, would require a plural or passive verb. Thus, many modern translators resort to emendation,[112] despite its lack of textual support,[113] whilst others rely on the less satisfactory translation "statute".[114] However, probably the best solution is to translate: "A boundary he has set (given), and it will not pass away";[115] the proximity in Hebrew of the conceptions of "boundary" and "command" are confirmed by Prov. 8:29, where חק stands in parallel to פֶּה, this latter term then being the object of עבר. Thus, the emphasis seems to be on the fixedness of the natural order, which shall endure for ever, without passing away or suffering infringement. There is no indication, however, that such balance is the outcome of any cosmic conflict, any more than it admits of the possibility that the structure of the universe could in some way be threatened. Rather, all of creation owes its existence to the command of God. Consequently, anxieties regarding the shakeable aspect of

111 Cf. Prov. 8:29, where חק is paralleled by פה (="command"), this latter term again being qualified by עבר; and Job 14:5 (there in a temporal sense, but with the same verb). The creation-association recurs again in Job 26:10, 38:10, whilst חק has the sense "boundary, limit" also in Job 14:13, Isa. 5:14, Mic. 7:11.

112 The plural is supplied by Kraus (II, p. 1140) and Wellhausen (p. 160), and the plural passive by RSV.

113 The singular verb is retained even by 11QPs[a].

114 Thus Cohen, in a distributive sense: "He hath given (each of them) a statute which it cannot transgress" (p. 475), explaining the reference as to the "laws of nature" which "were to the Psalmist the ordinances of God"; less clumsy, but entailing textual emendation, is Weiser's solution: "ein Gesetz gab er, das sie nicht übertreten" (p. 579; cf. Spieckermann, *Heilsgegenwart*, p. 50). Perhaps preferable, though still awkward, is Goulder's proposal, "He hath made a decree which none shall transgress" (*PR*, p. 293; thus also Kissane, II, p. 330; cf. Terrien, p. 918), which apparently assumes the expression of an indefinite personal subject by the third person masculine singular (GK, § 144 d).

115 Cf. the JPS translation, "establishing an order that shall never change", and Dahood's proposal (III, p. 351; cf. RSV mg., Allen, p. 311, Seybold, p. 541, Girard, III, p. 526): "he issued a decree, and it shall never pass away", comparing Ps. 33:11, Matt. 5:18, 24:35 (p. 353).

the cosmos, which occasionally appeared in view in the Zion psalms analysed in chapter 5[116] (characteristically in conjunction with political fears), seem so fully to have been resolved into a unified and joyful vision for the entire universe, that this composition freely and willingly embraces "all peoples", even the formerly threatening "rulers of the earth" (v. 11b).

3. Psalm 135

Finally, Psalm 135 must briefly be mentioned. This is a late[117] and frequently derivative[118] hymn, which in language, content and structure displays affinities to Ps. 136.[119] Of particular interest is v. 6, which corresponds programmatically to the creation section of Ps. 136, but in essential focus reflects the interests of the hymns considered in the present chapter. Once again, all spheres of existence are indicated in the quartet שָׁמַיִם and אָרֶץ, יַמִּים and כָּל־תְּהוֹמוֹת, the final כָּל ensuring total inclusivity. It is likely that כָּל־תְּהוֹמוֹת here indicates the subterranean waters[120] as opposed to the terrestrial sea.[121] In any case, all are affirmed to be within the realm of God, and subject to his total lordship;[122] as in Ps. 96, the command of creation is an attribute of the Most High God, and demonstrates his utter superiority to all deities (v. 5, cf. 96:4-5).[123] Once again, therefore, allusion to the *Chaoskampf* seems to be precluded.[124]

---

116 Notably in Pss. 46 and 65; cf. Ps. 93.

117 For dating evidence, see Cohen, p. 441, Oesterley, II, pp. 538-9, 541, Wellhausen, p. 214; a post-exilic provenance is advocated by virtually all writers, with the exception of Weiser (pp. 544-5), who seeks to admit of the possibility of a pre-exilic origin, in line with his proposed festal setting for the psalm.

118 The related passages are listed by Wellhausen, p. 214, Terrien, p. 858, and Allen, p. 224.

119 To be discussed in chapters 8 and 9 below.

120 But not necessarily the underworld, as Seybold suggests (p. 504).

121 Thus Cohen (p. 441), Allen (p. 223); see the discussion of תְּהֹמוֹת and its life-bestowing properties in relation to Ps. 148 above.

122 Thus also Oesterley: "All that happens in the world of Nature is according to his will (cf. Ps 115 3)" (II, p. 540; similarly Allen, p. 227).

123 Here, it is to be noted, in a rare monotheistic context (see vv. 15-18 and Oesterley's remarks on the psalm's "religious teaching", II, p. 541).

124 Yet cf. Kraus (II, p. 1075), who maintains that "verse 6 only indicates in catchwords the age-old story of the battle against chaos—the victory over the sea and the תהומות"; so also Dahood (III, p. 261). Schmidt discerns here an allusion to the same sphere of imagery, but in addition contends that v. 7 alludes to the annual re-manifestation of Yahweh's primal power in the rainy season, and thus is a liturgy of the autumn festival (p. 239); Weiser also associates the psalm with the autumn festival (p. 545), but is silent on the matter of the *Chaoskampf* theme. However, the glorification of Yahweh's power as exhibited in storm-phenomena is not usually associated with seasonal changes

4. Summary

In the joyful hymns Pss. 96, 98 and 148, all of which may be dated with unusual confidence to the late exilic or post-exilic periods, a highly unified view of creation as uniting in praise of Yahweh, or in jubilant anticipation of his advent, is evident, as befits the universalistic perspective of these psalms. Ps. 135 is to be distinguished in content from the others despite probably also emanating from the post-exilic period, since the cosmos here rather provides a passive or receptive forum for his action (v. 6). Although the articulation of the structure of the cosmos may vary slightly between different presentations, the inclusion of the sea(s), rivers or deeps in some form is a common, and indeed essential, element, with mention also often being made of marine life, either through the formula ומלאו ("and all that fills it", 96:11b, 98:7a) or through the specific mention of תנינים (148:7b). Hence, the wide inclusivity of the invocations to praise or description of the forum of God's activity offers no support for the postulation of an allusion to "chaos". As a result, commentators often acknowledge the absence of this theme or relegate it to a supposed subtext, which in turn is dependent on its putative presence in certain other biblical passages. However, the motif may be confidently excluded from the conscious agenda of any of these compositions.

---

and new year celebrations, but simply functions to demonstrate his supremacy and might: cf. Jer. 10:13, 51:16 and relevant theophany passages.

VIII. The Creation of "Chaos" in the Psalter? Psalms 24, 95, 146, 148, 136, 33 and 104

The theme of creation is of crucial relevance to any examination of the "*Chaoskampf*" motif in the Psalter, since chaos and creation are intrinsically related, both by definition and also in most reconstructions of the theme which have been based upon the Hebrew Bible. It is axiomatic in the studies of Gunkel and his successors that the divine combat with "chaos" in its original form resulted in creation, whether in the mythology of Babylon or (according to many, despite the lack of supporting evidence) of Canaan, or in that of Israel. So fundamental has this connection been deemed to be, that it has informed the title both of Gunkel's *Schöpfung and Chaos*, and of more recent monographs dedicated to the theme of "chaos", such as Anderson's *Creation versus Chaos* and Levenson's *Creation and the Persistence of Evil*. It is therefore the aim of this chapter to consider all those passages in the Psalter in which mention of any body of water—whether יַמִּים, נְהָרוֹת, תְּהוֹמוֹת, מַעְיָנִים or simply מַיִם—occurs in the context of an allusion to an originating creative act, with the intention of discerning whether the connection between "chaos" and creation is in any way justified. Although a number of the psalms discussed so far may contain a passing allusion to creation or related motifs, only Pss. 24 and 148 fulfil this criterion, as do also five further compositions to be discussed in this context, namely Pss. 95, 146, 136, 33 and 104.

However, besides the issue of the content of these psalms, the question of their date also emerges as of critical relevance, since if creation is to be regarded as the "original" context for "chaos" imagery, one should expect the connection to be present amongst some of the earlier psalms considered. In reality, the evidence seems to fail to correspond to the model of development which has occupied something of a consensus position among biblical scholars. The absence of interest in cosmic creation and lack of belief in *Chaoskampf* as a religious reality in the most archaic Hebrew compositions has been ably documented by D. J. McCarthy in his article, "'Creation' Motifs in Ancient Hebrew Poetry".[1] His conclusions are also corroborated by the evidence of the psalms so far analysed in the context of the present monograph. Although the motif of creation has been encountered, however transiently, in almost every category of psalms hitherto considered, the earliest group, the archaic theophany psalms examined in chapter 3, would seem to constitute an exception. Despite the fact that they celebrate Yahweh's power as manifested in and over nature, in storm and thunder, and through the provision of water, they

1 In B. W. Anderson (ed.), *Creation in the Old Testament* (Issues in Religion and Theology 6; London: SPCK, 1984) pp. 74-89.

remain silent on the subject of creation itself.[2] In fact, the theme of the establishment of the earth first surfaces among the selected psalms in Pss. 24:1-2 and 65:8; Yahweh's magisterial power and his control over the polarities of the cosmos—a typically exilic theme, which achieved especial prominence in the theology of Deutero-Isaiah—is then celebrated in the hymnic sections of Pss. 74 and 89 (74:16-17, 89:10, 12-13). Finally, all creation and peoples are seen joyfully to acknowledge Yahweh's universal sovereignty in the late psalms considered in chapter 7, the same motif recurring also in the concluding section of Ps. 69 (v. 35).

Thus, amongst the present group of psalms, the emergence of the creation theme may be placed probably in the mid- to late-monarchical period, since (if the dating conclusions advocated in chapter 5 are correct) the assertion that לַיהוָה הָאָרֶץ... כִּי־הוּא עַל־יַמִּים יְסָדָהּ in Ps. 24:1-2 may belong to the latest stratum of this tripartite hymn; similarly, Ps. 65 would appear to be late pre-exilic or later, whilst the remaining instances would seem to stem from the exile or subsequently. It may further be observed that Pss. 24:2 and 65:7 offer only brief declarations that Yahweh is creator, whereas more detailed treatments do not emerge until a later stage.[3]

Therefore, the issue of the time of origin of the psalms now to be considered in the present chapter is an important one, since the absence of the motif of creation in the earliest period—in continuity with the findings made so far—would undermine the consensus position of the course of emergence and original application of the "chaos" motif in Israel. It could rather suggest that the importation of the theme into leading Yahwistic religious circles occurred at a fairly late stage, or even that, in the form and with the content attributed to it by modern scholarship, the idea of *Chaoskampf* may not simply have pre-existed in the Israelite-Canaanite folk-traditions from the earliest times, as is commonly supposed. If it is further demonstrated that the motif of a divine conflict with "chaos" is altogether absent from "creation" portrayals, even in the later period, this would indicate, perhaps even more than in other cases where the theme has been thought to occur and found wanting, that regnant notions of the nature and development of the so-called *Chaoskampf* theme may be fundamentally misguided.

---

2 Pss. 29 and 68 and 2 Sam. 22:2-51 (// Ps. 18:2-51) are included by McCarthy in his analysis of ancient poetry; his conclusion that they are devoid of creation content is in accord with the present findings.

3 See W. Hermann, "Wann wurde Jahwe zum Schöpfer der Welt?" *UF* 23 (1991) 165-180, who places the emergence of a belief in Yahweh as creator of the world during the Babylonian exile.

1. Psalm 24

The date and content of this psalm have already received detailed treatment in chapter 5 above. It was concluded that the hymn would seem to be pre-exilic in origin, but that it may be composite in nature, vv. 1-2 probably belonging to the latest stratum if this is so. There seems to be no intrinsic connection between the respective sections of the psalm, and the logical consequence of the second and third parts on those preceding cannot therefore safely be presupposed.

As regards the creation portrayal of vv. 1-2, it appears to depend on a common ancient Near Eastern worldview, according to which the earth was supported on "foundations" or "pillars" that had their base in the subterrestrial waters feeding the world's water supply.[4] However, there is no indication of how this structure was achieved, or of any underlying narrative conception of the process of creation. Nor can Israel's dependence on the structural worldview of her time be assumed to indicate a commitment to a particular understanding of the cosmogonic process. The idea of "founding" and "establishing" suggests firmness and solidity, as if the present order and its watery base were perceived as firm and reliable, and the portrayal is devoid of combative overtones. On the other hand, the psalm does not specifically state that either the earth or the "sea" and "rivers" under it were actually formed by God. Nevertheless, it is probably incorrect to draw any significance from this, as there is no indication that God's formation of the world—as opposed to his ordering of its constituent elements—is in any way denied: rather, it is probably either presumed or (perhaps more likely) simply not yet conceived of in such an explicit form.

2. Psalm 95

The date of Ps. 95 is difficult to determine with certainty. However, affinities with Deuteronomy[5] and Deutero-Isaiah can be traced in the notion that the world-creator also "made" Israel (v. 6; cf., e.g., Deut. 32:6, Isa. 43:1,15 and often—though the motif also occurs elsewhere); the emphasis on הַיּוֹם, "this day" (v. 7), may also be compared with Deut. 4:40, 5:3, 6:6, 7:11 (and often). "Rest" as possession of land is a further deuteronomic feature—cf. Deut. 12:9.[6] Accordingly, Kraus may be correct when he places the psalm's origin

4 The "foundations" of the earth are mentioned in Pss. 104:5, 82:5, Job 38:4, Prov. 8:29, Isa. 24:18, 40:21, 48:13, 51:13, Jer. 31:37, Mic. 6:2, and its "pillars" in 1 Sam. 2:8, Job 9:6, Ps. 75:4. Their base in the subterrestrial waters may perhaps be in mind in Ps. 18:16 = 2 Sam. 22:16.

5 These are widely recognised: see Gerstenberger, II, p. 185 and the bibliography there.

6 Additional Deuteronomic characteristics are listed by J. Jeremias, *Kultprophetie und Gerichtsverkündigung in der späten Königszeit Israels* (WMANT 35; Neukirchen-Vluyn: Neukirchener Verlag, 1976), p. 126. He, however, thinks not of dependence on Deuteronomic sources, but of emanation from (Levitical) circles standing behind Deuteronomy (p. 126); see similarly A. R. Johnson, *The Cultic Prophet and Israel's*

between the emergence of Deuteronomy and the Chronicler's history,[7] a position which he further supports by reference to its possible Levitical associations.[8] Other scholars have discerned further links with the post-exilic community, for example, in the similarity of the psalm's preaching style to that of prophetic instruction in Chronicles,[9] or in the theme of the sins of the fathers, which is "a constant topic in postexilic sermons";[10] similarly, comparisons have been drawn between the underlying situation of the Psalm and the milieu of Trito-Isaiah.[11] In addition, the composition may display literary features which would be consistent with a later style: Seybold cites the rather forced "acrostic" play on א in vv. 4-5, 8-11 (אֲשֶׁר being repeated in vv. 4, 5, 9, 11) and the frequent alliteration, most impressively in v. 5b (י).[12]

These indications pointing towards an early post-exilic provenance are also broadly corroborated by a survey of the linguistic evidence relating to the psalm. For example, the image of Israel as a flock is especially encountered in late pre-exilic to early post-exilic contexts, the term מַרְעִית being applied to the nation only in Jer. 23:1, Ezek. 34:31, Ps. 74:1, 79:13, 100:3 and 95:7; the motif of Yahweh being "tested" or "tempted" by man (בחן, v. 9) recurs only in Mal. 3:10, 15, whilst כרע and השתחוה are combined outside v. 6 in 2 Chr. 7:3, 29:29 and Est. 3:2, 2, 5. Finally, the language of praise in vv. 1-2 may also reflect a predominantly late pattern of distribution (note especially רנן [Pi.], זָמִיר and תּוֹדָה in relation to songs of worship).

Therefore, it appears that an early post-exilic provenance may well be correct, although a more cautious assessment would endorse Kraus' broader parameters, and place the composition of the psalm between the latest pre-exilic times and the early post-exile, i.e., during the sixth or fifth centuries B.C.

As regards the content of Ps. 95, the motif of creation as "his, because he made it", encountered already in Ps. 24:1-2, recurs in v. 5, here, however, specifically in relation to הַיָּם. In contrast to Ps. 24:1-2, which concerns the foundation of the earth, in Ps. 95:4-5 the whole cosmos, from the depths of the earth to the heights of the mountains, both the sea and the dry land, are said to be Yahweh's (לוֹ), and are specifically acknowledged to have been created by him. The vocabulary employed in v. 4 is difficult. מֶחְקָר is a *hapax legomenon* from the root חקר, "search", comparable in usage to תְּהוֹם חֵקֶר in Job 38:16,

---

Psalmody (Cardiff: University of Wales Press, 1979), pp. 17-18, who even places the origin of the psalm as early as "the years of the settlement" (p. 19). This is in part prompted by the lack of reference to Zion (pp. 18-19), but also by the very influential rôle ascribed by Johnson to the cultic prophets in the pre-exilic cult, which he believes is directly reflected in the present psalm (vv. 7c-11; Johnson, p. 20).

7 II, p. 830.

8 II, p. 829; see also I, p. 529 and cf. Jeremias, *Kultprophetie und Gerichtsverkündigung*, p. 126.

9 Tate, p. 503.

10 Gerstenberger, II, p. 185; cf., besides Ps. 95:9, Jer. 44:9-10, Neh. 9, Ezra 9, 2 Chr. 29:6, Ps. 106.

11 Gunkel, *Die Psalmen*, pp. 419-420; Oesterley, II, p. 420.

12 P. 377.

which is translated by RSV as "recesses of the deep". It perhaps connotes the hidden parts, waiting to be explored. The parallel term תּוֹעָפָה has the opposite nuance, representing a "prominence" or "peak". It is also sparsely attested, denoting the "horns" or "humps" or a wild ox in Num. 23:22 and 24:8, and in Job 22:25 a "mound"[13] of silver. However, the general force of the pair is well-established, and there is no need to follow the Septuagint[14] in reading מֶרְחַקֵּי, "distant parts" in place of מֶחְקְרֵי, since this would destroy the merism with תּוֹעֲפוֹת. Weiser proposes that the verse may be understood as an affirmation that even realms sometimes considered to be outside the providence of Yahweh, the underworld and the abodes of the gods, are still his and subject to his jurisdiction.[15] However, although this is possible, such an implication is far from evident either here or in comparable expressions of the comprehensiveness of Yahweh's rule;[16] moreover, it is not clear that Sheol is connoted in the first part of the verse, whilst the supposition that unspecified mountains are to be associated specifically with deities other than Yahweh is particularly uncertain.

Traditional ascriptions of the deity as the Most High God, the "great king above all gods" and creator seem to have been influential, and may reflect ancient Canaanite notions of the supreme God, mediated most directly through the cultic traditions of Jerusalem. Kraus regards the formulae illustrating the extent of Yahweh's kingship in v. 4 as archaic, proposing that they constitute "a visualization of the title מלך על־כל־אלהים[17] (v. 3b). However, Jeremias[18] is surely right to emphasise, contra Mowinckel, that creation is in no way fundamental to the kingship of god in the Psalms, since it is absent from the oldest of these compositions; rather, his lordship over creation serves to demonstrate his superiority over other deities. At the same time, although it is not uniformly reckoned among the "divine kingship psalms",[19] this poem may also claim some affinities with them.

The direct declaration that Yahweh made the sea (הוּא עָשָׂהוּ, v. 5) is unusual.[20] Even in Gen. 1, God is not apparently unambiguously said to have brought the waters into being, though, of course, much depends on the

13 Thus Habel, *The Book of Job* (OTL; London: SCM, 1985), p. 332; cf. Pope, *Job* (Anchor Bible 15; New York: Doubleday, 3rd ed. 1973), p. 164, who translates the noun as "piled high".

14 With Gunkel (*Die Psalmen*, pp. 417, 420) and Oesterley (II, pp. 420, 421).

15 P. 428; see also Anderson, II, p. 678, Kraus, II, p. 830, Tate, p. 501; Dahood translates אֶרֶץ (v. 4b) as "nether world", as is his wont (II, p. 352).

16 Cf. Am. 9:2-3, Pss. 68:23, 139:8.

17 II, p. 830.

18 *Königtum*, p. 110, cf. Loretz, *UTT*, p. 312.

19 It is, however, classed as an enthronement psalm by some of the warmest advocates of the type of New Year festival envisaged by Mowinckel: see Mowinckel (*PIW*, I, pp. 32, 106, *PsSt* II, p. 56), Day (*God's Conflict*, pp. 21, 116, 118), Gray (*Biblical Doctrine*, p. 266) and Johnson (*SKAI*, p. 68); similarly also Loretz re vv. 1-7 (*UTT*, pp. 311-2), and Cohen (p. 312).

20 It recurs also in Ps. 146:6, to be discussed below.

interpretation of vv. 1-2.[21] One must also be aware that the distinction between "making" and "separating" or "founding", which seems so evident to moderns, may not originally have been a rigid one, and that apparently divergent creation accounts may effectively have been equated. Certainly, the frequent interchangeability of images employed in relation to creation would appear to suggest that they were not always understood literally, and that Israelite tradition was sufficiently fluid to encompass various modes of description without attributing great significance to their differences. In any case, the present portrayal offers no evidence of dependence on the mythic *Chaoskampf* view of creation, according to which the sea was not "made", but subdued and confined;[22] nor does it betray an awareness of a distinction in the intrinsic natures of the constituent elements of creation.

3. Psalm 146

This Psalm exhibits a number of characteristics pointing to a post-exilic origin, for example, the framing of the hymn with the call to praise הַלְלוּ־יָהּ (vv. 1, 10),[23] here in the context of the final series of "hallelujah" psalms, 146-150, which bring the תְּהִלִּים to an apt close. As is the case with Ps. 148, the influence of the final editing of the Psalter may therefore be in view. The "large number of Aramaisms"[24] in the psalm may also be remarked upon, e.g., עֶשְׁתֹּנָה (v. 4), שֵׂבֶר (v. 5) and זקף (v. 8). It is to be noted that in these cited examples, the evidence for lateness is does not rest merely on the known Aramaic connection, but is reinforced by the likely late provenance of the other biblical passages in

21 On this issue, see above Chapter 2, Section 1, "Chaos", and the bibliography cited there, together with the fuller analysis of the relevant section of Gen. 1 in Chapter 11 below.

22 Note especially Jeremias' recognition that this theme is not even in the background, since the moment the sea is mentioned it is immediately emphasised that Yahweh is its creator; however, "it is unthinkable that that one of the powers threatening creation should come from him"(*Königtum*, p. 110). Contrast Anderson's apprehension that "it is possible that we find an implicit allusion to the sea as the primeval opponent of God..., which is now fully under the divine control" (II, p. 678). This idea is expressed even more strongly by Mowinckel, who detects an echo of the "Drachenkampf-Schöpfungsmythus" here, citing vv. 3ff. as among those passages in which "Yahweh is King of the world because he has conquered Tiamat and created the world" (*PsSt*, II, p. 214). Girard even discerns a structural correspondence between the cosmogony of vv. 1-5 and "demogony" of vv. 6-7dα, hence fancying a parallel between the creation of the cosmos from "chaos" and the formation of a people from the "chaos" of Egyptian oppression (II, p. 565-7, especially p. 566; also p. 575); however, this implication is as self-evidently absent from the first cluster of verses as it is from the second.

23 All the psalms employing this phrase fall in the last third of the Psalter and are commonly placed in the post-exilic era, with the exception of Ps. 104, the date of which has baffled many commentators and will be discussed more fully below.

24 Kraus, II, p. 1132.

which this vocabulary occurs. In addition, the appearance of -שֶׁ (vv. 3, 5) is often typical of the later language,[25] as indeed is the use of עַל as a synonym of אֵל (v. 5), which may also reflect Aramaic usage.

Kraus' assertion that "Psalm 146 is a (late) compilation of older forms and formulations from Israel's songs of praise"[26] also has some justification, insofar as it has a number of close parallels with other poetic material, most notably in vv. 2, 3a, 6a, 7a and 10a.[27] However, most of these parallels are with late compositions, so one may think of a late renaissance of Israel's poetic tradition, rather than of extensive borrowing from identifiably earlier material. Thus, the evidence that this is a late composition stemming from post-exilic times, is fairly substantial, and is widely accepted amongst commentators.[28]

As regards its creation content, Ps. 146 offers little to distinguish it from Ps. 95. Here it is declared that Yahweh "made heaven and earth, the sea and all that is in them" (v. 6), so once again the whole of the cosmos is envisaged as owing its existence to God, and the depiction is balanced and inclusive. However, its also offers a minor addition to the creation lists so far considered in the mention of אֶת־כָּל־אֲשֶׁר־בָּם (v. 6b, cf. Ps. 24:1) i.e., the living inhabitants of heaven, earth and sea; in this respect, the ideology resonates with the inclusive calls to praise of Pss. 96, 98 and 148 discussed in the previous chapter, and would seem to be fully congruent with the psalm's post-exilic setting. Habel considers v. 6b to be an expansion of the traditional formula עֹשֶׂה שָׁמַיִם וָאָרֶץ, and identifiable as such by the difference in style between the two cola, most notably the absence of the article and object marker in the first part of the verse, and their appearance, together with אֲשֶׁר, in the second.[29] However, there is no reason to regard it as a redactional addition, since v. 6a, is a traditional formula, and thus not necessarily typical of the overall style of Ps. 146. אֶרֶץ commonly takes the article even in otherwise apparently archaic poetry (e.g., Pss. 18:8, 24:1, 68:33),[30] and -הַ is also prefixed to a participial attribute of God in v. 6c, the object marker, further, occurring in vv. 1b, 9a. Hence the difference in style between vv. 6a and 6b must, at least in part, be due to the archaic formulation of the first colon. Moreover, the second colon does not disrupt the rhythm or bicolonic structure which is sustained throughout vv. 3-6b,[31] and indeed it

---

25 Cf. the discussion of Ps. 124 in chapter 4 above.

26 II, p. 1131.

27 For details and additional examples, see J. S. Kselman, "Psalm 146 in its Context" *CBQ* 50 (1988), p. 589; he also stresses the wisdom elements in the psalm (which are probably a further indication of a relatively late origin), pp. 590-591.

28 See Anderson, II, p. 940, Kraus, II, p. 1132, Oesterley, II, p. 576, Terrien, p. 911, Allen, p. 302; it is classified as late post-exilic by Gunkel (*Die Psalmen*, p. 613) and Seybold (p. 536) and even as late Greek by Briggs (II, p. 530).

29 N. C. Habel, "'Yahweh, Maker of Heaven and Earth': A Study in Tradition Criticism" *JBL* 91 (1972), p. 330; see also Allen, pp. 300, 301, Briggs, II, p. 531.

30 A similar situation applies with יָם (v. 6b): compare, e.g., Ps. 114:3 and, in later poetry, Pss. 89:10, 96:11, 98:7.

31 V. 7c clearly belongs with v. 8a; v. 6c should likewise probably be read chiefly in conjunction with the following verse. See the layout in RSV and other modern

appears comparable to the prose formulations in Neh. 9:6 and Ex. 20:11,[32] both of which relate to creation. It also bears strong formal similarities to Pss. 69:35 and 96:11, in which heaven, earth, sea and all that is (or moves) within them are enjoined to praise or rejoice in Yahweh.[33]

Creation is here indirectly associated with the divine kingship (v. 10, cf. vv. 6c-9). The infinite power demonstrated by the formation of the cosmos stands in pointed contrast to the frailty and fallibility of man acknowledged in the previous verses (3-4), and invites trust in God (v. 5).[34] Verses 6c-9 elaborate on the practical benefits which ensue from God's rôle as creator, as manifested in his continued activity in the world, as he reliably "keeps faith" and "executes justice".[35] The motifs of Yahweh's "help" (עֵזֶר, v. 5) and blessing (אַשְׁרֵי, v. 5) are elsewhere associated with his rôle as "maker of heaven and earth".[36] Once again, however, there is no hint of a combat with chaos, and this is reflected in studies of this psalm.[37]

---

translations, and Kraus, II, pp. 1130-1, who categorises vv. 1-2, 6c-7b, 7c-8b as tricola, according to the sense.

32 According to Briggs, v. 6b (or, as he describes it, v. 6aβ) was actually added by a glossator from Ex. 20:11 (II, p. 531). However, given the late and tradition-dependent nature of Ps. 146, it seems more likely that a conflated recollection of the traditional formula עשׂה שׁמים וארץ, together with the expansion attested in Exodus, was included in v. 6ab of the original composition.

33 The three nouns are collocated also in Ps. 135:6, Hag. 2:6, Am. 9:6 (also in relation to creation), Ps. 8:9-10 and Job 12:7-8, as well as in further expanded combinations in Gen. 9:2, Ezek. 38:20 and Hos. 4:3.

34 The chiastic structure identified by Girard in vv. 3-5 (III, pp. 509-10) serves to emphasise this contrast.

35 Note the recurrence of keywords from v. 6 in vv. 7-9 (עֹשֶׂה, שֹׁמֵר), as identified by Girard (III, pp. 508, 510). Girard also refers to the use of לְעוֹלָם in vv. 6cβ and 10a, hence designating vv. 6-10b as a unit; however, since v. 10 (according to Girard, just v. 10c) seems to provide a structural counterpart to the opening hymnic section of the psalm (vv. 1-2), and since v. 6c seems to relate more clearly in content to the following verses than the preceding cola, the slightly different division advocated here seems preferable.

36 Cf. Pss. 121:2 and 124:8 for the former and Gen. 14:19, Pss. 115:15, 134:3 for the latter, and see Habel's analysis of the nexus of ideas associated with this formula in *JBL* 91 (1972), pp. 326-332. Lipiński has, further, shown how vv. 5-9 constitute a "homogeneous development of the beatitude of v. 5" ("Macarismes et psaumes de congratulation" *RB* 75 [1968], p. 349), and indeed, even viewed grammatically, the thought of v. 5 continues into the following lines (likewise Girard, III, p. 511).

37 It is notable, for example, that, despite Anderson's tendency to discern allusions to the primeval enmity of the sea, even where it is "now fully under divine control" (Ps. 95:5, II, p. 678) or participating in the praise of God (98:7, II, p. 693), he here distances the psalm from such motifs, merely remarking that "among the neighbouring peoples it often had a mythological significance, traces of which survive in the Old Testament, mainly in metaphors" (II, p. 942).

4. Psalm 148

Psalm 148 has already been subject to analysis in the previous chapter. As has been shown, it bears every indication of being a late composition, perhaps being one of the latest in the Psalter, and it reflects a very unified view of creation, in which the whole cosmos is invoked to praise its Lord.

Of particular interest for the present purpose are vv. 4-6. הַמַּיִם אֲשֶׁר מֵעַל הַשָּׁמָיִם are invited, together with the rest of the celestial realm, to praise God (vv. 1-4); at the conclusion of this section, it is declared (vv. 5-6):

יְהַלְלוּ אֶת־שֵׁם יְהוָה כִּי הוּא צִוָּה וְנִבְרָאוּ׃
וַיַּעֲמִידֵם לָעַד לְעוֹלָם חָק־נָתַן וְלֹא יַעֲבוֹר׃

The precise nature of the subject here referred to is slightly ambiguous, insofar as the verbs of vv. 5a, bβ, 6a could refer either to the entire heavenly sphere whose elements are enunciated in vv. 1-4, or merely to the immediate antecedent. However, since הַמַּיִם אֲשֶׁר מֵעַל הַשָּׁמָיִם stands at the end of the list of celestial creatures, for the present purpose, the issue is of no great significance. The setting of the boundary alluded to in v. 6[38] would, nevertheless, seem to be most consistent with the latter interpretation.

It is evident from the tone of this hymnic celebration that the creation of the heavenly ocean is an aspect of divine beneficence occasioning gratitude and praise from all sectors of the cosmos. That the waters are "established"[39] and are to remain so "for ever and ever" is an indication of their positive nature as an essential element in the universe; it is to be noted also that they were brought into being by the divine decree, and thus owe their existence to the will of God. Crucial also is the imposition of order and balance: the supercelestial zone has a place among others, and as such is limited: its boundary is set and cannot be passed, a restriction which shall be as enduring as its waters themselves. This does not imply an underlying conflict- and subjugation-dependent view of the universe or of the sea within it, but may rather reflect an obvious awareness that all bodies of water are contained: without a receptacle or boundary, they disperse, losing their essential identity and failing to fulfil the function for which they were formed. The idea of the "gathering" of the sea is depicted somewhat more colourfully in Ps. 33, which shall be examined further below.

Finally, it remains to be observed that the terrestrial order which is exhorted to join in exultation of Yahweh in the second part of the hymn is not specifically stated to owe its existence to God. Nevertheless, the creation-declaration at the midpoint of the psalm to some extent resounds outwards over both halves of the composition, and the createdness of the earth and its creatures is rather assumed than denied; notably, first among them, and

38 The interpretation of this ambiguous colon is discussed in the previous chapter.

39 Literally, "he has caused them to stand", יַעֲמִידֵם; a similar idea, though expressed in different vocabulary, appears in relation to the founding of the earth in Ps. 24:2.

therefore directly succeeding the creation affirmation of vv. 5-6, are תַּנִּינִים וְכָל־תְּהֹמוֹת, who are invoked to praise Yahweh מִן־הָאָרֶץ (v. 7).

5. Psalm 136

In the compositions examined thus far, little detail is offered concerning how the universe was formed, its precise layout and the methods employed. Rather, the declarations tend towards baldness and non-specificity, since the emphasis rests on the fact or celebration of creation, and there is no attempt to produce a complete and consistent narrative of the processes involved. However, Ps. 136 must be distinguished from these insofar as it comprises a sustained attempt to narrate the great deeds of חֶסֶד enacted by Yahweh of old, beginning, after a list of his glorious and supreme titles, with his originating acts.

i. The Date of Psalm 136

Psalm 136 is widely considered to be post-exilic.[40] It displays a high density of prose-style features, most notably ten occurrences of the definite article הַ־ and two of אֶת־, besides two examples of late linguistic usage, namely שֶׁ־[41] and לְ as a sign of the object.[42] The vocabulary and concerns of the psalm would likewise appear to corroborate this dating. For example, the first verse (which, of course, also informs the repeated refrain) is paralleled in full in Pss. 106:1, 107:1, 118:1, 29, 1 Chr. 16:34,[43] all of which are commonly assigned to the post-exilic period, and indeed the main constituents of the line seem to be predominantly late. Also typically exilic or later are the use of עֶבֶד to characterise Israel in its relationship to Yahweh (v. 22),[44] רוֹקַע / רֹקַע הָאָרֶץ (v. 6),[45] יַם־סוּף (vv. 13, 15)[46] and שֵׁפֶל (v. 23),[47] and the use of the verb פרק in its

---

40 Thus Allen ("evidently post-exilic", p. 231), Goulder (*PR*, p. 220), Terrien (p. 863) and Kraus (II, p. 1079). According to Anderson, it is "late post-exilic" (II, p. 894), a view endorsed by Gunkel, for who it "belongs... to the latest period of psalm-composition" (*Die Psalmen*, p. 577). Nevertheless, the argument is sometimes encountered that the psalm has undergone various phases of expansion (thus Briggs, II, p. 481, Seybold, p. 507, Oesterley, II, p. 542), though this has not commanded wide assent.

41 V. 23; this characteristically Aramaic feature is discussed above in relation to Pss. 124 and 146.

42 Vv. 19, 20; see Gunkel, *Die Psalmen*, p. 578, GK §117n.

43 Cf. also Ezra 3:11, Jer. 33:11, 2 Chr. 7:3, Ps. 100:4c-5a and, more loosely, though all the elements are still present, 2 Chr. 5:13.

44 Confined (in addition to the contentious Servant Songs of Deutero-Isaiah) to Isa. 41:8, 9, 42:19, 43:10, 44:21, 49:3; Ps. 136:22; cf., of יַעֲקֹב (often in parallel with יִשְׂרָאֵל), Isa. 44:1, 2, 45:4, 48:20, Jer. 30:10, 46:27, 28.

45 Yahweh is recognised as such elsewhere only in Isa. 42:5, 44:24, cf. Job 37:18 (Hiph., of spreading out clouds).

Aramaic sense, "rescue", in v. 24.[48] Also of interest is the title "God of heaven" in v. 26, since although it only occurs once in the Psalter, it is found (with אֱלֹהֵי for אֵל) quite commonly in literature of the Persian period (Ezra 1:2, 5:12, 6:9; Neh. 1:4, 2:4; Jon. 1:9, etc.).[49]

The psalm may presuppose the completion of the Pentateuch.[50] In particular, the section concerning creation (vv. 5-9) may reflect influence from Gen. 1:16 (cf. vv. 7-9) as well as from wisdom material (compare v. 5 with Prov. 3:19b; cf. Jer. 10:12)[51], whilst deuteronomic influence is probable in v. 12,[52] and perhaps also in v. 21.[53] The likelihood of dependence on familiar traditions is also raised in respect of v. 15, where the unusual verb נער, "shake off", is employed, apparently in a reminiscence of Ex. 14:27. Finally, the parallels between Ps. 136:10, 17-22 and Ps. 135:8, 10-12 are striking, and may indicate a direct relationship between them.[54]

---

46 This is applied to the Red Sea or its arms outside the Hexateuch only in Neh. 9:9, Pss. 106:7, 9, 22 and 136:13, 15.

47 It is confined to this verse and Eccl. 10:6.

48 Cf. Lam. 5:8, Ps. 7:3.

49 The only occurrence which may fall outside the post-exilic period is Gen. 24:7, where יהוה אֱלֹהֵי הַשָּׁמַיִם וֵאלֹהֵי הָאָרֶץ should be read, as in the LXX and v. 3.

50 Thus Kraus, II, pp. 1079, 1080, Noth, "Nu 21 als Glied der 'Hexateuch'-Erzählung" in *Aufsätze zur biblischen Landes- und Altertumskunde*, I (Neukirchen-Vluyn: Neukirchener Verlag, 1971) p. 99 n. 75, and Scharbert, "Das 'Schilfmeerwunder' in den Texten des Alten Testaments" in A. Caquot and M. Delcor (edd.), *Mélanges bibliques et orientaux en l'honneur de M. Henri Cazelles* (Kevelaer: Butzon & Bercker, 1981), p. 415. Contrast Norin, *Er spaltete das Meer*, p. 146, who maintains that the author uses the Pentateuchal traditions too freely—with the exception of Deuteronomy—for this to be the case; compare, however, his remarks on p. 147.

51 בִּינָה, "understanding" (v. 5), is a quality which is especially valued in wisdom literature, and indeed about two-thirds of the occurrences of this term are in a wisdom setting, e.g. Job 28:12, 20, 28, Prov. 4:5, 7, Dan 1:20; for "wisdom" or "understanding" as a divine attribute especially manifested in the works of creation, cf. Job 9:10, Ps. 104:24.

52 The phrasing recurs in Deut. 4:34, 5:15, 7:19, 11:2, 26:8, Jer. 32:21, Ezek. 20:33, 34, 1 Ki. 8:42 = 2 Chr. 6:32, and cf. Jer. 21:5; outside the Psalter, the זְרוֹעַ of Yahweh is especially characteristic of Deuteronomy, Jeremiah and Deutero-Isaiah.

53 Cf. Deut. 29:6-7, where נתן נַחֲלָה is employed immediately after mention of the defeat of Sihon and Og; also, e.g., Deut. 4:21, 15:4, 19:10, 20:16, Josh. 11:23. Further possible parallels with Deuteronomy are cited by Goulder, *PR*, p. 221.

54 For the dating of Ps. 135, see chapter 7 above. Comparisons have also been drawn between v. 4 and Pss. 72:18b, 86:10; v. 10 and Pss. 135:8, 78:51, Ex. 12:12, 29; v. 11 and Ex. 18:1, 20:2, Deut. 1:27, 4:20, 5:15, etc.; v. 14 and Ex. 14:22; v. 16 and Deut. 8:15, Jer. 2:6c, Am. 2:10b; and v. 25 and Pss. 104:27, 145:15. However, in these cases, the reliance may be on a common, probably oral and cultic, tradition, rather than on strict literary borrowing.

ii. The Theme of "Chaos" in Psalm 136

The description of Yahweh's act of creation is fairly prosaic, as may perhaps be expected from its influence by Genesis 1 and Wisdom literature. Nevertheless, the simple statement that he "spread out (רקע) the earth upon the waters" (v. 6) is interesting insofar as, uniquely in the Psalter, it employs the metaphor of beating out metal.[55] The utilisation of rather matter-of-fact, workmanlike terminology may perhaps be compared with the imagery of Ps. 33, and certainly suggests far removal from battle motifs.[56] The idea of the "founding" of the earth upon sea and rivers is already familiar from Ps. 24:1-2, the same cosmological structure being reflected also in Gen. 7:11, 49:25, Ex. 20:4 and Deut. 33:13.[57] Nevertheless, the assertion of Allen that v. 6 (together with v. 13) is dependent on "seemingly old, cultic material"[58] is not substantiated, and perhaps reflects the assumption that there is an underlying mythical (*Chaoskampf*) content which is essentially ancient (and probably ultimately Canaanite) in origin. In fact, despite the many affinities between Ps. 136 and various Old Testament traditions, v. 6 has its only close parallels with Deutero-Isaiah; similarly, v. 13 would seem to represent the end-point of the developed Exodus tradition, as shall be indicated in chapter 9 below. Nor is there any need to assume the dependence of v. 6 on Ps. 24:1-2, to which it bears only a general resemblance as regards its underlying structural worldview.[59]

55 Not the "image of the expanse of a tent or curtain spread upon the waters" as Briggs asserts (II, p. 483). Compare Isa. 42:5 and 44:24, where the same image of "beating out" occurs in parallel to the "stretching out" (נטה) of the heavens, and cf. Job 37:18, where the root רקע is applied to the "spreading" of the clouds.

56 T. M. Ludwig's assertion that "this creation tradition involved ordering the cosmos against chaotic forces" ("The Traditions of Establishing the Earth in Deutero-Isaiah" *JBL* 92 [1973], p. 348) is dependent on interpreting Isa. 44:24-28 such that "all the ongoing activity of Yahweh" described in vv. 25-28 is "include[d] within the sphere of his creative ordering of the cosmos in the face of chaotic, disruptive forces" (p. 349); this background is then projected onto the further occurrences of the expression רֹקַע הָאָרֶץ in Ps. 136:6 and Isa. 42:5, since Ludwig assumes that these associations are intrinsic to the history of the phrase itself, and applicable wherever it may occur. Allen's explanation (p. 233), that "the earth, culturally described as poised remarkably but firmly over the primeval waters (cf. 24:1), is a cosmos won out of chaos", similarly overreaches the evidence, whilst Girard's comparison of Yahweh's "mastery of the mythic waters of primordial chaos" with that of "the mythical waters of the Sea of Reeds" (vv. 6a, 13-15; Girard, III, pp. 405-6) lacks any linguistic foundation and is not supported by the content of either passage: see further the discussion of vv. 13-15 in Chapter 9 below.

57 Cf. also Job 26:10 and Jon. 2:7. A similar arrangement is envisaged in the celestial sphere in Ps. 104:3.

58 P. 231.

59 Contra Briggs, II, p. 482. Their vague similarity now perhaps appears exaggerated because of the unfamiliarity of their shared conceptions.

6. Psalm 33

i. The Date of Psalm 33

It is very difficult to determine any indication of the date of this psalm, or of any particular cultic setting.[60] Nevertheless, most who would venture to offer some form of estimate place the psalm in the post-exilic period.[61] Some of the arguments advanced in support of this are dubious, for example, the premise of an eschatological interpretation, which was sometimes advocated by the older scholars.[62] Bickell's apprehension[63] that it is an "acrostic song" on the grounds that there are the same number of lines as letters in the alphabet (i.e. twenty-two) could, if correct, also suggest a late origin for the hymn. However, as there is no sequential correspondence between the lines and letters and no trace of any alphabetic arrangement in the psalm, it is difficult to accredit its length to anything other than coincidence, and this approach must also therefore be rejected. On the other hand, the possible dependence of vv. 6, 9 on the "creation by word" theology, and even on the phrasing, of Gen. 1, may suggest that the psalm is fairly late,[64] perhaps post-exilic. Of course, the use of a related or antecedent tradition cannot absolutely be precluded, but, against the supposition of an early provenance, it may be noted that there is scant evidence for the appearance of the creation by word motif in pre-exilic Israelite material. Moreover, the language of v. 9a in particular seems to resonate with the current form of the priestly account.[65]

---

60 Anderson speaks of the Autumn Festival, or at least of a common theological background with it (I, p. 260), and Kraus of a "context of cultic obeisance" comparable with that of Pss. 95:6, 99:9, 100:4 (I, p. 409), whilst others (such as Craigie, p. 271) resist any attempt to determine such a precise worship context.

61 Thus Anderson (I, p. 260), Oesterley (I, p. 211), Oeming (I, p. 194), Zenger (HZ, I, p. 206), and Briggs (I, p. 286). Craigie thinks, on the other hand, that there are similarities between Ps. 33 and Judg. 5, "notably the episodic structure of the substance and the use of repetition", and concludes that the date of the psalm may be earlier than is commonly supposed: "While the date remains uncertain, there are no overwhelming reasons to oppose a general setting in the cult as practiced [*sic*] during the period of the Hebrew monarchy" (p. 271).

62 Such as Staerk, *Lyrik* (not available to me). This is not to deny that the presence of certain limited eschatological elements is still accepted by some (e.g., Kraus, I, pp. 410, 414-5, Anderson, I, p. 261).

63 *Carmina Veteris Testamenti Metrice* (Innsbruck: Libraria Academica Wagneriana, 1882), p. 21; followed by Gunkel, *Die Psalmen*, p. 139, Kraus, I, p. 409; see also Craigie, p. 271, Briggs, I, p. 286, Oeming, I, p. 191, Zenger, HZ, I, p. 206.

64 Thus, e.g., Kraus, I, p. 409; cf. Zenger, HZ, I, p. 206. Gerstenberger, by contrast, relates the emphasis on the "word of God" to "synagogal Scripture readings"(I, p. 144), but the consequences for dating are similar.

65 Thus, e.g., Wellhausen, p. 179, who discerns here "a clear reference to the story of creation as told in Gen. 1"; similarly Anderson, I, p. 264, Kraus, I, p. 411, Craigie, p.

In addition, a post-exilic dating is broadly supported by the linguistic profile of the psalm, for example, the use of the definite article no fewer than eleven times and of אֲשֶׁר twice. The employment of expressions such as שִׁיר חָדָשׁ (v. 3) and רנן (v. 1) have already been discussed above in relation to Pss. 96 and 98 and Ps. 95 respectively.[66] In addition, יְשָׁרִים as a designation of the upright among the people of God (v. 1) is confined to wisdom literature and to apparently late psalms, most of which also display indications of wisdom influence;[67] note also the distribution, e.g., of Qal כנס ("gather, collect", v. 7),[68] צוה of the divine action in creation (v. 9),[69] and the combination רַב־כֹּחַ (v. 16).[70] Indeed, even the mention of the creation of the heavens (with various verbs), especially outside the formula "heavens and earth", would appear to be typically Jeremianic or later.[71]

ii. The Theme of "Chaos" in Psalm 33

In the final psalms to be considered in this chapter, Pss. 33 and 104, the portrayals of creation are much more detailed than those discussed so far. Nevertheless, it cannot be presumed that such images are necessarily always literally consistent with those occurring elsewhere in the biblical tradition or even in their more immediate compositional context; they thus appear to have the character of imaginative depictions rather than firm doctrine.

Psalm 33 is a hymn inviting the faithful to join in praise of Yahweh. In the section of interest here, 33:4-9, the dependability of God's word is illustrated by his work of creation, and this invites confidence in the fulfilment of his promises and awe at his power. Thus, there is a correlation between Yahweh's might as creator and his activity as lord of history. The emphasis on the divine fiat has clear affinities with Gen 1.

---

273. Cf. Ps. 148:5. Briggs lists a further series of possible influences (I, p. 286), but they are not in general sufficiently exact as to demand direct dependence.

66 As sometimes occurs elsewhere, certain commentators have sought to relate the שִׁיר חָדָשׁ (v. 3) to a renewal of creation (Leslie, p. 84) or of the covenant (Weiser, pp. 41, 195), or to a recent act of deliverance (Oesterley, pp. 210, 211). However, such attempts are dubious, and are rightly eschewed by most scholars.

67 Namely, Pss. 94:15, 111:1, 112:2, 4, 107:42, 140:14. A further instance occurs in Dan. 11:17. Compare also Gerstenberger's relation of this and other terminology to the "ecclesiastical organization of the diaspora community"(I, p. 145).

68 1 Chr. 22:2, Est. 4:16, Neh. 12:44, Eccl. 2:8, 26, 3:5.

69 Isa. 45:12, Ps. 148:5.

70 Isa. 63:1, Job 23:6, 30:18.

71 The creation of the heavens is mentioned, besides Ps. 33:6, in Ps. 136:5, Prov. 3:19, 8:27, Isa. 40:12, 22, 42:5, 44:24, 45:12, 18, 48:13, 51:13, 16, Jer. 10:12, 51:15, 1 Chr. 16:26; that of the heavens and the earth occurs, apart from the possibly very primitive קֹנֵה שָׁמַיִם וָאָרֶץ in Gen. 14:19, 22 (perhaps with the meaning "possessor" there), in Ex. 20:11, 31:17 (P), 2 K. 19:15, Isa. 37:16, Jer. 32:17, 2 Chr. 2:11, Pss. 12:4, 124:8, 134:3; cf. the new heavens and new earth of Isa. 65:17, 66:22.

There is no implication of conflict, or even of a fearful response by the waters here. "Gathering" and "putting" (v. 7) are simple utilitarian terms, conveying a sense of daily human tasks magnified on a cosmic scale, and are without mythological overtones. The "bottling" of the sea (entailing the emendation of כַּנֵּד, "like a heap", to כְּנֹאד or כַּנֹּד, "as in a skin bottle") is supported by most of the versions[72] and modern commentators,[73] and would fit the context better than the well-known image of gathering into a heap; probably a copyist slipped into the familiar idiom here, hence its appearance in the MT.[74] There is no indication that an act of separation or of confining the waters behind barriers is envisaged; the "bottle" and "storehouses" alluded to would appear to be for the provision of water, most naturally in rain, in which case the waters "above the firmament" would be intended.[75] This may be compared with Job 26:8, 38:37 and Deut. 28:12; meteorological storehouses are also encountered in Jer. 10:13 = 51:16, Ps. 135:7 (of the wind, though rainfall is also implicated in each context) and Job 38:22 (of snow and hail). The use of the term יָם to denote the heavenly ocean is attested also in Am. 9:6, where the waters of the sea are said to be poured out, evidently in rain, whilst the process envisaged as underlying rainfall is further illuminated by Gen 7:11, and indeed by the structural arrangement established in Gen. 1:6-7. On the other hand, it is possible that subterranean waters are envisaged in v. 7b[76] as a counterpart to the heavenly ocean mentioned in the first part of the verse. תְּהוֹם is not elsewhere applied to the celestial sphere, but the "deeps" were frequently understood as a divinely bestowed reservoir nourishing the earth's water supply: see, e.g., Gen. 49:25, Deut. 8:7, 33:13, Ezek. 31:4, 15, Ps. 78:15, Prov. 8:24, 28 and (by

---

72 Greek, Targum, Latin, Symmachus, Origen, Syriac (there in the plural: "as if in skins").

73 Among them Day, *God's Conflict*, p. 56, Kraus, I, pp. 408-409, Seybold, pp. 137, 138, Gunkel, *Die Psalmen*, p. 138, Wellhausen, p. 30, Briggs, I, pp. 285, 287, and Oesterley, I, pp. 211-12. It is resisted by JPSA and Craigie, p. 270, the latter of whom accordingly sees an allusion to the Red Sea event, at which "God's creation of his people Israel" occurred, alongside the reference to the formation of the physical cosmos (p. 273). Dahood, in dependence on a tentative suggestion of J. Aistleitner (*Wörterbuch der ugaritischen Sprache* [Berlin: Akademie Verlag, 4th ed. 1974], No. 1337, p. 152) and followed by Anderson (I, p. 263), vocalises the noun as כַּנֵּד, identifying it with the Ugaritic *knd*, comparable to Akkadian *kandu*, "jug, pitcher"; he then explains the absence of a preposition "on the principle of a double-duty preposition", according to which "one preposition can suffice for two nouns in tandem" (I, pp. 201-2). However, Dahood's translation is extremely doubtful; see Dietrich and Loretz, "Die Ug. Gewandbezeichnungen *PǴNDR, KND, KNDPNṮ*" *UF* 9 (1977), p. 340, and likewise Craigie, p. 270.

74 Cf. Ex. 15:8, Ps. 78:13, Josh. 3:13, 16.

75 Thus, e.g., Kraus, I, p. 411, Anderson, I, p. 263, Seybold, p. 138, Gunkel, *Die Psalmen*, p. 140, Dahood, I, p. 201. Contrast Cohen, who thinks of the waters of the sea gathered together ready to perform great deeds at the behest of the divine (p. 96).

76 Thus, e.g. Oeming, I, p. 192.

implication) Am. 7:4.[77] The complementary rôle of the super- and subterrestrial seas in watering the earth is encountered most vividly in Gen. 7:11, 8:2, as well as in Prov. 3:20, 8:28 and Gen. 1:6-7.

Although the psalm is removed from theophany and warrior language, the assertion that fear and trembling are the proper response to Yahweh's mighty deeds still remains (v. 8). Nevertheless, awe, which is the natural response to these creative acts of God, is provoked by the magnitude of the work, and also by the fact that it happened in response to the divine command (v. 9), rather than by the simple "terribleness" of the deed or indeed of the divine presence.[78] Creation also indicates the power of God to work on a world scale (vv. 10ff.), frustrating human plans but protecting those who trust in him: the Creator is also the Lord of history.

In accordance with the lack of mythological content, most commentators remain silent on the issue of *Chaoskampf* or, as in the case of Anderson, emphasise that "whatever was the original mythological significance of the 'deep', in the *OT* passages it was largely 'demythologized'."[79] Nonetheless, some would prefer to go further: Kraus, for example, translates v. 7b as "he lays the primal seas up in storehouses",[80] "primal", in this context, being simply an explanatory gloss inserted in accordance with his favoured interpretation. He further comments[81] that the "foundational event" of the creation of the "powerful heavenly world ... is in v. 7 described with conceptual rudiments of myth ... The pictures, interlaced with mythical concepts, illustrate the sovereign way in which Yahweh overcomes the archetypal powers (תהומות) of chaos". The theomachic aspects of the passage are painted still more strongly by the Uppsala scholar Helmer Ringgren, according to whom it concerns "God's ... victory over the powers of chaos, represented by 'the ocean' or 'the deep' (*tehom*)... [T]he mighty God ... crushes all opposition and defeats all hostile powers, even the superhuman chaotic powers. Everything that stood in the way of the Creator's work was subdued by his mighty word".[82] In each case, the starting point for such imaginative reconstructions seems to be

77 Contrast Briggs (I, p. 293), who thinks of a special sense, "primal sea", for which he cites Ps. 104:6 and the present verse. However, since Hebrew nouns are not elsewhere temporally delimited, and the remaining uses of תְּהוֹם are not thus restricted, it seems unlikely that this should comprise a fundamental category of meaning, even though it may represent a genuine context of application for the word. In any case, the appearance of the term in relation to an act of creation strongly implies that the statement is forward-looking: the object "put into storehouses" is that entity now known and recognised as תְּהוֹמוֹת, an aspect which is still more apparent in Ps. 104:6.

78 "The 'fear of the Lord' includes both the experience of awe and the irresistible attraction to the graciousness of God, but it is *not* a state of anxiety" (Anderson, I, p. 210, on Ps. 25:12).

79 I, p. 263. See likewise Day (*God's Conflict*, p. 1; also p. 180).

80 "(Der)... in Speichern die Urfluten legt", I, p. 408; see similarly Briggs, I, p. 285, and Seybold, pp. 136, 138.

81 I, pp. 410-411.

82 *The Faith of the Psalmists* (London: SCM, 1963), p. 49.

the use of the word תְּהוֹמוֹת.[83] However, as has been shown by the careful examination of applications of the term conducted in relation to Ps. 77:17 in chapter 6 above, such an approach is entirely unnecessary. In the majority of cases, תְּהוֹמוֹת is unambiguously associated with the exodus or with the provision of fertile, life-sustaining water, as in Ps. 78:15 and Deut. 8:7;[84] often, the context is actually one of creation, as in Prov. 8:24, 3:20,[85] and this background would eminently suit the context of creating storehouses for the beneficent use of fresh water here. However, there is in the language employed in the present context no hint of resistance, subjugation or conflict; nor has any concretely been identified by proponents of the *Chaoskampf* interpretation.[86] It may, in addition, be observed that the mixing of images for creation in vv. 6-7 suggests that there may have been a conscious awareness that such language was essentially metaphorical. Though it could be confidently asserted that Yahweh alone made the heavens, all descriptions of the process involved were ultimately conjectural.

7. Psalm 104

i. The Date of Psalm 104

Psalm 104 is the most lengthy of the psalms to be examined in the present context, and the only one of these actually meriting the title "creation hymn", since this constitutes its primary concern. As in the case of Ps. 33, evidence regarding its provenance is scarce, as would be expected from a hymn celebrating such a universal theme. The data are also open to contradictory interpretations, with estimates ranging from the occasion of Solomon's dedication of the Temple[87] to the post-exilic period,[88] with many scholars expressing uncertainty regarding this issue.[89] The current debate has mainly

83 Note how Gunkel describes the term itself as "originally mythic", *Die Psalmen*, p. 140.

84 Cf. in the singular Gen. 49:25, Deut. 33:13, Prov. 8:28, Ezek. 31:4, 15.

85 Cf. Pss. 148:7, 135:6.

86 Craigie's discernment of "creation language... reminiscent of Canaanite and Mesopotamian cosmogonies involving conflict and the primeval waters" (p. 273) is heavily dependent on a perceived reliance on the "Song of the Sea" (Ex. 15:1-18). However, not only is MT נֵד (the keyword on which the putative relationship rests) dubious, though readily explicable as a scribal error: Craigie's use of the Song is also doubtful, since it contains no reference to any combat between Yahweh and the waters, either at a literal or a metaphorical level (see further the discussion of this poem in Chapter 11 below).

87 P. C. Craigie, "The Comparison of Hebrew Poetry: Psalm 104 in the Light of Egyptian and Ugaritic Poetry" *Semitics* 4 (1974), pp. 19-21.

88 Crüsemann, *Studien zur Formgeschichte von Hymnus und Danklied in Israel*, pp. 301-2, Seybold, p. 409, Briggs, II, p. 331.

89 E.g., Kraus, II, p. 881, Seybold, p. 409.

centred around the relationship of the psalm to other compositions or traditions with which it has clear affinities.

Firstly, some commentators have discerned a connection between this hymn and Ps. 103 (which is probably post-exilic), proposing that they emanate from the same author;[90] both begin and end with the self-exhortation, "Bless Yahweh, O my soul," and there are a number of stylistic similarities between them. On the other hand, the affinities could simply be attributable to a common cultic background or dependence on traditional formulae. Nevertheless, since Ps. 104 seems to take up the call of 103:22, one could imagine that it was composed to follow on from the preceding psalm, and therefore would be of the same or a later date. The other possibility is that the present arrangement could have been imposed by a compiler on two already-existing psalms, although this may not explain the similarity between them so well.

Some exegetes detect a further affinity with Genesis 1, although the putative correspondences are mainly sequential rather than verbal; thus, any such relation is surely very loose, and hardly provides a basis for speaking of a literary dependence, let alone for declaring which may be primary.[91]

Some ancient motifs are recognisable: Yahweh riding on his cloud-chariot (v. 3b) is familiar from theophany appearances,[92] but by now seems to be his customary mode of transport rather than a warning of his imminent manifestation. It still signals his glory, but as an indication of the scale on which he operates rather than as a feature of a specific act of salvation. Typical storm theophany language also occurs in vv. 7, 32, yet it is not sufficient to make the reader think in terms of a very early origin for the psalm.

A link with a still earlier poem is suggested by the indisputable similarities with the hymn to the Aton discovered at El-Amarna (c. 1375-1358 B.C.).[93]

---

90 E.g., Gunkel, *Die Psalmen*, p. 447, Schmidt, p. 188, P. E. Dion, "YHWH as Storm-god and Sun-god: The Double Legacy of Egypt and Canaan as Reflected in Psalm 104" *ZAW* 103 (1991) 43-71, pp. 43-4.

91 Gunkel, *Die Psalmen*, p. 453, Cohen, p. 337 and Briggs, II, pp. 330, 331 maintain the priority of the priestly creation account; on the other hand, Day (*God's Conflict*, pp. 34, 51-3), Levenson (*Creation and the Persistence of Evil*, p. 58), and A. van der Voort ("Genèse I,1 à II,4[a] et le Psaume 104" *RB* 58 [1951], p. 346) argue for the opposite direction of influence, whilst Terrien regards them as roughly contemporary (pp. 718-9). Thus many think in terms of a "common cultic tradition", e.g., Weiser, p. 456; cf. Kraus, II, pp. 880-881, P. Humbert, "La relation de Genèse 1 et du Psaume 104 avec la liturgie du Nouvel-An israélite" *RHPR* 15 (1953), 1-27, and B. W. Anderson, *Creation versus Chaos*, p. 91.

92 The expression כַּנְפֵי־רוּחַ (v. 3) recurs in Ps. 18:11 = 2 Sam. 22:11, and Hos. 4:19 may also be compared.

93 The dependence of Ps. 104 on this hymn is urged, among others, by Day, *God's Conflict*, p. 29, and Oesterley, II, p. 440. G. Nagel, however, thinks of the indirect exercise of Egyptian influence through Phoenician mediation ("À propos des rapports du Psaume 104 avec les textes égyptiens" in W. Baumgartner et al [edd.] *Festschrift für Alfred Bertholet* [Tübingen: J. C. B. Mohr (Paul Siebeck), 1950], p. 403); see likewise Dahood, III, p. 33, Terrien, p. 716, Kraus, II, pp. 880, 885 and Gerstenberger, II, pp.

How and when any connection may have been mediated is not known. However, the manifest wisdom influence in the Psalm—the emphasis on the ordering of creation, the placing of barriers and making provision (cf. Prov. 8) and indeed the mention of wisdom itself[94]—may suggest one possible channel of transmission which would be consistent with a relatively late date of composition. The hymn exhibits a number of features which would support this conclusion, most notably, the closing phrase, הַלְלוּ־יָהּ, which is consistently characteristic of late psalms; it also has a number of possible contacts with other parts of the Psalter: for example, Ps. 104:33 is practically identical to Ps. 146:2, whilst v. 34 is similar to Ps. 19:15.

Linguistically, the hymn displays both "archaistic" and apparently late features. In the former category are the notable density of ־ן terminations, the use of the old case ending in חַיְתוֹ (vv. 11, 20) and the appearance of the "archaic" form שָׂדָי in place of the more common שָׂדֶה in v. 11. However, the distribution of these nouns alerts one to consider the likelihood that they are essentially elements of "poetic" or possibly "archaising" style, since many occurrences of each are in literature considered to be exilic or later, and none are in compositions widely recognised as "archaic".[95] This is confirmed by the presence of a variety of "prose-style" features, such as אֲשֶׁר (vv. 16b, 17a), אֶת־ (v. 1) and הַ (which occurs sixteen times in the psalm, including many instances which are highly unusual in poetry, besides more common examples of its use, e.g., as prefixed to אֶרֶץ). In addition, there are a number of items of vocabulary which are predominantly late, among them קרה ("lay the beams of", v. 3)[96] רמשׂ (v. 20),[97] גוע (v. 29),[98] and רעד (v. 32),[99] as well as the apparent Aramaisms קִנְיָן (v. 24)[100] and II שׂבר (Pi., v. 27),[101]. Therefore, it would seem

---

224, 226 (the latter two urging a more general Canaanite route of transmission), whilst Uehlinger even posits a more exclusive Canaanite-Phoenician background ("Leviathan und die Schiffe in Ps 104,25-26", *Biblica* 71 [1990] 499-526). A lengthy bibliography on this topic is provided by Dion, "YHWH as Storm-god and Sun-god", p. 59 n. 65.

94 V. 24. The divine חָכְמָה is mentioned elsewhere only in Job, Prov. and Jer. 10:12 = 51:15 (in the latter case, and in Job 38:36, 37 and Prov. 3:1, in connection with creation).

95 Nor can the use of the short YIQTOL in past narrative in vv. 6-8 be taken as indicative of the archaic interchange of imperfect and perfect forms: see Gibson, *Davidson's Introductory Hebrew Grammar—Syntax*, §62, contra Robertson, *Linguistic Evidence*, pp. 14-17, 42-3.

96 Elsewhere in 2 Chr. 34:11, Neh. 2:8, 3:3, 6.

97 This verb is almost exclusively limited to "P", but appears also in the holiness code of Leviticus three times, and in Ezek. 38:20, Ps. 69:35, Deut. 4:18 (the latter probably being a deuteronomistic addition to be located in the exilic period: see Mayes, *Deuteronomy*, p. 148).

98 Besides the very numerous occurrences in "P" and eight in Job, it features also in Ps. 88:16, Zech. 13:8 and Lam. 1:19.

99 Elsewhere in Dan. 10:11, Ezra 10:9.

100 Elsewhere only in "P" (four times), Lev. 22:11 (H), Ezek. 38:12, 13, Ps. 105:21, Prov. 4:7.

that the psalm in its present form exhibits many indicators of late composition, although an earlier tradition-history in images such as the divine theophany and in the material shared with the Egyptian hymn to the Aton must also be acknowledged.

ii. The Theme of "Chaos" in Psalm 104

Psalm 104 is clearly a hymn praising the works of God in creation and, in particular, celebrating the dependence of the created order on Yahweh for its origin and sustenance. Various aspects of this psalm are especially worthy of attention. Firstly, the general observation may be made that the provision of water is a dominating concern, providing a supreme expression of the divine beneficence and of God's continuing care for his creation.[102] Especially notable in this regard are vv. 10-13, 16. The springs which "gush forth בַּנְּחָלִים" and provide drink to all the creatures (vv. 10-12) are presumably fed by the nourishing waters of the deep;[103] the same subterranean source may also be envisaged as "abundantly water[ing]" the trees of Yahweh in v. 16 (cf. Ezek. 31:4-5, 7).[104] This method of water-bestowal is then balanced by the sending of rain in v. 13, which of course is dropped from heaven: for the mechanism involved, compare Gen. 7:11, 8:2, and especially Mal. 3:10, which speaks of Yahweh opening the windows of heaven and pouring down an overflowing blessing.[105] The "fruit of thy work" alluded to in v. 13b may then either be the rain[106] or the produce resultant upon it.[107]

---

101 Otherwise limited to Isa. 38:18, Pss. 119:166, 145:15, Ru. 1:13, Est. 9:1, whilst the cognate noun שֵׂבֶר appears only in Pss. 119:116 and 146:5.

102 Oesterley's remark that "in a country like Palestine [water] was looked upon as one of the greatest of God's gifts" (II, p. 443) is apt.

103 The negativity of Anderson's assertion (II, p. 721; see likewise Kraus, II, p. 882) regarding v. 10, that "springs had their origin in the waters of the great abyss, so that destructive Chaos was utilised for the furthering of life", is undermined by the fact that "destructive Chaos" is not in evidence either here or in the preceding verses (see the discussion of the latter below). Oesterley finds an additional reference to Yahweh "caus[ing] moisture to come forth from the earth" in v. 14c (II, p. 441) by emending לֶחֶם to לַח (II, p. 442).

104 Though precipitation may be wholly or partially envisaged as providing this water (cf. Briggs, II, p. 335).

105 The attribution of rainfall to various deities is plentifully attested elsewhere: compare *KTU* 1.4.v.6-9 (of Baal) and the description of the provision of rain in the Hymn to the Aton; in Israel, it is most often associated with the theophany tradition.

106 This is the most popular interpretation, but is dependent on various proposed emendations; see, e.g., Briggs (II, p. 330), Weiser (p. 455), Schmidt (p. 188; cf. Oesterley, II, pp. 441, 442), Gunkel (*Die Psalmen*, p. 455), Dahood (III, pp. 31, 39), and Kraus (II, pp. 877-8).

107 Cohen, p. 339.

Secondly, in accordance with this interest in water-provision, the psalm is not content merely to celebrate the fact and resultant blessings of Yahweh's bestowal of water on his earth: it is first of all concerned to demonstrate that it was a primary concern in the foundation of the cosmos. The development of the theme of "cosmic ordering" in vv. 2b-3a, 5-9 is not, then, a mere recollection of Yahweh's originating acts, but is clearly focused on this central interest, the establishment of the superterrestrial (vv. 2b-3a) and terrestrial (vv. 5-9) oceans being related in turn. The latter section will be considered in more detail below. As regards the former, the idea that Yahweh's abode was above the celestial waters is encountered also in Pss. 29:10 (cf. also v. 3) and Am. 9:6, in both of which the link with rain or storm and thunder is evident.[108] The use of the word עֲלִיּוֹת in 104:3 is especially appropriate, because it denotes a room in an upper storey or on the flat roof of a house (cf. I Ki. 17:19, 2 Ki. 1:2, 4:10), and hence, as Kraus renders the phrase, a "lofty home".[109] However, the view that it reflects the idea of "successive heights or layers of heaven"[110] is probably to be rejected.[111]

Thirdly, a further outworking of the idea of water bestowal, namely the motif of the divine theophany, is in many ways closely related to these interests, and it is perhaps therefore not surprising that it finds expression in v. 3, in immediate succession to the description of the foundation of the divine chambers upon the waters. The idea of riding upon clouds is, of course, a particularly characteristic aspect of the storm deity.[112] Verse 7 is also to be understood within the context of the influence of storm-theophany language upon the psalm. The dominating concerns of Yahweh's self-manifestation in nature and provision of water have influenced the mode of expression here. The issue will be adverted to further below. Finally, stylised theophany language may be identified again in v. 32,[113] though here without such recognisable storm-characteristics, and the motif of smoking mountains may indicate the influence of Sinai traditions on the epiphany-portrayal.[114] The description is noteworthy for its exclusively terrestrial effects, since, as in Pss. 97:4-5, 99:1, 46:7 and Mic. 1:4, there is no portrayal of fleeing waters; the theophany is here

108 Cf. also Jer. 10:13 = 51:16.

109 ("Hochsitz"), II, p. 881.

110 Thus Briggs, II, p. 337; similarly Wellhausen, p. 203.

111 Nor is there any need to follow Dahood's translation, "who stored with water his upper chambers" (derived on analogy with Ugaritic *qryt* and Akkadian *qarîtu*, "granary"; III, p. 34), though it would adequately fit the context.

112 Cf. Deut. 33:26, 2 Sam. 22:11, Ps. 18:11, Isa. 19:1, Dan. 7:13; also Matt. 24:30; it is, further, a stock epithet of Baal in the Ugaritic tablets, e.g. *KTU* 1.2.iv.8, 29, 1.4.iii.11, 18, etc. Compare also Ps. 68:5, 34. For "wings of the wind", cf. Ps. 18:11b, 2 Sam. 22:11b, and compare the allusion to the "wing of the south wind" in the Akkadian myth of Adapa, B, l. 6 (*ANET*, p. 101).

113 Weiser's translation, "Blickt er grollend zur Erde, dann bebt sie;/ berührt er die Berge, so spielen sie Rauch" (p. 456), is highly interpretative, and is to be rejected.

114 Cf. Ex. 19:18. It is to be noted that this aspect of the divine epiphany features also in Ps. 144:5, but not in the almost certainly earlier parallel in Ps. 18:10 = 2 Sam. 22:10.

apparently regarded as an attribute of the deity *per se*, and is divorced from any purposeful impact in a context of historic intervention (as at the Exodus, cf. Ps. 77:15-21) or water-bestowal (cf. Ps. 68:8-11).[115] As Kraus perceives, "The incomparable power of Yahweh is only hinted at in v. 32... The conception of a forest fire or a volcanic eruption ... illustrates the infinite power of the Creator, who is above all worlds."[116] The "glory" (כָּבוֹד) of Yahweh alluded to in the previous verse (v. 31) is also often associated with his self-manifestation: compare Ps. 29:1, 2, 3, 9, 102:17, Ex. 16:7, 10, 24:16, 17, 33:18, 22, 40:34, 35, Ezek. 1:28, 3:23, 8:4, and the frequent instances of this usage in Ezekiel and the Pentateuch.

The presumption is sometimes made[117] that the storm theophany must be associated with the theme of *Chaoskampf*, both in Ugarit and in the Old Testament. However, it is not self-evident that Baal's action of "destroy[ing] Judge Nahar" (*KTU* 1.2.iv.27) with the clubs furnished for him by Kothar-wa-Khasis, and then "scattering"[118] his defeated foe, is to be associated with storm and thunder. Certainly, the characteristic elements of the storm theophany are not there explicitly alluded to.[119] Conversely, in *KTU* 1.4.v.6-9, when Baal "give[s] his voice in the clouds" and "flash[es] to the earth lightning", it is intimately associated with the provision of rain. The freedom of the thunder of Yahweh from *Chaoskampf* or any other combative overtones in many instances in the Old Testament should also by now be apparent. In addition to the passages so far considered, compare, for instance, Job 37:2-5 and following, where the intertwining of thunderstorm and water-bestowal, and the sense of wonder at the power and incomprehensibility of God, is tangible. In fact, the general content and wisdom-influenced tone of the passage have much in common with Ps. 104.[120]

Leviathan appears in v. 26 as one of God's creatures, dependent on him for sustenance (vv. 27-8) and even for life itself (vv. 29-30). The issue of the precise force of v. 26c has attracted some attention, since the phrase לְשַׂחֶק־בּוֹ could be rendered "to play in it", i.e., in the sea,[121] or "to sport with it", i.e. as

115 It communicates a sense of his overwhelming and terrible power, but need not be linked directly with "huge catastrophes" and Yahweh's destruction of all that opposes him, as Weiser supposes (p. 459, cf. Cohen, p. 342).

116 II, p. 886.

117 E.g., by John Day, *God's Conflict*, p. 30.

118 This verb has been variously interpreted, the different proposals being documented in Wyatt, *RTU*, pp. 68-9 n. 150. However, the dissociation from storm theophany language pertains whichever translation is adopted.

119 The closest approximation is in the use of the title *rkb 'rpt* in Athtart's injunction to Baal (ll. 28-29): "Scatter (him), o mightiest [Baal]! / Scatter (him), o rider on the clouds!" (*CML*, p. 44). However, as often, it stands in parallel to the name Baal and substitutes for it, rather than reflecting any immediate action.

120 Cf. especially Job 37:8 with Ps. 104:20, 22.

121 Thus RSV, JPSA, Cohen (p. 431), Kirkpatrick (p. 612), Seybold (p. 407), Allen (p. 25); for the idea of wild beasts playing, cf. Job 40:20.

a plaything, cf. Job 41:29.[122] Beyond certain resolution as the question may be, the verse in any case creates the impression that Leviathan is a playful creature in which God delights,[123] and whose existence man also is enjoined to celebrate. The idea of God sporting with Leviathan, if it is to be inferred here, would indicate God's freedom to play with massive beasts, just as men might with a bird or domestic pet (cf. Job 40:29); it would thus illustrate his great might and the scale of his operations, and evoke wonder at the divine providence and wisdom that he should find a place for creatures such as these. However, since the interest of the psalm would appear primarily to be on the astonishing diversity of nature and of God's care for his creatures, this would tend to support the alternative translation, according to which it is Leviathan who plays. In any case, Anderson's assertion that "the once mighty Leviathan appears as a grotesque figure—a plaything of Yahweh"[124] draws a wholly unwarranted inference from the verse, which is entirely out of keeping with the tone of the composition.

The view that Leviathan is to be recognised as some form of "chaos monster" (albeit perhaps in a considerably weakened form) is advocated also by Day.[125] According to him, "Leviathan in Ps. 104:26 may be understood as a remnant of the chaos powers whose conquest is described in highly mythological terms... in vv. 6-9." Yet, despite the fact that he asserts that "the mythological chaos monster has... undergone a process of depotentization", he also thinks that the author of Job "is directly dependent on Ps. 104:26"[126] for his rather more fearsome—one might say "repotentized"—portrayal of Leviathan. On the other hand, he considers that the writer of Gen. 1, in drawing on the same psalm, exhibited a greater "anti-mythological tendency" in substituting "great sea monsters (הַתַּנִּינִם הַגְּדֹלִים) for the more mythological term Leviathan of the parallel passage in Ps. 104:26". However, the notion that an originally "mythological" figure has been "depotentized", then variously "repotentized" or further "demythologized" by later, dependent authors, though the "mythological" understanding finally prevailed in later Jewish literature, does not sound entirely convincing. The argument that Leviathan was originally a "terrifying monster" who, following subjugation by Yahweh, became "humbled and under his control"[127] and hence (apparently) a relatively benign sea creature described in Ps. 104:26, is belied by the fact that it is said to

122 Thus, e.g., Wellhausen, p. 204, Weiser, p. 455, Day, *God's Conflict*, p. 72, Gunkel, *Schöpfung und Chaos*, p. 57, n. 4, *Die Psalmen*, pp. 446, 451, Dahood, III, pp. 32, 45, Kraus, II, p. 878, Schmidt, p. 188.

123 As recognised, e.g., by Weiser, pp. 458-9. Compare also Briggs' charming description (II, p. 336): "Leviathan..., too huge for man, is to God a dear little animal to sport with".

124 II, p. 724; see likewise Kraus, II, p. 885.

125 *God's Conflict*, p. 74.

126 *Ibid.*, p. 13.

127 Day, *God's Conflict*, p. 74.

have been created by God,[128] and by the reality that its existence and sustenance is here a subject of praise. The Tiamat analogy also collapses along with this model, since Leviathan is evidently a sea-creature, not the slain and cleft sea itself.

Others have sought to emend the reference to ships (אֳנִיּוֹת) in v. 26a to אֵימוֹת or אֵימוֹת, "terrors",[129] or to תַּנִּינִים, "sea monsters",[130] on the basis that the allusion is out of place in a celebration of the diversity of creatures made and sustained by God. However, the negative connotations of the proposed reading would likewise ill fit the context,[131] as well as lacking versional support; furthermore, the Hymn to the Aton, with which Ps. 104 has a number of similarities, makes reference to "the ships sailing north and south as well", again in a setting which is otherwise concerned only with the natural, rather than the technical, world.[132] The blurring of natural and mythological categories in Israelite speculative zoology has already been touched upon in relation to Ps. 74, and is still more evident in Job 40:15-41:26 (ET 40:15-41:34), which is discussed in Chapter 11 below.[133] Here in Ps. 104 Leviathan seems to equate with the great beasts which were known or presumed to inhabit the seas; we might think of the whale,[134] but it quite likely that their conceptions were no more refined than current day speculations regarding the "Loch Ness monster".

As regards the content of vv. 5-9, it appears that the situation envisaged is not entirely placid, since it is at Yahweh's rebuke that the waters flee; "rebuke"

---

128 Day, of course, has to acknowledge the formation of Leviathan by God (*God's Conflict*, p. 73). However, this is not integrated into his ensuing discussion of Leviathan as a depotentised monster, and it is questionable whether he has thought through its consequences fully. Even if Leviathan is a tamed plaything in Ps. 104:26, if it was in essence and personal origin (rather than merely in an early stage of the tradition) a "chaos" monster, there are two problems with the idea that it was created by God: first, there is the presumption reflected in, but not confined to, Gen. 1, that God created only that which was good; and, second, there is the evidence of history of traditions: it is certain that Baal did not create Yam or *Ltn*, nor Marduk, Tiamat, and indeed basic logic itself determines against a created pre-creation "chaos".

129 Gunkel, *Schöpfung und Chaos*, p. 57.

130 Oesterley, II, pp. 441, 442.

131 See Kraus' criticism of Gunkel that he "'mythologizes' and ... inserts into a picture full of friendliness and playful beauty the dark colours of that which is chaotic" (II, p. 885; cf. p. 879).

132 Dahood, further, compares *UT* 125:7-9 (*KTU* 1.16.i.8-9), where the collocation of "ship, bark" and "phoenix" is similarly seemingly mismatched (III, p. 45); however, contrast now Wyatt, *RTU*, p. 220, especially n. 200, and Greenstein, *UNP*, p. 31, p. 46 n. 109).

133 It is well exemplified by Seybold's description of Leviathan as "the mythical sea monster whom God had created", p. 410.

134 Thus Cohen, p. 341, Gunkel, *Schöpfung*, p. 58, Briggs, II, p. 336 (Briggs assumes identity also with the "great sea monsters" of Gen. 1:21, which he argues was the source for this verse).

(v. 7a) may here be understood as his "roar", the uttering forth of his terrible voice which parallels his thunder (v. 7b; cf. the expression "the thunder of his power" in Job 26:14, and see the discussion above at Ps. 18:16).[135] As Briggs explains, "The voice of God speaking in the thunder of the storm, as He rides in His chariot with His angelic winds and lightnings, frightens the Deep and fills it with terror—and the waters flee // haste away. This graphic poetic description takes the place of the calm command, Gn. 1[9]: 'God said, "Let the waters under the heaven be gathered together unto one place, and let the dry land appear"; and it was so.'"[136] However, the process envisaged in the poetic passage is no less accurate and subject to Yahweh's overall controlling design than that of Gen. 1, since God "with His thunder frightened the sea to the boundaries he had assigned it",[137] vv. 7-9. In fact, more fundamentally, "God's rebuke ... can be described as a 'word in action'";[138] it here signifies "the word of power uttered in primeval times".[139] It may thus perhaps be a particularly vigorous—and maybe rather primitive—outworking of the "word" theology, the focus being placed on the dynamic and efficacious aspects of the divine utterance. Compare, for a possible general parallel, the "Prayer for Uplifted Hands" for Nanna: "When your word roars by in the heavens like the wind, it brings abundant food and drink to the land; when your word goes out on the earth, it causes lush grass to grow...".[140] In the Prayer, further effects of the divine word, such as "mak[ing] sheepfolds and cattle pens fat" and "bring[ing] justice and righteousness" then follow. However, the ideas of the powerful word of God as a "roar" and the bounty of God in creation bear obvious similarities to Ps. 104:7, and make it clear that there is no necessary conflict here.[141]

135 Thus Dahood, III, p. 36, J. Day, *God's Conflict*, p. 29, n. 82; see the arguments, examples and bibliography cited there, and cf. the JPS translation "blast". Further literature on the issue includes F. Seely, "Note on G'RH with Especial Reference to Proverbs 13:8", *Bible Translator* 10 (1959), 20-21; P. van Zijl, "A Discussion of the Root gā'ar (rebuke)", *Biblical Essays: Proceedings of the 12th Meeting of "Die Ou-Testamentiese Werkgemeenskap in Suid-Afrika"* 1969, 56-63; and J. E. Hartley, "1721 גער", *NIDOTTE* I, 884-887.

136 II, p. 333; thus also Anderson, II, p. 720. See likewise Hartley's exposition of the verb גער in this context: "Often God delivers a loud blast by means of a storm, either a sharp clap of thunder (Ps 104:7), or strokes of lightning..., or a mighty gust of wind" ("1721 גער", *NIDOTTE* I, 884-887, p. 885). He continues: "At creation God drove the great, turbulent waters of the deep to their rightful place with a loud foreboding clap of thunder (Ps 104:6-7); the retreat of the waters enabled the dry land to appear (104:8-9)."

137 Briggs, II, p, 329; likewise p. 333.

138 Anderson, I, p. 108 (on Ps. 9:6).

139 Kraus, I, p. 290 (on Ps. 18:16).

140 Translation as in Kraus, I, p. 411, re Ps. 33:4-9; cf Pritchard, *ANET*, p. 386.

141 Indeed, the content of v. 7 "may be a more picturesque description of Gen. 1:9: 'And God said... And it was so!'" (Anderson, II, p. 720).

In contradiction to the *Chaoskampf* view of creation,[142] it is moreover notable that Yahweh himself is credited with covering the earth with the deep in an early stage of the process of creation;[143] further adjustments were then made in the relative heights of sea and land in order to form the ordered arrangement which is now familiar and established. The MT of v. 6a has caused some dispute, because the Hebrew כִּסִּיתוֹ presupposes a masculine suffix, whereas the antecedent אֶרֶץ is usually feminine. However, אֶרֶץ can sometimes be masculine;[144] possibly, then, the masculine suffix was intended to ensure that תְּהוֹם, which, like אֶרֶץ, is also feminine, was not mistaken as the object of the verb. Alternatively (and perhaps preferably, given the occurrence of אֶרֶץ as feminine in vv. 5, 24, 32), the masculine suffix may be explained as due to a textual corruption, and the feminine restored. However, reference back to the earth as the antecedent which is covered by the deep is strongly supported not only by the parallelism within the verse itself, but by the versions[145] and the Targum, suggesting the fundamental veracity of the Hebrew text. Some commentators have nevertheless sought to emend MT כִּסִּיתוֹ to כִּסַּתָּה in order to make תְּהוֹם the subject of v. 6a.[146] However, this reading is not offered by any of the versions, and it would seem primarily to be motivated by the prior assumption of the presence of the *Chaoskampf* motif in these verses, as indeed is explicitly acknowledged by Gunkel,[147] who states that the translation "you covered it" "is incorrect, since in what follows, the water is clearly represented as independent, and even as hostile to Yahweh".[148] In any case, the sense of the MT is retained by most modern versions, including RSV and JPSA, and the translation appears to be secure.

Throughout the process described in vv. 5-9, Yahweh remains wholly in command of the situation; the water and land are passive objects in his hands;

---

142 As advocated in relation to this passage by Weiser, p. 457, Day, *God's Conflict*, p. 30, Kraus, II, p. 882, Gerstenberger, II, pp. 222-3, and Clifford, II, pp. 148-9; cf. Oesterley, II, pp. 442-3, Seybold, p. 409, and Allen, p. 26. Terrien even speaks in terms of an allusion "to the Near Eastern myth of a cosmic fight of the God of light with the goddess of darkness" (p. 714).

143 In an interesting counterpart to this, the darkness (the other element present with תְּהוֹם in Gen. 1:2) is also said to be made by God, and to have a place in his natural order (v. 20).

144 See BDB, p. 75, *DCH*, I, p. 384, Gibson, *Davidson's Introductory Hebrew Grammar—Syntax*, p. 17, § 17b; and cf. LXX.

145 With the exception of the LXX, which reads περιβολαιον αὐτου, "his covering [i.e. Yahweh's]", which is clearly wrong.

146 E.g., Kraus, II, p. 879, Oesterley, II, p. 442, Weiser, p. 455, Day, *God's Conflict*, p. 29, Clifford, "A Note on Ps 104: 5-9" *JBL* 100 (1981) 87-9, p. 87.

147 *Die Psalmen*, p. 454.

148 To take תְּהוֹם as the object of the verb, with Girard (III, pp. 50, 53, yet cf. p. 55 n. 2), on the other hand, makes little sense and also suffers from the problem that תְּהוֹם is usually feminine.

and the image of the garment can scarcely be construed negatively.[149] In addition, even if "the waters are viewed as semi-personal... they are not divine, as Tiamat".[150] Most importantly, the image of the creator-god himself covering the earth with the deep is wholly in contravention to the Tiamat model of the deep as a pre-existent entity which was defeated and separated prior to the emergence of the earth;[151] moreover, there is no hint of a battle, since the waters simply flee at his coming.[152] As regards the content of the ambiguous v. 8, this may be interpreted in one of two ways: either the mountains and valleys are taken as the subject of the verbs יַעֲלוּ and יֵרְדוּ,[153] or as their objects ("they [the waters] went up to the mountains, they went down to the valleys").[154] The latter alternative would accord with the continued reference to the waters in v. 9, but reads rather oddly, as the waters would then be envisaged as flowing in the opposite direction from that which is customary.[155]

The slight awkwardness of the description in vv. 5-9—the idea that the waters were once above the mountains (v. 6b), the ambiguity of v. 8 as regards the subject of the verbs, and the surprising intrusion of language more familiar from the flood narratives in v. 9b (and indeed v. 6b)—may perhaps in part be

149 It may perhaps be reflective of the "birth" of the earth: cf. Job 38:9 (there in relation to the sea).

150 Anderson, II, p. 720.

151 Accordingly, it is necessary to quibble even with Anderson's fairly moderately stated précis of the supposed *Chaoskampf* content of vv. 5-9, according to which these verses "describe... the subjection of the Chaos waters which now serve Yahweh by serving his creatures who are sustained by him (verses 10-18)" (II, p. 718; cf. Weiser, p. 457).

152 As emphasised by Habel, *Yahweh versus Baal*, p. 66. One might compare, e.g., the trembling of the mountains at the divine rebuke in Job 26:11, where again the terrible power of God but no conflict is implied; and Ps. 114:3-4, where both the sea/the Jordan and the mountains/hills flee or skip before the theophany of God.

153 As by RSV, JPSA, Weiser (p. 455).

154 Thus Gunkel, *Psalmen*, p. 445, E. F. Sutcliffe ("A Note on Psalm CIV 8" *VT* 2 [1952], p. 179), Kraus (II, pp. 877, 879), NEB (poetically, "flowing over the hills, pouring down into the valleys; cf. Dion, "YHWH as Storm-god and Sun-god", p. 70); omitting the preposition 'to': Day (*God's Conflict*, pp. 29, 34-5), Girard (III, p. 50), Briggs (II, p. 333), Seybold (p. 406), Terrien (p. 707); cf. Spieckermann (*Heilsgegenwart*, p. 22), Podella ("Der 'Chaoskampfmythos'", p. 310). Scarcely probable is Dahood's rendering, "they went up to the mountains, they went down to the nether chasm" (III, p. 31), which is explained in terms of the waters being consigned to the "celestial mountains" and to the underworld, on analogy with Gen. 1:7, 7:11 (III, pp. 36-7). Verse 10 is then interpreted by Dahood as the release of the "destructive springs and torrents which Yahweh imprisoned in the subterranean chasm at the time of creation ... for the benefit of his creatures" (III, p. 37).

155 This is sometimes explained in terms of the waters "flowing up" to appear as mountain springs, and then as "running down" as streams (thus Sutcliffe, *VT* 2 [1952], p. 179, Anderson, II, p. 720, Kraus, II, p. 882). However, it could not then refer to the originating act of ordering the surface waters of the earth, as the context would seem to require, but only to its subsequent movements.

accounted for on the premise that the psalm is dependent on material known to us through the Hymn to the Aton,[156] and that the formulation of the Israelite creation tradition has here been influenced by the latter's striking mode of expression. According to the Egyptian hymn, the deity "makes a Nile in the underworld ... to maintain the people of Egypt", but for

> All the distant foreign countries, thou makest their life (also),
> For thou hast set a Nile in heaven,
> That it may descend for them and make waves upon the mountains,
> Like the great green sea,
> To water their fields in their towns.

The intention is evidently to describe the provision of rain, but the continued metaphor of "a Nile", and the description of the "waves upon the mountains" (cf. Ps. 104:6b) hardly provide a literal account of the gift of rainfall. In the Israelite poem, this image has instead been merged with a portrayal of an originating act of creation, through which the place of the waters on the earth was established. In addition, the description of vv. 6-9 may be understood as the result of a blending of Israelite rain-orientated concepts of water-provision as occurring through the direct action of the storm-god (discussed above, v. 7), and of the Egyptian premise of its source as a vast body of water on analogy with the Nile. This portrayal then leads into the celebration of the benefits stemming from this flowing water (vv. 10-12 and frequently), and it is this primary aspect of water provision which understandably informs the shape of the rest of the psalm; the watering of the mountains (in rain) is then mentioned in v. 13.[157]

V. 9b is reminiscent of the flood story, but here appears simply to indicate the situation prior to the separation of the waters (cf. Gen. 1:2). Despite the possible negative overtones here, there is no suggestion either that the waters are any more than semi-personified or that they offered any resistance. In each case, the covering (and uncovering) of the earth was in accord with God's purpose, and was not due to the aggressive instincts of the waters themselves. It is also noticeable that God is the agent determining every stage in the process—he covered, rebuked, appointed a place, set a bound, etc., so that the deep should be ordered and contained and "never again" cover the earth. At the same time, as Podella has highlighted, he is not actually the subject of the actions of vv. 7-8; hence, far from appearing as a warrior God engaged in battle, he remains more like a director controlling events from the background.[158] The motif of the containment of the sea is reflected elsewhere in Job 38:10-11, Prov.

156 Pritchard, *ANET*, pp. 369-371.

157 This is elsewhere the more fundamental and typical type of water-bestowal in the Old Testament, deriving from the very ancient divine theophany tradition: cf. Pss. 29, 68:8-11, 65:10-13.

158 "Der 'Chaoskampf' Mythos", p. 311.

8:29 and Jer. 5:22, and was obviously a cosmological necessity according to the ancient structural worldview.[159]

8. Summary

It may be concluded from the foregoing discussion that the "*Chaoskampf*" understanding of creation cannot be validated in respect to the psalms here considered. In fact, in many cases, an overtly positive and celebratory attitude to the establishment of the celestial and subterrestrial "reservoirs" of water, and to the ongoing provision of moisture to nourish the earth, may be detected. This is a particularly important result for the overall scope of the present monograph, since it suggests that—contrary to the currently dominant model of the origin and essential focus of the "*Chaoskampf*" theme in Israel—the Psalter nowhere celebrates the formation of the cosmos as resultant upon the defeat of powers of "chaos". This conclusion is further corroborated by the fact that none of the poetic passages considered in the present chapter is likely to antedate the late pre-exilic period, and some—perhaps all—of those specifically relating to the creation of water-reserves (as opposed simply to the foundation of the earth upon the seas) may be considerably later than this. It thus appears possible that interest as to how the cosmic oceans were established in their proper place may not fully have been awakened in Israel, or at least, have entered the hymnology of the Temple, until after the period of the exile.

159 Compare the Babylonian Creation Epic, IV, 139-40.

IX. The Crossing of ים־סוף: Psalms 78, 106 and 136

The psalms to be considered in the present chapter contain recollections of the Red Sea[1] event which may be regarded as 'historical' or 'credal' in intention: in each of them the two elements which came to define its essential and miraculous character, namely, the drying or division of the sea, and the crossing of the people of Israel, are explicitly stated. In this they are to be distinguished from the two psalms so far considered which also allude to the Red Sea miracle, Pss. 114 and 77,[2] since 114:3, 5 and 77:17-21 have the character of free and imaginative evocations, which are intended to convey the atmosphere and awesome aspects of the event, rather than concentrating on the historical details. Thus, there is a qualitative difference between the two groups of psalms. In Pss. 114 and 77, the miraculous is heightened through the medium of poetry and dramatic evocation. By contrast, in the compositions to be considered in the present chapter, as shall be seen, the opposite approach is adopted, one which stresses the 'historical facts' of the situation, and which, in time, or in differing contexts, increased the impact of the tale only by exaggerating the details of the story or portraying it in increasingly extravagant or striking language, without, however, ever abandoning the literalistic mould.[3]

Psalm 114 is archaic in style and possibly also in date, whilst Ps. 77, standing at the threshold of the exile, sought comfort from traditional modes of thought and from some of Israel's most deeply rooted religious ideas. Though Ps. 78 may be late pre-exilic and therefore possibly earlier than or approximately contemporary with Ps. 77, its didactic form is progressive, seeking to shock, challenge and re-express the sacred history in the service of a

---

1 Commonly translated "Reed Sea"; see J. Bright, *A History of Israel* (London: SCM, 3rd ed. 1981), p. 122; however, this has been disputed by N. H. Snaith, "יַם־סוּף: The Sea of Reeds: The Red Sea" *VT* 15 (1965) 395-8 and B. F. Batto, "The Reed Sea: Requiescat in Pace" *JBL* 102 (1983) 27-35, both of whom advocate the meaning "sea of the end". In the absence of certainty on this issue, the traditional designation "Red Sea" will here be retained.

2 Although Psalms 74 and 89 may also be associated with this event, they are primarily concerned with the defeat of the Egyptian foe (74:13-14, 89:11); thus, where the division of the sea is mentioned in Ps. 74:13a, it is perhaps to be connected with this aspect, rather than with the crossing (cf. Ex. 15:8-10).

3 There is a further example of an Exodus portrayal in Ps. 66; however, since it refers only to the "drying" of the sea, an allusion to the *Chaoskampf* is very rarely proposed (an exception is Curtis, who discerns here a reference to "Yahweh ha[ving] the waters in subjection", "The 'Subjugation of the Waters' Motif in the Psalms: Imagery or Polemic?" *JSS* 23 [1978], p. 255); hence the psalm will not be discussed in the present context.

wholly different intention. It successors, the historical psalms 106 and 136, are almost certainly post-exilic, and from this late vantage-point offer a mature expression of the miracle through which the special relationship between God and his people was inaugurated. From the perspective of the history of traditions, further insights may be offered: all of the three psalms to be considered in the present chapter display an awareness of the Exodus tradition preserved in the 'P' source of the Pentateuch, as it alone of the sources commonly identified in Ex. 14 seems unequivocally to know of the dividing and crossing of the sea, as opposed simply to the inundation of the Egyptian forces, which facilitated the Israelites' nocturnal escape. By the time of the composition of Pss. 106 and 136, the Exodus narrative may have achieved a more-or-less fixed form, and they may represent some of the latest biblical attempts to inject new life and vigour into the most familiar story of Israel's national religious epic.

Despite the 'prosaic' and intentionally literalist nature of these historical recollections, many scholars have sought to discern here an 'historicised' version of the chaos myth, in which, at the 'creation' of the nation Israel, God rent open the sea, just as Marduk cleft Tiamat's body in twain in the Babylonian epic *Enuma elish*. Obviously, there are immediate difficulties with this presumption: the historical contours identifiable from the prose narratives are not disrupted, and yet here the portrayals are supposed to adopt a significance which is less readily to be claimed for the parallel (and, at least in the case of some of these psalms, quite possibly the source) accounts in Exodus. Moreover, there is little to support the view that the Exodus was understood as a generative event: it was the crucial moment in the formation of Israel as a people, and the foundational event for her relationship with God, but there is no evidence that it was regarded as a "creation" *per se*. In addition, the foe defeated at the Red Sea is the Egyptian host, not the sea itself; the latter is evidently an instrument in the hand of God and employed in the service of his good purpose, and it could hardly be claimed that it was hostile or resistant, let alone the sole or chief combatant of God. Finally, of course, once parted, the sea was permitted to reform naturally and to return to its wonted flow: its cleft elements were not employed as the basis of a new creation, and it is never stressed that it was separated into two pieces or to be regarded—however transiently—as two independent parts. Interestingly, although the *Chaoskampf* interpretation of the Exodus pattern is relatively commonplace in the broader field of Old Testament scholarship, being promulgated, for example, by von Rad in his *Theologie des Alten Testaments*,[4] it is not much emphasised in specialist studies of the psalms here to be considered.[5] Nevertheless, the issue may only be resolved by a painstaking examination of the evidence in relation to each of these compositions.

---

4 I, pp. 179-180.

5 Mowinckel, for example, makes no mention of the theme in relation to these psalms in his *The Psalms in Israel's Worship*, and many of the commentators are similarly muted on this matter.

1. The Date of Psalms 78, 106 and 136

As is the case with the psalms discussed in Chapters 4 and 8, the compositions to be analysed in the present context have been selected according to their thematic coherence, rather than to considerations of date. Whereas the presence of the theme of creation in predominantly late contexts was found to be highly significant from the point of view of the putative origins of the *Chaoskampf* motif, the same import does not apply to allusions to the exodus, which one would expect to have occurred across a broad chronological span.

Nevertheless, it may be observed that Pss. 106 and 136, which employ highly exaggerated language in relation to the Red sea event, are likely to have emanated from the post-exilic period, and thus to represent a late flowering from an already well-established stem. The provenance of Ps. 136 has already been considered in the previous chapter. With regard to Ps. 106, it appears that the exile is presupposed in vv. 27 and 46.[6] It is possible (if uncertain) that v. 46 may perhaps allude to Cyrus' edict,[7] and that v. 47 may then follow on from this in the wish for a comprehensive ingathering surpassing the earlier small-scale returns which had hitherto taken place (cf. Deut. 30:3, 1 Ki. 8:50).[8] The

---

6 This is widely accepted, although it is questioned by Weiser (pp. 467, 468), who contends that it "can just as well be understood to refer to a calamity that has come upon the people, for instance after the destruction of the Northern kingdom" (p. 468); nevertheless, even he accepts that it refers to the hope that "God ... will bring together the members of the Covenant scattered amongst the nations" (*ibid.*), so his position seems unnecessarily contentious. Furthermore, there are various linguistic usages in the passage which are only or primarily associated with the experience of Babylonian exile: see Haglund, *Historical Motifs*, pp. 63, 69.

7 The perception of some of the older scholars that it refers to "the kind treatment which the Jews abroad experienced from Alexander's successors" (Wellhausen, p. 205), on the other hand, seems implausible.

8 "It is the part of the people which has already returned which prays that the rest of the people may also be gathered in the land", Haglund, *Historical Motifs in the Psalms* (CBOT 23; Lund: C.W.K. Gleerup, 1984), p. 63. Haglund substantiates this position on the basis that Hiph. ישע and Pi. קבץ are employed by the prophets of the exile in promises of deliverance (citing Isa, 43:5, 54:7, Jer. 23:3, 29:14, 31:8, 10, 32:37, Ezek. 11:7, 20:34, 41, 28:25, 34:13, 36:24, 39:27). The more specific differentiation between an exilic and post-exilic provenance is then provided by further linguistic considerations (p. 63), and especially by the attestation of the idea of having sinned like the fathers, which is confined to late contexts. He concludes that the composition is to be located in a time "before the Persian regime is stable in the country and parts of the people remain in the dispersion" (p. 63). Hence it is sometimes assigned to the "latter part of the exile" (thus Terrien, p. 733; similarly Seybold, p. 421, Allen, p. 52, Mitchell, *Message*, p. 295), though most locate its composition in the post-exilic period (e.g., Kraus, II, p. 901, Cohen, p. 351, Gerstenberger, II, p. 244, and Anderson, II, p. 736); in fact, however, the distinction may often largely be one of definition, since it seem to inhabit

replication of this verse in 1 Chr. 16:35 could indicate that it was a cliché of the second temple period, though this cannot confirm that the expression (or the psalm in which it is presently located) emanated from this time.[9] One may also imagine that the regret at the failure to destroy the nations on entry to the land (vv. 34-39) may have been influenced by a retrospective attribution of their present predicament to this earlier default on their part; moreover, the racial exclusivism of the post-exile (cf. v. 5, especially the designation of Israel as the בָּחִיר of God[10]) could perhaps almost as readily be inferred as the exile itself.[11] Verse 41, though ostensibly alluding to the period of the Judges as portrayed from a Deuteronomistic perspective (cf. Judg. 2:14, 13:1), similarly seems to presuppose at least the great power struggles of the late pre-exilic period, but would probably best reflect the experience of the returnees, or of those left in the land at the time of the exile.

The author of the psalm may have been familiar with the completed form of the Pentateuch,[12] although there are minor sequential variations;[13] he seems perhaps also to have been able to presuppose a familiarity on the part of his "audience" with the events to which he makes reference. Kraus here identifies a "Deuteronomistic structure"[14] and theology of history.[15] In addition, priestly influence is discernible in the description of Aaron as "the holy one of Yahweh" (v. 16), the rôle performed by Moses in v. 23 in averting the divine wrath, the prominence ascribed to Phinehas (v. 30), the apparent partial exoneration of Moses in vv. 32-3, and the non-mention of Korah's mutiny in

---

the borderland of the partial return. Anderson locates its composition between the completion of the Pentateuch and of the Books of Chronicles, and this seems plausible.

9 Compare Koenen's view that v. 48 (which is echoed in 1 Chr. 16:36) was added to the Psalm at a post-compositional stage (*Jahwe wird kommen*, p. 95).

10 A late expression—see Haglund, *Historical Motifs*, p. 63, Gerstenberger, II, p. 238.

11 Gerstenberger has, further, shown how the themes of the extermination of the inhabitants of the land, or the failure to carry this out, and of the sacrifice of sons and daughters according to the ways of the Canaanites, "seem to presuppose both D[eu]t[e]r[onomistic] and priestly writings" (II, p. 242): see further the references cited there.

12 Thus Kraus, who speaks of a literary dependence (II, p. 900; similarly Scharbert, "Das 'Schilfmeerwunder' in den Texten des Alten Testaments", *Mélanges bibliques et orientaux en l'honneur de M. Henri Cazelles*, p. 414), whilst Allen specifically argues that vv. 16-18 reflect a supplemented (and therefore later) version of Num. 16 (p. 51); cf. Norin, who assumes a familiarity with a form not very different from that of today, but recalled from memory (*Er spaltete das Meer*, p. 122). Contrast Weiser, p. 468.

13 Detailed by Haglund, *Historical Motifs*, p. 69.

14 II, p. 901; see similarly Allen, p. 51.

15 II, pp. 899-900. Specific deuteronomistic characteristics (for example, the use of the designation "Horeb" in preference to the more usual "Sinai" in v. 19) are outlined in more detail by Haglund, *Historical Motifs*, pp. 64-68. He concludes that deuteronomistic influence is most evident in the historiography of the psalm, as well as in the apostasy-punishment-penance-deliverance pattern familiar especially from the Book of Judges (p. 70).

vv. 16-18, in contrast to the record of Num. 16. There is also a persistent concern with cultic purity (e.g., in vv. 19ff., 28ff., 34ff.), whilst accumulations of expressions of sin (also a characteristically late feature) may be noted especially in v. 6.[16] Examples of vocabulary normally found in late contexts are Hiph. רשׁע with the meaning "act wickedly" (v. 6),[17] and the call to praise הַלְלוּ־יָהּ, which frames the poem (vv. 1, 48), the opening invocation (v. 1) being especially close to that of Pss. 107:1, 118:1, 136:1.[18]

The dating of Ps. 78 is more complex,[19] but it is worth pursuing because of the starkness of its language in comparison with Pss. 136 and 106 and, indeed, as contrasted also with the theophany portrayals of Pss. 77 and 114.[20] The psalm is silent on the matter of the Exile, which one might have expected to have been mentioned as the supreme example of the fruits of disobedience had it occurred prior to the time of composition; moreover, it seems to presuppose the continued existence of the Davidic monarchy (vv. 70-71)[21] and of the Solomonic Temple (v. 69).[22]

Verses 59-69 seem to reflect the Judahite view (encountered also, e.g., in Jer. 7:12, 14) that the fall of Shiloh and establishment of the Jerusalem sanctuary constituted the rejection of "Ephraim" by God and the choice of Jerusalem in its stead. Alongside this attitude of religious supremacy articulated especially in vv. 60, 67a, 68b, the same passage (vv. 67-9) also seems to reflect a sense of political hostility to Ephraim (v. 67b, presumably referring to Northern Israel) in favour of the rival leadership of Judah in the south (v. 68a). This would seem to indicate that the division between North and South had

---

16 See further Gerstenberger, II, p. 239.

17 It is otherwise confined to Job 34:12, Neh. 9:33, Dan. 9:5, 11:32, 12:10, and 2 Chr. 20:35, 22:3.

18 Further examples are listed in Haglund, *Historical Motifs*, p. 63.

19 It has been dated variously from the tenth century to the post-exilic period, with a more complex redactional history being proposed, for example, by Seybold (pp. 307-8): see further the summary of scholarship in Tate, pp. 284-6.

20 There is a sixth reference to the Red sea deliverance in Ps. 66, but this psalm is particularly unsympathetic to dating, not least because of its likely composite origin; hence, although it may be post-exilic (see Anderson, I, p. 473, Gunkel, pp. 277, 278, Oesterley, II, p. 314, Buttenwieser, pp. 354-7), the section pertaining to the exodus could be much earlier in origin (a pre-exilic date for the composition being contemplated by Cohen, p. 204, Scharbert, "Das 'Schilfmeerwunder'", p. 405, Norin, *Er spaltete das Meer*, pp. 123-4, and Kraus, II, p. 617).

21 This seems to be the most natural interpretation of the verse, and it is followed by most scholars, who see this assured celebration of the fact (not merely promise) of David's election as untarnished by the crisis of c. 587 B.C.; contrast, however, Hossfeld, who considers it to be comparable with certain passages in Ezekiel and hence to reflect the hope of restoration (HZ, II, pp. 429-30).

22 Compare the certainty of Weiser and Cohen on this issue: for the former, the lack of reference to the destruction of the temple constitutes "proof of the pre-exilic date of the psalm" (pp. 367-8), whilst for the latter, the reference to the Temple as still in existence in v. 69 is equally decisive (p. 249).

already taken place,[23] and some would contend, further, that "the general outlook suggests that the Northern kingdom was no longer in existence".[24] One might particularly imagine that the understanding and narration of past events has been informed by contemporary concerns, and that such recollected experiences, like the pattern of sin, punishment, repentance and renewal, were regarded as parabolic for the present (cf. vv. 1-2). Thus, it is possible that vv. 56-72, though ostensibly concerned with the fall of Shiloh and the election of Zion, primarily relate to the theology and practical implications of the fall of the northern kingdom, as understood from a Judaean perspective.[25] At the same time, the emphasis on the judgment on Ephraim, as opposed to the election of Judah (vv. 67ff., cf. v. 9), would provide a further indication that the composition antedated the exile. Therefore, a date in the late eighth century or shortly afterwards would appear most likely on the basis of historical considerations, and in fact this is broadly endorsed by the tradition-historical and linguistic data.

The psalm seems to draw on independent traditions regarding the early period (e.g., in vv. 9, 63-4), which, again, are perhaps more likely to have existed closer to the events themselves than to have appeared as a late innovation.[26] In

---

23 Compare Tate's remark that "the separation of North and South in Yahweh's eyes (and, therefore, in the eyes of his people) is certainly indicated" (p. 286), yet contrast Eissfeldt (*Das Lied Moses Deuteronomium 32, 1-43, und das Lehrgedicht Asaphs, Psalm 78, samt einer Analyse der Umgebung des Mose-Liedes* [Berichte über die Verhandlungen der Sächsischen Akademie der Wissenschaften zu Leipzig. Philologisch-Historische Klasse. Bd. 104, Heft 5; Berlin: Akademie Verlag, 1958], p. 36), and Freedman (*PPP*, p. 118).

24 Anderson, II, p. 562; see likewise Cohen, p. 249. Haglund interprets vv. 9-11 as anticipating and thus addressing the fall of the Northern Kingdom and vv. 67 ff. as confirming this interest (*Historical Motifs*, pp. 89, 98), and Hossfeld discerns a similar preoccupation in vv. 62-4 (HZ, II, p. 428). Contrast, however, on one hand, Day's apprehension that the psalm "knows nothing of the fall of the Northern Kingdom" (in Mayes, ed., *Text in Context*, p. 437) and, on the other, Spieckermann's claim that vv. 61ff. reflect the liquidation of both the Northern and Southern Kingdoms and the exile of their people (*Heilsgegenwart*, pp. 146-7; cf. Gerstenberger, II, p. 97, who wonders if "Shiloh" in v. 60 could be a pseudonym for Jerusalem).

25 This possibility seems to be discounted by Weiser (p. 368), who interprets the theological lessons of the psalm in an abstract and universally applicable sense, rather than concerning himself with the concrete realities which it may have sought to address. See, however, Haglund, for whom the whole presentation of history from Egypt to the kingdom "as a series of events where people have been disbelieving and apostate and God punishing and gracious ... is told as an explanation of the fall of the Northern Kingdom" (*Historical Motifs*, p. 99). Thus, the traditions "are used to prove and defend the advantages of Jerusalem and Judah over the fallen Northern kingdom and to propagate faith in God in order not to be stricken by a disaster similar to that of the people of Samaria" (*Ibid*., p. 101).

26 This is substantiated in detail by Goulder (*PAP*, pp. 114-7), who, further, makes a plausible case that Num. 11 represents a development and interpretation of Ps. 78:17-20 (*ibid*., pp. 116-7) and that Ps. 105:27 is derivative upon Ps. 78:43 (*ibid*., p. 121).

addition, a certain freedom of presentation and organisation may be detected, e.g., in the double allusion to the plague / exodus events (vv. 12ff., 43ff.), or in the reference to a defection by the Ephraimites (v. 9) made prior to the Exodus recollection.[27] All this would probably support an early setting. Fairly primitive Zion traditions also appear to be present, as in vv. 68-9 (note also the repeated use of the divine name עֶלְיוֹן, the combination אֵל עֶלְיוֹן being peculiar to v. 35 and Gen. 14:18 ff.; cf. אֱלֹהִים עֶלְיוֹן, v. 56), but particularly striking is the image of God awaking as from sleep "like a strong man shouting[28] because of wine" and routing his enemies on the battlefield (vv. 65-6). The association of the "power" and "glory" of God with the Ark (v. 61) may be compared with Ps. 132:8 and Sam. 4:21 respectively, as well as with the theophany imagery of Ps. 29, and this may also be a relatively primitive feature.

Despite these early indications, comparisons are also made with the interpretation of history encountered in the prophets,[29] or in Deuteronomy,[30] and with its attitude to Zion and high places.[31] Kraus relates the psalm to the Levitical sermons in the Chronicler's history, particularly emphasising the presence of claims to the election of Zion and David over against northern

---

Goulder draws the same conclusion from a comparison of the plague accounts (*ibid.*, pp. 121-3; see likewise Haglund, *Historical Motifs*, p. 95), but here the results seem to be less clear.

27 See the further examples cited by Goulder, *PAP*, pp. 114-5; variations from the "canonical" order are also brought clearly by Gerstenberger, II, pp. 95-6, who concludes that "when our psalm came into being… there had not yet been formed a fixed interpretation of Yahweh's history with Israel" (p. 98).

28 Taking מִתְרוֹנֵן as the Hithpo'el of רנן: "the Psalmist daringly compares Yahweh with a mighty warrior who is stirred to great deeds by strong wine", hence the rendering "stimulated by wine" (Anderson, II, p. 576); the same reading is also assumed by Haglund (*Historical Motifs*, pp. 97-8). However, many prefer a derivation from the root רון, "overcome" (e.g., Cohen, p. 258, Wellhausen, p. 83); cf. Dahood, "resting after" (II, p. 196). Kraus' translation "vom Rausch sich erhebt" (II, p. 701) depends on an emendation to מִתְרוֹמֵם.

29 Weiser compares Am. 1:9ff. (*sic*; cf. 2:9ff.), 4:6ff., Hos. 11:1f., Jer. 2:1ff. (p. 367), whilst Goulder thinks of the breadth of the historical references in Hosea and Amos, and the potential for variation from the Pentateuch in one case in Hosea (cf. also Am. 4:25), as a point of significant comparison (*PAP*, p. 24) and hence as suggesting a common era (and place) of origin. However, why he latches onto Hosea as providing an indication of Northern origin, rather than taking into greater account the southern milieu of Amos' ministry, remains unexplained but for its place within his overall thesis of the Northern provenance of the Asaph psalms. The negative interpretation of the Exodus and wilderness traditions in Am. 2:9-10 provides a particularly close parallel to the timbre of Ps. 78, with a flexible use of sequencing also being displayed.

30 E.g., by Junker, "Die Entstehungszeit des Ps 78 und des Deuteronomiums", *Biblica* 34 (1953) 487-500, Kraus, II, p. 704, and Norin, *Er spaltete das Meer*, pp. 132-3.

31 Cf. especially v. 58 with Deut. 32:16, 21, Judg, 2:12, 1 Ki. 11:7, 12:31, 15:14; and vv. 67-70 with 1 Ki. 8:16.

Israel, and locating it in the post-exilic period.[32] However, the deuteronomistic tendencies which he detects appear to be confined to the understanding of history, something which does not really present sufficient grounds for claims of dependence;[33] moreover, a deuteronomic understanding of history need be no later than Josiah[34] and may have derived from, or been influenced by, the cult, rather than *vice versa*.[35]

As regards the language employed to describe the exodus, there are resonances with a variety of traditions. Nevertheless, the use of בקע to describe the dividing of the waters, and the application of the verb עבר to the Red Sea event, rather than merely to the Jordan crossing, seems to reflect a mature stage in the evolution of the tradition, and to indicate at minimum a fairly late pre-exilic origin for the composition.[36] When this is balanced with the sometimes apparently quite primitive features of the psalm, a dating at a relatively advanced point in the pre-exilic era would seem to offer the only way of accommodating both of these aspects. This would also seem to corroborate the post-722 date arrived at on the basis of historical and ideological considerations. Both Haglund[37] and Junker[38] think of the reign of Hezekiah; interestingly, Cohen arrives at the same conclusion on the basis of entirely different considerations, maintaining that "the moral which the psalmist sought to impress upon his contemporaries would naturally apply to a period of religious decline, such as set in after the reign of Hezekiah".[39]

This convergence of evidence continues in the linguistic sphere, since Psalm 78 contains a few features which may be regarded as "archaic", but not in any great density, and it may therefore represent a transitional phase in the

32 II, pp. 703-4. However, as Goulder pertinently observes, a closer parallel to this Psalm than the Levitical sermons cited by Kraus is furnished by Deut. 32, which appears to be early (*PAP*, p. 108).

33 Hence compare Haglund's interpretation of the same data: although he concludes that "the traditions behind T [the Tetrateuch], Deut. and part of the D-work have obviously been known to the author" (*Historical Motifs*, p. 99), this is modulated by an appreciation that "the parallels to younger material... may be due to an adherence to a common stream of tradition which has continued" (p. 101). Goulder, further, emphasises that the deuteronomic understanding of history is crucially influenced by the disasters of c. 597 and 587 B.C., whereas in Ps. 78, although "things are bad... and [the psalmist] naturally attributes this to God's wrath, and so to national disobedience,... the message is one of hope" (*PAP*, p. 32).

34 The date advocated by Norin, *Er spaltete das Meer*, pp. 131-3.

35 See Weiser, p. 367. The further affinities with the concerns of the pre-exilic prophets would corroborate this view. For the possibility that deuteronomistic traditions may antedate Josiah, see Robertson, *Linguistic Evidence*, p. 152.

36 It cannot reasonably be claimed, however, with Scharbert, that the verb בקע actually derives from P, and that the author therefore knew the full form of the Pentateuch ("Das 'Schilfmeerwunder'", p. 414).

37 *Historical Motifs*, p. 101.

38 "Die Entstehungszeit des Ps 78", p. 493.

39 P. 249.

development of the conventions governing Hebrew poetry. In this case, Robertson’s judgment that Ps. 78 “may come from a period in which standard forms have only recently replaced the early ones”[40] and thus is to be dated “shortly before or sometime after the eighth century”[41] is to be observed. Hence a date in the late eighth century or shortly thereafter may be advanced as the most likely milieu in which the composition emerged.

It would appear, therefore, that the Psalter attests to exodus traditions as manifested over a wide chronological range, with considerable variation in the content and manner of presentation; such psalms would also seem to engage with other strata of material now preserved in the Pentateuch. However, the evidence suggests that Ps. 78 constitutes the earliest extant reference to the division of the sea within the Psalter, probably in the late pre-exilic period, and this would be consistent with the evidence preserved elsewhere in the biblical tradition. Thus, it appears that the motif of division is not among the earliest or most fundamental exodus traditions, but constitutes a development of it. However, it remains to be considered whether the *Chaoskampf* theme may be discerned in this imagery, and this shall now comprise the subject of the following discussion.

2. The Theme of “Chaos” in Psalms 78, 106 and 136

i. The Theme of “Chaos” in Psalm 78

The first mention of the Red Sea event, in v. 13, is expressed in highly conventional language, which immediately resonates with allusions elsewhere. Yahweh “divided” or “cleft open” the sea (בקע), the same verb being employed of the crossing in Ex. 14:16 (P), Neh. 9:11, Isa. 63:12, as well as in the Niph. in Ex. 14:21. In the present instance, the choice of vocabulary may, further, have been influenced by the cleaving of the rocks in v. 15 (Pi. בקע, cf. in the Qal Judg. 15:19, Isa. 48:21, Ps. 74:15). However, it is notable that the more forceful form of the verb, the Pi‘el, which, as BDB states in relation to this verb, is “oft. more complete or more violent than Qal”,[42] is applied to the activity of water-provision, not to Yahweh’s treatment of the sea. This is readily understandable, since not only does it suggest an intensification and sense of cumulation as, in the citing of Yahweh’s salvific activities, the same verbal root is repeated for the second time: it is also appropriate to the greater effort involved in splitting solid rock, as contrasted with parting the (possibly less resistant) liquid sea. In any case, the repeated use of the verb “underscores the wondrous rule of Yahweh”.[43] Both the modulation in usage between vv. 13 and 15 and the frequent repetition of the verb elsewhere in relation to the Exodus,

40 *Linguistic Evidence*, p. 150.

41 *Linguistic Evidence*, p. 54; cf. p. 150.

42 P. 132.

43 Kraus, II, p. 708.

including in "literalistic" prose contexts, militate against discerning any hint of "chaos" here.[44]

The crossing of the sea is then described by means of the verb עבר, which is also employed in the recollection of this event in Neh. 9:11, Isa. 51:10 and Num. 33:8; cf. also Zech. 10:11. However, it is more commonly used to the describe the fording of a river,[45] most often the Jordan,[46] and it is the key word used to denote the crossing which marked the people's entry into the land under Joshua.[47] Thus the simplicity of the action of "passing over" highlights the magnitude of Yahweh's deed, and binds the two crossings conceptually together, but it not a special term reserved for the Red Sea event.

Finally, יַצֶּב־מַיִם כְּמוֹ־נֵד provides a clear echo of Ex. 15:8b, נִצְּבוּ כְמוֹ־נֵד נֹזְלִים, here transformed into the Hiph.; it is especially interesting to note the probably oral-formulaic repetition of the poetic form כְּמוֹ. The reference to מַיִם in place of נֹזְלִים is not greatly significant: the former is anyway utilised in Ex. 15:8a, and it may have been introduced in Ps. 78:13 in reminiscence of this, or in the interest of clarification. However, the effect is a "prosaification" of the previously dynamic poetic cadences of Ex. 15, and once again renders any suggestion of mythologising highly improbable.

In the iteration of the Exodus theme in vv. 52-3, it is simply stated that Yahweh "led forth his people" from Egypt, with great emphasis being placed on his protection of them: he guided them like a flock (cf. Pss. 74:1, 77:21 and the discussion thereon) and led them to safety so they were not afraid. Then, standing in contrast to this, is the statement that the sea "overwhelmed", or more accurately, "covered" (Pi. כסה) their enemies.[48] This is perhaps one of the oldest Red Sea traditions, and may be compared with Ex. 14:28 (P), 15:5, 10, Josh. 24:7 (E), Ps. 106:11.

Alongside the first Exodus recollection and, as has been seen, echoing and intensifying its use of the verb בקע, is the memory of Yahweh's provision of water in the wilderness (vv. 15-16, cf. Ex. 17:6, Num. 20:8ff.). Here, the celebration of plenteous water is epitomised by the use of the noun תְּהֹמוֹת,

---

44 It moreover renders particularly unlikely Girard's assertion that the Reed Sea is a negative symbol "of imprisoned and imprisoning water, connoting evil, oppression, death" (II, p. 359). Similarly-worded assertions are a frequent refrain in his commentary, but they appear more as a "fixed idea" than as a reflection on a particular context: the same claim is repeated already by Girard in respect of v. 53 on p. 359 n. 8. Norin's apprehension that the absence of the definite article before יָם reflects the use of the noun as a title of the water deity (*Er spaltete das Meer*, p. 129), on the other hand, ignores the conventions of Hebrew poetry, according to which הַ is customarily omitted.

45 E.g., in Gen. 31:21, 32:23, Deut. 2:13, Judg. 8:4.

46 E.g., 1 Sam. 13:7, 25, 17:24, 19:19, 1 Chr. 12:15.

47 E.g., Num. 32:21, 29, 33:51, 35:10, Deut. 2:29, 3:27 and often, Josh. 1:2, 11, 3:1, 14, 17 and often; cf. 2 Ki. 2:8, 9, 14.

48 Some assume a double accusative or insert a preposition before הַיָּם to make God the subject: "He guided them safely,... but their foes he overwhelmed with the sea" (Wellhausen, p. 80).

which is synonymous with an abundance of fresh water.[49] The conjunction with רַבָּה is reminiscent of the expression מַיִם רַבִּים, which, as has been shown from the discussion in relation to Ps. 29:3, is fundamentally to be associated with the idea of a great volume of water.[50] The theme is adverted to again in v. 20, and even the provision of manna (vv. 23-5) and of meat (vv. 27-9)—here, contrary to the Pentateuchal tradition, subordinated to the provision of water—is described under the image of rain (vv. 24, 27),[51] for this is the essential manifestation of the divine beneficence.

ii. The Theme of "Chaos" in Psalm 106

The Red Sea event is recounted in vv. 7-12, and may possibly be further alluded to in vv. 21-22. Unusually, however, it is introduced by the statement that the people "rebelled against the Most High at the Red Sea"[52] even before the crossing (v. 7).[53] Accordingly, the divine motivation for the ensuing deliverance is said to be "for his name's sake, / that he might make known his mighty power" (v. 8),[54] and it is therefore the "wondrous" and "terrible" aspects of his works which are awarded prominence. The absolute and comprehensive nature of the event as a manifestation of Yahweh's power is highlighted in three important respects. Firstly, instead of merely "drying up" the sea, "he rebuked (יִגְעַר)[55] the Red Sea, and it became dry" (v. 9); thus, his personal dynamic intervention and efficacious word of power is evoked. The point is further emphasised in the second colon of the verse: Yahweh himself led the people

---

49 This is acknowledged by many commentators, but there is no need to stress, with Anderson, that the "primeval waters" are "now put to good use", or indeed to refer to discussions equating it with Tiamat (Anderson, II, p. 566; cf. I, p. 517, II, p. 720). The explanation that "its abundance is compared to the תהומות, the precreation, primeval waters that filled the universe" (Kraus, II, p. 708) quite mistakenly assigns a temporally restricted definition to the word. However, this is unwarranted by the Hebrew usage, which makes it quite evident that the תְּהוֹם persists and nourishes the earth from beneath up to the present day; see further the discussion of this term in relation of Pss. 42:8 and 77:17 above in Chapters 4 and 6 respectively.

50 Cf. Wellhausen's translation, "He gave them drink from out of the great deep" (p. 80).

51 The motif of manna "raining down" is encountered in Ex. 16:4; however, it is absent from the record of Ex. 16:13-14 and Num. 11:31-4, despite the fact that the psalm's description of the provision of quails and ensuing judgment is otherwise strikingly close to that of the latter presentation.

52 Emending the tautologous עַל־יָם of MT to עֶלְיוֹן, with most commentators. Contrast JPSA "But they were rebellious at the Sea, even at the Red Sea".

53 Reflecting the tradition preserved also in Ex. 14:11-12.

54 Cf., e.g., Ezek. 20:9.

55 Cf. the JPS translation, "he sent his blast against", and see the discussion of this root in respect of Pss. 18:16, 104:7 above (in Chapters 4 and 8 respectively); it recurs also in Job 26:11, to be considered in Chapter 11 below.

through and, further, instead of turning the "sea" into "dry land",[56] the "deeps" (תְּהֹמוֹת, the vast subterranean reserve of water feeding the earth's water supplies)[57] became כַּמִּדְבָּר. The thought here is probably the ease of passage, as if walking through "pasture-land" (the translation adopted by RV mg., Wellhausen,[58] Weiser,[59] Cohen[60]); thus, the exposed sea-bed is not merely envisaged as having become like "dry ground": rather, the land beneath the people's feet has become indistinguishable from the open country to which livestock were taken for pasture. There may also be a link with the frequent Exodus image of Yahweh guiding his people like a flock: "God conducted them across the bed of the sea like a shepherd who leads his flock across the fields where they graze".[61] Finally, when "the waters covered their adversaries",[62] the destruction was complete, for "not one of them was left" (v. 11). Not surprisingly, then, the response even of this sinful and rebellious people was to "believe his words"[63] and "s[i]ng his praise" (v. 12).[64]

Some have attempted to discern in this psalm an allusion to a divine combat with "chaos". However, there are a number of factors which seem to contradict this view. The root גער has already been discussed in relation to Pss. 18:16 and 104:7, where it was shown to be equivalent to Yahweh's "roar", the thunder of his voice, which often seems to give expression to a particularly tangible and vigorous outworking of his powerful word of command.[65] Here, the sea is not

---

56 Cf. Ex. 14:16, 21, 22, 29, 15:19.

57 Not the "chaos flood", as it is translated by Gerstenberger (II, p. 240).

58 P. 113.

59 P. 464.

60 P. 352.

61 Cohen, p. 352. Less probable is the translation "desert" adopted, for example, by RSV and Anderson (II, p. 739), for much as the contrast between "deeps" and "desert" is extremely apt, the overtones of the English term must be contrasted with that of the Hebrew: although the "wilderness" was uncultivated and could be rather barren, it was not truly arid, and in the biblical tradition may sometimes be associated with lush abundance (c.f., e.g., Ps. 65:13). The same congruence of תְּהֹמוֹת and מִדְבָּר in relation to a vivid portrayal of the Red Sea event is encountered also in Isa. 63:13.

62 Cf. Ex. 14:28, 15:5, 10, Josh. 24:7, Ps. 78:53.

63 Cf. Ex. 14:31.

64 Cf. Ex. 15:1, 21.

65 Others, of course, also compare the use of the verb with that in Ps. 104, thereby importing the notion that the waters here resisted God, though of course there is in reality no indication of this in either context (see the discussion of Ps. 104 in Chapter 8 above): thus Cohen (p. 352, referring to p. 338); compare Day's more diffident annexation of Ps. 106:9 (as an "also note") to a list of references in which גער "is a sort of technical term for the divine conflict with the sea" (*God's Conflict*, p. 127, cf. Lauha, "Das Schilfmeermotif im Alten Testament", *VT[S]* 9 [1963], p. 40); see also the tentative claims of Kraus (II, 902) and Wellhausen (p. 113). Haglund likewise proposes only that "v. 9a has a vague connexion with the dragon-fight myth" (*Historical Motifs*, p. 64), whilst Allen's claim that "the *Chaoskampf* is echoed in a historicized form relating to the Exodus" (p. 48) sounds similarly qualified; this link is still further

personified, and the theophany language of seeing (cf. 77:17) and fleeing (cf. 114:3, 5) is absent; nor is the water explicitly stated to obey his command: rather, the transformation of the sea is immediate and automatic (v. 9a). Thus, far from being met with resistance, God's rebuke seems to have an absolute authority: the sea immediately "became dry" and the people, together with their divine shepherd, passed through with ease. Moreover, the event is localised: it is clear that Yahweh is not here dealing with "יָם", but with "יַם־סוּף", just as it is evident that the focus of the recollection is not on the sea itself: indeed, the נוֹרָאוֹת which Yahweh performed were merely "by the Red Sea" (the most natural and obvious force of עַל, as indicated by the context, vv. 21-22). Finally, it must be noted that the motif of "cleaving" the sea, which some have compared with Marduk's division of Tiamat, is not in this case actually mentioned, though it is of course to be assumed from the fact of the crossing.[66] Such an interpretation is confirmed by the recognisable place of Ps. 106 in the exodus tradition, since in concept and vocabulary it has a number of affinities with other recollections of the event which have not been identified as concerned with the *Chaoskampf*.

iii. The Theme of "Chaos" in Psalm 136

The image for the splitting of the Red Sea in v. 13a is unique and, like the description of the hammering out of the earth upon the waters, is based on a colourful and rather physical articulation of the divine action, since Yahweh is depicted as "cutting" or "dividing" the sea in two (גזר לִגְזָרִים). This verb is usually applied to straightforward division or cutting (e.g., 1 Ki. 3:25, 2 Ki. 6:4), although it can also be used of being "cut off" in the sense of being excluded (e.g., Ps. 88:6; but this sense is clearly not appropriate here), and (rarely), by extension, of destruction (i.e., death: Lam. 3:54, Ezek. 37:11; cf. Isa.

---

weakened by Eichrodt (*TAT* 2/3, p. 72), who, despite considering the Red Sea here to be personified as "a monster which Yahweh by his rebuke frightens away or restrains", emphasises that this image has nothing to do with the *Chaoskampf* myth. Similarly, Norin thinks only in terms of a residual personification of the waters (*Er spaltete das Meer*, p. 123). Wyatt, on the other hand, deletes נער as a gloss and imparts conflict notions into the second verb, חרב, which he translates with the unusual root III meaning, "he smote" (*Myths of Power*, pp. 85-6). However, the first aspect of his proposal is unjustified and the second implausible given the especial frequency of the application of I חרב to waters, including in contexts where the meaning is indisputable. Quite distinct in the profundity which he assigns the *Chaoskampf* theme is von Rad, for whom the welding of "the creation myth, the struggle with chaos" into the Exodus narrative assumes critical doctrinal importance: "the event thus took on primeval dimensions, and was transferred from its historical setting to the beginning of the history... Thereafter it was only a short step to Deutero-Isaiah's characteristic equation of creation and redemption"; Ps. 106:9 is thus seen as a crucial preliminary step towards the insights articulated by the great prophet of the exile (*TAT*, I, pp. 179-180).

66 In this regard, Eichrodt's comment cited above is especially pertinent.

53:8). At root, the idea seems to be of incisive division—hence perhaps its association with the notion of "decreeing" (Job 22:28, Est. 2:1). It may therefore constitute a more forceful variation on the usual terms of "division", probably emphasising the straight path through the sea.

However, there is a further aspect to this image which must be considered, since גְּזָרִים occurs elsewhere only in Gen. 15:17, there in relation to the formation of the Abrahamic covenant: "When the sun had gone down and it was dark, behold, a smoking fire pot and a flaming torch passed between these pieces (הַגְּזָרִים הָאֵלֶּה). On that day Yahweh made a covenant with Abraham, saying, 'To your descendants I give this land...'"[67] In fact, there are a number of linguistic and thematic affiliations between the two passages. Most obviously, Ps. 136 is fundamentally concerned with Yahweh's eternal חֶסֶד. As Anderson has stated, "*Ḥeseḏ* is primarily a covenant word,... the unceasing outworking of the covenant relationship, the essence of which is summed up in "I will be your God and you shall be my people"... When referring to Yahweh, *ḥeseḏ* means, in the first place, his covenant promises and all that they imply... Consequently the meaning of this term is closely associated with the significance and interpretation of the covenant."[68] The effect of each phrase in the historical narration of Ps. 136 being followed by the averral, "indeed, his חֶסֶד endures for ever",[69] is that each aspect of the divine action is interpreted as an outworking of Yahweh's covenant relationship with his people.[70] This covenant relationship which is so continually evoked is especially presupposed in the concluding part of the psalm, since in v. 23 the verb זכר "points back to a previously existing relationship";[71] hence "it means not only 'to remember, call to mind', but also 'to act upon (something)'".[72] Psalm 136 is thus already fundamentally orientated towards the covenant, even before any direct contacts with Gen. 15:17-18 may be evoked. However, there are also many general resonances between the exodus-situation and that of the Abrahamic covenant-cutting, for example, the evening setting (Ex. 14:20)[73] and the theophany as manifested in fire (cf. Ex. 13:21-22, 14:24). Gen. 15:18 mentions the "River of Egypt" in relation to the gift of the land; Psalm 136 celebrates the defeat of the inhabitants of Canaan and the giving of the land as a heritage (vv. 17-22). More importantly, however, the linguistic congruities between Gen. 15:17 and Ps.

---

67 Gen. 15:17-18.

68 Anderson, I, p. 215; see further Nelson Glueck, *Das Wort Ḥesed in alttestamentlichen Sprachgebrauche* (1927), pp. 32-4, 35-67, especially pp. 45-6, M. Buber, *Der Glaube der Propheten* (1950), p. 164, K. D. Sakenfeld, *The Meaning of Ḥesed in the Hebrew Bible: A New Enquiry* (1978), pp. 165-168.

69 כִּי in this context should be interpreted in a deictic and emphatic sense, "surely, indeed" (Anderson, II, p. 750; Crüsemann, *Studien zur Formgeschichte*, pp. 32-35; Seybold, pp. 505-6, translating "ja", perhaps a more felicitous rendering than is possible in English).

70 See Glueck, p. 46.

71 Anderson, II, p. 539; see B. S. Childs, *Memory and Tradition in Israel* (SBT 37, 1962) p. 35-6, 41-2.

72 Anderson, II, p. 579.

73 Cf. the break with the tradition of Gen 1:16 in including the stars in Ps. 136:9.

136:13-14 extend beyond the unique nominal link to the verbal usage: the smoking fire pot and flaming torch עבר בֵּין הַגְּזָרִים הָאֵלֶּה, just as the Red Sea is divided (גזר לִגְזָרִים) .... וְהֶעֱבִיר יִשְׂרָאֵל בתוכו. The same usage recurs in Jer. 34:18, 19: here it is assumed that the covenant was made "when I brought them out of the land of Egypt, out of the house of bondage..." (v. 13), and it is clearly emphasised that when "the calf ... they cut in two and passed between its parts—the princes of Judah, the princes of Jerusalem, the eunuchs, the priests, and all the people of the land ... passed between the parts of the calf" (vv. 18-19).

Here it is not suggested that the Red Sea crossing is understood solely in terms of covenant-formation. However, the double context of a celebration of the sacred foundation-moment when God and people became bound together at the Red Sea, recited within a hymn of thanksgiving for Yahweh's חֶסֶד, determines that the nuances of this highly distinctive language could scarcely fail to enrich the significance of the recollection.[74]

Scholarly perceptions of the language of "division" are mixed; although many, including Mowinckel and Day, remain silent on the matter,[75] and Gunkel even thought of a folk-tale motif,[76] others have seen an echo of the *Chaoskampf*. Drawing on Ugaritic material, R. Dussaud,[77] followed by Kraus[78] and Terrien,[79] has compared the Ugaritic expression *agzr ym bn ym* (*KTU* 1.23.23, 58-59, 61), understood as "I divide the sea from the sea". However, this sense is contextually doubtful, and must be contrasted with most modern translations, in which *ym* is commonly understood to refer to the day.[80] It is, further, to be noted that the context is the Shachar and Shalim text, concerned with the birth of the "gracious gods", in which there is no discernible conflict. The proposed *Chaoskampf* interpretation must therefore be rejected.

---

74 Oesterley also considers that "this covenant-rite, of great antiquity, must have been in the mind of the psalmist" (II, p. 544).

75 Cf. Norin's consideration of the Psalm under the heading "Auszug ohne Mythos", *Er spaltete das Meer*, p. 138.

76 *Die Psalmen*, p. 577.

77 *Les Découvertes de Ras Shamra (Ugarit) et l'Ancien Testament* (Paris: Librairie Orientaliste Paul Geuthner, 1937), p. 61.

78 II, pp. 1080-1081.

79 P. 862.

80 Thus Lewis, *UNP*, pp. 209 ("Paired devourers of the day that bore them"), Wyatt, *RTU*, pp. 329 ("both gluttonous from birth"), Gray, *The Legacy of Canaan*, p. 98 ("those who cut off, i.e., delimit, the day, two born in one day"); cf. even Driver (*CML*, 1st ed., p. 123), "twin figures born in one day". Alternative renderings are cited in Gibson, *CML*, p. 124, Gray, *Legacy*, p. 98 n. 7, and Wyatt, *RTU*, p. 329, Gibson himself maintaining an unusual reference to the sea with his rendering, "'cleavers' of the sea, children of the sea" (*CML*, 2nd ed., p. 126). Dahood, with sensible reticence, merely notes "the material similarity" of the Hebrew and Ugaritic expressions, remarking that, as regards the later, the "interpretation, unfortunately, is uncertain" (III, p. 266).

Alternatively, some scholars have discerned an echo of Marduk's treatment of Tiamat.[81] However, any similarity is very remote: there is no indication that the Red Sea is personified, still less thought of as a dragon. Moreover, there is no interest in the use made of its parts: rather, the people pass through and the sea then "overwhelms" the enemy. Thus the differences are greater than any passing similarity that may pertain, and even Allen's moderation of Alonso-Schökel's interpretation, that "in the present context it has become a worn metaphor and appears to connote not hostility but divine power over nature",[82] is overstated. His further, more poetic, claim that "the sea was slashed open and the arch-enemy was easily disposed of, army and all"[83] exploits the nuances of the *Chaoskampf* theme without actually claiming its content. It appears, then, that once again, the theme of "chaos" is absent.

3. Summary

The putative evidence for the presence of the *Chaoskampf* motif in the psalms concerned with the Red Sea event is especially slender, and even some of the customary advocates for this type of interpretation avoid making such a claim here. A close examination of the evidence confirms that such an approach cannot be substantiated, but reveals a variety of images through which the familiar theme of the exodus is ever cast afresh according to different emphases.

81 See Alonso-Schökel, "Psalmus 136 (135)", *Verbum Domini* 45 (1967), p. 132, Gerstenberger, II, pp. 386-7. Seybold also considers the struggle with the chaos dragon to be in view, but makes no further comment as to its background or significance (p. 508; cf. similarly Eaton p. 453).

82 P. 230.

83 P. 233.

X. The Theme of "Chaos" in the Psalter: Summary of Results

It was proposed in the introduction of the present monograph that the diversity of motifs conventionally classified as being concerned with chaos, despite the lack of any corresponding term within the Hebrew language itself, indicated that this concept as applied to the Psalter was in need of reassessment. The results of a thorough critical analysis of the relevant psalm texts, considered individually without recourse to extra-biblical parallels, confirms that the traditional interpretation has grossly overplayed any indications which could be compatible with the presence of the *Chaoskampf* theme, and indeed that there is no unequivocal internal evidence pointing to its existence in any of the texts considered. The foregoing discussion, further, corroborates the critique of the standard treatments of this image made in Chapter 2, namely that the term "chaos" cannot legitimately be applied to the cluster of Old Testament texts hitherto classified under that label; that there is no clear causal link between this motif and that of creation, but that any connection between the two is relatively late and probably a secondary development from that of Yahweh's control of the cosmic waters; and that in none of the passages here examined can it properly be stated that any form of combat is depicted as taking place.

It was, further, suggested that the application of the *Chaoskampf* as an overarching theme encompassing such a variety of biblical motifs has, in part, at least, been a product of the comparative method, which has tended to overemphasise putative similarities between religious systems and cultures but, as a result, has obscured the distinctiveness of the imagery and beliefs contained within the Hebrew Bible; equally significantly, it has effectively suppressed the linguistic and theological diversity encapsulated within the texts with which we are concerned.

Thus, a careful re-examination of the psalms which have conventionally been associated with "chaos", eschewing either the tendency to seek a unifying theme or to make exegetical recourse to extra-biblical material, gives rise to an appreciation of a diverse spectrum of imagery. Through figures such as Leviathan, Rahab, storms, oceans, deeps, and rivers, occurring either alone or in different combinations, are conjured up depictions of theophany, creation, exodus, conquest, death and universal joy—a whole spectrum of human experience, individual, national and cosmic—yet all are embraced within the tremendous power of God.

Accordingly, within this range of motifs, there are important theological contrasts. The theophanic appearance of God often evokes an anguished response to his terrible power, as evidenced by the disruption of the natural order in the quaking mountains and fleeing seas (Ps. 114, cf. Pss. 18, 68).

Indeed, his terrible manifestation in the thunderstorm is sometimes conceived as directly destructive, as in Psalm 29. On the other hand, rather than making the terrestrial structures shake, Yahweh sometimes is the one who makes steady its pillars and prevents the sea from fleeing or from breaking its bounds. He is the founder and stabiliser rather than the destroyer, the one who is resident in Zion, protecting his holy city from within (Pss. 24, 65, 93), rather than the rider on the clouds who performs a more dynamic and aggressive function. (Psalm 46 seems to contain elements of both motifs, though the latter is uppermost.) Indeed, in certain late hymnic evocations of the coming of Yahweh, his arrival elicits a joyous response from the whole cosmos—heavens and earth, sea and dry land, the inhabitants of all these spheres together with the nations, which collectively welcome his just rule (Pss. 96, 98, cf. Ps. 148).

Yet the saving / destructive dynamic of God's work may be experienced in a more personal context, too. Within individual and royal laments and thanksgiving psalms, he is sometimes experienced in the spectacular theophanic deliverance of a suppliant, rescuing him from his enemies and from the waters of death (Pss. 18, 144; cf. Pss. 69, 124). Elsewhere, it appears that it is he who actually afflicts the sufferer, overwhelming him with his waves and billows (Pss. 42-3, cf. Ps. 88). Possible explanations for this dichotomy were considered in Chapter 4, in which it was suggested that the suppliant's confidence in divine support or, conversely, his feeling of alienation from God, could be a factor. Also influential here is the temporal focus of the composition: thanksgivings looking back retrospectively on the experience of deliverance reflect joyful confidence in divine salvation, whereas laments uttered from the midst of pain and suffering frequently betray a sense of bewilderment and uncertainty with regard to God's activity. It is, however, difficult to discern whether this is simply a product of the individual's sense of isolation from God, or whether it is the result of his inability to explain the source of his suffering within his customary apprehension of the world; whether accusation is a rhetorical device intended to elicit a decisive divine response, or whether the image of persecution by Yahweh reflects belief in suffering as the result of sin; and indeed aspects of some or all of these factors may be operative. Nevertheless, one common tendency manifests itself, namely that "enemy" imagery predominates in situations where divine support is forthcoming and deliverance assured, whereas the predicaments from which God himself appears to be hostile to the suppliant are coloured by the *Wortfeld* of Sheol.

Equally striking are the contrasts between the forms of depiction of individual and national crises. It appears that it is only an individual who may experience extreme suffering as a threat to his personal existence, understood in terms of the encroachment of the underworld, though this motif also features in communal or royal thanksgiving psalms in which, however, enmity assumes equal or greater prominence. In communal laments, the historical reality of the nation's suffering—the destruction of the temple, exile of the people, failure of prophecy, mocking of the enemies, and so forth—is graphically portrayed, and more "mythical" pictorial language is harnessed in such contexts only in relation to historical retrospects, chief among them the exodus (Pss. 77, 74, 89).

The treatment of the exodus motif well illustrates the flexibility of themes and motifs as expressed in an Israelite context, yet also the conventionality of many forms of expression. There is here a clear dichotomy between historical recollections within national laments, and those in hymnic and didactic settings. In the former, God's saving theophany may be vividly portrayed (Ps. 77), or the enemy cast in the form of a monstrous beast (Pss. 74, 89), but in the latter, by contrast, the language is characteristically far more concrete, the details of the event being related in a more-or-less direct way (Pss. 66, 78, 106, 136). The only exception to this is the fragment Ps. 114, in which exodus and entry are conflated into a portrayal of the distress of nature at his coming.

Finally, mention of Yahweh's creative work is slightly less diverse, yet ranges from simple statements of the foundation of the earth (Ps. 24, cf. Pss. 95, 146), to descriptions of the creative processes (Pss. 33, 104, 136), or evocations of praise by his creatures (Ps. 148). However, the focus is often not on the *Urzeit* as such, but on the continuing stability of the earth and Yahweh's gracious provision (cf. Ps. 65).

Very often, differences in theology and emphasis may be explained in terms of context and genre, yet the issue of chronology may also exert an influence. Clearly, the issue of dating is highly complex and contentious, and the core findings of the present monograph stand independently of any specific dating conclusions. Nevertheless, certain tendencies are suggested by a consideration of the thematic classification of particular psalms in combination with an appreciation of their likely era of emergence, usually considered according to very broad relative categories.

Arguably, perhaps the earliest of the compositions here considered concern the divine theophany. This is highly significant, since this complex of ideas is perhaps one of the furthest removed from any notion of *Chaoskampf* among those here examined. In such contexts, the distress of nature at Yahweh's coming is common to all of creation, both earth and seas, even trees and animals. There is no interest in the confining or subjugation of waters, but rather with Yahweh's provision of rain and his abode over the heavenly ocean (see especially Ps. 29). The theophany motif persisted long into Israel's creative literature, sometimes appearing in short "ossified" phrases (Pss. 104, 46), elsewhere continuing to be deployed dynamically in imaginative evocations of his salvific work (Pss. 18, 77), the water provision aspect often fading even where the characteristics of storm and thunder are clearly present.

Probably a little later in origin than the earliest theophany psalms are those concerned with cosmic stability and the security of Zion, which were seen most probably to derive from the pre-exilic Jerusalemite cult. Here, the dominant themes of the upholding of the cosmos, protection of the holy city, relations with the nations, the kingship and power of God, and his gracious provision for his people, may be seen to reflect the concerns of the Davidic monarchy as it sought to preserve the Judahite state in an often turbulent world. However, as was stressed in Chapter 5, the motif of "chaos" is nowhere made explicit in these hymns, and it is methodologically unacceptable simply to presume its presence on the basis of putative cross-cultural parallels. Although Israel evidently shared her basic cosmology with neighbouring peoples, entailing a flat earth supported on pillars and surrounded (and probably threatened) by waters, it is a grave error on the basis of a world-view which appears to us to be "mythological" to attribute to the Israelites the whole associated "mythology" as it was found in Canaan or Babylon. Even where parallels occur between two different contexts (as does not to any great extent pertain here), the same internal and contextual significance cannot be presumed to accompany a particular linguistic or narrative form.

Another clearly identifiable meeting-point between historical situation and poetic image is in the figures of Rahab and Leviathan, who are depicted in the Psalter as being overcome by God only in Psalms 74 and 89, which would appear to have been composed in response to the fall of Jerusalem in 587 B.C. The significance of this is, however, harder to discern: were these "dragons" inventions of a period of crisis, or a reapplication of folk-mythology for the first time in the temple cult? Does the imagery reflect a sudden identification with wider Canaanite culture when all was under threat by the Babylonian monolith, or a counterblast to Babylonian Marduk theology? Was it a widespread part of pre-exilic worship in Israel, perhaps excluded from wider mention by the orthodox compilers of the biblical material, or even perhaps a central part of the Jerusalem cult, which just happens not to have been more widely expressed in the Old Testament, due to historical accident or to later aversion to such imagery? These questions are easier to pose than to answer. However, the foregoing analysis has raised a number of crucial objections to the existence of the type of pre-exilic enthronement festival associated with this theme by Mowinckel and many subsequent scholars, not least on grounds of methodology. As regards the question of the time of emergence of "dragon" imagery, it may be noted that the occurrences elsewhere in the Old Testament are also confined to the time of the Babylonian crisis or subsequently (Isa. 27:1, 51:9; Job 3:8, 7:12, 9:13, 26:12-13, 40:25-41:26 [ET 41:1-34]). Its development, either in expansion of detail and detachment from a clear historical focus (as in Job) or in heightening and eschatologisation (see Isa. 27) in the subsequent period, and especially in post-biblical literature (not least in Revelation), belies the assumption of late editorial aversion to this motif. One must therefore assume the absence of the dragon motif from the circles of pre-exilic worship which contributed to the collections of psalms now extant and perhaps in general from official cultic circles, at least as attributed to Yahweh himself. A rather less likely possibility is its existence in pre-exilic times in a form which was later seen to be objectionable, despite its subsequent transformation into an acceptable mode. This would require highly effective suppression and rigorous exclusion from an early stage in the tradition, and is plausible only in the form that the slaying of Leviathan was originally attributed in Israel to another deity, most likely Baal or his consort, and then later transferred to Yahweh.

The line of development of the figure of Rahab outlined in Chapter 6 would lend further corroboration to this reconstruction, since it was there shown that the earliest occurrences of this term (in Isa. 30:7, Ps. 87:4) are in reference to the nation of Egypt, without any mythological overtones being present. Thus, the usage in Ps. 89:11, where Rahab may represented as some form of draconic being, seems to constitute a development away from the original use of the term, but one which is explicable in the context of representations of Egypt as a crocodile or other form of monstrous creature (e.g., in Ezek. 29:3, 32:2).

The apparently post-exilic hymns considered in Chapter 7 exude a positive and unified view of creation, according to which the whole world, the sea included, is called to join in exuberant praise of its maker and king. Such compositions may perhaps best be understood to reflect a background in which the universalist and monotheistic implications of the theological revolution of the exile have been worked out to their fullest extent. Likewise, it appears that the evocations of God's creative work incorporating portrayals of the confining of the sea (considered in Chapter 8) are equally unsupportive of the notion of cosmic combat: in Ps. 148, the creation of the sea even occasions joyful celebration. Moreover, it seems that this motif is restricted— as far as may be discerned from the limited evidence available—to the later literature. This is especially significant insofar as it undermines the presumption accepted by the majority of scholars that Israelite theologians were directly dependent for the imagery of "chaos" on earlier Babylonian or Canaanite creation accounts.

Finally, the two remaining "synchronic" groups of psalms considered in the present monograph, those relating to the Exodus and Red Sea crossing, or which speak of threatening waters in the context of individual or royal lament and thanksgiving psalms, constitute perhaps the clearest examples of passages in which the assumption of *Chaoskampf* influence is surely mistaken. The latter group, in particular, must be distinguished from those contexts which relate to the cosmic waters of the deep sourcing the world's water supply, since here the waters of the underworld are in view. Consequently, a distinct vocabulary and imagery adheres to this sphere of reference, frequently including mention, for example, of "mire" or "the pit" alongside clear allusions to Sheol and more familiar maritime language. Particularly distinctive is the way in which such waters thinly veil the action of the suppliant's enemies or even embody the hostile activity of God.

As has been mentioned above, the manner of presentation of the Exodus events is extremely variable, and context and genre play an highly influential rôle. The theophany (Pss. 77, 114) and dragon (Pss. 74, 89) motifs have already been adverted to in some detail; as regards the more "prosaic" depictions, as occur in Pss. 66, 78, 106 and 136, even some of the most enthusiastic exponents of the "*Chaoskampf*" interpretation of certain psalms are muted in their claims in respect of these compositions. In fact, unless one is to assume *a priori* that any reference to cutting or division must necessarily entail the implication of mythical combat, this type of interpretation here becomes very difficult to sustain.

To summarise the chronological aspects of the present survey, it appears that the image-complexes encountered here seem to have grown out of the theophany tradition, with input from ancient motifs such as the kingship of the high God, and Zion traditions. Contrary to expectation, and despite clear Canaanite influence in language, image and poetic forms, the so-called "chaos" imagery is often absent from the earliest hymns, or present only to a very limited extent; sometimes the interest is merely cosmological. The major impetus for the use of these images comes with the devastating experience of the exile and being engulfed and destroyed by hostile powers. A stabilising influence is seen in the post-exilic era. There is an interest in a benign, well-ordered creation, and images of "division" have become standardised in Red Sea allusions. Running alongside this, and perhaps operative over a long period, is the characterisation of the threat of death as the waters of Sheol in the individual lament form.

The most significant conclusions resulting from this investigation are twofold. First, the terminology of "chaos" should be abandoned in relation to the texts here considered, since it obscures the diverse spheres of imagery and reference displayed within them. Second, even the specific content ascribed to the motif of "chaos" has been shown to be inappropriate. In addition, the present findings suggest the likelihood that the imagery of divine combat is absent from the earliest layers of the Old Testament. This has important ramifications for the understanding of the development of Yahwism and its relation to the cults of Baal and other Canaanite deities. It has frequently been assumed that influences from the wider ancient Near Eastern environment were greater in the earliest period, and indeed that the religion of Israel effectively emerged out of a Canaanite background from which, in the pre-monarchic era or earlier, it—or some of its constituent elements—may have been scarcely distinguishable. The results of the present investigation would, however, suggest a very different model of influence, namely that, whilst the language of theophany or of cosmic stability is very ancient, and may perhaps have been presumed from ancient times to have adhered to the attributes of God or to the structure of the universe, the motif of the overcoming of a dragon by Yahweh may have been consciously imported and adapted at a relatively late period in the history of Israel, namely in association with, or perhaps subsequent to, the events of c. 587 B.C. Thus, it is to be viewed as a coherent theological development rather than a redundant or quasi-redundant echo of the past, and one which was to gain increasing importance in later centuries.

XI. The Theme of "Chaos" in the Wider Old Testament

Having established that the presence of the theme of "chaos" has been overstated in relation to the Psalter, and indeed that it may be absent from most or all instances where it has conventionally been assumed, this clearly raises the question of whether the same may be said of the rest of the Old Testament. This is important for three main reasons. First, although the theme may appear to be absent from the Psalter, if it were found explicitly elsewhere, this might raise the possibility that some of the conclusions already reached here should be reviewed, since the notion of "chaos" might then reasonably be understood to be in the background in some of those passages where it is not actually expressed. A muted or modified allusion, on the other hand, might encourage the view that the theme was transformed or suppressed in formal Israelite religious circles, but would confirm at least a residual presence in some spheres. If, however, the theme were absent elsewhere, this would further strengthen the thesis so far advanced, especially in those cases where the evidence may be perceived as equivocal or more readily subject to competing interpretations. Second, much of the present monograph has been concerned not simply with assessing the presence or absence of the imagery of "chaos", but with reviewing how it should be understood, for example in questioning the presumed connection with creation or in highlighting various clusters of imagery conventionally subsumed within the "chaos" theme. Hence should the differing spheres of allusion which have been detected in place of the prevalent "chaos" interpretation be found outside the Psalter in similar contexts, this would further advance, and hopefully allow the nuancing of, the case here presented. Third, the diachronic aspect of the analysis completed thus far suggested that there was a developmental aspect to the range of imagery here considered, for example in the prevalence of thunderstorm and theophanic motifs in the earlier period, or the apparent use of references to draconic figures only after the events of 587 B.C. This also would benefit from being tested against a wider range of material, not least because the dating of extra-Psalteric texts is often less uncertain and more readily set against known events. Once again, the modification or strengthening of the proposed developmental model should result.

Nevertheless, despite the clear benefits of conducting such a further survey, a certain amount of pragmatism must be exercised as regards to space. I propose therefore to focus on those passages where the case for a *Chaoskampf* reading has been most frequently urged, and is perhaps at its strongest, namely those passages in Job and Isaiah which concern draconic or beastly figures. The case for seeing the representation of Pharaoh as a crocodile in Ezek 29, 32 or of Nebuchadrezzar in Jer. 51:34 in the light of the "chaos" motif, though sometimes made, is based on a more distant form of dependence, relying on the idea that what is expressed more mythically elsewhere is here transformed into a historicized form. Hence, such an interpretation would become difficult to sustain if it were shown that the *Chaoskampf* reading of the related but more "mythical" texts of the Bible is found to be unsatisfactory, and it is chiefly by this means that I hope to proceed. In any case, the depiction of Nebuchadnezzar in Jer. 51:34 lacks those features which are found elsewhere in relation, e.g., to Rahab or Leviathan, and indeed his insatiable appetite seems more redolent of Mot; hence it should probably be understood independently of the texts conventionally bracketed under the "chaos" label.[1] Similarly, Ezekiel's love of parodying quotation, combined with the Egyptian convention of representing the Pharaoh as a crocodile,[2] besides the influence of the Israelite Rahab traditions, must be seen as dominant factors behind the imagery employed in 29, 32.

Since references to the roaring sea or a flooding river (as in the simile of Isa.17:12-13 and metaphors of Isa. 8:5-8, Jer. 47:2) and allusions to the setting of boundaries for the containment of the sea (Prov. 8:29ab,[3] Jer. 5:22[4]) may simply be understood naturalistically, and since much of the vocabulary employed in such contexts, as well as the general type of imagery, has already been encountered in relation to the Psalter,[5] I hope little will be lost by sparing the reader the exegesis of such passages, the results of which may perhaps occasion little surprise to anyone familiar with the approach here taken.[6] Similarly, the exact phrase of Jon. 2:4cd כָּל־מִשְׁבָּרֶיךָ וְגַלֶּיךָ עָלַי עָבָרוּ has

1 See further the brief discussion of this allusion undertaken below in relation to the exegesis of Job 7:12.

2 On which see further below.

3 This reference is, of course preceded by explicit mention of the "establish[ment of] the fountain of the deep" (v. 28b), before which "there were no depths...no springs abounding with water" (v. 24). The primacy of the creation of these sweet waters (which probably also feed the sea) and their place among other vital aspects of creation is thus affirmed.

4 Note how, in Jeremiah, Yahweh's manifestation of power in containing the sea (5:22) is balanced by his skill in stirring it up so that its waves roar (31:35).

5 Compare Isa. 17:12-13 with Ps. 46:4, 7, 65:8; Isa. 8:7-8, Jer. 47:2 with Ps. 124:4; and Jer. 5:22cd, Prov. 8:29ab with Ps. 104:9a.

6 Congruences in content with Psalteric material seem to follow the same broad chronological pattern: the turbulent floods or waves of the roaring nations in the monarchic passages Isa. 17:12-13, 8:7-8, Jer. 47:2 correspond with the probable date of Pss. 46 and 65 which seem to reflect a similar situation and employ the same type of imagery. The creation passage of Prov. 8 is often dated late, and Jer. 5:22 is also frequently regarded as secondary, as is congruent with the apparent absence of an interest in the event of creation in the earlier Psalms. Allusions to Pharaoh or

already been analysed in detail in respect of Ps. 42:8, whilst further aspects of the portrayal are clarified by the explicit mention of Sheol in v. 3 and the allusion to the oceanic יַמִּים and נָהָר in v. 4a, so detailed exegesis of this passage will also be omitted. An exception has, however, been made in the case of Job 38:8-11, since in this passage the sea is personified, and the description is unusually vivid, employing imagery not encountered elsewhere in relation to the confining of the sea. Job 9:8 will also be considered because of its proximity to another putative "chaos" allusion in v. 13 and its use of the very distinctive expression דרך עַל בָּמֳתֵי יָם.

Brief consideration must also be made of Nah. 1:4, in which the allusion to Yahweh's rebuking of the sea and making it dry has sometimes been seen as an expression of the *Chaoskampf* theme. However, the context is the terrible theophanic manifestation of Yahweh in wrath and judgment in which mountains and hills, the earth and its inhabitants are also "laid waste" before him (v. 5), so the reference in v. 4 cannot be interpreted as an act of hostility directed specifically at the waters. Moreover, the essential negativity and destructiveness of the divine action against the sea, rather than any salvific value, is confirmed by the consequence in the withering of vegetation (v. 4cd).

Another notable prophetic passage in which a conflict with the sea has often been discerned is Hab. 3; however, in view of the length and complexity of this chapter and the difficulty it presents for dating, I intend to treat it elsewhere in more detail than would be possible here. The reader is therefore temporarily referred to the brief note on Hab 3:8 in the Introduction (Chapter 1).

Finally, there are two formative contexts in which the presence of the "chaos" motif has more often been denied than affirmed: these are Gen. 1 and Ex. 15. In the case of the latter, which is likely to be one of the earliest representations of the Red Sea miracle, and possibly even the earliest,[7] it is significant that, in the words of John Day,

---

Nebuchadrezzar as a תַּנִּין (or תַּנִּים) in Ezek. 29, 32 and Jer. 51:34 also correlate with the apparent association of dragon language in the Psalter with the disaster of 587 B.C.

7 Despite continued debate, the evidence seems to favour an early provenance: see the summaries in Childs, pp. 245-247, Durham, p. 203, and note, besides the treatments by the Albright "school", Lohfink, *Das Siegeslied am Schilfmeer*, pp. 108-9, and Robertson, *Linguistic Evidence*, especially p. 155; his analysis is helpfully summarised by Kloos, *Yhwh's Combat with the Sea*, pp. 130-132, both Kloos and Cross (*CMHE*, p. 121) considering the issue to be decided by Robertson's study. Efforts to discern secondary redactional layers (as by Norin, *Er Spaltete das Meer*, pp. 77-107, or Zenger, *VT[S]* 32 [1981] 452-83) have produced variant results on the basis of rather doubtful methods, such as an overdependence on metrical analysis, whilst Brenner's advocacy of a post-exilic origin (in *The Song of the Sea*) is characterised by an excessive reliance on history of traditions evidence, and a marked tendency both to classify comparative material as exilic or later and to assume that contacts between sources indicate contemporaity. See further the summary of scholarship in Zenger, "Tradition and Interpretation in Exodus XV 1-21", *VT[S]* 32 (1981) 452-483, pp. 456-8.

> There is here no divine conflict with the waters, nor do the waters symbolize a foreign nation or nations; rather Yahweh's victory at Yam Suph is over Pharaoh and his armies, and the waters, which are in no way personified, are merely the passive instrument used by Yahweh in accomplishing his purpose.[8]

Some have nevertheless discerned here the replication of a Canaanite "victory pattern", in which conquest is followed by the establishment of a temple / palace (cf. vv. 13, 17) and an affirmation of the kingship of the victor (cf. v. 18).[9] Such associations should occasion no surprise and are readily attributable to the general common cultural milieu, the lack of a fixed order of events being especially notable. Moreover, the supposed pattern probably relates to the motif of victory *per se* rather than necessarily being restricted only to the conflict with Yam, and indeed it is the sort of sequence which one might imagine occurring independently within that culture, perhaps also echoing historical realities.[10] In any case, even if its fundamental setting were that of the conflict with the sea, the emphases of the present passage, with its interest in the rôle of the waters in crushing the Egyptians, indicates that this original content has been radically transformed and subverted even in this probably very early Hebrew context.

---

8 *God's Conflict*, p. 98; see similarly, e.g., Cross, *CMHE*, pp. 131-2, Habel, *Yahweh versus Baal*, p. 60, Anderson, *Creation versus Chaos*, pp. 50, 128, Childs, *The Book of Exodus* (OTL; Louisville, KY: Westminster, 1974), p. 251. Vestigial traces of a struggle with the sea are nevertheless claimed by Cassuto (pp. 177-181), in line with his theory that there was an Israelite epic poem concerning a revolt by the sea: with obvious circularity, he reconstructs the content of the epic from biblical phrases he associates with this theme, then claims vestiges in Ex. 15 on the basis of a version of the Song which is supplemented by his epic reconstruction. For example, he assumes that the exaltation (גאה) of Yahweh (vv. 1, 21) should be associated with the rising up (גאה) of the sea, even though this verb is not applied to the waters here. However, even thus enhanced, the evidence for such a reading still appears remarkably thin. Wyatt's urging of a dual reference in vv. 6-8 (*Myths of Power*, pp. 172-9) is similarly dependent on imaginative reconstruction (e.g., replacing בְּלֵב with כְּלֵב in v. 8c and proposing that תְּהֹמֹת [vv. 5a, 8c] should have the same force as the Ugaritic *thmtm*) since, unlike the allusion to Egypt, the notion of a battle with the sea can claim no direct support from the MT; moreover, Wyatt still has to admit that in v. 10b "Sea... has become Yahweh's agent of destruction" and that, as it stands "it is no longer a version of the *Chaoskampf* at all; it is on the contrary a poem about the saving of Israel from the power of Egypt".

9 Thus, e.g., Cross, *CMHE*, p. 142, Forsyth, *The Old Enemy*, p. 95, Day, *God's Conflict*, p. 98, Fretheim, p. 166. Cf. (with kingship preceding construction) *KTU* 1.2.iv.10, 32; 1.3-4; and (with kingship prior even to the victory) *Enuma elish* IV.13-15, 28; VI.49-58.

10 One might compare the emphasis on the establishment of the city of David and building of the palace and Temple there as the cementing of David's kingship; the concern with the Davidic origin of the Temple, despite the fact that it was not constructed until the reign of his successor, is especially notable. For the kingship overtones of military prowess, cf., e.g., 1 Sam. 18:7-8.

Similarly, in the crucial statement of Israel's creation faith in Gen. 1, notwithstanding the debate over the precise significance of the first two verses,[11] and despite the continued assumption by some that v. 2 refers to "chaos",[12] the absence of any reference to cosmic combat is now widely affirmed. Thus Mark Smith represents the view of many when he states that:

> Genesis 1 omits not only the conflict but also any personification of the cosmic waters. With no hint of conflict or even hostility, God speaks (not even rebukes), and the divine will is achieved...The watery creatures are now not monstrous, and they are contained in the created order in Genesis 1:21, characterized repeatedly in Genesis 1 as good.[13]

The fact that תֹהוּ וָבֹהוּ does not appear to denote "chaos" but "emptiness, waste" or the like has already been explored above in Chapter 2. Moreover, the non-mythological and impersonal aspects of תְהוֹם in v. 2 are also frequently acknowledged, and have been subjected to a particularly thorough etymological and comparative study by Tsumura. It is impossible to rehearse all of his findings here, but some of his key conclusions are as follows:

> [1]...It is very unlikely that Hebrew *tĕhôm* is a borrowing from a Canaanite divine name... [2]...Since the Hebrew term *tĕhôm* is most probably a common noun in origin, like the Ugaritic, Akkadian and Eblaite terms, there is no strong reason why we should take *tĕhôm* as a depersonification of the original divine name... [3] The Canaanite Sea-dragon is Yam, not Tahām ... Therefore it is almost certain that even if there should be an undiscovered myth in which a 'creator' god had to fight a Canaanite sea-dragon, the dragon was not Tahām... [4] Baal is not a creator god...[5]... If the Genesis account were the demythologization of a Canaanite dragon myth, we would expect in the initial portion of the account, the term *yām* 'sea', the counterpart of the Ugaritic sea-god Yam who corresponds to the god ^{d}A.AB.BA (=*Ti'āmat* or *Ayabbu*?) in the official pantheon list from ancient Ugarit. However, the term *yām* does

---

11 On which, see above Chapter 2, Section 1, "Chaos".

12 Even where mention is made of "chaos" in the present connection, it is usually merely to denote a formless, empty, or disordered state prior to or as the first stage of creation. As a result, it is often accompanied by an acknowledgement of the "absence of the battle theme" (S. Niditch, *Chaos to Cosmos*, p. 20) and a stress on the lack of personification of תְהוֹם (e.g., Vawter, p. 40, Wenham, p. 16). Thus the term "chaos" is employed by such authors only in a general sense without much of the specific content usually intended in reference to Old Testament contexts.

13 *The Memoirs of God*, p. 97. See similarly, e.g., Day, *God's Conflict*, p. 50, Cassuto, I, pp. 24, 31-33, 49-51, Steck, *Der Schöpfungsbericht der Priesterschrift* (Göttingen: Vandenhoeck & Ruprecht, 1975), pp. 231-2, 63-4, Wyatt, *Myths of Power*, p. 200, Hamilton, pp. 111, 130, and Wakeman's description of Gen. 1:21 as "a deliberate effort to contradict the battle myth" (p. 78).

> not appear in Gen 1 until v. 10 where the plural form *yāmmîm* appears as the antithesis of the 'land' (*'ereṣ*).[14]

He concludes,

> This Hebrew term *tĕhôm* is simply a reflection of the Common Semitic term *tihām- 'ocean' and there is no relation between the Genesis account and the so-called *Chaoskampf* mythology.[15]

Such results are supported by the contextual analysis of the use of תְּהוֹם in Gen. 1:2. Tsumura has shown convincingly that הָאָרֶץ and תְּהוֹם comprise a hyponymous pair (the latter being included within the former) and that the qualifying expressions תֹהוּ וָבֹהוּ and חֹשֶׁךְ signify "'not yet' normal, i.e. 'not yet productive and inhabitable and without light'".[16] This coheres also with Westermann's apprehension that:

> The function of the word in the present case is obviously to describe the situation which preceded creation, parallel to darkness as the first sentences of the cosmogony of Berossus (quoted by Eusebius...): "There once was a time, so he says, when every thing was darkness and water." The phrase "over the face of the waters" at the end of the verse has the same meaning and shows that תהום in Gen 1:2 cannot be intended to signify a mythical person or even a personified power...[17]

Accordingly, as Westermann maintains, following W. H. Schmidt,[18] "one should not make too much of the absence of the article: חשך too is without the article."[19] Moreover, following a survey of occurrences of the word תְּהוֹם

---

14 *The Earth and the Waters*, pp. 62-65.

15 *Ibid.*, p. 65.

16 *Ibid.*, p. 78. The "primal situation" is thus aptly characterised by van Wolde as "not 'nothing', far less a chaos which has yet to be ordered, but a situation of 'before everything' or 'not yet' in respect of what is to come" (*Stories of the Beginning*, p. 22). See further the bibliography cited at Chapter 2 n. 27 and the more extensive bibliography in Wenham, pp. 10-11. One might, further, compare Lambert's suggestion that Gen. 1:2 may reflect cosmogonies beginning with the earth ("Old Testament Mythology in its Ancient Near Eastern Context" [VT(S) 40, 1988] 124-143. pp. 137-8), since this would distance it further from the idea of a pre-existent watery "chaos".

17 P. 145. The non-mythological use of תְּהוֹם here is very widely acknowledged: see, e.g., Wenham, p. 16, Vawter, p. 40, Steck, *Schöpfungsbericht*, p. 64.

18 *Die Schöpfungsgeschichte der Priesterschrift* (WMANT 17; Neukirchen-Vluyn: Neukirchener Verlag, 1964), p. 81.

19 P. 145; Tsumura makes the further point that several other common nouns appear without the article in Gen. 1, whilst others occur with it; hence, its omission from תְּהוֹם "is no proof of personification, since this form (sg.) appears either as a part of an idiomatic expression or in the poetic texts," Indeed, the occurrence of תְּהוֹם elsewhere either in the plural or with the article encourages the view that it is a common noun, as in the cognate languages (*The Earth and the Waters*, pp 57-8).

in the Old Testament, he draws a conclusion, based on this wider Hebrew usage, which exactly corroborates the results of a similar analysis conducted at an earlier stage in the present monograph:

> תהום in the Old Testament has no other meaning than the deep or the waters of the deep. It can mean that which blesses or destroys just as can water... The evidence does not allow us to speak of a demythologizing of a mythical idea or name... When P inherited the word תהום, it had long been used to describe a flood of water without any mythical echo.[20]

These results are very significant, since they are wholly in accord with the findings of the present study. Here is a highly monotheistic creation account in which there is no trace of combat, and no personification of the waters, yet at the same time it understandably reflects a common ancient cosmological structure in which there was water and darkness at the beginning of the world, the waters being separated from the waters for the dry land to appear. Such cosmology was a "given" within that ancient cultural context:[21] it was probably the only available model which fitted with the perceived reality of the world. However, this stands independently of the mythology—and indeed theology—attached to its formation and maintenance. In a reflection of the same theological and cosmological worldview, the Priestly writer could similarly portray the disaster of the Flood in terms of a reincursion of the

---

20 *Genesis 1-11*, pp. 104-5. Moreover, as is now widely recognised, the Hebrew תהום is not actually derived from the Akkadian Tiamat, as Gunkel had thought, so this distances Gen. 1 further from its Babylonian antecedents (see e.g., Day, *God's Conflict*, p. 50, and references there). Thus, as Tsumura emphasises (*The Earth and the Waters in Genesis 1 and 2*, p. 47), "the idea that the Akkadian Tiamat was borrowed and subsequently demythologized is mistaken and should not be used as an argument in a lexicographical discussion of Hebrew *tĕhôm* ... The Akkadian term *ti'āmtum>tâmtum* normally means 'sea' or 'ocean' in an ordinary sense and is sometimes *personified* as a divine being in mythological contexts. Therefore, the fact that *tĕhôm* is etymologically related to Tiamat as a cognate should not be taken as an evidence for the mythological dependence of the former on the latter." The result is what von Rad describes as "an increasing disinclination to interpret the concepts contained in v. 2 in terms of the mythological conceptions of neighbouring religions" (*Genesis*, OTL [based on the 9th German edition], p. 50), Day, for example, explicitly stating that "it is improbable that the account of creation in Gen. 1 is dependent on Enuma elish at all" (*Ibid.*, p. 51; cf. Dalley's assessment that "Differences between *Enūma Eliš* and Genesis 1 make it hard for us to know if the biblical author was familiar with the Babylonian account" ["The Influence of Mesopotamia upon Israel and the Bible", in *The Legacy of Mesopotamia*, p. 65]).

21 On the primacy of the waters in Egyptian and some Greek cosmologies, see Lambert, *JTS* 16 n.s. (1965), p. 293, whilst the creation traditions of Sumer, Babylon, Egypt and Greece are surveyed in Schmidt, *Schöpfungsgeschichte*, pp. 21-9. The possible links between Gen. 1 and Egyptian precedents has been the subject of various studies: see e.g. V. Notter, *Biblischer Schöpfungsbericht und ägyptische Schöpfungsmythen* (Studies in Biblical Theology 68; Stuttgart: Katholisches Bibelwerk, 1974).

waters (one might say, as a reversion to "primeval chaos"), in which "all the fountains of the great deep burst forth, and the windows of the heavens were opened" (Gen. 7:11). However, this is again entirely at the instigation of, and within the control of, God and is thus comparable to the description of the smaller-scale destruction of the Egyptian foe at the Red Sea as it is portrayed in Ex. 15, but wholly at variance with the world-view which may result within a polytheistic system.

Nevertheless, the high monotheistic theology and solemn liturgical cadences of P need not merely be contrasted with extra-biblical polytheistic systems, since, on a more limited scale, it stands at one end of the variegated spectrum of Old Testament theology, at the other end of which may be placed the intense eschatological utterances of Isa. 24-27 and, in a different sense, the poetic outpourings of Job. Since each of these, together with Isa. 51:9-11, contains allusions which have frequently been explained as relating to "chaos", it remains to be determined whether there is any validity in these claims, and whether the Old Testament indeed contains both passages which deny or ignore the possibility of a struggle with "chaos" and others which affirm it. The texts to be analysed include two relating to the sea (Job 38:8-11, 9:8), a brief allusion to the sea and a dragon (Job 7:12), four occurrences of "Rahab" (Isa. 51:9-11, Job 26:12, 9:13, besides Isa. 30:7, where a literalistic use is usually recognised), and two of Leviathan (Isa. 27:1, Job 3:8), in addition to the very extended portrayal of Behemoth and Leviathan in Job 40-41. These shall each be considered in turn. However, in view of the broad developmental schema advanced in Chapter 10 above, it remains first to comment briefly on the date of the material here to be analysed, before embarking on the exegesis proper.

1. The Dating of the "Chaos" References of Job and Isaiah 27, 30, 51

The texts to be analysed may, with the exception of Isa. 30:7,[22] be dated with confidence subsequent to the fall of Jerusalem in c. 587 B.C., probably in the case of Isa. 27:1 and quite possibly also in that of Job, to a time considerably later than this, perhaps even near the close of the Old Testament era. Though the dating of Job is unlikely to be resolved with certainty and a wide spectrum of proposals have been made, there are few who would attempt to date the book of Job prior to the exile, even if some underlying traditions of the story of Job may be considerably more ancient. Although there are linguistic characteristics of the book which might seem to be consonant with a very early origin, they are probably more plausibly to be explained as due to conscious archaising in a late period, or to dialectic influence from the north, to which it may owe its authorship. Thus, Robertson, in his survey of *Linguistic Evidence*, recognised that his findings might seem to suggest a very early date for the book of Job, but at the same time acknowledged the

22 On which see below and the briefer remarks made above in Chapter 6.

unlikelihood that this would gain acceptance, emphasising instead the "extremely tenuous" nature of chronologies based on the relative density of standard and archaic verbal forms.[23]

The occurrence of the literalistic reference to Egypt-Rahab in the pre-exilic context of Isa. 30:7, whilst the remaining extra-Psalteric references to Rahab and Leviathan appear in literature to be dated post-587 B.C., is consonant with the conclusions drawn in respect of the Psalter. However, whether the absence or underplaying of the theme of a combat with "chaos" pertains in these passages also is still to be determined. Nevertheless, irrespective of these findings, the conclusions drawn with respect to the absence of the *Chaoskampf* theme in the earliest period and the ramifications of this for the understanding of the history of religion in Israel, remain.

2. The Theme of "Chaos" in Job and Isaiah 27, 30, 51

Most of the passages to be considered make allusion either to Rahab or to Leviathan. Such references sometimes appear quite disparate, with Leviathan, for example, on one hand being associated with darkness and death (Job 3:8), and on another apparently appearing as a creature of the natural world (Job 40:25-41:26), whilst in a third passage he appears in a more representative inimical guise (Isa. 27:1). Elsewhere, connections may be more apparent, with the use of "Rahab" as a simple nation-name in Isa. 30:7 paralleling the usage in Ps. 87:4, whilst comparisons are frequently drawn between Isa. 51:9-10 and Ps. 89:10-11 (again referring to Rahab), and more obscure links emerge between Job 3:8 and 26:12-13 (the first mentioning Leviathan, the second Rahab). It therefore seems profitable to organise the discussion according to the figure named therein, in order to attempt to discern any patterns which may emerge and to determine the associative spheres of each. At the same time an openness to any interconnections between Leviathan and Rahab also needs to be maintained, and it will be necessary to reflect carefully on this once the detailed analysis of the pertinent passages has been concluded.

The corpus here considered also includes three references to the sea (Job 38:8-11, 9:8, 7:12), in the last, brief, instance, also in connection with an unnamed תַּנִּין. In Job 7:12 and 38:8-11 the idea of the confinement of the sea may be present, whilst an association with creation seems likely both in this latter case and in 9:8. Each of these passages shall now be examined, before the material relating to Rahab and Leviathan is discussed in detail.

---

23 *Linguistic Evidence*, pp. 155-6.

i. Passages including an Allusion to the Waters: Job 38:8-11, 9:8, 7:12

Job 38:8-11

Job 38:8-11 has been widely cited as a prime example of the "chaos" motif, but close attention to the language of this passage, or even a relatively cursory consideration of its imagery, indicates that this assumption plays scant heed to its essential force and extraordinary mode of expression. Any interpretation must take account of the obvious fact, already identified by Newsom, that "this pericope radically departs from traditional imagery... in that it does not cast the sea as God's opponent in battle... but instead represents God as the midwife who births the sea and wraps it in the swaddling bands of darkness and cloud."[24] Hence, if it is to be understood in relation to the *Chaoskampf* theme, it must be as a challenge to its assumptions, either as a conscious rewriting of the motif of the confining of the sea or through the expression of an alternative, but otherwise unattested, tradition.[25]

In couching the familiar motif of the confinement of the sea in terms of its birth, with God as the midwife tending to its needs, the writer skilfully expresses himself in language which is appropriate both to the care of a newborn infant and to the nature of the sea itself. The idea of "hedging about" (סוך) echoes the accusation made by the Satan in 1:10 that God had "put a hedge about [Job] and his house and all that he has, on every side" (1:10); the infant sea is here subject to the same protective care,[26] even as the language employed might also be employed to denote limitation (3:23).[27]

24 *The Book of Job*, p. 244. It is this caring aspect of God's interaction with the sea and the very nature of dependent infancy that renders particularly improbable Day's claim that "the allusion to the sea as a newborn child with swaddling clothes in vv. 8b-9 ... hints at the personification of the sea in the underlying myth" (*God's Conflict*, p. 43). Similarly the clothing of this metaphorical infant suggests a human form which undermines Habel's assumption (p. 534) of a reference to a "baby chaos monster" here.

25 See similarly Alter, *The Art of Biblical Poetry*, p. 99: "In God's own words that martial story [of the Canaanite cosmogonic myth of a triumph by force over an archaic sea monster] is set aside, or at the very least left in the distant background, so that the cosmogony can instead be rendered in terms of procreation". Compare also Fuch's description of the passage as "a loving ironical treatment; the sea is integrated and civilised" (*Mythos*, p. 200).

26 Thus, as Alter recognises (*The Art of Biblical Poetry*, p. 100), "The verb, in its various conjugations,... generally suggests a shading or sheltering act, as with a wing or canopy... The Creator... is actively blocking off, bolting in, the surge of the sea, but the word carries after it a long train of associations having to do with protection and nurture... What results is a virtual oxymoron, expressing a paradoxical feeling that God's creation involves a necessary holding in check of destructive forces and a sustaining of those same forces because they are also forces of life."

27 In fact, if the normative, positive sense is encountered in 1:10, and the Job of 3:23, characteristically, takes up a received idea only to distort it, Yahweh in 38:8

Similarly, יָצָא, though a common verb used in a variety of contexts, is applicable both to flowing water (cf., e.g., Gen. 2:10, Ex. 17:6, Judg. 15:19) and to the context of birth (Job 1:21, 3:11, 38:29, Gen. 38:28, 29, 30 and frequently). Although the verb גִּיחַ may be utilised in relation to gushing water (Job 40:23; cf. the name of the spring גִּיחוֹן, 1 Ki. 1:33 etc.), it too is particularly familiar from the language of birth. In each case, the verb is applied to the agent bringing the child to birth, either the divine "midwife" "drawing forth" the child from the womb (Ps. 22:10), or the mother "pushing it forth" in labour at the moment of birth (Mi. 4:10). It is likely, therefore, that such an idea may be present here, in which case, the personal involvement of Yahweh would be envisaged, and the suffixal form should be interpreted as in Ps. 22:10 as referring to the drawing forth of the infant.[28] Consonant with this ambience of care, the womb is here denoted by רֶחֶם, cognate with רַחֲמִים, "compassion" and רחם, "love", Pi. "have compassion".

The divine parent, further, clothes the infant sea, עָנָן and עֲרָפֶל being particularly the covering of God:[29] perhaps it is in his own robe that he clothes this baby, the cloud (עָנָן) of the Exodus (normally perceived as a sign of the divine presence) being spread as a protective covering also in Ps. 105:39. However, clouds and darkness are undoubtedly also appropriate to the cosmic scale envisaged here. A locale above the heavens, referring to the celestial ocean, may also be implied by this terminology, since this is the only likely setting for clouds, whilst the space above the firmament, on which the luminaries were set, was presumably shrouded in darkness.[30] Swaddling continues the double applicability to a baby and to the unruly sea, since it restrains and calms the child in a reassuring manner akin to the confines of the womb. At the same time, it is a mark of care and compassion: compare Ezek. 16:4-5.

---

reformulates the motif in order to undermine Job's governing assumptions, reinstating the positive where the negative might be expected, or revealing that protection and restriction are not incompatible alternatives, but may be operative at the same time.

28 This certainly seems more plausible than the interpretation of this Qal verb in terms of an isolated occurrence referring, in the Hiph'il, to men "rushing out" in ambush (Judg. 20:33; see Habel, p. 539, Gordis, p. 444), especially given the self-evident context of birth.

29 E.g., Deut. 4:11, 5:22 (19), Ps. 97:2.

30 Contrast the apprehension of Tromp (*Primitive Conceptions*, p. 131) that the reference is here to the netherworld. However, although support could be offered for his interpretation if the "womb" of v. 8 were to be envisaged subterrestrially, as in the Qumran Targum, it cannot be assumed that a specific cosmic location is intended in this probably rather conceptually-grounded image; compare the questions relating to the birth and parentage of rain, dew, ice and frost in vv. 28-29, which should probably similarly be understood without reference to a precise geographical origin. Another possibility is that it is from "the primordial mists over the surface of the deep" that the swaddling bands are formed (Alter, *The Art of Biblical Poetry*, p. 99); cf. the idea of a "cloud of mist" (עָב טַל; RSV "cloud of dew"), Isa. 18:4.

However, no responsible parenting is complete without the setting of boundaries, and this is not least the case as regards the role of the ancient father. In the words of Prov. 13:24, "He who spares the rod hates his son, but he who loves him is diligent to discipline him". Here such harsh enforcement is not seen as necessary, and indeed safety barriers akin to the modern playpen or stairgate may well be all that is envisaged. Clearly, in an ancient household, where a wife was expected to continue her domestic responsibilities whilst simultaneously guarding her children from its numerous hazards, such as open fires, livestock and potentially dangerous tools, barriers, whether verbal or physical, were essential to the toddler's safety and no doubt firmly applied.[31] At the same time, as is consonant with the focus of the opening challenge of 38:2, the ordering of the cosmos is in chapter 38 expressed through the lens of the setting of boundaries and limits, those structural elements which are essential to the cosmic design of Yahweh.[32] Such barriers are in any case particularly applicable to the nature of the sea and the necessity of its confinement, and the same idea is encountered elsewhere in such passages as Ps. 104:9, Prov. 8:29 and Jer. 5:22. What is striking, however, is that it should be couched in terms of parental care and protectiveness, and prefaced by the presentation of the sea as a newborn. As a result, as Carol Newsom observes, "The metaphorical filter diminishes the sense of the sea as a hostile, alien power and associates it rather with the vigor of new life."[33]

Verse 11b is awkward, since the force of the preposition בְּ as prefixed to גְּאוֹן is difficult to discern, unless a complement, such as חֹק from v. 10, is to be assumed.[34] Though it is possible this consonant should simply be omitted, its transference into the preceding word, resulting in the reading יִשְׁבֹּת גְּאוֹן, would make good sense, the MT then being explicable as having arisen through a scribal error.[35] Fortunately, however, the general meaning, referring

31 Note, for example, Meyers' perception that "women's productive work was largely unaffected by maternal activities" ("The Family in Early Israel" in L. G. Perdue, J. Blenkinsopp, J. J. Collins and C. Meyers, *Families in Ancient Israel* [The Family, Religion and Culture; Louisville, KY: Westminster John Knox Press, 1997] 1-47, p. 28) and her comments on their "extraordinarily large workload" (*Ibid*., p. 25).

32 This has often been noted elsewhere: see, e.g., Newsom, *The Book of Job*, pp. 241-2, 243-4, Habel, p. 532.

33 *The Book of Job*, pp. 244. At the same time, "V. 10f. removes any basis for the battle with the sea. The imperial divine word is enough" (Fuchs, *Mythos*, p. 200).

34 For the difficulties with this, see Dhorme, p. 529.

35 This emendation, which was originally proposed by Bickell, is noted in *BHS*, and followed also by Gordis, p. 445; the same meaning is achieved by Blommerde (*Northwest Semitic Grammar and Job* [Biblica et Orientalia 22], 1969), p. 133; followed by Habel, p. 521) by proposing a verb *šbb* "break" [(Ugaritic *ṯbb*)] with infixed *-t-* (vocalised as יִשְׁתַּבֵּ), but the existence of this verb is doubtful (see Pope, p. 294). Various alternatives are documented in Rowley, p. 243. The LXX and Vulgate seem to translate as if the verbs of 10a and 11b should be transposed, and this may also be implied by the Syriac; the same reading is followed also by Merx (pp. 175-7), Wright (pp. 96-7) and Fuchs (*Mythos*, p. 194; cf. similarly Ewald in respect of v. 11, p.

to the placing of limits on the surging of the waves of the sea, is clear. It has nevertheless been claimed that the reference to גְּאוֹן גַּלֶּיךָ (translated as "your proud waves") "hints at the personal conflict existing between the sea and Yahweh".[36] However, the verb גאה actually means "rise up", hence Ezek. 47:5 "the waters had risen", and the meaning "rising up, swelling" as applied to the sea is evident for two cognate nouns, גַּאֲוָה in Ps. 46:4 and גֵּאוּת in Ps. 89:10. It therefore seems most likely that a similar force, referring to the lifting up of the waves or to the high tide, is operative here, as suits the context.[37] Hence the Vulgate translates *tumentes fluctus tuos* ("your swelling waves"), whilst the LXX κυματα (literally "swells [of the sea]", i.e. waves) probably reflects the same idea, one which is made explicit by Symmachus (το ἐπαρμα των κυματων σου).

Job 38:8-11 thus encapsulates both the potential unruliness of the sea, which necessitates firm governance and the setting of boundaries, and the importance of this body as a child nurtured by God with a valued part in creation. This has already partially been grasped, for example by Alter, who recognises that "God's creation involves a necessary holding in check of destructive forces and a sustaining of those same forces because they are also forces of life."[38] Thus, "what we are invited to imagine... is creation not as the laying low of a foe but as the damming up and channeling of powers nevertheless allowed to remain active."[39] Although restraint is depicted, and the dangerous power of the sea is recognised (as it is universally), the

---

291), whilst Gordis makes a plausible case for translating שׁבר itself as "decree, decide" (p. 444). Is it possible that conventional phrases referring to the setting of boundaries and the breaking of waves have deliberately had their verbs transposed in order, in "festive and incongruous" mode (Habel's terminology to describe the "celebrative" aspects of this speech, p. 532), to hint at the divine maximisation of the sea and limitation of the land, where the "boundary" is "broken" for the sea and its uplifted waves "set" to reach a fixed point?

36 Day, *God's Conflict*, p. 43.

37 Moreover, when applied personally, this semantic group can have both positive and negative implications, communicating such qualities as "majesty" or "exaltation" as well as the more pejorative "pride". Attestations of the term גָּאוֹן, unlike those of גַּאֲוָה, employed in 40:11-12, fall in the vast majority of cases into the former category, so even a negative subsidiary nuance of "pride" cannot be assumed in preference to a more celebratory term such as "exalted" or "majestic" here. (Cf. Habel's very apt highlighting of the celebratory motifs of this speech, p. 532.) In any case, reference to the swelling waves must take precedence as the chief, or possibly the sole, focus of allusion.

38 *The Art of Biblical Poetry*, p. 100. Compare similarly Balentine's statement that Job is here "invited to understand that God intends not to eliminate or banish forces of opposition and challenge but to preserve and direct them, because they are vital elements in the architecture of life" ("'What are Human Beings, That You Make So Much of Them?' Divine Disclosure from the Whirlwind: 'Look at Behemoth'" in T. Linafelt, and T. Beal, [edd.], *God in the Fray. A Tribute to Walter Brueggemann* [Minneapolis, MN: Fortress, 1998] 259-78, p. 267).

39 Alter, *The Art of Biblical Poetry*, pp. 99-100.

language of combat is absent; rather, the depiction of God's protective care of the newborn sea represents the antithesis of *Chaoskampf*, both in its appreciation of the need to nurture this great body of water and in the assumption of God's unchallenged parenting and ordering of the world, before which the sea stands not in antagonism but in infantile dependence.

Job 9:8

A further context in which an allusion to "chaos" in its oceanic manifestation has been claimed is Job 9:8b. Albright proposed[40] that the colon "should be read as though it were in a Ugaritic context, with *bmt* meaning 'back', and rendered, 'and Who treads on the back of Yam'", and this has been reflected in a number of subsequent translations.[41] In fact Ugaritic seems to attest to both anatomical and topographical senses,[42] as does Akkadian,[43] so this cannot be viewed as offering a constraint upon the interpretation of the present verse. Anyway, the reference should most naturally be interpreted in

40 In a review of Hölscher, *Das Buch Hiob*, *JBL* 57 (1938) p. 227, and iterating the same essential point in "The Psalm of Habakkuk" in H. H. Rowley (ed.), *Studies in Old Testament Prophecy* (Edinburgh: T. & T. Clark, 1950) 1-18, p. 18.

41 E.g., RSV mg., NEB, Newsom (*NIB*, IV, p. 410), M. K. Wakeman ("The Biblical Earth Monster in the Cosmogonic Combat Myth", *JBL* 88 [1969] 313-320, p. 314; *God's Battle with the Monster*, p. 118), Vaughan (*The Meaning of 'Bāmâ*, p. 10), Clines (p. 213), Pope (p. 68), Gordis (p. 96), Good (*In Turns of Tempest*, p. 71), and Michel (*Job in the Light of Northwest Semitic*, I, p. 205), the latter of whom, unusually, but rather awkwardly, follows the implication of the Hebrew form בָּמֳתֵי in translating with the plural, "backs". Others retain the term "back" but eschew draconic personification by rendering יָם as "the sea" (thus Hartley, p. 168, and, with a further variation for בָּמֳתֵי, Tur-Sinai ["treadeth upon the body of the sea"], pp. 156, 157-8). Reference to the "waves" of the sea is still made by Crenshaw, "'Wedōrēk 'al-bāmŏtê 'āreṣ'" *CBQ* 34 (1972) 39-53, p. 47, Day, *God's Conflict*, p. 40, Terrien, p. 94, Guillaume (translating "high storm waves"), p. 27, and Dhorme, p. 118, whilst "heights" ("*Höhen*") are mentioned, e.g., by Horst (p. 137).

42 Contra the assertions of Pope (p. 70: "The cognate word in Ugaritic texts always designates the 'back' of an animal or a god.") and Gordis (p. 103); cf. P. H. Vaughan, *The Meaning of 'Bāmâ' in the Old Testament: A Study of Etymological, Textual and Archaeological Evidence* (Society for Old Testament Study Monograph Series; Cambridge: CUP, 1974), pp. 5-6. In fact, although the former meaning is more common, there is wide agreement that the latter is attested in *KTU* 1.4.vii.34 (thus, e.g., Smith in *UNP*, p. 137, Wyatt, *RTU*, p. 109, Gibson, *CML*, p. 65, Driver, *CML*, p. 101).

43 See especially the discussion of Vaughan, *The Meaning of 'Bāmâ' in the Old Testament*, pp. 7-9, where he suggests the meaning "hilly slopes or foot-hills surrounding cities" for Akkadian *bamâtu*, and states that "the Hebrew expression *bāmoṯê 'ereṣ* is generally accepted as being equivalent to Akkadian *bamât šadî*."

the light of the other biblical occurrences of the form בָּמֳתֵי,[44] which almost invariably occurs in the stock poetic context of Yahweh treading (דרך) upon בָּמֳתֵי אֶרֶץ, or the like, or causing another to do so. The fact that such expressions occur some dozen times suggests that they comprise a set, and probably very ancient, poetic formula.[45] As Vaughan recognises, their "exact significance...is no doubt lost to us now; but it is clear that treading upon *bām°tê 'ereṣ* is essentially a divine activity, possible [*sic.*] indicating ownership of the land."[46] However, there is no reason to regard such phraseology as anything other than metaphorical, as shown by Crenshaw.[47] For the idea of ownership, one might compare, for example, Deut. 11:24, "every place on which the sole of your foot treads shall be yours" (cf. also Gen. 13:17, Deut. 1:36, 11:25, Josh. 14:9, Mic. 5:4-5).[48] That it is the idea of possession (rather than of trampling a foe) which pertains, is evident from the context in which such phrases occur (there being only one other, uncertain, instance in which the meaning "back" might be possible),[49] and from the accompanying verbs employed. Although דרך[50] may be subject to either interpretation (ownership or subjugation), the idea of motion is conveyed by

---

44 This should normally be contrasted with the alternative, but distinct, construct form בָּמוֹת, applied to cultic installations: see P. H. Vaughan, *The Meaning of 'Bāmâ' in the Old Testament*, pp. 9-13.

45 Thus similarly Vaughan, *The Meaning of 'Bāmâ'*, p. 9.

46 *The Meaning of 'Bāmâ'*, p. 9. The nuance of kingship or dominion may also (though perhaps more as an undertone) be implied by דרך, since, as noted by Crenshaw ("'Wedōrēk 'al-bāmŏtê 'āreṣ'", p. 39, n. 1), the Ugaritic "*drkt* occurs a number of times in the sense of sovereignty, power, and throne", and this seems to provide the most plausible interpretation of certain biblical instances of the noun, some of which would otherwise be found problematic, e.g. in Prov. 8:22, 19:16, Hos. 10:13; see also Prov. 31:3, Am 8:14, Job 26:14, 40:19. The issue is discussed further in M. Dahood, "Ugaritic Drkt and Biblical Derek" *ThSt* 15 (1954) 627-631, *Psalms I, 1-50* p. 2, and Michel, *Job in the Light of Northwest Semitic*, I, pp. 205-6, the latter also providing a bibliography (n. 28, pp. 205-6).

47 "'Wedōrēk 'al-bāmŏtê 'āreṣ'" *CBQ* 34 (1972) 39-53: see especially his concluding summary, pp. 52-3.

48 This is a fundamental aspect to territorial claims, reflected in such diverse spheres as animal behaviour, children's play, military conflict and even the old law of possessory title.

49 Namely Deut. 33:29, where, unusually, the subject is human (Israel) and בָּמוֹתֵימוֹ independent of any construct relation; compare Ezek. 36:2 for the idea of taking possession of the במות of another nation, walking upon the mountains and possession again being connected in Ezek. 36:12. Vaughan (*The Meaning of 'Bāmâ'*, p. 10) further translates Isa. 14:14a (אֶעֱלֶה עַל־בָּמֳתֵי עָב) as "I will rise upon the back of a cloud", but there the choice of English terminology simply reflects the analogy with riding which may be the subject of the allusion, rather than the attribution of anatomical characteristics to, or the personification of, the clouds.

50 Which occurs in conjunction with בָּמֳתֵי, besides the present verse, in Deut. 33:29, Amos 4:13, Mic. 1:3, and Hab. 3:19.

the alternatives רכב[51] and עלה.[52] Treading, riding, and ascending are congruent with sovereign possession and the freedom of this territory, but the latter two activities seem incompatible with the crushing of a foe. In the context of Job 9:8, therefore, the idea conveyed by the parallelism seems to be akin to Ps. 95:5, "his, for he made it": God spread out the heavens and, as its owner, has the undisturbed freedom of the sea, most probably, given the continued reference to the celestial sphere in the following verse, that of the heavens. Some have suggested here the emendation of יָם to עָב ("clouds"), following the evidence of three manuscripts,[53] and this would indeed suit the context admirably, being comparable to Isa. 14:14 and related also to the motif of God as riding on the clouds (as in Deut. 33:26, Isa. 19:1, Ps. 68:5, 34). In either case, the association with the theophany tradition already alluded to in the preceding triplet (vv. 5-7) is evident.[54]

It has been claimed by Wakeman that underlying biblical references to the trampling of the בָּמֳתֵי־אָרֶץ is the idea of a divine conflict with an "earth-monster", akin to the battle with the "chaotic" sea.[55] However, such a

---

51 Deut. 32:13, Isa. 58:14.

52 Isa. 14:14 may have the sense "go up upon", i.e., "mount", here reflecting the divine attribute of riding on the clouds: see Vaughan, *The Meaning of 'Bāmâ'*, pp. 10-11. However, the alternative translation, "I will ascend above the בָּמֳתֵי עָב", expressed, e.g., in the RSV, is no less dynamic. עמד, which is applied to the psalmist (stated to be David), in Ps. 18:34 = 2 Sam. 22:34, perhaps reflects the more limited aspirations (or potential) of the human subject, and belongs to a different sphere of imagery, where the focus is on security, akin to the surefootedness of a hind; cf. Hab. 3:19.

53 E.g., Fohrer, p. 198, de Wilde, pp. 137, 141-2; cf. K.-D. Schunck, "בָּמָה", in G. J. Botterweck and H. Ringgren (edd.), *TWAT*, I (Stuttgart: W. Kohlhammer, 1973) 662-7, p. 662. Fohrer considers that this type of terminology is required by the sequence of vv. 5-9 (mountains, earth, sun and stars, sky, [clouds], stars), although were the sea of v. 8 to be regarded as the celestial one, the apparent incongruity would be substantially abated.

54 The theophanic associations of vv. 5-6 have been highlighted especially by Jeremias (*Theophanie*, pp. 23-4, 89, 123-4, 161; cf. also, e.g., Crenshaw, "'Wedōrēk 'al-bāmŏtê 'āreṣ'", p. 47), and similarly pertinent is Vaughan's assertion, made in respect of Mic. 1:3, that בָּמֳתֵי־אָרֶץ "refers to some mythological mountains on which Yahweh was visualised as walking, when he appeared in theophany" (*The Meaning of 'Bāmâ' in the Old Testament*, pp. 11-12; the wider theophanic contexts of occurrences of the phrase such as Deut. 33:29, Hab. 3:19 and Ps. 18:34 = 2 Sam. 22:34 are also evident). This is particularly important insofar as the same background pertains to the parallel colon, v. 8a, since Habel has concluded ("'He Who Stretches out the Heavens'", *CBQ* 34 (1972) 417-430, p. 430) that "the formula 'stretching out the heavens' in the context of Pss 18, 104, 144 and Job 26 suggests that the *Chaoskampf* motif itself is not the primary element in the meaning of this formula. Rather, the heavens are 'pitched' as a sacred world tent where Yahweh 'comes' to reveal himself in theophanic splendour and exercise his kingship as creator, lord and redeemer."

55 M. K. Wakeman, "The Biblical Earth Monster in the Cosmogonic Combat Myth" *JBL* 88 (1969) 313-320, pp. 319-320, and *God's Battle with the Monster*, pp. 118-120; cf. Michel, *Job in the Light of Northwest Semitic*, I, p. 206.

proposal appears superfluous to the biblical passages in which אֶרֶץ occurs, since nowhere is reference to a monster required by the context, and the same may also be stated in respect of the Ugaritic and Mesopotamian data.[56] Not surprisingly, therefore, her thesis has been widely dismissed as implausible. As regards the idea of the trampling down of the enemy sea, this has found more supporters, but of course on the basis of the presupposition that the subjugation of the sea is a motif attested in a number of other instances in the Old Testament, an assumption which the present study has found to be questionable. Such an interpretation would seem to distance this allusion from the related occurrences of דרך עַל בָּמֳתֵי, and is tenable also only on the basis that בָּמֳתֵי comprises a "plural of local extension" or that the monster Sea had "many loops ('backs')".[57] It therefore seems preferable here, as apparently is the case in all other contexts in the Old Testament, to understand יָם in its straightforward, geographical sense, rather than in relation to a mythological or divine entity.

Job 7:12

As in other sections of the speeches of Job, chapter 7 expresses extreme negativity and cynicism concerning the nature of human existence and the ways of God in a manner which represents a distortion of the traditions which the author had inherited. Thus v. 17 ("What is man, that thou dost make so much of him...?") may be contrasted with Ps. 8:5 ("what is man, that thou art mindful of him...?"); similarly, the description of God as "thou watcher of men (הָאָדָם נֹצֵר)" in v. 20 is here employed negatively to characterise him as a persecutor, in contrast to the protective rôle usually denoted by this verb (cf., e.g., Deut. 32:10, Isa. 49:8, Ps. 31:24, Prov. 2:8).[58] Probability and context therefore strongly suggest that the accusatory outburst against God in v. 12 should be regarded not as a mere restatement of received ideas, but as a heightening or original reinterpretation of pre-existing material in line with

---

56 See, e.g., Day, *God's Conflict*, pp. 84-5, Vaughan, *The Meaning of 'Bāmâ'*, p. 59 n. 28.

57 As proposed by Vaughan, p. 60 n. 33, though favouring the former option; for the latter, see Michel, *Job in the Light of Northwest Semitic*, I, p. 205. Vaughan has maintained that since the term בָּמָה is etymologically unconnected to the meaning "heights", it is therefore not applicable to the sea viewed as a topographical entity. However, since he has argued for the meaning "flank" or the like, understood as "hilly slopes or foot-hills" (p. 8), "[mountain] slopes" (p. 12) or even "mountains" (p. 24) in respect of the phrase בָּמֳתֵי אָרֶץ, it is difficult to imagine why this could not be transferable to the waves of the sea, especially given the heavily traditional nature of the term in such a context. In any case, "the primary sense" identified by Vaughan as "the concept of 'ribcage'" (p. 10) seems superbly fitted to the idiom of Job 9:8, since waves may be thought of as shaped—in cross-section—like one side of a rib cage, or the sea, viewed aerially, might appear "ribbed" with waves.

58 On this aspect of the Book of Job, see K. J. Dell, *The Book of Job as Sceptical Literature* (BZAW 197; Berlin: de Gruyter, 1991).

the speaker's peculiarly negative purpose, or as a free composition. Clearly the gist of the sufferer's words is to the effect: am I something really harmful or dangerous, which might need to be watched over, that I am subject to your ceaseless persecutions?

However, the more precise significance of the verse is uncertain, since the absence of the article for יָם and תַּנִּין, compounded with the lack of any qualifying personal name which might offer a clue to the identity of the תַּנִּין here mentioned, leaves open the question of whether these should be understood as common or proper nouns, and whether תַּנִּין (and even יָם)[59] is definite or indefinite. Normally, one might hope to resolve this issue on the basis of the context, but the reference itself is so terse and isolated from any adjacent allusion which might offer illumination that the task of interpretation is to a great extent dependent on "reading between the lines". In practice, this entails reliance on evidence adduced from texts thought to offer some parallel to the reference here. Inevitably, most have sought to find a reference to the confining (and even imprisonment) of powers of "chaos". In the absence of appropriate Canaanite parallels, this has involved adducing mainly Babylonian material, and suggesting that since the theme occurs elsewhere in the Old Testament it should be recognised here also.

Of course, especially in the absence of clear internal evidence, of itself, adducing inner-biblical material which seems to offer a real parallel in its language and sphere of reference seems methodologically appropriate. However, the results of the current analysis of Old Testament passages thought to manifest the "chaos" theme indicates that at the very least its presence has been very significantly overplayed and that it may be absent from this material altogether. Moreover, the terms יָם and תַּנִּין rarely occur in close proximity, and where they do, there appears to be no intrinsic connection between them. In Ps. 74:13, the most often-cited reference made in this connection (even though תַּנִּין is there in the plural), it seems that sequential action is described in relation to one particular historical event, and the same applies in Isa. 51:9-10. In Isa. 27:1, "the dragon" is simply said to be "in the sea", so there is no implication of their confederation; one might compare similarly Ezek. 32:2 (כַּתַּנִּים בַּיַּמִּים). Yet if this analysis is correct, it seriously undermines the supposition that יָם and תַּנִּין are paired keywords which may confidently be associated with "chaos" in every instance. The extra-biblical material cited in support of the discernment of an allusion to "chaos" in Job 7:12 is also of doubtful assistance in ascertaining the meaning of the verse, as shall be shown below.

However, it must at the same time be acknowledged that if there is little intrinsic to the verse which might encourage a *Chaoskampf* interpretation, its brevity also entails that the refutation of such an approach or the offering of an alternative sphere of reference inevitably has a narrower basis than is the case elsewhere. This is especially so if the tendency to seek exegetical leads outside the biblical material is eschewed and an attempt is made to confine

59 Cf. Ewald, p. 111, who mentions "a sea, or a living monster of the sea" as the two elements here depicted as under watch.

the interpretation as narrowly as possible to the Hebrew context itself. Nevertheless, even here, there are indications that an allusion to "chaos" cannot be assumed and indeed that it does not present itself as the most probable sphere of reference, as the following analysis of the verse will indicate.

The sense of the phrase תָּשִׂים עָלַי מִשְׁמָר seems to be fairly clear, as מִשְׁמָר is commonly employed to refer to a watch or guard.[60] As Newsom states, this image "appears not to be drawn specifically from a myth but represents [Job's] interpretation of his own situation."[61] Although in certain contexts, מִשְׁמָר may denote a prison, this is evidently not the case here, as it would ill correlate with the expression שִׂים עַל;[62] moreover, the nature of Job's complaint is that he finds himself under constant surveillance, not that he is in any sense imprisoned. Where the meaning "watch" pertains, this is nowhere in relation to those in captivity, whereas "the aspect of surveillance is very much a part of the concept".[63] It is therefore surprising that certain commentators have sought to draw a comparison between this verse and the reference to the taking captive, imprisonment and binding of the forces of Tiamat in *Enuma elish*, IV.111-120.[64] Since it is thought by recent writers that the source of the Bible's conflict allusions is not Babylonian, but Canaanite, it is then claimed, at risk of circularity, that "one may presume that the Canaanite myth used similar language".[65] However, it appears that an

60 Cf. Jer. 51:12, Neh. 4:3, 16, 17, 7:3, 12:24, 25, 1 Chr. 26:16, Prov. 4:23.

61 Newsom, *NIB*, IV, P. 395. See similarly Diewert, "Job 7:12", pp. 210, 215.

62 Also unlikely is Dahood's proposal, adduced from *KTU* 1.3.iii.40, that מִשְׁמָר should here be translated "muzzle" ("Mišmār 'muzzle' in Job 7 12", *JBL* 80 [1961] 270-1; followed by Habel, p. 153), since this has been widely rejected both on the grounds of its inapplicability to Job, and of its dubious etymology: see further J. Barr, "Ugaritic and Hebrew '*šbm*'?" *JSS* 18 (1973) 17-39, Pope, p. 61, Grabbe, *Comparative Philology and the Text of Job* (SBLDS 34; Scholars, Press, 1977), pp. 55-8. Moreover, as Diewert aptly states, "whatever the precise meaning of *šbm* in Ugaritic, its relevance for Job 7:12 seems peripheral. *Mišmār* is a perfectly common word in biblical Hebrew stemming from the familiar root *šmr*. There is no compelling reason to replace it with a substantive from the root *šbm*, which is not attested in biblical Hebrew, nor to propose a unique meaning for *mišmār* supported solely by a desire to create a parallel with the Ugaritic passage, which is itself uncertain" ("Job 7:12: *Yam, Tannin* and the Surveillance of Job", *JBL* 106 [1982], 203-215, p. 207). Likewise, Dhorme's translation "barrier", made on the basis of Jer. 51:12 (p. 94), is questionable even in that isolated instance; moreover, although it may be congruent with the motif of the confining of the sea behind a barrier (Jer. 5:22), it would ill fit the situation of Job and should therefore be rejected.

63 Thus Newsom, *NIB*, IV, p. 395, comparing Neh. 4:16-17 (ET 4:22-23). Diewert convincingly draws out the importance of this theme by showing the close structural relationship between vv. 12 and 17, which indicates that they should be read together ("Job 7:12", pp. 210-15).

64 *ANET*, p. 67. Thus, e.g., Day, *God's Conflict*, p. 45.

65 Thus Day, *God's Conflict*, p. 43, comparing the reference to Yam as "our captive" in *KTU* 1.2.iv.29-30, from which state he is "immediately afterwards killed" (*Ibid.*, p. 44).

influencing factor here, as explicitly stated by Day,[66] is the presupposition that "the expressions used, *yām* and *tannīn*, indicate that we are in the realm of Canaanite mythology". Hence, it seems probable (especially given the very doubtful nature of the putative connection with *Enuma elish*) that the line of reasoning has in this case gone from the acceptance of the presence of an allusion to "chaos", here considered to have derived from outside Israel, to the seeking of points of contact with ancient Near Eastern material thought to manifest the same theme, even where such parallels might not be apparent from an exegetically "neutral" perspective. In fact, the frequency with which the association is made between *ym* and *tnn* as agents of "chaos" renders it easy to overlook the fact that in the extant Ugaritic material these two common nouns appear in proximity, besides *KTU* 1.83, only in a list of the conquests of Anat (*KTU* 1.3.iii.38-40) and (if *yām* is to be understood by *ym*, rather than *yōm*) in reference to *tnn* as "in the sea" (*KTU* 1.6.vi.50). In neither case does there seem to be an intrinsic connection between *ym* and *tnn*. Moreover, although *KTU* 1.83 is too fragmentary for any certain conclusion to be drawn from it, the fact that ll. 11-12 may actually constitute an appeal to Yam to restrain the *tnn* referred to in the previous lines[67] could work against the notion of their confederacy.

But if the Ugaritic data offers little encouragement to the view that *ym* and *tnn* are virtually synonymous manifestations of cosmic "chaos", the form of Job 7:12 itself ensures that their near equivalence cannot merely be assumed,[68] since the construction אִם... הֲ, which is used to express disjunctive interrogation, may be employed to denote real, as well as merely formal, alternatives. In fact, Job 7:12 constitutes an unparalleled example in the Old Testament of the use of this formula to present a single nominal alternative in place of the standard conjunction וְ (or אוֹ, "or"); more importantly, elsewhere when the second interrogative term is followed only by a single word, in every case the contrast is a genuine one.[69] Similarly, when אִם is followed

---

Pope cites the same lines in making the similar claim that "we may safely assume that Prince Sea was not annihilated, but, as OT tradition attests, made captive and kept under guard" (pp. 61-2). However, as Diewert recognises, "It seems more likely... that Yam was indeed destroyed by Baal, as the repeated announcement 'Yam is indeed dead'... would indicate" ("Job 7:12", p. 205).

66 *God's Conflict*, p. 43.

67 Thus S. B. Parker, *UNP*, p. 192.

68 Contra, e.g., Dhorme, who states that "Tannîn...symbolise[s] the sea" (p. 94), and Gordis, who conversely claims that "יָם is the god of the sea...identified with the primordial monster (תַּנִּין...)" (p. 81; see similarly Davidson, p. 54, who refers to "the raging sea itself as a furious monster"). Fohrer seems to retain no distinction all, instead claiming that "they symbolise the chaotic sea, which is chiefly represented as a mythical monster" (p. 179).

69 The most obvious examples are the expressions אִם לֹא ... הֲ (Gen. 24:21, 27:21, 32, Ex. 16:4, Num. 11:23, Deut. 8:2, Judg. 2:22) and אִם אַיִן ... הֲ (Ex. 17:7, Num. 13:20), but compare also Num. 13:18, 19 (twice), 20; Josh. 5:13; Judg. 20:28; 1 Ki. 22:6, 15 = 2

merely by a nominal clause, in all but one instance some distinction between the sequential questions remains.[70] Hence, this calls into question any simplistic assumption of near-identity between the two alternatives here presented, and raises the possibility that יָם and תַּנִּין are distinct objects occurring sequentially in the poet's mind as potential entities over which a guard may be set, without there necessarily being an implied connection between them.

The reference to the sea[71] in the present context should not occasion surprise, and is readily explained. Although guarding of the sea is not an idea which is attested elsewhere in the Old Testament, its dangerous potential is obvious, whilst the related motif of its being confined is familiar from Job 38:8-11, Ps. 104:8-9, Prov. 8:29 and Jer. 5:22. Thus, the reference should be regarded as no more than a negative intensification by the Joban poet of the more familiar motif. Many commentators compare here *Enuma Elish*, IV.139-40,[72] in which it is stated that Marduk set up half of Tiamat as the sky, then "pulled down the bar and posted guards. He bade them not to allow her waters to escape." It would certainly be in keeping with the radical challenge to orthodoxy and provocative talk about God expressed in the speeches of Job (and not least in this one) for the imagery used to steer daringly close to the Babylonian myth. However, notable is the absence of any linguistic contact (i.e., תְּהוֹם rather than יָם) which might encourage us to think of a direct reference. Moreover, recent advocates of the theme of "chaos" in the Old Testament emphasise the closer relation of Yahwism to the mythology of ancient Ugarit, in the extant texts of which both the idea of the guarding of Yam and its cosmogonic basis seem to be absent.[73] Therefore, any connection, though not surprising of itself, may be very remote,[74] and certainly it cannot offer any justification for imputing the idea of a conflict with a personified monster or deity of the sea as its antecedent. Rather, the

Chr. 18:5, 14; 2 Chr. 18:17; and (in the structure אִם... [וְ]אִם) Jer. 42:6, Ezek. 2:5, 7, 3:11, Job 37:13. The distinction remains also, in a rather different sense, in Am. 3:3, 4.

70 Besides the pertinent references cited in the preceding note, see Mic. 2:7, Jer. 2:14, 31. Only in Jer. 31:20 may the sequential questions be said to be synonymous, whilst in Hab. 3:8b, the repetition is due to staircase parallelism and must not be considered a genuine disjunction.

71 The form used is יָם, but of course omission of the definite article is usual in poetry: cf., e.g., Job 11:9, 38:8, 16, 41:23 (ET v. 31). Hence Clines' note that "without the article[ ] it is effectively a proper name" (p. 165; see similarly Diewert, "Job 7:12", p. 204 n. 4, Terrien, p. 86, Fohrer, p. 179, Horst, p. 118) is surprising and insufficient to substantiate this irregular translation.

72 *ANET*, p. 67; thus, e.g., Fohrer, p. 179 n. 40, Perdue, *Wisdom in Revolt*, pp. 123-4, Clines, pp. 189-90.

73 This lack of interest in creation is mentioned in connection with the issue of the Ugaritic antecedents of Job 7:12 by Pope, p. 61 and Clines, p. 189; see further the discussion in Chapter 2 above.

74 Thus similarly Newsom, *NIB*, IV, p. 395, Diewert, "Job 7:12", p. 204.

motif may form part of only very distantly related traditions, in Job probably in departure from standard forms of expression.

No parallel to the guarding of תַּנִּין can be claimed even from within the Bible, and indeed the exact referent of this term needs to be explored. Although there are three instances where תַּנִּין occurs in connection with a named "dragon", Rahab (Isa 51:9) or Leviathan (Isa. 27:1, Ps. 74:13, cf. "Leviathan", v. 14), in the majority of cases, as here, the term stands without such qualification. Most commonly, a zoological creature such as a serpent (Ex. 7:9, 10, 12, Deut 32:33, Ps. 91:13) or (in the plural) great sea creatures (Gen. 1:21, Ps. 148:7) seem to be denoted. Of the remaining references, the original sense of תַּנִּין in Neh. 2:13 is unclear, since it appears there only in the name of a well, so this is of little assistance to the discussion. In Lam. 4:3, it seems that תַּנִּים, "jackal", should be read, since the animal referred to is clearly a negatively perceived mammal, and the consonants could easily have become confused. Conversely, for תַּנִּים in Ezek. 29:3, 32:2, one should presumably read תַּנִּין, here in reference to a crocodile (or, in the view of some, a dragon). Finally, and perhaps most pertinently, in Jer. 51:34 there is a reference to "Nebuchadrezzar the king of Babylon...ha[ving] swallowed me like a monster (בְּלָעַנִי כַּתַּנִּין)".[75]

The exact significance of תַּנִּין in this last reference is not certain; however, it is notable that the verb בלע is not generally applied to animals, an exception being Jon. 2:1, where it is stated that "Yahweh appointed a great fish to swallow up Jonah". It is possible that this should be compared with the use of תַּנִּין to denote "great sea monsters", as in Gen 1:21, Ps. 148:7; however, whether a fish should be regarded as included in this category is uncertain, and doubtful also is whether what is described in Jonah was ever regarded as anything other than exceptional. A more likely basis for an animal comparison is Ex. 7:12, the swallowing up of the Egyptians' serpent-rods by that of Aaron. Since the capacity of the snake to swallow whole is notorious and the meaning "snake, serpent" is the most heavily represented sense for תַּנִּין, not least when employed in an indefinite, generic sense, as may be the case also in Job 7:12, this has much to commend it. The resultant reading would be "he has swallowed me like a snake / serpent (i.e. whole)", the parallel colon similarly emphasising the totality of destruction with the idea of being made like an empty vessel. Also possible is the interpretation reflected in the translation "monster", that Nebuchadrezzar is here represented as like a "dragon" in a general sense. Since the frequency with which the verb בלע is applied to שְׁאוֹל, אֶרֶץ, or מוֹת is very striking,[76] and the personification of death or Sheol as a monster may underlie such references (note especially Isa. 25:8), it may be that this kind of association is implied. However, the appropriateness of the same verbal terminology to the

75 Following Qr; Kt בלענו.

76 שְׁאוֹל in Prov. 1:12; אֶרֶץ in Num. 16:32, 34, 26:10, Deut. 11:6, Ps. 106:17 (cf. אֲדָמָה, Num. 16:30 and note the proximate mention of Sheol in Num. 16:30, 33); cf. מוֹת, Isa. 25:7, and מְצוּלָה, Ps. 69:16 (there parallel to בְּאֵר).

experience of destruction or the action of enemies or the wicked,[77] as described in Jer. 51, ensures that this thanatotic aspect cannot be presumed to operate on an unequivocal level. Thus the senses "snake" or "monster" (possibly to be associated, if with any specific sphere at all, with Sheol) seem here to be the most plausible.

In Job 7:12, therefore, various possible interpretations apply. An allusion to a specific dragon, Rahab or Leviathan, seems least likely, since no appellative is given or particular identity implied by the context; moreover, the present or open-tense nature of the reference in Job 7:12 stands in contrast to the past recollections of Isa 51:9 and Ps. 74:13-14 and the precise future anticipation of Isa. 27:1, but is consonant with the remaining occurrences of תַּנִּין. In addition, notwithstanding the frequent assumption made by many advocates of a *Chaoskampf* interpretation of the verse that יָם and תַּנִּין are here virtually synonymous, this is by no means a necessary interpretation of the verse itself, as has been shown above: rather the rare disjunction between the two items would seem to tend towards a distinction between them.

At the same time, the "(great) sea monsters" (perhaps "sea serpents"?), to which reference is made in Gen. 1:21 and Ps. 148:7, are described in the former as creatures of God and part of a "good" creation, and in the latter as being enjoined to participate in the praise of God. On this basis, an allusion to a need to guard them carefully seems unlikely, although it is possible that these extant references may represent only one half of a dual tradition which recognises them not only as part of God's creation, but as fearsome as well. However, the other alternatives, an allusion to a "serpent" or to a non-specific "monster" may be more promising. This would seem to suit the present or non-time-specific orientation of the reference, as well as the lack of any qualification for the indefinite noun employed. In fact, unless it can be assumed that there is one dragon which may be regarded as *the* dragon *par excellence*, and that it is referred to here,[78] the beast of 7:12 must be an indeterminate monster or snake. Against the view that a specific draconic referent is intended, and favouring the indefinite translation "a dragon", it may be recalled that the noun תַּנִּין is applied to both Leviathan and Rahab

77 Isa. 49:19, Hos. 8:8, Hab. 1:13, Lam. 2:16, Ps. 35:25; cf. Ps. 124:3.

78 The translation "the dragon" is followed by a number of scholars (e.g., Day, *God's Conflict*, p. 43, Dhorme, p. 94), whilst some, notwithstanding the apparent absence of a parallel elsewhere in the Old Testament, even interpret תַּנִּין as a proper name (thus Habel, p. 152, Clines, p. 157 and "Job's God" in E. van Wolde, (ed.), *Job's God* [Concilium 2004/4; London: SCM, 2004], p. 44). Nevertheless, agreement is lacking as to its identity, whether it is Leviathan (Day, *God's Conflict*, p. 43), either Leviathan or Rahab (Habel, p. 162, Rowley, p. 68), the "monster[]... Tannîn", to be distinguished from Leviathan and Rahab (Dhorme, p. 94, Kissane, p. 41), or equivalent to Yam from the Ugaritic myth (an alternative view cited by Rowley, p. 68; see Gordis, p. 81, and cf. Dhorme, p. 94, Fohrer, p. 179); essentially, however, these deliberations seem to have in common the view that it is "the chaos monster" (Perdue, *Wisdom in Revolt*, p. 123, n. 3; cf. Gordis, p. 81: "the primordial monster").

(and hence it is not peculiar to one of them), whilst the plural occurs in Ps. 74:13, and a more general reference to a non-specific monster is assumed by most translators for Jer. 51:34. On the other hand, the alternative rendering, "snake", can claim the most numerous attestations for תַּנִּין, as well as being a possible interpretation for Jer. 51:34. Within the context of Job 7:12, this would simply constitute an allusion to the presumably common practice of keeping a close (but distant) watch on any snake which entered areas of human activity in order to prevent it from being inadvertently disturbed and provoked.[79] Certainty in choosing between these alternatives is elusive. However, neither offers any encouragement to the view that a reference to "chaos" is intended here.

It may therefore be concluded that this verse is without close parallel either from within the Bible or without, and seems to represent an idiosyncratic adaptation or distortion of a familiar idea in line with the persona of Job created by the poet. Putative parallels with extra-Israelite material are of doubtful relevance, and encouragement for the discernment of the theme of "chaos" here cannot be claimed from Old Testament occurrences of its key terms. Indeed, יָם and תַּנִּין should perhaps be regarded as more distinct than has generally been thought. The latter term may denote an indeterminate monster or snake, and there is no need to associate it with named תַּנִּינִים like Rahab or Leviathan, as encountered elsewhere. The use of the term in a generic sense in Jer. 51:34 encourages the view of a תַּנִּין as a devouring beast, perhaps akin to Sheol, but not clearly related to the specific characteristics of named draconic individuals, so this may well be the case here. The portrayal of יָם as subject to surveillance, on the other hand, appears to be a negative articulation of a more familiar and relatively well-attested motif of the confining of the sea. Although this necessary aspect of cosmic ordering is not intrinsically to be associated with any notion of "chaos" in its expression elsewhere in the Old Testament, it has to be conceded that the formulation in Job 7:12, with the implied element of surveillance, particularly when coupled with the picture of the harassment of Job in vv. 13-15, steers closer to the idea of hostility on the part of the divine protagonist. This is wholly consonant with the accusatory and cynical attitude of the plaintiff Job, but is without clear precedent in the extant biblical or extra-biblical traditions from which it may have drawn. It thus seems to be a free distortive expression, attributed only to the sufferer Job, which does not necessarily allude to the idea of "chaos" or draw directly on any previous expression of the theme. This nevertheless crucially finds its corrective in the speeches of Yahweh, which attribute to him (and hence more widely commend) a celebratory and inclusive view of all aspects of the cosmos.

---

79 The necessity of being on one's guard in case of such an encounter is emphasised, for example, by the *SAS Survival Guide* (Collins Gem Series; Glasgow: HarperCollins, 1999), which urges the need to avoid confrontation with a snake, and hence to "watch...look closely...check..." and so on (p. 342).

Summary

It may be concluded that these disparate allusions from the Book of Job can lend little encouragement to the view that they refer to a combat with "chaos". Although 38:8-11 admits the need to confine the sea, this is depicted not through battle language, but through its antithesis, the image of the protective care of a newborn child. A connection with the time of creation is possible also in 9:8. However, here the chief idea seems to be that of God's sovereign ownership of the sea, and a careful examination of occurrences of the phrase דרך עַל בָּמֳתֵי distances it from the motif of combat. Job 7:12 is more open to a negative interpretation, since the speaker is clearly seeking to cast God in an oppressive rôle. However, not only is this attitude unparalleled in the other references considered in the present monograph: this apparent distortion of tradition for rhetorical purposes finds its corrective in the divine speeches out of the whirlwind, and is thus ultimately rejected by the Joban author. More importantly, despite the brevity of the allusion contained here and the negative tone in which it is conveyed, it provides several indicators that the common interpretation of this verse in terms of "chaos" is misguided, both on the grounds of its linguistic structure and phrasing and on the evidence of references elsewhere to a תַּנִּין or the restraint of the sea.

ii. Passages Relating to Rahab: Isa. 30:7, 51:9-11, Job 26, 9:13

Isa 30:7c

In this brief and difficult reference, the text and translation are uncertain, with many scholars resorting to emendation,[80] and some even removing mention of Rahab from the reference altogether[81] or (rarely) dismissing the final colon of the verse as a gloss.[82] Perhaps the best option is to try to extract a meaning from the MT,[83] although it is possible that the consonants of הֵם שָׁבֶת should be retained and reformulated, e.g., into הַמָּשְׁבָּת,[84] or some other minor emendation

80 See Kaiser, II, p. 229 n. 6, or Day, *God's Conflict*, p. 89, for various possibilities.

81 Thus BHS footnote (proposing either רַהַב הַמָּשְׁבָּת or רְהָבָה מָשְׁבָּת); O. Procksch, *Jesaja*, I (Leipzig 1930), p. 387 (רְהָבָה מָשְׁבָּת).

82 F. Huber, *Jahwe, Juda und die anderen Völker beim Propheten Jesaja* (BZAW 137; Berlin: de Gruyter, 1967), pp. 119-120. However, this is widely rejected: see Williamson, *The Book Called Isaiah*, p. 84, and the further references there.

83 Thus, e.g., Kaiser, II, p. 229 ("'Are they Rahab?'—Sitting still!"), following H. Donner, *Israel unter den Völkern* (VT[S] 11: Leiden: Brill, 1964), p. 158 ["Rahab sind sie? Untätigkeit!"]; Delitzsch, "Boasting that sits still" ("Großmaul das still sitzt"), p. 330.

84 This is perhaps the most commonly advocated emendation, being followed, e.g., by *BHS*, Auvray, p. 264, Fohrer, II, p. 89, Wildberger, III, p. 1157, 1158-9, Kissane, I, p. 329, and Clements, p. 245.

adopted. In either case, it seems there may be an implied contrast between the two elements of this colon (Rahab and the accompanying term rendered in MT as שבת), with a play on the root meaning of "Rahab": "the silenced (or silent) boaster", "the boisterous one who sits still", "static turbulence", "the arrogant Do-nothing", "A mover and shaker, are they? Inertia, more like!" Jer. 46:17 offers a good general parallel to a variety of renditions, but, more specifically, it may provide a guide to the original force of the reference, since the sentiments of the MT of Isa. 30:7c here find their striking echo, again in relation to Egypt:

> Call the name of Pharaoh, king of Egypt,
> "Noisy one who lets the hour go by."

This seems to favour the preservation of the sense of inactivity conveyed by the MT, either through the retention of the current Hebrew text or (perhaps better) through its replacement by a slightly emended form based on the same verbal root, e.g., (ה)ישֶׁבֶת.

In view of this parallel, and indeed the immediate context of the allusion in Isa. 30:7, it is not surprising that there is wide agreement regarding the fact that Egypt comprises the subject of reference, and indeed this conclusion seems unavoidable, even when some mythological connection is claimed.[85] Conversely, evidence that "Rahab" should be interpreted as alluding to a mythological beast, rather than as a simple nation name, is lacking.[86] Consonant with the use of Rahab to refer directly to Egypt, rather than to a personification of the nation conceptualised as a monster, is the use of the masculine plural הֵם which, if correct, suggests a nation conceived as a plurality of individuals. The feminine forms of the more secure text of the surrounding cola also suggest that a nation (which would usually be regarded as feminine) is envisaged: particularly to be noted are the feminine singular suffixes of the following verse, which may refer back to Rahab,[87] whilst the antecedent זֹאת is also feminine. שָׁבֶת, of course, is difficult, and in its present form can yield no data relating to the gender of Rahab. However the reading (ה)ישֶׁבֶת, suggested by the combination of the apparent parallel in sense with Jer. 46:17 and the existing consonants of the MT, is feminine, as indeed are most verbs derived by emendation of the MT (with the exception of forms of שׁבת). This use of the name "Rahab" as a proper name for Egypt, occurring in

85 As by Kaiser, II, p. 231, Wildberger, III, pp. 1159, 1164, Brueggemann, I, p. 242, Seitz, p. 218. Many (e.g., Blenkinsopp, pp. 413-4; Day, *God's Conflict*, p. 88; cf. p. 90 n. 9) write as if the reference is simply to Egypt, but assume in the wider context that a name given to the dragon of "chaos" has here been applied to this nation.

86 Gunkel proposed that *bhmt* in v. 6 refers to Behemoth and should therefore be equated with Rahab, but this is widely rejected; see, e.g., the refutation in Day, *God's Conflict*, p. 90.

87 See Williamson, *The Book Called Isaiah*, p. 84.

a text which seems to date from c. 705-1 B.C.,[88] tallies with the same usage in Ps. 87, which may also emanate from the same or a not far distant period.[89] It is also consonant with the diachronic results of this study, which suggest that reference to a dragon Rahab or Leviathan in the Old Testament is only attested from the exile or subsequently, and that the appellative "Rahab" may have originated as a personal name for Egypt.[90]

Many scholars, following *BHS*, delete ומִצְרַיִם in v. 7a as a gloss on grounds of metre and of content, Wildberger, for example, stating that "mentioning Egypt detracts from the flow of the poem. The strategy is to mention the country only in paraphrases, so that the hearer is informed of the country's identity only when the phrase רהב המשבת... is used."[91] However, if this is correct, perhaps the most plausible explanation is that such a gloss may have arisen either in order to clarify the meaning of term "Rahab" in a later period when its use as a designation for Egypt had been superseded by a more mythological understanding, or to clarify the referent of the foregoing verse once its (previously adequate) crystallisation as Rahab = Egypt was no longer widely understood. Such a development would cohere with the wider results of this study.

Isaiah 51:9-11

Psalm 89:10-11 has often been seen as relevant to the interpretation of Isaiah 51:9-11, since there are indisputable similarities between the respective passages. First, both seem to emanate from a time following the destruction of Jerusalem, Isa. 51:9-10 emulating a type of appeal often found in psalms of lament (e.g., Ps. 44:2-4, 24; 80:3, 9-12, 15-16), which urges God to intervene in the present urgent situation as he had in days of old. Moreover, although Ps. 89:6-19 takes the form of praise of Yahweh, celebrating his incomparable power and faithfulness, v. 11 does seem to constitute just such a threnodic recollection, here, as in Isa. 51:9, mentioning the destruction of

88 According even to such an advocate of limited Isaianic authorship as O. Kaiser (II, p. 230); compare Clements' statement that the "authenticity [of 30:6-7] to Isaiah, and to the situation of 705-1, cannot... be in doubt" (p. 244).

89 See the discussion thereon in Chapter 6 above.

90 Contrast Schunck's advocacy of the opposite line of development ("Jes 30 6-8 und die Deutung der Rahab im Alten Testament", *ZAW* 78 [1966] 48-56, pp. 53-4), based on the acceptance of a post-exilic date for Ps. 87 (following Kraus) and a tenth-century one for Ps. 89:11 (following Albright). However, he offers no direct evidence in support of this dating, instead merely citing the conclusions of an earlier scholar in each case; moreover, he makes this schema foundational for his exegesis, and thus assumes that Isaiah, in mentioning Rahab, "can only have been thinking in the first instance of the well-known monster". Even so, he is still compelled to conclude that the term is here employed symbolically to designate Egypt in a way which gave rise to the later use as a nation-name.

91 III, p. 1158.

Rahab, in this case in conjunction with the scattering of Yahweh's enemies with his mighty arm. The linguistic affinities between both may especially be noted.[92] In addition, Psalm 74:12-14, though concerning Leviathan rather than Rahab, also occurs in the same type of form-critical context as Ps. 89:11 and, like Isa. 51:9-11, places the destruction[93] of the (heads of the) dragon next to the division of the sea and "salvation"[94] worked by God.

Nevertheless, although this type of correspondence necessarily entails that the interpretation of these passages should be compatible, this does not obviate the methodological imperative to examine each context openly and independently, before bringing it to bear on the understanding of the other. In particular, those who have considered Ps. 89:10-11 to refer to a battle with chaos at creation have sometimes assumed that Isa. 51:9-10 must therefore also refer to the same sphere of allusion, John Day, for example, making a direct claim to this effect.[95] However, the careful analysis undertaken above in Chapter 6 has indicated that the interpretation of Psalm 89 as referring to the theme of *Chaoskampf* is at the very least questionable, and that the focus of vv. 10-13 is not on an originating act of creation, but rather on Yahweh's incomparability among the gods and exalted power (as is clearly signalled in vv. 6-9); this includes his lordship of creation (power over creation being the supreme manifestation of the greatest god and the greatest reassurance of his ability to act on a global scale), but the prime issue at stake is Yahweh's ability and commitment to act in the world arena (vv. 14-15).[96]

Moreover, the putative "chaos" content of Ps. 89:10-11 constitutes the primary basis of interpreting Isa 51:9-10 as referring to creation, since no evidence in its favour can be cited from the prophetic passage itself.[97] The most that can be maintained on the basis of Isa. 51 is that the mention of creation in vv. 13, 16 might allow for this thought also to be included in vv.

---

92 Compare the language of Ps. 89:11 (אַתָּה... כֶחָלָל רָהַב בִּזְרוֹעַ עֻזְּךָ...) with Isa. 51:9, where much of the same vocabulary recurs, albeit in a different order (עֹז זְרוֹעַ ... אַתְּ... רַהַב מְחוֹלֶלֶת...). Some have thought these similarities sufficient to claim the dependence of Deutero-Isaiah on the Psalm, e.g., H. L. Ginsberg, "The arm of YHWH in Isaiah 51-63 and the text of Isa 53 10-11", *JBL* 77 (1958), p. 153, A. Schoors, *I am God your Saviour* (VT[S] 24, 1973), p. 123, Day, *God's Conflict*, p. 92.

93 Crushing, as in Ps. 89:11, but using a different verb, רצץ instead of דכא.

94 Ps. 74:12; cf. the content, but not the vocabulary, of Isa. 51:11.

95 *God's Conflict*, p. 93.

96 Hence the interest of vv. 12-13 is not on a series of sequential acts but on God's ownership of and acknowledgment by the whole cosmos, and it is complemented by two further illustrations of his power: first over the sea, which is a supreme manifestation of might but also indicative of the reassuring stabilising force which he provides (v. 10); and, second, in an archetypal situation of victory (v. 11, cf. vv. 14, 18-19, cf. v. 16a). However, all is directed cogently at the central concerns of the Psalm: the maintenance of the covenant and upholding of God's promises, as manifested in his powerful acts which provide his people with victory and political stability under their Davidic king.

97 See further below.

9-10,[98] but the difficulties with this view will become apparent below. As a result, there is disagreement as to exactly where the reference to creation is supposed to lie, and indeed some scholars simply interpret the passage in relation to the flight from Egypt.[99] Of those who discern a battle with "chaos", some contend that v. 9 simultaneously[100] or sequentially[101] alludes to the Exodus and creation, or that the thought of the Exodus is conveyed through the imagery of creation myth,[102] whilst others maintain that this verse is focused solely on creation.[103] In a like manner, some commentators would regard the whole of v. 10 as concerning the Exodus,[104] whilst others propose that v. 10a may refer to creation and v. 10b to the Exodus,[105] or that v. 10a comprises a transitional colon encompassing both themes prior to the definite statement of the Exodus motif in v. 10b.[106]

As has already been indicated, it is highly significant for the understanding of Isa. 51:9-10 that these verses and their immediate context

---

98 Thus, e.g., Day, *God's Conflict*, p. 93.

99 Thus, e.g., H. G. M. Williamson, *The Book Called Isaiah*, pp. 84, 86; W. Schmidt, *Königtum Gottes in Ugarit und Israel*, p. 40; A. Heidel, *The Babylonian Genesis*, pp. 109-110; M. Görg, "'Chaos' und 'Chaosmächte' im Alten Testament", *BN* 70 (1993) 48-61, pp. 53-4; W. G. Lambert, "Old Testament Mythology in its Ancient Near Eastern Context" (VT[S] 40, 1988) p. 129; cf. P.-E. Bonnard, who suggests that the subject of reference is the Exodus, but that the terminology employed is intended to imply an identity between Yahweh's creative and redemptive power, pp. 252-3.

100 Thus Day, p. 92, hesitantly including Babylon in the picture as well.

101 Thus Baltzer, who advocates an allusion to creation myth in v. 9b, despite his recognition of the Exodus language of v. 9a (pp. 447-450), and similarly Kissane (II, p. 163). Compare Koole's advocacy of a reference only to the Exodus in v. 9aβ (p. 170) but to both in v. 9b (pp. 172-3), and see his detailed survey of scholarship on this issue.

102 E.g., Oswalt, pp. 341-2.

103 E.g., Westermann, p. 195, and Whybray, p. 159, though the latter acknowledges that "this is not specifically stated".

104 Thus very definitely Oswalt, p. 342; similarly also Koole, pp. 173-5 (again with a comprehensive survey of scholarly opinion), Kissane, II, p. 163, and Whybray, the latter still also finding "mythological overtones" in v. 10a, p. 159.

105 Thus Day, p. 93.

106 Thus Westermann, p. 195 n. 5, following Volz; see similarly Miscall, p. 121; cf. Childs, p. 403, and Brueggemann, II, p. 130. Blenkinsopp here perceives an allusion to "the old myth of the victory of the god over the forces of chaos at the beginning of time" which he associates with creation (p. 332-3), yet also acknowledges the permeation of exodus associations in the mention of the "arm" of Yahweh (p. 332) and of the sea (p. 333), i.e., in vv. 9a, 10ab. Thus he presumably envisages the simultaneous activation of different levels of meaning. If the chief thrust of the passage spoke merely of "chaos" as the dissolution of order without specifically recollecting the events of creation, one could understand the intertwining of the exodus motif, or the recollection of the latter idea couched in terms of the former. However, the interaction and active association of two independently-outplayed events, certainly in a way that might allow the understanding of one through allusion to the other, may be felt to stretch credibility beyond a reasonable point.

do not make any allusion to creation (unless, of course, it is to be presupposed through the mention of Rahab *per se*).[107] The nearest references to this theme (one much favoured by Deutero-Isaiah) occur in vv. 13 and 16, both of which describe Yahweh, in closely parallel doxological phrases, as the one "who stretched out the heavens and laid the foundations of the earth",[108] that in verse 13 also being preceded by the attribution of Yahweh as the "Maker" of Israel. These verses may be relevant insofar as they seem to belong to the same section as 51:9-11 within the wider tripartite editorial unit 51:9-52:12.[109]

However, vv. 13, 16 are most naturally to be understood, like similar occurrences elsewhere in Deutero-Isaiah, as conveying reassurance in God's redemptive power to save his people from their oppressors, as befits its immediate context, rather than (somewhat distantly) alluding back to v. 9.[110] Verse 16 is, moreover, immediately preceded by the description of "Yahweh your God... Yahweh Sebaoth" as the one "who stirs up the sea so its waves roar" (רֹגַע הַיָּם וַיֶּהֱמוּ גַּלָּיו, v. 15b; cf. Jer. 31:35),[111] a divine attribute which is completely counter to the supposed suppression of the sea. At the same time, it can hardly be suggested that these ideas have been set in immediate contrast to each other as a collective indicator of the scope of this deity's

107 In this respect, comparison may be made with the Ugaritic myth of the vanquishing of *tnn* (*KTU* 1.3.iii.40), since the extant texts also fail to make a specific connection between this and the creation of the world.

108 V. 16 uses infinitive constructs rather than participles, and has נטע for נטה, though the Syriac offers support for reading לנטת, in line with v. 13, and indeed this is the usual word employed in relation to the creation of the heavens: cf. Isa. 40:22, 42:5, 44:24, 45:12.

109 The structural device both uniting and delineating the sections has long been recognised, since the first and last begin with the call, "Awake, awake, put on strength" (51:9, addressed to the "arm of Yahweh"; 52:1, addressed to Zion), whilst the central one takes up the same verbal root, עור, and double imperatival form in the demand, "Rouse yourself, rouse yourself, stand up, O Jerusalem" (51:17).

110 Contra Brueggemann, II, p. 132. Of course, if v. 9 is definitely to be understood as an unambiguous reference to creation, it could potentially be claimed that vv. 13, 16 continue the same thought (although, as should become clear, there are difficulties with this view when it is considered in detail). However, if the content of vv. 9-10 is to be understood as fluid and ambiguous in its sphere of reference, perhaps alluding to creation, perhaps to the Exodus, then the occurrence of the former theme in the later, separated verses cannot be claimed to guide the reader or hearer to discern it in the earlier context: a theme can only be carried forward in the consciousness from where it is introduced, and is not ordinarily transposed back.

111 The suggestion that רֹגַע should be emended to גֹּעֵר, "rebukes", is rightly rejected by most commentators, since the proposal is entirely conjectural, and indeed, evidence from other contexts where the latter verb is employed suggests that roaring is an unlikely response for the sea to make to Yahweh's "rebuke" (contrast Ps. 106:9, Na 1:4, Isa. 50:2, in which it is dried up, and Ps. 18:16 = 2 Sam. 22:16, Ps. 104:7 in which it is exposed or flees). Moreover, רגע appears again in relation to the sea in Isa. 5:30, which Williamson attributes also to Deutero-Isaiah (*The Book Called Isaiah*, p. 136).

power, since it is the defeat of a dragon, not of the sea, which is mentioned in v. 9, and "drying up" is a very benign means of expressing the feat at the Red Sea if it is intended to be read as a manifestation of Yahweh's defeat of chaotic powers. However, v. 15b would furnish an excellent counterpart to the drying of the Red Sea in v. 10, since it is compatible, and naturally resonates back, with this recollection, without having to be directly connected to it.

Psalm 89:10-11 is moreover not the only occurrence of the mention of "Rahab" which may be brought to bear on Isa. 51:9-11. H. G. M. Williamson cites the use of "Rahab" to refer to Egypt in Isa. 30:7, a passage about which "there is virtual unanimity in ascribing... to Isaiah of Jerusalem, writing during the period 705-701 B.C.",[112] as a possible example of the influence of Proto-Isaiah on the remainder of the Isaianic tradition as a whole. A primary basis for this is simply that "Isa 51:9... by its clear allusion to the deliverance of the Israelites at the Red Sea, identifies the mythical monster with Egypt".[113] In this respect, according to Williamson, it seems to bear stronger similarities to the application of Rahab to Egypt in Isa. 30:7 than to the usage in Ps. 89.[114] He also identifies the equation or comparison of Pharaoh with תַּנִּין in Ezek. 29:3 and 32:2 as "moving in the circle of closely associated ideas". He proposes, either, that "the equation of Rahab with Egypt was in wider circulation and that the fact that before the time of Deutero-Isaiah it occurs only in Isa. 30:7 is a matter of coincidence" or, his preferred option, it "is first attested by, and quite probably was first coined by, Isaiah of Jerusalem, that it may have been developed in a slightly different, because personalized, way by Ezekiel, and thus that the use of it by Deutero-Isaiah is most likely to have been inspired by his reading of the earlier work of Isaiah".[115] However, influential in Williamson's conclusion is his assumption that Ps. 87, although dated by "most scholars" to the pre-exilic period, must refer to proselyte or Diaspora Jews or to an eschatological vision of Zion as the world centre for Yahweh worship, and hence be placed in the post-exilic period. If a pre-exilic date is accepted, as was urged above in Chapter 6, then, of course, Isa. 30:7 no longer provides the sole extant reference to Rahab from the pre-exilic period, and hence it might be inferred that its use to refer to Egypt may have been more general in this period than Williamson allows. This is indeed supported by the fact, cited by Wildberger, that "in Egypt itself, the crocodile [was] symbolic of the power of the king (as seen in hieroglyph I 3, which uses the image of the crocodile in duplicate as a way to refer to the Pharaoh); a hymn says about Thutmose III, 'I permit them to see your majesty as a crocodile, which is feared in the water, which a person does not approach too closely.'"[116]

112 *The Book Called Isaiah*, p. 83.

113 *Ibid.*, p. 84.

114 *Ibid.*, p. 86.

115 *Ibid.*, p. 86.

116 Wildberger, *Jesaja*, II, p. 1003; see *ANET*, p. 374.

Moreover, if Egypt is seen as the primary subject of allusion in Pss. 89:10-11 and 74:12-14, as was argued above in Chapter 6, then Isaiah 51:9-11 may be understood in relation to both groups of passages. Nevertheless, Williamson's contribution is important in highlighting the necessity of taking into account these more literalistic passages, and in showing how Isa. 51:9 is clearly to be understood in relation to the Red Sea deliverance. At the same time, despite the value of such inner-biblical comparisons, the proper place for them is after a close analysis of the text in question has taken place, and primacy must be awarded to exegesis of the passage in and of itself. It is to this which we shall now turn.

The most immediately striking element of Isa. 51:9-11 is the close mirroring of vv. 9c and 10a, which suggests that they should be understood as referring to the same event. Both begin with the phrase הֲלוֹא אַתְּ־הִיא, the sound and form of הַמַּחְצֶבֶת and הַמַּחֲרֶבֶת then closely echoing each other. A recognition of the common focus of the lines is only one stage towards its interpretation: few would dispute that, taken in isolation, v. 10a sounds like an Exodus allusion: the motif of the Red Sea crossing entailing the "drying up" (Hiph. חרב) of the sea is a well attested in the Old Testament,[117] and this indeed is unmistakably the subject of reference in v. 10b.

Nevertheless, many would wish to contend that v. 10a also continues the thought of a battle with a chaos dragon which they regard as the subject of v. 9c. In fact, it is unclear why such a conflict should entail the drying up of the sea, especially if creation should ensue, since this required the ordering and proper provision of water, not its eradication. Moreover, as Koole recognises, "the mythology of the ancient East does not talk about a 'drying up' of the chaos monster..., and the question whether something of the kind coincided with or followed the destruction of Rahab... is therefore rather unrealistic."[118] Nor is the further claim which is sometimes encountered that תְּהוֹם רַבָּה (v. 10a) is an especially "mythological" term[119] supported by the evidence: it never elsewhere appears in connection with any putative *Chaoskampf* passages, but rather is consistently applied to indicate the great depth of water beneath the earth (Gen. 7:11, Am. 7:4, Ps. 36:7).[120] As such, its employment in the present context apparently serves to maximise the extent of the miracle described, in much the same way as the use of תְּהוֹמוֹת in Ps. 106:9 (again in relation to the Red Sea crossing), and in a manner consistent with the other occurrences of תְּהוֹם רַבָּה. Indeed, this maximising heightened language is characteristic of Isa. 51:9-11 as a whole (note, e.g., "cut in

117 See Ps. 106:9 (Qal), Josh. 2:10, 4:23 (יבשׁ) and cf. Ex. 14:21 (חָרָבָה), 16, 22, 29, 15:19, Ps. 66:6, Neh. 9:11 (יַבָּשָׁה). The second Exodus is envisaged as entailing the drying of the sea also in Isa. 11:15, which belongs to a passage which may be attributed to Deutero-Isaiah (Williamson, *The Book Called Isaiah*, pp. 125-133).

118 P. 174.

119 Thus, e.g., Whybray, p. 159, Westermann, p. 195, Baltzer, p. 449. These authors also suggest that יָם has mythological overtones here, but since it is the commonplace Hebrew term for the sea, this can hardly be presumed.

120 Cf. similarly Koole, p. 174.

pieces... everlasting joy... sorrow and sighing shall flee away"); hence, it must be understood as reflecting the character and thrust of the passage, rather than as requiring an explanation in terms of a putative mythological background. This interpretation is further supported by the fact that מַעֲמַקֵּי־יָם (v. 10b) appears to be comparable in meaning,[121] although here the subterrestrial element is not evident. It finds its closest parallel in the phrase מַעֲמַקֵּי־מָיִם found in Ps. 69:3, 15 (discussed above in Chapter 4) and Ezek. 27:34. Though in the former instance, the expression is employed metaphorically as figurative of the suffering experienced by the psalmist, in the latter, a literal level of meaning, connoting the depths of the sea, is apparent, as indeed is consistent with its placement parallel to יַמִּים.[122] It must therefore be concluded that, in contrast to the self-evident exodus overtones of v. 10a, the case for seeing a mythological reference here seems very weak. Yet if v. 10a cannot readily constitute a *Chaoskampf* reference – and indeed commentators are uncertain on this issue – it raises the question as to whether it is appropriate to claim that this is the primary focus of v. 9c.

Particularly significant in this regard is the consideration that Isaiah 51:9-10 as a whole may very readily be understood solely in relation to the Exodus. Thus, in v. 9a, the arm of Yahweh acting in power to save his people is chiefly an Exodus attribute.[123] The divine "arm" is not associated with any other event in the same way, and even occurs in connection with the hope of a second Exodus, especially pertinently, in the climactic part of the section to which Isa. 51:9 belongs, 52:10; cf. also Ezek. 20:34. [124] The allusion to יְמֵי קֶדֶם דּוֹרוֹת עוֹלָמִים (v. 9b) is also particularly consonant with this sphere of

121 The reading found in IQIsa is במעמקי־ים, but this makes little difference to the general point here being made.

122 There is one further instance of מַעֲמַקִּים, in Ps. 130:1, there in the absolute, but it does not much assist in determining its precise object of reference.

123 It is especially characteristic of Deuteronomy, e.g., Deut. 4:34, 5:15, 7:19, and often; however, it is also found elsewhere, e.g., Ex. 6:6, 15:16, 2 Ki. 17:36, Isa. 63:12, Jer. 32:21, Pss. 77:16, 136:12, and most notably, in Ps. 89:11, where it stands in parallel with a mention of Rahab.

124 The only exceptions to this are significant to the present context, since, beside one occurrence in connection with the closely-related motif of the gift of the land in Ps. 44:4, they are two similarly-phrased allusions to creation in Jer. 27:5 and 32:17. It is interesting, however, first, that these verses constitute a very small proportion of the numerous references to Yahweh's arm, and therefore, although reflecting a possible sphere of allusion, it is not a common one; and second, that these verses, though perhaps reflecting deuteronomistic influence, are to be distinguished from the standard deuteronomistic cliché, "with a mighty hand and outstretched arm" (and variations) (thus, e.g., Carroll, p. 527) and hence are unusual developments from the core tradition. Jer. 27:5, moreover, is addressed to the nations, hence perhaps the unusual appeal to "natural" theology rather than received Israelite traditions, and Jer. 32:17 leads straight into Exodus allusions, in v. 21 again in relation to Yahweh's arm. The remaining instances of the "arm" of Yahweh employed with present reference are either ambiguous in what they refer to or indicate a general divine attribute (Isa. 40:10, 53:1, 59:16, 63:5, Pss. 89:14, 98:1, Job 40:9).

reference, since the motif of "days of old" is in the Hebrew Bible elsewhere applied only to historical time,[125] whilst עוֹלָם is also never used in relation to creation, mention of דּוֹרוֹת, in common with other biblical usage, similarly implying a time known to humanity, and Israel in particular.[126] The expression דּוֹרוֹת עוֹלָמִים is unparalleled elsewhere in the Old Testament; however, the Exodus and settlement generations are probably to be regarded as the archetypal "generations of long ago", the Pentateuch having an unusual and striking emphasis on these generations (e.g. Num. 1, 3:1, and cf. especially Deut. 32:17) and their legacy to those to come (e.g. Ex. 12:42, 16:32-33, 31:13). Collectively, this evidence indicates that the primary focus of v. 9ab is historical, rather than mythical; it has also already been shown that v. 10a, with which v. 9c is closely connected, most naturally refers to the Red Sea crossing, and that this is indisputably the case in v. 10b. V. 11 then looks forward to a second Exodus. This suggests, therefore, that, in common with the rest of the passage, the Exodus should be understood as the chief sphere of allusion in v. 9c, even if mythical forms of expression have been adopted, or a prior myth perhaps have furnished the vehicle for the tenor of the *Heilsgeschichte* to be expressed anew.[127] This type of interpretation has already been advanced above in Chapter 6 in respect of Ps. 89:11, which of course bears important similarities to Isa. 51:9, and for which one might expect a compatible interpretation. Indeed Rahab stands for Egypt not only there, but in a solely-literal sense in Ps. 87:4 and Isa 30:7, whilst Egypt / Pharaoh is represented as a dragon in Ezek. 29:3, 32:2;[128] one might compare also Jer. 51:34 re Nebuchadrezzar.

The Exodus theme is not only dominant in the immediate context under examination: it also resonates further through the wider passage. This has already been delineated above as 51:9-52:12: see further, e.g., Korpel and de Moor,[129] Williamson,[130] and Westermann.[131] However, one should probably

---

125 It seems to be applied to the Exodus and wilderness period in Deut. 32:7 (which furnishes the closest parallel to the language of Isa. 51:9 in its use of יְמוֹת עוֹלָם... שְׁנוֹת דּוֹר־וָדוֹר), Isa. 63:9, 11, Pss. 44:2, and probably in Ps. 77:6 (cf. v. 12 where פִּלְאֶךָ מִקֶּדֶם most naturally refers to this period) and Mal. 3:4; cf. Ps. 74:2. The remaining occurrences are in 2 Ki. 19:25, Isa. 23:7, 37:26, Am. 9:11, 7:14, 20, and Ps. 143:5; see also the related expressions in Mic. 5:1, Lam. 5:21 and Neh. 12:46. References to Yahweh "plan[ning] from days of old" (2 Ki. 19:25, Isa. 37:26) should not, of course, be understood in terms of the much later doctrine of predestination, but as occurring within the course of history. Contrast Westermann's contention that the phrase may "represent both the primaeval creation and the first beginnings of the nation's history" (p. 195).

126 See similarly Heidel, *Babylonian Genesis*, p. 109.

127 Cf. the discussion of Ps. 74 in Chapter 6 above.

128 Indeed, according to Oswalt, "The Arabic word for 'crocodile' is a derivative of 'Pharaoh'" (p. 341 n. 45).

129 Pp. 542-4.

130 Williamson recognises the same tripartite structuring in 51:1-8, hence classifying 51:1-52:2 as a unit climaxing with 52:7-12 (*Variations on a Theme*, pp. 156-7, *The Book*

also include 51:1-8 under consideration, both because the present ordering of these chapters of Isaiah shows signs of being a deliberate construct and, more specifically, because the parallel structuring of the two tripartite sections 51:1-8 and 51:9-52:2 suggests, as Williamson proposes, that they belong together; Oswalt indeed envisages the cry of 51:9 as being "sparked by" what precedes.[132] The dominant theme introduced in 51:1-8 is "salvation" and "deliverance" (vv. 5, 6, 8), and this is a classic Exodus (and second Exodus) concern (e.g., Ex. 3:8, 14:13, 15:2, 18:8, 9, 10, 11), which reaches its culmination in 52:7, 10. Oswalt is thus surely correct in commenting on 52:11-12: "Whenever Isaiah or any other Hebrew prophet begins to talk about deliverance, it is the exodus to which their minds turn sooner or later", p. 372).[133] The idea of the "ransomed" (v. 11;[134] "redeemed without money" 52:3; cf. 35:10, Jer. 31:11) returning then clearly expresses the important Deutero-Isaianic theme of the return from exile as a second Exodus. The motifs of foreign oppression (51:12-13, 52:4, cf. Gen. 15:13, Ex. 1:12, 3:9, Deut. 26:7) and of "your tormentors, those who have said to you, 'Bow down...'" (v. 23) are also important, and are accompanied by the promise of "release[]" (v. 14), and the reassurance that "You are my people" (v.16, cf. Ex. 3:7, 10, 5:1, 6:7, etc.). The Exodus language reaches its climax, however, in 52:3-6, the message to captive Jerusalem whose bonds are to be loosed, most unmistakably in v. 3, and explicitly in v. 4, the whole passage then attaining its finale in the twofold command, "Depart, depart, go out thence" (v. 11a) in which the people are called upon to participate in a new and

---

Called Isaiah, p. 229); Bonnard, too, takes 51:1-52:12 as a unit, with the complementary sections 51:1-8 and 51:9-52:12 being bound together by certain common vocabulary (pp. 244-5).

131 Westermann follows the view that 51:9-52:2 (6) is a "single, consciously-designed unit", "the entire poem [leaving aside the hymn of praise in 52:7-10] represent[ing] the preparation of the way for the final summons in 52:11f., 'depart, depart'" (p. 194); thus the shape of the whole shows real coherence. 51:9-52:12 is taken as a unit also by Oswalt (pp. 339-340) and Kissane (II, p. 157), although 52:2 is sometimes taken as a delimiting point, e.g., by Watts (pp. 210-211). Others, such as Duhm (e.g., pp. 386, 387), followed by Whybray (p. 158), acknowledge the deliberate conjoining of material, but regard the present arrangement as due to an editor, whilst alternative units have also occasionally been proposed: Coffin (*IB*, V, p. 588-9) and Kuntz ("The Contribution of Rhetorical Criticism to Understanding Isaiah 51:1-16" in *Art and Meaning: Rhetoric in Biblical Literature* [JSOT(S) 19; Sheffield: JSOT, 1982], pp. 140-171) see 51:1-16 as a bipartite unit, Coffin then taking 51:17-52:12 as the next section (*ibid.*, p. 602), whilst another minority view is to read 51:1-11 together (F. Holmgren, "Chiastic Structure in Isaiah 51:1-11", *VT* 19 [1969], pp. 196-201).

132 P. 340.

133 However, it is difficult to see a call for the fulfilment of that hope in the recollection of a slaughter of a dragon prior to creation. Though an extraordinary act of power and deity, it is doubtful if one should interpret it as providing salvation where there is nothing yet created to be saved.

134 Following MT, with Whybray, p.159, Day, p. 91, Oswalt, p. 339; 1QIsa reads ופזורי, "and the dispersed, scattered".

greater Exodus which surpasses the redemption of old (vv. 11-12). Thus Isa. 51:9-52:12 is infused with this overriding concern, the Exodus hope in particular emphatically providing the pinnacle of its vision for the future at the end of this passage.

It has already been shown that the domination of the Exodus theme in 51:9-10 can scarcely be denied, and that v. 9 is suffused with Exodus language, as well as being compatible with the imagery apparently applied to the Red Sea crossing in Pss. 74 and 89. Once read in this way, a powerful correspondence is unleashed between the plea in 51:9-10 for God to re-enact the great miracle of Exodus salvation, and the answering promise in chapter 52 of a new and greater redemption. Moreover, placed in a context where the identity between the Exodus situation and the people's present affliction is such a central motif, the couching of the Red Sea recollection in terms of the overcoming of Rahab provides a further means of drawing the nation's enemies together into a single identity as the foe vanquished by Yahweh.

Turning to v. 9c itself, the verbs employed here do not seem to offer evidence in favour of a particular interpretative strategy for the colon. The language of piercing (חלל) occurs also in Ps. 89:11 (there as a noun), and Job 26:13, in each case in relation to Rahab, so it may be presumed that this language may to some extent be traditional. Hiph. חצב, "hack in pieces", may perhaps be compared with Pi. שׁבר in Ps. 74:13, since this may be taken to mean "shatter, break in pieces". The use of חצב in this type of context is unusual, since it is normally applied to digging or hewing through stone; however, the close echoing of sound between this verb and הַמַּחֲרֶבֶת in v. 10a may be considered as having exercised an influence on the choice of vocabulary, and the general sense is unsurprising.[135] It has already been maintained above in Chapter 6 that the Exodus comprises the chief sphere of allusion in Pss. 74 and 89, so the commonality of expression in Isa. 51 would be compatible with a similar interpretation here. On the other hand, the presence of what may be traditional language, including a term shared with Job 26:13, where the focus seems to be more mythical and a reference to Egypt is improbable, suggests that traditions of mythical dragon-figure under the name of Rahab are at least employed symbolically here; if so, this would again result in a compatibility of interpretation with that advanced in respect of Pss. 74 and 89 above. However, this does not mean that the motif of a conflict with Rahab should be associated with the theme of "chaos", nor that v. 9c should be read in a manner that isolates it from the Exodus-focused cola which surround it.

---

135 Alternatively, the variant reading, found in 1QIsa, הַמֹּחֶצֶת, "the one who smote through, shattered", like חלל, again takes up a verb applied to Rahab in Job 26:12 and may offer evidence for a common reliance on the same traditional language. However, in view of the unusual application of the verb חצב in MT, and indeed the fact that it is less common in Hebrew than מחץ, a later assimilation to Job in preference to this reading is perhaps the most likely explanation for the variants having occurred. See similarly, e.g., Korpel and de Moor, p. 490 n. 1, Blenkinsopp, p. 330, Koole, pp. 171-2; the same root occurs also in 51:1.

In fact, a careful examination of the passages concerned with this dragon-figure suggests that, although real reconstruction of an underlying myth is not feasible (one simply cannot go beyond the evidence one has without resorting to conjecture), they may furnish some indication as to the nature and setting of the story with which it is concerned. Job 26:8ff. is set in the heavens, as is Ps. 89:6-12a, whilst, in more distant connection, there is mention of the creation of the heavens and earth in Isa. 51:13, 16, which seems to belong to the same wider textual unit as vv. 9-11; moreover, even the subsidiary allusion to Rahab in Job 9:13 is not far removed from a reference to the heavenly sphere (vv. 7-9). Of even greater significance may be the parallelism in Job 26:13, since it implies that the result of the piercing of the "fleeing serpent" was the "mak[ing] fair" of "the heavens": thus to pierce the serpent is perhaps tantamount to, or the same act as, making the heavens fair. Since in the previous verse, the stilling of the sea is parallel to the smiting of Rahab, it thus appears that the destruction of Rahab by Yahweh was set in the region of the heavenly ocean and that it somehow effected the calming of what may have been a storm or some form of turmoil in that ocean, the result being the "making fair" of the heavens. Perhaps one might think of Rahab as a type of storm-causing agent, the result of the overcoming of which is the replacement of dark stormy skies with fair. Such a reconstruction is, of course, conjectural. However, the general point of the locus for the "smiting" of Rahab is firmly grounded in the textual evidence itself. This may have important ramifications in the re-evaluation of the presence of the theme of "chaos" in the Hebrew Bible, since the heavens may comprise a surprising setting for a precreation battle between the creator God and a monster of chaos. The evidence seems rather to suggest a localised battle with a localised effect. It therefore remains to examine in more detail Job 9 and 26, which contain the most mythological allusions to Rahab, in order to substantiate the preliminary remarks offered here. This is important not only for the understanding of these passages of themselves, but also insofar as they, and the fuller reference in chapter 26 in particular, may provide an insight into an underlying aspect of the allusions in Isa. 51 and Ps. 89.

Job 26

Verses 12-13 of the present chapter have often been cited as a *locus classicus* for the presence of the so-called *Chaoskampf* theme, since a number of its perceived keywords, such as הַיָּם, רַהַב and נָחָשׁ בָּרִיחַ, are present here. Nevertheless, the proponents of such an interpretation have experienced difficulty in attaining a coherent understanding of these lines as a whole without resorting to textual emendation or conjectural etymology, since v. 13a seems to defy inclusion within the expected pattern. As Habel states,[136] "The meaning of *špr* as "be beautiful, fair" seems irrelevant in connection with the chaos battle". One might add that the mention of שָׁמַיִם itself would be

136 P. 365; similarly Newsom, *NIB*, IV, p. 519.

surprising if the passage is to be read in terms of a supposed *Chaoskampf*, since even if a suitable verb is furnished, an allusion to the creation of the heavens would stand rather oddly in its present position between, rather than after, the two dragon-slaying references, and would thus seem to deny any form of chronological or logical sequence to vv. 12b-13. Habel's own proposal, following Gordis, that שפר relates to the Akkadian *šuparraru*, "spread out (a canopy)",[137] suffers from the further weakness that the spreading out of the heavens[138] is normally mentioned in conjunction with the founding of the earth, e.g., in Isa. 44:24;[139] Job 26:13 would therefore provide a rare instance where this close linkage is not in evidence, and the sole case where the earth is not mentioned in very close proximity to this idea.

Various other proposals have been made by scholars striving to maintain a *Chaoskampf* reading of this passage. Pope, for example, having first established that MT שִׁפְרָה is supported by the Qumran Targum,[140] appeals to *Enuma elish* in support of his proposed reading (entailing an otherwise unattested translation and minor emendation) of the text. Noting that Marduk used both a mighty wind (cf. v. 13a) and a net against Tiamat, he suggests that, given the similarity of the Akkadian word for "net" (*saparu*) to the last word of v. 13a (שִׁפְרָה), one should follow Tur-Sinai in adopting such a sense here, שָׁמַיִם then being divided into two words to read שָׂם יָם, "he put sea"; "thus 'By his wind he put Sea (in) a bag'".[141] However, besides the weaknesses of relying on the sort of reconstruction which it is methodologically preferable to avoid, Pope also takes as his starting-point an assumption that this passage is closely related to the Assyrian material, presuming also that Rahab should be equated with Tiamat, and the sea more-or-less with Rahab, without seeking to demonstrate these points first. In thus prioritising an extra-biblical "chaos" motif, he interprets יָם here as a proper noun, despite its occurrence in

---

137 Habel, p. 365, Gordis, p. 280, citing in support Jer. 43:10 Kt שפרור, Qr שַׁפְרִיר "tent". However, the subject of reference is here uncertain, and it may, at root, refer to something beautiful or brightly coloured, rather than to an object which is "spread out".

138 The most common verb used is נטה, but טפח also occurs. In addition, it is possible that נטה may be intended in Isa. 51:16 for MT נטע (thus, e.g., RSV; cf. Isa 51:13).

139 In eight instances, plus Isa. 51:16, these motifs occur consecutively; in addition, in the lengthy creation hymn Ps. 104, the spreading out of the heavens introduces an expanded section on this realm, and is thus separated from the succeeding reference to the founding of the earth, but the fundamental link remains intact. Cf. also Ps. 136:6, where the stretching out of the earth is coupled with the making of the heavens. In two further instances, the earth is nevertheless mentioned either in the same verse, and then also in the succeeding one, or is separated from reference to the heavens by a single verse.

140 This Pope restores as "[*d*]*nḥ*, 'shine,' cognate with Heb. *zrḥ* (**ḏrḥ*)" (p. 185).

141 Pope, pp. 185-6; Tur-Sinai, p. 382, 383-4; similarly Wyatt, *Myths of Power*, p. 95; cf. Greenstein, "The Snaring of Sea in the Baal Epic", *MAARAV* 3/2 (1982) 194-216, pp. 207-8, for whom this translation provides a justification for seeking a similar reference in a Ugaritic context, *KTU* 1.2.iv.27, notwithstanding "certain linguistic difficulties" and the peculiar syntax which results.

the preceding line with the definite article, and moreover ignores the fact that the idea of capturing a personified sea, as opposed to storing up the waters of the heavenly or subterrestrial ocean,[142] is unattested in the Hebrew Bible and seems alien to its traditions. One might note also how "net" has, in Pope's translation (and contrary to the listing for *saparru* A in *CAD*),[143] become "bag" – the capturing of water in a net being an unsustainable proposition indeed! Weaker still is Perdue's related rendering, "By his wind he ensnared Sea in a net,"[144] since the reading שׂים ים ("place sea") for MT שׁמים[145] sounds particularly forced; despite Perdue's proffered translation, the Hebrew of this colon is also left without a verb.[146]

Perhaps most damaging to such proposals, however, is the fact that they have been made not because of any difficulty with the received text itself, but on the basis of the *a priori* presupposition that the passage must be drawn into relation, and if necessary, made to conform, with other ancient Near Eastern (in this instance, chiefly Assyrian), material perceived as manifesting the *Chaoskampf* motif. However, as has already been indicated in relation to Isa. 51, mention of Rahab in contexts other than a literalistic allusion to Egypt (Isa. 30, Ps. 87) either occurs in connection with a heavenly setting (Ps. 89:6-12a) or, in Isa. 51:9-11, where the national use of the term is uppermost, close to a mention of the creation of the heavens (Isa. 51:13, 16).[147] Here, in Job 26:12-13, the most mythological reference to Rahab, and the only one where the thought of Egypt is not in evidence, it is perhaps therefore not surprising that the heavens both provide the focus of the preceding verses (vv. 8-11) and seem to register an effect of the slaying of the dragon (v. 13a).

Although a *Chaoskampf* reading of vv. 12-13 falters in failing to explain adequately the content of v. 13a, this type of interpretation may still be salvaged in respect of v. 12 alone if it is maintained that the dragons referred to in each verse should be distinguished, and this has indeed occasionally been attempted. However, a close analysis of chapter 26 and these verses in

---

142 Ps. 33:7; cf. Job 26:8 of the binding up of water in clouds, and similarly 38:22 (of the storehouses of snow and hail).

143 XV, p. 161-2.

144 *Wisdom in Revolt*, p. 175.

145 *Wisdom in Revolt*, p. 175 n. 2.

146 In another appeal to *Enuma elish*, Fohrer claims that v. 13 refers to the removal of the remains of the monster, comparing the carrying away of Tiamat's blood by the north wind in IV. 131-2 (p. 385). However, the assumption of dependence on Babylonian precedents is a governing factor; the putative correspondence with *Enuma elish* is very inexact; and the resulting sequence of thought in v. 13 is confused, since the dispersal of remains precedes the piercing of the serpent. As a result his proposal should be rejected.

147 The passing mention of the "helpers of Rahab" in Job 9:13 is merely illustrative of a point which may be presumed to be tangential to the main focus of the Rahab narrative itself, yet even here, it is not far removed from reference to the heavenly sphere (vv. 7-9).

particular indicates that this approach runs counter to the natural grain of the passage. The disputed lines stand within a carefully-structured speech, within which the established pattern is for each block of verses to allude to the same subject, or to scarcely differentiable subjects; it is not the case that individual lines refer to related but independent events or divine qualities. Within this structure, it is clear that vv. 12-13 must be read together.[148]

In fact, the initial position within each line of the mention of God's activity in nature, either in stilling the sea or in making the heavens fair, suggests that it was actually these actions which provided the first perceived point of contact between the two verses.[149] This is important, because this is most naturally to be explained by their forming part of the same event, possibly occurring sequentially; the appearance of a dragon-name in each of the paired cola therefore only confirms that impression, and indicates that רָהַב and נָחָשׁ בָּרִחַ are to be understood as the same being. The integration of the elements of these verses into one conceptual whole is further created by the occurrence of the related agents of God's power (כֹּחַ) and his hand (יָד) in 12a and 13b,[150] and of another pair, רוּחַ and תְּבוּנָה, in 12b and 13a,[151] and by the structuring of vv. 12b and 13b in such a way as to assume the appearance of effective parallels.

Even apart from such exegetical evidence, it should be considered that if נָחָשׁ בָּרִחַ is an appellation referring to a specific being other than Rahab, then that being must be Leviathan, if the commonly-held view that Isa. 27:1 refers to one creature, not three, is accepted.[152] Rahab and Leviathan are never mentioned together (even in the book of Job, though both are there alluded to in separate contexts) despite the fact that their core qualities in a mythic setting seem to be indistinguishable.[153] Hence, it appears most likely that the motifs of the slaying of Rahab and Leviathan were not regarded as

148 The speech begins, according to one's viewpoint, either with 25:2-6 or 26:2-4; then vv. 5-6 concern the vulnerability of the underworld and its inhabitants before God, before the focus moves on in vv. 7-10 to the creation, the interest being placed especially on the heavenly realm in vv. 8-11. Within the tightly-structured unit vv. 7-10, vv. 7, 10 and vv. 8-9 are each paired lines, the former alluding to the creation and placing of the circles of the earth and of the firmament, the latter to the clouds. V. 11 then seems to comprise a bridge to vv. 12-13, expressing with them the devastating power of God in the heavens, but standing before the tense break in v. 12 which marks this and probably also the subsequent verse off from the rest. The tricolonic v. 14 clearly functions to bring the speech to its close.

149 Conversely, the colonic ordering indicates that the lines are not to be read as a comparison between two independent dragon-slaying incidents.

150 Cf., e.g., Ex. 32:11, Isa. 50:2, Neh. 1:10; compare also יָמִין Ex. 15:6; זְרוֹעַ Deut. 9:29, 2 Ki. 17:36, Jer. 27:5, 32:17.

151 Cf. Ex. 31:3, 35:31, Isa. 40:13-14; compare also בִּינָה Isa. 11:2.

152 See the discussion of this passage below.

153 Of course, in certain respects, and quite possibly in origin, they may be differentiated, most notably, insofar as Rahab sometimes functions as a prosaic nation-name for Egypt, whilst Leviathan on occasion assumes a "natural" rôle as an animal living and encounterable in present historical time within God's created order.

concerning independent events which might be presented sequentially, but rather that they existed as separate traditions which had, at least in part, acquired the same content and which were regarded as alternative presentations of the same event. נָחָשׁ בָּרִיחַ is therefore probably not to be interpreted as a fixed attribute exclusive to a particular dragon, but rather as describing the behaviour of the one to which it is applied; alternatively, it may be that in one of these passages a phrase attached more particularly to one monster has been applied allusively to the other in a deliberate echo of this tradition or its poetic forms of expression as a means of drawing a parallel between them.

Thus, given that רָהַב and נָחָשׁ בָּרִיחַ are to be understood as the same being, the most probable line of interpretation is to find a locus for Rahab in the heavens themselves. This explanation was long pursued by scholars prior to the publication of Gunkel's *Schöpfung und Chaos*, and finds much support in the Joban context itself. It finds its ultimate context in the opening reflection of 25:2, and a more immediate one in the location of interest in the celestial realm from v. 8; here the binding of water in the clouds and the obscuring of the moon with cloud[154] (v. 9) is conjoined with the creation of the firmament, possibly seen under the lens of control over light and darkness (v. 10), and the trembling of the heavens at God's mighty roar in thunder (גער; v. 11). The result of this latter action may be understood thus:

> When he utters his voice there is a tumult of waters in the heavens
> (Jer. 10:13a, 51:16a).

But if vv. 8-11 envisage God as performing the negative functions of causing celestial turbulence and obscuring the light of the luminaries, vv. 12-13 then seem to reflect a time when the same—or similar—effects resulted from the activity of Rahab; however, God slew this monster, and restored calm[155] and brightness. The inference is presumably to be made that henceforth the state of the skies and celestial waters has been attributable only to God himself.

Verse 12 may at first glance appear to describe the calming of the heavenly ocean[156] after the upset caused by God himself, and in fact there are indicators of links with v. 11 which might in themselves render the passage

---

154 Reading כֶּסֶה for MT כִּסֵּה, with RSV and many modern translators.

155 The interpretation of the verb of v. 12a, רגע, is difficult since it may be understood either as "still" or "stir up", and both translations have their advocates. It is true that the stirring up of the sea is the meaning required in Isa. 51:15 and Jer. 31:35, and it might seem in place after the disturbing act of God just described in the previous line, but here one would expect a sense compatible with that of v. 13a, which seems to be a restorative action. Hence, unless vv. 12a, b, 13a are to be interpreted as a consecutive narrative describing a sequence of three acts in which the stirring up of the sea was somehow a necessary prelude to the slaying of its inhabitant, Rahab, the meaning "still" is to be preferred.

156 Or indeed the opposite, the stirring up of the sea, as either an ensuing or a related disruptive act following the trembling of the heavens. However, see the previous note.

sympathetic to such a reading. Thus, there is a fine parallel between the reaction of the pillars of heaven in v. 11b and the sea in v. 12a, since תָּמַהּ, though often translated "astound", is, at root, "to be conceived of as a torpidity which follows the divine impulse, without offering any resistance whatever";[157] conversely, the verb רגע, though often translated "still," more fundamentally means "be startled",[158] a state which may similarly result in immobility. "Power" and "rebuke = thunderous roar" are also credible conceptual parallels, despite the difference in the structuring of the lines; and there seems to be a sense in which there is an increase in intensity in the transition from indirectly- to directly-described divine action in vv. 11 and 12, before the sought-for brightening of the heavens is achieved in v. 13.

However, although such a connection may be in view on a subsidiary level, the sudden change to the perfect at the beginning of v. 12 after the long series of imperfects and participles in vv. 5-9, 11 seems to indicate that the main focus is now on a past event, rather than on a habitual act,[159] i.e., on a single and presumably particularly decisive stilling of the sea, which occurred in conjunction with the slaying of Rahab, rather than on the quietening of a storm in the heavens whenever that may arise. Indeed, the mention of the smiting of the serpent in itself seems most naturally to imply a recollection of a past event (even if, for argument's sake, cyclically renewed), rather than a repetitive action. Nevertheless, just as aquatic turbulence may only be a subsidiary effect of God's thunderous roar, it may be that it is a secondary result and indicator of Rahab's activity, the focus of which may be directed elsewhere, i.e., in darkening or clouding the heavens in some way (cf. v. 13). This is indicated in particular by the apparent paralleling of the twin functions of God's control of light and darkness in the heavens (vv. 9 [-10?]) and effect in causing celestial turmoil (in this case, the trembling of the pillars of heaven, v. 11) with the similar action and effect on the part of Rahab (thus apparently vv. 13b, 12b). It is further supported by the close links between vv. 11 and 12,[160] thus ensuring that v. 12 is read under the lens of the heavenly context provided by v. 11, v. 13 then providing the climax of these verses by drawing both elements (the skies and the dragon) together in the final resolution.

However, the question still remains as to precisely what effect Rahab may have caused in the heavens, and how the divine רוּחַ is envisaged as making the heavens fair. Here nothing more may be offered than imaginative proposals formulated largely through a combination of what the text seems to imply (or at least allow as feasible), and ideas drawn from extra-biblical texts which seem to illustrate possible objects of reference or means of understanding relevant celestial phenomena which were open to inhabitants

157 Franz Delitzsch, II, p. 57.

158 *Ibid.*, p. 58.

159 Compare similarly חָק in v. 10, which seems also to be a perfect referring to a past event.

160 These are outlined above.

of the ancient Near East.[161] Nevertheless, suggestions have not been lacking, the two main possibilities being that either the obscuring of the sky with dark stormclouds or the effects of an eclipse are envisaged.[162] The former explanation engages well with v. 13, which has been understood as describing the brightening of the heavens after a storm, the dispersing wind-blown clouds assuming the shape of a "fleeing serpent". Such an interpretation of the verse has a natural appeal, almost exactly the same sort of picture of the wind brightening and clearing the skies occurring in Job 37:21 (there in a more routine sense); likewise, the perceiving of the shape of strange creatures in the clouds may be presumed to be a universal human experience. A reference to the clearing of a storm here would also cohere well with the content of v. 11, especially if v. 12 is read in conceptual sequence with v. 11, and as describing the stilling of a storm in the heavenly ocean, though in this case, as has already been shown, the perfect seems to indicate turbulence which may be presumed chiefly to have been caused by the movements of Rahab, rather than by the divine thunder.

Satisfactory as this explanation may appear to be, like any other proposal concerning the exact movements and impact of Rahab on its environment, it is necessarily tentative, and it is therefore appropriate to consider the alternative possibilities. The other main suggestion made in this connection is to understand Rahab as some form of eclipse-dragon, which swallowed, or wrapped itself around, the sun or moon, נָחָשׁ בָּרִיחַ sometimes then being taken by the earlier writers as a constellation into which the eclipse-dragon was

161 In the present study, detailed exegesis of the Joban text itself remains of primary importance, supplemented, as far as is possible from the meagre data available, by any relevant biblical evidence. Any extra-biblical material is cited merely as providing an attested, concrete example of the sort of background one would expect to supply on the basis of Job 26 alone.

162 These suggestions are not necessarily seen as mutually exclusive. Before the preference for emending v. 13a developed among the more recent commentators, a reference to the dispersal of storm clouds in v. 13a used to be widely perceived (thus, e.g., Davidson, p. 185, Franz Delitzsch, II, p. 61, Dillmann, p. 227, Driver, p. 75, Ewald, p. 243, Kissane, p. 199, Strahan, p. 222), the "fleeing serpent" then sometimes being explained as a storm-dragon (Strahan, p. 222) or personification of the clouds (Kissane, p. 199), both Strahan and Kissane understanding this monster in relation to powers of chaos. Alternatively, v. 13b was accounted for in terms of a dragon who swallowed or encircled the heavenly bodies, which might be either in storm or eclipse (Davidson, p. 185, Driver, p. 75, Dillmann, p. 228), though many writers preferred not to be too precise about exactly which was intended. Another permutation is for Rahab to be understood as an eclipse-dragon (Delitzsch, II, p. 61) with the clearing of the skies by the wind of God following in v. 13a, נָחָשׁ בָּרִיחַ then being taken as a constellation "formed" by God (p. 59). Surprising, however, is the prevalence of the assumption that these allusions are prefaced by reference to powers of chaos in v. 12 (Strahan, p. 222, Dillmann, p. 227, Kissane, p. 199; cf. Driver, p. 75, Davidson, p. 54), notwithstanding the proximity of Rahab and נָחָשׁ בָּרִיחַ, which one might expect to be identified in these verses.

turned as a punishment and example.[163] Although the latter part of this proposal is dubious, and often rejected even by advocates of an eclipse reading, evidence for the draconic explanation of the phenomenon of eclipse is widespread, and it seems to have the character of a spontaneously-arising and universal explanation.[164] It is therefore perhaps surprising that so much have modern scholars taken the presence of the *Chaoskampf* theme in this passage for granted, despite the manifest difficulties of sustaining this type of interpretation in respect of the Masoretic text, that the suggestion of an allusion to an eclipse-causing agent, though sometimes cited, is rarely considered as a serious possibility, and is even occasionally subjected to unsubstantiated ridicule.[165] However, one has to pause to ask whether the explanation in terms of eclipse is intrinsically less plausible than the *Chaoskampf* alternative, or whether it is simply the conventions of scholarly interpretation that have guided exegetes' judgment, and whether greater familiarity with the "chaos" myth has somehow rendered it more plausible or attractive than the more obscure alternative. As has been demonstrated, the setting of the overcoming of Rahab in the heavens is well-attested; hence a result of the piercing of this dragon which impacts positively on the heavens should occasion no surprise within this context, and v. 13 must in some such way be explained, if the MT is to be taken seriously.

In fact, although שפר may be interpreted in terms of the brightening of the sky, and thus plausibly restoration after an eclipse, the agency of the wind[166] (v. 13a) may perhaps be of less certain relevance in such a connection. It is also unclear whether the action of an eclipse-causing dragon in the heavens would create a need to calm the celestial sea, though such a connection is clearly possible. However, this difficulty may be resolved by the related, but distinct, proposal that in vv. 12-13 Rahab is to be regarded as operating within, or to the advantage of, the underworld in swallowing, or otherwise endangering, the sun. This luminary was conceived of as crossing the sky from east to west, and then passing through the netherworld in order to resurface once more in the east. The motif of a dragon posing a threat to the sun as it travelled through the waters of this subterrestrial realm is reflected in a wider context in the Egyptian Apophis myth[167] and in the Ugaritic Baal-

---

163 Cf. Ewald, pp. 243-4 (re both Rahab and נָחָשׁ בָּרִיחַ, as "formerly raging monsters"), and Franz Delitzsch, II, pp. 59-61.

164 For examples drawn from various parts of the world, see Gaster, *Thespis*, pp. 228-9.

165 E.g., by Pope, p. 185.

166 If, following the majority of translators, this, or the "breath of God", rather than his "spirit", is to be understood by רוּחוֹ. (Generally, "wind" is preferred by the more modern commentators [Fohrer, p. 382, Perdue, p. 175, Rowley, p. 174, Day, p. 38, Pope, p. 181, RSV, JPS; also Strahan, p. 222; cf. REB "winds"], and "breath" by slightly earlier writers [Davidson, p. 185, Driver, p. 75, Kissane, p. 199, Dillmann, p. 227, Dhorme, p. 342, Friedrich Delitzsch, p. 73; also NEB, Gordis, p. 274]; but the rendering "Spirit" [KJV, RV] is rare.)

167 See especially *ANET*, pp. 6-7, 11-12, and the many briefer allusions there, e.g., on pp. 253, 263, 366, 367; note also the discussion of Perdue, *Wisdom in Revolt*, pp. 47-48.

Mot cycle. Although *KTU* 1.6.vi.45-53 has been subject to a variety of different translations[168] a common position is that the latter part of these lines refers to the nightly journey of the sun-god, Shaphash, through the netherworld, during which she had to negotiate her way through the waters of the underworld, inhabited by *'arš wtnn*, [169] and indeed the mention of the shades, the ghosts, the gods, and the dead (ll. 45-7) would seem to be compatible with such a focus. It may safely be presumed that this view of the sun's course—across the sky from east to west, then dipping below the horizon to travel through the world beneath the earth before rising in the east once more—may be presupposed in Israel; further, it would be natural for the underworld to be viewed as in some sense a dangerous region through which to travel, it being somewhere from which no man could hope to return as well as the abode of death. It is consequently represented through a variety of negative images, which characterise it, for example, as a dark[170] wasteland,[171] or as a hungry beast waiting open-mouthed to devour its victim.[172]

In fact, the context of Job 3:8 suggests that the association of a dragon, in this case Leviathan, with darkness and/or the underworld may have been present in Israel. Here the wish for the cursing of the day of Job's birth by those "who curse the day, who are skilled to rouse up Leviathan" is immediately followed by the hope of a lightless dawn for the same day (v. 9), this providing the climax to an oppressively dense series of images for darkness, much of it apparently associated with the *Wortfeld* of death (vv. 4-9), and framed by the explicit curse "Let the day perish wherein I was born... because it did not shut the doors of my mother's womb" (vv. 3a, 10a).[173] Some form of connection between Leviathan / נָחָשׁ בָּרִיחַ and death may also be in evidence in Isa. 26:19-27:1.[174] If this were the case with respect to Rahab / נָחָשׁ בָּרִיחַ in Job 26:12-13, as seems possible, it may offer an explanation of the parallelism in v. 5 between "the shades" and "the waters

---

168 Compare, e.g., those of *CML*, *UNP*, *RTU*, *CS*, I, Margalit, *A Matter of "Life" and "Death"*, and Dijkstra, *UF* 17 (1986), p. 149.

169 Thus M. Smith, *UNP*, pp. 175-6 n. 206; Gibson, *CML*, p. 81 n. 9; de Moor, *Seasonal Pattern* (1971), pp. 243-4; Lipiński, "The Goddess Aṯirat in Ancient Arabia, in Babylon and in Ugarit: Her Relation to the Moon-god and the Sun-goddess", *OLP* 3 (1972) 101-119, pp. 106-110; W. G. E. Watson, *UF* 9 (1977), pp. 275-6; in a variation on this, Dijkstra sees an allusion to the nightly journey of Shaphash to the underworld in ll. 44-46, there as offering reassurance that the sun goddess will guide the Shades back there after a communion meal with worshippers (*UF* 17 [*UF* 17 (1986), 1986], p. 151). Contrast, however, Margalit, *A Matter of "Life" and "Death"*, pp. 194-202.

170 For the darkness of Sheol, see the discussion thereon in relation to Job 3:8.

171 See, e.g., Jer. 2:6, 31; this imagery is discussed further in Tromp, *Primitive Conceptions of Death and the Netherworld*, pp. 131-3.

172 Thus Isa. 5:14; the notorious appetite of Sheol is subject to comment also in Prov. 30:15-16, Hab. 2:5; cf. Isa. 25:8, Ps. 141:7.

173 See further the discussion of this passage below.

174 Compare also the reference to the "swallow[ing] up" of death in Isa. 25:8, still within the so-called "Isaiah Apocalypse".

and their inhabitants" which has long puzzled scholars. (A similar idea as is expressed here in Job 26:5 seems also to be reflected in *KTU* 1.6.vi.51, where, if *ym* is translated "in the sea (of / [are])", as appears probable, it may most readily be understood as a reference to the waters of the underworld, inhabited by *'arš wtnn*;[175] one might note also the concern with the shades in the same context, *KTU* 1.6.vi.45-47).

From this perspective, the structure of the chapter as a whole assumes particular significance; thus, in Job 26, God's power to arouse fear in the realm beneath (vv. 5-6) is followed by the laudation of his disturbing power in the realm above (i.e., in v. 7 the earth, but subsequently, in vv. 8-11, the heavens). V. 12 may then return to the subterrestrial ocean, the home of Rahab, that monster's actions there causing an effect in the heavens. Verses 12-13 would thus integrate beautifully the dual netherworldly and heavenly focus of the chapter at its conclusion. Nevertheless, it has to be admitted that despite the coherence such a reading would lend to the chapter as a whole, the netherworldly location of v. 12 is not evident from the immediate context. If to the original audience it were a known aspect of the Rahab myth as referred to here, this would not have presented a problem; however, this connection is uncertain and a heavenly setting seems more probable both on the grounds of context and of the known connections of Rahab.[176] Certainly the orientation has turned once more to the celestial realm by v. 13. In fact the Baal-Mot cycle from Ugarit seems to provide evidence for an implied connection between *ltn bṯn brḥ* and an effect on the heavens, this occurring in possible association with Mot, even though the context lacks a clear subterrestrial setting.

---

175 The main alternative, that *ym* be translated "on the day (of)", though perhaps less likely, and more obscure to the modern reader in its reference, at the same time seems to invite comparison with Job 3:8, especially if *ydy* is understood to be a technical term for exorcism (see Dijkstra, *UF* 17 (1986), p. 149; Avishur, *UF* 13 (1981), pp. 15-17; de Moor, *UF* 9 [1977], pp. 366). Dijkstra even ponders in an echo of the issues raised by Job 3:8: "Was the *yam 'arš wtnn* a special black day of the Ugaritic calendar?" (p. 151).

176 Of course, were vv. 12 and 13 to be read as alluding to separate dragons, a sea-monster Rahab in v. 12 and darkness-causing cohort of death נָחָשׁ בָּרִיחַ-Leviathan in v. 13, the problem might seem to be solved. However, this is a highly doubtful means to proceed, not least for the reasons already outlined in favour of identifying these beasts above. Moreover, it would partially alienate Rahab from the heavenly context which is required in Job 26:11, 13 and which seems to be implied for this figure elsewhere; at the same time, it would entail the attribution of a celestial background to Leviathan / נָחָשׁ בָּרִיחַ, which would be highly unexpected and difficult to accommodate in relation to any of the other references to this monster found elsewhere. (In fact, if נָחָשׁ בָּרִיחַ is to be understood as an appellative especially used of Leviathan but applied here to Rahab, it is possible that it has brought with it some of this related sphere of association; or conversely, it may be that the term especially associated with Leviathan has been applied to Rahab because of the unusual relation with the realm of death made here. However, in neither case is this likely to account fully for the presence of the connection in the first place.)

The precise translation and interpretation of the relevant passage, *KTU* 1.5.i.1-5 = (26-27), 27-32, is uncertain.[177] However, it is translated by Gibson[178] thus:

> [Have you forgotten, Baal, that I can surely transfix you],
> [you][179]
> For all that you smote Leviathan the slippery serpent,
> (and) made an end of the wriggling serpent,
> the tyrant with seven heads?
> The heavens will burn up (and) droop (helpless),
> For I myself will crush you in pieces,
> I will eat you....

If this rendering of ll. 1-5 were repunctuated as a single sentence ("For all that you smote Leviathan... the heavens will burn up (and) droop (helpless)"),[180] it would seem to provide a neat counterpart to the thrust of Job 26:13, i.e., in the latter, the piercing of נָחָשׁ בָּרִיחַ is associated with the brightening of the heavens, whilst in the former, it is threatened that despite the slaying of *bṯn brḥ*,[181] (and presumably contrary to the anticipated effect of this) the heavens will still suffer harm. On the other hand, the translation of Mark Smith,

> When you killed Litan, the Fleeing serpent,
> Annihilated the Twisty Serpent,
> The Potentate with Seven Heads,
> The heavens grew hot, they withered,[182]

177 As Margalit states, "The text is famous, and infamous, at once for its virtually unique OT parallels... and its philological intractability" (*A Matter of "Life" and "Death"*, p. 87).

178 *CML*, pp. 68, 69.

179 These lines, found in damaged form in ll. 26-7, are supplied by Gibson as an antecedent to ll. 1ff., and presumed to be the final lines of the preceding tablet.

180 Cf. Wyatt (*RTU*, pp. 115-6):
Though you smote Litan the wriggling serpent,
finished off the writhing serpent,
Encircler-with-seven-heads,
the skies will be hot, they will shine
when I tear you in pieces...
The description of Ltn as an "encircler" adopted here could tally with the motif of a serpent encircling the sun as a form of entrapment which causes an eclipse.

181 In this instance, identified as Ltn. However, in view of the considerable temporal gulf between the Ugaritic and Joban texts, and indeed the absence of any mention of Rahab in Ugaritic, or any other extra-Israelite material, there seems no reason to assume that what is said of *Ltn bṯn brḥ* should necessarily be applied to the biblical Leviathan (in any of its various occurrences) rather than, or even as well as, to the נָחָשׁ בָּרִיחַ Rahab.

182 *UNP*, p. 141.

seems to imply the opposite, namely damage to the heavens at the slaying of this dragon, though the connection between the destruction of the fleeing serpent and an effect in the heavens remains. Presumably, such damage would have to be rectified; indeed, given that the slaying of the dragon was perceived as a past event, to the reader or hearer entering imaginatively into the scope of the story, it must have appeared self-evident, if only on the basis of the present *status quo*, that the heavens were made good. If so, Job 26:13 could be understood as supplying this stage in the sequence, the restoring, or "making fair", of the heavens by the רוּחַ (wind?) of God. The proposal is, inevitably, like any other made in this regard, conjectural, but, on the basis of the structural and interpretative signals of Job 26 as a whole, seems to provide a plausible explanation. Further, although it appears that the heating of the heavens may be associated with Mot (*KTU* 1.4.viii.21-24), in view of the aspects in which there is a close identity between Mot and *bṯn brḥ*,[183] and indeed the dense darkness and underworld associations of Leviathan in Job 3:8, this does not nullify the possibility of a link between an effect on the heavens and the "fleeing serpent" as well. Rather it is a subject which may not yet be fully understood and which merits further research.

Thus, of the possible means of reconstructing the precise underlying content of Job 26:12-13, the presence of Rahab in the celestial ocean causing the heating and even withering of the heavens provides a plausible explanation. It moreover fits the known relations of this monster from elsewhere, requires no textual emendation or unusual etymology and can even boast nearer extra-biblical support than may be claimed for a *Chaoskampf* reading. However, the same, but for its more distant comparative support, could be claimed also for the idea of stilling a storm in the heavens and blowing away the remnants of cloud. The only possible difficulty for this reading is a slight uncertainty as to whether a single decisive past storm-stilling is a likely narrative construct. At the same time, there is nothing to preclude it, and it would admirably fit the sequencing from v. 11, as well as explaining the close interweaving of motifs between vv. 11 and 12. In the absence of more certain evidence, it is therefore difficult to decide between these two alternative interpretations, although the negative agency of Rahab in the heavens seems well established. By contrast, the *Chaoskampf* interpretation of the passage fails to provide a unitary reading of the text of vv. 12-13 without resorting to emendation or questionable etymology or creating a false division between the two verses, and is therefore to be rejected.

---

183 See the remarks of Margalit, *A Matter of "Life" and "Death"*, p. 90, and cf. *tnn* in *KTU* 1.6.vi.51.

Job 9:13

Chapter 9 constitutes perhaps the most negative, distorted picture of God in the whole composition, since here he is portrayed as a destructive force in the world both on a cosmic scale and personally in relation to Job, as well as his dealings with humanity in general. In anti-creation mode, he overturns mountains (v. 5) and causes earthquakes (v. 6) and utter darkness (v. 7),[184] whilst in acts of apparently random violence, he suddenly snatches away, yet with impunity because of his unrivalled power (v. 12). Vis-à-vis Job, he "multiplies [his] wounds without cause" (v. 17b) and though "[Job is] blameless, he would prove [him] perverse" (v. 20). On a wider scale, "the earth is given into the hand of the wicked; he covers the faces of its judges" (v. 24). Even where something positive appears to be said about God, this is immediately extrapolated negatively: thus, that "he is wise in heart, and mighty in strength" (v. 4a) is elucidated by the ironical aside, "Who has hardened himself against him, and succeeded?" (v. 4b); and that he "does great things beyond understanding, and marvellous things without number" (v. 10) receives its expansion in the theme of God's invisible presence, under the cover of which he snatches away, unseen and unchallenged (vv. 11-12).

It is immediately after this particular example of violent and unpredictable divine action that it is stated that "God will not turn back his anger",[185] this being exemplified by the fact that "beneath him[186] bowed the helpers[187] of

184 Here as an expression of the anger of God, rather than theophany or salvific intervention: compare, e.g., the closely parallel imagery of Isa. 13:10, 13, and the causative rôle of the divine anger in Ps. 18:8, and contrast Clines, p. 230.

185 The translation "even a god cannot turn back his (i.e. Yahweh's) anger", as is occasionally proposed (e.g., by Pope, p. 68, Terrien, p. 95, Kissane, pp. 49, 54, Tur-Sinai, pp. 162, 163-4), has been aptly refuted by Gordis (p. 105), who emphasises that הֵשִׁיב אַף always means to "withdraw one's own anger". Moreover, of the thirty-seven instances of אֱלוֹהַּ in Job, there is only one, famously difficult, instance in which the meaning "a god" is possible (12:6), and this is highly debated, whilst divine beings are habitually referred to by alternative means (e.g., 1:6, 2:1, 4:18, 5:1, 15:8, 15, 25:2, 38:7).

186 Dahood's proposal (*Psalms*, III, p. 330; see further I, pp. 51, 272), that תַּחְתָּו should be rendered "at his feet" seems plausible in a small number of passages, e.g., Ps. 45:6, Ex. 24:4, but there seems no compelling reason to depart from the far commoner meaning of "under him" in this instance.

187 The meaning "helpers" is the one preferred by most translators, although occasionally a derivation from a root עזר II, better known in its Ugaritic form of *ǵzr*, is advocated, resulting in the rendering "warriors, heroes" or the like. This interpretation was expounded by H. L. Ginsberg, "A Ugaritic Parallel to 2 Sam. 1:21" *JBL* 57 (1938) 209-213, n. 5, pp. 210-211, but has gained only sparse acceptance, occurring in M. J. Dahood, Review of Friedrich Horst, *Hiob, Biblica* 43 (1962) 225-6, p. 226, Pope (rendering "cohorts", p. 68), Terrien, p. 95, and Wakeman, *God's Battle with the Monster*, p. 58; see further the detailed bibliography and discussion of possible occurrences in P. D. Miller, "Ugaritic *ǴZR* and Hebrew *'ZR* II" *UF* 2 (1970) 159-175, and the briefer summary of Michel, *Job in the Light of Northwest Semitic*, I, pp. 211-2,

Rahab". Verse 13 therefore seems to provide an example of unrelenting aggression. Certain scholars have commented that the nature of the allusion invites one to expect an historical subject of reference even despite the fact that this might seem contrary to the expected pattern in the book of Job.[188] However, although the very nature of this composition ensures that its focus remains elsewhere, this is not to preclude the possibility of historical allusion: cf. 22:15-18. Similarly, the apparent antique setting (the so-called "patriarchal" background) may not offer a guarantee that the author literally confined himself to the primeval or patriarchal era only in his references. This, of course, is especially (but not exclusively) the case if the prose frame and poetic dialogues are to be regarded as originally independent, since we are reliant for the setting almost exclusively on the former, whereas in the intense verbal debates of the latter it seems scarcely of relevance. Indeed, reference to the gift of the land may already be made in 15:18. It is, moreover, notable that Job and his friends appeal readily enough to "bygone ages" or "the fathers" (e.g., 8:8, 15:18), yet this tendency is otherwise manifested only in accounts of the Exodus generation or later, but, understandably, is not an interest attributed to the patriarchs.

Advocates of a *Chaoskampf* interpretation have sought to compare an allusion to the subjugation of the helpers of Tiamat in *Enuma elish*,[189] but this can hardly be thought of as the only possible context for an adversary to have confederates.[190] In fact, a more immediate parallel to the phrase עֹזְרֵי רָהַב is afforded by the allusion to the "helpers" of Egypt (מִצְרַיִם... כָּל־עֹזְרֶיהָ) in Ezek. 30:8,[191] which in view of the apparent origin of "Rahab" as a proper name for

especially n. 67. In fact, although either translation is possible in Job 9:8, probability, in terms of the wider Old Testament usage, favours the traditional rendering, and it is consistently preferred by those who have made a detailed study of this terminology: see P. D. Miller, *ibid.*, p. 164, Michel, *ibid.*, pp. 211-2, A. F. Rainey, "Institutions: Family, Civil, and Military" in L. R. Fisher (ed.), *Ras Shamra Parallels* (Analecta Orientalia 50; Rome: Pontifical Biblical Institute, 1975), II 69-107, pp. 74-5, 105-6. At the same time, further arguments adduced in favour of the meaning "helpers" verge on the subjective, such as a perceived compatibility with extra-Israelite references to the helpers of various deities (e.g., Baal, Marduk; Miller, *ibid.*, p. 164) or a wish "to emphasise the vassal character of the forces allied with Rahab" (Michel, p. 212), so certainty is by no means assured, and indeed a derivation from עזר II might distance the verse further from perceived ancient Near Eastern parallels.

188 Thus, e.g., A. B. Davidson, p. 69.

189 *Enuma elish*, IV.107-109; *ANET*, p. 67. Thus Newsom, *NIB*, IV, p. 411, Michel, *Job in the Light of Northwest Semitic*, I, p. 206, Fohrer, p. 207, Pope, p. 71, Clines, p. 233, Rowley, p. 78, Good, *In Turns of Tempest*, p. 418 n. 48, Strahan, p. 98 (asserting that "Rahab... was a Hebrew name for the Babylonian Tiâmat"; similarly Kissane, p. 54; cf. S. R. Driver, p. 24).

190 One might note, e.g., the reference to the "gods who help Baal" in *KTU* 1.47.26, 1.148.25, which may signify something akin to the "divine assistants" (*RTU*, p. 124) or "pages" (*CML*, p. 72) alluded to in 1.5.v.8-9.

191 Cf. also Nah. 3:8-9, where mention is made of the helpers of Thebes (נֹא אָמוֹן) and Isa. 31:1-3, where Egypt itself is cast in the rôle of a "helper".

this nation, could prove a possible line of interpretation. Of course, the signification of "Rahab" here cannot be derived solely from examples of the idiom "helpers of" which happen to be extant, since this expression could potentially be applied to a variety of subjects. Nevertheless, the known application of the appellative "Rahab" to Egypt elsewhere would further encourage this identification here, if (as seems plausible) an historical subject of reference may be accepted in this instance.[192] It may be pertinent to compare also the references to the breaking of the heads of the dragons (note the plural) and crushing of the heads of Leviathan in the context of an allusion to the Egyptian foe, conceived in plurality, at the Red Sea, in Ps. 74:13b, 14a, and similarly the "enemies" mentioned parallel to Rahab in Ps. 89:11.[193]

If, on the other hand, a mythical background is to be pursued, a further possible context may be hinted at (though only remotely) in Job 25-26, since 25:2 refers to the establishment of peace in the heavens through domination, with the concomitant implication that there may be opposing forces in that setting. Alternatively, though perhaps more conjecturally, it is possible that 26:5b may allude to Rahab and others as inhabiting the underworld (for which, perhaps compare the reference to *'arš wtnn* in *KTU* 1.6.vi.51), though the precise force of this verse is less clear, and a celestial location for Rahab seems more likely.[194] Little more than this may be said, except to observe that

192 In fact, an allusion to the Pharaoh of the Exodus is also sometimes perceived in v. 4b (see Rowley, p. 76), whilst Heidel reads 9:13 itself in terms of the Red Sea crossing, explaining "the helpers of Rahab" as "either the gods of Egypt (cf. Exod. 12:12; also 15:11) or her mighty warriors [cf. the paralleling of 'Rahab' with 'thine enemies' in Ps. 89:11], [who], unable to avert the disaster, had to admit defeat and, as it were, bow under the god of the Hebrews" (*The Babylonian Genesis*, p. 105; cf. Norin, *Er Spaltete das Meer*, p. 73). Guillaume also perceives a possible identity between Rahab and Egypt, but, in line with his postulated (yet widely rejected) sixth-century Arabian background to the book, wonders whether the "helpers" may constitute a thinly veiled allusion to Nabonidus and his allies (*Studies in the Book of Job*, p. 88).

193 Another possible source of comparison might be the allusion to the "fish of your streams" that are to be destroyed together with הַתַּנִּים הַגָּדוֹל Pharaoh in Ezek. 29:4-5.

194 By contrast, Day's contention that "Behemoth... is certainly one of the helpers" (*God's Conflict*, p. 41) is highly conjectural, being founded merely on the mention of Arš or *'gl 'il 'tk* in proximity to *Ltn* or *tnn* in two Ugaritic passages (*KTU* 1.3.iii.43-4, 1.6.vi.51), since he finds the prototype for Behemoth in the former, and proposes that Rahab should probably be identified with the latter. However, there is no indication that the foes named as conquered by Anat in *KTU* 1.3.iii.43-4 should be regarded as the confederates of a leader *Ltn* and as overcome within the same conflict, since they merely appear in a list form, with no connection between its members, whilst they are also very diverse, ranging from Yam (the first-mentioned and probably the most important) to Fire and Flame. In *KTU* 1.6.vi.51, Arš is actually mentioned prior to *tnn*, so one might expect this to be the dominant partner if they are to be regarded as standing in a leader-helper relationship, whilst the mention of only two names can offer no encouragement to the hypothesis of a wider circle of confederates. In addition, the association between Behemoth and Arš or *'gl 'il 'tk* is very tenuous: see the discussion

when God is the agent of the verb שׁחח, the object which is "bowed down" is effectively always something "high" or "proud" which must be brought low.[195] Hence, in view of the etymology of Rahab, it seems likely that the nuance of arrogance is dominant here. Given the sweeping arguments of the Book of Job about God's exercise of justice in the world as it impinges on humanity or on its various groupings, such as the righteous and the wicked, it is not inconceivable that the adjective רָהָב, "(the) proud, defiant (one[s])" should be understood.[196] However, if this is so, given Job's insistence on God's perversion of justice, the term should most probably have a specific referent,[197] rather than representing a generalised class of proud people (whom, according to his perspective, are likely to be beneficiaries of divinely-induced disorder).

Finally, it remains to be emphasised that the picture portrayed by the verses surrounding v. 13 is of God acting arbitrarily and unjustly (see especially v. 12 and note v. 22, "he destroys both the blameless and the wicked"). Thus the reader's sympathies are set against this hostile God even if they are not specifically adduced (or assumed) in respect of the casualties of his anger here. For God to refuse to turn back his anger speaks of the exercise of an uncompromising, ruthless intent to destroy (Jer. 4:23-28; 2 Ki. 23:26-7; Isa. 9:7-10:4; cf. 2 Chr. 29:8-9) that will not be deflected "until he has executed and accomplished the intent of his mind" (Jer. 23:20 = 30:24) and which is impervious to efforts at propitiation.[198] The point at issue is clearly the persistence of the divine "anger" which, one may suppose, may have been excessive or (credibly within the context of the book of Job, though this is not a judgment made elsewhere) unwarranted, or have failed to relent despite the submission, pleas or other efforts of these "helpers". Possibly the "anger" of God was necessarily prolonged in order to accomplish his purpose, i.e., overcoming these helpers may have been a protracted affair. Use of the term "helpers" may be significant insofar as the

---

of this issue below in relation to the identity of Behemoth in Job 40. Finally, since no extra-Israelite reference to Rahab is known, and the biblical tradition never mentions this figure in conjunction with Leviathan even where they are both alluded to within the same work, any simplistic identification between them seems ill-advised.

195 Isa. 2:[9], 11, 17; 25:12; 26:5; and 5:15 (where "the haughty" are named in the parallel colon). In Hab. 3:6, such terminology is not employed, but as it is the "everlasting hills" (paralleling "eternal mountains") which here "sink low", the same principle may pertain.

196 Cf. רְהָבִים in Ps. 40:5, and the KJV of Job 9:13 "even the proud helpers stoop beneath him".

197 The pride of various enemy nations is a frequent prophetic theme; for that of Egypt, see Ezek. 30:6, 18, 31:10, 32:12; Ex. 9:17.

198 As by lamentation (Jer. 4:8), supplication (Dan. 9:16), beseeching (Ex. 32:11-14), humbling oneself (2 Chr. 12:12), repentance (Jon. 3:9), obedience (Deut. 13:19), atonement (Num. 25:11, 13), turning to Yahweh to serve him (2 Chr. 30:8), the making of a covenant with him (2 Chr. 29:10) or the eradication of evildoers (Num. 25:4, Josh. 7:26).

term עֹזֵר normally has a positive ambience, and suggests reduced culpability as compared with that which may have pertained to Rahab itself; to exercise sustained ruthlessness towards such secondary parties may therefore speak of moral questionability on the part of God.[199]

Most have assumed that the reference here is to an especially notable "bowing" of unusually substantial opponents, as may be implied by the following phrase (אַף כִּי, "How much less...",[200] v. 14a). Nevertheless, this aspect is often perhaps overstated,[201] since it merely seems to constitute a possible subtext to the further reflections commencing from v. 14, whereas in v. 13, which seems to belong structurally with vv. 11-12,[202] the explicit point made (that God will—and in this instance did—not turn back his anger) is quite distinct. Hence Newsom, in distinguishing between the allusion of v. 13 and the contextualisation which follows, interprets v. 14 without reference to the power of the "helpers of Rahab", seeing the point of comparison rather in terms of "God's superiority in strength and cleverness" which would prevent Job from making an adequate legal response.[203] Moreover, were the power of the "helpers" the primary point intended, one might think it might better be made by reference to the leader, Rahab itself. This is, of course, not least the case if Rahab is to be identified as the primeval chaos monster.

As regards the nature of Rahab, nothing can be assumed from the present passage itself, even concerning its mythical or historical status, barring the fact that this entity had helpers who were the recipients of the anger of God; for further elucidation, the reader is dependent on additional occurrences of the same name. The assumption that since Tiamat is named as having helpers, reference must be to an equivalent monster, is clearly unwarranted, not least if it is no longer realistic to claim dependence on Babylonian prototypes, except in a very indirect sense. Moreover, although combat may be a relatively common and widespread motif, conflict with "chaos" is not by any means its only possible form. An alternative proposal, the relating of the "helpers of Rahab" to constellations, as favoured by some of the older

199 The formulation in Job 9:13 stands in marked contrast to the normal pattern of judgment being passed on the helper only in conjunction with the helped, as in Isa. 31:2 (cf. also v. 3), Ezek. 12:14, 30:8, the assistants being mentioned together with (and usually after) the ringleader and as an adjunct to him; cf. similarly 1 Chr. 12:18.

200 RSV, "How then".

201 Clines' translation of v. 13b, "beneath it *even* Rahab's supporters were laid prostrate" (p. 214; my italics), for example, seems unwarranted.

202 The theme of God's "anger" in v. 13 even seems to comprise an *inclusio* with v. 5, framing the triplets on God's terrible power, vv. 5-7, 8-10, 11-13, before the transition to first-person reflections from v. 14; compare similarly Hartley's placing of the division here between the larger units 9:5-13 and 9:14-24 (pp. 168, 173), Rowley's demarcation between 9:2-13 and 9:14-21 (p. 75), and Terrien's, between vv. 2-13 and 14-24 (pp. 93, 96). Others, such as Clines (p. 224) recognise at least a strophic division here, contra Fohrer, pp. 201-2 (who perceives 9:11-14 as a strophic unit within the larger section 9:2-24), and Horst, p. 137 (who takes vv. 11-17 as a strophe).

203 *NIB*, IV, p. 411.

commentators,[204] seems to have its basis in the antecedent description of the formation of the heavens and constellations, yet it can command no clear support from the text. Nevertheless, it is notable that the celestial connection which elsewhere prevails in respect of the biblical Rahab may also be operative here, albeit in a less direct fashion. This may therefore be of significance for its interpretation, in which case an allusion similar to that in Job 26 may pertain, though nothing more precise may be claimed. However, there is nothing in the verse which would seem to offer direct encouragement to the view that it concerns a battle with "chaos".

Summary

Reference to Egypt is indisputable in Isa. 30:7, and the context offers no indication that anything other than a recognised name (or perhaps nickname) is here employed. The portrayal of the Red Sea crossing and new exodus in Isa. 51:9-11 is also widely acknowledged. Moreover, a close examination of the pericope also provides powerful reasons for interpreting v. 9 as alluding to the same event, and indeed there is nothing here to suggest a connection with creation. The mention of the bowing of the "helpers of Rahab" in Job 9:13 is too terse to offer any internal guidance as to the subject of reference; the modern reader is left to supply the likely content on the basis of allusions to Rahab elsewhere. The colon has usually been interpreted mythically, in which case Job 26:12-13 offers the best hope of illumination, but a historical subject of reference might appear to be suggested by the form of words, and this cannot be excluded. Finally, Job 26:12-13 furnishes the most detailed allusion to Rahab in a context which suggests an effect in the heavens for the slaying of this monster. Although it is possible that Rahab should be regarded as an inhabitant of the underworld which presents a threat to the sun as it passes through this region each night, it seems more likely that it was understood as inhabiting the heavenly ocean, either as a storm-causing agent or as somehow effecting the heating and even withering of the skies, analogous to the description of *KTU* 1.5.i.1-5, there in association with *ltn bṯn brḥ*. Such an interpretation coheres with the frequent mention of the heavens in association with Rahab (Ps. 89:6-12a, Isa. 51:13, 16, Job 9:7-9) and indeed suggests that there may be a similar mythological background in the passages where this occurs.

Particularly striking is the way the interpretative conclusions reached here dovetail so closely with the results of the study of Pss. 87 and 89. The only references likely to derive from the pre-exilic period, Ps. 87:4 and Isa. 30:7, employ "Rahab" as a name for Egypt; this is developed in the probably exilic use of the appellative in reference to the destruction of the host at the Red Sea (Ps. 89:11, Isa. 51:9-10), though in each a symbolic use of the name, alluding to an extant mythological tradition, must be considered, and indeed this seems to be confirmed in Isa. 51:9 by the reference to the "dragon".

204 E.g. Ewald, p. 126.

Finally, Job 26:12-13 tantalisingly hints at this mythic content, apparently filling out the implications of the repeated setting in or association with the heavens which is evidenced elsewhere. This rather seems to suggest that "Rahab" originated as a name for Egypt, but that it later came to be envisaged as having a monstrous form, and ultimately came to be associated with a particular mythology, perhaps derived from another dragon figure. If this is so, it may explain the "liminal" nature of the allusion in Isa. 51:9-10, where the reference is historical but Rahab is referred to as a dragon, since it may be transitional in the development of the understanding of this figure and the thought of Egypt may anyway have run parallel to or dominated any mythological connotations. The same applies also to Ps. 89:11, where the form of Rahab is not indicated and it may chiefly have been conceptualised as an embodiment of the "enemies" overcome at the Red Sea, and it is possible even in Job 9:13. Here a dual signification would aptly balance the historical tone of the reference against the general sparsity of such allusions in the book as a whole. However, in none of these passages does a struggle with "chaos" appear to be connoted. This is nowhere more so than in Job 26, the chief source for the mythical associations of this figure, since there this theme may be extracted from the MT only with great difficulty, either though emendation or dubious etymology, and this approach is therefore to be rejected.

iii. Passages Relating to Leviathan: Job 3, Isa. 27:1, Job 40-41

Job 3

Job 3 has been understood in relation to the theme of chaos on two levels: first, in a surprisingly often-quoted article, Fishbane proposed that vv. 3-13 are a "counter-cosmic incantation" intended to effect a systematic reversal of the process of creation itself;[205] and second, v. 8 has been seen by many scholars, following Gunkel, to constitute a very direct allusion to the powers of chaos, Yam and Leviathan, יוֹם in v. 8a being emended to יָם in order to secure the desired parallel. However, there are considerable difficulties with both of these proposals, as will now be demonstrated.

Fundamental to Fishbane's thesis is his detection of points of contact between the Joban curse and the Priestly creation narrative of Gen. 1:1-2:14, which generally follow the same order. By imitating the thought (though interestingly, it appears, rarely the terminology) of the P account within the same general structure, it is maintained that Job thereby harnesses and simultaneously undermines the power of creation inherent in the divine fiat. Fishbane seeks credence for this idea by recourse to Akkadian incantations, which were often prefaced with cosmologies, apparently with the purpose of

205 M. Fishbane, "Jeremiah 4:23-26 and Job 3:1-13: A Recovered Use of the Creation Pattern", *VT* 21 (1971) 151-167, p. 153.

participating in this primordial power. In Egypt, too, divine "words of power" were deemed efficacious, though it seems only through assimilation to the prototypic event.

However, there are a number of inherent weaknesses in Fishbane's thesis. First, it must be recognised that there are certain natural resonances between the particular creation language of Gen. 1 and Hebrew curse formulae in general, insofar as both are informed by a theology of the word, according to which emphasis is placed on the efficacy of the command itself. This finds its characteristic expression in the jussive tense;[206] hence certain external conceptual and structural features adhere to both genres without there necessarily being any intrinsic relationship between the two. Thus, in order to support a theory of literary dependence, a close resemblance to the terminology of the primal narrative must be demonstrated. How far Fishbane actually achieves this will be considered below.

Second, West Semitic curses differed significantly from those typically employed in the Eastern (Akkadian) tradition, where the deities themselves were invoked to execute the curse. (Thus, in Fishbane's paradigm, the "Cosmological incantation against a Toothache", Ea is called upon to smite the toothache worm.) This has important ramifications for the understanding of the *modus operandi* of the creation accounts employed in such contexts. In the Akkadian and Egyptian examples, it appears that a recitation of the primal deeds formed an important basis for the divine action in the present; that this recitation preceded the invocation, albeit with some overlap, due primarily to the close relation between the two; and that the present situation of need could be closely identified with that in the corresponding *Urzeit*. By contrast, any allusion to creation in Job 3:3-13 is subsumed into the curse itself, rather than recited, and thus there is no indication that it is intended to form a basis for the present invocation; nor indeed is there a named addressee for the curse. Furthermore, to unravel this text into a logic parallel to that cited, one would have nothing less than a call for creation to discreate itself, or, on the Akkadian model, for God himself (who is in Job 3 deliberately not addressed) to destroy on the basis of his creative work.

This indeed is a paradox of which Fishbane is aware, and he acknowledges that the Joban curse, if assigned his interpretation, would be anomalous on three counts: first, because it seeks to effect a reversal of the cosmicising act in which it has its basis (the only parallel he can locate for this is in the Black Mass perpetrated by witches in the Middle Ages); it moreover is purported to be cosmic in its scope, whereas magic is usually an egocentric act, designed to have effect only in a limited sphere;[207] and finally,

206 Perdue, perhaps the most enthusiastic exponent of creation theology in Job, has discovered no fewer than sixteen instances of this verbal form, together with prohibitions, in 3:1-10, as opposed to the fifteen jussives and imperatives in Gen. 1; he concludes that this may reflect an attempt to "overcome the creative structure of the divine language" in the primal narrative (*Wisdom in Revolt*, p. 98).

207 Of course, the cursing of the day of one's birth and the wish for personal annihilation which infuses the whole of this speech must also be placed in this category. Thus, if

there is a significant temporal difference. The imperfects of Job 3:3ff. have a past conditional or past optative force, as contrasted with the present-future orientation of the Akkadian precative, characteristic of magical contexts. However, Fishbane does not address the immediate corollary of this observation, namely the efficacy of a *post facto* curse.

A number of other factors support this reserve. First, a close parallel to Job’s curse is furnished within the Old Testament itself, in Jer. 20:14-18. Both texts incorporate four primary themes of cursing the day of birth (Jer. 20:14a), announcement of a male child (20:15), closure of the womb (20:17), and the experience of life as עָמָל (20:18), the content of Jeremiah’s incantation providing a “frame” for that in Job (3:3, 10).[208] This is suggestive of a tradition of cursing the day of one’s birth, of which only these two examples have been preserved.[209] Foremost among the reasons for regarding this genre as operating on a strictly literary, rhetorical level, as an expression of extreme distress, must be the manifest ineffectiveness of Job’s curse (it does not bring about his sought-for release); furthermore, if the curse were seriously believed to be imbued with sinister powers, one may question whether it would have been recorded.[210]

But if Job’s curse is to be interpreted as a poetic expression of extreme anguish and hopelessness, this is not to negate any hypothesised reversal of the Genesis account on a literary level. In Fishbane’s judgment, Job 3:1-13 exhibits parallel elements from all but one of the seven days of creation. Nevertheless, the extent and distribution of allusion within the passage is variable. The reversal of the language of Gen. 1:3, יְהִי אוֹר, in Job 3:4, הַיּוֹם הַהוּא יְהִי חֹשֶׁךְ, has frequently been noted,[211] and provides a plausible correspondence. Similarly, the concept of the division of time into days and years[212] is a common element, though applied differently. However, Fishbane finds no reference to the third day of creation (the separation of the dry land

Fishbane’s detection of counter-cosmic significance in Job’s words is correct, it is in stark tension with the explicit agenda of the passage.

208 This structural point is noted also by Habel, p. 103.

209 Cf. also Sir. 23:19 (ET v. 14).

210 Compare the reticence to quote curses levelled against David in 1 Sam. 17:43, 2 Sam. 16:5-6, 1 Ki. 2:8-9, and the transmission of words of power in the cited Egyptian texts, and even the Gospels, for the purpose of application. On the ineffectuality of the Joban imprecation, see further Clines, I, pp. 76-7, 79-80. Of course, the reasons for recognising that Job did not utter an effective curse of the type envisaged by Fishbane are still more numerous: among them may be mentioned the integrity of Job (as of Jeremiah) and his relentless quest for meaning in his suffering, which would always stop short of negation (mere release could in any case presumably be achieved by cursing God “to his face”); the fact that Job perceives himself as impotent before God and too innocuous to merit constant punishment (7:12); the total non-mention of the curse and its supposed consequences in the subsequent narrative; and indeed Job’s ultimate vindication before God (42:7).

211 See, e.g., Dhorme, p. 23, Habel, p. 107, Clines, I, p. 81, Perdue, *Creation versus Chaos*, p. 98.

212 יְמֵי שָׁנָה, Job 3:6b; יָמִים וְשָׁנִים Gen. 1:14.

and seas, and the bringing forth of vegetation), and detects only a tentative allusion to its precursor, the separation of the waters above and below the earth on the second day (the waters מֵעַל the firmament paralleling God מִמַּעַל). He then reads Leviathan in v. 8 as the correspondent of הַתַּנִּינִם הַגְּדֹלִים created amongst the animals on the fifth day (Gen. 1:21), despite the fact that the logical corollary of his proposed restitution of יָם in the parallel line, as well as his wider interpretation of Job's curse as an invocation of chaos, would be for comparison to be made rather with the second or third day of creation.

The final counterparts to the creation narrative of Genesis 1 can then be detected only outside this strophe,[213] with the creation of man mirroring the opening line of Job's lament in v. 11; and the rest (שָׁבַת) after the work of creation balancing release from suffering in the underworld (which, despite using four distinct roots—נוח, ישן, שקט and שכב—, still does not pick up the verb of Gen. 2:2). Fishbane declares this a "consistent unit", though it bridges two different metrical units and even different literary forms before terminating in the midst of what is conventionally regarded as one sentence. Within the curse itself, the theme of human generation is present in the fact of Job's birth (primarily intended, if one were to seek a source, in the sense of the blessing conferred by God in Gen. 1:28). However, this operates in tandem with the postulated creation allusions, thus causing a further disruption to the sequential correspondence with the Priestly creation narrative sought by Freedman. One is then left with none of the acts of generation, but only those of division. Furthermore, the only linguistic parallels between Job 3:6 and Gen. 1:14 are the expressions יְמֵי שָׁנָה and יָמִים וְשָׁנִים (which are virtually unavoidable), but again the keynote of the creation of the luminaries is absent, as indeed is any mention of acts of separation, still less of God himself. Thus, given the misplacing of the reference to Leviathan from its sequential order, besides the questionable nature of any attempt to draw a direct association between the reference in v. 8 and the second or third days of creation, all that remains is the possible parody of the יְהִי אוֹר of Gen. 1:3 in Job 3:4. This is entirely consonant with the limited scope of Job's malediction, which is explicitly directed only against the day of his birth and night of his conception, and motivated by the simple desire for personal annihilation expressed throughout the chapter. Hence Job 3:3-10 constitutes not a systematic dismantling of creation but rather expresses the much more limited wish never to have been born, uttered by a man undergoing immense suffering.

As regards the interpretation of v. 8, which has been much discussed as purporting to employ the theme of chaos, this is best executed within an analysis of the unit vv. 3-10 within which it stands. The structure of the passage is unusually clear, and there is wide agreement among scholars as to

213 The delimitation of which is clearly marked in the Hebrew and perhaps universally recognised by contemporary scholars: note the opening כִּי clause, v. 10, and the sudden move to questions focused on death at birth commencing at v. 11.

its basic constituents.[214] After the motif of the cursing of the day of birth and night of conception is introduced in the tricolon v. 3, there follow two tricola on the day (vv. 4-5) and two on the night (vv. 6, 9), these last two framing the paired bicola vv. 7 and 8, before the whole unit is rounded off with the final bicolonic "motive" line in v. 10. As Clines states,[215] "The presence of five tricola in the first strophe (but nowhere else in the poem) is remarkable (vv. 3-6, 9); it can only signify a relentless aggregation of the maledictions". Hence the release of the intensive tricolonic structure in vv. 7-8 allows these lines to stand out as peculiarly significant and climactic within the structure of the unit vv. 3-10, just as the other bicolon in v. 10 acts as a concluding formula. (Often, tricola are used in the opposite way, as occasional inserts into prevailing bicola, often in concluding motive clauses, or to express especially significant thoughts, but here the standard practice is reversed). That vv. 7-8 should thus be interpreted, rather than as a parenthesis, as Freedman proposes,[216] is further supported by the employment of an initial extra-metrical הִנֵּה in v. 7, which provides in Freedman's view the only disruption in the symmetry of the text (note also the logically superfluous repetition of the expression הַלַּיְלָה הַהוּא) thus drawing particular attention to this couplet. Moreover, from almost unbroken terminology of darkness, verse 8 seems to exhibit language which moves away from metaphor into a more mythological (and at the same time, in its reference to human agents, more concrete) realm of allusion. Viewed contextually, then, v. 8 provides the climax of Job's consignment of "that night", and indeed also "that day", unto darkness. It seems reasonable, therefore, to expect that its subject of reference should be consonant with the prevailing language of darkness, which dominates not only the wider context, but also the paired bicolon v. 7.

However, before the content of v. 8 is analysed in detail, the force of the surrounding darkness imagery must first be determined. An indication is furnished by the consistent theme of the passage, Job's wish that he had never lived. This is developed in the rest of the speech through the expression of a desire that he had died at birth (vv. 11-12, 16) interspersed with positive images of Sheol (vv. 13-15, 17-19), and through the articulation of a longing for death to be available to those, such as him, for whom life has become unbearable (vv. 20-26). Hence in vv. 16, 20, 23, "light" is tantamount to "life", these terms standing in parallel in v. 20. The corollary of this, that "darkness" might signify death or Sheol, finds further support in the use of the same terminology in this way elsewhere in the Book of Job. 10:18-22 is extremely close in thought and tone to 3:3-10, vv. 18-19 expressing a wish to

214 See, e.g., Freedman, "The Structure of Job 3", *Biblica* 49 (1968) 503-8, followed by Habel, p. 103; and Clines, p. 76, who also acknowledges the similarity of his analysis to that of Freedman.

215 I, p. 176.

216 "The Structure of Job 3", p. 504.

have died *in utero*,[217] before a dense concentration of language held in common with 3:4-6, 9 follows in vv. 21-22. Replicated terms include חֹשֶׁךְ (3:4, 5; 10:21; cf. יֶחְשְׁכוּ, 3:9), צַלְמָוֶת (3:5; 10:21, 22), אֹפֶל (3:6; 10:22a, c) and תּוֹפַע / תֹּפַע (3:4; 10:22), yet the application of these lexemes to a "land" (אֶרֶץ) ensure that the reference to Sheol is unmistakable. Nor is the language of darkness as applied to the underworld confined to these passages. One might compare, e.g., חֹשֶׁךְ in 17:13,18:18, Pss. 88:7, 13, 143:3 and אֹפֶל in Job 28:3 and perhaps also 23:17. The vocalisation of צַלְמָוֶת as a compound, צֵל + מָוֶת, is supported by all the ancient versions, and, as has been noted by Michel, is preferred by those who have undertaken a detailed study of the term.[218] Even apart from this, the employment of the word in relation to death is irrefutable in 10:21, 22, 38:17[219] and likely also in 24:17,12:22, 28:3, so this sphere of association must be considered in relation to Job 3:5 irrespective of the translation adopted.

The pervasiveness of the motif of darkness throughout the passage, and the many indicators that it should be understood in relation to the sphere of death thus create an expectation that v. 8 has a similar frame of reference. This is especially the case when the continued darkness imagery, both in the paired bicolon v. 7 and in the succeeding line, v. 9, is taken in to consideration. Certainly, some form of continuity of thought is required, and it is not difficult to imagine how the idea of cursing the day might cohere with what precedes, as being inimical to light (cf. Gen. 1:5a: וַיִּקְרָא אֱלֹהִים לָאוֹר יוֹם). The most plausible explanation of v. 8a is thus that it refers to the cursing of a chosen day in order to make it ill-omened, probably in order to give rise to an eclipse,[220] though it may possibly be a generalised allusion to those evil ones who would curse the day(light), preferring to have all consigned to darkness (cf. 24:13-17). Less likely is the proposal of Dhorme[221] that the allusion is to those who would curse the day of their birth (cf. Job

217 Note how even the form of v. 18a mirrors that of 3:11, whilst its content, with its apparent expression of the wish to have died in the womb, supplements that of 3:3-10, and plugs the tiny niche between this and the idea of death at birth found in vv. 11ff.

218 W. L. Michel, "ṢLMWT, 'Deep Darkness' or 'Shadow of Death'?" *BR* 29 (1984) 5-20, p. 12. Space prohibits the rehearsal of the arguments surrounding the pointing and translation of this term; however, the reader is referred to Michel's article; other advocates of the reading "shadow of death" include Clines (p. 69), Newsom (*NIB* IV, p. 367), and Tromp (*Primitive Conceptions*, pp. 140-2); compare D. Winton Thomas, "צַלְמָוֶת in the Old Testament" *JSS* 7 (1962) 191-200, who retains the traditional pointing, but understands מָוֶת as a negative superlative and thus renders "very deep shadow, thick darkness" (p. 197). The pointing צַלְמוּת, which is presumed to be derived from a root צלם, "be dark", is preferred, e.g., by Dhorme (p. 24), and Gordis (p. 33), although the existence of such a root is disputed (see Clines, "The Etymology of Hebrew Ṣelem", *JNWSL* 3 [1974] pp. 23-5, Michel, *BR* 29 [1984], p. 8), as is its meaning (Michel, *BR* 29 [1984], p. 13, p. 14 n.1).

219 LXX even translates here "Hades".

220 Thus Clines, p. 86, Driver and Gray, p. 33.

221 P. 27.

3:1, Jer. 20:14), since it is doubtful whether a retrospective curse would have been deemed to be effectual, and, as has been shown above, cursing the day of birth is probably to be understood as a private expression of despair rather than as a genuine malediction.

Consonant with this, reference to an eclipse-causing dragon seems likely in v. 8b, as many have perceived.[222] In this way, the darkness and possible underworld associations of נָחָשׁ בָּרִיחַ (an epithet of Leviathan in Isa. 27:1, a context where there may also be an association with Sheol), discussed above in relation to Job 26:12-13,[223] may come into play here. A number of other scholars have also recognised the connection between the two Joban passages; some have additionally cited *KTU* 1.6.vi.45ff. (cited above, again in relation to 26:12-13) as relevant to the discussion.[224] Thus, as Clines has already appreciated, cursing the day (v. 8a) and rousing Leviathan (v. 8b) are complementary skills, "for if the dragon had swallowed up the moon, the night would have belonged unequivocally to the realm of the underworld and conception of a life would either have been impossible or ill-omened."[225] This type of interpretation finds further corroboration in the continuation of Job's malediction in v. 9, which describes the failure of the light of dawn, which would of course be the consequence of the swallowing of the sun as it passed through the netherworld on its diurnal round. Hence, in the words of Clines once again, "If the night of his conception has been consigned to the power of the underworld by the ministrations of Leviathan..., it could have remained dark for ever, never giving place to day... It would then have been no ordinary night, one in which a mortal could be conceived, but would have taken on a wholly new quality as a monstrous manifestation of the dark powers of Sheol."[226]

It is therefore surprising that some scholars follow Gunkel[227] in emending יוֹם to יָם in order to create a parallelism between the sea and Leviathan. An Aramaic incantation from Nippur, "I will enchant you with the spell of the sea and the spell of Leviathan the sea-monster",[228] is often quoted as lending

---

222 E.g., de Wilde, p. 98, Clines, p. 87, Day, *God's Conflict*, p. 46, and most of the older commentators (e.g. Ewald, p. 82, Davidson, p. 20, Dillmann, p. 25, Franz Delitzsch, p. 52, Driver and Gray, p. 34).

223 The mutual relevance of Job 3:8 and 26:12- 13 to the understanding of each other has already been recognised, e.g., by Davidson, p. 20.

224 This connection is probably correct; however, the qualification that such observations should be consequent upon, rather than foundational for, exegesis, remains.

225 Clines, p. 87.

226 Clines, p. 87.

227 *Schöpfung und Chaos*, p. 59; cf., e.g., Horst, pp. 36-7, Perdue, *Wisdom in Revolt*, p. 92, Pope, pp. 26, 30, Good, *In Turns of Tempest*, pp. 54-5, Fuchs, *Mythos*, p. 66.

228 Translation as in C. D. Isbell, *Corpus of the Aramaic Incantation Bowls* (SBLDS 17; Missoula, MT: Scholars Press, 1975) Text 2, ll. 3-4 (p. 19).

credence to this idea.[229] However, in their conviction that Leviathan must necessarily be associated with watery "chaos", and in their desire to create such a connection where none may exist, even where the logical progression of thought within the verse and MT present no problems, such scholars have overlooked the fact that they have thereby created an opposition within the verse, since cursing the sea is an act inimical to "chaos", whereas rousing Leviathan constitutes its activation.[230] Others, recognising the contradiction, undeterred, resort to further emendation or creative etymology in order to create uniformity between the verbs of each cola, whilst retaining the coveted Yam–Leviathan parallel. Thus, Gordis chooses to replicate the verb of v. 8b in 8a, reading עֹרְרֵי יָם, "Let them curse it who rouse the Sea, those skilled in stirring up Leviathan";[231] G. R. Driver derives ערר from "an unknown Hebrew root" עיר, "revile" proposed on the basis of a putative Arabic cognate;[232] and Ullendorff achieves a rendering of v. 8a as "Let the light-rays of day pierce it", by taking אררי as the plural construct of אוֹר, and deriving יקבוהו from נקב "to pierce" instead of קבב "to curse".[233] Such views have been adeptly critiqued elsewhere,[234] so there is no need to replicate the arguments here, but suffice it to say that they have not commanded wide assent.

An alternative suggestion, that one is rather to perceive here an implied wordplay between יוֹם and יָם, "a clever paratactic device for preserving two mythologems of the dragon"[235] is more sensitive to the subtleties of the Hebrew text, and would obviate the need for potentially clumsy emendation. Nevertheless, it is still subject to the same objections as advanced above; in addition, since יוֹם actually precedes rather than succeeds לִוְיָתָן in the structure of the line, and since there is no evidence that יָם was associated with cursing in ancient Israel, the probability that this type of literary nuance should be detected here is considerably diminished. Likewise, Day's proposal that Leviathan should be associated with the darkness of precreation is founded on questionable assumptions made in relation to three further passages. First, he maintains that the reference to the making fair of the heavens in Job 26:13 concerns creation, and that this theme should therefore be perceived here; however, the foregoing analysis of this passage has found that this interpretation is unlikely to be accurate. Second, he quotes the idea of darkness being "upon the face of the deep" prior to the creation of light in

229 Thus G. R. Driver, "Problems in the Hebrew Text of Job" (VT[S] 3, 1960), p. 72; Perdue, *Wisdom in Revolt*, p. 92 n. 8, p. 105; Fishbane, "Jeremiah 4:23-26 and Job 3:1-13", p. 160, Wakeman, *God's Battle*, pp. 63, 67; cf. Habel, p. 107.

230 This point has been made frequently before: see, e.g., Dhorme, p. 27, Gordis, pp. 34-5, Day, *God's Conflict*, pp. 46-7, Fohrer, p. 108, Clines, p. 86.

231 Pp. 28, 35.

232 "Problems in the Hebrew Text of Job", *VT[S]* 3 (1960), p. 72.

233 E. Ullendorff, "Job 3:8", *VT* 11 (1961) 350-351.

234 See Clines, p. 71 and Day, *God's Conflict*, pp. 47-48 (the latter in respect of Driver and Ullendorff only).

235 Fishbane, "Jeremiah 4:23-26 and Job 3:1-13", p. 161; cited approvingly by Habel, p. 101 and Michel, *Job in the Light of Northwest Semitic*, pp. 54-5.

Gen. 1:2 as supporting his exegesis, but fails to show how this might be the case; and finally his statement that *KTU* 1.6.vi.45ff. offers a "remarkable parallel" to the association of Leviathan with precreation darkness in Job 3:8 is dependent on his contention that since this passage is situated at the end of the Baal-Mot cycle, it may thus be associated with the New Year. This proposal itself rests on a number of doubtful premises, and has not attracted assent elsewhere. In particular, the transference of a connection inferred from the postulated calendric and cultic setting of a reference in a Ugaritic text onto the interpretation of an allusion in another, Hebrew, context, entails a whole series of dependent assumptions, all of them questionable, and it is only required for one of these assumptions to be mistaken for the whole theory to collapse. Moreover, the need for a differentiation between the external details of a myth and its theological, cultic or literary significance, especially where there is a significant geographical and temporal separation between the cultures concerned, cannot be overemphasised. See further the critique of Day's use of *KTU* 1.6.vi.45ff., which is crucial to his overall thesis, above in Chapter 1.

Thus, one must conclude that the attempt to seek (or create) a reference to "chaos" in this verse, howsoever this is achieved, seems particularly dubious, and should be rejected. By contrast, if Job 3:8 is read, as seems highly probable, as referring to the swallowing of the sun as it passes through the netherworld, this depends only on the most straightforward translation of the Masoretic text, without emendation and following well-established etymologies, yet it results in a highly effective parallelism between the two cola, as well as an impressively direct continuity of thought across the neighbouring lines. It thus seems satisfactory on all levels.

Isaiah 27:1

Despite differences over the exact genre-classification of Isaiah 24-27,[236] its distinctive style and interests which mark it out from prophecy in general and the rest of the book of Isaiah in particular, have long been noted by scholars:[237] the coming intervention of God is envisaged as a final solution acted out on a world scale, encompassing both heavenly and earthly powers, and even entailing the "swallowing up" of death. Characteristic of this type of writing, however, is the obscurity of its references, and the difficulty of

236 Some have affirmed its apocalyptic (or, perhaps better, proto-apocalyptic) status, whilst others have insisted that it is merely eschatological in character, and hence perhaps closer to prophecy than has often been assumed; thus, Sweeney has even concluded that "the generic character of the whole is a Prophetic Announcement of Salvation that focuses on the establishment of YHWH's new world order" (p. 315). For summaries of research on this issue, see Millar, *Isaiah 24-27 and the Origin of Apocalyptic*, pp. 1-9, Sweeney, pp. 313-4.

237 Thus even Jerome, *Commentariorum in Esaiam*, VIII, xxiv, 1/3, ll. 9-15 (Corpus Christianorum, Series Latina LXXIII; Turnholti: Brepols, 1963, p. 316).

connecting it to specific historical circumstances, despite the general picture of the oppression of God's people which may be derived from its content. Hence, there is a considerable diversity of opinion over an enormous range of issues connected with this passage, among them its date,[238] textual divisions and literary unity,[239] and indeed the section to which 27:1 belongs. Many scholars read it together with 26:20, 21, and this seems the most persuasive option,[240] though some widen these parameters,[241] whilst a few take 27:1 alone.[242]

Fortunately, for the present purpose, resolution of these complex, and perhaps insoluble, issues is not vital. Nevertheless, it is in keeping with the proto-apocalyptic context of Isa. 27:1, but a tangible departure to the usage elsewhere in the Old Testament, that the slaying of Leviathan is here projected into the future. The various epithets for the dragon have sometimes

---

238 Most regard Isaiah 24-7 as post-exilic, and although advocates for every century within this epoch may be found, the more recent trend tends towards reversing the enthusiasm for a very late date within this band that was displayed by many earlier scholars. A time later than the second century, which has in the past sometimes been proposed, now seems excluded by the Qumran discoveries, whilst a pre-exilic and Proto-Isaianic origin, although occasionally advocated, seems similarly improbable and has consequently failed to command wide assent. For summaries of scholarship on this issue, see Gray, pp. 403-4, Millar, *Isaiah 24-27 and the Origin of Apocalyptic*, pp. 15-21, Johnson, *From Chaos to Restoration*, pp. 11-14, and Wildberger, II, pp. 905-6; note especially Wildberger's helpful analysis of some of the key issues, II, pp. 907-911, and Polaski's evaluation of the difficulties with the most commonly advanced evidence (*Authorizing an End: The Isaiah Apocalypse and Intertextuality* [Biblical Interpretation Series, 50; Leiden: Brill, 2001], pp. 51-56).

239 For the history of research on this issue, see Wildberger, II, pp. 893-897 (and his own proposals on pp. 904-5), Kaiser, II, pp. 141-143 (he sets forth his own reconstruction on pp. 144-5), and Johnson, *From Chaos to Restoration*, pp. 14-15; cf. the analyses of Vermeylen, *Du prophète*, I, pp. 349-81, Clements, pp. 197-200, and Sweeney, pp. 316-7.

240 See especially B. W. Anderson, "The Slaying of the Fleeing, Twisting Serpent: Isaiah 27:1 in Context" in *Uncovering Ancient Stones*, 3-15, pp. 9-10; this position is accepted also, e.g., by Oswalt, p. 490, Johnson, *From Chaos to Restoration*, p. 81, Auvray, p. 237, and Millar, *Isaiah 24-27 and the Origin of Apocalyptic*, p. 69, though the latter simultaneously claims an independent origin for 27:1, which he describes as a "Divine Warrior Hymn" (p. 105).

241 Thus Gray, who describes 24, 25:6-8, 26:20-21, 27:1, 12-13 as "An Apocalyptic Poem" (p. 404); contrasts Watts' highly unconventional understanding of 27:1 as part of the supposed unit 27:1-13 (pp. 348-9).

242 E.g., Brueggemann, I, p. 210, Wildberger, II, p. 903, Kaiser, II, p. 177, and Clements, p. 218, the latter of whom however thinks of it as "sum[ming] up the message of assurance given in 26:19", and hence as "a further response to the lament of 26:7-18"; cf. Childs' description of v. 1 as "a separate oracle that is joined thematically with the rest of the chapter" (p. 194), and similarly Sweeney, pp. 350-1.

been read as alluding to three (or occasionally two) world kingdoms,[243] but more often in recent times (especially in the light of Ugaritic parallels) they have been interpreted as appositional clauses, and hence as referring to one nation or city,[244] and indeed the single nature of the dragon and its referent may now almost be taken for granted. A slight variation on this is the credible proposal that Leviathan is here intended to signify world powers in general. Alternatively (or perhaps simultaneously) the strong emphasis on the "iniquity" of "the inhabitants of the earth" in the preceding verse and in chapter 24 may be compatible with the idea of Leviathan as a symbol for the enemy of God which is ultimately overcome by God; hence it may even possibly represent that evil, or cause or agent of evildoing, in whatever form it may take, which must be eradicated.[245] However, to suggest that he represents the originating source of evil,[246] which must be dealt with once its specific manifestations have been despatched,[247] though attractive and in keeping with later apocalyptic usage, may possibly be to extend the point too far. It is interesting to note in this context the plausible proposal that 26:20 may contain an echo of the Exodus tradition reflected in Ex. 12, especially Ex. 12:23,[248] since mention of Leviathan, together with other allusions to a

---

243 The various proposals which have been made in this regard are documented by Day, *God's Conflict*, p. 143, Polaski, *Authorizing an End*, pp. 53, 281 n. 4, and Gray, p. 450.

244 The most common candidates are Babylon (Johnson, *From Chaos to Restoration*, p. 84; Seitz, p. 198) and Egypt (thus Wildberger, II, p. 1004, and Day, *God's Conflict*, pp. 144-5, the latter also regarding Persia or Babylon as possibilities), though Assyria (Hayes and Irvine, p. 315) and Tyre (Watts, p. 348) have also been proposed

245 Thus Stacey appropriately describes Leviathan as "the symbol of all rebellion" (p. 162) and "in the present verse as the ultimate enemy of Yahweh" (p. 163), whilst Clements is more specific, stating that "the dragon expresses the power of evil and oppression throughout the world... By [slaying the dragon] Yahweh would remove the cause of social disorder and silence the voice of oppression and contempt which threatened the lives of Jews" (p. 218); cf. also Anderson, p. 7 (who characterises Leviathan as "a monster who symbolizes powers of evil at work in human history, manifest in any of the oppressive nations") and Oswalt, p. 491 (who refers to "the monster of moral evil"). Brueggemann's claim that Leviathan represents "a real, live, objective power of evil, without regard to human goodness" (I, p. 211), however, may take insufficient account of the mention of "iniquity" in the preceding verse.

246 Thus Childs: "the imagery... serves to address the basic ontological problem of primordial evil" (p. 197).

247 Thus Kaiser, II, p. 179: "Behind 26:20f. we saw Yahweh's judgment upon the nations; and it follows from the logic of mythical thinking that after the incarnations of evil the evil itself must be conquered, and that God has to destroy the last enemy, if 'that day' is really to bring the final turning point in history." See likewise Childs: "[God] will destroy not only historical forms of evil, but strike against its cosmic source once and for all" (p. 196).

248 See Johnson, *From Chaos to Restoration*, pp. 81-2 for detailed arguments relating to matters of context, language and content, which, though of varying strength, may be offered in support of this idea; the connection is also made by Gray, p. 449, and Fischer, I, p. 179.

dragon, is frequently encountered in relation to the same tradition.[249] Though this could be adduced in support of understanding Egypt as the subject of reference in 27:1, it is possible that the recollection is rather due to the history of usage and traditions associated with Leviathan itself.

The likely post-exilic date of Isa. 27:1, and the possibility that it may even be the latest of the passages considered in the present monograph, is significant from a diachronic perspective, since here "mythical" language is at its most explicit. Congruent with this are the linguistic affinities between Isa. 27:1 and *KTU* 1.5.i.1-3,[250] which have often been noted, and which are all the more remarkable for the immense time-span between the production of the texts. The fact that it is in this very late text that the greatest affinities to Canaanite literature are present should act as a salient warning against the assumption that such points of contact are indicative of an early provenance. Rather, it may indicate that the acceptance, or possibly appropriation for Yahweh, of such mythic material in formal religious circles may have been late and gradual, all the draconic references here considered seeming at least to be exilic or later.

The presence of such parallels with Ugaritic literature may well indicate the existence of a common west-Semitic tradition of the slaying of Leviathan by the leading deity. However, it cannot be assumed from the limited extant references that the motif had a central place within any religious system, and indeed it may perhaps better be classified as of the nature of popular religious tradition, dragon-slaying myths having a central place in folk stories throughout the world.

Of course, the crucial issue here is not merely the presence of the motif, but its signification. By most modern commentators the connection of Leviathan with a primordial chaos-battle preceding creation is taken for granted.[251] However, the analysis of relevant passages in the present monograph would suggest that there is no reason to posit an identification between Leviathan (or indeed Rahab) and the sea,[252] still less to associate it

---

249 If so, it is not impossible that there may be a more remote connection between the sphere of thought encountered in Isa. 26:21 and Ps. 74:14b, the uncovered slain being comparable to the body of Leviathan left in the open to be consumed.

250 The wording of this latter passage is: *ktmḫṣ ltn bṯn brḥ / tkly bṯn ʿqltn / šylt d šbʿt rašm* ("for all that you smote Leviathan the slippery serpent (and) made an end of the wriggling serpent, the tyrant with seven heads"). The appellative נָחָשׁ בָּרִחַ occurs also in Job 26:13, there applied to Rahab, but עֲקַלָּתוֹן, "crooked, twisting" is a *hapax legomenon* in the Old Testament, though different forms of the same root are found on three other occasions.

251 Thus Wildberger, II, p. 903, Johnson, *From Chaos to Restoration*, p. 100, Gray, p. 449, Miscall, p. 71, Sweeney, p. 344; the identification of Leviathan with Yam is also often presumed (e.g., by Kaiser, II, p. 177).

252 Indeed, the statement here that הַתַּנִּין is *in* the sea suggests a distinction between the two; however, since the final clause of the verse, אֲשֶׁר בַּיָּם, is omitted from the LXX, even this connection may not be original. Note also in a Ugaritic context Loewenstamm's observation ("The Ugaritic Myth of the Sea and its Biblical Counterparts", *Eretz Israel*

closely with creation or "chaos", in either the extant Ugaritic or biblical literature. Hence, whatever the import of references to Yam and the deity's engagement with it, the same significance cannot be assumed to pertain to draconic contexts. Indeed, in Ugarit, the allusion to the slaying of *Ltn*[253] is slightly briefer than that in Isa. 27:1, and although a detailed description of Leviathan is offered in the second divine speech of Job, the varied and diversely-developed biblical allusions do not do much to assist in the quest for the form and meaning of any "original" Leviathan myth. However, in both Ugaritic and biblical contexts the overcoming of this dragon is understood as conveying the power and supremacy of the victorious deity, and perhaps this is the fundamental extent of its import, despite the variety of applications of the theme manifested in the Old Testament. Alongside this, as in Pss. 74, 89, Isa. 51:9 and Job, the power of the dragon motif is in Isa. 27:1 felt as a metaphor for suffering or embodiment of experienced evil, here, as often elsewhere, primarily encountered in the form of political oppression.

Wildberger, in his discussion of the extent of apocalypticism in Isa. 24-7, lists those elements found in true apocalyptic, but absent here; among them, he includes "a Satan figure who is a personification of evil".[254] The assessment that this motif is not present in Isaiah 24-7 is undoubtedly correct, and indeed it would be wrong to suggest that "Satan" or related ideas are in any way envisaged. Nevertheless, the futuristic and – in the sense that its significance is not revealed - apocalyptic-symbolic use of the dragon image, and even perhaps the moral overtones of the verb פקד (brought out particularly strongly in Gray's translation, "visit iniquity upon"[255]), could be viewed as an advance in this direction, and as laying the foundations for the fuller imagery found in Revelation, where the dragon, as a symbol of evil, is identified with Satan (Rev. 12:9).

Finally, although the foregoing analysis has failed to find any basis for associating Leviathan with the theme of "chaos", it is worthy of notice that Isa. 24 has sometimes been described as delineating a return to precreation

---

9 [1969], English summary, p. 136) that "in Gordon 68, 129, 137, the god of the sea appears without monsters", whilst "text 67 refers to Baal's victory over *ltn bṯn brḥ // ltn bṯn 'qltn* alone"; hence it is only in relation to Anat that the overcoming of *ym* and *tnn* are conjoined, in what this scholar describes as "an older stratum of the myth" (*KTU* 1.3.iii.38-46, there in a list where a number of monsters are mentioned, and PRU II no. 3, ll. 7-8). Loewenstamm also emphasises that Yam is portrayed as having a human form, "his relation to the waters hinted at only by name", and that his struggle with Baal is understood as "strife between members of the royal court", not as an attempt by the waters to conquer the dry land.

253 *KTU* 1.5.i.1-3; cf. 1.3.iii.40-42, where mention of *tnn* is followed by that of "the wriggling serpent, / the tyrant with seven heads" (*bṯn 'qltn / šylṭ d šb't rašm*, the same appellatives as are employed in 1.5.i.2-3), there in a list of conquests.

254 II, p. 910.

255 P. 407. The more common translation, "punish", obviously has the same import.

chaos,[256] and indeed in v. 10 mention is made of the קִרְיַת־תֹּהוּ (cf. תֹהוּ וָבֹהוּ, Gen 1:2), whilst v. 18e clearly echoes Gen. 7:11. However, here in Isaiah it is made explicit that the desolation of the earth is effected by Yahweh (v. 1) and is due to the guilt of the inhabitants of the earth (vv. 5-6, 20). This seems to reflect a totally different form of thinking from that which speaks of an earth cosmologically threatened by a chaos-dragon,[257] since the cause is to be found within the terrestrial, and particularly the human, realm itself. Moreover, a careful reading reveals that this desolation is expressed in the language of aridity and drought, even to the extent that the clear echo of Gen 7:11 is employed to indicate divine intervention, but one which results in an earthquake, not a deluge of water. If comparison were to be made with the Ugaritic Baal cycle, such aridity would have to be found, though without close parallel, in the results of the reign of Mot (*KTU* 1.5.ii.5-6, 1.6.iv.1-3), as indeed may be compatible with the overcoming of death which is described in Isa. 25:8, 26:19. However, the language of desolation and infertility is also closely comparable with that employed elsewhere in prophetic passages of judgment, and is bound up with concepts of kingship and divinity, fertility being the result of a strong, good king and deriving from a beneficent deity, whilst drought and disaster are its opposite.

John Day makes comparison between the mention of "the dragon" (*tnn*) at the end of the Ugaritic Mot cycle and the reference to resurrection beyond the grave in Isa. 26:19, shortly before the allusion to the destruction of Leviathan;[258] Ltn is, of course, actually mentioned by name in *KTU* 1.5.i.1-3 in the opening lines of the myth, where Mot makes reference to Baal's destruction of this dragon in language comparable to Isa. 27:1. It is difficult to assess how much, if anything, should be made of this observation, without moving into the realm of conjecture and hypothetical reconstruction. However, if there is a connection between Leviathan and Mot this might explain the reference to Leviathan in Job 3:8,[259] which seems to operate within the *Wortfeld* of death, even though this connection does not seem to be widely applicable to the biblical allusions and does not feature in the extant lament psalms, despite their frequent use of the imagery of Sheol. At the same time, if this is correct, it would further distance Leviathan from the association with primordial, cosmic "chaos" which has conventionally been made by the majority of modern scholars.

256 Thus Miscall, p. 71, Millar, *Isaiah 24-27 and the Origin of Apocalyptic*, e.g., p. 118, Johnson, *From Chaos to Restoration*, e.g., p. 16.

257 Contrast Miscall's apprehension that in Leviathan "chaos is overcome and the cosmic destruction [of chapter 24] reversed" (p. 71; cf. Johnson, *From Chaos to Restoration*, p. 84); however, judgment by God is not an enemy to be externalised and overcome by him, and as Miscall himself says in relation to 27:6-13 (which he describes as "summariz[ing] the preceding"), "salvation and judgment, sin and its removal" "[are] combin[ed]" (p. 72).

258 *God's Conflict*, pp. 150-1.

259 See the discussion thereon, and compare also the analysis of the use of נָחָשׁ בָּרִיחַ in Job 26:13.

Job 40-41

Much of the debate concerning Behemoth and Leviathan has centred on the question of whether they are "real" or "mythological" animals. The majority view is that Behemoth is the hippopotamus and Leviathan the crocodile, and certainly this is more persuasive than the opposing "mythological" interpretation.[260] Nevertheless, it is not always found compelling, since Leviathan is depicted as breathing fire, which is difficult to explain in naturalistic terms and hence must be attributed to poetic hyperbole if a non-mythological understanding is to be pursued. Although this explanation is in many ways persuasive, it is not immediately appealing to all commentators.

However, it must be appreciated that the distinction between "real" and "mythological" creatures is not one which the ancient Israelites would have been likely to have recognised.[261] In the ancient world, descriptions of animals were often reliant on reports, with the concomitant risk of inaccuracy, misunderstanding and embellishment. Just as early seafarers returned with tales of monsters of the deep, likewise desert-dwellers, hunters ranging through little-explored forests or areas of wilderness, travellers and others might tell of strange animals seen from afar but not actually captured. Egyptian art contains many examples of composite animal figures, these in turn probably having a Mesopotamian origin, but since they are represented as living in the wild among real animals such as lions and antelopes, it

260 G. R. Driver's identification of Behemoth as a crocodile (G. R. Driver, "Mythical Monsters in the Old Testament", *Studi orientalistici in onore di Giorgio Levi della Vida* I [Rome, 1956] 234-49, pp. 234-8) and Leviathan as a whale (*Ibid.*, pp. 238-42) or dolphin (G. R. Driver, Review of H. H. Rowley, *Job*, *JTS* 22 n.s. [1971] 176-9, pp. 177-8) may be discounted, since it is reliant on dubious emendations in respect of Behemoth, combined with the transposition of a large section of text (40:31-41:26, ET 41:7-34) from the second description to the first, in order to facilitate the attribution of Leviathan's crocodilian features to Behemoth ("Mythical Monsters", p. 242). Likewise, the notion that the Leviathan of 40:25-41:3 (ET 41:1-11) is a hippopotamus (E. Ruprecht, "Das Nilpferd im Hiobbuch", *VT* 21 [1971] 209-31, pp. 221-222), rests on the dubious premise that it reflects methods of capture which were applicable to this animal (even though the rhetorical point being made is that capture by these means was not possible), as well as entailing the dismissal of the bulk of the Leviathan passage, 41:4-26 (ET 41:12-34), as an incompatible addition, and thus this is also to be rejected. Another suggestion, that Behemoth should be understood to be the buffalo (B. Couroyer, "Qui est Béhémoth?", *RB* 82 [1975], pp. 418-43; Duck-Woo Nam, *Talking about God: Job 42:7-9 and the Nature of God in the Book of Job* [Studies in Biblical Literature 49; New York: Peter Lang, 2003], p. 150), is undermined by the fact, acknowledged by Couroyer himself, that the buffalo, or wild ox, has already been considered in 39:9-11. Note also the treatment of these and other minority views in Day, *God's Conflict*, pp. 66-68, 78-80, and the systematic rebuttal of Couroyer's case in Keel, *Jahwes Entgegnung an Ijob* (Göttingen: Vandenhoeck & Ruprecht, 1978), pp. 128-131.

261 A similar point is made by Fuchs, *Mythos*, pp. 227-8.

appears that they were considered actually to have existed in nature.[262] In one example, on the walls of the tomb of the nomarch Baqet III of Beni Hasan, is "a detailed hunting scene in which there [are] fantastic animals... On the same wall [is] a whole catalog of real birds, represented in color, with their names—indicating the extent and accuracy of Baqet's knowledge of the fauna. There, as in all contexts already mentioned, fantastic animals were perceived as an integral part of the natural environment."[263] Other strange animals are portrayed in a domestic setting together with tame creatures such as dogs and monkeys. The discovery at Gaza and Megiddo of so-called magic wands which depict fantastic animals considered to have protective powers indicates the attractiveness of these animals for the people of Palestine and also the migration of these traditions through the Fertile Crescent.

A similar situation seems to pertain in Herodotus' account of the natural history of Egypt: he describes the crocodile and hippopotamus successively in some depth, but then provides similar detail concerning the phoenix, an animal which he had never seen since, as he was informed, it visited Egypt only once every five hundred years. He then includes further legendary information about this creature, before providing an account of horned snakes, and then of winged flying snakes which, he records, were killed *en masse* by ibises at a certain pass in Arabia where he himself saw their skeletons piled up.[264] He thus seems to mix legendary and factual material without any apparent awareness of the distinction between the two. Yet the context for these descriptions, which may be roughly contemporary with the book of Job, is one of informative prose travel writing, which was apparently carefully researched and produced within one of the more advanced and sophisticated cultures of the day.

Inaccurate medieval depictions (e.g. the misplaced elephant trunk on the Hereford Mappa Mundi) and cartographic practices (e.g., the decoration of the sea with strange sea serpents, or the marking of locations such as Alexander's barrier against Gog and Magog or, on Eastern medieval maps, the Land of the Wāqwāq), and indeed modern claims regarding encounters with UFOs, the Loch Ness monster, big-foots, or yetis, among others, suggest that this is not a phenomenon which was confined to one setting. Hence, if the creature which is described at what is presumably intended to be the climax of God's answer to Job out of the whirlwind (and indeed of the whole book) were a fantastic animal, believed to have existed in the wild, but not actually fully recognisable as a "real" species, this would hardly be surprising, such creatures being the most impressive and striking that could be recalled. However, this background also suggests that the typical assumption in relation to the identity of Behemoth and Leviathan, that they should either wholly correspond to a known species or be regarded as

262 See D. Meeks, "Fantastic Animals" in D. B. Radford, *The Ancient Gods Speak: A Guide to Egyptian Religion* (Oxford: OUP, 2002), 117-120.

263 D. Meeks, "Fantastic Animals" in D. B. Radford, *The Ancient Gods Speak*, p. 118.

264 Herodotus, *The Histories*, II.68-71.

mythological embodiments of chaos, is inappropriate.[265] Fantastic creatures could be believed both to exist as real animals and, at least on occasion, to have a supernatural quality, one which was characteristically beneficent. Conversely, accounts of natural creatures were sometimes embellished or simply mistaken or inaccurate. Presumably, in either case, belief in the existence of such animals in the present may be taken for granted. This is certainly demanded for Behemoth and Leviathan—whether they are natural or not—by their immediate context within the divine speech, where Yahweh's address to Job would have little impact if they were thought merely to be the subject of fiction, defunct religion, or historical interest.[266] Moreover, even were either of these beasts thought of as supernatural, it is another issue again as to whether they may be perceived as embodiments of "chaos", as detrimental in some other way, or as accepted members of the natural order.

In fact, there is evidence that Behemoth and Leviathan should here be regarded as "natural" creatures. At the outset, the content of the first divine speech creates this expectation for the animals described in the second, though of course this does not exclude *per se* the possibility that such an expectation could be thwarted or challenged. Nevertheless, the description of Behemoth correlates well with what is known of the hippopotamus, and more importantly reflects a peaceable creature at home in its environment and finding particular favour with God. Thus the portrayal begins with mention of his herbivorous diet (v. 15), and this is iterated again in v. 20, before his sedentary habits are outlined (vv. 21-22). Just as crucial to the understanding of Behemoth is the highly positive divine attitude to him, since he is said not only to have been created by God, as was Job (v. 15),[267] but even to be the foremost among his ways (v. 19).[268] The generous provision of nature for his needs (stated in the active, rather than the passive, vv. 20, 22) is probably also to be understood as a further outworking of the divine blessing of this creature. His impressiveness lies in his powerful form (vv. 16-18) and

265 Compare Carol Newsom's insight that "although [Behemoth and Leviathan] are unquestionably creatures of God (40:15; 41:25-26 [ET vv. 33-34]; cf. Ps. 104:26), they partake of the primordial... and the mythic... These are liminal beings who belong to the boundaries of the symbolic world." (*The Book of Job*, p. 248).

266 For this reason, Habel's claim that "Leviathan is the great primordial seamonster portrayed...as if he could be observed today" (p. 573) seems dubious.

267 This is the most natural interpretation of עִמָּךְ, although alternatives have been proposed, and are helpfully summarised in Nam, *Talking about God*, p. 151. Day's omission of אֲשֶׁר עָשִׂיתִי in 40:15a and translation as "Behold Behemoth before you" (*God's Conflict*, p. 75 n. 37, following LXX; cf. similarly Fuchs, *Mythos*, pp. 230, 234, Fohrer, pp. 521-2), is unpersuasive, since the proposed rendering of עִמָּךְ as "before you" would be highly unusual in any context, and moreover deletion on the grounds of metre is always uncertain. The desirability of excising this phrase for someone seeking to sustain a mythological interpretation is evident.

268 On this, see below.

(presumably related to this) his fearlessness in turbulent water (v. 23).[269] He is unsusceptible to control, or perhaps capture, by two described means (v. 24).[270] As such, he is to be held in awe, and God's pride in the creation and provision for this creature, as well as the idea that Behemoth is foremost among his works of creation, and hence of particular importance to him, is to be wondered at. All this strongly indicates that Behemoth is a valued part of the natural world, and not some form of monster subdued before creation or in some sense adversarial to God's purpose within it. In terms of its physical characteristics, there is a great deal to support the commonly held view that Behemoth is to be identified with the hippopotamus, and nothing to preclude it.

The idea that Behemoth is the "first of the ways of God" is presumably intended to indicate especial divine pride in this creature,[271] the phrase "the ways of God" probably referring to the way Yahweh orders the world, the overarching design informing its creation and governance.[272] Behemoth is thus a primary expression or example of this, and hence reveals something of God's values, perspective and intention. This is an impressive claim to make, and would doubtless have caused surprise in relation to such a feared beast as the hippopotamus. However, it is entirely consonant with the challenging and vivid nature of the poetry of the divine speeches, and thus is probably to be understood as eliciting a change of perspective in its human recipient by undermining simplistic anthropocentric assumptions about God's provenance and activity in the world. In view of Prov. 8:22, this verse might be

---

269 This seems to be the general force of the Hebrew, although the exact sense of the verb is uncertain, as עשק normally means "oppress", which ill suits the context here. Many commentators therefore resort to emendation, for examples of which see Dhorme, p. 569, Rowley, p. 257. Dhorme himself proposes a root עשק, "be strong", comparing Assyrian *ešqu*, "strong", hence "swells violently" ("est violent", p. 569), whilst Guillaume ("The Arabic Background of the Book of Job" in F. F. Bruce [ed.], *Promise and Fulfilment*, p. 126) finds an Arabic sense for the verb, "rise and fall", and either of these possibilities would suit the context adequately; other translations, of varying credibility, are documented by Fuchs, *Mythos*, p. 234 n. 71. However, to conclude on the basis of this verse, with Habel (p. 567), that "Behemoth seems to represent lordship amid the chaos waters" seems wholly unwarranted. In fact, hippopotami are strong swimmers and may sometimes be seen with mouths agape in the water; special mention of this creature's mouth is particularly apt, since it is the largest of that of any land creature, and may be opened 180°.

270 On this, see further below.

271 "First" thus indicating pre-eminence (so also Gordis); alternatively, chronological primacy could be indicated, but even then this might be regarded as a means of indicating this creature's superior importance. However, to conclude, with Habel (p. 566), that "The world apparently began with the chaos God created, personified here, as in other mythic traditions, by a monster he then overcame and controlled" is to overreach the evidence and to supply an idea from elsewhere which is not apparent here.

272 Cf. Fuchs' paraphrase as "plans and leadership", *Mythos*, p. 238. The nuance of kingship or dominion may also be present, as discussed above in relation to Job 9:8.

tantamount to saying that this animal epitomises God's wisdom, but it is not as man's. The world is made on a scale which man cannot comprehend, and contains, with God's blessing, not only the genuinely beautiful and beneficial, but also what from a human perspective appears dangerous and ugly, yet which to God may nevertheless be especially pleasing.

The parallel colon, v. 19b, is rendered in the RSV "let him who made him bring near his sword".[273] According to Day, this half-verse "coher[es] with the idea implicit in Job 40:9ff. and 24 that God, but not man, can overcome Behemoth".[274] However, although 40:9ff. is a challenge to Job to don divinity, and right all the wrongs in the world, this is not necessarily to imply that to capture or overcome Behemoth is straightforwardly to be equated with crushing the proud and wicked, since such groups seem very much to be located in the human sphere, both here and elsewhere,[275] whereas no connection is made between them (or such qualities as pride or wickedness) and Behemoth.[276] Indeed, were one to understand that Behemoth is an example of such a being which Job would wish to see "brought low", the unfolding passage shows that to do this is not God's way: God is the creator of this mighty creature, and Behemoth is a source of especial pride, not the subject of fear or hostility. Nor is the overcoming of Behemoth presented as

---

273 Habel's translation, "His Maker draws his sword against him" (p. 550), seems to create a direct opposition with the parallel colon, and so can hardly be correct; scarcely better is that of Day, *God's Conflict*, p. 75, "He that made him may bring near his sword." Another possibility which would at least be intelligible is that of RV margin (advocated also by Rowley, pp. 256-7, and many older commentators, e.g., Franz Delitzsch, pp. 488-9, Dillmann, pp. 345-6), "He that made him hath furnished him with his sword", referring to the hippopotamus' teeth or tusks. (Congruent with this, the central incisors may be described as "spear-shaped", whilst the lower tusks may be up to 50cm long ["Hippopotamus: hippopotamus amphibius" (On-line. Reprinted from "The Safari Companion" by Richard Estes), (Nature-wildlife.com). Accessed 14 September, 2004 at http://www.nature-wildlife.com/hipptxt.htm]). Alternatively, a number of commentators emend יַגֵּשׁ חַרְבּוֹ to נֹגֵשׂ חֲבֵרָו, hence "made to dominate his companions" (Nam, *Talking about God*, p. 151; similarly Dhorme, p. 567, Fohrer, p. 522, Jean Lévêque, "L'Argument de la Création dans le Livre de Job" in L. Derousseaux [ed.], *La Création dans L'Orient Ancien* [Paris: Les Éditions du Cerf, 1987], p. 294). For a survey of other proposals, see Rowley, pp. 256-7.

274 Day, *God's Conflict*, p. 75, n. 39. Compare similarly Habel's apprehension that "The image here is of threatening or intimidating [the Beast] to keep it under control" (p. 567). However, this sits ill with God's attitude to Behemoth and transcendently confident style of governance, which hardly needs to resort to physical intimidation to maintain order within the cosmos, and which exerts control, where necessary, by the setting of appropriate limits (cf., e.g., Ps. 148:6, Job 38:10-11).

275 Cf., e.g., Isa. 2:11-17, Ps. 94:2-3 and Westermann, *Der Aufbau des Buches Hiob*, pp. 92-3.

276 A similar point is made by Westermann, *Aufbau*, p. 93, who stresses that "there is no talk about God's sovereignty over these mighty ones [Behemoth and Leviathan], specifically that he topples them or forces them back within their own domains"; rather they are his creatures.

necessary or desirable: one should presumably not assume that the answer to the question, "Can one take him...?" (v. 24)[277] is "No: you cannot, and neither can God." Hence, if one is rather to assume "You cannot, but God can", one is confronted with the reality that God does not and that to do so (or to have done so) would be contrary to God's attitude to him. Thus, Job's (or humanity's) inability to take Behemoth with rings[278] speaks of man's insignificance and impotence even within the scale of the natural, created world of which he is a part. This may be stated in order to suggest that he is therefore in no position to challenge God, or, perhaps more likely, in order to undermine Job's own simplistic, anthropocentric assumptions about God's governance in the world. Man may find the existence of such a creature as Behemoth uncomfortable and undesirable, but God created him as he did Job, and, through the words of the passage, betrays evident pride—and this is something expressed, not merely inferred from what is written—in Behemoth, as the foremost of the creatures. God's ways and God's values and decisions in running the world are not as man's. This may both provide assurance in God's ultimate control and providence in the world in situations, such as Job's, where it may not be in evidence, but it also shames Job's presumption in making accusations against God when his capacities, perspective and understanding can only be so very limited. Hence, were the MT of v. 19 to be accepted as original (and many have thought emendation necessary), it must be have the force of, "Leave him who made him to bring near his sword", i.e., it is not your place to pre-empt the rôle of God in pontificating on how the world should be and in passing judgments on how God should act. The prerogative remains only with God, and it appears that God will not exercise that prerogative.[279]

Fairly minor points of detail have been queried in their applicability to the hippopotamus. The comparison of the animal's tail with the cedar[280] has been

---

277 It is reasonable to suppose that the interrogative should here be understood, as it is often left unstated (hence RSV, "Can one take him...?") although some commentators (e.g., Dhorme, p. 570) actually prefer to insert מִי־הוּא, since this could have fallen out by haplography with פִּיהוּ at the end of v. 23. More involved is Habel's translation of the verse, "El takes him by the mouth with rings, / he pierces his nose with hooks", since it depends on the transposition of the final phrase of the previous line, אֶל־פִּיהוּ, to this verse, and the repointing of the preposition in order to obtain the divine name. However, a further preposition then has to be supplied for פִּיהוּ, and, more importantly, the sense obtained seems to be at odds with the tenor of the remaining description.

278 For the nature of the implements referred to in this verse, see further below.

279 Possibly also the thought is included that as God's primary creation, Behemoth has been made such that no-one could bring near his sword, or God has decreed that no-one should touch him (cf. Cain, Gen. 4:15). Alternatively, it may even constitute a challenge to Job: you bring near your sword, if you are setting yourself up as God.

280 The exact force of the verb is uncertain. The translation "he (i.e., Behemoth, or even perhaps God) delights in his tail like a cedar" is not impossible; however, most feel a better sense is obtained by relating it to the Arabic *hafaṣa*, "bend down" (thus BDB, explaining, "extendeth down stiffly"), which, however, seems strange as applied to a

thought to be inappropriate on the grounds that the hippopotamus' tail is short.[281] However, this has been massively overstated. In fact, its tail is approximately 56cm in length, i.e., rather more than one third of its height,[282] and is broad and muscular,[283] being used as a paddle and rudder, and for a number of characteristic behavioural gestures. It thus answers the parallel with the cedar very exactly, since the point seems to be its strength and rigidity. In any case, in a country where hippopotami were outside the experience of most, the expectation of cedar-like proportions could easily have been aroused by this animal's otherwise unusually substantial frame.[284] More importantly, the tail is raised and stiffened in aggression, and perhaps to anyone who had witnessed the charge of an irate hippopotamus, that posture would be unforgettable.[285] In this case, the signification of the gesture would be the main point, and indeed if it is an oblique reference to the animal's dangerous potential, the reticence shown on this issue here would be in keeping with the rest of the description.

Alternatively, a euphemistic use of זנב has also been proposed. Having assembled evidence for the translation of פַּחֲדָיו (v. 17b) as "his testicles" (thus the Syriac and Vulgate of v. 17b; Gordis cites Arabic *afḥadh*, which may mean "thighs" or "his testicles," and Syriac *pḥdyn*, "testicles"), and drawn

---

cedar. Gordis, having observed that "the content requires the meaning 'stretch out'", makes the attractive suggestion that "if our root is identical with that of the verb 'desire,' it would offer the only instance in biblical Hebrew of the original, concrete meaning of the verb" (p. 476). Rigidity seems to be the point at issue, and accordingly it is usually rendered "stiffen" (thus Gordis, p. 468), or "makes erect" (Day, *God's Conflict*, p. 75, claiming support from LXX, Syr., the Arabic version and Ibn Ezra.)

281 Thus G. R. Driver, *JTS* 22 n.s. (1971) p. 177, "absurdly short and curly"; followed by John Day, *God's Conflict*, p. 77. This latter point is simply wrong. One must question, therefore, what standard of accuracy one can reasonably expect for an ancient poetic passage, where rhetoric is dominant over zoological precision, and a background of direct observation cannot be presumed. For comparison, it is worth noting that in *The Histories*, Herodotus attributes the hippopotamus with having "a horse's mane and tail". In fact, although literalistic accuracy is perhaps least to be expected in the Joban passage, it compares very favourably with these sources, as should become apparent from the ensuing discussion.

282 See N. Shefferly, "Hippopotamus amphibius" (On-line), (Animal Diversity Web, 2001). Accessed September 14, 2004 at http://animaldiversity.ummz.umich.edu/site/accounts/information/Hippopotamus_amphibius.html.

283 Thus "Hippopotamus: hippopotamus amphibius" (On-line. Reprinted from "The Safari Companion" by Richard Estes), (Nature-wildlife.com). Accessed 14 September, 2004 at http://www.nature-wildlife.com/hipptxt.htm.

284 Moreover, comparison with a cedar may well have been something of a Hebrew cliché, in which case one should not expect to take it too literally, but for the general point, since it would be excusable within a context of evident poetic hyperbole.

285 Despite their massive bulk, they are surprisingly agile on land, and can reach speeds of up to 18 mph (30 kmph): see "Hippopotamus: hippopotamus amphibius" (On-line. Reprinted from "The Safari Companion" by Richard Estes), (Nature-wildlife.com). Accessed 14 September, 2004 at http://www.nature-wildlife.com/hipptxt.htm.

attention to the fact that און (v. 16b) is elsewhere used in the Bible of sexual vigour (Gen. 49:3, Deut. 21:17, Ps. 105:36), Gordis points out that זָנָב was "a colloquial term for the *membrum virile* in postbiblical Hebrew".[286] However, although this may be linguistically possible, it is biologically difficult, since hippopotami have internal testes and a recurved penis. This translation would therefore only work if the knowledge of ancient Israelites about hippopotamus genitalia was as scant as that of most modern biblical scholars, which of course may be so; such a subject of allusion in a context of gratuitous observation would also, however, be without parallel in the Hebrew Bible, and would therefore be surprising here. If genuine, it may speak of the frightening procreative powers of Behemoth, but the manner of expression might perhaps suggest the intrusion of the deliberately grotesque or even parodic into the portrayal of the beasts of the second divine speech, to which the exaggerated divine praise of these animals and hyperbolic peroration on Leviathan's fearsome attributes may also attest. Whether this is the intended force of the verse nevertheless remains uncertain, and therefore a more literal application to the tail, which renders an entirely satisfactory sense and relies only on the more obvious translation values of the terms employed, seems preferable.[287] At the same time, the existence of this possible alternative further undermines the attempt to deny an original perceived applicability of v. 17a to the hippopotamus.

It has also sometimes been suggested that v. 24 could not properly be applied to the hippopotamus, since these animals were hunted in the ancient world. However, besides the fact that knowledge of the hunting achievements of an élite within another culture (or an acceptance of the truth or wider applicability of such accounts) cannot be assumed for ancient Israel, such denials by modern scholars ignore the hyperbolic possibilities of poetry and rhetoric. More importantly, a careful reflection on the content of v. 24 suggests that only specific, and probably widely used, methods of controlling, or possibly entrapping, animals in general are referred to, and that these are indeed not applicable to the hippopotamus. עֵינָיו should probably be interpreted in the light of the Keṯîḇ of Hos. 10:10 as alluding to "rings", either as an instrument used when working with domestic animals,[288]

286 Pp. 476-7; thus also Habel, p. 553, Nam, *Talking about God*, p. 152, Newsom, "The Book of Job", *NIB*, IV, p. 618, Balentine, "'What are human beings...'", p. 270, Alter, *The Art of Biblical Poetry*, p. 108, and Pope, pp. 323-4, who, further, suggests a possible connection between שְׁרִירֵי (v. 16b) and Arabic *sirr*, plural *asrār*, "secret[s], pudenda" (p. 323).

287 The alternative urged by Fuchs (*Mythos*, pp. 235-6), that the reference to the cedar is to be understood in relation to earth-mother symbolism, is unlikely to command assent.

288 Hence possibly, "Can you take (= lead?) him with rings?". Compare the interpretation of Hos. 10:10 Kt advocated by G. I. Davies, following the Targum: "'like the binding of the team [sc. of oxen] to its two rings [sc. of the yoke]'" (*Hosea* [NCBC; Grand Rapids, MI: Eerdmans, 1992], p. 245).

or as a form of trap.[289] This type of translation would furnish a more exact parallel with מוֹקְשִׁים in the following colon than the more common meaning of עַיִן, "eye", as well as being supported by the fact that the letter *'ayin* was originally circular in form.[290] מוֹקֵשׁ, literally a lure or bait, is commonly employed synecdochically to denote a trap, and thus would provide an excellent correspondence with the understanding of עֵינָיו as the rings of a trap advanced by Gordis. Such a reference would engage with the hunting methods employed by ordinary Israelites to catch small animals and birds, and would display a sense of the ridiculous in expressing the idea that one might attempt to capture a hippopotamus in this way, and in aiming to snare (or perhaps just being capable of snaring) only its nose. Alternatively, since "piercing" does not accurately describe the action of a trap, it has been proposed that בְּמוֹקְשִׁים may have arisen through a slight metathesis of the consonants from בְּקִמּוֹשִׁים, "with thorns",[291] in which case it would correspond well with the meaning of עֵינָיו advanced by Davies, in representing a method of control. Again, a sense of the ludicrous may be in evidence, since "the hippopotamus has nothing in common with those animals which man captures and holds by the simple device of a barb stuck in the nose".[292] In either case, the methods described are probably those available to the ordinary Israelite farmer or trapper (trapping being no doubt a common activity in an essentially rural situation), and the point would be that Behemoth cannot be treated either like בְּהֵמוֹת (cattle) or בְּהֵמוֹת הַשָּׂדֶה (i.e., wild animals).[293] Certainty in choosing between the alternative interpretations outlined here is elusive, in view of our limited knowledge of Hebrew

289 Thus Gordis (p. 480), who translates Hos. 10:10 Kt as "when they are caught by the double ring", which he explains as a circular trap.

290 The lexical value "eye" is nevertheless advocated by a number of commentators, who understand בְּעֵינָיו either as "before his eyes" (i.e. while he is looking, rather than by stealth; thus, e.g., Driver and Gray, p. 331), or as "by his eyes" (i.e., by doing something to his eyes. Herodotus mentions the plastering of the crocodile's eyes with clay in order to make capture possible, and Dhorme, p. 570, recommends this type of reference here, whilst Pope prefers an allusion to the grasping of a fish by the eyes in order to cause paralysis [pp. 327-8] More commonly, however, the reference is understood in relation to harpooning: see, e.g., Fohrer, p. 524). Various other related options are documented by David Wolfers (*Deep Things*, p. 177) who, in an unusual permutation, and eschewing the interrogative, interprets the phrase as "in one's own opinion", hence, "In his opinion, he (Behemoth) can seize him (Nahar)" (*Ibid.*, pp. 177, 371, 458-9). Alternatively, a number of emendations have been proposed, one of the most popular being that advanced by Ball, בְּצִנִּים, "with thorns, i.e., hooks" (thus Rowley, p. 258).

291 Thus Ehrlich, *Randglossen*, VI, p. 339, followed by Dhorme, p. 570, Pope, p. 328, Rowley, p. 258.

292 Thus Dhorme, p. 570.

293 Habel's suggestion (p. 568) that "'piercing the nose' of Behemoth... may also connote tempering its 'anger/rage,' and 'holding its mouth' may connote muzzling its 'authority'", together with his further application of this to the control of Job's "rage", seems unduly sophisticated and can command little encouragement from the context.

technical vocabulary; however, the agricultural imagery of Hos. 10:11ff. and in particular the sustained allusion to yoked oxen in Hos. 10:11 might favour a reference there to the treating of Israel as a draught animal, an instrument of restraint also being more appropriate to the wider theme of servitude and exile under a foreign overlord than one of entrapment. Such an interpretation of Job 40:24 would also provide the closest correlation with the continuation of this theme in the questioning of whether Leviathan could be employed for human advantage in the succeeding verses. However, neither understanding of 40:24 would offer any support to the view that what is here described is inapplicable to the hippopotamus.[294]

However, if Behemoth may be identified with much confidence as the hippopotamus, and in any case is envisaged as wholly naturalistic and, most importantly, as a creature of God, this strongly indicates that Leviathan is to

294 Comparison is sometimes made between the description of 40:24b and the Egyptian hunting practice of seeking to harpoon the hippopotamus' nose first, in order to sever the nostrils and prevent it from submerging; it would then flee to the land, where it would be easier to kill. (Ruprecht, *VT* 21 [1971], p. 222; Keel, *Jahwes Entgegnung an Ijob*, p. 131; p. 134, Abb. 74; p. 135 Abb. 75b and 76; see further Säve-Söderbergh, *On Egyptian Representations of Hippopotamus Hunting as a Religious Motive*, p. 11; p. 14, fig. 5). However, the sources attesting to this method typically relate to the idealised achievements of a divine or royal-divine hunter *par excellence* and are "absolutely impossible in practice" (see Säve-Söderbergh, *Ibid.*, p. 12). The depictions from Old Kingdom graves (and one from the First Intermediate Period) which may stand outside this royal tradition portray a highly treacherous attack on the hippopotamus, involving the participation at close range of a number of slaves, whilst the lord watches, or is otherwise occupied, a safe distance away (see Säve-Söderbergh, *Ibid.*, pp. 12, 21; Keel, *Ibid.*, pp. 132-6). Hence the point of impossibility (especially viewed poetically) still stands for one, such as Job, who is presumably not skilled in this type of hunting, a mere individual, who has lost both his servants and his heath, as well as being of sufficient social standing as not to consider engaging directly in the hunt, and indeed the point is clearly applicable to anyone not willing seriously to imperil his life. Even more importantly, there is no indication that hippopotamus hunting was attempted by the Israelites, and indeed recreational hunting of large game by the upper classes was probably the preserve of more sophisticated societies; hence the cultural limitation on the perception of what was possible should not be underestimated. Further, it is doubtful whether קִמּוֹשׁ, the emended reading of the MT applicable here, might be understood to represent a harpoon-point: this meaning cannot claim support from elsewhere (cf. the translation of קִמּוֹשׁ in LXX and Vulgate respectively as ἀκανθαι and *urtica*, hence BDB "thistles or nettles"), and knowledge of Israelite technical vocabulary is simply too sparse for the extant content of the verse to be questioned (or conjectural emendations proposed) with any confidence. However, since the first half of the verse seems to describe something which is inapplicable to the hippopotamus, sense requires that the same must pertain in v. 24b also. Of course, if the subject of reference is trapping or if v. 24a were to be taken as alluding to a direct approach "before the eyes" of a wary hippopotamus, the point of impossibility would still stand.

be understood in the same way.[295] Or to express the same point slightly differently, the nature of Leviathan is not likely to be radically different from that of Behemoth, whether its description is recognisable in every detail or not, and this important point seems to have been widely grasped by the commentators, even where it has not been made explicit. One can discount the idea that one is a natural creature celebrated on that level, and the other a mythological beast liable to cause cosmic interruption, not least because it would entail a different rhetorical force for the divine words in respect to each of these creatures. The style of writing and rhetorical voice of the section concerning Leviathan is recognisably the same as in the first part of the speech, and the same type of characteristics (physical strength, impossibility of capture and subjection to human control) are highlighted as in respect to Behemoth. At the same time, as the climactic animal of the divine speeches, Leviathan is portrayed at greater length and in still more impressive and heightened terms, and hence in the latter part of the description in particular, the speech strives to the outer limits of poetic expression as it builds to its zenith. Thus, the reflections on the impossibility of controlling Leviathan by close-handed and primitive means, and on the danger of stirring him up in the attempt (40:25-41:2; ET 41:1-10), give way via a celebration of his physical attributes (41:4ff.; ET vv. 12ff.), to an intensified recollection of these two earlier themes. Now his invincibility applies even in the face of a comprehensive range of weapons (41:18-21; ET vv. 26-29), whilst a variety of interspersed statements portray him not merely as dangerous when provoked, but as intrinsically fearsome and aggressive (vv. 6b, 14b, 17; ET vv. 14b, 22b, 25). Such is the poetic character of the second part of the Leviathan passage that even where details are not especially controversial in their applicability to the crocodile, an expression such as "his eyes are like the eyelids of the dawn" (41:10; ET v. 18) can leave commentators straining to determine a precise prose paraphrase. Hence, there is much here which, despite probably having its origin in genuine physiological or behavioural characteristics, owes more of its expression to poetic hyperbole. At the same time, however, the divine pride in this creature, though expressed less fulsomely than in respect to Behemoth (perhaps because the point has already been made so strongly in the former case, and

---

295 In fact, the idea of Leviathan as a God-created creature of the natural world is already found in Ps. 104:26, and one might compare also the creation of the "great sea monsters" (אֶת־הַתַּנִּינִם הַגְּדֹלִים) in Gen. 1:21 and the call for תַּנִּינִים to praise Yahweh in Ps. 148:7, since (הַ)תַּנִּינ(ִים) is used in connection with Leviathan in Ps. 74:13 and Isa. 27:1, and "Leviathan" in Job 40:25-41:26 (ET 41:1-34) is itself translated in the Syriac as *tnyn'*, 11 Q Targ Job *tnyn*. Moreover, when the Pharaoh is described, in the same language, as (הַ)תַּנִּין (הַגָּדוֹל) in Ezek. 29:3, 32:2 (thus many manuscripts of Ezek. 29:3, and two in respect of 32:2; cf. Syriac, Targum), the crocodile seems to be in mind. For *tnyn* as "crocodile", see similarly Keel, *Jahwes Entgegnung an Ijob*, p. 143 n. 398 and the further bibliography there; note also such circumstantial evidence as the fact that the stream Crocodilion referred to by Pliny (*Naturalis Historia* V, 17) became known as *naḥal tanninīm* (Keel, *Jahwes Entgegnung an Ijob*, n. 424, p. 156).

so is less in need of iteration),[296] is still in evidence, most particularly in 41:4 (ET v. 12), where scholars even now baulk at applying the word "grace" to a beast which is still, to the human perception, so feared and ugly.[297]

Much of the portrayal of Leviathan is especially appropriate to the crocodile. For example, the detailed description of this creature's closely-abutting scales (41:7-9; ET vv. 15-17) precisely reflects the non-overlapping scales of the crocodile (as contrasted with the overlapping scales of many reptiles), whilst the emphasis on their impenetrability is biologically accurate, correlating also with the statement of Herodotus[298] that the crocodile has "a scaly hide, which on its back is impenetrable" (δερμα λεπιδωτον ἀρρηκτον

---

296 Conversely, it is notable that Behemoth is not portrayed as an aggressive creature: although his relaxed behaviour and fearlessness even in turbulent water may hint at a latent invincibility, as may also the questioning of whether he may be captured in the ways described, it is not actually made explicit. However, it is commonly assumed, largely on the basis of the succeeding Leviathan passage, and perhaps not least because of the smooth transition made between them through the theme of capture, which invites a projection back of the aggression motif. Nevertheless, the sustained absence of this idea throughout the first description firmly establishes the divine perspective, which is to delight in such strength, rather than to fear or seek to overcome it.

297 The received text means, literally: "I will not keep silent about his limbs (or 'body parts, members') or the matter of [his] great strength and the grace of his arrangement (= 'form / proportions / structure')." The pointing of חִין is not paralleled elsewhere, but the most obvious explanation is that it is equivalent to חֵן, probably as a *plene* spelling; see Gordis p. 484 for examples of this form utilised in respect to other nouns. Proposed emendations both of this word and of other aspects of this verse have been many, varying from the superfluous though satisfactory (such as חִין → חֵיל, "strength" – G. Beer, *Der Text der Buches Hiob* [Marburg, 1895], pp. 251-2, followed e.g., by Day, *God's Conflict*, p. 63) to the highly creative and widely rejected (thus Pope, p. 335: "Did I not silence his boasting by the powerful word Hayyin prepared?", Hayyin being explained as an epithet of the god Kothar-wa-Khasis; further possibilities are documented by de Wilde, p. 388). Habel, in an impressive *tour de force* which follows on from the precedent of the JPS translation, extracts the following from the MT, by rendering בַּדָּיו "his boasting", but otherwise retaining the same etymologies as advanced above: "Did I not silence his boasting, / his mighty word and persuasive case?" (p. 551). However, reference to his commentary is necessary for the possible significance of this to become clear, and indeed the meaning he accords it depends on the highly dubious identification of Leviathan with the Yam of the Ugaritic texts (Habel, p. 571). Moreover, besides the fact that Habel's proposed reading would constitute the only past-tense reference of a passage otherwise firmly focused on the present, the translation values he accords to many of the words here used are unusual. Thus, גְּבוּרָה, like גִּבּוֹר, is always outside this verse applied to physical strength; the meaning "case" is not elsewhere attested for עֵרֶךְ; and the sense "appealing, persuasive" for the noun חֵן again stretches probability; so the cumulative effect of the constituents of this proposal remains unpersuasive.

298 *The Histories*, II.68.4.

ἐπι του νωτου).[299] Similarly, the description of 41:22 (ET v. 30) may reflect the belief held in the ancient world that the scales of the underside of this reptile were ridged, like those on its back. Although this is not in fact the case, except in a small number of species, it is true that crocodiles leave slide marks in the mud along river banks (cf. 41:22b; ET v. 30b), which could have given rise to this idea.

The reference to Leviathan "spread[ing] himself... on the mire" (41:22a; ET v. 30a) may relate to the fact that entering the water entails a significant change in the manner of locomotion adopted by the crocodile. When moving on land, crocodiles are capable of an almost mammalian "high walk", with the limbs positioned virtually beneath it, which among reptiles is unique to the crocodile, but on entering the water, a more lizard-like "belly crawl", in which the legs are splayed out to the side, would be employed, the crocodile actually sliding into the water (except on rough ground) on its belly, with chest, stomach and tail all in contact with the ground.[300]

Mention of Leviathan "rais[ing] himself up" so that "the mighty are afraid" (41:17; ET v. 25)[301] would cohere very well with perhaps the most frightening and spectacular of the crocodile's attributes: the ability to leap suddenly out of the water to capture prey. The propensity of the Nile crocodile to lunge from a stationary position in the shallows, "its feet acting

---

299 Nam's assertion in relation to 41:5-6 (ET v. 13-14) that "the sea god has been transformed into the dragon-like Leviathan" (p. 182, n. 252), made merely on the basis of the recurrence of the terms "garment" and "doors" here and in 38:8-11, is unwarranted, not least because in the former case they describe armour intrinsic to the crocodile which keeps enemies out, whereas in the latter, the barriers external to the sea keep it in.

300 See Crocodilian Biology Database (On-line), accessed September 14, 2004 at http://www.flmnh.ufl.edu/cnhc/cbd-gb8.htm, and Heinz Fritz Wermuth, "Crocodile" (On-line), (*Encyclopædia Britannica* from Encyclopædia Britannica Premium Service, 2004), accessed September 10, 2004 at http://www.britannica.com/eb/article?eu =121030.

301 The translation of אֵלִים as "the mighty" is followed by most (e.g., RSV, Fohrer, p. 526, Groß, p. 143, de Wilde, p. 412), and is supported by Aquila, Symmachus, Targum, and Syriac; cf. 2 Ki. 24:15, Ezek. 17:13, 31:11, 32:21. Some (e.g. Fuchs, *Mythos*, p. 231, Pope, pp. 336, 344, Nam, *Talking about God*, p. 158, Good, *In Turns of Tempest*, p. 368, Perdue, *Wisdom in Revolt*, p. 228) prefer to render "the gods" (cf. Day, *God's Conflict*, p. 64, "the angels", following the Vulgate *angeli*), but this does not seem probable within the theological context of the book of Job: compare "sons of God" (בְּנֵי אֱלֹהִים) in 38:7. Habel, further, takes מִשֵּׂתוֹ (defective spelling for מִשְּׂאֵתוֹ), not as an infinitive construct, "when he raises himself up", but as a noun, reading "at his majesty" (p. 556; thus also Nam, *Talking about God*, p. 158). However, a nominal derivation would probably more appropriately result in the translation "at his 'uprising'", i.e., "at his rising up"; although the nuance of the terrible nature of Leviathan may be present, to employ the word "majesty" imparts overtones of an exalted status which ill correlates with the animal and physical expression of intimidating power which is the focus of both cola of this verse, and which conforms with the context as a whole.

like spring-loaded pistons to push the crocodile's body forward at high speed"[302] in order to capture prey by surprise, is well known, but crocodilians are also capable of vertical leaps out of the water (achieved in deeper water through sinusoidal undulations of the tail) in order to capture flying prey or animals resting on overhanging branches, and even a "tail-walk", like that of the dolphin, in which the head and body are held out of the water.[303] Similarly, the allusion in the parallel colon to שְׁבָרִים,"the crashings",[304] may pertain either to the sound of the crocodile landing back in the water from such a leap, or to the habit of "mark[ing] their territory by loudly slapping their head down on the water or snapping their jaws on the surface of the water."[305]

Comparison with 3:9 suggests that the point of the reference to Leviathan's eyes being "like the eyelids of the dawn" in 41:10b (ET v. 18b) is the emanation of light from the crocodile's eyes. This is highly appropriate to the crocodile since the layer of tapetum (the so-called tapetum lucidum) at the back of its eyes, which greatly enhances its night vision, also causes its eyes to glow in the dark.[306] Such an understanding would, moreover, fit the

---

302 Crocodilian Biology Database (On-line). Accessed September 14, 2004 at http://www.flmnh.ufl.edu/cnhc/cbd-gb8.htm.

303 "Crocodilia" (On-line), (Animal Diversity Web, 2002). Accessed September 14, 2004 at http://www.animaldiversity.ummz.umich.edu/site/accounts/information/Crocodilia.html.

304 For this meaning of שֶׁבֶר, lit. "breaking", compare especially Zeph. 1:10, Jer. 50:22, 51:54, though sound is often also in mind elsewhere. It is advocated also, e.g., by Habel, p. 556, although some prefer to emend the MT, e.g., to מִשְׁבְּרֵי יָם (thus Dhorme, p. 584, Fohrer, pp. 526-7, Day, *God's Conflict*, p. 64), without necessarily improving the sense. Gunkel elected to impart a more mythological nuance by emending to בִּשְׁמֵי מָרוֹם יִתְחַבָּאוּ, "In the highest heaven they hide themselves" (*Schöpfung*, p. 55), but here clearly the argument has pre-empted the conclusion. Pope (p. 345, followed by Fuchs, *Mythos*, p. 233) remains within the same allusive sphere by understanding מִשְּׁבָרִים in relation to the "breaking of the loins" as an expression of fear; however, although he claims that this is achieved without emendation, his interpretation entails both taking the verb according to the Arabic root *ḫṭ'*, meaning "cast down", instead of in relation to the common Hebrew verb meaning "miss (a goal or way)", and explaining the noun of the MT as elliptical for שֶׁבֶר מָתְנַיִם, even though support for this longer phrase can be claimed only from a single occurrence of שִׁבְרוֹן מָתְנַיִם in Ezek. 21:11 (ET v. 6). Moreover, his English translation, "with consternation prostrate" (p. 336), is a rather loose rendition of the elements he has described.

305 "Crocodilia" (On-line), (Animal Diversity Web, 2002). Accessed September 14, 2004 at http://www.animaldiversity.ummz.umich.edu/site/accounts/information/Crocodilia.html.

306 On this, see Heinz Fritz Wermuth, "Crocodile" (On-line), (*Encyclopædia Britannica* from Encyclopædia Britannica Premium Service, 2004). Accessed September 10, 2004 at http://www.britannica.com/eb/article?eu=121030; and "Crocodilia" (On-line), (Animal Diversity Web, 2002). Accessed September 14, 2004 at http://www.animaldiversity.ummz.umich.edu/site/accounts/information/Crocodilia.html. The other distinctive aspect of the crocodile's eyes which contribute to its ability to see in

context and parallelism of the verse (where the reference is to sneezings flashing forth light) and would in turn support a naturalistic interpretation for the "fiery" imagery of the surrounding lines.

Mention of "terror" "round about his teeth" (41:6; ET v. 14) may relate to another highly distinctive, but well-known, feature of the crocodile: the fact that its sharp teeth, which may number more than one hundred on each jaw,[307] are visible on the outside of the mouth, even when it is shut. The idea of the impossibility of pressing this animal's tongue down with a cord (40:25b; ET 41:1b) may be a wry allusion to the fact that the crocodile's tongue is virtually immobile or, as was widely thought in the ancient world, that it did not have a tongue at all.[308]

A further point of contact with perceptions of the crocodile in the ancient world is found in the power of Leviathan to terrify. This pervades much of the passage, being expressed especially in 41:1-2, 6, 14, 17 (ET vv. 9-10, 14, 22, 25), and epitomised by the idea that "man... is laid low even at the sight of him" (41:1; ET v. 9),[309] but it also closely correlates with the image of crocodiles eloquently conveyed in The Teaching of Khety[310] and other Egyptian sources.[311]

---

the dark may also have been called to mind by this reference, namely its unnerving, vertical, slit-shaped pupils, like those of a cat.

307 I am dependent for this information on Heinz Fritz Wermuth, "Crocodile" (On-line), (*Encyclopædia Britannica* from Encyclopædia Britannica Premium Service, 2004). Accessed September 10, 2004 at http://www.britannica.com/eb/article?eu=121030.

308 S. R. Driver, "Mythical Monsters in the Old Testament", *Studi orientalistici in onore di Giorgio Levi della Vida* 1, p. 238, cites in this connection Herodotus, Diodorus Siculus, Plutarch, Pliny, and Ammianus Marcellinus, though without giving precise references.

309 Thus MT. A number of scholars have sought to change the preposition אֶל to אֵל or אֵלִים in order to introduce nuances compatible with the theme of "chaos" into the passage; thus, e.g., Gunkel, "his appearance casts down even a god" (*Schöpfung*, p. 55); Cheyne, גַּם־אֵלִם מֹרָאוֹ יָטִל (i.e., "even divine beings the fear of him lays low", "The Text of Job", *JQR* 9 [1896-7] 573-80, p. 579); Pope, "were not the gods cast down at the sight of him?" (pp. 335, 336-7). Pope in particular emphasises that "the text has suffered some sabotage intended to obscure gross pagan allusions", and cites references to the cowering of the gods in the Babylonian creation epic (*ANET* p. 64, ll. 86-91) and the Ugaritic Baal-Yam cycle (*KTU* 1.2.i.21-4). However, as Rowley states (p. 260), "there seems no need to bring mythological material to a text which is intelligible as it stands".

310 "I will tell you about the fisherman. He is made feebler than any other profession—whose labour is on the river, who consorts with crocodiles. Even when the total of his reckoned catch comes to him, he is still lamenting; he cannot even realise that the crocodile's waiting, being blinded by fear. Even if he comes out of the flowing water, he's as if smitten by God's anger." (translation from R. B. Parkinson, *The Tale of Sinuhe and other Ancient Egyptian Poems 1940-1640 BC* [Oxford: Clarendon, 1997], p. 279; cf. *ANET*, pp. 433-4). Even given a certain amount of exaggeration in order to highlight the superiority of the scribal profession, it was true that, if his canoe capsized, even the best swimmer could not hope to escape the jaws of a crocodile.

311 Cf. "A Dispute over Suicide", ll. 74-5, *ANET*, p. 406.

With so many details which appear to apply specifically to the crocodile, it seems difficult to attribute this to coincidence and to deny that Leviathan is envisaged as crocodilian, not only in form, but in his behavioural characteristics. As the description becomes progressively more intense, poetic heightening of Leviathan's natural attributes is in evidence, for example in the exaggeration of his innate and impressive impermeability (41:18-21; ET vv. 26-29) and in the enhancing of the impact made on the water by his activity (41:23; ET v. 31). However, this is most in evidence in the fire and light imagery of vv. 10-13 (ET vv. 18-21). Such descriptions appear to be broadly compatible with the biological crocodile, given the poetic context in which they occur, as the following discussion will indicate. Nevertheless, the exact classification of the animal described is not important to the question of the presence of "chaos" imagery in the present passage, and a more "fantastic" identity would be possible, and indeed perhaps more appealing to those who prefer to place a relatively low limit on the imaginative and hyperbolic capacities of poetry. The critical issue is that Leviathan is a creature of God which, despite its animalic strength and ferocity, is presented as possessing a wild beauty (41:4, 10; ET vv. 12, 18) and transforming luminosity (41:10, 24; ET vv. 18, 32), its role sanctioned and appointed by God (41:25-26; ET vv. 33-34). This is not compatible with the idea of this beast as some form of pre-creation monster inimical to cosmic order and overcome (or overcomable) by God, but it is supported by a close reading of the verses concerned.

Extraordinarily, the light and fire passage, vv. 10-13 (ET vv. 18-21), begins on a highly positive note with Leviathan as a source of light, the verb הלל, "shine, give forth light" (v. 10a; ET v. 18a), being applied elsewhere to the sun (Job 31:26) and stars (Isa. 13:10), and to God's lamp, figuring his grace (Job 29:3). אוֹר also has an overwhelmingly positive sphere of association, since besides being used in relation to such objects as daylight, the dawn, the luminaries, a lamp and God's lightning, it also often stands for goodness, justice, hope, salvation, and so on. Thus even the sneezes of Leviathan are viewed favourably by its creator, whilst its eyes, which might be unnerving for man, are to God like a new sunrise (v. 10b; ET v. 18b). The interpretation of the first colon in terms of the effect of sunlight on the spray created by this creature's sneezes is reflected in ancient traditions cited by Bochart, and may perhaps be supported by modern observations of water being "sprayed high into the air from each side" as the crocodile's flanks vibrate violently as it roars (roaring possibly being mistaken for a sneeze).[312] It would also, of course, cohere with the allusion in the parallel colon to Leviathan's eyes emanating light.[313] The following verse can be rendered,

312 Heinz Fritz Wermuth, "Crocodile" (On-line), (*Encyclopædia Britannica* from Encyclopædia Britannica Premium Service, 2004). Accessed September 10, 2004 at http://www.britannica.com/eb/article?eu=121030.

313 Presumably by glowing in the dark: see the discussion above, and contrast the view of Habel (p. 572) that "the intensity of the heat [from within Leviathan] is such that his eyes light up red", and of Pope (p. 341) that it might be possible for fire to emanate

"Out of his mouth come torches (= shining / flickering lights), sparkles of fire slip out", which, in continuity with v. 10 (ET v. 18), may portray water running out of the sides of the crocodile's mouth and sparkling in the sunshine. (The crocodile's mouth is lipless and thus water leaking out would be a common sight). Similarly, v. 12 (ET v. 20) may readily be understood in terms of water-vapour from the crocodile's breath, just as one might speak of "smoking breath" in modern English parlance. This is especially suggested by the second colon, which may literally be translated, "like a blown[314] pot and rushes [אַגְמֹון]." However, the reference to "rushes" reads rather awkwardly here (presumably they would be burning rushes, but this would perhaps comprise an unlikely fuel over which to boil a pot), and so it has plausibly been suggested, following the Syriac and Vulgate, that one should read אֹגֵם, as cognate with the Arabic *ajam*, meaning "to be hot, boiling", and Assyrian *agâmu*, "to be boiling with anger", the final ן- being deleted as an anticipation of the following word.[315] Hence the crocodile's breath is "like a pot blown and boiling", this evocation of rising water vapour corroborating a similar interpretation of the first colon.

However, the destructive, devouring nature of the crocodile is progressively brought into view in these last two verses: a "torch" (לַפִּיד, v. 11; ET v. 19) is often simply a source of light, or employed in metaphors or similes to denote something that gleams or shines (even salvation, Isa. 62:1), yet in one instance a "flaming torch" (לַפִּיד אֵשׁ) might "devour to the right and to the left... round about" (Zech. 12:6; note the parallel, "blazing pot", כִּיּוֹר אֵשׁ), and in the present verse there may be a certain ambivalence as regards which aspect, shining, or flaming, should be drawn out. "Smoke" and "fire" are difficult to comment on because they are such everyday phenomena, but certainly the former might be associated with destruction, as in smoke rising from a burning city (e.g., Josh. 8:20, 21, Judg. 20:38, 40) or in divine judgment (e.g., Nah. 2:14, Isa. 34:10), and this is still more the case for fire: compare the expression of the anger of God in 2 Sam. 22:9, Ps. 18:9: "Smoke went up from his nostrils, / and devouring fire from his mouth;/ glowing coals flamed forth from him." However, it is only in the last of this series of four verses (v.13; ET v. 21) that the language moves unequivocally to that of Leviathan not just as emanating light, but fire, with power to ignite (להט). Compare especially Joel 2:3 and 1:19, where this verb is used of the devouring fires of locust plague and drought, and similarly לַהַב, "flame", in Isa. 29:6, 30:30, 66:15. Thus, in the striking poetic evocation of Job 41:10-13 (ET 18-21), the perspective broadens from the divine to the human as

---

from the eyes of a dragon, despite the lack of any clear allusion to such a phenomenon. (He refers to the appearance of the emissaries of Yam, *KTU* 1.2.i.32-3, where the reference seems rather to be to their tongues as a sharp sword: see Gibson, *CML*, p. 42, N. Wyatt, *Religious Texts from Ugarit*, p. 61, M. S. Smith in *UNP*, p. 100 and *The Ugaritic Baal Cycle*, I, p. 307).

314 I.e., fanned, so well-heated, boiling; cf. Job 20:26 (Pu'al), Jer. 1:13, Sir. 43:4.

315 Thus Dhorme, p. 581, followed, e.g., by Fuchs, *Mythos*, pp. 231, 233, Fohrer, pp. 286-7, Groß, p. 143, de Wilde, p. 412, and Day, *God's Conflict*, p. 64.

what is at first portrayed as beautiful is transformed into the terrible, and sparkling light and steaming breath give way to flames with all their consuming potential. Since this type of language is used metaphorically elsewhere, especially in Joel, where another devouring animal, the locust, is portrayed,[316] there is no need to insist that this should be interpreted literally rather than as a product of the poetic hyperbole which is so much in evidence in Hebrew poetry in general and not least in the present context.[317] Probably, the rather more imaginative language encountered here should be understood as having its basis in the same realities as expressed in the earlier verses, but as further expressing the ferocity of this creature and as emphasizing as strongly as possible the danger it presents.[318] Its origin may perhaps further be found in a local legend or in ideas attached to a particular fantastic animal which was essentially crocodilian but also owed something to the imagination, despite being perceived as an extant creature of the natural world.

As regards the portrayal of Leviathan in his aquatic environment in 41:23-24 (ET vv. 31-2), several elements are here skillfully blended. The most obvious aspect may be the behaviour of the crocodile in stirring up the water, as similarly described of the Pharaoh-תַּנִּין in Ezek. 32:2: "You burst forth in your rivers, / trouble the waters with your feet, / and foul their rivers"; the term מְצוּלָה (v. 23; ET v. 31) further resonates with the idea of the יְוֵן מְצוּלָה encountered also in Ps. 69:3, mire (טִיט) being the last word of the previous verse. In a similar vein, as may be expected from the crocodile's large but streamlined form, it leaves a wake behind it as it swims (v. 24; ET v. 32).[319]

316 Note especially Joel 2:3a: "Fire devours before them / and behind them a flame burns".

317 It is notable that the supposed mythical content of the Hebrew description has even here appeared sufficiently doubtful that proponents of this type of interpretation have sometimes been tempted to enhance it further. For example, Pope renders לַפִּידִים יַהֲלֹכוּ as "flames leap" in v. 11a (ET v. 19a) (p. 335), whilst Habel translates 41:12b (ET v. 20b) as "flames, fanned and fierce" (p. 552), repointing כְּדוּד (literally, "like a pot"), with Pope, as כִּידוֹד, "flame, spark" (p. 556; Pope, p. 342), but then gratuitously pluralizing it, as well as seeking an "off-centre" translation of אֹגֵם in order to maximize the force of the verb and thus support his understanding of the verse.

318 If a naturalistic explanation were to be sought, one might think in terms of an origin in the sundried or blackened remains of carcasses stored by the crocodile, which suggested the effect of heat or charring; an alternative inspiration could be the crocodile's very red mouth, which might liplessly leak blood as it consumed its prey. However, the explanation that fire conveys the idea of the crocodile devouring all before it, as with the effect of locusts in Joel 1:19-20, 2:3, 5, would seem to offer a more convincing way forward.

319 It has sometimes been objected that the terms employed here are inappropriate to the environment of the Nile crocodile. However, מְצוּלָה and יָם are applied to the Nile (the former in Zech. 10:11, the latter in Isa. 19:5—where it is often translated as "the Nile"—and Ezek. 32:2, Nah. 3:8), whilst תְּהוֹם occurs in a number of freshwater contexts, as nourishing the earth's water supply, and it has often been thought that its occurrence in Ps. 42:8 alludes to the Jordan; cf. also Ezek. 31:4, 15, where it is used in relation to the Egyptian Pharaoh. In any case, the prime focus here is not on pure

However, more profound than this is Leviathan's beautifying and ennobling of the aquatic environment which was viewed as treacherous by the Israelites. Etymologically, צול and its derivatives may be related to the idea of a basin or hollow (cf., with BDB, p. 846, "*miṣwal* [in Syria], stone-lined hollow, or basin, for washing grain", and probably מְצֻלָה, Zech 1:8) and, thus conceptualized as a container, it is susceptible to domestication as a "pot", a common household or cultic item (v. 23a; ET v. 31a). The comparison with an ointment- or spice-pot (v. 23b; ET v. 31b) introduces a further element, since the art of perfumery and its results were particularly to be associated with the holy oil and incense of the sanctuary (Ex. 30:22-38, 37:29, 1 Chr. 9:30; cf. Isa. 57:9), and with the royal sphere (1 Sam. 8:13, 2 Chr. 16:14), as sensually delightful (Cant. 5:13, 8:2) and even worthy of analogy with such virtues as wisdom and honour (Eccles. 10:1). Leviathan's positive transformational impact is still more in evidence as he swims, since he thereby "makes a pathway light up / shine behind him", the resultant foam giving the impression of the deep as "hoary". The radiant goodness of the first image is perhaps self-evident, but of course it must not be overlooked that the "hoary head", which could be synonymous with, or indicative of, old age, was regarded with the greatest of respect (Prov. 20:29, Lev. 19:32), as "a crown of glory... gained in a righteous life", Prov. 16:31 and as synonymous with wisdom (Job 15:10).[320]

The sustained evocation of Leviathan then ends with a final impression of him as a magnificent creature – incomparable (v. 25, ET v. 33a),[321] fearless (v. 25b, ET v. 33b) and king of the wild beasts (v. 26b, ET v. 34b; cf. 28:8), yet also one who was made (v. 25b, ET v. 33b; cf. Behemoth, 40:15, 19), and hence, presumably, a creature of God. However, the statement that Leviathan is "one made without fear" (v. 25b, ET v. 33b), thus expressed, further conveys the important idea that his fearlessness is the product of divine intentionality: it is God's purpose that Leviathan should be thus.[322] The

---

natural history, and hence the choice of vocabulary must serve other, more important, rhetorical interests.

320 Contrast the inevitable association with "chaos" often made in respect of these verses, e.g., by Nam, who states that "this picture seems to be the culmination of the universal chaos and cosmic upheaval, affirming that Leviathan is the embodiment of chaos" (*Talking about God*, p. 158). Typically, however, this link is merely affirmed rather than demonstrated.

321 The most natural derivation of מָשְׁלוֹ, followed by most commentators, is from I משל, "represent, be like", hence "his likeness" (thus, e.g., Fohrer, p. 526, de Wilde, p. 413, Fuchs, *Mythos*, p. 231, Gordis, p. 472). However, some (e.g. Habel, pp. 552, 557) prefer to translate "his rule", from III משל, "rule, have dominion, reign" (for which, cf. Zech. 9:10, Dan. 11:4), since the resultant reading, "none can dominate him", would also adequately suit the context. Newsom even sees both meanings here ("The Book of Job", *NIB*, IV, p. 625).

322 The proposal of A. C. M. Blommerde *(Northwest Semitic Grammar and Job* p. 139, following Dahood, *Biblica* 45 [1964], p. 410; *Ugaritic-Hebrew Philology*, p. 10), that the verse should be translated, "On earth is not his equal, / made as he is without flaw"

reason for this seems to be indicated in the following verse. בְּנֵי־שָׁחַץ is rendered by BDB "majestic wild beasts"; they are those that may be paralleled with שַׁחַל, "lion", Job 28:8, and hence are probably the greatest wild beasts. This thus resonates with the pairing of the lion and תַּנִּין in Ezek. 32:2: both are possibly contenders of the title of "king over the proud beasts", but it is here in 41:26 (ET v. 34) awarded to Leviathan. However, there is a further aspect to be drawn out here, which closely links with the divine intentionality underlying v. 25b (ET v. 33b): Leviathan's kingship is not merely indicated in the construct form, as is usual when referring to the monarch of a particular nation or group,[323] but by the preposition עַל, the term employed to indicate the accession or appointment of a king.[324] Hence, once again, the form of expression points to a divinely instituted role for Leviathan.

As regards the force of v. 26a (ET v. 34a), יִרְאֶה is ambiguous and may be variously interpreted.[325] Probably foremost is the implication that to look on something exalted requires an exalted status for Leviathan himself, and this is elucidated in the next colon. At the same time, kingship entails "having regard for" those subject to the monarch's rule, and this should possibly be read back retrospectively into this colon from the next, as a subsidiary nuance. However, another royal function is the administration of justice, and this is reflected in the divine-royal sphere in the challenge to Job in 40:11b-12a, to "look on (ראה) all the proud (כָּל־גֵּאֶה) and abase them / bring them low". Thus it is possible that Leviathan is here accorded a rôle in the administration of justice in the world, exercised in his own context, which Job is incapable of performing.[326] As a result, by the conclusion of the second divine speech, Job is induced to recognize not only his own physical incapability of answering this initial challenge of God, but his ignorance even of the workings of divine justice in the world, where a proud beast such as

---

(entailing the emendation of MT חַת to חַתְאֹת, derived from Ugaritic *ḫtu* "scatter, crack") further develops the idea of the peerlessness of Leviathan established by Yahweh, but it is doubtful if this reading should be preferred.

323 Cf. Gen. 14:1, 2, Ex. 1:5, Judg, 3:8, 10, 2 Ki. 15:19, 20, 29; 18:14, Ezra 1:1 and often.

324 This is the case whether it is by popular demand, anointing by a priest, or election by Yahweh; see, e.g. Deut. 17:14, Judg. 9:8, 2 Sam. 4:12, 1 Ki. 1:34, 2 Chr. 2:10, 1 Chr. 11:3, Neh. 9:37. Hence מֶלֶךְ עַל is employed after several characteristic verbs, as with משח, נתן, Hiph. כון, Hiph. קום. The difference between this type of expression and the construct form is particularly exemplified by a comparison of Ex. 1:8 and 15.

325 This is the case even apart from the suggestion that it should be emended to יִירָא, and אֵת at the beginning of the verse to אוֹתוֹ, hence "all that is proud fears him" (thus Gordis, p. 490; similarly Fohrer, pp. 526, 527, and de Wilde, p. 413, following Gunkel, Driver and Gray and others).

326 Compare Balentine's perception that "in this final acclamation of Leviathan as king, God offers Job a worthy example of how to enact the very assignment he has been given" ("'What are Human Beings...'", p. 273), and Nam's statement that "here Leviathan the symbol of evil takes the place of Job the supposed judge" (*Talking about God*, p. 158).

Leviathan has a valid and valued role. He is moreover brought to a clear realization of his own overweening pride in presuming to pontificate about that which he did not understand.[327] As a result, instead of abasing the proud (40:11-12), he humbly confesses that he despises himself; and rather than hiding them in the dust (עָפָר) together (40:13), he repents in dust (עָפָר) and ashes (42:6).

An examination of the Leviathan passage as a whole thus suggests that it begins with the human perspective, which is to seek to overcome such a beast, or to be overcome by it, to bend it to his will, or to attempt to slay it (40:25-32; ET 41:1-8). However, the final section of the speech (41:23-26; ET 41:31-34) invites one to consider Leviathan in his natural environment, to appreciate his part in creation and to wonder at his wild beauty and magnificence, thus finally to adopt a God's-eye view. It is this obvious divine pride in both Behemoth and Leviathan, even apart from evidence suggesting that they are intended as creatures of the natural world, which determines that the motif of divine conflict cannot be of central interest here. This being so, it renders highly unlikely the proposal that the theme of *Chaoskampf* is implied here. Nevertheless, it remains for the chief arguments advanced in its favour to be considered.

One claim which is made fairly frequently is that the Leviathan of Job 40:25-41:26 (ET 41:1-34) must be a mythological monster because it is presented as insusceptible to capture, whereas the crocodile was actually hunted in the ancient world.[328] However, a number of objections may be raised against this view. First, it presupposes that there are only two possible identities for Leviathan: zoologically accurate Nile crocodile or mythological chaos monster; but it excludes the possibility of Leviathan as a fantastic or quasi-fantastic creature or as a crocodilian which has been enhanced in conception and/or in poetic portrayal.[329] In fact, 40:31 (ET 41:7) and 41:18-

327 Pride epitomises the negative aspect of Job's deportment in the dialogues: he would condemn God that he would be justified. An implication of v. 26 (ET v. 34) may be that Job should be recognised as the "proud" who is not only impotent before Leviathan but possibly also subordinate in terms of the order of creation or divine perception of him.

328 See, e.g., Day, *God's Conflict*, p. 65, Habel, p. 561; and compare similarly Keel, *Jahwes Entgegnung an Ijob*, pp. 143-4, for whom Leviathan is a mythological crocodile symbolising evil.

329 It moreover ignores the fact that the idea of crocodile-hunting may have been unfamiliar, or perceived as unachievable, to the original audience of the book, since there is no firm evidence for it having been practised in Israel, even though there were crocodiles in Palestine, at least on the coastal plain; moreover, if Ruprecht is correct, crocodile-hunting was confined in Egypt to the south, whereas in Thebes and further north this animal was subject to cultic worship (*VT* 21 [1971], p. 221; compare similarly Herodotus, *The Histories*, II.69.1) so this would place the practice even further away from Israel. Keel (pp. 141-2, n. 389) can cite counter-evidence for crocodile-hunting only from Dendera, some 70 km north of Thebes, i.e., still relatively far south, but interestingly not from elsewhere, which seems to imply that Ruprecht's general point still holds true. Even more important, perhaps, is the distinction between what might be achieved in theory or by certain individuals and that which might be

21 (ET vv. 26-29) seem to be the only verses concerned with the possibility of killing Leviathan, but these are focused around the general issue of impenetrability, which of course is wholly valid for the crocodile, the same point being made by Herodotus (*The Histories*, II.68.4, quoted above), whilst Ruprecht likewise maintains (though unfortunately without acknowledging his sources) that the crocodile's hide was impenetrable to harpoons, so it could only be killed with a spear directed down its open throat.[330] Certainly, at the very minimum, it has to be conceded that the softer underparts of the crocodile would have to be exposed for there to be much hope of penetration by a pointed weapon, since the piercing of the bony plates of the back or head would require extreme force exercised from extraordinarily close range. The passage also tallies with the theme of the invincibility of the crocodile found especially in Egyptian literature. Gordis appropriately compares the Egyptian "Hymn of Victory", which says of Pharaoh Thutmose III: "The lands of Mitanni are trembling under the fear of thee; I cause them to see thy majesty as a crocodile, the lord of fear in the water, who cannot be approached".[331] The portrayal of 40:31, 41:18-21 (ET 41:7, 26-29) therefore seems wholly applicable to the crocodile, even appearing to fit a recognisable pattern attested elsewhere, and this is especially the case once the poetic and hyperbolic context within the Book of Job is taken into consideration.

40:25-31 (ET 41:1-7), on the other hand, concern the impossibility of subjecting Leviathan to a variety of uses which might apply to agricultural, domestic or wild animals (farm work, being played with as a pet, sale by merchants, hunting),[332] vv. 25-6 (ET 41:1-2) apparently relating to methods of control and perhaps also capture which would prove unsuccessful with this creature. As is the case with 40:25 (ET 41:1), lack of knowledge of Hebrew technical vocabulary is a barrier to an exact understanding of these verses. However, the claim, made on the basis of the mention of a "hook" or "fishhook" in vv. 25a, 26b (ET 41:1a, 2b), that the same procedure is reflected here as is outlined in Herodotus' account of "the most interesting" method of catching crocodiles,[333] entailing capturing it on a hook baited with

---

regarded as personally attainable by the majority. One might compare certain achievements within the modern world, such as splitting the atom, space-travel, or climbing Everest, which the vast majority of people would unhesitatingly confess their inability to emulate. Given the social and geographical, and probably cultural, specificity of crocodile-hunting in the ancient world, the same situation is highly likely to pertain in relation to this practice, should the question be raised.

330 *VT* 21 [1971], pp. 221-2.

331 Gordis, pp. 479-480; *ANET*, p. 374.

332 Alternatively, it is possible that 40:31 should be taken to allude to the culinary preparation of Leviathan: although the verse is interpreted by most commentators as referring to harpoons and spears or the like, Tur-Sinai has suggested that שְׂכוֹת should be translated as "cloves" and בְּצִלְצַל related to the Mishnaic בְּצַלְצוֹל, "(small) onion", hence, "Couldst thou stud his body with cloves, / with fish-onions his head?" (Tur-Sinai, pp. 564, 565-6).

333 *The Histories*, II.70.

pork, ignores the unreliability of Herodotus and the considerable implausibility of what he describes.[334] If an animal the size of a crocodile were taken with a hook, its weight would be such that the risk of the flesh tearing, the hook or line breaking or the huntsmen having the line wrenched from their hands or being pulled into the water, would be considerable and would render the method wholly impracticable. This is all the more the case in a situation without the benefit of the strong, lightweight equipment at the modern fisherman's disposal, with no reel and, in all probability, with only a short rod or no rod at all. A dangerous tug-of-war with a thrashing crocodile by crocodile-infested waters with a real likelihood of being pulled in is not a feasible method nor a probable sport for kings. One might contrast caiman-hunting in Guyana, where the priority is to attempt to rope the mouth shut, not to cause aggravated snapping with a hook; and big-game fishing (of fish such as tuna, marlin and shark), which was made practicable only with the advent of the motor boat, from which "big-game anglers fish from fighting seats into which they can be strapped. Rods are massive, and the butts fit into a socket mounted on the chair".[335]

In fact, a close examination of 41:25-6 (ET 41:1-2) suggests that both verses may in fact allude to methods of control employed elsewhere in relation to animals and even human captives. Two basic types of instrument seem to be referred to: hooks (vv. 25a, 26b; ET 41:1a, 2b) and ropes (vv. 25b, 26a; ET 41:1b, 2a). חַכָּה in v. 25a (ET 41:1a) seems to refer specifically to the fishhook, which one might expect to be an instrument of capture (cf. Isa. 19:8, Hab. 1:15). However, although חוֹחַ in v. 26b (ET 41:2b) could possibly also allude to a method of catching an animal, in the only other occurrence of חוֹחַ and most of the cognate term חָח it is a means of control (see חוֹחַ in 2 Chr. 33:11, and חָח in Isa. 37:29 = 2 K. 19:28, Ezek. 19:4, 9, 38:4), so this seems to be the more likely interpretation, especially given the parallelism of the context.[336] Moreover, v. 25b (ET 41:1b) seems to describe

334 Similarly the explanation of 40:25-32 (ET 41:1-8) as an account of a hippopotamus-hunt (Ruprecht, *VT* 21 [1971], pp. 221-2) must be rejected if the unity of the Leviathan passage and its differentiation from that concerning Behemoth is to be upheld.

335 "Fishing" (On-line), (*Encyclopædia Britannica* from Encyclopædia Britannica Premium Service, 2004). Accessed November 9, 2004 at http://www.britannica.com/eb/article?tocId =2333.

336 The idea of חָח (and hence possibly, though hardly necessarily, חוֹחַ) as a means of catching an animal could garner support only from Ezek. 29:4. However, there it is God, not an ordinary hunter such as Job might be, who is the captor of the Pharaonic תַּנִּין / crocodile, so this would not substantiate any claim for this as a more widely applicable method which might be reproduced elsewhere. Since in the equivalent reference in Ezek. 32:3, God is said to take the Egyptian king with nets (חֵרֶם elsewhere usually, and always in Ezekiel—cf. 26:5, 14, 47:10—being a fishing net), Ezekiel may in both passages be conveying the idea of the helplessness of the Pharaoh before God, that he should be subject to the humiliation of being captured like a mere fish, although it is possible that in the latter reference a method appropriate to the capture of wild beasts in general (though not normally the crocodile) might be envisaged. In any case, a

a means of leading or restraining a wild animal or even human captives, so it is possible that חַכָּה in the parallel line (v. 25a, ET 41:1a) should also thus be understood. In fact, Egyptian and Assyrian reliefs depict prisoners being held or led by a hook drawn through the lips, nose or jaws,[337] so this practice may be reflected in v. 25a (ET 41:1a). If this is the case, it should probably be translated, "Can you lead Leviathan along (or drag him off) with a (fish)hook?", the same idea possibly being alluded to in Am. 4:2; compare also חוֹחַ in v. 26 (ET 41:2). Verse 26a (ET 41:2a), with its reference to putting a rope in Leviathan's nose, likewise reflects the control of animals or slaves: Ruprecht refers to the practice of driving an ox with a rope through its nose,[338] and one might also compare the statement that Ea "laid hold on Mummu, holding him by the nose-rope" in the *Enuma elish* I.72.[339] Thus vv. 25-6 (ET 41:1-2) as a whole seems to refer in different aspects to the same practice of leading prisoners by a rope attached to a hook impaled in the facial area. This is clearly the interpretation followed by the Qumran Targum, which is translated by Pope thus:

Can you drag Drake[340] with a hook,
Or with rope string[341] his tongue?
Can you put a ring in his nose,
Or with your gimlet string his cheek?[342]

It may therefore be concluded that the reference is likely to be to control rather than capture. In any case, the implausibility of capturing a crocodile with a hook in its mouth ensures that it is doubly improbable that a case could be made for seeing an allusion to the hunting of this animal here. As a result, the claim that Leviathan must be a mythological beast cannot be upheld in this way.

---

subtextual motif of Job 40:25-31 (ET 41:1-7), which rises to the surface in 40:29 (ET 41:5), is that of unfavourable comparison with other animals which might variously be caught, restrained, tamed, enslaved and set to work, made a pet of, sold, or hunted. Hence mention of methods of capture or control which might ordinarily be applicable to other creatures regularly handled in Israel, but not the crocodile, would be fully congruent with the context. Note especially the attention given to the mouth, and in one case, the nose, of Leviathan, in these verses, the snapping jaws of the crocodile being its most fearsome weapon, and close work with this part of the creature (vv. 25b, 26a; ET 41:1b, 2a) being what one would most wish to avoid.

337 See e.g., the stela of Esarhaddon, *ANEP* no 447; also no. 296.

338 *VT* 21 (1971), p. 222.

339 *ANET* p. 61.

340 *Tnyn.*

341 *Thrz*, "push through, poke through, pierce", cognate with Arabic *ḫrz*, used of sewing with an awl. The verb of MT, שׁקע, usually means "sink", hence perhaps "press down", but, as Dhorme has indicated (p. 571), it is employed in the Samaritan text of Lev. 8:13 to translate חבשׁ, "bind". This is also the meaning followed by the Vulgate, Aquila and Theodotion, so it should perhaps be accepted here.

342 Pope, p. 332.

Nevertheless, in an alternative approach to the same issue, Day has maintained that the questions of Job 40:25ff. (ET 41:1ff.) "impl[y] that God can, or more precisely, has captured Leviathan", since the ability of God to do what is impossible for man is the force of the interrogatives in the first divine speech; he also thinks that "Job 40:9ff. suggests that Job would need divine power to overcome Leviathan (and Behemoth)",[343] whilst "it is probable that [Job 40:29 (ET 41:5)] is directly dependent on Ps. 104:26"[344] , and should similarly be read as implying a contrast between what God is capable, and Job incapable, of doing. He concludes that "the message therefore presupposes a battle in which God defeated Leviathan."[345]

However, there are a number of difficulties with this view, and in particular with the assumption that the point of the questioning of whether Job could capture or tame Leviathan is to imply that God has so acted. The form of the second divine speech is so different from the first in terms of the sparsity of questions there employed and the great preponderance of description, that the issue of authenticity of authorship has frequently been raised. Whichever way this is resolved, it certainly suggests caution before assuming that the force of the interrogatives in each speech is the same. In fact, chapter 39 already represents a step towards the second divine speech in offering more lengthy descriptions of selected animals in a passage less punctuated by questions. This is then carried to a fuller extent in the Leviathan and Behemoth passages. More importantly, when the questioning is set in a form comparable with that of chapters 40-41, with the focus being on the behaviour of a particular animal towards Job, and the possibility of its tameability or use to man (39:9-12), it cannot be said that the implication is that God does, or has, done what Job cannot, in this case, in utilising the wild ox as a domestic animal. Rather, it should be read in the light of the questions which open the previous description ("Who has let the wild ass go free?...") and the accompanying outline of God's provision of its natural habitat: Yahweh is Lord over this animal, which is useless to man, and made it and provides for it as it is.

Day's second point, regarding the impact of 40:9ff. on the interpretation of 40:15-41:26 (ET 40:15-41:34), has already been discussed above in respect of 40:19b; however, more broadly, it touches on the vital issue of the overall message of the second divine speech (and hence of the book as a whole), without a consideration of which the problem of the identities of Behemoth and Leviathan cannot be solved. Permutations are almost as numerous as scholars writing on this issue, so space determines that a full treatment cannot be given here; at the same time, it is inevitable also that certain aspects of the present discussion will coincide with what has already been raised above in relation to specific interpretative issues. Crucial to the understanding of this speech is the nature of the challenge with which it commences: "Will you

343 Day, *God's Conflict*, p. 69.

344 Day, *God's Conflict*, p. 73.

345 Day, *God's Conflict*, p. 69.

even put me in the wrong?[346] / Will you condemn me that you may be justified?" (v. 8). Accordingly, Job's reply in chapter 42 is far more forthcoming and wide-ranging than his response to the first divine speech (40:4-5), since here he acknowledges the absolute power of God to do as he wills, confessing that he had spoken in ignorance, but now had a new vision of God and repented utterly. Any interpretation of Job 40:6-41:26 (ET 40:6-41:34) must therefore cohere with this dominant theme of divine justice and cosmic ordering.[347]

It is exactly in accordance with this theme of justice that, following the initial accusation, God challenges Job to don divinity (40:9-10) and mete out judgment in the world himself (vv. 11-13). Think of Behemoth, a created creature like Job, but so powerful. He is a source of pride to God, but would Job bring near his sword? Job, it may be presumed, may not feel comfortable with his existence, but he is not capable of asserting control over him; more importantly, it is emphasised how Behemoth is as much a creature of God as Job (v. 15), the first of God's works (v. 19), fearless and confident in his environment (v. 23). To God, he is a blessed part of the created order, not something which should be excised from it. "Let him who made him bring near his sword" (v. 19b) therefore seems to have the force of: only he who made him (and no-one else) may do so. It is the prerogative of the maker (albeit not one which he will chose to exercise), but not of anyone else. Nor could Leviathan be tamed or made useful to humanity;[348] he is far too fierce for that! How much less, then, can one challenge God (thus perhaps 41:2; ET

346 Note here, however, that מִשְׁפָּט may be equivalent to "governance": see S. E. Balentine, "'What are Human Beings that You Make so Much of Them?' Divine Disclosure from the Whirlwind: 'Look at Behemoth'" in T. Linafelt and T. Beal (edd.), *God in the Fray. A Tribute to Walter Brueggemann* (Minneapolis, MN: Fortress, 1998), 259-78, p. 267 and S. Scholnick, "The Meaning of *Mišpaṭ* in the Book of Job", *JBL* 101 (1982) 521-9, pp. 522-3.

347 Of course, the centrality of the issue of divine justice and ordering mirrors its importance in the speeches of Job (see e.g. 9:22-4). To perceive a "complete evasion of the issue [of divine justice and mercy] as Job had posed it" in the divine speeches is a corollary of the *Chaoskampf* interpretation proposed by Pope which even to him comes as "something of a surprise and, on the face of it, a disappointment" (p. LXXX).

348 As has been shown above, 40:25-31 (ET 41:1-7) seem to concern Leviathan's insusceptibility to human control or use for human benefit: vv. 25-6 (ET 41:1-2) appears to refer to the control of Leviathan as one might restrain or lead an animal or human captive, and the theme of making a servant or captive pet of Leviathan is continued in vv. 27-9 (ET 41:3-5). Nor may he be sold for profit (v. 30; ET 41:6; the second half of the verse is likely to refer to the division of the proceeds of the sale: see Habel, p. 554, Dhorme, pp. 572-3) or hunted (v. 31; ET 41:7). As has been indicated, it is likely also that the instruments described in relation to Behemoth in v. 24 are chiefly those of restraint. Thus these passages should not be related to the "defeat" or "overcoming" of these beasts, but to Job's inability to control them for his own ends. The continuation of the Leviathan description then makes a further point, that man rather has reason to fear this mighty animal, which has a range of dangerous attributes, is resistant to human weaponry, and is wholly without fear.

v. 10).[349] "Whatever is under the whole heaven is mine" (41:3b; ET v. 11b) seems to say more or less the same as 42:2:[350] it is not just an affirmation of the power of God, but of his absolute ability to do as he wills and to order the world as he wills. The implication seems to be that these animals are there because he wants them to be, and are subject to his protection. Job cannot change the world or remove from it those aspects which he does not like. Yet God celebrates Leviathan's strength, his imperviousness to attack and fearsome characteristics. Nothing compares with him, and like Behemoth he is without fear.

Just as the description of the wild ox is a continuation of the idea expressed in relation to the wild ass, so that the two should be read together, similarly the divine pride in the creation of Behemoth and his provision for him should be read forward into the Leviathan passage, where the same favourable overtones recur in vv. 4, 10, 23-26 (ET vv. 12, 18, 31-34), thus indicating that Leviathan's physical attributes there outlined are viewed positively by, and indeed are due to, God.[351] The fearlessness of Behemoth (40:23) and indeed Leviathan (41:25; ET v. 33) is developed into the idea of Leviathan as king over all the sons of pride (41:26b; ET v. 34b). This may have a double nuance: positively, he is the chief or greatest beast (and kingship is awarded by God, so he may be understood to owe his status to the divine will; note especially the use of the preposition עַל). Yet if Job had aspirations to insist on the exercise of strict justice in the world according to his perceptions and epitomised by the idea of abasing the proud, he may here be challenged further to revolutionise his thinking. The foregoing has already emphasised his physical incapability when faced with such creatures as Behemoth and Leviathan, whilst the nature of their presentation calls into question the propriety of acting in hostility towards them. In this final verse of the second divine speech, the association of Leviathan with the בְּנֵי־שָׁחַץ may be intended to indicate both similarity and difference as compared with the גֵּאֶה of 40:11b, 12a: despite the conceptual overlap between the terms, the distinction in terminology indicates that the king appointed over the "proud,

349 Following MT and the continuing first-person singular prepositional suffixes of the following verse. However, many MSS read here לְפָנָיו and this is preferred by some commentators.

350 Hence there is no justification for following Pope (pp. 335, 338) in emending לִי to מִי, in order (in combination with his own suffixual alteration of הִקְדִּימַנִי from the first to third person and the widely-followed emendation of וַאֲשַׁלֵּם to וַיִּשְׁלָם, following the LXX) to obtain the reading, "Who could confront him [i.e. Leviathan] unscathed, / Under the whole heaven, who?" Compare similarly Day, who makes the same changes to the first colon, but reads לֹא הוּא or לֹא אֶחָד for לִי הוּא, resulting in the translation, "There is not one under the whole heaven" (*God's Conflict*, p. 63), whilst others (e.g., Fuchs, *Mythos*, p. 23, Fohrer, pp. 525, 527, de Wilde, pp. 356, 388, and Groß, p. 142) achieve the same meaning by following the above-cited emendations, but substituting קִדְּמוֹ for הִקְדִּימַנִי.

351 See especially v. 25b (ET v. 33b) and the discussion thereon.

exalted"[352] beasts is not to be identified with the "proud, arrogant" wicked who should be cast down. Thus the presentation of Behemoth and Leviathan indicates that this is not about beasts epitomising evil which God can or has overcome, but about their positive divinely hallowed place in creation, contrary to men's limited, simplistic and anthropocentric perspective and expectations of good and evil and of how the world and God should be. God is Lord of all and the world is under his absolute control. The second divine speech enables Job to come to a recognition of this, having spoken out of such ignorance, and having had little understanding of the true nature of God.

As regards the proposal of dependence on Ps. 104, there is a similarity between the idea and vocabulary expressed in v. 26b of this Psalm and Job 40:29a (ET 41:5a), as well as a general correspondence in content and ambience between the two compositions, each considering the cosmic aspects of God's work before focusing on his care for the living creatures. Nevertheless, it may be rather simplistic to assume direct dependence is operative here, even if a similar milieu in the genre of (probably post-exilic) creation psalms is likely. However, the positive character of the notion of Leviathan's playfulness in Ps. 104:26 should be noted;[353] hence, even if Job 40:29a (ET 41:5a) were to be interpreted as Day recommends, in the light of Ps. 104, this would not imply any basis in an earlier divine conflict and subjugation of Leviathan.[354] In fact, the celebratory tone of the creation psalms with respect to all aspects of creation, including that of the "sea monsters", and their delight in the diversity of the natural world as manifesting God's power and care, must be recognised. Thus, as Day states, "a strong case may be made that the description of Leviathan inherently belongs with the previously mentioned works of creation in Chapters 38-9"[355]; however, it is literally as a *work* of creation that Behemoth and Leviathan appear, both here (40:15, 41:25 [ET v. 33], and cf. 40:19 in respect of Behemoth) and in Ps. 104, so Day's assumption that this is "the mythological ... dragon... overcome at the time of creation"[356] appears rather as a reflection of his own expectation rather than a statement of how they are presented by the divine speaker of chapters 40-41.[357]

---

352 Thus BDB explains בְּנֵי־שָׁחַץ as "majestic wild beasts", translating שַׁחַץ as "dignity, pride" and comparing late Hebrew "act proudly", Arabic "rise, be elevated" and "be a person of rank", Aramaic שַׁחֲצָא, "lion".

353 Though of course, the exact translation of the verse is uncertain, and "Leviathan which thou didst form to play in it" (i.e. the sea) may be the more likely reading: see the discussion thereon in Chapter 8 above.

354 See further the discussion of Ps. 104 above, Chapter 8.

355 Day, *God's Conflict*, p. 70.

356 Day, *God's Conflict*, p. 71.

357 He also makes comparison with the mention of Rahab in Job 9:2-14; however, since this is an anti-creation, rather than creation passage, one can hardly expect the same orientation as in the divine speeches or Ps. 104 with respect to the mention of Rahab (assumed by Day to be more-or-less equivalent to Leviathan). Moreover, 9:13 may well mark the beginning of a new section, rather than belonging closely with vv. 2-12, so

The concluding plea of Ps. 104:35, that sinners be consumed from the earth and the wicked be no more, forms a striking correspondence with the challenge of Job 40:11-13, and indicates that a correlation should be assumed between the natural and moral orders in each case. In the second divine speech, there are three possible ways in which this could be interpreted. The first is that God has crushed Behemoth and Leviathan, but Job cannot. However, this is belied by the divine pride in and creation of these creatures. The second, that Job cannot control them, and neither can God, would comprise a surprising and unparalleled conclusion for a work in the Hebrew Bible, and is also subject to the same objections as the first possibility just considered. The third option, that Job might wish to overcome these animals (possibly to render them useful to man, rather than simply through a desire to exterminate such fearful beasts) but cannot, whilst God will not, but rather delights in them no less than he might in man, follows the grain of the text, and results in a startling challenge to Job's blithe certainties and anthropocentricity.[358]

Some have nevertheless sought to justify a *Chaoskampf* interpretation of Job 40:25-41:26 by appealing outside the text to the mythological nature of Leviathan or *Ltn* in passages such as Isa. 27:1 and KTU 1.3.iii.41, 1.5.i.1-22.[359] However, the relationship of the Joban portrayal to this material is extremely difficult to reconstruct, since there Leviathan is portrayed as a serpent, as twisting, and in the Ugaritic, as having seven heads. By contrast, although the Leviathan of Job 40-41 is presented as scaly, his impenetrability (41:5-9, 18-21; ET vv. 13-17, 26-29) and the mention of his limbs (41:4; ET v. 12) and emphasis on his muscular frame (41:4, 14, cf. v. 15; ET vv. 12, 22, cf. v. 23) militate against a serpentine form. Likewise, although the name Leviathan may etymologically derive from a root *lwh* "to twist" and this

---

this would further undermine the comparison Day seeks to draw. See further the discussion of Job 9 above.

358 For this reason, the attempt made by Keel and others (e.g., V. Kubina, *Die Gottesreden im Buch Hiob* [Freiburg, 1979], pp. 68-75 [re Behemoth and Leviathan]; E. Ruprecht, *VT* 21 [1971] p. 228, B. Lang, "Job xl 18 and the 'Bones of Seth'" *VT* 30 [1980] pp. 360-1 [re Behemoth only]) to relate the content of the second divine speech to the understanding of the crocodile and hippopotamus in certain aspects of Egyptian religion as the form adopted by Seth as the enemy of Horus, and as an embodiment of evil, is implausible: the divine attitude to these beasts is not antagonistic and there is no indication of a divine combat, past, present or future. Moreover, since such proposals are merely a variation on the *Chaoskampf* understanding of the second divine speech, many of the specific criticisms pertaining to a putative northwest Semitic or Babylonian origin for the imagery still apply, for example in relation to the capturability of the hippopotamus and crocodile.

359 Thus, e.g., Pope, claiming that "the supernatural character of Leviathan is abundantly clear from [such] data" (p. 331). Contrast, however, the far more perceptive understanding of Newsom that, notwithstanding "the temptation... to read these speeches... along the lines of Psalms 74 and 89 and Isaiah 51,... although this speech may draw on materials from those traditions, it does not 'say' the same thing" (*The Book of Job*, p. 248).

would be compatible with the crocodile's ability suddenly to lunge sideways to capture prey,[360] this is not a theme which is explored in the Joban passage, despite its mention in even very brief allusions to Leviathan elsewhere. Finally, although the motif of the "heads of Leviathan" recurs in Ps. 74:14 (after רָאשֵׁי תַנִּינִים in the preceding colon) as well as being a firm feature of the two Ugaritic passages here cited, the lengthy description of Leviathan in Job 40:25-41:26 (ET 41:1-34) remains silent on this point, and indeed mention is rather made of "his head" (40:31; ET 41:7), "his nose" (40:26; ET 41:2), "his jaw" (40:26; ET 41:2), "his tongue" (40:25; ET 41:1), "his face" (41:6; ET v. 14), "his mouth" (41:11, 13; ET vv. 19, 21) and "his neck" (41:14; ET v. 22) in the singular. It may therefore safely be concluded that Leviathan is not here envisaged as polycephalic.[361]

The relationship between the Leviathan of Job 40:25-41:26 (ET 41:1-34) and that of 3:8 is similarly unclear. The latter, it will be recalled, occurs in a context of oppressive darkness imagery, whereas the former is associated with light (41:10-11, 24; ET vv. 18-19, 32), and this cannot readily be reconciled, unless the light from Leviathan might be due to his swallowing of the sun as it passed through the underworld on its diurnal course. However, even if the issuing forth of light from his mouth and eyes might potentially be explained in this way, thus to attribute the shining wake which he leaves behind him seems to stretch probability too far. Moreover, the divine positivity towards this animal and the apparent earthly context of Job's potential encounter with him speaks further against this interpretation, even if Leviathan might possibly be "roused" (3:8; 41:2 [ET v. 10]). Similarly, although there might be a tentative correlation in the idea of there being none like Leviathan "on the dust", insofar as in Job this term can be employed not just to denote the earth (14:19; 39:14) or mortality (4:19), but burial (7:21) and the underworld itself (within the second divine speech, in 40:13; also 17:16), it is difficult to discern how this might illuminate the current issue. The reference may here only be interpreted as referring to earthly, or mortal, life and hence, unless a conscious denial of similarity with a Leviathan of the underworld is intended, it can offer no hope of a connection. It therefore appears to be the case that there is an incompatibility in all the available concrete details between the portrayal of Job 40:25-41:26 (ET 41:1-34) and the biblical and Ugaritic references sometimes cited in support of perceiving an allusion to a monster of "chaos" in the Leviathan of the second Divine Speech. This being so, it is inadmissible to persist in imparting the perceived, but more nebulous, "mythological" nature of Leviathan to the Joban passage, not least when Job 40:29 (ET 41:5) seems to be related to Ps. 104:26, a context in which, as in Job 40-41, Leviathan is apparently portrayed naturalistically and as a source of delight to his maker, and all within the context and ambience of a wisdom-inspired celebration of God's care for the

360 Thus also Keel, *Jahwes Entgegnung*, p. 143, contra, e.g., Day (*God's Conflict*, p. 66), who states that "the crocodile... has great difficulty in turning its body rapidly".

361 This is a point acknowledged even by some proponents of the theory that Leviathan is here a chaos dragon: see e.g. Day, *God's Conflict*, p. 72.

natural world which bears many affinities to the divine speeches of Job.

Nevertheless, the question of the relationship of the different references to Leviathan still stands, not least in respect of the two allusions within the Book of Job itself. One is therefore presented with a number of alternative conclusions. The first is that the notion of "Leviathan" was perceived in more than one form or was envisaged very fluidly to the degree that even one author could refer to it in different ways within the course of the same composition. This seems to be required by the apparent association of Leviathan with the underworld only in Job 3:8 but not elsewhere in the Old Testament, and by the physical differences in its appearance which seem to pertain between Job 40:25-41:26 (ET 41:1-34) and other passages offering any detail in this regard. A proposal of Uehlinger may here be suggestive: he maintains that Leviathan was fundamentally serpentine, although the seven heads may be derivative from some other monster and "are at best secondary elements".[362] However, the representations of Horus (who was identified in MBA Palestine with the Syrian weather-god Baal / Hadad) as "spearing a crocodile... represents a precedent for the biblical association of Leviathan with the crocodile", whilst it is possible that Leviathan may in a later period have been assimilated to Apophis, the netherworld serpent who attempts to hinder the sun's course.[363] Alternatively, or perhaps additionally, one might surmise that the term "Leviathan" was employed to refer both to a particular species and to an animal of that species as embodying certain other forces (cf. "the Bear", "British bulldog", "Frogs", even "The Hun"). Of itself, this second hypothesis would not explain the differences in physical characteristics between the portrayal in Job and Isa. 27:1 or Ps. 74:14, but it might offer an account, or partial account, of the two Joban allusions. Another possibility which should be considered in respect of Job 3:8 and Job 40:25-41:26 (ET 41:1-34) is that it should be explained by the frequently-proposed suggestion that the portrayal of Behemoth and Leviathan in the second divine speech were not part of the original composition of the book of Job, and this is not impossible.[364]

If the relationship of the Leviathan of Job 40-41 to other allusions to a beast of this name is a natural question to consider, the issue of the origin and identity of Behemoth is far more opaque, since clear allusions to this creature are otherwise lacking. Nevertheless, some have sought to draw a connection with comparative mythological material, thus justifying the attribution of mythological, "chaotic" elements to Behemoth itself. However, Pope's proposed connection of Behemoth with *'gl il 'tk* (*KTU* 1.3.iii.44), the "Eaters" and "Devourers" of *KTU* 1.12 and the Sumero-Akkadian "bull of heaven" of the Gilgamesh Epic[365] is widely rejected, since it is highly conjectural and seems to have its basis only in the apparent bovine nature of each of these beings, rather than in any evidence for a relationship between

362 "Leviathan לִוְיָתָן" in *DDD*, p. 512.

363 *Ibid.*, p. 513.

364 See, e.g., Ewald, pp. 312-4, for arguments in favour of secondary authorship.

365 Pp. 321-2; cf. Nam, *Talking about God*, p. 150.

them. In fact, even this aspect of the figures from Ugaritic myth is questionable, since the "Eaters" and "Devourers" are only likened to cattle in parallel similes pertaining to limited physical characteristics (their horns and humps[366]), and a variety of identities have been proposed for them, ranging from goats to flies.[367] Similarly, as Mark Smith has indicated, "calf" in the phrase *'gl il 'tk* (*KTU* 1.3.iii.44), like the proximate denotations "dog, "beloved" and "daughter", "may be applied as titles to someone to denote his or her subservience and belonging to another person".[368] Moreover, as Pope himself admits, "there is no intimation of the bovine character of Behemoth apart from the reference to its herbivorous nature in v. 15c";[369] there, however, the comparison with an ox actually implies that Behemoth is a wholly different type of animal. Similarly, since בְּהֵמָה means not just "cattle" in a general sense, but also "beast", this does not assist in the species-identification of Behemoth, "the great beast". Pope's interpretation would, further, necessitate the transposition of v. 23 to the passage concerning Leviathan, since it is not compatible with a bovine animal.

In a further permutation of the same theory, Day proposes an identity between *Arš* and *'gl il 'tk*, claiming that the postulated bovine nature of the latter and the mention of the former, together with "the dragon" (*tnn*), as being "in the sea" in *KTU* 1.6.vi.51, provides a significant point of contact with Behemoth.[370] However, besides the uncertainty regarding the bovine character of both Behemoth and *'gl il 'tk*, Wyatt is surely correct in stating that "there is nothing in the text [*KTU* 1.3.iii.43-44] to justify supposing that Arsh is bovine in form or is another name for 'El's calf Atik'", whilst "Day's broader argument, that Arsh is the prototype of Behemoth... seems to go beyond the evidence."[371] Similarly, M. K. Wakeman's theory of a biblical and Ugaritic earth monster called both Ereṣ (*arṣ* in Ugaritic) and Behemoth, which is also to be identified with Arš and *'gl il 'tk*,[372] has been found wholly unconvincing, since it is implausible on many levels. Most notably, the interpretation of אֶרֶץ as referring to a monster, rather than concretely to "the earth" or "land", is in every instance unnecessary.[373] It must be concluded that explanations of the origin of Behemoth deriving from comparative

366 Or "bulk"? Thus Mark Smith in *UNP*, p. 189.

367 See Wyatt, *RTU*, p. 163, n. 9.

368 *UNP*, p. 168, n. 71.

369 P. 322.

370 Day, *God's Conflict*, pp. 81-2; followed also by Batto, "Behemoth בהמות", in *DDD*, p. 168.

371 *RTU*, p. 79, n. 50.

372 "The Biblical Earth Monster in the Cosmogonic Combat Myth" *JBL* 88 (1969) 313-320; *God's Battle with the Monster*, pp. 108-117.

373 Here the arguments against identifying Behemoth with *Arš* and *'gl il 'tk* pertain once more. See further the detailed critique by Day (*God's Conflict*, pp. 84-6), which is still valuable, despite the fact that Wakeman's theory is in certain respects vulnerable to the same criticisms as his, and note also the more general evaluation of her methodology above in Chapter 2.

studies are highly conjectural and indeed dubious on many counts. They also appear superfluous, insofar as the simple and widely accepted etymological explanation of Behemoth as "great beast" or "the beast *par excellence*" seems to account adequately for the use of the name in the present context.

However, if the attempt to interpret Behemoth and Leviathan as representations of chaos to the exclusion of the positive aspects of their portrayal proves inadequate, presentations which claim that they are to be regarded as at once embodiments of evil and valued creatures of God are also unsatisfactory. Nam, for example, on one hand talks of Behemoth as "the chaos monster" yet on the other acknowledges him as "peaceful"[374] and as "hav[ing] the capacity for giving the order of life in his divinely ordained space";[375] and he likewise regards Leviathan as a "symbol of evil",[376] whilst also recognising that this creature "is the object of Yahweh's praises"[377] and that "Leviathan is not destructive in action, especially against God".[378] Hence Nam perceives that Behemoth and Leviathan "have a positive value as God's creatures"[379] and "display what the beauty and wonders of creation are like in their domains".[380] However, it is questionable whether such extremes may be embodied within the same creature: the very createdness and divinely endorsed rôle of Behemoth and Leviathan seem to exclude the possibility that these beasts should represent "chaos" or have an implied anti-creation function themselves.[381] Clearly, Behemoth and Leviathan are fearsome, but to describe them as "representing all the proud and wicked of the world"[382] and as "evil" or as embodying "chaos" is to overreach the evidence, especially given the positive aspects which should be balanced against this. Nam surely comes closer to the truth when he recognises that these animals "are fascinating and beautiful, though fearsome to ordinary humans"[383] and acknowledges their didactic function in showing a pattern of working in the world on a "totally different level from anthropocentric-moral categories".[384] That is, their fearsomeness lies on the human and not on the cosmic level; though dangerous to man, they present no threat to God but are instead valued by him.

It thus appears from the foregoing discussion that the characteristics of Behemoth are compatible with identifying him as a hippopotamus, and that Leviathan is essentially crocodilian, having many features which are

374 *Talking about God*, p.153.

375 *Ibid.*, p. 152.

376 *Ibid.*, p. 158.

377 *Ibid.*, p. 158.

378 *Ibid.*, p. 157.

379 *Ibid.*, p. 160.

380 *Ibid.*, p. 163.

381 Nam refers to "universal chaos and cosmic upheaval" in respect of Leviathan as "the embodiment of chaos" (*Ibid.*, p. 158).

382 *Ibid.*, p. 159.

383 *Ibid.*, p. 183, n. 267.

384 *Ibid.*, pp. 159-60.

distinctive to this creature, despite the heightened and hyperbolic poetic language in which the description is couched. However, it should occasion no surprise in such a context if this most impressive and fearsome animal is a "liminal" being, having fantastic, as well as natural, attributes, though presented as a member of the created order and a work of God. Clearly, however, it is not a creature which is confined to the "divine" world, but one which exists within the present, physical, world, and which (potentially, at least) is encounterable by humanity.

The crucial distinction in ascertaining whether these are monsters of "chaos" is in the divine presentation of and attitude towards them. Here the createdness of both Behemoth and Leviathan, their exalted status within creation, and the evident divine pride in them and delight in their fearsome beauty, indicates that the thought of theomachic combat is not present here. Nevertheless, within the theological argument of the book of Job, this presentation of Behemoth and Leviathan constitutes a profound comment on God's ordering of the world and on the place within it of elements which are outside the control of man and indeed threatening and dangerous to him. The second divine speech thus offers a stark challenge to the "faultfinder" Job, the man who "would put [God] in the wrong", by decimating Job's simple certainties: it presents a vision of the works of God in which the heightened portrayal of the wild strength of Behemoth and inconquerable ferocity of Leviathan is exceeded only by the hyperbolic expression of their primacy within creation. It thus leaves an impression of the rule of God, and of the nature of the world, which is far deeper and more complex than Job (or the reader) might previously have imagined; here anthropocentricity is pushed to the margins, and what to man seems marginal or inimical is centralised. Job's acknowledgement that he had "uttered what [he] did not understand, things too wonderful for [him], which [he] did not know" seems a natural and wholly appropriate response.

Summary

Although only three passages concerning Leviathan have been discussed here, they are very disparate in their content, one being mythological, another apparently relating to an extraordinary creature of the natural world, and the third having what may be described as an eschatological-historical referent. To these may also be added the historical and natural allusions of Pss. 74 and 104 respectively. However, despite these considerable variations, it seems that in none of these settings is the theme of "chaos" implied. Indeed, in Job 3:8, the one passage which appears to have a purely "mythological" referent, the relation of Leviathan to the underworld has already been recognised, and indeed is difficult to ignore. In Isa. 27:1, as in Ps. 74, any underlying mythical narrative seems only to provide a "frame" from which to display other interests, and its original reference (if it ever was fixed) is probably not of concern, except as a matter of religio-historical interest, since it is not directly connoted. Indeed, it is possible that—in respect of Israelite traditions relating to Yahweh—it was only ever a story evoking the deity's power and supremacy, but that it could derive its content from the immediate context. Lastly, it is perhaps in Job 40-41 that the motif of Leviathan as a "chaotic" monster finds its most direct refutation, since the createdness of this animal and even its exalted status within creation is explicitly claimed.

As a result, the absence of any direct concern with an originating act of cosmic creation in the three passages here considered can scarcely be questioned. The same has already been maintained above in Chapter 6 with respect to Ps. 74, whilst in Ps. 104, the celebration of Leviathan as one of the animals formed by God, rather than as an entity to be related to the establishment of the cosmic structure (as described in earlier in the Psalm, vv. 2b-9/10), seems actually to contravene the *Chaoskampf* idea. Its createdness, especially with a specific intent in mind, also undermined the suggestion that the primeval monster has somehow been overcome and "naturalised": according to this portrayal, Leviathan was an animal of the natural world from the start. This wholly coheres with the interpretation advanced in respect of Job 40-41.

As regards the interrelation of the various allusions to this figure, it appears that the Leviathan motif was utilised to denote Yahweh's overcoming of his enemy as a manifestation of power (Ps. 74, Isa. 27), with considerable flexibility allowed in the denotation of that enemy. Job 3:8 seems to provide a more purely mythological, and hence perhaps more original, application, with Leviathan there being associated with the underworld, possibly as a monster which threatened the sun. The reference to the slaying of Ltn in the context of the Ugaritic Baal-Mot cycle (*KTU* 1.5.1-4), and especially the allusion to a *tnn* which seems to present a danger to Shaphash at its close (*KTU* 1.6.vi.45-53), may perhaps provide further corroboration for this from a source which is considerably earlier than those in the Hebrew Bible. Wyatt has drawn attention to the possibility that in Israel Egypt was mythologically conceived as signifying death, hence perhaps the rather anomalous expression "go down to Egypt".[385] If this is correct, it could provide a ready explanation of the application of the name "Leviathan" to Egypt, and from there, of the broader use evidenced in Isa. 27:1. Finally, the more naturalistic allusions in Ps. 104 and Job 40-41 may possibly offer later, monotheising reflections on the motif, although it is also conceivable that the concept of monsters as the "beloved" ones of El has left an influence.[386]

The apparent dissociation of Leviathan from the theme of "*Chaoskampf*" which emerges from this analysis is thus in accord with the conclusions reached in respect of Rahab and (as designated through various terminology) the waters. The fact that the same type of results emerge consistently from the whole range of material here considered does much to strengthen the thesis advanced here as a whole. Moreover, this has highly significant ramifications, not only for the understanding of the putative theme of

385 *Myths of Power*, pp. 87-8.

386 See Mark S. Smith, *The Origins of Biblical Monotheism*, p. 37.

"chaos", but also in respect of the development of Israelite religious thought and its relation to wider Canaanite beliefs and religious practice. The cumulative case built up throughout the present monograph will therefore be summarised in the concluding chapter, before some of these wider diachronic and history-of-religion implications are discussed.

Conclusion

There are two distinct types of conclusion which may be drawn from the present monograph. The first is a semantic one: that the language of "chaos" has been inappropriately applied to the material here considered, and that there is therefore a strong case for abandoning it in respect of the Old Testament. The second aspect to the present findings may be of still wider significance, and this concerns its diachronic results and their implications for the history of Israelite religion. The reasons for proposing the abandonment of the terminology of "chaos" shall therefore first be explained through the systematic evaluation of the varied allusions contained within these passages. Then the implications of these findings for the history of Israelite religion shall be considered, and certain tentative proposals advanced.

1. Reassessment of the Applicability of "Chaos" Language to the Hebrew Bible

In the initial review of the "State of the Question" of research into the theme of "chaos" undertaken in Chapter 2, the putative theme was characterised as having three essential elements, namely chaos, creation and combat. The results of the present monograph pertaining to the issue of the applicability of the imagery of "chaos" to the passages here considered may therefore most helpfully be summarised under each of these headings, which shall be taken in reverse order.

1.1. Combat

If "combat" is properly defined as entailing a struggle between opponents of relative parity for whom the outcome is genuinely open and victory hard-won, then there is no hint of this in the interaction of God with any other entity in the passages examined in the present context. The common combat pattern of the enemy gaining ascendancy before the victor finally triumphs, perhaps with the aid of another, finds no echo here. Beyond this, the interactions between Yahweh and the waters, or between Yahweh and a dragon or possibly-draconic being, need to be distinguished.

In the former case, Yahweh may be said to terrify, dominate or control the waters, which are referred to by a variety of terminology. However there is never any clear indication that the sea or deep is ever seen as a genuinely personal power or deity, rather then merely being subjected to metaphorical personification as a figure of speech (as, e.g., in Job 38). Moreover, one might look in vain for any indication that Yahweh slew the sea: the expected actions of combat, such as slaying, hacking in pieces, piercing, entrapping and so on, are absent. Even mention of Yahweh's sword, stated in Isa. 27:1 to be the instrument with which he was to slay Leviathan, is lacking. The sole possible allusion to any form of weaponry is in the highly imaginative Red Sea evocation of Psalm 77, described under the imagery of a storm theophany, in which it is stated that "thy (lightning) arrows flew hither and thither"[1] (v. 18c), the previous and following two cola similarly describing storm phenomena (vv. 18ab, 19ab). There is no indication of a target, whilst the crossing itself is described solely in terms of a "way... through the sea" (v. 20a), without mention even of the division of the sea.

Similarly, although it has occasionally been claimed that the ascription to Yahweh of dividing the Red Sea in Pss. 78:13 and 136:13 reflects the idea of cleaving a monster in two as Marduk did to Tiamat, the motif comprises a very firm aspect of the tradition, the verb בקע being applied to the waters, besides Ps. 78:13, in Ex. 14:16, 21 and Neh. 9:11; one might compare also Isa. 63:12. In Ps. 136, the use of the verb גזר seems in addition to reflect the idea of covenant formation (the noun גְּזָרִים being confined to v. 13 and Gen. 15:17) since this coheres so well with the theme of the חֶסֶד of Yahweh which pervades the Psalm. Now clearly it could be claimed that the dividing and crossing of the Red Sea was a construct based on a mythological prototype of the slaughter of a god or dragon Sea, but there are few who would wish to support such a radical solution. In particular, it meets with two very significant problems. First, it is clear that, howsoever the motif of the dividing of the Red Sea originated, before long (and indeed probably from the beginning) it was accepted as an historical tradition and any mythological background was forgotten or subsumed under the more literalistic perspective. Second, and perhaps more importantly, it might be noted that the Ugaritic deity Yam is not cleft in two, and nor is יָם etymologically or conceptually equivalent to Akkadian Tiamat, so the whole basis for the claim remains highly dubious.

Yahweh's relation to the waters is well exemplified by a catalogue of his actions towards them and these shall therefore be discussed in turn in order to determine whether some form of combat may be implied. First, he created the sea and established boundaries for it:

> The sea is his, for he made it (Ps. 95:5)
>
> [He] made... the sea, and all that is in [it] (Ps. 146:6)
>
> He commanded and [the waters above the heavens] were created. And he established them for ever and ever; he fixed their bounds which cannot be passed (Ps. 148:5b-6)
>
> He established the fountains of the deep,... He assigned to the sea its limit, so that the waters might not transgress his command (Prov. 8:28-9)
>
> [He] didst cover [the earth] with the deep as with a garment...

1 Translation mine.

> [He] didst set a bound which they should not pass, so that they might not again cover the earth (Ps. 104:6, 9)
>
> [He] placed the sand as the bound for the sea,
> A perpetual barrier which it cannot pass;
> Though the waves toss, they cannot prevail,
> Though they roar, they cannot pass over it. (Jer. 5:22)
>
> He gathered the waters of the sea as in a bottle; he put the deeps in storehouses (Ps. 33:7)
>
> [He] shut in the sea with doors, when it burst forth from the womb; [He] made clouds its garment, and thick darkness its swaddling band, and prescribed bounds for it, and set bars and doors, and said, "Thus far shall you come and no farther, and here shall your proud waves be stayed." (Job 38:8-11)
>
> And God... separated the waters which were under the firmament from the waters which were above the firmament. And it was so... And God said, "Let the waters under the heavens be gathered together into one place, and let the dry land appear." And it was so... and the waters that were gathered together he called Seas. And God saw that it was good... And God said, "Let the waters bring forth swarms of living creatures..." (Gen. 1:7, 9-10, 20).

In general, no reaction of the sea is recorded, except insofar as the effectiveness of the boundaries set up by God is implied or stated (Ps. 148:6, Prov. 8:29, Ps. 104:9; Jer. 5:22, Job 38:10-11). Compliance is particularly implied in the account of the separation and ordering of the waters in Gen 1, which is punctuated by the refrain, "And it was so" and concluded with the reflection that "God saw that it was good." Only in Jer. 5:22 is the sea depicted as behaving in a way that might imply an attempt to transcend the boundaries established by God. However, since the portrayal is heavily naturalistic (for example in mentioning the sand), and personification seems to be discounted by the fact that it is only the waves which toss, observation of the reality of nature seems to provide the best explanation of this description. The repeated celebration of God's creation of the sea is also notable (Pss. 95:5, 146:6, 148:5-6; cf. Prov. 3:20; the creation of the deep is probably also implied in Gen. 1:1-2), whilst its permanence is important in Ps. 148:6 and implied also in Prov. 8:28.

In addition to God's direct action towards the sea mentioned in the context of creation, in Ps. 104:7, it is stated, "at thy rebuke [i.e., roar, as the parallelism implies] they [the waters] fled; at the sound of thy thunder they took to flight". Although it is not stated that God's roar in thunder is aimed at the waters, its effect is to make them flee. Here a graphic portrayal of a storm theophany is in evidence, and the fleeing of the waters is accompanied by the rising and sinking of the earth in order for the mountains and valleys to find their appointed places. This thus seems to constitute a particularly vivid depiction of the process of creation which has been cast in the theophanic mould, the fleeing of the waters and movement of the earth being especially common aspects of the divine appearing, in conjunction with God's rebuke/roar and thunder. However, it is notable that it was God who covered the mountains with the deep in the first place, whilst the image of a garment suggests a protective covering; moreover, it is only "the waters" which are presented as fleeing, even though they are not generally viewed as imbued with mythological significance or elsewhere (even in the wider ancient Near Eastern background) presented as the enemy of God.

The next group of allusions relates to Yahweh's calming or stirring up of the sea, obviously as an indication of his great power over creation; its compliance seems to be assumed:

> [He] do[es] still the roaring of the seas, the roaring of their waves (Ps. 65:8)
> [He] do[es] rule the raging of the sea; when its waves rise [he] still[s] them (Ps. 89:10)
> By his power he stilled the sea (Job 26:12)
> [He] stirs up the sea so that its waves roar (Isa. 51:15, Jer. 31:35)

Collectively, such allusions seem to find their echo in the sentiment of Ps. 135:6, "Whatever Yahweh pleases he does,... in the sea and all deeps"; he both withholds the waters and sends them out (Job 12:15), and his power over them is not in question. Of these references, only Job 26 seems to concern a specific event rather than God's ongoing work; the calming of the celestial ocean may have been necessary after the presumed turbulence caused by the trembling of the pillars of heaven at God's rebuke/roar (cf. Jer. 10:13), but a more immediate connection might be with the slaying of Rahab, who may also have caused some oceanic disturbance, quite probably in the heavens (cf. v. 13a).

Another obvious forum for God's action in respect of the sea is the crossing of the Red Sea, the waters here being said to be divided or dried:

> [He] did[] divide the sea by [his] might (Ps. 74:13)
> He divided the sea and let them pass through it,
> He made the waters stand like a heap (Ps. 78:13)
> [He] divided the Red Sea in sunder (Ps. 136:13)
> He turned the sea into dry land (Ps. 66:6)
> He rebuked the Red Sea, and it became dry (Ps. 106:9)
> [He] did[] dry up the sea, the waters of the great deep (Isa. 51:10)

In addition, in Ex. 15, the waters are not the subject of God's direct action, but he seems to control them (and their effects) by less direct means, as passive agents in his hands:

> At the blast of thy nostrils the waters piled up,
> The floods [נֹזְלִים] stood up in a heap;
> The deeps congealed in the heart of the sea...
> Thou didst blow with thy wind, the sea covered them;
> They sank as lead in the mighty waters. (Ex. 15:8, 10)

Still less directly,

> Pharaoh's chariots and his host he cast into the sea...
> The floods cover them... (Ex. 15:4-5)

Full, though apparently passive, compliance is also seemingly assumed in the remaining references, as is implied by the statements, following the drying of the sea, that "men passed through the river on foot" (Ps. 66:6b), or that "he led them through the deep as through a desert" (Ps. 106:9b). In the latter case, it is further remarked that "the waters covered their adversaries; not one of them was left" (v. 11). It is notable that the sea is not here personified and the event is localised at the "Red Sea"; hence the mention in v. 9a of the divine rebuke / roar as instigating the drying of the sea should probably be understood as a particularly graphic presentation of God's direct personal action as he blows back the water with a strong wind (cf. Ex. 14:21) and as an indication of his "mighty power", as is anticipated in v. 8b. This detail is also congruent with the absolute and comprehensive nature of the event as portrayed here (v. 9b, v. 11b, and cf. v. 7 with v. 12). However, it leaves scant ground for assuming some form of combat.

In addition, in Nah. 1:4 there is an echo of the language of Ps. 106:9, though here as a general assertion of God's action in context of judgment:

> He rebukes the sea and makes it dry,
> He dries up all the rivers.

Here God's destructive power is in evidence, in a context where his theophanic advent in judgment may be presumed (v. 3cd, 6). However, it is clear from the context that the "adversaries" (v. 2) referred to are human, whilst the action against the sea has an effect which is adverse to human life: "Bashan and Carmel wither, the bloom of Lebanon fades" (v. 4cd). It has its counterpart in the quaking and melting of the mountains and hills and laying waste of the earth, and here "the world and all that dwell therein" are also mentioned, in accordance with the human target. Very similar language occurs also in Isa. 50:2, where the consequence is the death of fish, and there is a counterpart in Yahweh's blackening of the heavens. Indeed, the drying of the sea or rivers and its devastating effects is a recurrent theme in such contexts (cf. Isa. 19:5, Jer. 50:38, 51:36, Ezek. 30:12), and there can be no doubt that in each case this was perceived as a negative action which was inimical to life. The use of the waters as an instrument of judgment occurs also, apart from allusions to the Red Sea crossing or the Flood, in passages such as Ps. 78:44 ("He turned their rivers to blood"), Ezek. 32:14 ("Then I will make their waters clear, and cause their rivers to run like oil"), or, in a metaphorical sense, Isa. 8:7 ("The Lord is bringing up against them the waters of the River, mighty and many, the King of Assyria and all his glory"). In each case, the reference to the waters as an impersonal and non-resistant agent in God's hands is obvious.

Also to be considered are two brief allusions to the trampling of the sea:

> [He] trampled the waves of the sea (Job 9:8).

[He] did[] trample the sea with [his] horses (Hab. 3:15)

Here set poetic phrases seem to be used, probably to indicate ownership and sovereign possession. However, a careful examination of the contexts in which this language is employed indicates that the idea of the trampling of a foe is not present. In Habakkuk the idea of combat with the sea seems to be precluded by the context (see the comments in Chapter 1 on verse 15; I intend to discuss this passage further elsewhere), whilst in Job, the parallel reference to creation suggests a thought akin to that expressed in Ps. 95:5, "his, for he made it".

A further allusion, in this case from the speeches of Job, has a distinctively negative perspective which sets it apart from the other references here considered. Here it is claimed that God sets (or might potentially set) a guard over the sea (Job 7:12). Of course, this negativity is ultimately rejected in the integrative portrayal of all that is great and terrifying in creation in the speeches of God out of the whirlwind. Even so, in Job's bitter recasting of the rôle of God here in 7:12, the underlying tradition of confining of the sea is apparent; moreover, if guarding and treading its waves are the most destructive and tyrannical images which might be within reach of the poet's imagination without overstepping too far the boundaries of acceptability, then presumably the thought of a battle was a far remove away indeed.

Finally, in one royal psalm, there is an invocation for God to rescue the suppliant from "many waters, from the hand of aliens" (Ps. 144:7; cf. Ps. 18:17-18 = 2 Sam. 22:17-18), whilst in the individual lament Ps. 69:16, there is a plea, "Let not the flood sweep over me, or the deep swallow me up, or the pit close its mouth over me." A contrasting perspective is in evidence in Pss. 42-3 and 88, where the suppliant objects, "all thy waves and thy billows have gone over me" (42:8), or, more strongly, "Thou hast put me in the depths of the Pit, in the regions dark and deep...Thy wrath lies heavy upon me, and thou dost overwhelm me with all thy waves" (88:7-8). The metaphorical use of this language is indicated by the close parallelism with "the land of aliens" (144:7) or "thy wrath" (88:8) in certain instances, whilst the overwhelming thought of Sheol is clearly indicated by the mention of "the pit" (69:16, 88:7). The fact that God is understood as actively subjecting the suppliant to the aquatic terrors of the pit, and using his waves and billows, indicates that the deity's opposition to such forces is not in such cases implied, but rather he utilises them for his own purposes; even in Ps. 69, there may be an underlying thought that the flood is of God. In any case, it is within his control whether the suppliant is swept away and swallowed up or not. The personal nature of the experience here described, and of the oppression or deliverance by God, further distances this very specific type of imagery from the thought of cosmic combat.

Yet if scant support can be claimed for the view that the action of God towards the waters is indicative of combat, there is still less evidence for hostility on their part towards God, as their responses to him (where they are described) indicate. Nowhere is there any indication of aggression or hostility by the waters towards God, still less of an open combat: a consistent factor in presentations of Yahweh's intimidating or controlling power towards the waters is their submission and obedience, or fear and/or flight, which seems rather to indicate a situation in which their aggression or active opposition to God or the created order is excluded. It is sometimes claimed that the fleeing of the waters is indicative of a combative situation, but such a position is clearly untenable when the frequent mention in the same contexts of a comparable reaction (usually fear and trembling or melting) by the earth or mountains is taken into consideration. Indeed, in certain instances, there is mention of a terrestrial reaction to the advent of Yahweh where no such response by the seas is recorded. In addition, and independent of descriptions of God's direct action involving the waters or his theophany, there are various invocations to the seas, waters or deeps to participate in the spontaneous and joyous praise of God (Pss. 96:11, 98:7, 148:4, 7).

Clearly to be distinguished from these allusions are the references to God's action towards Leviathan and Rahab. Of the former, it is most notably stated in Isa. 27:1 that "Yahweh with his hard and great and strong sword will punish Leviathan the fleeing serpent, Leviathan the twisting serpent, and he will slay the dragon that is in the sea", and the picture is complemented by the description in Ps. 74:14 of Yahweh crushing the heads of Leviathan and giving him as food for the creatures of the wilderness. Similarly, Rahab is said to be crushed like a carcass (Ps. 89:11), cut in pieces (Isa. 51:9), smitten (Job 26:12) and pierced (Isa. 51:9, Job 26:13), whilst its helpers are described as having bowed beneath God (Job 9:13). In addition, in Psalm 74:13b, God is stated to have "shatter[ed][2] the heads of the dragons" in a context which is directly followed by mention of the crushing of the heads of Leviathan. (Perhaps if the second colon reflects a received phrase which may no longer fully have been understood, the first might have been intended to explain the polycephalicity of Leviathan, though both expressions were probably taken primarily in relation to the commanders of the Egyptian host). It seems also to be implied in Job 7:12 that God might "set a guard over" a תַּנִּין.

At the same time, however, this is balanced by benign portrayals of Leviathan as among the created works of God (Ps. 104:26, Job 41:25 [ET v. 33]; cf. אֶת־הַתַּנִּינִם הַגְּדֹלִים, Gen. 1:21, and אֶת־הַיָּם וְאֶת־כָּל־אֲשֶׁר־בָּם, Ps. 146:6), a playful creature sporting either simply in the sea or with God (Ps 104:26), and in whom God takes especial pride. In addition, the lack of any recorded aggression or hostility, still less of an open combat, which pertained in respect of the waters, holds here too. The consistent portrayal in the negatively orientated presentations of Leviathan and Rahab is of God's forceful and destructive activity, which seems wholly and unequivocally successful, whilst there is no hint of resistance by the dragon who is the recipient of his aggression. This consistent omission of any resistance, let alone active opposition to God suggests an element of conscious exclusion, whatever the pre- or popular history of the motif may have been.

---

2 Pi. שׁבר; RSV "break".

Thus, to summarise: it appears that although Leviathan and Rahab are sometimes portrayed as recipients of Yahweh's antagonism, the lack of resistance (or even acknowledged provocation or hostility) precludes speaking of a "combat" proper. In the case of the waters, although in various guises they might be commanded, rebuked, divided, dried up, or confined before God, and although they might sometimes flee from before him, antagonistic action by the deity is insufficient to merit even talking about a one-sided combat.

1.2. Creation

The association of "chaos" with creation has from the beginning been axiomatic and was foundational for Gunkel's comparative study of *Enuma elish* and its supposed biblical parallels. However, the widening knowledge-base afforded by the intervening one hundred and ten years has served, first, to reveal that any connection between "chaos" and creation is not necessarily inevitable or intrinsic: in Babylon and elsewhere in the ancient Near East (as in the Bible), creation is not necessarily the result of combat, and combat does not always result in creation. Even *Enuma elish* is probably more interested in the glorification of Marduk than in creation *per se*, whilst the independence of the Ugaritic myths of Baal's combats with Yam and Mot from any discernible creation-connection is especially notable. A second trend since Gunkel has been the distancing of the Bible from the supposed parallels with *Enuma elish*, influencing factors in this sphere being the subsidence of the initial rush of "pan-Babylonism" and the corresponding recognition of the very significant differences between the "Babylonian creation account" and that of Genesis 1, and also the emergence of other finds which have both contextualised *Enuma elish* and revealed closer parallels to the biblical material in the nearer geographical environs of Israel, especially in Ugarit. Moreover, the lack in the Ugaritic material of any association of Baal with an originating act of cosmic creation, and the apparent attribution of the rôle to El, calls into question the expectation of an intrinsic connection between "*Chaoskampf*" and creation in the extant Israelite texts, although in any case the situation should be judged on its own merits and not on the basis of prior assumptions drawn from comparative data.

Nevertheless, such a background ensures that it should occasion little surprise even among advocates of a "*Chaoskampf*" interpretation of the biblical material here considered that the Old Testament seems to lack a sequential portrayal of the originating acts of creation involving a combat between God and a draconic being. At the same time, although there are depictions of creation which include the confining of the waters, sometimes presented in quite dramatic and graphic terms, this interest seems—as far as it is possible to date the relevant passages—in general, and perhaps always, to be a late inclusion in Israelite theology. Moreover, it is balanced by the idea of "establish[ing][3] the fountains of the deep" as a vital part of God's providential order (Prov. 8:28b; cf. 3:20): that the sea was made by God is a theme repeated in various contexts (Pss. 95:5, 146:6; cf. Ps 148:5b-6 of the waters above the heavens, and Gen. 1:[1-2], 9-10) and the same is true also of תַּנִּינִים (Gen. 1:21; cf. Ps. 104:26, Job 41:25 [ET v. 33] re Leviathan, and Ps. 146:6 "all that is in [the sea]"). It is particularly to be noted that the most heightened portrayals of the ordering of the deeps at creation (in Job 38:8-11, Ps. 104:5-9) are both proximate to the (possibly related) characterisations of Leviathan as one of God's creatures with a recognised place in creation and God's providential order (Ps. 104:26, Job 40:25-41:26 [ET 41:1-34]). The essential rôle of water-provision in the sustenance of the cosmos is an undergirding theme in Ps. 104 (vv. 3, 10-13, 16), and in evidence also in Job 38:25-30, 34-38; cf. Ps. 65:10-13, Prov. 3:20, 8:24, 28.

Of the passages considered here, in the vast majority of cases where there is a putative expression of the "chaos" motif, the theme of creation is not in any way touched on in the proximate verses (thus Pss. 18, 29, 32, 42-3, 44, 66, 68, 69, 77, 78, 87, 88, 98, 106, 114, 124, 144; Isa. 8:5-8, 17:12-14, 27:1, 30:7, Jer. 51:34, Ezek. 29, 32, Jon. 2, Nah. 1:4, Hab. 3, Job 3:8,[4] 7:12, Dan. 7); in addition, although Behemoth and Leviathan in Job 40-41 are presented as creatures of God and part of the wonders of the created order, there is no real interest in the originating acts of creation here. Even where there is a concern with cosmic stability, the events of creation are not normally recalled (Pss. 46, 93), the most that occurs being a passing mention of God having "established the mountains" (Ps. 65:7) or having founded and established the earth (Ps. 24:2), this interest being echoed also in Ps. 96:10. There are a small number of instances where an allusion to creation has been claimed, chiefly, one suspects, or as is sometimes stated, on the basis of the presumed connection, but without clear evidence in its favour., e.g. in Ex. 15 (where the verb קנה—usually translated "acquire, purchase" or the like—occurs in respect of Israel in v. 16, though much separated from allusions to the waters and clearly not in any case relating to cosmic creation) and in Isa. 51:9-10. This leaves, besides references to the ordering of the seas at creation, only a very few cases where "combat" with a dragon occurs in proximity to the creation theme, namely Pss. 74, 89 and Job 9:13, 26:12-13. However, in Job 9 and 26, the attributes of God in creation actually precede mention of the dragon, and in each case are separated from it by allusions which are not concerned with an originating act of creation, whilst Ps. 74:16-17 (which is separated from the reference to Leviathan by one verse[5]) seems to be concerned with the ordering of the polarities of creation rather than with its formation as such. In each of these contexts, the citation of God's wonders in

---

3 MT has בַּעֲזוֹז, "when they grew strong", but probably בְּעַזְּזוֹ, "when he made firm, fixed fast", should be read, with most translators.

4 Unless one is to insist on interpreting the birth and conception of Job as a creation theme.

5 There have been efforts to relate v. 15 to creation, but these have not proved convincing: see the discussion in Chapter 6 above.

creation (in Job 9, chiefly works of "anti-creation", and in Job 26, *creatio continua*), together with the slaying of the dragon, are manifestations of his power and supremacy, in Job 9 generally in a destructive sense, and in Ps. 74 (as in Ps. 89) in answer to the disaster which is the subject of the lament. However, there is no interest in rehearsing the sequential acts of creation. Even in Ps. 89, the one instance where an allusion to creation does follow on from the crushing of Rahab, the first interest is in God's ownership of the heavens and the earth, a sure indication that the rhetorical focus is placed other than on a simple recollection of the events of primeval times. Indeed, in this passage, vv. 6-15, the attributes and "wonders" of Yahweh as the incomparable and supremely powerful Most High God, the global deity who is also the reliable covenant partner of the davidic king, are densely compressed in sequence, and it is highly doubtful if Yahweh's ownership and foundation of all creation should be regarded as a direct result of the crushing of Rahab.

Similarly, in the passages which are directly concerned with creation, there is no indication that the origination of the cosmos should itself be thought of as resultant upon the confining of the waters, except in the most obvious physical sense, i.e. dry land and seas had to be separated and made distinct in order for certain further creative acts to take place. It is moreover notable that the creation or confining of the waters is usually mentioned among the works of creation, rather than prior to them: for example, the heavens and earth are created before the latter is covered "with the deep as with a garment" in Ps. 104:2, 5-6, and the same sequence is reflected more briefly in Ps. 146, whilst the making of heavens precedes the "gather[ing of] the waters of the sea as in a bottle" in Ps. 33:6-7, and the "depths of the earth" and "heights of the mountains" are also mentioned prior to the sea in Ps. 95:4-5 (the formation of the dry land in v. 5b perhaps presenting an alternative aspect of the creative act through which the sea was brought into being). Similarly, in Prov. 8:27-28, the sequence seems to be heaven, earth, skies and fountains of the deep, though it is possible that the second pair might mirror the first here. One might reasonably deduce that these passages provide declarations of the createdness of the various parts of the cosmos without exhibiting a desire to relate a narrative sequence of events. However, it may be that a broad "order of creation" is reflected in Pss. 104 and 148; and in any case, these allusions do not seem to know of a pattern of creation in which the cleaving of an aquatic "chaos" monster is an initial act. Even in the two instances where a creation allusion occurs after a mention of Rahab or Leviathan (i.e. Pss. 74, 89), there is no indication of a connection between the two, and we are left to imagine why the putative victory over "chaos" (if that is what it is) had to happen in order for creation to take place: it might occasion surprise to note that, far from the corpse providing the raw material for the cosmos, in Ps. 74:14b it provides food for the inhabitants of the wilderness.

In addition, the lack of any connection between the battle of Yam and Baal and the creation of the cosmos in Ugaritic myth may once again be of relevance. Whatever its precise significance, the outplaying of the myth seems probably to be reflected in the ongoing (perhaps meteorological and/or seasonal) phenomena of the world through time, but not to have any connection with its origination. This type of focus struggles to find an echo in the Old Testament material, but perhaps the closest (though contrastive) parallel is the description in Isa. 51:15 and Jer. 31:35 of Yahweh as the one "who stirs up the sea so that its waves roar", combined with statements that he stills the sea (Pss. 65:8, 89:10). However, the monotheistic undergirding of such a presentation is obvious: one God controls the behaviour of the sea as an instrument in his hands. The coherence of this within the overarching theological system open to us from the Hebrew Bible is clear, but it seems to stand in sharp contrast to the tensions and struggles between the active deities of the Ugaritic pantheon.

This survey therefore seems to indicate that the association of the supposed "*Chaoskampf*" theme with creation seems not to be original or central in the Hebrew Bible. Although God did order—and continues to restrain—the oceans, this cannot really be described in terms of "combat" and indeed the waters appear as an essential aspect of creation more often in such contexts than as frightening elements. The absence of a concern with creation in the earliest material here considered is especially notable (see, e.g., Pss. 29, 68, 114, 18, 24, 46), the seas and rivers even providing the foundation of the earth in Ps. 24:2, 136:6. Furthermore, it is clear from even quite a superficial reading that the dragon imagery is applied in many situations other than creation, and indeed this is true also of the majority of cases where the sea is mentioned.

1.3. "Chaos"

If the theme of creation is not fundamental to the material here considered, this raises the question of whether it is possible to speak of "chaos" in this context. If "chaos" is defined as the chaotic mass or power(s) preceding creation, it seems that even the most determined "*Chaoskampf*" advocate could squeeze only a handful of passages into this definition. Though the waters might be powerful and frightening to humanity, God's absolute control of them and the permanence and stability of the created order is affirmed. A rational, detached examination of the evidence can offer little to support the idea of the waters as "rebellious", though their fear and compliance before God is often enough made explicit. Yahweh's absolute mastery is not in question.

Similarly, if "chaos" is defined more broadly as that which is adverse to creation including in the continuing order, although this might seem to offer more latitude, it is difficult to force much under this heading. Though dragons might often be inimical, the threat they present never seems to be cosmic. (If Leviathan is a sun-swallowing monster in Job 3:8 and the same, or something similar, is true of Rahab in Job 26:12-13, the term might apply, but this is hardly the sense or context generally assumed by those who speak of "chaos" in this connection). Likewise, although the deeps, rivers, and so on, are mentioned in a variety of contexts, literal references (whether the waters are personified or not) are relatively infrequent, whereas metaphorical allusions, where the interest is not simply physical and cosmological, are more numerous. It therefore remains to evaluate the content of the putative "chaos" references in order to determine whether this interest is actually likely to be present. The relevance of the ideas of creation and combat to such definitions should be apparent, and some of the results of the foregoing discussion may therefore be brought to bear where appropriate.

1.3.1. Aquatic Imagery

As regards the aquatic imagery here considered, these fall into two main categories, the literal and the metaphorical.

A. Literal Allusions

The literal types of allusion may be classified as follows:

a) Red Sea Event

In the references to the Red Sea event listed above in relation to the putative theme of combat with the waters, fairly graphic language might sometimes be employed to describe God's action, but there is a good correspondence with the prose traditions, sometimes even to the point of close linguistic contact. The waters are not personified, and it seems clear—and indeed virtually indisputable in most instances—that Yahweh's hostility is not against the sea. The motif of creation, or the ideas of a cosmic threat or of the waters as oppositional to Yahweh, are not apparently in view. It is therefore not surprising that claims for discernment of a *Chaoskampf* are relatively rare and muted, and, when made, are usually related to the prehistory of the motif. The use of the waters to achieve God's salvific purpose is especially clear in Ex. 15.

There seem to be two further, more metaphorical, allusions to the Red Sea in contexts which have not already been discussed with respect to Yahweh's action towards the waters (Pss. 77, 114), since his direct engagement with them is not mentioned. In Psalm 77:17-21, although the waters (as indicated by any of the whole range of terms) do not occur as a direct object of God's action, it is stated "thy way was through the sea", and the reference to the Red Sea event is clear both from the terminology of the preceding verses (vv. 12-16) and from the concluding reference to the "lead[ing of] thy people like a flock by the hand of Moses and Aaron" (v. 21). Far from acting in a way which might be viewed as "chaotic", the waters reacted in fear and trembling at the sight of God, and there is no mention of the dividing or drying of the sea, although this may be presumed from the mention of the crossing. In Ps. 114, again God does not engage directly with the sea or Jordan, but their fearful reaction before his presence entails their fleeing, which presumably facilitates a safe passage for his people. The absence of mention of divine action in relation to the waters, as well as the inclusion of a parallel reaction by the mountains and hills (despite the irrelevance of this detail to a strict historical recollection) and the invocation to the earth to tremble before God, indicates that hostile action specifically towards (let alone by) the waters is not in view here. There is no implication of a threat to creation, except insofar as the divine appearing induces cosmic distress.

b) As the Base on which the Earth or Yahweh's Throne is Set

In two passages, the earth is said to be "founded" or "spread out" on the seas (נְהָרוֹת commonly stands in parallel with יַמִּים, and seems to indicate the channels of the sea) or waters, these presumably providing its base:

Psalm 24:2
He has founded it [the earth/world] upon the seas,
And established it upon the rivers.

Psalm 136:6a
...who spread out the earth upon the waters

In a third, "the waters" provide the base for Yahweh's heavenly abode:

Psalm 104:3a
... who hast laid the beams of thy chambers on the waters.

The same idea is apparently attested also in Ps. 29:10, where Yahweh is said to "sit" over the flood (לַמַּבּוּל):

Yahweh sits [יֹשֵׁב; RSV: sits enthroned] over the flood;
Yahweh sits [יֹשֵׁב; RSV: sits enthroned] as king for ever.

This seems to reflect the locus of his abode over the heavenly ocean or in the temple (cf. v. 9c); the latter is perhaps most vividly represented as resting upon the waters in Ezekiel's vision of the new Temple, whilst the description of El's abode as "at the springs of the rivers, amid the streams of the deeps" in the Ugaritic texts is also particularly called to mind. There is, however, no parallel for the enthronement of the victor deity over the corpse of his slain foe, either in the extant Ras Shamra material or in *Enuma elish*, so such a construct appears fanciful.

Thus, in these three passages, far from having an anti-cosmic rôle, the waters actually seem to act as the foundations for further structures. This is unequivocal in Pss. 24 and 136, and in Ps. 29, such an understanding seems to be implied by the mention of Yahweh sitting "as king" (presumably in a temple/palace or on a throne) in v. 10b. It does not therefore seem likely that "chaos" is referred to here.

c) Creation

This theme has been discussed fairly extensively in its own right above. Related to this is the theme of *creatio continua*, God's control over the natural world, which includes both the stirring up and stilling of the sea as indicative of his power. In the case of allusions to an originating act of creation, the temporal setting might permit reference to a struggle with "chaos", but it is doubtful whether the seas are presented in such passages as a counter-cosmic power, rather than merely being viewed, in accordance with their nature, as a sometimes frightening and boisterous force. In fact, in most cases where mention is made of the creation of the waters, the allusion is so celebratory and devoid of an indication of combat that the thought of "chaos" can confidently be excluded (Pss. 95:5, 146:6, 148:4-7; cf. Prov. 3:20 re the breaking forth of the deeps, and Ps. 136:6 re the spreading out of the earth on the waters, besides Gen. 1). Moreover, the inclusion of the fixing of the bounds of the sea next to a declaration that they were created by God's command and "established... for ever and ever" in Ps. 148:5-6 clearly indicates that this motif is to be understood as an aspect of the ordering of creation rather than as expressing a concern with "chaos" as a mythological idea, and this encourages a similar interpretation of other passages expressing the same motif. In fact, the affirmation of the createdness of the "fountains of the deep" in Prov. 8:28, which is then followed by a description of the confining of the seas, similarly seems to exclude the idea of any pre-existent "chaos", and the rather vivid presentation of the birth of the seas and their nurture by God in Job 38:8-11 appears also to reflect the same essential background. In Ps. 104:6, the deep is notably made to cover the earth by God, before it fled at his roar in thunder. This is not the behaviour of a rebellious monster, and nor is the covering of the earth with the deep a likely action for its vanquisher. Finally, in Ps. 33:7, the "put[ting of] the deeps in storehouses" suggests that they were here reserved for use by God, and this again does not seem consistent with their being viewed as an inimical power. Rather they should probably be understood in connection with the provision of rain (cf. Job 26:8, 38:37, Deut. 28:12) or with the deeps as a subterrestrial water source (cf., e.g., Deut. 8:7, 33:13, Prov. 3:20a, 8:24, Ps. 78:15).

In Jer. 5:22, the sea is represented as a vigorous force, tossing against the barriers erected by God. However, what is first stressed is that the sand forms "a perpetual barrier which it cannot pass"; moreover, "[the waves] cannot prevail... they cannot pass over it". It is consistent with this aspect of God's supreme control that in the same book, God is also depicted as the one who "stirs up the sea so that its waves roar" (31:35; cf. Isa. 51:15), this being viewed as part of the "fixed order" of creation (31:36) which God has undertaken to maintain. The picture of absolute control and security is sustained throughout the allusions to the confinement of the sea, God's mastery, further, being well expressed in the claim that "whatever Yahweh pleases he does, in heaven and on earth, in the seas and all deeps" (Ps. 135:6). Similarly the createdness and/or recognised place of the sea within the created order is in most cases acknowledged. It therefore seems that it is not viewed as presenting a cosmic threat: at the very least, this seems to be excluded by the power of Yahweh and by the permanence of the barriers he has erected. However, more than this, the compliance of the sea to the extent that its reaction is generally not recorded (except to say that it fled in Ps. 104, or to explain that God confined it "that it might not" cover the earth or transgress his command), and God's consistent and unquestionable control of these forces elsewhere (for example, in the flood or exodus narratives, or in allusions to his calming or stirring up of the sea), together with their frequently positive presentation as part of the created order or as participating in the praise of God, indicates that, in a reading in which any of these allusions is contextualised within the Old Testament as a whole, the thought of "chaos" should be excluded. At the most (though perhaps plausibly) the idea of the sea as a "chaotic" anti-creation force may be conjectured as providing a possible history-of-religions background to such an interest. However, the most natural interpretation of the allusions to the confining of the sea or to the "roaring" or "tossing" of its waves is to understand them, within their present context, as a reflection of nature and of the awe in which the ocean was held.

d) The Distress of Nature at the Divine Appearing (this sometimes overlaps with other classes of use)

Under this heading may be included allusions to the anguish of the waters at divine theophany, as a response to which they flee or tremble. Characteristically, a comparable reaction by the earth or mountains is also recorded, as in Pss. 114:3-4, 5-7, 77:17, 19c, Nah. 1:4-5, Hab. 3:6-7, 10, and perhaps Ps. 104:7-8; compare Pss. 29:5-9b, 68:9, 97:4-5, Job 26:5-6, 11, where there is no marine parallel to the terrestrial reaction to the divine appearing. It therefore seems clear that the fearful behaviour of the sea is held in common with the rest of creation, and it is not an indication of especial divine hostility directed at it. The motif is a reflection on the terrible presence of God rather than on the nature of the waters, and in such contexts there is no allusion to antagonistic action by them. As a result, such passages cannot provide evidence for the "chaotic" nature of the sea.

B. Metaphorical Allusions

The references to the waters in metaphorical contexts may be defined as follows:

a) Allusions to the Underworld and Related Ideas in Individual and Royal Laments and Thanksgiving Psalms

A wide variety of waters imagery is employed in such contexts as Jon. 2 and Pss. 18, 32, 42-3, 69, 88, 124 and 144. Often the frightening and threatening aspects of "the pit", "thy waves and thy billows", "the regions dark and deep", and so on, are apparent. However, the metaphorical denotation, not only of the underworld and threat of death, but of the action of the Psalmist's enemies or of the hostile hand of God is frequently made clear. At the same time, the perceived threat is viewed as a personal and individual one, as is the rescue (most notably in Ps. 18:5-20 = 2 Sam. 22:5-20), so the thought of cosmic "chaos" can be excluded. Moreover, although God might "dr[a]w [the suppliant] out of many waters" or (presumably) lift his heavy hand of wrath and cease overwhelming the sufferer with his waves, contrary to any indication of combat, he does not engage with the aquatic threat directly. Indeed, in certain instances, God is attributed with utilising these waters in order to afflict the psalmist, even to the extent that they are referred to as "thy waves and thy billows" (Ps. 42:8) or "thy waves" (Ps. 88:8).

Although in Ps. 18 a spectacular theophanic rescue is depicted in which "the channels of the sea were seen, and the foundations of the world were laid bare", this seems to comprise part of an action directed against a collective "them" (v. 15ab), for which the most obvious antecedent is the psalmist's foes; in addition, the suppliant is delivered not only from his strong enemy, but from "the cords of death" and "the torrents of perdition" in the realm beneath, and this has also doubtless influenced the presentation. The exposure of the "foundations of the world" provides an essentially terrestrial correspondent to the laying bare of the "channels of the sea" (i.e. the channels feeding the sea from beneath, hence its very lowest part), both being affected by the roar and stormy blast of God in storm and thunder, and relating to the psalmist's depicted location in the underworld. However, the implication is that there is no interest in "cosmic chaos" or in forces oppositional to God himself here or in any of the other comparable allusions.

b) The nations

Here there are two main groups of imagery, although they cannot in every case be clearly distinguished.

1) In the first group, hostile enemy action is described through the image of a flooding river. This is particularly apposite to the expansionist behaviour of Assyria "sweeping" through the neighbouring countries, so "its outspread wings will fill the breadth of [the] land" (Isa. 8:6-8). However, the explicit

use of metaphor, with reference being made only to a river rather than to an agent posing a wider, "cosmic" threat, and the mention of these "waters" as having been brought up against Judah by God himself, all militate against seeing an allusion to "chaos" here. In a second passage, Ps. 124:1-5, flooding "waters" comprise one of a series of vivid metaphors to depict the predicament from which the people were delivered. The idea of Sheol may have been an influencing factor in the choice of imagery, and it is not clear whether the "men" who "rose up against us" with kindled anger is a group of individuals rather than a nation posing a military threat. Again, the localised effect of the "torrent" described and the use of metaphorical language should guide the interpretation of this passage: there is no "cosmic" aspect to the experience described. In addition, as has already been indicated above, in neither case is an association with creation appropriate, and, despite the deliverance effected in Ps. 124, there is no hint of Yahweh engaging in combat with these waters.

2) In two passages, the roaring of the sea is paralleled with that of the nations (Ps. 65, Isa. 17), and in another the same link may perhaps be understood, though it is not made explicit (Ps. 93). In a fourth context, Ps. 46, the mirroring of cosmic and political concerns is expressed in a similar way, though here the question of stability is raised in addition to vocal aspects.

In Isa. 17:12-13, the roaring of the nations is compared in a simile to that of the seas, the same basis for comparison being reflected in Jer. 6:23, 50:42 (of an army) and Ezek. 1:24 (of the sound of the wings of the "four living creatures" of Ezekiel's vision). This motif occurs again in Ps. 65:6-9, where the stilling of the seas may be metaphorical for the roaring nations or be viewed as a parallel sphere of action, God's control in one sphere then providing reassurance for his capacity to act in the other. The obvious aptitude of the comparison, and its use in situations, like the first vision of Ezekiel, where an allusion to "chaos" is not suspected, suggests that such a reference cannot be presupposed here. The mere calming of the sea in Ps. 65:8 does not sound like an action to be associated with combat, whilst in Isa. 17, the "rebuke / roar" of God is only directed against the nations, and not against the waters at all. The response of the nations mirrors the allusions found elsewhere to the waters fleeing in terror before the theophanic appearance of God, but, as has been seen, this (or a comparable reaction) is common to creation as a whole, and the motif has no apparent association with "chaos" in the Hebrew Bible. Moreover, in the present context, the idea is immediately connected with another image from the natural world, that of chaff being blown on the wind, so it is presumably in relation to this (and the following) connected simile and not the preceding allusion to the waters that it should chiefly be interpreted. It is clear also that in neither Isa. 17:12-13 nor Ps. 65:8 is the interest fundamentally cosmic, whereas the overarching political concerns informing these allusions are obvious. This, together with the absence of mention of combat with the waters, encourages an understanding of these references as a simple and apposite comparison with a well-known but dramatic feature of the natural world, the roaring sea.

The passage from Ps. 65 may also reflect the motif of cosmic stability which is more strongly in evidence in Pss. 93 and 46, since v. 7 alludes to the establishment of the mountains. Nevertheless, even in Ps. 46 the fundamentally political interests of the psalmist are evident from the linguistic parallels linking the actions of the "waters" and "nations" and "kingdoms", and the same concern may also underlie Ps. 93. In any case, it is clear that the latter composition celebrates Yahweh's eternal, unchanging rule which is the guarantee of stability, but there is no allusion to his engagement with the sea in primeval time.

It might appear that, at last, in Pss. 46 and 93 the advocate of the discernment of references to "chaos" in the Old Testament may find brief comfort, since—despite the overarching political concerns—the underlying imagery is cosmic and entails a perception of the structure of the cosmos according to which the waters may (potentially, if not in reality) present some form of threat to the cosmic structure. However, significant as this point of contact may seem from a modern perspective, it of course reflects the only cosmology (i.e., understanding of the structure of the cosmos) available in the ancient context in which the authors of these compositions lived. It does not imply a correspondence to the mythology attached to its formation as exhibited, for example, in *Enuma elish*. What is clearly emphasised in each of these psalms is that "the world is established; it shall never be moved" (Ps. 93:1; cf. 24:2); though the waters may lift up their voice and roar and foam, "Yahweh on high is mighty" (Ps. 93:4), and there is no need to fear (Ps. 46:3). In all four of the passages here discussed, there is only one occasion where there is reference to the waters doing any more than lifting up their voice and roaring: this is in Ps. 46:4, where, however, what is described is hypothetical and hyperbolic. It is unlikely that this "worst case scenario", entailing the earth "chang[ing]" and the "mountains trembl[ing]"at the tumult of the sea, would have been regarded as a real possibility; at the most, it depicts the very worst that could be imagined. This is highly significant, because although the mountains might shake, the cosmic structure does not crumble, the waters do not inundate the land, and the psalmist has no need to fear. It may therefore be concluded that although the seas may appear as tumultuous, they pose no threat in world in which Yahweh is king. Indeed, Psalm 93 might be understood as a polemical exaltation of Yahweh's permanent kingship and the enduring stability which results, in contrast to the cyclical or changeable rule of a deity such as Baal. Even use of the plural נְהָרוֹת (Ps. 93:3) contrast this statement of faith very directly from a theology which understands "Prince Sea" and "Judge Nahar" as a god. Thus the most plausible explanation of these allusions is that they constitute metaphorical references to the sea, understood according to the cosmology of the time, and reflecting the threatening potential of this vast body of water which is obvious in any age and culture. The seas reveal an inimical aspect, and in this limited respect these allusions are open to being regarded as the remote relatives, albeit many generations removed, of the story of a struggle with Yam. However, the lack of a primeval orientation or need for combative action towards the waters, still less of a concern with the event of creation, combined with the absence of a genuine threat to the cosmic order, should call into question whether it is appropriate to speak of "chaos" here. The political, rather than cosmic, interest, certainly in three of these passages, and possibly in all four, further removes them from the sphere of allusion conventionally attributed to them.

It may therefore be concluded that there is a very substantial body of evidence which calls into question the view that the various aquatic entities in the Old Testament are to be understood as embodiments of "chaos". In addition to the absence of a combat or hostile action by the waters towards God, the lack of a connection with creation in the majority of allusions, and the positive attitude to the createdness of the waters in many instances where such a link is made, may all be cited in support of this assessment. Although the sea is viewed as inimical in certain contexts, this is chiefly metaphorical, and nowhere is it understood to present a real threat. Its power and volume is apparently heightened in order to magnify still further the greatness of the God in whose control it lies. Although in a small number of cases, such allusions may be viewed as ultimately related to the theme of a battle with Yam, this does not do justice to their meaning even in their immediate context, still less to the sense lent to them when the likely range of interpretations is narrowed by a consideration of the totality of such references; moreover, nearly all of the specific content associated with the Baal-Yam saga is absent, and the creation-bound conception of "chaos" may be inapplicable even there. Indeed, with the possible exception of certain references to the underworld in which there seem to be a mixing of images, the allusions to the seas or other bodies of water may be interpreted wholly naturalistically. This is the interpretation which dominated for many centuries before the publication of Gunkel's influential study, and which, the evidence suggests, may well have pertained even from the point of composition.

1.3.2. References to Rahab, Leviathan or a תַּנִּין *or* תַּנִּינִים

It now finally remains to evaluate the putative "chaos" content of the references to Rahab, Leviathan or an unnamed תַּנִּין or תַּנִּינִים, before the wider results of this monograph are evaluated from a developmental and history-of-religions perspective. It is self-evident that certain allusions to one of these figures view the dragon there mentioned as inimical and as the object of God's destruction; however, the ascertainment of the signification of these entities is vital to the assessment of whether they may be thought to resemble or embody "chaotic" forces. An important aspect of this will be the attempt to establish how the negative portrayals should be related to the contrary traditions of Leviathan as a playful creature with a valued place in creation, Rahab as a simple name for Egypt with no apparent draconic associations, or תַּנִּינִים as created by God and as offering him praise. Clearly here a crucial issue will be the essential significance of these entities, from which the other uses may have derived and to which they may be related; no less pertinent are the theological influences on the development of the understanding of Rahab,

Leviathan and תַּנִּינִים in general. The following discussion will therefore attempt to uncover the interrelation of the various portrayals; this may on occasion suggest a particular diachronic schema, which in the present study may be tested against (or substantiated by) the careful dating undertaken above of the sources in which the allusions occur.

Although the nature of the references, whether historical, naturalistic, or mythical, is in most cases clear (notwithstanding debate over the precise mythological ideas reflected in the latter case), the subject alluded to in Isa. 51 and Pss. 74 and 89 remains a particular topic of dispute. The reasons for advancing the interpretation adopted here in respect of these passages, namely that they refer to the Red Sea event, shall therefore be summarised before wider conclusions are drawn concerning each of the entities here referred to.

An important consideration is the fact that in two of these three occurrences, mention is made of Rahab or Leviathan in conjunction with what in any other context would be regarded as an unmistakable allusion to the Red Sea crossing: it is declared that Yahweh "did[] divide the sea" (74:13a) and that he was the one that "did[] dry up the sea… that did[] make the depths of the sea a way for the redeemed to pass over" (Isa. 51:10). In Isa. 51, this is preceded by mention of Yahweh's "arm" as "in days of old, the generations of long ago" (all fine Exodus and historical language, but not applicable to a primeval event) cutting in pieces and piercing Rahab. Taken contextually, with close attention to the language of vv. 9-10, this appellative must, as often elsewhere, refer to Egypt; but by contrast, direct mention of creation is absent from the immediate context. Rahab features again in Ps. 89:11 in a briefer allusion, there parallel not to תַּנִּין but to "thy enemies". The many verbal echoes in vv. 6-14 of Ex. 15 and Ps. 77:12-16, taking up the key motifs of the Deuteronomic manifesto, are particularly striking, and again imply that the exodus experience should be understood. The subject of reference in Ps. 74:13b-14b is also indicated by its context, not least by attention to the terminology of vv. 1-2, 11 and to the structural relationship of these verses to vv. 12ff. However, the allusion to the dividing of the sea even before mention of the תַּנִּינִים clearly introduces the familiar theme, whilst v. 15 is most naturally taken as alluding to the "cleav[ing] open" of springs in the wilderness and "dry[ing] up" of the perennial streams of the Jordan (and/or Red Sea). In addition, the giving of Leviathan "as food for the עָם לְצִיִּים", although understandable in reference to the leaving of the bodies of the Egyptian host to be consumed by wild animals, has no affinity with any known account of cosmic combat. This is not least with one which purports to result in creation, since, besides the difficulty of the existence of "inhabitants of the wilderness" in primordial time, the corpse of Leviathan is here ignominiously disposed of rather than being utilised as the raw material from which the cosmos may be formed.

It is especially striking that such firm links with the exodus traditions should occur in all three of these passages, and this correspondingly strengthens the interpretation here advanced. However, if the destruction of the Egyptian foe at the Red Sea is referred to, then the idea of cosmic combat, and hence "chaos", would seem to be excluded from these recollections. It is moreover to be noted that if the language of an existing mythic tradition of the overcoming by Yahweh of a draconic foe is here employed, then the usage in the present context is only metaphorical, Rahab and/or Leviathan then standing for the archetypal foe of Yahweh which he spectacularly overcame, but probably having no further representative function. In any case, the reasons for dissociating these allusions from an intrinsic connection with an originating act of creation have already been outlined above (in relation to this theme); as regards any further underlying mythic signification, the evidence from other references to Rahab and Leviathan supports this separation, as will be indicated in the ensuing discussion.

a) Rahab

Probably the earliest occurrences of the name "Rahab" are as a literal denotation of Egypt, in Isa. 30:7 and Ps. 87:4. In two further instances, the term is used in reference to Egypt at the time of the Exodus (Isa. 51:9, Ps. 89:11). In Job 9:13, where there is an allusion to the helpers of Rahab bowing beneath God, there is insufficient detail for the original referential context to be discerned; however, it appears that "Rahab" is here understood as a (possibly mythical) opponent of Yahweh. Finally, in Job 26:12-13 the slaying of Rahab is associated with the "making fair" of the heavens.

It therefore remains to explain the relation between the different uses of the term, both historically and conceptually, taking into account the content of each of these references, together with their likely relative dates. Obviously, the date of a particular occurrence cannot simplistically be assumed to reflect the time of emergence of the ideas it expresses, yet this datum must, together with other evidence, form some kind of basis for any developmental model. It is certainly unsatisfactory, as is the current tendency, to assert a pattern of development which contravenes the diachronic evidence without actually engaging with it. In fact, the attested references seem to fall into a coherent pattern corresponding to their apparent relative dates, and this lends support to the model proposed here.

It appears that "Rahab" was probably originally an epithet of Egypt referring to its legendary pride and dominating behaviour. It was conceptualised at some stage (not necessarily from the first) as draconic. In Ps. 89, Rahab is not actually described as a dragon, though it is possible it was conceived in this way, the personified nation being concretised into a single bestial entity. In Isa. 51, which is probably roughly contemporaneous (or perhaps slightly later), very similar language is used again in allusion to the Red Sea deliverance, and here Rahab is referred to as a dragon. The reference in Job 26:12-13 is certainly and that in 9:13 perhaps also mythological. Once characterised as the draconic enemy, Rahab could then have absorbed features from other dragon myths, though the only evidence for this is in the sole and late context of the book of Job. The likely association of Rahab with darkness in 26:13 seems to tally with the portrayal of Leviathan in Job 3:8, although it is interesting that the two figures are never identified despite the fact that each occurs in the Book of Job and is described as נָחָשׁ בָּרִחַ (Job 26:13, Isa. 27:1) and תַּנִּין (Isa. 51:9, Isa. 27:1, cf. Ps. 74:13). Therefore a distinction in origin and probably also in significance should be maintained even if in certain respects they might appear to belong to parallel traditions. The allusion in Job 9:13 is too terse for its content to be discerned on the basis of this passage alone, and hence it must be understood in conjunction with other references to the same figure, whether historical (cf. Isa. 30:7, 51:9, Pss. 87:4, 89:11) or mythical (as again in the Book of Job in 26:12-13). However, in none of these passages does Rahab appear to embody the personified sea or pose an aquatic threat to the land. Moreover, if one wished to reconstruct an underlying mythological content for the allusions in Isa. 51:9 and/or Ps. 89:11, the obvious source would be the specific application of the imagery in Job 26:12-13, in which Rahab seems to present some form of threat to the heavens. This link is suggested further by the frequent reference to the heavens in connection with Rahab (Job 26:11, 13; Ps. 89:6, 12a; Isa. 51:13, 16; cf. Job 9:7-9). If this is correct, the sequence in Ps. 89:10-12 would flow in an admirably coherent pattern from the ruling of the sea, through the overcoming of Rahab (once, it is suspected, in, or in relation to an effect in, heaven) to God's lordship over both heaven and earth (the latter, or course, including the seas). Therefore the specific "chaos" content usually claimed in respect of Rahab seems at the very least to be questionable, and indeed, most probably, inapplicable.

b) Leviathan

References are diverse although it is likely that none antedate the exile, whilst that in Isa. 27:1 has sometimes been thought to belong among the latest strata in the Hebrew Bible. Ltn, which is thought to be etymologically equivalent, is in the Ugaritic texts described in a list of Baal's conquests (*KTU* 1.5.i.1-4), although the overcoming of the same monster is apparently also claimed by Anat in *KTU* 1.3.iii.38-40, where Ltn is not mentioned by name, but his epithets are. However, beyond the firm idea that Ltn is a conquered dragon, nothing more is known about this motif. In contrast to Baal's struggles with Yam and Mot, where it is evident that the gods of sea and death are referred to, it is not clear that Ltn has any particular representative function; indeed, of his epithets, *'qltn* (wriggling, writhing, twisty) merely seems to affirm his serpentine form and *šlyṭ*, usually translated "tyrant, potentate", is scarcely more informative. An association with a constellation (perhaps one had a serpentine form) or, if the *tnn* of *KTU* 1.6.vi.51 is to be identified with Ltn (which cannot be assumed), as a sun-threatening dragon,[6] or even some form of sea-monster, is possible, though this is unclear. In any case, the content(s) given to it in a Ugaritic context cannot be assumed to have any direct bearing on its presumed significance in the Hebrew texts of the Bible some eight hundred years or more later.

6 Note the association with Shaphash here.

However, the essential points of Leviathan / Ltn as a dragon and as overcome by the deity as a manifestation of power remains, though in some biblical passages, in accordance with the tendency towards monotheisation, and perhaps in association with other uses of the term תַּנִּין, Leviathan becomes a creature of Yahweh in the natural world with no antagonistic overtones remaining. It therefore seems to have the character of a received and flexible motif applicable in various circumstances.

1) Psalm 74
The motif of the draconic enemy slain by God is evident, and in this passage alone of the biblical occurrences, the motif of the heads of Leviathan echoes the seven-headedness of Ltn. However, in the Psalm, this may be equivalent to "the heads of the dragons", suggesting a reinterpretation of the original motif, possibly when the allusion to Ltn's / Leviathan's polycephalicity was no longer recognised, or perhaps to impart a new content into an old idea. Here, in the recital of Yahweh's salvific acts, Leviathan represents his most characteristic foe, the enemy Egypt from whom he redeemed his people. Leviathan thus retains its character as "the enemy" conquered by God, its slaying being cited as a manifestation of his power.

2) Isaiah 27
In a striking echo of *KTU* 1.5.i.1-4, and in the only application of the term נָחָשׁ to an entity here or elsewhere termed draconic, Leviathan is characterised as נָחָשׁ בָּרִחַ and נָחָשׁ עֲקַלָּתוֹן, who shall be slain by Yahweh's hard and great and strong sword. Both the draconic aspect and Leviathan as the enemy of the deity are clearly in evidence, and it is possible that Leviathan here is no longer employed merely to denote a specific nation or nations, but the power of evil as such. Thus in a late maturation of the motif (which itself is only manifested in the formal circles preserved in the Bible from the exile on), the heightening and dualising to which it is subjected brings it full circle back to the language employed among the earliest known pre-Israelite antecedents. What is especially striking is that this traditional pre-Israelite language was still known, preserved, and available to be reused, despite its apparent incompatibility with the conceptualisation or application of such imagery in formal "orthodox" Yahwistic circles prior to this point. However the abstract representative function of Leviathan and the projection of his slaying into the future eschatological resolution is a development which seems to distance it substantially from its apparent Ugaritic antecedent, and reflects the theological transitions and developments absorbed in the intervening centuries. Nevertheless, in Revelation, the concretisation of evil powers in Satan, who was also called "the dragon", entailed the dualistic pattern of the world temporarily being in his power before the final decisive battle in which God will have the ultimate victory and establish his reign. Such a sequence, though applied to a wholly different category of evil either from the cosmological or from that manifested in Ugaritic or pre-apocalyptic Israelite thinking, as well as distinctively being projected into the future, reflects the combat pattern of the ascendancy of the enemy prior to the final victory

which is exhibited not only in Ugaritic mythology but in various combat narratives (including those not connected with "chaos") throughout the wider cultural area.

3) Job 3:8
Leviathan appears in a rather different setting in Job 3, where there is no historical application, and Leviathan is not explicitly presented as a dragon (no information about his physical appearance is revealed), although this is not precluded either. The association with darkness and death may reflect the usage exhibited earlier in Ugaritic (cf. *tnn*, *KTU* 1.6.vi.51) and indeed may tally with expressions of this interest in Isa. 25:8 and 26:19, as well as, in due course, being associated with Satan and with "the enemy" destroyed on the cross. More immediately, it may be linked with Job 26:13, where the clearing of the skies seems to result from the piercing of the "fleeing serpent" (again in a reflection of the language of Isa. 27:1 and *KTU* 1.5.i.1-4, 1.3.iii.38-40). Probably this connection originally belonged to Ltn / Leviathan and was later transferred onto Rahab.

4) Ps. 104:25, Job 40:25-41:26 (ET 41:1-34)
Finally, there are those passages where Leviathan is viewed as a creature which, though perhaps extraordinary and even fantastical, was thought of as existing in the known physical world and as created and valued by God and having a rightful place in the current world order. Leviathan is named in this way in Ps. 104:26 and Job 40:25-41:26 (ET 41:1-34), in descriptions which may be related, but it is possible that this beast was also thought of as included in statements that God created the תַּנִּינִים or in invocations for them to offer him praise. Probably such passages, when compared, for example, to Isa. 27:1, should be understood as alternative responses to received traditions about Leviathan. This apparently mirrors the competing voices of the Old Testament regarding the origin of that which is negative in the world in creation and history, since both the option of God's pan-causality (as in Isa. 45:7) and dualistic schemas (as in apocalyptic thinking) are attested.

Physiological descriptions of Leviathan seem to be varied and no single pattern emerges. For example, this creature is described as multi-cephalic in Ps. 74, but this idea receives no support from the other allusions, and indeed seems to be inapplicable to Job 40:25-41:26 (ET 41:1-34) and inappropriate also in Ps. 104:25; similarly, it is portrayed as a "serpent" (נָחָשׁ) in Isa. 27:1, which might appear to conflict with the heavy bodily frame and limbs celebrated in the second divine speech of Job. Indeed, in this latter passage, Leviathan appears to be crocodilian, but in Isa. 27:1 and Ps. 104:25, it is described as a creature of the sea, in the Psalm, one would imagine, as a rather large one, if Yahweh is understood as having formed this animal in order to play with it. Collectively, such disparities suggest that traditions concerning the appearance of Leviathan were flexible and were therefore probably chiefly known from verbal rather than pictorial sources, where his fearsome nature was known but the detail of his appearance was often unstated or expressed only briefly. There seem to be two main strands here, one regarding him as draconic (Ps. 74, Isa. 27:1, probably also Job 3:8), the other as a creature of the natural world (Ps. 104:25, Job 40:25-41:26 [ET 41:1-34]). The description of Leviathan as both a תַּנִּין and a נָחָשׁ in Isa. 27:1 suggests that these ideas were viewed as at some level compatible, though it is not impossible that some level of harmonisation between different traditions has occurred. However, the likely differences in perception between Ps. 104:25 (where no detail is forthcoming except what may be implied from his oceanic abode) and Job 40:25-41:26 (ET 41:1-34) may indicate that the concepts of Leviathan as a תַּנִּין and a creature of the sea may here have been differently interpreted, perhaps in separate monotheisations and naturalisations of an originally mythical theme.

However, as regards the content of that mythical core, the clearest evidence comes from what may be the only purely mythical allusion to Leviathan in the Hebrew Bible, Job 3:8, and here it is apparent that it is to be associated with the underworld. This would cohere with the depiction of Nebuchadrezzar as a devouring תַּנִּין in Jer. 51:34, as well as tallying with the allusion at the end of the Baal-Mot cycle to the *tnn* which seems to pose a threat to the sun as it passes through the underworld (KTU 1.6.vi.48-53). As has been seen, it also seems to reflect a possible correspondence to the נָחָשׁ בָּרִיחַ of Job 26:13b. However, this seriously undermines the idea that Leviathan embodies the "chaotic" sea overcome at creation and which might wish to engulf the land once more.

c) תַּנִּין

In addition to those passages where תַּנִּין occurs in conjunction with Rahab or Leviathan, there are several instances of interest to the present discussion where it (or the plural תַּנִּינִים) occurs alone.

1. as the "great sea monsters" made by God and offering him praise (Gen. 1:21, Ps. 148:7; cf. Pss. 96:11, 98:7, 146:6).
2. as representative of Pharaoh / Egypt, possibly as a crocodile, that archetypal Egyptian creature which in Egypt itself could be used to stand for the Pharaoh (Ezek. 29, 32).
3. as a "monster" in a general sense (Jer 51:34 [re Nebuchadrezzar, possibly influenced by death/Sheol language], Job 7:12)

Although the content of Job 7:12 is so brief as to require infilling by data drawn from other references, even here there are indications pointing away from an allusion to the guarding of a monster of "chaos", and this is corroborated by the remaining references to a תַּנִּין or תַּנִּינִים, where no such association pertains. In the majority of cases, it is clear that a creature of the natural world is intended, whilst the apparent denotation both of the crocodile and creatures of the sea, as well as serpents, mirrors an aspect seen already in relation to Leviathan. The use of language which echoes the idea of death as a devouring monster constitutes a further possible point of contact with traditions associated with Leviathan, but which again call into question the putative link with the "chaotic" sea.

It therefore seems clear from the foregoing analysis of the supposed references to "chaos" that there are many weaknesses with presuming that they should be interpreted in the light of this theme. That this holds true in so many cases and on so many different grounds does much to strengthen the overall results of this thesis and to encourage a similar understanding even in those cases where the evidence is less clear or where a passage may be perceived to be open to competing interpretations. However, before any final conclusions may be drawn, one further aspect of the present monograph remains to be considered, namely its diachronic results and their implications for the understanding of the history of Israelite religion.

2. Diachronic Results and Implications

One of the firmer results of the present monograph seems to be the absence of references to the overcoming of a dragon prior to c. 587 B.C. and the concentration of such allusions around, and directly following, that time (Pss. 74, 89, Isa. 51:9-10; possibly Job 26:12-13, 9:13 and 7:12; and, probably somewhat later, Isa. 27:1. Cf. also Ezek. 29, 32; Jer. 51:34). Another fairly clear result is the use of theophany language, entailing the fearful reaction of the waters along with other elements of creation, in the earliest material considered; this is combined with a lack of any apparent aquatic threat, either from flooding or from the rocking of the foundations of the earth, in such passages. A concern with cosmic stability, often as expressive of political anxieties, seems also to manifest itself in the pre-exilic period, with the imagery of flooding characteristically appearing in similes or metaphors for imperial expansionism from around the time of proto-Isaiah, whilst similar language (among various forms of aquatic imagery) is applied also to the terrors of Sheol.

In the latest period, there are a number of examples of a highly monotheistic perspective, in which the whole of creation, including the seas and תנינים, are invoked to praise God or celebrate his rule (Pss. 96, 98, 148). Perhaps the most monotheistic theological statement, however, occurs in the priestly presentation of creation encapsulated in Gen. 1, although many of the other creation portrayals have a broadly compatible outlook, in accepting the createdness of the sea and/or its valued place in the world.

How is such a distribution of ideas and imagery to be explained? One key factor must surely be that the Old Testament is a product and expression of orthodox Yahwism, and that most books within it were compiled or reached their final (or near-final) form during the exile or later. It is therefore far from offering us a clear window into earlier expressions of Israelite faith and practice, even where earlier sources have been preserved within it; these, too, may have been subject to adaptation and editing, even apart from the process of selection which has been so influential on the content of the Hebrew Bible as we know it.

The archaeological evidence increasingly indicates the polytheistic nature of Israelite religion until at least a relatively late stage in the pre-exilic era and perhaps (in a reduced form) beyond. It therefore seems that the most plausible explanation of the absence of the motif of the slaying of a dragon prior to the time of the exile is that this feat was in Israel originally attributed to another deity. This mythical theme was probably simply received in a form in which the divine protagonist was not Yahweh, but another deity, probably Baal (or possibly Anat), and the transference of this attribute seems to have been made—or accepted in formal circles—around the time of, or probably not long prior to, the exile. The apparent relative prevalence of this motif during the exilic period is testimony to its relevance to the theological crisis which the fall of Jerusalem had provoked. However, it may also be indicative that it had the power of a new idea to speak afresh in a challenging situation. In any case, when the motif does appear, it is in a distinctively Israelite form, insofar as it is characteristically employed to speak of the dynamics of a historical situation, chiefly the exodus and hope of redemption after c. 587 B.C. (Pss. 74, 89, Isa. 51), though the final overcoming of "the enemy" in a more eschatological setting (Isa. 27) comprises a particularly impressive, and perhaps later, example. Nevertheless, the line of continuity with Israel's Canaanite forebears is suggested by the presence of highly traditional language in Isa. 27:1; although this of itself cannot suggest its attribution and date of transfer, one might think that had this motif of the slaying of Leviathan been applied to Yahweh earlier, such language is perhaps more likely, over time, to have been supplanted by peculiarly Israelite modes of expression, and the motif may even have assumed a more central theological rôle.

As has already been observed, for evidence of the mythic form of the story in Israel, the reader is chiefly dependent on the brief allusions in Job 26:12-13 and 9:13 re Rahab, 3:8 re Leviathan and 7:12 re the guarding of a תַּנִּין. 7:12 and 9:13 are so brief as to be unhelpful and to require elucidation from other, fuller allusions. Job 3:8 suggests a firm association of Leviathan with the underworld and death. A similar sphere of allusion may also be implied by the reference to the "making fair" of the heavens in connection with the destruction of Rahab in Job 26:12-13, although it is possible that this monster was viewed as celestial rather than subterrestrial (cf. vv. 8-11; also Ps. 89:12a, Isa. 51:13b, Job 9:7-9).

It is conceivable, as Mark Smith suggests, that the motif of Leviathan as the plaything of Yahweh (Ps. 104:26; cf. Job 40:29 [ET 41:5]) is a reflection of the idea found in the Ugaritic texts that various monsters were the "beloved" ones of El. If Yahweh was identified with, or assumed the attributes of, El, before absorbing the combative aspects of Baal, this might explain the presence of both positive and negative portrayals of Leviathan in the Hebrew Bible. However, a clear influence on at least some of the presentations of תַּנִּינִים as divinely-originated members of the created order is the monotheistic framework that is so much in evidence in Gen. 1, Deutero-Isaiah and certain of the later Psalms. Whatever the original provenance of the brief allusion in Job 40:29 (ET 41:5), clearly the more immediate and significant motivation for its employment is the theological debate is over divine justice (theodicy).

However, if Yahweh assumed the mantle of the deity who slew the dragon relatively late, the Old Testament has no direct allusion to his overcoming of the sea; despite occasional references to its "lifting up", "roaring", and so on, such allusions are characteristically employed metaphorically in the service of other interests, chiefly political. The reason for this is not hard to find: theomachic combat, or the struggle of the chief, creator deity with an aspect of his creation has no place within a monotheistic system. Hence, even had such a myth once been applied to Yahweh, it should occasion no surprise if it left no trace within the formal corpus of the Hebrew scriptures. If any such hints may remain (as some have maintained), they are interpretable within that monotheistic framework, and indeed with the supremacy of Yahweh and the unity of the created world presupposed, the allusions to roaring or flooding waters could hardly otherwise be understood except as references to natural phenomena. However, an influence in that direction may already have taken place if Yahweh was identified as El, the creator deity and head of the pantheon, who takes no active part in such struggles but perhaps supports such parties as may be necessary to maintain stability. Certainly those passages concerned with the secure maintenance of the cosmos, as, e.g., Ps. 24:1-2, would seem to take its fundamental stability for granted, notwithstanding any minor tremors which might arise. The apparently late development of Israelite thinking on creation is a further factor which may have contributed to the absence or muted expression of any notion of conflict with the sea.

References to fleeing waters in theophany portrayals, or to the aquatic aspects of Sheol or distress and divine hostility seem to belong to further, distinct, spheres of imagery which must be distinguished from that which may pertain to control or confinement of the sea. The failure of the so-called "*Chaoskampf*" imagery to leave its mark on either *Theophanieschilderungen* or the core exodus traditions may readily be explained: such motifs in Israel probably antedate the appropriation for Yahweh of any so-called "*Chaoskampf*" attributes; moreover, the early association of the theophany and exodus themes with the sea, but not (except, apparently, in certain lamenting circles of the exile) with a dragon, further distances them from any combative association, since the idea of Yahweh as the vanquisher of the sea was probably never appropriated in Israel, at least in the circles that left their mark on the Old Testament, and quite possibly at all.

Such an understanding of the evolution and interrelation of the ideas here considered paradoxically implies a closer identity with the religion of Canaan in the early period of Israelite religious history than has often been assumed in respect of the "chaos" theme. At the same time, it draws a sharper demarcation between the content of the Hebrew Bible and the religious texts of Israel's neighbours, especially as regards the mythological motifs often attributed to them. However, even here, the results of this study point to the need to examine each "comparative" text independently, without regard to postulated parallels, before any comparisons with texts derived from other contexts are made. This pertains as much to the Baal epic, the contents of which have sometimes been "biblicised" in order to extract a presumed connection between "*Chaoskampf*" and creation, as it does to the Old Testament itself.

Indeed, one of the results of the present monograph, not least if a close continuity between the religion of ancient Israel and its Canaanite forebears is accepted, is that it suggests a need to rethink the concept of "chaos" as it has been applied outside Israel, and perhaps most especially to the literature of Ugarit. In particular, it confirms the separation between theomachic combat and creation already recognised by many scholars in relation to the struggles of Baal with Yam and Mot, and encourages the interpretation of the feat of slaying the dragon independently from the Baal-Yam conflict. The chief—and most obvious—import of dragon-slaying by a deity is in any context as a manifestation of power and supremacy, which may perhaps illuminate its apparent attribution to both Baal and Anat, though it is possible that the influence of variant traditions is responsible for this. However, the understanding of Ltn simply as an extension of Yam, either as effectively synonymous or as a cohort and confederate, needs to be revisited and its validity reassessed, since it is likely that the whole connection has simply been assumed and imported on the basis of existing scholarly presuppositions about the almost inevitable association of combat (especially with a draconic and/or marine figure) with "chaos" and creation. More widely, even though it is true to say that in ancient Near Eastern combat narratives the conquered deity or monster is the enemy of the victor and indeed is often more broadly conceived as inimical or at least as potentially threatening, there may still be a general need to question the almost automatic use of the term "chaos" to denote the power overcome by the warrior god. There is a risk that "chaos" may be an idea which more accurately encapsulates our own conceptual framework and mythological heritage (especially through the Greek world) than those of the ancient peoples whose beliefs we are trying to understand. However, any firm conclusions in this sphere are beyond the scope of the present thesis, in which comparative methodology has been avoided, except as subsequent to the main exegetical task; nevertheless, they suggest promising avenues for further research.

Finally, the core result of the present monograph may be summarised by stating that the term "chaos" should be abandoned in respect of the Old Testament, since this literary collection does not seem to possess a clear expression of the idea that Yahweh engaged in combat with the sea or a sea monster in primordial times, whereas it contains much that contravenes this view. There is a further problem that the label of "chaos" has been applied by many scholars not only to allusions to the control or confinement of the sea or to the overcoming of a dragon, but to a wide variety of references which have no intrinsic connection to these ideas and which should be properly defined under a variety of distinct categories. For example, the overcoming of the sea seems to have no place in relation to the theophany and exodus themes, whilst the language associated with Sheol and enmity is another sphere which should properly be distinguished.

However, even apart from this, the concept of a monolithic "chaos" theme which is expressed through a variety of terminology, but without there being any clear distinction between its different forms, must be called into question. For example, it seems likely that the figures of Leviathan and Rahab may have originated and developed independently, despite certain apparent overlaps between them, and indeed there may be other traditions of unnamed תַּנִּינִים which may be crocodilian or perhaps associated with Mot or other mythic or non-mythic spheres. Moreover, ideas relating to draconic figures seem to be a relatively late and theologically reflective appropriation within Israel, although Rahab may have originated there as a designation for Egypt prior to any envisagement of it having a draconic form. Even Leviathan seems not to have been "chaotic" as such, despite its varied manifestations in the literature of Israel.

As regards allusions to the sea, one certainly could not claim the absence of ideas relating to this body of water before a certain period, since it is an essential and familiar aspect of the cosmos. However, the notion of combat with or the suppression of the sea is nowhere clearly expressed in the Old Testament and indeed there could be no place for such a notion within the monotheistic framework of which it is ultimately an expression. Probably if there ever was a belief in a combat with the sea in Israel, it was attributed to Baal, whilst Yahweh / El(ohim) never engaged in such a struggle. In the Hebrew Bible, where the question of cosmic stability is alluded to it is strongly affirmed and the strength of Yahweh to uphold the existing order is not questioned; it is never really threatened. Similarly, the Old Testament does not propagate a view of creation other than one in which the waters were ordered with ease and securely (and permanently) confined. Thus although there are various references to the roaring of the sea or flooding, such imagery is not employed on a literal level, and there is no indication that it should be understood other than in relation to the natural world.

It must be emphasised that the breadth of the evidence relating to the lack of a clear expression of the theme of "chaos" in the Hebrew Bible, either in relation to a dragon or to the sea, and its clear explicability within the framework of orthodox Yahwism itself, does much to strengthen the overall results of this study. It has previously often been claimed that a reference to "chaos" is present in a certain instance, not because of the strength of the evidence in that case, but because it was generally accepted that such allusions occurred in the Hebrew Bible and that they could therefore be presupposed in many instances when they were less than apparent. However, the consistency of the results of the present monograph over such a wide range of references and the decisive nature of some of the evidence means that such an assumption should now no longer be regarded as acceptable; this is moreover not least the case insofar as the equivalence of different types of so-called "chaos" allusion can no longer be presumed. Thus even were an argument to be formulated for an allusion to "chaos" in relation to, say, a particular reference to Leviathan, this could not be taken to indicate an association between the same theme and the sea or Rahab: such a conclusion would rather have to be independently determined.

The present monograph began with the disorganised mass of material which, in a rather undifferentiated form, was commonly supposed to refer to "chaos". However, when this *rudis indigestaque moles* is separated out into its constituent elements, and its individual themes and concerns distinguished, the idea of "chaos" is itself uncreated, transformed into a coherent yet varied theological system of sometimes interconnected yet fundamentally distinct ideas. The Gunkelian version of "chaos" has held sway almost unaltered for over one hundred years, and its precursors in the discussion of Genesis 1 have a history reaching back to the earliest Christian era. I nevertheless hope that this present version of order out of "chaos" will prevail for some time to come.

Bibliography

Aartun, K., "Neue Beiträge zum Ugaritischen Lexicon (I)" *UF* 16 (1984) 1-52.

— —, "Neue Beiträge zum Ugaritischen Lexicon (II)" *UF* 17 (1986) 1-47.

Abrams, M. H., *A Glossary of Literary Terms* (Chicago, IL: Holt, Rinehart & Winston, 5th ed. 1988).

Ahlström, G. W., *Psalm 89: Eine Liturgie aus dem Ritual des leidenden Königs* (Lund: C.W.K. Gleerup, 1959).

Aistleitner, J., *Wörterbuch der ugaritischen Sprache* (Berichte über die Verhandlungen der Sächsischen Akademie der Wissenschaften zu Leipzig, Philologisch-historische Klasse, Band 106 Heft 3; Berlin: Akademie-Verlag, 4th ed. 1974).

Albertz, R., *Religionsgeschichte Israels in alttestamentlicher Zeit*, 2 vols. (Grundrisse zum Alten Testament, Das Alte Testament Deutsch Ergänzungsreihe 8; Göttingen: Vandenhoeck & Ruprecht, 1992). English translation: *A History of Israelite Religion in the Old Testament Period*, 2 vols. (London: SCM, 1994).

Albright, W. F., "Gilgameš and Engidu, Mesopotamian Geni of Fecundity" *JAOS* 40 (1920) 307- 335.

— —, "More Light on the Epic of Aleyân Bal and Môt" *BASOR* 50 (1933) 13-20.

— —, Review of Gustav Hölscher, *Das Buch Hiob, JBL* 57 (1938) 226-7.

— —, *Archaeology and the Religion of Israel* (The Ayer Lectures of the Colgate-Rochester Divinity School 1941; Baltimore, MD: John Hopkins, 1942).

— —, "The Chronology of the Divided Monarchy of Israel" *BASOR* 100 (1945) 16-22.

— —, "The Psalm of Habakkuk" in H. H. Rowley (ed.), *Studies in Old Testament Prophecy Presented to Professor Theodore H. Robinson Litt.D., D.D., D.Th., by the Society for Old Testament Study on his Sixty-fifth Birthday August 9th 1946* (Edinburgh: T. & T. Clark, 1950) 1-18.

——, "A Catalogue of Early Hebrew Lyric Poems (Psalm LXVIII)" *HUCA* 23 Pt 1 (1950-51) 1-39.

——, *Yahweh and the Gods of Canaan: A Historical analysis of Two Contrasting Faiths* (Jordan Lectures in Comparative Religion VII, 1965; London: Athlone Press, University of London, 1968).

Allen, L. C., *The Books of Joel, Obadiah, Jonah, and Micah* (NICOT; Grand Rapids, MI: Eerdmans, 1976).

——, *Psalms 101-150* (Word Biblical Commentary 19; Waco, TX: Word Books, 1983).

——, "The Value of Rhetorical Criticism in Psalm 69", *JBL* 105 (1986) 577-598.

Alonso-Schökel, L., "Psalmus 136 (135)" *Verbum Domini* 45 (1967) 129-138.

——, "The Poetic Structure of Psalm 42-43" *JSOT* 1 (1976) 4-11.

——, "Psalm 42-43. A Response to Ridderbos and Kessler" *JSOT* 3 (1977) 1-65.

Alter, R., *The Art of Biblical Poetry* (Edinburgh: T. & T. Clark, 1985).

Anderson, A. A., *Psalms*, 2 vols. (NCBC; London: Marshall, Morgan and Scott, 1972).

Anderson, B. W., "Creation", *IDB* I (Nashville, TN: Abingdon Press, 1962) 725-732.

——, (ed.), *Creation in the Old Testament* (Issues in Religion and Theology 6; London: SPCK, 1984).

——, *Creation versus Chaos: The Reinterpretation of Mythical Symbolism in the Bible* (Philadelphia, PA: Fortress, reprinted with a new afterword on the cosmic dimensions of the biblical creation faith 1987).

——, "The Slaying of the Fleeing, Twisting Serpent: Isaiah 27:1 in Context" in L. M. Hopfe (ed.) *Uncovering Ancient Stones: Essays in Memory of H. Neil Richardson* (Winona Lake, IN: Eisenbrauns, 1994) 3-16.

Anderson, G. W., (ed.), *Tradition and Interpretation: Essays by Members of the Society for Old Testament Study* (Oxford: Clarendon Press, 1979).

Archbishops' Commission to Revise the Psalter (ed.), *The Revised Psalter: the Amended Text as Approved by the Convocations of Canterbury and York in October 1963 with a View to Legislation for its Permissive Use* (London: SPCK, 1964).

Aristophanes, *The Birds* (trans. G. Murray; London: George Allen & Unwin, 1950).

——, *The Clouds* (trans. W. Arrowsmith; the Mentor Greek Comedy; London: the New English Library, 1962).

Arnold, A., *Dr. Friedrich Tuch's Kommentar über die Genesis* (Halle: Verlag der Buchhandlung des Weisenhauses, 2nd ed. 1871).

Auvray, P., *Isaïe 1-39* (Sources Bibliques; Paris: J. Gabalda, 1972).

Avishur, Y., "The Ghost-expelling Incantation from Ugarit (Ras Ibn Hani 78/20)" *UF* 13 (1981) 13-25.

——, *Studies in Hebrew and Ugaritic Psalms* (Publications of the Perry Foundation for Biblical Research; Jerusalem: Magnes Press, Hebrew University, 1994).

Baethgen, F., *Die Psalmen übersetzt und erklärt* (Handkommentar zum Alten Testament II, 2; Göttingen: Vandenhoeck & Ruprecht, 3rd ed. 1904).

Baldwick, C., *The Concise Oxford Dictionary of Literary Terms* (Oxford: OUP, 1990).

Balentine, S. E., "'What are Human Beings that You Make so Much of Them?' Divine Disclosure from the Whirlwind: 'Look at Behemoth'" in T. Linafelt and T. Beal (edd.), *God in the Fray. A Tribute to Walter Brueggemann* (Minneapolis, MN: Fortress, 1998) 259-78.

Baltzer, K., *Deutero-Jesaja: Kommentar zum Alten Testament* (Kommentar zum Alten Testament 10, 2; Gütersloh: Gütersloher Verlagshaus, 1999). English translation: *Deutero-Isaiah: A Commentary on Isaiah 40-55* (Hermeneia; Minneapolis, MN: Fortress, 2001).

Barker, M., *The Older Testament: The Survival of Themes from the Ancient Royal Cult in Sectarian Judaism and Early Christianity* (London: SPCK, 1987).

——, *The Gate of Heaven: The History and Symbolism of the Temple in Jerusalem* (London: SPCK, 1991).

——, *On Earth as it is in Heaven: Temple Symbolism in the New Testament* (Edinburgh: T. & T. Clark, 1995).

Barr, J., *The Semantics of Biblical Language* (Oxford: OUP, 1961).

——, "Ugaritic and Hebrew '*šbm*'?", *JSS* 18 (1973) 17-39.

——, *The Variable Spellings of the Hebrew Bible* (Schweich Lectures of the British Academy 1986; Oxford: OUP, 1989).

——,"'Thou art the Cherub': Ezek. 28:14 and the Post-Ezekiel Understanding of Genesis 2-3" in E. Ulrich, J. W. Wright, R. P Carroll, and P. R Davies (edd.), *Priests, Prophets and Scribes: Essays on the Formation and Heritage of Second Temple Judaism in Honour of Joseph*

Blenkinsopp (JSOT[S] 149; Sheffield: Sheffield Academic Press, 1992) 213-223.

Barton, J., *Isaiah 1-39* (OTG; Sheffield: Sheffield Academic Press, 1995).

— —, *Reading the Old Testament: Method in Biblical Study* (London: DLT, 2nd ed. 1996).

Batto, B. F., "The Reed Sea: Requiescat in Pace" *JBL* 102 (1983) 27-35.

— —*Slaying the Dragon: Mythmaking in the Biblical Tradition* (Louisville, KY: Westminster John Knox, 1992).

— —, "Behemoth בהמות" in K. van der Toorn, B. Becking, and P. W. van der Horst, *Dictionary of Deities and Demons in the Bible* (Leiden: E. J. Brill; Grand Rapids, MI: Eerdmans, 2nd extensively revised ed. 1999) 165-9.

Baumann, E., "Struktur-Untersuchungen im Psalter I" *ZAW* 61 (1945/1948) 114-176.

Baumgartner, W., "Hermann Gunkel" in W. Baumgartner, *Zum Alten Testament und seiner Umwelt: ausgewählte Aufsätze* (Leiden: E. J. Brill, 1959) 371-378.

— —, "Zum 100. Geburtstag von Hermann Gunkel" in G. W. Anderson et al. (edd.), *Congress Volume: Bonn 1962* (VT[S] 9; Leiden: E. J. Brill, 1963) 1-18.

Beer, G., *Der Text der Buches Hiob* (Marburg: N. G. Elwertsche Verlagsbuchhandlung, 1895).

Begrich, J., "Mabbul. Eine exegetisch-lexicalische Studie" *ZS* 6 (1928) 135-153.

— —, *Chronologie der Könige von Israel und Juda und die Quellen des Rahmens der Königsbücher* (BHT 3; Tübingen: J. C. B. Mohr, 1929).

Bellinger, W. H., Jr., *Prophecy and Psalmody* (JSOT[S] 27; Sheffield: JSOT, 1984).

Bergant, D., *Job, Ecclesiastes* (Old Testament Message 18; Wilmington, DL: Michael Glazier, Inc., 1982).

Berry, D. K., *The Psalms and Their Readers: Interpretative Strategies for Psalm 18* (JSOT[S] 153; Sheffield: JSOT Press, 1993).

Bertholet, J., *Deuteronomium* (Leipzig: J. C. B. Mohr, 1899).

Beyerlin, W., "Die tôdā der Heilsverkündigung in den Klageliedern des Einzelner" *ZAW* 89 (1967) 208-24.

Bezold, C., *Catalogue of the Cuneiform Tablets in the Kouyunjik Collection of the British Museum*, 2 vols. (London: by order of the Trustees of the British Museum, Longmans et al., 1889-1891).

Bickell, G., *Carmina veteris Testamenti Metrice. Notas Criticas et Dissertationem de re Metrica Hebraeorum Adjecit* (Oeniponte [Innsbruck]: Libraria Academica Wagneriana, 1882).

Blank, S. H., "Curse", *HUCA* 23 (1950-51) 73-95.

Blenkinsopp, J., *Isaiah 1-39: A New Translation with Introduction and Commentary* (Anchor Bible 19; New York: Doubleday, 2000).

— —, *Isaiah 40-55: A New Translation with Introduction and Commentary* (Anchor Bible 19A; New York: Doubleday, 2000).

Blommerde, A. C. M., *Northwest Semitic Grammar and Job* (Biblica et Orientalia 22; Rome: Pontifical Biblical Institute, 1969).

Blythin, I., "A note on Genesis I 2" *VT* 12 (1962) 120-121.

Bochart, S., *Hierozoicon*, 2 vols. (London: John Martyn and James Allestry, 1663).

Boling, G., "'Synonymous' Parallelism in the Psalms" *JSS* 5 (1960) 221-55.

Bonnard, P.-E., *Le Second Isaïe, son disciple et leurs éditeurs: Isaïe 40-66* (Paris: Librairie Lecoffre, 1972).

Bouzard, W., Jr., *We Have Heard with our Ears, O God: Sources of the Communal Laments in the Psalms* (SBLDS 159; Atlanta, GA: Scholars Press, 1997).

Brenner, Martin L., *The Song of the Sea: Ex. 15:1-21* (BZAW 195; Berlin & New York: Walter de Gruyter, 1991).

Brettler, M. Z., *God is King: Understanding an Israelite Metaphor* (JSOT[S] 76; Sheffield: Sheffield Academic Press,1989).

— —, "Images of YHWH the Warrior in Psalms", *Semeia* 61 (1993) 135-65.

Briggs, C. A., and E. G. Briggs, *A Critical and Exegetical Commentary on the Book of Psalms*, 2 vols. (ICC; Edinburgh: T. & T. Clark, 1906-7).

Bright, J., *A History of Israel* (London: SCM, 3rd ed. 1981).

Brockelmann, C., *Hebraïsche Syntax* (Neukirchen: Kreis Moers, 1956).

Brown, F., S. R. Driver, and C. A. Briggs, *A Hebrew and English Lexicon of the Old Testament with an appendix containing the Biblical Aramaic* (Oxford: Clarendon, 1907).

Broyles, C. C., *The Conflict of Faith and Experience in the Psalms: A Form-Critical and Theological Study* (JSOT[S] 52; Sheffield: JSOT, 1989).

Brueggemann, W., "Trajectories in Old Testament Literature and the Sociology of Ancient Israel" *JBL* 98 (1979) 161-185.

— —, *Genesis* (Interpretation; Atlanta, GA; John Knox, 1982).

——, *The Message of the Psalms: A Theological Commentary* (Minneapolis, MN: Augsburg, 1984).

——, *Israel's Praise: Doxology against Idolatry and Ideology* (Philadelphia, PA: Fortress, 1988).

——, *The Psalms and the Life of Faith* (edited by P. D., Miller; Minneapolis, MN: Fortress, 1995).

——, *Theology of the Old Testament: Testimony, Dispute, Advocacy* (Minneapolis, MN: Augsburg, 1997).

——, *Isaiah*, 2 vols. (Westminster Bible Companion; Louisville, KY: Westminster John Knox, 1998).

Buber, M., *Der Glaube der Propheten* (Zürich: Manesse Verlag, 1950).

Budge, E. A. W., and L. W. King, *Annals of the Kings of Assyria: The Cuneiform Texts with Translations, Transliterations, etc., from the Original Documents in the British Museum* (London: Trustees of the British Museum, 1902).

Buttenwieser, M., *The Psalms Chronologically Treated with a New Translation* (Chicago, IL: University of Chicago Press, 1938).

Calvin, J., *Commentaries on the First Book of Moses Called Genesis. Translated from the Original Latin, and Compared with the French Edition by the Rev. John King, M.A....* (Vol. 1; Edinburgh: Printed for the Calvin Translation Society, 1847).

Carroll, R. P., *Jeremiah: A Commentary* (OTL; London: SCM, 1986).

Cassuto, U., *A Commentary on the Book of Genesis*, 2 vols. (Jerusalem: Magnes Press, Hebrew University, 1st English ed. 1961-1964).

——, *A Commentary on the Book of Exodus* (Jerusalem: Magnes Press, Hebrew University, 1st English ed. 1967).

Cheyne, T. K., "Notes on Genesis I., 1, and XXIV., 14" *Hebraica* 2 (1885-6) 49-50.

——, *The Book of Psalms or the Praises of Israel: A New Translation, with Commentary* (London: Kegan Paul, Trench, & Co., 1888).

——, "The Text of Job", *JQR* 9 (1896-7) 573-80.

Childs, B. S., "The Enemy from the North and the Chaos Tradition" *JBL* 78 (1959) 187-198.

——, *Myth and Reality in the Old Testament* (SBT 27; London: SCM, 1960).

——, *Memory and Tradition in Israel* (SBT 37; London: SCM, 1962).

——, *Exodus: A Critical, Theological Commentary* (OTL; Louisville, KY: Westminster, 1974).

——, *Isaiah* (OTL; Louisville, KY: Westminster John Knox, 2001).

Clements, R. E., *Isaiah 1-39* (NCBC; Grand Rapids, MI: Eerdmans; London: Marshall, Morgan and Scott, 1980).

——, *A Century of Old Testament Study* (Guildford: Lutterworth, revised ed. 1983).

Clifford, R. J., "A Note on Ps 104: 5-9" *JBL* 100 (1981) 87-9.

——, *Deuteronomy: with an Excursus on Covenant and Law* (Old Testament Message: A Biblical-Theological Commentary 4; Wilmington, DL: Michael Glazier, Inc., 1982).

——, "Cosmogonies in the Ugaritic Texts and in the Bible" *Or* 53 (1984) 183-201.

——, *Creation Accounts in the Ancient Near East and in the Bible* (CBQ Monograph Series 26; Washington: The Catholic Biblical Association of America, 1994).

——, *Psalms*, 2 vols. (Abingdon Old Testament Commentaries; Nashville, TN: Abingdon Press, 2002-3).

Clines, D. J. A., "The Etymology of Hebrew Ṣelem", *JNWSL* 3 [1974] 19-25.

——, "The Evidence for an Autumn New Year in Pre-exilic Israel Reconsidered" *JBL* 93 (1974) 22-40.

——, *The Theme of the Pentateuch* (JSOT[S] 10; Sheffield: JSOT, 1978).

——, *Job 1-20* (WBC 17; Dallas, Texas: Word Books, 1989).

——, "A World Established on Water (Psalm 24)..." in D. J. A. Clines, and J. C. Exum, *The New Literary Criticism and the Hebrew Bible* (JSOT[S] 143; Sheffield: JSOT, 1993), 79-90.

——, (ed.), *The Dictionary of Classical Hebrew*, I-IV (Sheffield: Sheffield Academic Press, 1993-1998).

——, "Job's God" in E. van Wolde (ed.), *Job's God* (Concilium 2004/4; London: SCM, 2004).

Clines, D. J. A., and J. C. Exum, "The New Literary Criticism" in D. J. A. Clines and J. C. Exum, *The New Literary Criticism and the Hebrew Bible* (JSOT[S] 143; Sheffield: JSOT, 1993) 11-25.

Coffin, H. S., Exposition to Isaiah, Chs. 40-66 in Buttrick, G. A. (ed.), *The Interpreter's Bible*, V (Nashville, TN: Abingdon, 1956) 419-773.

Cohen, A, *The Psalms: Hebrew Text and English Translation with an Introduction and Commentary* (Soncino Books of the Bible; London & New York: Soncino Press, 1945).

Colenso, J. W., *The Pentateuch and Book of Joshua Critically Examined*, Part IV (London: Longman, Green, Longman, Roberts, and Green, 1863).

Collins, T., "Decoding the Psalms: A Structural Approach to the Psalter" *JSOT* 37 (1987) 41-60.

Cooke, G. A., *A Critical and Exegetical Commentary on the Book of Ezekiel* (ICC; Edinburgh: T. & T. Clark, 1936).

Cooper, A., "The Life and Times of King David According to the Book of Psalms" in R. E. Friedman (ed.), *The Poet and the Historian: Essays in Literary and Historical Criticism* (Harvard Semitic Studies 26; Chico, CA: Scholars Press, 1983) 117-31.

——, "Ps. 24:7, Mythology and Exegesis" *JBL* 102 (1983) 37-60.

Cornford, F. M., *Plato's Cosmology: the* Timaeus *of Plato Translated with a Running Commentary* (International Library of Psychology, Philosophy and Scientific Method; London: Kegan Paul, Tranch, Trubner & Co.; New York: Harcourt, Brace & Co., 1937).

Cowley, A. E., *Gesenius' Hebrew Grammar as edited and enlarged by the late E. Kautzsch* (Oxford: Clarendon, 2nd ed. 1910).

Craigie, P. C., "The Comparison of Hebrew Poetry: Psalm 104 in the Light of Egyptian and Ugaritic Poetry" *Semitics* 4 (1974) 10-21.

——, *Ugarit and the Old Testament* (Grand Rapids, MI: William B. Eerdmans, 1983).

——, *Psalms 1-50* (Word Biblical Commentary 19; Waco, TX: Word Books, 1983).

——, "Job and Ugaritic Studies" in W. E. Aufrecht (ed.) *Studies in the Book of Job* (Studies in Religion Supplements 16; Waterloo, Ont., Canada: W. Laurier University Press, 1985).

Crenshaw, J. L., "'W[e]dōrēk 'al-bāmŏtê 'āreṣ'" *CBQ* 34 (1972) 39-53.

Croft, S. J. L., *The Identity of the Individual in the Psalms* (JSOT[S] 44; Sheffield: Sheffield Academic Press, 1987).

Cross, F. M., "Notes on a Canaanite Psalm in the Old Testament" *BASOR* 117 (1950) 19-21.

——, "The Song of the Sea and Canaanite Myth" in R. W. Funk (ed.) *God and Christ: Existence and Providence* (*Journal for Theology and the Church* 5; New York: Herder & Herder, 1968) 1-25. *Canaanite Myth and*

Hebrew Epic: Essays in the History of the Religion of Israel (Cambridge, MA: Harvard University Press, 1973).

——, *From Epic to Canon: History and Literature in Ancient Israel* (Baltimore & London: John Hopkins University Press, 1998.

Cross, F. M., and D. N. Freedman, "The Song of Miriam" *JNES* 14 (1950) 237-50.

——, *Early Hebrew Orthography: A Study of the Epigraphic Evidence* (AOS 36; New Haven, CT: American Oriental Society, 1952).

——, "A Royal song of Thanksgiving: II Samuel 22 = Psalm 18" *JBL* 72 (1953) 15-34.

——, *Studies in Ancient Yahwistic Poetry* (Biblical Resource Series; Grand Rapids, MI & Cambridge: William B. Eerdmans, 1997).

Crüsemann, F., *Studien zur Formgeschichte von Hymnus und Danklied in Israel* (WMANT 32; Neukirchen-Vluyn: Neukirchener Verlag, 1969).

Cunchillos, J.-L., "Peut-on parler de mythes de création à Ugarit?" in L. Derousseaux (ed.), *La Création dans L'Orient Ancien* (Lectio Divina 127; Paris: Éditions du Cerf, 1987) 79-96.

Curtis, A. H. W., "The 'Subjugation of the Waters' Motif in the Psalms: Imagery or Polemic?" *JSS* 23 (1978) 245-256.

——, *Ugarit (Ras Shamra)* (Cities of the Biblical World; Cambridge: Lutterworth Press, 1985).

——, "The Psalms Since Dahood" in G. J. Brooke, A. H. W. Curtis, and J. F. Healey (edd.), *Ugarit and the Bible: Proceedings of the International Symposium on Ugarit and the Bible. Manchester, September 1992* (UBL 11; Münster: Ugarit-Verlag, 1994).

——, *Psalms* (Epworth Commentaries; Peterborough: Epworth, 2004).

Dahood, M. J., "Ugaritic Drkt and Biblical Derek" *ThSt* 15 (1954) 627-631.

——, "Mišmār 'muzzle' in Job 7 12", *JBL* 80 (1961) 270-1.

——, Review of Friedrich Horst, *Hiob*, *Biblica* 43 (1962) 225-6.

——, "Hebrew-Ugaritic Lexicography II" *Biblica* 45 (1964) 393-412.

——, *Ugaritic-Hebrew Philology* (Biblica et Orientalia 17; Rome: Pontifical Biblical Institute, 1965).

——, *Psalms: Introduction, Translation, and Notes*, 3 vols. (Anchor Bible 16-17A; Garden City, NY: Doubleday, 1966-70).

——, "A New Metrical Pattern in Biblical Poetry" *CBQ* 29 (1967) 574-582.

Dalley, S., "The Influence of Mesopotamia upon Israel and the Bible" in S. Dalley (ed.) *The Legacy of Mesopotamia* (Oxford: OUP, 1998) 57-83.

Davidson, A. B., *The Book of Job with Notes, Introduction and Appendix* (The Cambridge Bible for Schools and Colleges; Cambridge: CUP, 1899).

— —, *Introductory Hebrew Grammar: Syntax* (Edinburgh: T. & T. Clark, 3rd ed. 1902).

Davidson, R., *The Vitality of Worship: A Commentary on the Book of Psalms* (Grand Rapids, MI: Eerdmans, 1998).

Davies, G. I., *Hosea* (NCBC; Grand Rapids, MI: Eerdmans, 1992).

Davies, P. R., "'Take it to the Lord in Prayer': The Peasant's Lament" in P. R. Davies, *Whose Bible is it Anyway?* (JSOT[S] 204; Sheffield: Sheffield Academic Press, 1995) 114- 126.

Davis, E. F., "Psalm 98: Rejoicing in Judgment" *Int* 46 (1992) 171-5.

Day, J., *God's Conflict with the Dragon and the Sea: Echoes of a Canaanite Myth in the Old Testament* (University of Cambridge Oriental Publications 35; Cambridge: CUP, 1985).

— —, *Psalms* (OTG; Sheffield: Sheffield Academic Press, 1990).

— —, "Ugarit and the Bible: Do They Presuppose the Same Canaanite Mythology and Religion?" in G. J. Brooke, A. H. W. Curtis, and J. F. Healey (edd.), *Ugarit and the Bible: Proceedings of the International Symposium on Ugarit and the Bible. Manchester, September 1992* (UBL 11; Münster: Ugarit-Verlag, 1994) 35-52.

— —, *Yahweh and the Gods and Goddesses of Canaan* (JSOT[S] 265; Sheffield: Sheffield Academic Press, 2000).

Deissler, A., *Die Psalmen*, 3 vols. (Die Welt der Bibel; Düsseldorf: Patmos Verlag, 1963-5).

Delitzsch, Franz, *Die Genesis ausgelegt* (Leipzig: Dörffling und Franke; London: Williams and Norgate, 1852).

— —, *Biblischer Commentar über die poetischen Bücher des Alten Testaments. Das Buch Iob* (Biblischer Commentar über das Alte Testament 4; Leipzig: Dörffling und Franke, 1864). English translation: Biblical Commentary on the Book of Job, 2 vols. (Clark's Foreign Theological Library, Fourth Series 10, 11; Edinburgh: T. & T. Clark, 1866).

— —, *Neuer Commentar über die Genesis* (Leipzig: Dörffling und Franke, 1887). English translation: *A New Commentary on Genesis*, Vol. 1 (Clark's Foreign Theological Library, New Series 36; Edinburgh: T. & T. Clark, 1888).

——, *Biblischer Commentar über die Psalmen* (Biblischer Commentar über das Alte Testament 4, Bd. 1; Leipzig: Dörffling und Franke, 4th ed. 1883). English translation: *Biblical Commentary on the Psalms* (Foreign Biblical Library; London: Hodder & Stoughton, 1887-1889).

——, *Commentar über das Buch Jesaia* (Biblischer Commentar über das Alte Testament, III, 1; Leipzig: Dörffling & Franke, 1889). English translation: *Biblical Commentary on the Prophecies of Isaiah*, 2 vols. (Foreign Biblical Library; London: Hodder & Stoughton, 1891-2).

Delitzsch, Friedrich, *George Smith's Chaldäische Genesis. Keilinschriftliche Berichte über Schöpfung, Sündenfall, Sintfluth, Thurmbau und Nimrod, nebst vielen anderen Fragmenten ältesten babylonisch-assyrischen Schriftthums. Mit 27 Abbildungen. Autorisirte Übersetzung von Hermann Delitzsch. Nebst Erläuterungen und fortgesetzten Forschungen von Dr. Friedrich Delitzsch* (Leipzig: J. C. Hinrichs'sche Buchhandlung, 1876).

——, *Das babylonische Weltschöpfungsepos* (Leipzig: S. Hirzel, 1896).

——, *Das Buch Hiob neu übersetzt und kurz erklärt* (Leipzig: J. C. Hinrichs'sche Buchhandlung, 1902).

——, *Babel und Bibel: ein Vortrag* (Leipzig: J. C. Hinrichs'sche Buchhandlung, 1903).

——, *Zweiter Vortrag über Babel und Bibel* (Stuttgart: Deutsche Verlags-Anstalt, 1903).

Dell, K. J., *The Book of Job as Sceptical Literature* (BZAW 197; Berlin: de Gruyter, 1991).

Dhorme, E., *Le Livre de Job* (Études Bibliques; Paris: Librairie Victor Lecoffre, 2nd ed. 1926). English translation: *A Commentary on the Book of Job* (London: Nelson, 1967).

Dietrich, M., and O. Loretz, "Die Ug. Gewandbezeichnungen *PGNDR, KND, KNDPNṮ*" *UF* 9 (1977) 340.

——, "Schriftliche und Mündliche Überlieferung eines 'Sonnenhymnus' nach KTU 1.6 VI 42-53" *UF* 12 (1980) 399-400.

——, "*Šb, Šbm* und *Udn* im Kontext von KTU 1.3 III 35B—IV 4 und KTU 1.83:3" *UF* 14 (1982) 77-81.

Dietrich, M., O. Loretz, and J. Sanmartin, *Die keilalphabetischen Texte aus Ugarit: Einschliesslich der keilalphabetischen Texte außerhalb Ugarits. Teil 1: Transkription* (AOAT 24; Kevelaer: Butzon & Bercker; Neukirchen-Vluyn: Neukirchener Verlag, 1976).

Diewert, D. A., "Job 7:12: *Yam, Tannin* and the surveillance of Job" *JBL* 106 (1982) 203-215.

Dijkstra, M., "Once again: The closing lines of the Ba'al-cycle (KTU 1.6.VI.42ff)" *UF* 17 (1986) 147-152.

Dillmann, C. F. A., *Hiob* (Kurzgefasstes exegetisches Handbuch zum Alten Testament 2; Leipzig: S. Hirzel, 4th ed. [of the work by L. Hirzel] 1891).

Dion, P. E., "YHWH as Storm-god and Sun-god: The Double Legacy of Egypt and Canaan as Reflected in Psalm 104" *ZAW* 103 (1991) 43-71.

Domeris, W. R., "דכא" in W. VanGemeren (ed.) *NIDOTTE*, I (Carlisle: Paternoster, 1997) 943-946.

Donner, H., "Ugaritismen in der Psalmenforschung" *ZAW* 79 (1967) 322-350.

Doxey, D. M., "Sobek" in D. B. Radford, *The Ancient Gods Speak: A Guide to Egyptian Religion* (Oxford: OUP, 2002) 336-7.

Driver, G. R., "Textual and Linguistic Problems of the Book of Psalms" *HTR* 29 (1936) 171-195.

——, "Mythical Monsters in the Old Testament", *Studi orientalistici in onore di Giorgio Levi della Vida* I (Pubblicazioni dell'Istituto per l'Oriente 52; Rome: Istituto per l'Oriente 1956) 234-49.

——, *Canaanite Myths and Legends* (OTS 3; Edinburgh: T. & T. Clark, 1956).

——, "Problems in the Hebrew Text of Job" in M. Noth, and D. Winton Thomas (edd.), *Wisdom in Israel and in the Ancient Near East* (VT[S] 3; Leiden: E. J. Brill, 1960) 72-93.

——, "The Resurrection of Marine and Terrestrial Creatures" *JSS* 7 (1962) 12-22.

Driver, Review of H. H. Rowley, *Job*, *JTS* 22 n.s. (1971) 176-9.

Driver, S. R., *Sermons on Subjects Connected with the Old Testament* (London: Methuen, 1892).

——, *The Book of Job in the Revised Version edited with Introductions and Brief Annotations* (Oxford: Clarendon, 1906).

——, *Introduction to the Literature of the Old Testament* (International Theological Library; Edinburgh: T. & T. Clark, 9th ed. 1913).

Driver, S. R., and G. B. Gray, *A Critical and Exegetical Commentary on the Book of Job Together with a New Translation* (ICC; Edinburgh: T. & T. Clark, 1921).

Duhm, B., *Das Buch Jesaja übersetzt und erklärt* (Göttinger Handkommentar zum Alten Testament, III.1; Göttingen: Vandenhoeck & Ruprecht, 4th ed., 1922).

——, *Die Psalmen* (Kurzer Hand-Kommentar zum Alten Testament 14; Tübingen: J. C. B. Mohr [Paul Siebeck], 2nd ed. 1922).

Durham, J. I., *Exodus* (WBC 3; Waco, TX: Word Books, 1987).

Dussaud, R., *Les Découvertes de Ras Shamra (Ugarit) et l'Ancien Testament* (Paris: Librairie Orientaliste Paul Geuthner, 1937).

Eakin, F. E., Jr., "The Reed Sea and Baalism" *JBL* 86 (1967) 378-384.

Eaton, J. H., "The Origin and Meaning of Habakkuk 3" *ZAW* 76 (1964) 144-171.

——, *Psalms: Introduction and Commentary* (Torch Bible Commentary; London: SCM, 1967).

——, "The Psalms and Israelite Worship" in G. W. Anderson (ed.) *Tradition and Interpretation* (Oxford: Clarendon, 1979) 238-273.

——, *Vision in Worship: The Relation of Prophecy and Liturgy in the Old Testament* (London: SPCK, 1981).

——, *Kingship and the Psalms* (The Biblical Seminar; Sheffield: JSOT, 2nd ed. 1986).

——, *Psalms of the Way and the Kingdom: A Conference with the Commentators* (JSOT[S] 199; Sheffield: Sheffield Academic Press, 1995).

——, *The Psalms: A Historical and Spiritual Commentary with an Introduction and New Translation* (London: T. & T. Clark, 2003).

Ehrlich, A. B., *Randglossen zur hebräischen Bibel*, Vol. 6: *Psalmen, Sprüche und Hiob* (Leipzig: J. C. Hinrichs'sche Buchhandlung, 1918).

Eichrodt, W., *Der Prophet Hesekiel*, 2 vols. (Das Alte Testament Deutsch 22/1-2; Göttingen: Vandenhoeck & Ruprecht, 1956-66). English translation: *Ezekiel: A Commentary* (OTL; London: SCM, 1970).

——, "In the Beginning: A Contribution to the Interpretation of the First Word of the Bible" in B. W. Anderson, and W. Harrelson (edd.), *Essays in Honour of James Muilenberg* (New York: Harper & Brothers, 1962) 1-11; reprinted in B. W. Anderson (ed.) *Creation in the Old Testament* (Philadelphia, PA: Fortress; London: SPCK, 1984) 65-73.

——, *Theologie des Alten Testaments*, 3 parts in 2 vols. (Stuttgart: Ehrenfried Klotz Verlag; Göttingen: Vandenhoeck & Ruprecht, Part 1, 5th ed. 1957, Parts 2/3, 4th ed. 1961). English translation: *Theology of the Old Testament*, 2 vols. (OTL; London: SCM, 1961-7).

Eissfeldt, O., "Der Gott des Tabor und seine Verbreitung" *ARW* 31 (1934) 14-41.

——, *Das Lied Moses Deuteronomium 32, 1-43, und das Lehrgedicht Asaphs, Psalm 78, samt einer Analyse der Umgebung des Mose-Liedes* (Berichte über die Verhandlungen der Sächsischen Akademie der Wissenschaften zu Leipzig. Philologisch-historische Klasse. Band. 104, Heft 5; Berlin: Akademie Verlag, 1958).

——, *Kleine Schriften* (Dritter Band; Tübingen: J. C. B. Mohr [Paul Siebeck], 1966).

Elliger, K., and W. Rudolph (edd.), *Biblia Hebraica Stuttgartensia* (Stuttgart: Deutsche Bibelgesellschaft, 4th ed. 1990).

Emerton, J. A., "'Spring and Torrent' in Psalm LXXIV 15" in G. W. Anderson, P. H. A. de Boer et al. (edd.), *Volume du Congrès: Genève 1965* (VT[S] 15; Leiden: E. J. Brill, 1966) 122-133.

Engnell, I., *Studies in Divine Kingship in the Ancient Near East* (Uppsala: Almqvist & Wiksell, 1943).

Ewald, G. H. A. von, *Die Dichter des Alten Bundes erklärt. Zweiter Theil. Die Psalmen* (Göttingen: Vandenhoeck & Ruprecht, 2nd ed. 1840). English translation: *Commentary on the Poetical Books of the Old Testament. Division I. Commentary on the Psalms*, 2 vols. (Theological Translation Fund Library 23, 24; London & Edinburgh: Williams and Norgate, 1880-1881).

——, *Die Dichter des alten Bundes erklärt. Dritter Theil. Das Buch Ijob übersezt und erklärt* (Göttingen: Vandenhoeck & Ruprecht, 1854). English translation: *Commentary of the Book of Job with Translation* (Theological Translation Fund Library 28; London and Edinburgh: Williams & Norgate, 1882).

Fenton, T., "Differing Approaches to the Theomachy Myth in Old Testament Writing" in Y. Avishur, and J. Blau (edd.), *Studies in the Bible and the Ancient Near East: Presented to Samuel Loewenstamm on his Seventieth Birthday*, 2 vols. (Jerusalem: E. Rubinstein's Publishing House, 1978), I, 337-381 [Hebrew], English summary, Vol. II, 191-192.

——, "Chaos in the Bible? Tohu vavohu" in G. Abramson, and T. Parfitt (edd.), *Jewish Education and Learning: Published in Honour of Dr. David Patterson on the Occasion of his Seventieth Birthday* (London: Harwood Academic Publishers, 1993).

——, "Nexus and Significance: Is Greater Precision Possible?" in G. J. Brooke, A. H. W. Curtis, and J. F. Healey (edd.), *Ugarit and the Bible: Proceedings of the International Symposium on Ugarit and the Bible.*

Manchester, September 1992 (UBL 11; Münster: Ugarit-Verlag, 1994) 71-91.

——, "Baal au foudre: of Snakes and Mountains, Myths and Message" in N. Wyatt, W. G. E. Watson, and J. B. Lloyd (edd.), *Ugarit, Religion and Culture: Proceedings of the International Colloquium on Ugarit, Religion and Culture: Edinburgh, July 1994; Essays Presented in Honour of Professor John C. L. Gibson* (UBL 12; Münster: Ugarit-Verlag, 1996) 49-64.

Field, F., *Origenis Hexaplorum quae supersunt; sive Veterum interpretum graecorum in totum Vetus Testamentum fragmenta: post flaminium nobilium, drusium, et montefalconium, adhibita etiam versione Syro-hexaplari, concinnavit, emendavit, et multis partibus auxit*, II (Oxford: Clarendon, 1875).

Fishbane, M., "Jeremiah 4:23-26 and Job 3:1-13: A Recovered Use of the Creation Pattern", *VT* 21 (1971) 151-167.

Fischer, J., *Das Buch Isaias übersetzt und erklärt*, 2 vols. (HSAT VII, 1, 1-2; Bonn: Peter Hanstein Verlagsbuchhandlung, 1937).

Fisher, L. R., "Creation at Ugarit and in the Old Testament" *VT* 15 (1965) 313-324.

Fohrer, G., *Das Buch Hiob* (Kommentar zum Alten Testament 16; Gütersloh: Gütersloher Verlagshaus Gerd Mohn, 1963).

——, *Das Buch Jesaja*, Vols. 2 and 3 (Zürcher Bibelkommentare; Zürich: Zwingli Verlag, 1964).

Forsyth, N., *The Old Enemy: Satan and the Combat Myth* (Princeton, NJ: Princeton University Press, 1987).

Frankfort, H., *Kingship and the Gods: A Study in Ancient Near Eastern Religion as the Integration of Society and Nature* (Chicago, IL: University of Chicago Press, 1948).

Freedman, D. N., "The Structure of Job 3", *Biblica* 49 (1968) 503-508.

——, *Pottery, Poetry, and Prophecy: Studies in Early Hebrew Poetry* (Winona Lake, IN: Eisenbrauns, 1980).

——, "Acrostic Poems in the Hebrew Bible: Alphabetic and Otherwise" *CBQ* 48 (1986) 408-431.

Freedman, D. N., and C. F. Hyland, "Psalm 29: A Structural Analysis" *HTR* 66 (1973) 237-256.

Fretheim, T. E., *Exodus* (Interpretation; Louisville, KY: John Knox, 1991).

Fuchs, G., *Mythos und Hiobdichtung: Aufnahme und Umdeutung altorientalischer Vorstellungen* (Stuttgart: Kohlhammer, 1993).

Gaster, T. H., *Divine Kingship in the Ancient Near East: a Review Article* (The Review of Religion [offprint], March 1945; New York: Columbia University Press, 1945).

——, “Psalm 29” *JQR* 37 (1946/47) 55-65.

——, *Thespis: Ritual, Myth and Drama in the Ancient Near East* (New York: Doubleday Anchor, 2nd ed. 1961).

——, “Chaos”, *IDB* I (Nashville, TN: Abingdon Press, 1962) 552.

——, “Cosmogony”, *IDB* I (Nashville, TN: Abingdon Press, 1962) 706.

——, “Dead, Abode of the”, *IDB* I (Nashville, TN: Abingdon Press, 1962) 787-788.

——, *Myth, Legend, and Custom in the Old Testament: A Comparative Study with Chapters from Sir James G. Frazer’s* Folklore in the Old Testament (London: Duckworth, 1969; New York: Harper & Row, 1975).

Gelb, I. J., et al. (edd.), *The Assyrian Dictionary of the Oriental Institute of the University of Chicago* (Chicago, IL: The Oriental Institute, Chicago; Glückstadt: J. J. Augustin Verlagsbuchhandlung, 1956-).

Gelston, A. G., “A note on יהוה מלך” *VT* 16 (1966) 507-512.

Gelander, S., *The Good Creator: Literature and Theology in Genesis 1-11* (South Florida Studies in the History of Judaism 147; Atlanta, GA: Scholars Press, 1997).

Gerstenberger, E. S., *Der Bittende Mensch: Bittritual und Klagelied der Einzelnen im Alten Testament* (WMANT 51; Neukirchen-Vluyn: Neukirchener Verlag, 1980).

——, *Psalms, Part 1 with an Introduction to Cultic Poetry* (FOTL 14; Grand Rapids, MI: Eerdmans, 1988).

Gerstenberger, E. S., *Psalms, Part 2, and Lamentations* (FOTL 15; Grand Rapids, MI: Eerdmans, 2001).

Gevirtz, S., “Curse”, *IDB* I (Nashville, TN: Abingdon Press, 1962) 749-750.

Gibson, J. C. L., *Canaanite Myths and Legends* (Edinburgh: T. & T. Clark, 2nd ed. 1978).

——, *Davidson’s Introductory Hebrew Grammar*: *Syntax* (Edinburgh: T. & T. Clark, 4th ed. 1994).

——, “The Kingship of Yahweh against its Canaanite Background” in G. J. Brooke, A. H. W. Curtis and J. F Healey (edd.), *Ugarit and the Bible:*

Proceedings of the International Symposium on Ugarit and the Bible. Manchester, September 1992 (UBL 11; Münster: Ugarit-Verlag, 1994) 101-112.

Gillingham, S. E., *The Poems and Psalms of the Hebrew Bible* (Oxford Bible Series; Oxford: OUP, 1994).

——, "Psalmody and Apocalyptic in the Hebrew Bible: Common Vision, Shared Experience" in J. Barton, and D. J. Reimer (edd.), *After the Exile: Essays in Honour of Rex Mason* (Macon, GA: Mercer University Press, 1996) 147-169.

Ginsberg, H. L., "A Phoenician Hymn in the Psalter" in International Congress of Orientalists, (edd.) *Atti del XIX Congresso Internazionale degli Orientalisti: Roma, 23-29 settembre 1935 - XIII* (Rome: Tipografia del Senato, G. Bardi, 1935) 472-476.

——, "A Ugaritic Parallel to 2 Sam. 1 21" *JBL* 57 (1938) 209-213.

——,"The arm of YHWH in Isaiah 51-63 and the text of Isa 53 10-11", *JBL* 77 (1958) 152-6.

Girard, M., *Les Psaumes redécouverts de la structure au sens*, 3 vols. (Quebec, Canada: Bellarmin, Vol. 1 2nd ed.1996, Vols. 2 and 3, 1st ed. 1994).

Glueck, N., *Das Wort Ḥesed in alttestamentlichen Sprachgebrauche als menschliche und göttliche gemeinschaftgemäße Verhaltungsweise* (BZAW 47; Giessen: Alfred Töpelmann, 1927).

Good, E. M., *In Turns of Tempest: A Reading of Job with a Translation* (Stanford, CA: Stanford University Press, 1990).

Gordis, R., "The Asseverative Kaph in Ugaritic and Hebrew", *JAOS* 63 (1943) 176-178.

——, *The Book of God and Man: A Study of Job* (Chicago, IL: University of Chicago Press, 1965).

——, *The Book of Job: Commentary, New Translation and Special Studies* (Moreshet 2; New York: The Jewish Theological Seminary of America, 1978).

Gordon, C. H., "Leviathan: Symbol of Evil" in A. Altman (ed.) *Biblical Motifs* (Cambridge, MS: Harvard University Press, 1966) 1-10.

——, *Ugaritic Textbook* (Analecta Orientalia 38; Rome: Pontifical Biblical Institute, 1969).

Gordon, C. H, and G. A. Rendsburg, *The Bible and the Ancient Near East* (New York & London: W. W. Norton & Co., 4th ed. 1997) [previous editions having been entitled *Introduction to Old Testament Times*, 1953; *The World of the Old Testament*, 1958; and *The Ancient Near East*, 1965].

Görg, M., "'Chaos' und 'Chaosmächte' im Alten Testament" *BN* 70 (1993) 48-61.

Gottwald, N. K., "Poetry, Hebrew, *IDB* III (Nashville, TN: Abingdon Press, 1962) 829-838.

Goulder, M. D., *The Psalms of the Sons of Korah* (JSOT[S] 20; Sheffield: JSOT, 1982).

——, *The Prayers of David (Psalms 51-72): Studies in the Psalter, II* (JSOT[S] 102; Sheffield: Sheffield Academic Press, 1990).

——, *The Psalms of Asaph and the Pentateuch: Studies in the Psalter, III* (JSOT[S] 233; Sheffield: Sheffield Academic Press, 1996).

——, *The Psalms of the Return (Book V, Psalms 107-150)* (JSOT[S] 258; Sheffield: Sheffield Academic Press, 1998).

Grabbe, L., *Comparative Philology and the Text of Job: A Study in Methodology* (SBLDS 34; Missoula, MT: Scholars Press, 1977).

Grätz, H., *Kritischer Commentar zu den Psalmen nebst Text und Übersetzung*, 2 vols. (Breslau: S. Schottlaender, 1882-3).

Gray, G. B., *A Critical and Exegetical Commentary on The Book of Isaiah I-XXVII* (ICC; Edinburgh: T. & T. Clark, 1912).

Gray, J., "The Hebrew Conception of the Kingship of God: its Origin and Development" *VT* 6 (1956) 268-85.

——, "The Kingship of God in the Prophets and Psalms" *VT* 11 (1961) 1-29.

——, *I and II Kings* (OTL; London: SCM, 1964).

——, *The Legacy of Canaan: The Ras Shamra Texts and their Relevance to the Old Testament* (VT[S] 5; Leiden: E. J. Brill, 2nd ed.1965).

——, "The Book of Job in the Context of Near Eastern Literature", *ZAW* 82 (1970) 251-269.

——, "A Cantata of the Autumn Festival: Psalm LXVIII" *JSS* 22 (1977) 2-26.

——, *The Biblical Doctrine of the Reign of God* (Edinburgh: T. & T. Clark, 1979).

Greenfield, J. C., "*'attā pōrartā bĕ'ozkā yam* [Ps. 74:13a]" in S. E. Balentine, and J. Barton (edd.), *Language, Theology, and the Bible: Essays in Honour of James Barr* (Oxford: Clarendon, 1994) 113-119.

——, "The Hebrew Bible and Canaanite Literature" in R. Alter and F. Kermode (edd.), *The Literary Guide to the Bible* (London: Fontana, 1997) 545-60.

Grønbæk, J. H., "Baal's Battle with Yam—A Canaanite Creation Fight" *JSOT* 33 (1985) 27-44.

Groß, H., *Ijob* (Die Neue Echter Bibel: Kommentar zum Alten Testament mit der Einheitsübersetzung 13; Würzburg: Echter, 1986).

Gruber, M. I., (trans.), *Rashi's Commentary on Psalms 1-89 (Books I-III) With English Translation, Introduction and Notes* (South Florida Studies in the History of Judaism 161; Atlanta, GA: Scholars Press, 1998).

Guillaume, A., "The Arabic Background of the Book of Job" in F. F. Bruce (ed.) *Promise and Fulfilment: Essays Presented to Professor S. H. Hooke in Celebration of his Ninetieth Birthday* (Edinburgh: T. & T. Clark, 1963)106-127.

——, *Studies in the Book of Job with a New Translation* (Supplement II to the Annual of Leeds University Oriental Society; Leiden: E. J. Brill, 1968).

Gunkel, H., *Schöpfung und Chaos in Urzeit und Endzeit: eine religionsgeschichtliche Untersuchung über Gen 1 und Ap Joh 12* (Göttingen: Vandenhoeck & Ruprecht, 1895).

——, *Ausgewählte Psalmen übersetzt und erklärt* (Göttingen: Vandenhoeck & Ruprecht, 1904).

——, *Die Psalmen* (Göttinger Handkommentar zum Alten Testament II, 2; Göttingen: Vandenhoeck & Ruprecht, 4th ed. 1926).

——, *Das Märchen im Alten Testament* (Religionsgeschichtliche Volksbücher für die deutsche christliche Gegenwart, 2nd Series: Die Religion des Alten Testaments 23/26; Tübingen: J. C. B. Mohr [Paul Siebeck], 1917).

——, "The 'Historical Movement' in the Study of Religion" *ExpT* 38 (1927) 532-536.

Gunkel, H., and J. Begrich, *Einleitung in die Psalmen: die Gattungen der religiösen Lyrik Israels*, 2 vols. (Göttinger Handkommentar zum Alten Testament; Göttingen: Vandenhoeck & Ruprecht, 1928-33).

Habel, N. C., *Yahweh versus Baal. A Conflict of Religious Cultures: A Study in the Relevance of Ugaritic Materials for the Early Faith of Israel* (New York: Bookman Associates, 1964).

——, "'Yahweh, Maker of Heaven and Earth': A Study in Tradition Criticism" *JBL* 91 (1972) 321-337.

——, "'He Who Stretches out the Heavens'" *CBQ* 34 (1972) 417-430.

——, *The Book of Job: A Commentary* (OTL; London: SCM, 1985).

——, "The verdict on/of God at the End of Job" in E. van Wolde (ed.) *Job's God* (Concilium 2004/4; London: SCM, 2004).

Haglund, E., *Historical Motifs in the Psalms* (CBOT 23; Lund: C.W.K. Gleerup, 1984).

Halévy, J., *Documents Religieux de l'Assyrie et de la Babylonie* (Paris: Maisonneuve, 1882).

Hamilton, V. P., *The Book of Genesis Chapters 1-17* (Grand Rapids, MI: Eerdmans, 1990).

Hammond, N. G. L., and H. H. Scullard (edd.), *The Oxford Classical Dictionary* (Oxford: Clarendon, 2nd ed., 1970).

Handy, L. K., *Among the Host of Heaven: The Syro-Palestinian Pantheon as Bureaucracy* (Winona Lake, IN: Eisenbrauns, 1994).

Hartley, J. E., *The Book of Job* (NICOT; Grand Rapids, MI: Eerdmans, 1988).

——, "1721 גער" in W. VanGemeren (ed.), *NIDOTTE*, I (Carlisle: Paternoster, 1997) 884-887.

Hauge, M. R., *Between Sheol and Temple: Motif Structure and Function within the I-Psalms* (JSOT[S] 178; Sheffield: Sheffield Academic Press, 1995).

Hayes, J. H., and S. A. Irvine, *Isaiah the Eighth Century Prophet: his Times and his Preaching* (Nashville, TN: Abingdon, 1987).

Heidel, A., *The Babylonian Genesis: The Story of the Creation* (Phoenix Books; Chicago, IL: University of Chicago Press, 2nd ed. 1951).

Heim, K. M., "The (God-) Forsaken King of Psalm 89: A Historical and Intertextual Enquiry" in J. Day (ed.) *King and Messiah in Israel and the Ancient Near East: Proceedings of the Oxford Old Testament Seminar* (JSOT[S] 270; Sheffield: Sheffield Academic Press, 1998).

Held, M., "The *YQTL-QTL* (*QTL-YQTL*) Sequence of Identical Verbs in Biblical Hebrew and in Ugaritic" in M. Ben-Horin, B. D. Weinryb and S. Zeitlin (edd.), *Studies and Essays in Honor of Abraham A. Neuman. President, Dropsie College for Hebrew and Cognate Learning, Philadelphia* (Leiden: E. J. Brill for the Dropsie College, Philadelphia, 1962) 281- 290.

——, "Rhetorical Questions in Ugaritic and Biblical Hebrew" *Eretz-Israel* 9 (1969) 71-79.

Hempel, J., "Hermann Gunkels Bücher und Schriften" in H. Schmidt (ed.) *ΕΥΧΑΡΙΣΤΗΡΙΟΝ, Studien zur Religion und Literatur des Alten und Neuen Testaments, Herman Gunkel zum 60. Geburtstage, dem 23. Mai 1922 dargebracht von seinen Schülern und Freunden...* Vol. 2: zur Religion und Literatur des Neuen Testaments (Forschungen zur Religion und Literatur des Alten und Neuen Testaments 36 [neue Folge 19]; Göttingen: Vandenhoeck & Ruprecht, 1923) 214-225.

——, "Hallelujah", *IDB* II (Nashville, TN: Abingdon Press, 1962) 514-5.

——, "Psalms, Book of", *IDB* III (Nashville, TN: Abingdon Press, 1962) 942-958.

Hendel, R. S., *The Text of Genesis 1-11: Textual Studies and Critical Edition* Oxford: OUP, 1998).

Herder, J. G. von, *Vom Geist der Ebräischen Poesie: Eine Einleitung Für die Libehaber derselben und der ältesten Geschichte des menschlichen Geistes*, Vol. 1 (Leipzig: Johann Ambrosius Barth, 3rd ed. 1825). English translation: *The Spirit of Hebrew Poetry*, Vol. 1 (Burlington: Edward Smith, 1833).

——, *Against Pure Reason: Writings on Religion, Language, and History* (translated, edited, and with an introduction by M. Bunge; Fortress Texts in Modern Theology; Minneapolis, MN: Fortress, 1992).

Herdner, A., *Corpus des tablettes en cunéiformes alphabétiques découvertes à Ras Shamra-Ugarit de 1929 à 1939* (Bibliothèque archéologique et historique 79; Mission de Ras Shamra 10; Paris: Imprimerie Nationale, 1963).

Hermann, W., "Wann wurde Jahwe zum Schöpfer der Welt?" *UF* 23 (1991) 165-180.

Herodotus, *Historiae* (Oxford: Clarendon, 3rd ed., 1927). (English translation: *The Histories* [Harmondsworth: Penguin, 1954])

Hertlein, E., "Rahab" *ZAW* 38 (1919/20) 113-154.

Hess, R. S., "One Hundred and Fifty Years of Comparative Studies on Genesis 1-11: An Overview" in R. S. Hess, and D. T. Tsumura (edd.), *I Studied Inscriptions from Before the Flood: Ancient Near Eastern, Literary, and Linguistic Approaches to Genesis 1-11* (Sources for Biblical and Theological Study 4; Winona Lake, IN: Eisenbrauns, 1994) 3-26.

Hess, R. S., and G. J. Wenham (edd.), *Zion, City of Our God* (Cambridge & Grand Rapids, MI: Eerdmans, 1999).

Hieronymus, *Presbyteri Opera: Pars I: Opera Exegetica. 2 Commentariorum in Esaiam, Libri I-XI* (Corpus Christanorum, Series Latina LXXIII; Turnholti: Brepols, 1963).

Hillers, D. R., "Ritual Procession of the Ark and Ps 132" *CBQ* 30 (1968) 48-55.

——, "A Study of Psalm 148" *CBQ* 40 (1978) 323-334.

Hoffmann, G. E., *Hiob* (Kiel: C. F. Haeseler, 1891).

Hoffman, Y., *A Blemished Perfection: The Book of Job in Context* (JSOT[S] 213; Sheffield: Sheffield Academic Press, 1996).

Holmgren, F., "Chiastic Structure in Isaiah LI 1-11", *VT* 19 (1969) 196-201.

Hooke, S. H., (ed.), *Myth and Ritual: Essays on the Myth and Ritual of the Hebrews in relation to the Culture Pattern of the Ancient East by A. M. Blackman, C. J. Gadd, F. J. Hollis, S. H. Hooke, E. O. James, W. O. E. Oesterley, T. H. Robinson* (London: OUP, 1933).

——, *The Labyrinth: Further Studies in the Relation Between Myth and Ritual in the Ancient World* (London: SPCK; New York: Macmillan, 1935).

Horst, F., *Hiob*, Vol. 1 (BKAT 16/1; Neukirchen-Vluyn: Neukirchener Verlag, 1968).

Hossfeld, F.-L., and E. Zenger, *Die Psalmen: Psalm 1-50* (Die Neue Echter Bibel: Kommentar zum Alten Testament mit der Einheitsübersetzung 29; Würzburg: Echter Verlag, 1993).

——, *Psalmen 51-100* (HThKAT; Freiburg: Herder, 2000).

Howard, D. M., Jr., *The Structure of Psalms 93-100* (Biblical and Judaic Studies from the University of California, San Diego 5; Winona Lake, IN: Eisenbrauns, 1997).

Howard, V., "Psalm 104" *Int* 46 (1992) 176-180.

Hrozný, F., *Sumerisch-babylonische Mythen von dem Gotte Ninrag (Ninib) herausgegeben, umschrieben, übersetzt und erklärt* (Mitteilungen der Vorderasiatischen Gesellschaft 1903.5, 8 Jahrgang; Berlin: Wolf Peiser, 1903).

Huber, F., *Jahwe, Juda und die anderen Völker beim Propheten Jesaja* (BZAW 137; Berlin: de Gruyter, 1967).

Humbert, P., "'Qânâ' en Hébreu Biblique" in W. Baumgartner, O. Eissfeldt et al. (edd.), *Festschrift Alfred Bertholet zum 80. Geburtstag gewidmet von Kollegen und Freunden* (Tübingen: J. C. B. Mohr [Paul Siebeck], 1950) 259-266.

——, "La relation de Genèse 1 et du Psaume 104 avec la liturgie du Nouvel-An israélite" *RHPR* 15 (1953) 1-27.

Hunter, A. G., *Psalms* (Old Testament Readings; London & New York: Routledge, 1999).

Hunter, J., "Theophany Verses in the Hebrew Psalms" *Old Testament Essays* 11/2 (1998) 225-270.

Hurvitz, A., "The Chronological Significance of Aramaisms in Biblical Hebrew", *IEJ* 18 (1968) 234-40.

Innes, M. M. (trans.), *The Metamorphoses of Ovid* (Harmondsworth, Middx.: Penguin, 1955).

Isbell, C. D., *Corpus of the Aramaic Incantation Bowls* (SBLDS 17; Missoula, MT: Scholars Press, 1975).

Jacobsen, T., "The Battle between Marduk and Tiamat" *JAOS* 88 (1968) 104-8.

Jaki, S. L., *Genesis 1-11 through the Ages* (London: Thomas More Press, 1992).

Jefferson, H. G., "Psalm LXXVII" *VT* 13 (1963) 87-91.

Jeremias, J., *Theophanie: Die Geschichte einer alttestamentlichen Gattung* (WMANT 10; Neukirchen-Vluyn: Neukirchener Verlag, 1965).

——, *Kultprophetie und Gerichtsverkündigung in der späten Königszeit*

——, *Israels* (WMANT 35; Neukirchen-Vluyn: Neukirchener Verlag, 1976).

——, *Das Königtum Gottes in den Psalmen: Israels Begegnung mit dem kanaanäischen Mythos in den Jahwe-König-Psalmen* (Forschungen zur Religion und Literatur des Alten und Neuen Testaments 141; Göttingen: Vandenhoeck & Ruprecht, 1987).

——, *Der Prophet Amos* (Das Alte Testament Deutsch; Göttingen: Vandenhoeck & Ruprecht, 1995). English translation: *The Book of Amos* (OTL; Louisville, KY: Westminster John Knox, 1998).

——, "Die Erde 'wankt'", in R. Kessler *et al.* [edd.], "*Ihr Völker alle, klatscht in die Hände!": Festschrift für Erhard S. Gerstenberger zum 65. Geburtstag* (Münster: LIT Verlag, 1997) 166-180.

Jewish Publication Society of America (ed.), *The Book of Psalms: ספר תהלים: A New Translation According to the Traditional Hebrew Text* (Philadelphia, PA: Jewish Publication Society of America, 1972).

——, *JPS Hebrew-English Tanak: The Traditional Hebrew Text and the New JPS Translation—Second Edition* (Philadelphia: JPS, 1999).

Johnson, A. R., *The Cultic Prophet in Ancient Israel* (Cardiff: University of Wales Press, 2nd ed. 1962).

——, *The Vitality of the Individual in the Thought of Ancient Israel* (Cardiff: University of Wales Press, 2nd ed. 1964).

——, *Sacral Kingship in Ancient Israel* (Cardiff: University of Wales Press, 2nd ed. 1967).

——, *The Cultic Prophet and Israel's Psalmody* (Cardiff: University of Wales Press, 1979).

Johnson, D. G., *From Chaos to Restoration: an Integrative Reading of Isaiah 24-27* (JSOT[S] 61; Sheffield: JSOT, 1988).

Johnstone, W., *Exodus* (OTG; Sheffield: JSOT, 1990).

Joüon, P., "Notes de lexicographie hébraique" *Biblica* 6 (1925) 311-21.

Joyce, P. M., "The Kingdom of God and the Psalms" in R. S. Barbour (ed.) *The Kingdom of God and Human Society: Essays by Members of the Scripture, Theology and Society Group* (Edinburgh: T. & T. Clark, 1993) 42-59.

Junker, H., "Die Entstehungszeit des Ps 78 und des Deuteronomiums" *Biblica* 34 (1953) 487-500.

Kaiser, O., *Die Mythische Bedeutung des Meeres in Ägypten, Ugarit und Israel* (BZAW 78; Berlin: Alfred Töpelmann, 1959).

——, *Das Buch des Propheten Jesaja, Kapitel 1-12* (Das Alte Testament Deutsch 17; Göttingen: Vandenhoeck & Ruprecht, 5th ed. 1981).

——, *Der Prophet Jesaja Kapitel 13-39 übersetzt und erklärt* (Das Alte Testament Deutsch 18; Göttingen: Vandenhoeck & Ruprecht, 1973). English translation from 5th German edition 1981: *Isaiah 1-12* (OTL; London: SCM, 1983) and from the first German edition: *Isaiah 13-39* (OTL; London: SCM, 1974).

Kapelrud, A. S., *The Ras Shamra Discoveries and the Old Testament* (Oxford: Basil Blackwell, 1965).

——, "Creation in the Ras Shamra Texts" *StTh* 34 (1980) 1-11.

Keel, O., *Jahwes Entgegnung an Ijob: Eine Deutung von Ijob 38-41 vor dem Hintergrund der zeitgenössischen Bildkunst* (Göttingen: Vandenhoeck & Ruprecht, 1978)

——, *Die Welt der altorientalischen Bildsymbolik und das Alte Testament: Am Beispiel der Psalmen* (Neukirchen: Neukirchener Verlag; Zürich: Benziger Verlag, 1972). English translation: *The Symbolism of the Biblical*

World: Ancient Near Eastern Iconography and the Book of Psalms (Winona Lake, IN: Eisenbrauns, 1997).

Keel, O., and C. Uehlinger, *Göttinnen, Götter und Gottessymbole: Neue Erkenntnisse zur Religionsgeschichte Kanaans und Israels aufgrund bislang unerschlossener ikonographischer Quellen* (Quaestiones Disputatae 134; Freiburg: Herder, 2nd ed. 1993). English translation: *Gods, Goddesses, and Images of God in Ancient Israel* (Edinburgh: T. & T. Clark, 1998).

Keet, C. C., *A Study of the Psalms of Ascents: a critical and exegetical commentary upon Psalms CXX to CXXXIV* (London: The Mitre Press, 1969).

Kessler, M., "Response to L. Alonso-Schökel" *JSOT* 1 (1976) 12-15.

——, "A Methodological Setting for Rhetorical Criticism" in D. J. A. Clines, D. M., Gunn and A. J. Hauser (edd.), *Art and Meaning: Rhetoric in Biblical Literature* (JSOT[S] 19; Sheffield: JSOT, 1982) 1-19.

Kinnier Wilson, J. V., "A Return to the Problems of Behemoth and Leviathan" *VT* 25 (1975) 1-14.

Kirk, G. S., *Myth: Its Meaning and Function in Ancient and Other Cultures* (Cambridge: CUP; Berkeley & Los Angeles, CA: University of California Press, 1970).

Kirkpatrick, A. F., *The Book of Psalms*, 3 vols. (The Cambridge Bible for Schools and Colleges; London: C. J. Clay, 1891-1901).

Kissane, E. J., *The Book of Job Translated from a Critically Revised Hebrew Text with Commentary* (Dublin: Browne & Nolan, 1939).

——, *The Book of Psalms Translated from a Critically Revised Hebrew Text with a Commentary*, 2 vols. (Dublin: Browne & Nolan, 1952-1954).

——, *The Book of Isaiah Translated from a Critically Revised Hebrew Text with Commentary*, 2 vols. (Dublin: Browne & Nolan; Vol. 1 revised ed. 1960; Vol. 2 1943).

Kittel, D. R., *Die Psalmen übersetzt und erklärt* (Kommentar zum Alten Testament 13; Leipzig: A. Deichertsche Verlagsbuchhandlung, 3rd & 4th editions 1922).

Klatt, W, *Hermann Gunkel: zu seiner Theologie der Religionsgeschichte und zur Entstehung der formgeschichtlichen Methode* (Göttingen: Vandenhoeck & Ruprecht, 1969).

Kloos, C., *Yhwh's Combat with the Sea: A Canaanite Tradition in the Religion of Ancient Israel* (Amsterdam: G. A. van Oorschot; Leiden: E. J. Brill, 1986).

Knight, G. A. F., *Isaiah 40-55: Servant Theology* (International Theological Commentary; Edinburgh: The Handsel Press; Grand Rapids, MI: Eerdmans, revised ed. 1984).

Koch, K., "Gibt es ein Vergeltungsdogma im Alten Testament?" *ZTK* 52 (1955) 1-42.

Koehler, L., and W. Baumgartner, *Hebraïsches und Aramaïsches Lexikon zum Alten Testament*, 5 vols. (revised by W. Baumgartner with the collaboration of B. Hartmann et al.; Leiden: E. J. Brill, 3rd ed. 1967-95). English translation: *The Hebrew and Aramaic Lexicon of the Old Testament*, 1-3 (revised by W. Baumgartner and J. J. Stamm; Leiden: E. J. Brill, 1994-6).

Koenen, K., *Jahwe wird kommen, zu herrschen über die Erde* (Bonner Biblische Beiträge 101; Weinheim: Beltz Athenäum, 1995).

König, E., *Die Psalmen eingeleitet, übersetzt und erklärt* (Gütersloh: C. Bertelsmann, 1927).

——, *Die moderne Babylonisierung der Bibel: in ihrer neuesten Erscheinungsform (Delitzschs "Babel und Bibel" 1921)* (Stuttgart: C. Belsersche Verlag, 1922).

Koole, J. L., *Isaiah. Part 3 Volume 2: Isaiah 49-55* (Historical Commentary on the Old Testament; Leuven: Peeters, 1998).

Korpel, M. C. A., and J. C. de Moor, *The Structure of Classical Hebrew Poetry: Isaiah 40-55* (Oudtestamentische Studiën 41; Leiden: E. J. Brill, 1998).

Kraus, H.-J., *Die Königsherrschaft Gottes im Alten Testament: Untersuchungen zu den Liedern von Jahwes Thronbesteigung* (BHT 13; Tübingen: J. C. B. Mohr [Paul Siebeck], 1951).

——, *Psalmen*, 2 vols. (BKAT 15; Neukirchen-Vluyn: Neukirchener Verlag, 2nd ed. 1961).

——, *Psalmen*, 2 vols. (BKAT 15; Neukirchen-Vluyn: Neukirchener Verlag, 6th ed. 1989). English translation from 5th German edition 1978: *Psalms: A Commentary*, 2 vols. (Minneapolis, MN: Augsburg, 1988-9).

——, *Gottesdienst in Israel: Grundriß einer Geschichte des alttestamentlichen Gottesdienstes* (Munich: Chr. Kaiser Verlag, 2nd revised ed. 1962).

——, *Theologie der Psalmen* (Biblischer Kommentar; Neukirchen-Vluyn: Neukirchener Verlag, 1979). English translation: *Theology of the Psalms* (Minneapolis, MN: Augsburg, 1986).

Kselman, J. S., "Psalm 77 and the Book of Exodus" *JANES* 15 (1983) 51-58.

——, "Psalm 146 in its Context" *CBQ* 50 (1988) 587-599.

Kubina, V., *Die Gottesreden im Buche Hiob: Ein Beitrag zur Diskussion um die Einheit von Hiob 38,1-42,6* (Freiburger Theologische Studien 115; Freiburg: Herder 1979).

Labuschagne, C. J., *The Incomparability of Yahweh in the Old Testament* (Pretoria Oriental Series 5; Leiden: E. J. Brill, 1966).

Lacocque, A., "Job and the Symbolism of Evil", *BR* 14-15 (1979-80) 7-19.

Lambert, W. G., "A New Look at the Babylonian Background of Genesis" *JTS* 16 n.s. (1965) 287-300. Reprinted with a Postscript in H.-P. Müller, *Babylonien und Israel: Historische, religiöse und sprachliche Beziehungen* (Darmstadt: Wissenschaftliche Buchgesellschaft, 1991) 94-113; and then with the first and a second Postscript (September, 1994) in R. S. Hess and D. T. Tsumura (edd.), *I Studied Inscriptions from before the Flood: Ancient Near Eastern, Literary, and Linguistic approaches to Genesis 1-11* (Sources for Biblical and Theological Study 4; Winona Lake, IN: Eisenbrauns, 1994).

——, "Babylonien und Israel", *Theologische Realenzyklopädie* 5 (1979) 67-79.

——, "Old Testament Mythology in its Ancient Near Eastern Context" in J. A. Emerton (ed.), *Congress Volume, Jerusalem 1986* (VT[S] 40; Leiden: E. J. Brill, 1988) 124-143.

Lang, B., "Job xl 18 and the 'Bones of Seth'" *VT* 30 (1980) 360-1.

Lauha, A., *Die Geschichtsmotive in den alttestamentlichen Psalmen* (Annales Academiae Scientiarum Fennicae LVI, 1; Helsinki: Druckerei A.-G. der Finnischen Literaturgesellschaft, 1945).

——, "Das Schilfmeer Motiv im Alten Testament" in G. W. Anderson et al. (edd.), *Congress Volume: Bonn 1962* (VT[S] 9; Leiden: E. J. Brill, 1963) 32-46.

Legrand, L., "La Création, triomphe cosmique de Yahvé" *Nouvelle Revue Théologique* 83 (1961) 449-470.

Leichty, E., *A Bibliography of the Cuneiform Tablets of the Kuyunjik Collection in the British Museum* (London: Trustees of the British Museum, 1964).

Lelièvre, A., "YHWH et la mer dans les psaumes" *RHPR* 56 (1976) 256-63.

Lenormant, F., *La Magie chez les Chaldéens et les Origines Accadiennes* (Paris: Maisonneuve, 1874).

Leslie, E. A., *The Psalms Translated and Interpreted in the Light of Hebrew Life and Worship* (New York & Nashville, TN: Abingdon, 1949).

Levenson, J. D., *Creation and the Persistence of Evil: the Jewish Drama of Divine Omnipotence* (San Francisco, CA: Harper & Row, 1988).

Lévêque, J., "L'Argument de la Création dans le Livre de Job" in L. Derousseaux (ed.), *La Création dans L'Orient Ancien* (Lectio Divina 127; Paris: Éditions du Cerf, 1987) 261-299.

Liddell, H. G., and R. Scott, *A Greek - English Lexicon* (Oxford: Clarendon Press, 8th ed. 1897).

Limburg, J., *Psalms* (Westminster Bible Companion; Louisville, KY: Westminster John Knox, 2000).

Lindars, B., *Judges: A New Translation and Commentary* (Edinburgh: T. & T. Clark, 1995).

Lindström, F., *God and the Origin of Evil: A Contextual Analysis of Alleged Monistic Evidence in the Old Testament* (CBOT 21; Lund: CWK Gleerup, 1983).

— —, *Suffering and Sin: Interpretations of Illness in the Individual Complaint Psalms* (CBOT 37; Stockholm: Almqvist & Wiksell, 1994).

Lipiński, E., *Les Psaumes de la Royauté de Yahvé dans l'exégèse Moderne* (Sylloge excerptorum e dissertationibus ad gradum doctoris in Sacra Theologia vel in Iure canonico consequendum conscriptis 38.3; Louvain: Publications Universitaires de Louvain, 1962).

— —, *La royauté de Yahwé dans la poésie et le culte de l'ancien Israël* (Verhandelingen van de Koninklijke Vlaamse Academie voor Wetenschappen, Letteren en schone Kunsten van België XXVII, 55; Brussels: Paleis der Academiën, 1965).

— —, *Le poème royal du Psaume LXXXIX 1-5. 20-38* (Cahiers de la Revue Biblique 6; Paris: Gabalda, 1967).

— —, "Macarismes et psaumes de congratulation" *RB* 75 [1968], 321-367.

— —, "The Goddess Aṯirat in Ancient Arabia, in Babylon and in Ugarit: Her Relation to the Moon-god and the Sun-goddess", *OLP* 3 (1972) 101-119.

Loewenstamm, S. E., "The Expanded Colon in Ugaritic and Biblical Verse" *JSS* 14(1969) 176-196.

— —, "The Ugaritic Myth of the Sea and its Biblical Counterparts" (English summary), *Eretz Israel* 9 (1969), 136.

— —, *The Evolution of the Exodus Tradition* (Jerusalem: Magnes Press, Hebrew University, 1972).

——, "The Expanded Colon Reconsidered" *UF* 7 (1975) 261-264.

Lohfink, N., *Das Siegeslied am Schilfmeer: Christliche Auseinandersetzungen mit dem Alten Testament* (Frankfurt am Main: J. Knecht, 1965). English translation: *The Christian Meaning of the Old Testament* (Milwaukee, Wisc.: The Bruce Publishing Co., 1968).

Lohfink, N., and E. Zenger, *The God of Israel and the Nations: Studies in Isaiah and the Psalms* (Collegeville, MN: Michael Glazier [The Liturgical Press], 2000). Translated from *Der Gott Israels und die Völker: Untersuchungen zum Jesajabuch und zu den Psalmen* (Stuttgarter Bibel-Studien 154; Stuttgart: Katholisches Bibelwerk, 1994).

Long, G. A, "חלל" in W. VanGemeren (ed.), *NIDOTTE*, II (Carlisle: Paternoster, 1997) 151- 152.

Loretz, O., "Ugaritisch-hebräisch in Job 3, 3-26. Zum Disput zwischen M. Dahood und J. Barr", *UF* 8 (1976) 123-127.

——, *Psalm 29: Kanaanäische El- und Baaltraditionen in jüdischer Sicht* (UBL 2; Altenberge: CIS-Verlag, 1984).

——, *Ugarit-Texte und Thronbesteigungspsalmen: die Metamorphose des Regenspenders Baal-Jahwe (Ps 24, 7-10; 29; 47; 93; 95-100 sowie Ps 77, 17-20; 114). Erweiterte Neuauflage von "Psalm 29. Kanaanische El- und Baaltraditionen in jüdischer Sicht" (UBL 2. 1984)* (UBL 7; Münster: Ugarit-Verlag, 1988).

Ludwig, T. M., "The Traditions of Establishing the Earth in Deutero-Isaiah" *JBL* 92 (1973) 345- 357.

Luyster, R., "Wind and Water: Cosmogonic Symbolism in the Old Testament" *ZAW* 93 (1981) 1- 10.

Macintosh, A. A., "A Consideration of Hebrew נער" *VT* 19 (1969) 471-9.

Macmahon, J. H., and S. D. F. Salmond (trans.), *The Writings of Hippolytus*, Vol. 1 (Ante- Nicene Christian Library, Vol. VI; Edinburgh: T. & T. Clark, 1868).

Malamat, A., "The Amorite Background of Psalm 29"*BZAW* 100 Sup. (1988) 156-160.

Margalit, B., *A Matter of "Life" and "Death": A Study of the Baal-Mot Epic (CTA 4—5—6)* (AOAT 206; Kevelaer: Butzon & Bercker; Neukirchen-Vluyn: Neukirchener Verlag, 1980).

——, "The Ugaritic Creation Myth: Fact or Fiction?" *UF* 13 (1981) 137-145.

Margulis, B., "The Canaanite Origin of Psalm 29 Reconsidered" *Biblica* 51 (1970) 332-348.

Mauch, T. M., "Aaron", *IDB* I (Nashville, TN: Abingdon Press, 1962) 1-2.

May, H. G., "Some Cosmic Connotations of Mayim Rabbîm, 'Many Waters'" *JBL* 74 (1955) 9- 21.

— —, (ed.), *Oxford Bible Atlas* (New York & Toronto: OUP, 3rd. ed. revised by J. Day, 1984).

Mayes, A. D. H., *Deuteronomy* (New Century Bible; London: Oliphants, 1979).

— —, ed.), *Text in Context: Essays by Members of the Society for Old Testament Study* (Oxford: OUP, 2000).

Mays, J. L., *Hosea* (OTL; London, SCM, 1969).

— —, *The Lord Reigns: A Theological Handbook to the Psalms* (Louisville, KY: Westminster John Knox Press, 1994).

— —, "The Centre of the Psalms" in S. E. Balentine and J. Barton (edd.), *Language, Theology, and the Bible: Essays in Honour of James Barr* (Oxford: Clarendon, 1994) 231- 246.

McCann, J. C., *A Theological Introduction to the Book of Psalms: The Psalms as Torah* (Nashville, TN: Abingdon Press, 1993).

— —, (ed.), *The Shape and Shaping of the Psalter* (JSOT[S] 159; Sheffield: JSOT, 1993).

— —, "The Book of Psalms: Introduction, Commentary, and Reflections", *NIB*, IV (Nashville, TN: Abingdon Press, 1996) 639-1280.

McCarthy, D. J., "'Creation' Motifs in Ancient Hebrew Poetry" in B. W. Anderson (ed.), *Creation in the Old Testament* (Issues in Religion and Theology 6; London: SPCK, 1984) 74-89 (a revised reprint of the article originally published in *CBQ* 29/3 [1967] 393-406 [Pt. 3, 87-100]).

— —, "Compact and Kingship: Stimuli for Hebrew Covenant Thinking" in T. Ishida (ed.) *Studies in the Period of David and Solomon and Other Essays: Papers Read at the International Symposium for Biblical Studies, Tokyo, 5-7 December, 1979* (Tokyo: Yamakawa-Shuppansha, 1982) 75-921.

McCullough, W. S., W. R. Taylor et al., "The Book of Psalms" in G. A. Buttrick et al., *The Interpreter's Bible: The Holy Scriptures in the King James and Revised Standard Versions with General Articles and Introduction, Exegesis, Exposition for Each Book of the Bible in Twelve Volumes* , 4 (New York & Nashville, TN: Abingdon Press, 1955) 1-763.

McCullough, W. S., "Jackal", *IDB* II (Nashville, TN: Abingdon Press, 1962) 781.

——, "Land Crocodile", *IDB* III (Nashville, TN: Abingdon Press, 1962) 66.

——, "Mule", *IDB* III (Nashville, TN: Abingdon Press, 1962) 456.

McCurley, F. R., *Ancient Myths and Biblical Faith: Scriptural Transformations* (Philadelphia, PA: Fortress, 1983).

McKane, W., *Studies in the Patriarchal Narratives* (Edinburgh: The Handsel Press, 1979).

——, *A Critical and Exegetical Commentary on Jeremiah*, 2 vols. (ICC; Edinburgh: T. & T. Clark, 1986-1996).

McKenzie, S. L., and M. P. Graham (edd.), *The Hebrew Bible Today: An Introduction to Critical Issues* (Louisville, KY: Westminster John Knox, 1998).

Meeks, D., "Fantastic Animals" in D. B. Radford, *The Ancient Gods Speak: A Guide to Egyptian Religion* (Oxford: OUP, 2002) 117-120.

Merx, A., *Das Gedicht von Hiob: Hebräischer Text, kritisch bearbeitet und übersetzt, nebst sachlicher und kritischer Einleitung* (Jena: Mauke's Verlag [Hermann Dufft], 1871).

Mettinger, T. N. D., "Fighting the Powers of Chaos and Hell - Towards the Biblical Portrait of God" *StTh* 39 (1985) 21-38.

——, "YHWH SABAOTH - The Heavenly King on the Cherubim Throne" in T. Ishida (ed.) *Studies in the Period of David and Solomon and Other Essays: Papers Read at the International Symposium for Biblical Studies, Tokyo, 5-7 December, 1979* (Tokyo: Yamakawa-Shuppansha, 1982) 109-138.

Michel, L. W., *The Ugaritic Texts and the Mythological Expressions in the Book of Job, Including a New Translation and Philological Notes on the Book* (Ph.D. Dissertation, University of Wisconsin, 1970).

Michel, W. L., "SLMWT, 'Deep Darkness' or 'Shadow of Death'?" *BR* 29 (1984) 5-20.

——, *Job in the Light of Northwest Semitic*, I (Biblica et Orientalia 42; Rome: Biblical Institute Pres, 1987).

Milik, J. T., "Fragment d'une source du Psautier (4Q Ps 89) et fragments des Jubilés, du Document de Damas, d'un phylactère dans la grotte 4 de Qumran" *RB* 73 (1966) 94-106.

Millar, W. R., *Isaiah 24-27 and the Origin of Apocalyptic* (HSM 11; Missoula, MT: Scholars Press, 1976).

Miller, P. D., Jr., "Two Critical notes on Ps 68 and Dtn 33" *HTR* 57 (1964) 240-3.

——, “El the Warrior” *HTR* 60 (1967) 411-431.

——, “Ugaritic *ǴZR* and Hebrew “*ZR* II” *UF* 2 (1970) 159-175.

——, *The Divine Warrior in Early Israel* (Cambridge, MA: Harvard University Press, 1973).

——, “El, The Creator of Earth” *BASOR* 239 (1980) 43-46.

——, “Psalms and Inscriptions” in J. A. Emerton (ed.), *Congress Volume, Vienna 1980* (VT[S] 32; Leiden: E. J. Brill, 1981) 311-332.

——, *Interpreting the Psalms* (Philadelphia, PA: Fortress Press, 1986).

——, “The Sovereignty of God” in D. G. Miller (ed.), *The Hermeneutical Quest* (Allison Park, PA: Pickwick Publications, 1986) 129-44.

——, “The Theological Significance of Biblical Poetry” in S. E. Balentine and J. Barton (edd.), *Language, Theology, and the Bible: Essays in Honour of James Barr* (Oxford: Clarendon, 1994) 213-230.

Miscall, P. D., *Isaiah* (Readings: A New Biblical Commentary; Sheffield: JSOT, 1993).

——, *Reading Isaiah: Poetry and Vision* (Louisville, KY: Westminster John Knox, 2001).

Mitchell, D. C., *The Message of the Psalter: An Eschatological Programme in the Book of Psalms* (JSOT[S] 252; Sheffield: Sheffield Academic Press, 1997).

Moor, J. C. de, *The Seasonal Pattern in the Ugaritic Myth of Ba‘lu According to the Version of Ilimilku* (AOAT 16; Kevelaer: Butzon & Bercker; Neukirchen-Vluyn: Neukirchener Verlag, 1971).

——, “Some Remarks on U 5 V, no. 7 and 8 (KTU 1.100 and 1.107)” *UF* 9 (1977) 366-7.

——, (ed.), *Synchronic or Diachronic? A Debate on Method in Old Testament Exegesis* (Oudtestamentische studiën; Papers from the Ninth Joint Meeting of the “Oudtestamentisch Werkgezelschap in Nederland en België” and the British “Society for Old Testament Study”, held at Kampen, Aug. 1994; Leiden: E. J. Brill, 1995).

Moore, R. D., “The Integrity of Job”, *CBQ* 45 (1983) 17-31.

Morgan, D. F., *Wisdom in the Old Testament Traditions* (Oxford: Basil Blackwell, 1981).

Morgenstern, J., “Biblical Theophanies” *ZA* 25 (1911) 139-193, *ZA* 28 (1914) 15-60.

——, “The Sources of the Creation Story - Genesis 1:1-2:4” *AJSLL* 36 (1920) 169-212.

——, "Jerusalem - 485 B. C." *HUCA* 27 (1956) 101-79.

Motyer, J. A., *The Prophecy of Isaiah* (Leicester: Inter-Varsity Press, 1993).

Mowan, O., "Quattuor montes sacri in Ps. 89, 13?" *Verbum Domini* 41 (1963) 11-20.

Mowinckel, S., *Psalmenstudien*, 6 vols. (Oslo: J. Dybwad 1921-4).

——, *The Psalms in Israel's Worship*, 2 vols. (Oxford: Blackwell, 1962). Revised and translated from *Offersang og Sangoffer* (Oslo: Aschehoug, 1951).

——, *Der achtundsechzigste Psalm* (Avhandlinger utgitt av Det Norske Videnskaps- Akademi i Oslo. II. Historisk - Filosofisk Klasse 1953, No. 1; Oslo: I Kommisjon hos Jacob Dybwad, 1953).

——, *Real and Apparent Tricola in Hebrew Psalm Poetry* (Avhandlinger utgitt av Det Norske Videnskaps-Akademi i Oslo. II. Historisk - Filosofisk Klasse 1957. 2; Oslo: I Kommisjon Hos H. Aschehoug, 1957).

——, "G. W. Ahlström, *Psalm 89. Eine Liturgie aus dem Ritual des leidenden Königs*." *JSS* 5 (1960) 291-298.

——, "Drive and / or Ride in the Old Testament" *VT* 12 (1962) 278-299.

Muilenburg, J., Introduction and Exegesis to Isaiah, Chs. 40-66 in G. A. Buttrick (ed.), *The Interpreter's Bible*, V (Nashville, TN: Abingdon, 1956) 381-773.

Murphy, R. E., "A Consideration of the Classification 'Wisdom Psalms'" in G. W. Anderson et al. (edd.), *Congress Volume: Bonn 1962* (VT[S] 9; Leiden: E. J. Brill, 1963) 156-167.

Murray, Robert, *The Cosmic Covenant: Biblical Themes of Justice, Peace and the Integrity of Creation* (Heythrop Monographs 7; London: Sheed & Ward, 1992).

Nagel, G., "À propos des rapports du Psaume 104 avec les textes égyptiens" in W. Baumgartner, O. Eissfeldt et al. (edd.), *Festschrift Alfred Bertholet zum 80. Geburtstag gewidmet von Kollegen und Freunden* (Tübingen: J. C. B. Mohr [Paul Siebeck], 1950) 395-403.

Nam, D.-W., *Talking about God: Job 42:7-9 and the Nature of God in the Book of Job* (Studies in Biblical Literature 49; New York: Peter Lang, 2003).

Nel, P. J., "משל" in W. VanGemeren (ed.), *NIDOTTE*, II (Carlisle: Paternoster, 1997) 1136-1137.

Newsom, C. A., "The Book of Job: Introduction, Commentary, and Reflections", *NIB*, IV (Nashville, TN: Abingdon Press, 1996) 317-637.

——, *The Book of Job: A Contest of Moral Imaginations* (Oxford: OUP, 2003).

Nicholson, E. W., *The Pentateuch in the Twentieth Century: The Legacy of Julius Wellhausen* (Oxford: Clarendon, 1998).

Niditch, S., *Chaos to Cosmos: Studies in Biblical Patterns of Creation* (Scholars Press Studies in the Humanities 6; Chico, CA: Scholars Press, 1985).

——, *Oral Word and Written Word: Orality and Literacy in Ancient Israel* (London: SPCK, 1997).

Norin, S. I. L., *Er spaltete das Meer: Die Auszugsüberlieferung in Psalmen und Kult des Alten Israel* (CBOT 9; Lund: C. W. K. Gleerup, 1977).

Noth, M., *Das zweite Buch Mose: Exodus* (Das Alte Testament Deutsch 5; Göttingen: Vandenhoeck & Ruprecht, 1959). English translation including revisions for the 2nd German edition: *Exodus: A Commentary* (OTL; London: SCM, 1962).

——, *Geschichte Israels* (Göttingen: Vandenhoeck & Ruprecht, 2nd ed. 1954). English translation: *The History of Israel* (London: Adam and Charles Black, 2nd ed. 1960).

——, "Nu 21 als Glied der "Hexateuch"-Erzählung" in M. Noth, *Aufsätze zur biblischen Landes- und Altertumskunde* I (Neukirchen-Vluyn: Neukirchener Verlag, 1971) 75-101.

——, *Überlieferungsgeschichte des Pentateuch* (Stuttgart: Kohlhammer, 1948). English translation: *A History of Pentateuchal Traditions* (Scholars Press Reprint Series 5; Atlanta, GA: Scholars Press, 1981).

Notter, V., *Biblischer Schöpfungsbericht und ägyptische Schöpfungsmythen* (Studies in Biblical Theology 68; Stuttgart: Katholisches Bibelwerk, 1974).

Obermann, J., "An Antiphonal Psalm from Ras Shamra" *JBL* 55 (1936) 21-44.

Oeming, M., *Das Buch der Psalmen: Psalm 1-41* (Neuer Stuttgarter Kommentar Altes Testament 13/1; Stuttgart: Verlag Katholisches Bibelwerk, 2000).

Oesterley, W. O. E., *The Psalms Translated with Text-critical and Exegetical Notes*, 2 vols. (London: SPCK, 1939).

Olshausen, J., *Die Psalmen erklärt* (Kurzgefasstes exegetisches Handbuch zum Alten Testament 14; Leipzig: S. Hirzel, 1853).

O'Neill, J. C., *The Bible's Authority: A Portrait Gallery of Thinkers from Lessing to Bultmann* (Edinburgh: T. & T. Clark, 1991).

Oswalt, J. N., *The Book of Isaiah, Chapters 1-39* (New International Commentary on the Old Testament; Grand Rapids, MI: Eerdmans, 1986).

——, "שבח" in W. VanGemeren (ed.) *NIDOTTE*, IV (Carlisle: Paternoster, 1997) 26-27.

——, *The Book of Isaiah Chapters 40-66* (New International Commentary on the Old Testament; Grand Rapids, MI / Cambridge: William B. Eerdmans, 1998).

Otzen, B., H. Gottlieb, K. Jeppesen, *Myths in the Old Testament* (London: SCM, 1980). Translated from the Danish *Myter i Det gamle Testamente* (Copenhagen: G. E. C. Gads Forlag, 2nd ed. 1976).

Ouro, R., "The Earth of Genesis 1:2: Abiotic or Chaotic? Part 1" *Andrews University Seminary Studies* 35 (1998) 259-276.

Pardee, D., "Will the Dragon Never be Muzzled?" *UF* 16 (1984)251-5.

——, "West Semitic Canonical Compositions" in W. W. Hallo with J. L. Younger, Jr., *The Context of Scripture. I. Canonical Compositions of the Biblical World* (Leiden: E. J. Brill, 1997) 239-375.

Parker, S. B., (ed.), *Ugaritic Narrative Poetry* (SBLWAW 9; Atlanta, GA: Scholars Press, 1997).

Parkinson, R. B., *The Tale of Sinuhe and other Ancient Egyptian Poems 1940-1640 BC. Translated with Introduction and Notes* (Oxford: Clarendon, 1997).

Patton, J. H., *Canaanite Parallels in the Book of Psalms* (Baltimore, MD: John Hopkins, 1944).

Pelikan, J., (ed.), *Luther's Works: Vol. 1. Lectures on Genesis Chapters 1-5* (Saint Louis, MO: Concordia, 1958).

Pelt, M. V. van, and W. C. Kaiser, "ירא" in W. VanGemeren (ed.), *NIDOTTE*, II (Carlisle: Paternoster, 1997) 527-533.

Perdue, L. G., *Wisdom in Revolt: Metaphorical Theology in the Book of Job* (JSOT[S] 112, Bible and Literature Series 29; Sheffield: JSOT [Almond], 1991).

Perdue, L. G., et al., *Families in Ancient Israel* (The Family, Religion and Culture; Louisville, KY: Westminster John Knox Press, 1997).

Perry, T. A., "A Poetics of Absence: The Structure and Meaning of Genesis 1.2" *JSOT* 58 (1993) 3-11.

Petersen, A. R., *The Royal God: Enthronement Festivals in Ancient Israel and Ugarit?* (JSOT[S] 259; Copenhagen International Seminar 5; Sheffield: Sheffield Academic Press, 1998).

Phillips, A., *Deuteronomy* (Cambridge Bible Commentary; Cambridge: CUP, 1973).

Piper, O. A., "Light, Light and Darkness", *IDB* III (Nashville, TN: Abingdon Press, 1962) 130-132.

Plato, *The Symposium* (trans. W. Hamilton; London: Penguin, 1951).

——, *Timaeus and Critias* (trans. H. D. P. Lee; London: Penguin, revised ed. 1977).

Podella, T., "Der 'Chaoskampfmythos' im Alten Testament: Eine Problemanzeige" in M. Dietrich and O. Loretz, *Mesopotamica—Ugaritica—Biblica: Festschrift für Kurt Bergerhof zum Vollendung seines 70. Lebensjahres am 7. Mai 1992* (AOAT 232; Kevelaer: Butzon & Bercker; Neukirchen-Vluyn: Neukirchener Verlag, 1993) 283-329.

Polaski, D. C., *Authorizing an End: The Isaiah Apocalypse and Intertextuality* (Biblical Interpretation Series, 50; Leiden: E. J. Brill, 2001).

Polzin, R., *Biblical Structuralism: Method and Subjectivity in the Study of Ancient Texts* (Semeia Supplements; Philadelphia, PA: Fortress; Missoula, MT: Scholars, 1977).

——, *Moses and the Deuteronomist: A Literary Study of the Deuteronomic History. Part One: Deuteronomy, Joshua, Judges* (New York: Seabury, 1980).

Pope, M. H., *El in the Ugaritic Texts* (VT[S] 2: Leiden: E. J. Brill, 1955).

——, *Job: A New Translation with Introduction and Commentary* (Anchor Bible 15; New York: Doubleday, 3rd ed. 1973).

Prévost, J.-P., *Petit Dictionnaire des Psaumes* (Cahier Evangile 71; Paris: Éditions du Cerf, 1990).

Pritchard, J. B., *The Ancient Near East in Pictures Relating to the Old Testament* (Princeton, NJ: Princeton University Press, 1954).

——, (ed.), *Ancient Near Eastern Texts Relating to the Old Testament* (Princeton, NJ: Princeton University Press, 3rd ed. with Supplement, 1969).

Propp, W. C., *Exodus 1-18: A New Translation and Commentary* (Anchor Bible; New York: Doubleday, 1998).

Pyeon, Y., *You Have Not Spoken What Is Right About Me: Intertextuality and the Book of Job* (Studies in Biblical Literature 45; New York: Peter Lang, 2003).

Quinn-Miscall, P. D., see P Miscall.

Rad, G. von, "מַלְאָךְ im AT" in G. Kittel (ed.), *Theologisches Wörterbuch zum Neuen Testament*, I (Stuttgart: W. Kohlhammer, 1932) 75-79.

——, "Das Theologische Problem des alttestamentlichen Schöpfungsglaubens" in P. Volz, F. Stummer, and J. Hempel (edd.), *Werden und Wesen des Alten Testaments: Vorträge gehalten auf der internationalen Tagung Alttestamentlicher Forscher zu Göttingen vom 4.-10. September 1935* (BZAW 66; Berlin: Alfred Töpelmann, 1936) 138-147; reprinted in G. von Rad, *Gesammelte Studien zum Alten Testament* (Theologische Bücherei Neudrucke und Berichte aus dem 20. Jahrhundert 8; Munich: Chr. Kaiser Verlag, 1958) 136-147. English translation: "The Theological Problem of the Old Testament Doctrine of Creation" in B. W. Anderson (ed.), *Creation in the Old Testament* (Issues in Religion and Theology 6; London: SPCK, 1984) 53-73.

——, *Das formgeschichtliche Problem des Hexateuch* (Beiträge zur Wissenschaft vom Alten und Neuen Testament, 4th Series 26; Stuttgart: W. Kohlhammer, 1938) 1-72; reprinted in G. von Rad, *Gesammelte Studien zum Alten Testament* (Theologische Bücherei Neudrucke und Berichte aus dem 20. Jahrhundert 8, Altes Testament; Munich: Chr. Kaiser Verlag, 1958) 9-86. English translation: "The Form-Critical Problem of the Hexateuch" in G. von Rad, *The Problem of the Hexateuch and Other Essays* (Edinburgh and London: Oliver & Boyd, 1984) 1-78.

——, "Das Judäische Königsritual" *Theologische Literaturzeitung* 72 (1947) 211-216; reprinted in G. von Rad, *Gesammelte Studien zum Alten Testament* (Theologische Bücherei Neudrucke und Berichte aus dem 20. Jahrhundert 8, Altes Testament; Munich: Chr. Kaiser Verlag, 1958) 205-213. English translation: "The Royal Ritual in Judah" in G. von Rad, *The Problem of the Hexateuch and Other Essays* (Edinburgh and London: Oliver & Boyd, 1966) 222-231.

——, *Theologie des Alten Testaments,* 2 vols. (Munich: Chr. Kaiser Verlag, 1957-1960). English translation: *Old Testament Theology*, 2 vols. (London: SCM, 1975).

——, *Das erste Buch Mose: Genesis* (Das Alte Testament Deutsch 2/4; Göttingen: Vandenhoeck & Ruprecht, 5th ed. 1958).

——, "Hiob xxxviii und die altägyptische Weisheit" in M. Noth, and D. W. Thomas (edd.), *Wisdom in Israel and in the Ancient Near East* (VT[S] 3; Leiden: E. J. Brill, 1960) 293-301.

——, *Das fünfte Buch Mose: Deuteronomium* (Das Alte Testament Deutsch 8; Göttingen: Vandenhoeck & Ruprecht, 1964). English translation: *Deuteronomy* (OTL; London: SCM, 1966).

——, *Weisheit in Israel* (Neukirchen-Vluyn: Neukirchener Verlag, 1970). English translation: *Wisdom in Israel* (Nashville, TN: Abingdon; London: SCM, 1972).

Rahlfs, A., (ed.), *Septuaginta: id est Vetus Testamentum Graece iuxta LXX Interpretes*, vol. II Libri poetici et prophetici (Stuttgart: Privilegierte Würtembergische Bibelanstalt, 4th ed. 1950).

Rainey, A. F., "Institutions: Family, Civil, and Military" in L. R. Fisher (ed.), *Ras Shamra Parallels: The Texts from Ugarit and the Hebrew Bible* (Analecta Orientalia 50; Rome: Pontifical Biblical Institute, 1975) II, 69-107

Reif, S. C., "A note on נער" *VT* 21(1971) 241-4.

Rendsburg, G. A., "Double Polysemy in Genesis 49:6 and Job 3:6", *CBQ* 44 (1982) 48-51.

Rendsburg, G., R. Adler, M. Arfa, N. H. Winter (edd.), *The Bible World: Essays in Honour of Cyrus H. Gordon* (New York: KTAV and the Institute of Hebrew Culture and Education of New York University, 1980).

Rendtorff, R., *Das überlieferungsgeschichtliche Problem des Pentateuch* (BZAW 17; Berlin: W. de Gruyter, 1977).

Renfroe, F., "Methodological Considerations Regarding the Use of Arabic in Ugaritic Philology" *UF* 18 (1986) 33-74.

Reuchlin, J., *De rudimentis hebraicis* ([Phorce]: Thomas Anshelm, 1506).

Reventlow, H. G., *Hauptprobleme der alttestamentlichen Theologie im 20. Jahrhundert* (Erträge der Forschung 173; Darmstadt: Wissenschaftliche Buchgesellschaft, 1982).

——, *Hauptprobleme der Biblischen Theologie im 20. Jahrhundert* (Erträge der Forschung 203; Darmstadt: Wissenschaftliche Buchgesellschaft, 1983).

Ricoeur, P., *Philosophie de la Volonté: Finitude et Culpabilité II. La Symbolique du Mal* (*Philosophie de la Volonté* Vol. 3, Philosophie de l'Esprit; Paris: Aubier, éditions montaigne, 1960). English translation: *The*

Symbolism of Evil (Religious Perspectives 17; Boston, MA: Beacon Press, 1969).

Ridderbos, N. H., "Response to L. Alonso-Schökel" *JSOT* 1 (1976) 16-21.

Rignell, G., *The Peshitta to the Book of Job Critically Investigated with Introduction, Translation, Commentary and Summary* (edited by K.-E. Rignell; Kristianstad: Monitor Förlaget, 1994).

Ringgren, H., *The Faith of the Psalmists* (London: SCM, 1963). Translated from *Psaltarens Fromhet* (Stockholm: Svenska Kyrkans Diakonistyrelses Bokförlag, 1957).

——, *Israelitische Religion* (Der Religion der Menschheit 26; Stuttgart: W. Kohlhammer, 1963).

Roberts, A., and J. Donaldson (edd.), *The Writings of Methodius, Alexander of Lycopolis, Peter of Alexandria, and Several Fragments* (Ante-Nicene Christian Library: Translations of the Writings of the Fathers down to A.D. 325, Vol. XIV; Edinburgh: T. & T. Clark, 1869).

——, *The Writings of Tertullian, Vol. III. with the Extant Works of Victorinus and Commodianus* (Ante-Nicene Christian Library: Translations of the Writings of the Fathers down to A.D. 325, Vol. XVIII; Edinburgh: T. & T. Clark, 1870).

Roberts, J. J. M., *Nahum, Habakkuk, and Zephaniah: A Commentary* (OTL; Louisville, KY: Westminster John Knox, 1991).

——, "Zion in the Theology of the Davidic-Solomonic Empire" in T. Ishida (ed.) *Studies in the Period of David and Solomon and Other Essays: Papers Read at the International Symposium for Biblical Studies, Tokyo, 5-7 December, 1979* (Tokyo: Yamakawa-Shuppansha, 1982) 93-108.

Robertson, D. A., *Linguistic Evidence in Dating Early Hebrew Poetry* (SBLDS 3; Missoula, MT: Society of Biblical Literature, 1972).

Robinson, H. W., *Deuteronomy and Joshua: Introductions, Revised Version with Notes, Maps and Index* (The Century Bible; Edinburgh: T. C. & E. C. Jack, 1907).

——, "The Council of Yahweh" *JTS* 45 (1943) 151-157.

Robinson, J. M., and H. Koester, *Trajectories through Early Christianity* (Philadelphia, PA: Fortress, 1971).

Rogers, R. W., *The Religion of Babylonia and Assyria especially in its Relations to Israel: Five Lectures delivered at Harvard University* (New York: Eaton and Maines; Cincinnati, OH: Jennings and Graham, 1908).

Rogerson, J. W., "The Hebrew Conception of Corporate Personality: A Re-examination" *JTS* 21 n.s. (1970) 1-16.

——, *Old Testament Criticism in the Nineteenth Century: England and Germany* (London: SPCK, 1984).

——, *Genesis 1-11* (OTG; Sheffield: JSOT, 1991).

——, *Anthropology and the Old Testament* (The Biblical Seminar; Sheffield: JSOT, 1984).

Rogerson, J. W., and J. W. McKay, *Psalms*, 3 vols. (Cambridge Bible Commentary; Cambridge: CUP, 1977).

Rose, H. J., "Chaos" in N. G. L. Hammond and H. H. Scullard (edd.), *Oxford Classical Dictionary* (Oxford: Clarendon Press, 2nd ed. 1970).

Rowley, H. H., *The Book of Job* (NCBC; London: Marshall, Morgan & Scott, 2nd ed. 1976).

Ruprecht, E., "Das Nilpferd im Hiobbuch: Beobachtungen zu der sogenannten zweiten Gottesrede ", *VT* 21 (1971) 209-231.

Rylaarsdam, J. C., "The Book of Exodus: Introduction and Exegesis" *Interpreter's Bible*, I (New York & Nashville, TN: Abingdon Press, 1952) 832-1099.

Sabourin, L., *The Psalms: Their Origin and Meaning* (New York: Alba House, new, enlarged, updated ed. 1970).

Saggs, H. W. F., *The Encounter with the Divine in Mesopotamia and Israel* (School of Oriental and African Studies, University of London: Jordan Lectures in Comparative Religion XII [1976]; London: Athlone Press, University of London, 1978).

——, *Babylonians* (Peoples of the Past; London: British Museum, 1995).

Sakenfeld, K. D., *The Meaning of Ḥesed in the Hebrew Bible. A New Enquiry* (HSM 17; Missoula, MT: Scholars Press, 1978).

Sanders, J. A., *The Dead Sea Psalms Scroll* (Ithaca, N.Y.: Cornell University Press, 1967).

Sarna, N. M., *Songs of the Heart: An Introduction to the Book of Psalms* (New York: Schocken, 1993).

——, "Exodus, Book of" in D. N. Freedman et al (edd.), *The Anchor Bible Dictionary* (New York: Doubleday, 1992), Vol. 2, 689-700.

——, *Exploring Exodus: The Heritage of Biblical Israel* (New York: Schocken, 1987).

Sasson, J. M., "On Relating 'Religious' Texts to the Old Testament" *MAARAV* 3/2 (1982) 217-225.

Saussure, Ferdinand de, *Cours de Linguistique Générale* (ed. Charles Bally, Albert Sechehaye, with the collaboration of Albert Riedlinger; Paris: Payot, 1922). English translation: *Course in General Linguistics*, translated and annotated by Roy Harris (London: Duckworth, 1983).

Säve-Söderbergh, T., *On Egyptian Representations of Hippopotamus Hunting as a Religious Motive* (Uppsala: Appelbergs Boktryckeri, 1953).

Savignac, J. de, "Le sens du terme Ṣâphôn" *UF* 16 (1984) 273-8.

Sayce, A. H., *Lectures on the Origin and Growth of Religion as Illustrated by the Religion of the Ancient Babylonians* (Hibbert Lectures, 1887; London: Williams & Norgate, 1887).

Schaefer, K., *Psalms* (Berit Olam. Studies in Hebrew Narrative and Poetry; Collegeville, MN: The Liturgical Press, 2001).

Scharbert, J., "Das 'Schilfmeerwunder' in den Texten des Alten Testaments" in A. Caquot, & M. Delcor (edd.), *Mélanges Bibliques et Orientaux en L'honneur de M. Henri Cazelles* (Alter Orient und Altes Testament: Veröffentlichungen zur Kultur und Geschichte des Alten Orients und des alten Testaments 212; Kevelaer: Butzon & Bercker; Neukirchen-Vluyn: Neukirchener Verlag, 1981) 419-38.

Schmidt, H., *Die Thronfahrt Jahves am Fest der Jahreswende im Alten Israel* (Sammlung Gemeinverständlicher Vorträge und Schriften aus dem Gebiet der Theologie und Religionsgeschichte 122; Tübingen: J. C. B. Mohr [Paul Siebeck], 1927).

——, *Das Gebet der Angeklagten im Alten Testament* (BZAW 49; Giessen: A. Töpelmann, 1928). Previously published (much abridged) as "Das Gebet der Angeklagten im Alten Testament" in *Old Testament Essays: Papers Read Before the Society for Old Testament Study at its 18th Meeting, Held at Keble College, Oxford, September 27th to 30th, 1927* (London: Charles Griffin, 1927) 143-156.

——, *Die Psalmen* (HAT 15; Tübingen: J. C. B. Mohr [Paul Siebeck], 1934).

Schmidt, W. H., *Königtum Gottes in Ugarit und Israel: zur Herkunft der Königsprädikation Jahwes* (BZAW 80; Berlin: Alfred Töpelmann, 1961).

——, *Die Schöpfungsgeschichte der Priesterschrift* (WMANT 17; Neukirchen-Vluyn: Neukirchener Verlag, 1964).

Scholnick, S., "The Meaning of *Mišpaṭ* in the Book of Job", *JBL* 101 (1982) 521-9.

Schoors, A., *I am God your Saviour* (VT[S] 24; Leiden: E. J. Brill, 1973).

Schrader, E., *Studien zur Kritik und Erklärung der Biblischen Urgeschichte: Gen. Cap. I-XI: Drei Abhandlungen mit einem Anhange: Die*

Urgeschichte nach dem Berichte des Annalischen und nach dem des Prophetischen Erzählers (Zurich: Meyer & Zeller, 1863).

— —, *Die Keilinschriften und das Alte Testament* (Giessen: J. Ricker, 1872).

Schunk, K.-D., "Jes 30 6-8 und die Deutung der Rahab im Alten Testament", *ZAW* 78 (1966) 48-56.

— —, "בָּמָה" in G. J. Botterweck and H. Ringgren (edd.), *Theologisches Wörterbuch zum Alten Testament*, I (Stuttgart: W. Kohlhammer, 1973) 662-7. English translation: "בָּמָה *bāmāh*" in G. J. Botterweck and H. Ringgren (edd.), *Theological Dictionary of the Old Testament*, II (Grand Rapids, MI: Eerdmans, revised ed., 1977) 139-145.

Scott, R. B. Y., Introduction and Exegesis to Isaiah, Chs. 1-39 in G. A. Buttrick (ed.), *The Interpreter's Bible*, V (Nashville, TN: Abingdon, 1956) 381-773.

Seely, F., "Note on G"RH with Especial Reference to Proverbs 13:8" *Bible Translator* 10 (1959) 20-21.

Seitz, C. R., *Isaiah 1-39* (Interpretation; Louisville, KY; John Knox, 1993).

Seybold, K., "Die Geschichte des 29. Psalms und ihre theologische Bedeutung", *ThZ* 36 [1980] 208-219.

— —, *Introducing the Psalms* (Edinburgh: T. & T. Clark, 1990). Translated from *Die Psalmen, Eine Einführung* (Stüttgart: W. Kohlhammer, 1986).

— —, *Die Psalmen* (HAT 1/15; Tübingen: J. C. B. Mohr [Paul Siebeck], 1996).

Sheppard, G. T., *Wisdom as a Hermeneutical Construct: A Study in the Sapientalizing of the Old Testament* (BZAW 151; Berlin & New York: Walter de Gruyter, 1980).

Skinner, J., *A Critical and Exegetical Commentary on Genesis* (ICC; Edinburgh: T. & T. Clark, 1930).

Smelik, K. A. D., *Writings From Ancient Israel: A Handbook of Historical and Religious Documents* (Edinburgh: T. & T. Clark, 1991). English translation from *Behouden Schrift: historische documentation uit het Oude Israël* (Baarn: Ten Have, 1984).

Smick, E., "Another Look at the Mythological Elements in the Book of Job", *Westminster Theological Journal* 40 (1978) 213-228.

Smith, G., *The Chaldean Account of Genesis Containing the Description of the Creation, the Fall of Man, the Deluge, the Tower of Babel, the Times of the Patriarchs, and Nimrod; Babylonian Fables, and Legends of the Gods; From the Cuneiform Inscriptions* (London: Sampson, Low, Marston, Searle, & Rivington, 4th ed. 1876).

Smith, G. A., *The Historical Geography of the Holy Land* (London: Hodder & Stoughton, 25th ed., 1931).

Smith, G. V., "שַׁחַץ" in W. VanGemeren (ed.) *NIDOTTE*, IV (Carlisle: Paternoster, 1997) 786-789.

Smith, G. V., and V. P. Hamilton, "גאה" in W. VanGemeren (ed.), *NIDOTTE*, I (Carlisle: Paternoster, 1997) 786-789.

Smith, J. M. P., W. H. Ward, and J. A. Bewer, *A Critical and Exegetical Commentary on Micah, Zephaniah, Nahum, Habakkuk, Obadiah and Joel* (ICC; Edinburgh: T. & T. Clark, 1911).

Smith, M. S., "Interpreting the Baal Cycle" *UF* (1986) 312-339.

——, "Mythology and Myth-making in Ugaritic and Israelite Literature" in G. J. Brooke, A. H. W. Curtis, and J. F. Healey (edd.), *Ugarit and the Bible: Proceedings of the International Symposium on Ugarit and the Bible. Manchester, September 1992* (UBL 11; Münster: Ugarit-Verlag, 1994) 293-341.

——, *The Ugaritic Baal Cycle. Volume I: Introduction with Text, Translation & Commentary of KTU 1.1-1.2* (VT[S] 55; Leiden: E. J. Brill, 1994).

——, *The Origins of Biblical Monotheism: Israel's Polytheistic Background and the Ugaritic Texts* (Oxford: OUP, 2001).

——, *The Memoirs of God: History, Memory, and the Experience of the Divine in Ancient Israel* (Minneapolis, MN: Fortress, 2004).

Snaith, N. H., "יַם־סוּף: The Sea of Reeds: The Red Sea" *VT* 15 (1965) 395-8.

——, *The Book of Job: Its Origin and Purpose* (SBT Second Series 11; London: SCM, 1968)

Sparks, H. F. D., *The Apocryphal Old Testament* (Oxford: Clarendon, 1984).

Speiser, E. A., *Genesis* (Anchor Bible 1; Garden City, NY: Doubleday, 1964).

Spieckermann, H., *Heilsgegenwart: Eine Theologie der Psalmen* (Forschungen zur Religion und Literatur des Alten und Neuen Testaments 148; Göttingen: Vandenhoeck & Ruprecht, 1989).

Stacey, D., *Isaiah 1-39* (Epworth Commentaries; London: Epworth, 1993).

Staerk, W., *Lyrik (Psalmen, Hoheslied und Verwandtes) übersetzt, erklärt und mit Einleitungen versehen* (Die Schriften des Alten Testaments 3/1; Göttingen: Vandenhoeck & Ruprecht, 2nd ed., 1920).

Starbuck, S. R. A., *Court Oracles in the Psalms: The So-called Royal Psalms in their Ancient Near Eastern Context* (SBLDS 172; Atlanta, GA: SBL, 1999).

Steck, O. H., *Der Schöpfungsbericht der Priesterschrift* (Göttingen: Vandenhoeck & Ruprecht, 1975).

— —, "Theological Streams of Tradition" in D. A. Knight (ed.) *Tradition and Theology in the Old Testament* (London: SPCK, 1977) 183-214.

Stonehouse, G. G. V., *The Book of Habakkuk: Introduction, Translation, and Notes on the Hebrew Text* (London: Rivingtons, 1911).

Stonehouse, G. G. V., and G. W. Wade, *The Books of the Prophets Zephaniah, Nahum and Habakkuk* (Westminster Commentaries; London: Methuen, 1929).

Strahan, J., *The Book of Job Interpreted* (Edinburgh: T. & T. Clark, 2nd ed. 1914).

Streibert, C., *Schöpfung bei Deuterojesaja und in der Priesterschrift: Eine vergleichende Untersuchung zu Inhalt und Funktion schöpfungs-theologischer Aussagen in exilisch-nachexilischer Zeit* (Beiträge zur Erforschung des Alten Testaments und des Antiken Judentums 8; Frankfurt am Maine: Peter Lang, 1993).

Sutcliffe, E. F., "A Note on Psalm CIV 8" *VT* 2 (1952) 177-9.

Sweeney, M. A., *Isaiah 1-39: with an Introduction to Prophetic Literature* (FOTL 16; Grand Rapids, MI & Cambridge: Eerdmans, 1996).

Talmon, S., "The 'Comparative Method' in Biblical Interpretation - Principles and Problems" in J. A. Emerton, W. L. Holladay et al. (edd.), *Congress Volume Göttingen 1977* (VT[S] 29; Leiden: E. J. Brill, 1978) 320-356.

Talstra, E., *Solomon's Prayer: Synchrony and Diachrony in the Composition of 1 Kings 8, 14-61* (Contributions to Biblical Exegesis and Theology 3; Kampen: Kok Pharos, 1993). English translation from *Het Gebed van Salomo: Synchronie en Diachronie in de Kompositie van I Kon. 8, 14-61* (Amsterdam: Amsterdam University Press, 1987).

Tate, M. E., *Psalms 51-100* (Word Biblical Commentary 20; Dallas, TX: Word, 1990).

Terrien, S., *Job* (Commentaire de l'Ancien Testament 13; Neuchatel: Éditions Delachaux & Niestlé, 1963).

— —, *The Psalms: Strophic Structure and Theological Commentary* (Eerdmans Critical Commentary; Grand Rapids, MI: Eerdmans, 2003).

Thomas, D. W., "צַלְמָוֶת in the Old Testament" *JSS* 7 (1962) 191-200.

Thompson, J. A., "Horse", *IDB*, II (Nashville, TN: Abingdon Press, 1962) 646-8.

Tournay, R., "Recherches sur la Chronologie des Psaumes" *RB* 65 (1958) 321-57.

——, *Seeing and Hearing God with the Psalms: The Prophetic Liturgy of the Second Temple in Jerusalem* (JSOT[S] 118; Sheffield: JSOT, 1991).

Trèves, M., "The Date of Psalm 24" *VT* 10 (1960) 428-437.

Tromp, N. J., *Primitive Conceptions of Death and the Nether World in the Old Testament* (Biblica et Orientalia: Sacra Scriptura Antiquitatibus Orientalibus Illustrata 21; Rome: Pontifical Biblical Institute, 1969).

Tropper, J., and E. Verreet, "Ugaritisch *ndy*, *ydy*, *hdy*, *ndd* und *d(w)d*" *UF* 20 (1988) 339-350.

Tsevat, M., *A Study of the Language of the Biblical Psalms* (JBL Monograph Series 9; Philadelphia: SBL, 1955).

Tsumura, D. T., "'The Deluge' (*mabbûl*) in Psalm 29:10", *UF* 20 (1988) 351-5.

——, *The Earth and the Waters in Genesis 1 and 2: A Linguistic Investigation* (JSOT[S] 83; Sheffield: Sheffield Academic Press, 1989).

——, "The Earth in Genesis 1" in R. S. Hess, and D. T. Tsumura (edd.), *I Studied Inscriptions from before the Flood: Ancient Near Eastern, Literary, and Linguistic approaches to Genesis 1-11* (Sources for Biblical and Theological Study 4; Winona Lake, IN: Eisenbrauns, 1994).

——, "Genesis and Ancient Near Eastern Stories of Creation and Flood: An Introduction" in R. S. Hess, and D. T. Tsumura (edd.), *I Studied Inscriptions from Before the Flood: Ancient Near Eastern, Literary, and Linguistic Approaches to Genesis 1-11* (Sources for Biblical and Theological Study 4; Winona Lake, IN: Eisenbrauns, 1994) 27-57.

Tubb, J. N., *Canaanites* (Peoples of the Past; London: British Museum, 1998).

Tur-Sinai, N. H., *The Book of Job: A New Commentary* (Jerusalem: Kiryath Sepher, revised ed. 1967).

Uehlinger, C., "Leviathan und die Schiffe in Ps 104,25-26", *Biblica* 71 (1990) 499-526.

——, "Leviathan לויתן" in K. van der Toorn, B. Becking, and P. W. van der Horst, *Dictionary of Deities and Demons in the Bible* (Leiden: E. J. Brill; Grand Rapids, MI: Eerdmans, 2nd extensively revised ed. 1999) 511-515.

Ullendorff, E., "Job 3:8", *VT* 11 (1961) 350-351.

——, "Is Biblical Hebrew a Language?" in E. Ullendorff, *Is Biblical Hebrew a Language? Studies in Semitic Languages and Civilizations* (Wiesbaden: Otto Harrassowitz, 1977) 3-17.

Van der Voort, A., "Genèse I,1 à II,4[a] et le Psaume 104" *RB* 58 (1951) 321-347.

Van Wolde, E., *Stories of the Beginning: Genesis 1-11 and Other Creation Stories* (London: SCM, 1996). Translated from *Verhalen over het begin. Genesis 1-11 en andere scheppingsverhalen* (Baarn: Uitgeverij Ten Have, 1995).

Vaughan, P. H., *The Meaning of "Bāmâ" in the Old Testament: A Study of Etymological, Textual and Archaeological Evidence* (Society for Old Testament Study Monograph Series; Cambridge: CUP, 1974).

Vaux, R. de, *Histoire ancienne d'Israël*, I (Paris: Gabalda, 1971). English translation: *The Early History of Israel*, I (London: DLT, 1978).

——, *Les Institutions de l'Ancien Testament*, 2 vols. (Paris: Les Éditions du Cerf, 1958- 60). English translation: *Ancient Israel: Its Life and Institutions* (London: DLT, 1961).

Vawter, B., *On Genesis: A New Reading* (London: Geoffrey Chapman, 1977).

Veijola, T., *Verheissung in der Krise: Studien zur Literatur und Theologie der Exilszeit anhand des 89. Psalms* (Suomalaisen Tiedeakatemian toimituksia. Annales Academiae Scientiarum Fennicae Sarja B., 220; Helsinki: Suomalainen Tiedeakatemia, 1982).

——, "Davidverheißung und Staatsvertrag: Beobachtungen zum Einfluß altorientalischer Staatsverträge auf die biblische Sprache am Beispiel von Psalm 89" *ZAW* 95 (1983) 9-31.

——, "Das Klagegebet in Literatur und Leben der Exilsgeneration am Beispiel einiger Prosatexte" in J. A. Emerton (ed.), *Congress Volume Salamanca 1983* (VT[S] 36; Leiden: E. J. Brill, 1985) 286-307.

Velde, H. te, "Seth" in D. B. Radford, *The Ancient Gods Speak: A Guide to Egyptian Religion* (Oxford: OUP, 2002) 331-4.

Vermeylen, J., *Du prophète Isaïe à l'Apocalyptique: Isaïe, I-XXXV, mirroir d'un demi-millénaire d'expérience religieuse en Israël*, vol. 1 (Études Bibliques; Paris: Librairie Lecoffre, J. Gabalda, 1977).

Vlastos, G., *Plato's Universe* (Oxford: Clarendon, 1975).

Vogt, E., "Der Aufbau von Psalm 29", *Biblica* 41 [1960] 17-24.

Volz, P., *Das Neujahrsfest Jahwes (Laubhüttenfest)* (Sammlung Gemeinverständlicher Vorträge und Schriften aus dem Gebiet der Theologie und Religionsgeschichte 67; Tübingen: J. C. B. Mohr [Paul Siebeck], 1912).

Vosberg, L., *Studien zum Reden vom Schöpfer in den Psalmen* (Beiträge zur evangelischen Theologie 69; Munich: Chr. Kaiser Verlag, 1975).

Wakeman, M. K., "Chaos", *IDB* Supplementary Vol. (Nashville, TN: Abingdon Press, 1976) 143-145.

——, "The Biblical Earth Monster in the Cosmogonic Combat Myth" *JBL* 88 (1969) 313-320.

——, *God's Battle with the Monster: A Study in Biblical Imagery* (Leiden: E. J. Brill, 1973).

Ward, J. M., "The Literary Form and Liturgical Background of Psalm LXXXIX" *VT* 11 (1961) 321-339.

Watson, W. G. E., "Ugaritic and Mesopotamian Literary Texts", *UF* 9 (1977), 273-284.

——, *Classical Hebrew Poetry: A Guide to its Techniques* (JSOT[S] 26; Sheffield: Sheffield Academic Press, 2nd ed. 1995).

Watts, J. D. W., *The Books of Joel, Obadiah, Jonah, Nahum, Habakkuk and Zephaniah* (Cambridge Bible Commentary; Cambridge: CUP, 1975).

——, *Isaiah 1-33* (WBC 24; Waco, TX: Word Books, 1985).

——, *Isaiah 34-66* (WBC 25; Waco, TX: Word Books, 1987).

Weber, R., et al. (edd.), *Biblia Sacra iuxta Vulgatam Versionem*, 2 vols. (Stuttgart: Würtembergische Bibelanstalt, 1969).

Weidener, E. F., "Jojachin, König von Juda, in babylonischen Keilschrifttexten" in Haut-commissariat de la République Française en Syrie et au Liban, Service des Antiquités (ed.), *Mélanges Syriens offerts à Monsieur René Dussaud. Secrétaire Perpétuel de l'Académie des Inscriptions et Belles-Lettres, par ses Amis et ses Élèves*, II (Bibliothèque Archéologique et Historique 30; Paris: Librairie Orientaliste Paul Geuthner, 1939) 923-35.

Weiser, A., *Die Psalmen übersetzt und erklärt* (Das Alte Testament Deutsch 14/15; Göttingen: Vandenhoeck & Ruprecht, 5th revised ed. 1959). English translation of 5th revised ed. 1959: *The Psalms: A Commentary* (OTL; London: SCM, 1962).

——, "Zur Frage nach den Beziehungen der Psalmen im Kult" in W. Baumgartner, O. Eissfeldt et al. (edd.), *Festschrift Alfred Bertholet zum*

80. Geburtstag gewidmet von Kollegen und Freunden (Tübingen: J. C. B. Mohr [Paul Siebeck], 1950) 513-531.

Wellhausen, J, *Psalms* (The Polychrome Bible; London: James Clarke, 1898).

——, *Prolegomena zur Geschichte Israels* (Berlin: Georg Reimer, 3rd. ed. 1886). English translation: *Prolegomena to the History of Israel with a Reprint of the Article* Israel *from the "Encyclopaedia Britannica"* (Edinburgh: Adam & Charles Black, 1885).

Wender, D., (trans.), *Hesiod Theogony, Works and Days; Theognis Elegies* (Harmondsworth, Middx.: Penguin, 1973).

Wenham, G. J., *Genesis 1-15* (WBC 1; Nashville, TN; Thomas Nelson, 1987).

Westermann, C., *Schöpfung* (Themen der Theologie 12; Stuttgart & Berlin: Kreuz-Verlag, 1971). English translation: *Creation* (Philadelphia, PA: Fortress, 1974).

——, *Genesis: I. Teilband Genesis 1-11* (BKAT; Neukirchen-Vluyn: Neukirchener Verlag, 1974). English translation: *Genesis 1-11: A Commentary* (London: SPCK, 1984).

——, *Lob und Klage in den Psalmen* (Göttingen: Vandenhoeck & Ruprecht, 1977 [fifth, expanded, edition of *Das Loben Gottes in den Psalmen*]). English translation: *Praise and Lament in the Psalms* (Atlanta, GA: John Knox, 1981; Edinburgh: T. & T. Clark, 1987).

——, *Der Aufbau des Buches Hiob* (BHT 23; Tübingen: J. C. B. Mohr [Paul Siebeck], 1956). English translation of 2nd ed. 1977: *The Structure of the Book of Job: A Form-Critical Analysis* (Philadelphia, PA: Fortress, 1981).

——, *Ausgewählte Psalmen übersetzt und erklärt* (Göttingen: Vandenhoeck & Ruprecht, 1984). English translation: *The Living Psalms* (Edinburgh: T. & T. Clark, 1989).

——, *Das Buch Jesaja: Kapitel 40-66 übersetzt und erklärt* (Das Alte Testament Deutsch Neues Göttinger Bibelwerk 19; Göttingen: Vandenhoeck & Ruprecht, 5th ed. 1986). English translation: *Isaiah 40-66* (OTL: London: SCM, 1969).

Wevers, J. W., "A Study in the Form Criticism of Individual Complaint Psalms" *VT* 6 (1956) 80- 96.

White, H. G. (trans.), *Hesiod, the Homeric Hymns and Homerica* (Loeb Classical Library; London: Heinemann, 1914).

Whybray, R. N., *Isaiah 40-66* (NCBC; London: Oliphants, 1975).

——, *The Second Isaiah* (OTG; Sheffield: JSOT Press, 1983).

Wifall, W., "The Sea of Reeds as Sheol" *ZAW* 92 (1980) 452-483.

Wilcox, J. T., *The Bitterness of Job: a Philosophical Reading* (Ann Arbor, Michigan, IL: University of Michigan Press, 1994).

Wildberger, H., *Jesaja*, 3 vols. (BKAT 10-10/3; Neukirchen-Vluyn: Neukirchener Verlag, 1972-1982). English translation: *Isaiah: A Continental Commentary*, 3 vols. (Continental Commentaries; Minneapolis, MN: Fortress Press, 1991-2002).

Wilde, A. de, *Das Buch Hiob eingeleitet, übersetzt und erläutert* (Oudtestamentische Studiën 22; Leiden: E. J. Brill, 1981).

Willesen, F., "The Cultic Situation of Psalm lxxiv" *VT* 2 (1952) 289-306.

Williamson, H. G. M., *The Book Called Isaiah: Deutero-Isaiah's Role in Composition and Redaction* (Oxford: Clarendon, 1994).

——, *Variations on a Theme: King, Messiah and Servant in the Book of Isaiah* (The Didsbury Lectures 1997; Carlisle: Paternoster Press, 1998).

Wilson, G. H., *The Editing of the Hebrew Psalter* (SBL Dissertation Series 76; Chico, CA: Scholars Press, 1985).

——, "The Use of the Royal Psalms at the 'Seams' of the Hebrew Psalter" *JSOT* 35 (1986) 85-94.

Wilson, W., (trans.), *The Writings of Clement of Alexandria*, Vol. II (Ante-Nicene Christian Library, Vol. XII; Edinburgh: T. & T. Clark, 1869).

Wiseman, J., *SAS Survival Guide* (Collins Gem Series; Glasgow: HarperCollins, 1999).

Wolfers, D., *Deep Things out of Darkness. The Book of Job: Essays and a New Translation* (Grand Rapids, MI: Eerdmans, 1995).

Wolff, H. W., "Prophecy from the Eighth through the Fifth Century" *Int* 32 (1978) 17-30.

Wolverton, W. I., "The Psalmists' Belief in God's Presence" *Canadian Journal of Theology* 9 (1963) 82-94.

——, "Sermons in the Psalms" *Canadian Journal of Theology* 10 (1964) 166-176.

Wright, G. H. B., *Book of Job: A New Critically Revised Translation, with Essays on Scansion, Date, etc.* (London: Williams and Norgate, 1883).

Wyatt, N., "The Theogony Motif in Ugarit and the Bible" in G. J. Brooke, A. H. W. Curtis, and J. F. Healey (edd.), *Ugarit and the Bible: Proceedings of the International Symposium on Ugarit and the Bible. Manchester, September 1992* (UBL 11; Münster: Ugarit-Verlag, 1994) 395-419.

— —, *Myths of Power: a study of royal myth and ideology in Ugaritic and biblical tradition* (UBL 13; Münster: Ugarit-Verlag, 1996).

— —, *Religious Texts from Ugarit: The Words of Ilimilku and his Colleagues* (The Biblical Seminar 53; Sheffield: Sheffield Academic Press, 1998).

— —, "Arms and the King: The earliest allusions to the *Chaoskampf* motif and their implications for the interpretation of the Ugaritic and biblical traditions" in M. Dietrich and I. Kottsieper (edd.), *"Und Mose schrieb dieses Lied auf": Studien zum Alten Testament und zum Alten Orient. Festschrift für Oswald LORETZ zur Vollendung seines 70. Lebensjahres mit Beiträgen von Freunden, Schülern und Kollegen* (AOAT 250; Munich: Ugarit-Verlag, 1998) 833-882.

Yadin, Y., (ed.), *Jerusalem Revealed: Archaeology in the Holy City 1968-1974* (Jerusalem: The Israel Exploration Society, 1976).

Young, I., *Diversity in Pre-Exilic Hebrew* (FAT 5; Tübingen: Mohr, 1993).

— —, (ed.), *Biblical Hebrew: Studies in Chronology and Typology* (London: Continuum [T. & T. Clark], 2003).

Zenger, E., "Tradition und Interpretation in Exodus XV:1-21" in J. A. Emerton (ed.), *Congress Volume, Vienna 1980* (VT[S] 32; Leiden: E. J. Brill, 1981) 452-483.

Zijl, P. van, "A Discussion of the Root gāʻar (rebuke)" in A. van Zyl (ed.) *Biblical Essays: Proceedings of the 12th Meeting of Die Oud-Testamentiese Werkgemeenskap in Suid-Afrika: held at the University of Potchefstroom, 28th - 31st January 1969* (Potchefstroom, SA: University of Potchefstroom, 1969) 56-63.

Zimmerli, W., "The Place and Limit of the Wisdom in Old Testament Theology", *Scottish Journal of Theology* 17 (1964) 146-158.

On-line Sources

"Crocodile" (On-line), (*Encyclopædia Britannica* from Encyclopædia Britannica Premium Service, 2004), accessed September 10, 2004 at http://www.britannica.com/eb/article?eu=121030.

"Crocodilia" (On-line), (Animal Diversity Web, 2002). Accessed September 14, 2004 at http://www.animaldiversity.ummz.umich.edu/site/accounts/information/Crocodilia.html.

Crocodilian Biology Database (On-line), accessed September 14, 2004 at http://www.flmnh.ufl.edu/cnhc/cbd-gb8.htm

"Fishing" (On-line), (*Encyclopædia Britannica* from Encyclopædia Britannica Premium Service, 2004). Accessed November 9, 2004 at http://www.britannica.com/eb/article?tocId=2333.

"Hippopotamus: hippopotamus amphibius" (On-line. Reprinted from "The Safari Companion" by Richard Estes), (Nature-wildlife.com). Accessed 14 September, 2004 at http://www.nature-wildlife.com/hipptxt.htm).

"The Safari Companion" by Richard Estes), (Nature-wildlife.com). Accessed 14 September, 2004 at http://www.nature-wildlife.com/hipptxt.htm]).

Shefferly, N., "Hippopotamus amphibius" (On-line), (Animal Diversity Web, 2001). Accessed September 14, 2004 at http://animaldiversity.ummz.umich.edu/site/accounts/information/Hippopotamus_amphibius.html.

Wermuth, Heinz Fritz, "Crocodile" (On-line), (*Encyclopædia Britannica* from Encyclopædia Britannica Premium Service, 2004). Accessed September 10, 2004 at http://www.britannica.com/eb/article?eu=121030.

Wermuth, Heinz Fritz, "Crocodile" (On-line), (*Encyclopædia Britannica* from Encyclopædia Britannica Premium Service, 2004). Accessed September 10, 2004 at http://www.britannica.com/eb/article?eu=121030.

Index of Subjects

Index of Biblical, Ancient Near Eastern and Classical References

1. Biblical References

1.1 Old Testament

1.2 Apocrypha

2. Ancient Near Eastern References

3. Classical References

Index of Modern Authors

Index of Hebrew and Ugaritic Terms

Hebrew

Ugaritic